UNITED STATES HISTORY

Preparing for the Advanced Placement Examination

Jessica Marciello

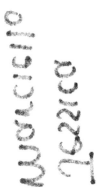

John J. Newman, Ed.D., has served as Adjunct Assistant Professor of History Education at Illinois University and Adjunct Professor of History at the College of DuPage. He was for many years Department Coordinator of Art, Foreign Language, and Social Studies and teacher of Advanced Placement U.S. history at Naperville North High School, Napervile, Illinois.

John M. Schmalbach, Ed.D., is Adjunct Assistant Professor at Temple University. He was for many years Social Studies Department Head and teacher of Advanced Placement U.S. history at Abraham Lincoln High School, Philadelphia, Pennsylvania.

UNITED STATES HISTORY

Preparing for the Advanced Placement Examination

(Second Revised Edition)

John J. Newman

John M. Schmalbach

AMSCO SCHOOL PUBLICATIONS, INC.
315 Hudson Street/New York, N.Y. 10013

This book is dedicated to our wives,
Anne Newman and Rosemarie Schmalbach;
our children, Louise Newman,
and John, Suzanne, and Robert Schmalbach;
and our students, who share our study of America's past.

Reviewers

William McKee
Chairperson, Social Studies, Brockport High School, Brockport, N.Y.

Stephen A. Shultz
Social Studies Coordinator, Rocky Point Public Schools, New York

Composition: Monotype Inc.
Printing: Maple-Vail Book Manufacturing Group

Please visit our Web site @ **www.amscopub.com**

When ordering this book, please specify:
either **R 785 P** *or* U.S. HISTORY: ADVANCED PLACEMENT

ISBN 978-1-56765-660-2
NYC Item 56765-660-1

Preface

United States History: Preparing for the Advanced Placement Examination has been revised and updated to include recent historical events and interpretations. It also reflects the latest changes in the Advanced Placement United States History examination format and question structures. This book was designed so that teachers and students could use it in a number of ways. The book may be used as a guide to accompany a yearlong course in AP or honors U.S. history. It may be used to bridge the gap between the typical textbook used in these courses and the needs of AP history candidates. Some teachers also may use the book in conjunction with their own materials and extensive readings and primary sources in lieu of a traditional U.S. history textbook. Students may use the book as a review text in the weeks before taking the May AP U.S. history exam. In all instances, the purpose is to assist students and teachers in dealing successfully with a challenging examination.

The book offers students a concise, accessible, and easy-to-review survey of the course content. The framework for this historical narrative is based on the course outline and guide to test coverage in the College Board's *Advanced Placement Course Description: History.*

While the concise presentation of the essential content for Advanced Placement U.S. history is the heart of this book, a number of features have been integrated into the book to help students prepare for the AP examination. In the Introduction, the latest AP examination format and the methods of grading the exam are explained. A brief explanation of historical methodology introduces students to the analytical demands of college-level history. Finally, a step-by-step guide to developing essay-writing skills is provided, together with AP-based evaluation rubrics that are used in grading students' work.

In the text, following the historical narrative is a Historical Perspectives section, which analyzes a historical issue or question and briefly introduces students to changing interpretations of history. The section Key Names, Events, and Terms provides a list of important terms to aid in the review of the chapter content. Each chapter has ten multiple-choice questions similar in style and content to those found on the AP exam, which provide for ample review and practice. The five essay questions in each chapter simulate the essay questions in the free-response section of the AP exam. These questions are designed to promote the critical-thinking skills needed for the exam.

Each chapter concludes with either a section of Documents and Readings or a Document-Based Question (DBQ). These readings, pictures, cartoons, graphs, and historical data will help promote analysis of primary sources, understanding of different points of view, and skills of synthesis and writing that are needed for answering the Document-Based Question on the AP exam. In addition to the ten DBQs provided for practice in this book, activities identified as Guide to Writing the DBQ are incorporated into Chapters 4, 8, 12, 13, and 17.

Following the final chapter is a complete practice examination that follows the format of the Advanced Placement Examination. It has 80 multiple-choice questions, a document-based question, and four standard essay questions.

A separate Answer Key is available. It contains the answers to the multiple-choice questions and suggested responses for the essays, the document-based questions, and the Practice Exam.

Probably the most rewarding aspect of teaching Advanced Placement classes is to be part of the amazing growth that students are capable of over the year, as they strive to meet the challenges of a college-level course. If this book can support their effort, it has accomplished its goal.

John J. Newman
John M. Schmalbach

Contents

Introduction

Preparing for the Advanced Placement Examination in U.S. History

High school students take over 2 million Advanced Placement (AP) examinations each year. Advanced Placement U.S. History is the most popular of the exams with nearly 300,000 students participating yearly. The growth of Advanced Placement programs in many states and school often reflects an effort to raise academic standards on the high school level. For students, the benefits of Advanced Placement frequently cited are:

- Earning college credit for work done during high school
- Testing out of introductory college courses for placement in courses appropriate for the student's ability and interests
- Saving on college tuition costs or gaining additional time to pursue other studies
- Demonstrating academic motivation and performance to colleges and universities
- Enriching one's high school experience

While most colleges and universities recognize the Advanced Placement program and its examinations, the amount of college credit offered and the advanced placement granted will vary from college to college. A list of the colleges that use Advanced Placement grades in determining credit and advanced placement is given in the annual edition of the College Board's "Acorn" booklet, *Advanced Placement Course Description: History.* Students can receive additional information on the policies of specific colleges and universities from their high school guidance or counseling department or by writing to the directors of admissions of the colleges that they are interested in attending.

Each Advanced Placement examination, including the United States History exam, grades student performance on a five-point scale:

5: Extremely well qualified; *4:* Well qualified; *3:* Qualified; *2:* Possibly qualified; *1:* No recommendation.

The AP grade reflects the level of student proficiency on an examination based on the AP U.S. History course description. An AP grade of *3* or higher is usually considered evidence of mastery of course content similar to that demonstrated in a college-level introductory course in the same subject area. However, since the content of these introductory courses varies from college to college, it is difficult to relate a grade on an AP exam to a grade given in a specific college or university. Some colleges may accept a *2* on the AP history exam, while more selective institutions may require a score of *4*.

Overview of the AP Exam in U.S. History

The AP exam in U.S. History is designed to evaluate the knowledge, understanding, and thinking and writing skills that would be demonstrated in a yearlong introductory-level college course in U.S. history. A combination of factual knowledge and ability to analyze historical questions in a critical manner is the key to successful performance on the exam.

The AP exam lasts three hours and five minutes and consists of two sections: (1) multiple choice and (2) free response. The free-response section consists of two parts: (a) a document-based question (DBQ) and (b) two standard essay questions.

The U.S. History exam is administered in the high schools on the same day sometime during a two-week AP exam schedule from early May through mid-May. For example, in 2007 and the AP U.S. history is scheduled for May 11, but in 2008, it is on May 9. The exam dates often do not match school calendars and classroom instruction. Therefore, AP students should be prepared to do some preparation for the exam on their own.

Multiple-Choice Section

The multiple-choice part of the exam consists of 80 questions and accounts for 50 percent of students' grades. The questions assess the depth and breadth

Section	Format	Number of Items	Time Allowed (minutes)	Percent of Grade
I	Multiple choice	80	55	50
II	Free response			
Part A	Document-Based Question (DBQ)	1	60 (advised)	22.5
Parts B and C	Standard essays	2	70 (advised)	27.5

of students' factual knowledge and their ability to interpret quotations, maps, graphs, and visual sources, including political cartoons. The content is drawn from a full-year course in United States history. The College Board gives the following approximate breakdown for its selection of questions:

Pre-Columbian to 1789	20%
1790–1914	45%
1915 to the present	35%

Students should expect only a few questions from the period after the early 1980s. The use of any questions about the history of the past ten years is even rarer. The College Board has announced an increased emphasis on social history in recent years, but it cautions that even social and economic history questions often deal with the impact of public policy and legislation. While history cannot be neatly divided into categories, the recommended allocation for the multiple-choice questions for the AP U.S. History exam is as follows:

Political institutions, behavior, and public policy	35%
Social change, cultural and intellectual developments	40%
Diplomacy and international relations	15%
Economic developments	10%

Unlike most classroom exams designed to measure mastery of specific content, the AP exams are deliberately constructed to provide a wider distribution of scores and high reliability (likelihood that test-takers repeating the same exam will receive the same scores). A "qualified" or level 3 grade on the multiple-choice section is usually around 60 percent. Only a small percentage of students will answer more than 80 percent of the questions correctly. Therefore, students who are having real difficulty with a third or more of the questions should not be discouraged.

Performance on the multiple-choice section has proved a strong predictor of the student's overall success on the examination. While an above-average score on the multiple-choice section cannot guarantee an overall score of 4 or 5, most students who do well on this section also do well on the essay, or free-response, section. The breadth and depth of knowledge and understanding of U.S. history needed to answer the multiple-choice questions will also support the students' efforts at writing historical essays.

Free-Response (Essay) Section

The free-response, or essay, section of the AP United States History exam is divided into two parts. Part A, a document-based question (DBQ), counts for

45 percent of the free-response grade (22.5 percent of the total test grade); Parts B and C, two standard essays, count for 55 percent of the free-response grade (27.5 percent of the total). Current directions for the exam give the test-takers 130 minutes to complete the free-response section. In the College Board's directions, the time allotment is divided into the following mandatory and advised time periods:

> 15 minutes (mandatory) to read the document-based question (Part A)
> 45 minutes (advised) to write the response to the DBQ

> 5 minutes (advised) to plan one essay from Part B (to 1865)
> 30 minutes (advised) to write the response to one essay from Part B

> 5 minutes (advised) to plan one essay from Part C (after 1865)
> 30 minutes (advised) to write the response to one essay from Part C

Of course, students have some flexibility during the mandatory 15 minutes to make notes in the Section II question booklet and to look ahead at the standard essay questions. They cannot, however, start writing in the sealed free-response composition booklet until the mandatory 15 minutes are over. The mandatory reading and advised planning time may seem to complicate the process, but it is the College Board's way of saying STOP AND THINK before you write. The short time taken in the prewriting stage to think through the question and formulate a response is critical if the exam-taker is to write a well-organized, coherent essay.

Students who answer the ten multiple-choice questions and five essay questions in each chapter and take the practice AP U.S. history exam included in this text will be well prepared for both the format and pacing of the exam. It is a good idea to practice writing the sample DBQs and standard essays within the time frame of the AP history exam. In past years the College Board has made changes in the time allocation and number of questions. Any future changes will be announced and explained in the annual updates of the two College Board publications: (1) The "Acorn" booklet for history and (2) *A Guide to the Advanced Placement Program*. Updates for the format and exam dates can also be found on the College Board's web site: http://www.collegeboard.com.

To better understand the free-response section of the exam, let's first look at the composition and grading of the standard essay questions before dealing with the more complex document-based question.

Standard Essay Questions

AP U.S. history candidates are required to answer two standard essay questions, one question from Part B, which generally deals with topics through the Civil War era, and one question from Part C, which covers the period after the Civil War. These essay questions often ask you to explain, analyze, or evaluate

different influences from different periods of history. The following questions
are samples from AP exams:

> Part B: Choose ONE question from this group. You are advised to spend 5
> minutes planning and 30 minutes writing your answer.
> 1. Analyze the ways in which TWO of the following influenced the devel-
>   opment of American society:
>   Puritanism during the 17th century
>   The Great Awakening during the 18th century
>   The Second Great Awakening during the 19th century
> 2. Evaluate the relative importance of domestic and foreign affairs in
>   shaping American politics in the 1790s.
> Part C: Choose ONE question from this group. You are advised to spend 5
> minutes planning and 30 minutes writing your answer.
> 3. Analyze the ways in which the Great Depression altered the American
>   social fabric in the 1930s.
> 4. Analyze the influence of TWO of the following on American-Soviet
>   relations in the decade following World War II:
>   Yalta conference
>   Communist revolution in China
>   Korean War
>   McCarthyism

The essay questions are designed to probe your understanding of the complexity of historical events and issues, and your ability to marshal relevant evidence behind a strong thesis. How broad and deep your understanding is of history, including
varying interpretations of key events, will determine how well yo are able to understand the question and to develop historical arguments to support your analysis.

The scoring guides developed by the College Board to evaluate the standard essay are shaped by the content of the question, but certain criteria are
found in each:

- A clear and well-developed thesis
- Thesis supported with relevant and substantial historical evidence
- Understands the complexity of the question
- Effectively analyzes all parts of the question, does not simply describe
- Essay is free of significant errors

Understanding and internalizing these criteria can help the student write better essays and heighten awareness of the kind of historical topics that become
the subject of essay questions. A sample, or generic, 0–9 point scoring guide is
found on pages xxvii–xxviii.

Document-Based Question

For many students, the DBQ is the most challenging section of the AP history exam. Others find the variety of documents provided with the question a great help in writing their essay. The DBQ in United States history usually has about eight documents to interpret. They are mainly short readings and two or three visual resources, such as charts, maps, cartoons, and photographs.

The question part of a DBQ often reads very much like a regular essay. Here is an example from a recent AP exam:

> What were the Cold War fears of the American people in the aftermath of the Second World War? How successfully did the administration of President Dwight D. Eisenhower address these fears?

> Use the documents and your knowledge of the years 1948–1961 to construct your response.

The DBQ directions ask you to "construct a coherent essay that integrates your interpretation of the documents . . . *and* your knowledge of the period referred to in the question." The directions emphasize the need to use *both* the documents *and* one's knowledge of the history of the era. "High scores will be earned only by essays that both cite key pieces of evidence from the documents and draw on outside knowledge of the period."

You will have a mandatory 15 minutes to study the DBQ and the documents and then 45 minutes to write your response. You may not begin to write in the sealed composition booklet until a signal is given by the proctor. Use the 15-minute preparation period to analyze the documents, take notes, decide on a thesis, and outline your DBQ essay.

This book gives you a wide variety of documents to analyze from all the eras of United States history and ten sample Document-Based Questions to practice your skills. These DBQs are found at the end of Chapters 4, 8, 12, 13, 17, 19, 22, 25, and 28, and in the Practice Exam following Chapter 30.

Writing a strong DBQ essay demands the same skills that a well-written standard AP essay requires: a strong and well-developed thesis, use of substantial relevant information, and ability to analyze all parts of the question. At the same time, a DBQ also requires the ability to (1) interpret the documents, (2) recognize conflicting viewpoints, and (3) use and refer to the documents effectively in the context of an essay. The current grading standards for a DBQ are very similar to the 0–9-point scale used for AP essay questions, but include the added standard: "effectively uses a substantial number of documents." Readers do not expect students to use every document, but the number of documents that can be used effectively in the essay is usually an indication of the depth of the student's understanding.

The DBQ tests the skills needed by historians or any serious students of history. It calls for an ability to read primary sources in their historical context and integrate them into one's understanding of history. While the DBQ may be the most challenging part of the exam, it also comes closest to measuring the skills associated with the study of history.

Grading of the U.S. History Examination

Essays are graded in June at one central site by college and high school teachers, who are trained to grade the essay answers with a high degree of consistency. AP readers develop a level of consistency and speed which would amaze most untrained teachers. However, the task of grading nearly 900,000 essays in itself explains why it is essential for AP candidates to learn how to write a clear and well-organized essay that focuses on a strong thesis.

After the multiple-choice and the free-response sections have been graded, each candidate receives a composite-score that gives equal weight to the multiple-choice section (50 percent) and free-response section (50 percent) of the exam. This formula is available to the students at www.collegeboard.com/ap-students. Finally, each composite score is converted into an AP grade of 1 to 5. Each year, the Chief Reader and the staff of the Educational Testing Service (ETS), a nonprofit organization that develops student tests, determine the range of the composite scores needed for the AP grades from 1 to 5. The percentage students who receive each grade varies from year to year, because the grades are based on objective standards of performance, not a standard grading curve. Therefore, students who wish to qualify with a 3 or higher need to achieve a level of performance that the College Board associates with a college-level U.S. history course.

Some students equate the study of history with memorizing names, dates, and events. History becomes "a confused heap of facts." Not only is this a poor description of history, but also it will not get you very far in the AP exam. To become a successful AP history student, it helps to understand the nature of history as practiced by historians.

What Is History?

Historians attempt to give meaning to the facts by explaining the connections among them. The job of the historian is to evaluate, organize, and interpret a wide variety of facts from a wide variety of sources in an effort to understand the past. While the analysis, evaluation, and organization of historical evidence has many aspects of a science, many historians would argue that the reconstruction of the past, especially in narrative form, is also an art. Many of the great historians of the narrative style would agree with the comment of Bernard

De Voto: "There is no boundary between history and literature; each holds a large part of its field in common with the other."

Is history a science or an art? This interesting philosophical question cannot be resolved here, but it helps us explore the issue of what kind of history the AP history exam requires. It does *not* require or even encourage a narrative style of historical writing. What the AP readers hope to find in a student's essay is some awareness of the complexity of history, of conflicting interpretation of the facts, and of the kind of decisions that historians make about the evidence.

The sarcastic observation of Samuel Butler, "God cannot alter the past but historians can," was a reflection not on divine power, but on the limitations of historians and the nature of history. The influential African American historian John Hope Franklin, writing about the era after the American Civil War, identified the tentative and changing character of history.

> If every generation rewrites its history, then every generation since 1870 has written the history of the Reconstruction. And what historians have written tells us as much about their own generation as about the Reconstruction period itself.

The practice of historians to revise and rewrite history is not a perverse plot to confuse students, but a result of changes in society, changing perspectives of historians, the discovery of new sources and information, and, above all, the asking of new questions.

The history of the American Civil War, for example, was obviously influenced for years by the regional origin of the historian, but in time, contemporary events, such as World Wars I and II and the civil rights movement of the 1950s and 1960s, had more influence on historians than their place of birth. Historians were also encouraged by the active role of African Americans in the civil rights movement to ask new questions about African Americans' role in their emancipation and in the Civil War itself. Historians asked whether Lincoln freed the slaves by proclamation or whether the slaves freed themselves by escaping to Union lines and forcing the issue of emancipation. Historians' views of Abraham Lincoln, the most analyzed subject in American history, also continue to undergo change. The recent discovery and study of Lincoln's early legal work in Illinois gives historians new insights into the man.

New questions have often led to significant revision of our understanding of the past. Charles A. Beard, one of the most famous "revisionist" historians, created a lasting controversy in the early 20th century by asking what were the economic interests of the nation's Founders. In *An Economic Interpretation of the Constitution of United States* (1913), Beard concluded that the writing of the

Constitution was motivated by the economic self-interests of the framers, not by political idealism.

In our own time, there has been renewed debate over the U.S. government's decision to drop two atomic bombs on Japan in 1945. The traditional interpretation accepted President Truman's public explanation that the atomic bomb was used to shorten the war and to save lives. In a later era, a few historians suggested that the bomb may have been intended as the first shot of the Cold War. Revisionist historians argued that the bomb was aimed at stopping Joseph Stalin and the Soviet Union from overrunning Eruope and Asia. The debate over the decision to drop the bomb goes on, and in fact this issue became the subject of the document-based question on an exam:

> The United States' decision to drop an atomic bomb on Hiroshima was a diplomatic measure calculated to intimidate the Soviet Union in the post-Second-World War era rather than a strictly military measure designed to force Japan's unconditional surrender.
>
> Evaluate this statement, using the documents and your knowledge of the military and diplomatic history of the years 1939 through 1947.

Obviously, it would have helped the students dealing with this question if they had some knowledge of the controversy among historians.

The AP history exam is designed to measure students' knowledge and understanding of the issues, controversies, and complexity of history. The "correct" answers to essay questions and DBQs cannot be found in any answer booklet, no more than ultimate historical truth can be found in any one history book. The quality of the students' demonstration of their understanding of history is the issue. Part of the understanding of any historical era is knowledge of the differing perspectives both of the participants and of later historians. AP candidates should have some awareness that historians differ in their interpretation of events. The study of the works of historians and their changing methodologies and interpretations is called *historiography.*

Each chapter of this text concludes with a section headed Historical Perspectives. Its purpose is to introduce you to some of the issues and questions raised by historians, both traditional and revisionist. The AP history exam does not call for advanced knowledge of historiography, or "the history of history." Nevertheless, the richness of historical thought can provide added depth to students' analysis of historical questions.

Themes in AP U.S. History

Recently, the College Board recommended the use of themes in the study of history to promote higher level thinking skills. The following 12 general themes are suggested as a starting point by the AP U.S. History Development Committee:

1. *American Diversity:* relationships among different groups; race, ethnicity, gender, and class
2. *American Identity:* regional differences; views about the American character
3. *Culture:* arts, literature, philosophy, and popular culture
4. *Demographic Changes:* changes in birth, marriage, and death rates; internal migration and immigration.
5. *Economic Transformation:* trade, markets, capital, technology; the role of government in the economy
6. *Environment:* impact of population growth, industrialization, consumption, and conservation
7. *Globalization:* economic and cultural relationships with the rest of the world, from the colonial era to the present
8. *Politics and Citizenship:* political traditions, democracy, citizenship, and civil rights struggle
9. *Reform:* movements to improve society
10. *Religion:* diverse religious beliefs; influence on politics and society
11. *Slavery and Its Legacies:* origins of slavery, economic and racial dimensions, resistance
12. *War and Diplomacy:* impact on politics, the economy, and society

The tracing of multiple themes through U.S. history is an effective way to review both during your studies and before the AP exam. A thematic approach encourages one to think about specific events in a larger framework, and to make judgments about change over time, change and continuity, and similarities and differences. Historical perspective also recognizes the complexity of historical causation, the difference between fact and opinion, and the important and the inconsequential. Critical thinking in history avoids interpreting the past in terms of the present, and understands the tentative nature of many of our judgments about the past.

Preparing for the Exam

Under the best conditions, preparation for the AP U.S. History exam takes place within the context of an Advanced Placement or Honors course. However, whether this textbook is used in conjunction with the course or as a review book before the exam, it is recommended that the teacher or students organize a review schedule before the exam. Many AP candidates find that the study groups are helpful, especially if the students bring to the group a variety of strengths.

The following is a sample of the kind of review schedule using this text that either teachers or students might construct to organize their preparation:

Week 1: Exploration, Colonial, and Revolution, to 1800 (Chapters 1–6)
Week 2: 1800 to 1861 (Chapters 7–13)
Week 3: 1861 to 1900 (Chapters 14–19)
Week 4: 1900 to 1945 (Chapters 20–25)
Week 5: 1945 to present (Chapters 26–30)
Week 6: Complete and review practice test

Staying with such a schedule requires discipline. This discipline is greatly strengthened if a study group chooses a specific time and place to meet and sets specific objectives for each meeting. For example, students might divide the material by chapters and prepare outline responses to key terms and essay questions. Some individuals may find it more productive to create a review schedule for themselves. If this review text has been used in conjunction with a history course, your familiarity with the essential content and skills developed in this book should make it an even more convenient and efficient review tool.

Writing the Standard Essay Questions

AP candidates will most benefit from starting the practice of writing AP history essays as early as possible. Instead of writing and rewriting complete essays until all elements are mastered, break down the skills needed to write an effective AP history essay into sequential steps. The following steps have proved useful in developing the skills needed to answer AP essay questions:

1. Analyze the question
2. Organize the information
3. Develop a thesis
4. Write the introductory paragraph
5. Write the supporting paragraphs and conclusion
6. Evaluate your AP essay

Let's look at some of the activities and skills that you can practice to develop essay-writing skills for the AP test. (See also the Guides to essay and DBQ writing, in Chapters 1, 4, 8, 13, and 17.)

1. Analyze the question. Taking the time to consider what the question *really* asks is often overlooked in the rush to start writing. Stop and ask yourself, What is the key word or phrase in the question? Underline it. It could be a verb such as "evaluate," "assess," "analyze," "apply," "compare," or "account." Often AP history questions ask, "To what extent" is a given statement valid? "In what ways" did one event or condition relate to another? All questions have one thing in common: They demand judgments about the historical evidence. Therefore, be on your guard for questions that start out with the verbs "identify," "describe," or "explain." An AP question is *never* satisfactorily answered by simply reporting information. Such a question is usually followed by "analyze" or some other more demanding mental activity. Consider, for example, this AP essay question:

> Describe THREE of the following and analyze the ways in which each of the three has affected the status of women in American society since 1940:
> Changing economic conditions
> Rebirth of an organized women's movement
> Advances in reproductive technology
> Persistence of traditional definitions of women's roles

For this essay, it is not enough simply to describe changing economic conditions, women's organizations, and so on. You must also *analyze* the effect that these factors had on the status of women. Here is a fairly sure guideline for any AP essay question: *If you think that you can write an essay without making some judgment that results in a thesis statement, you have not understood the question.*

After the kind of judgments needed to complete the essay are clear, all the parts of the question need to be identified. In recent years, the AP history exam has made some questions easier to understand by clearly structuring the question's parts, as in the above question on the status of women. More often, however, the two, three, or more aspects of the question are embedded in one sentence, as in this example:

> Evaluate the relative importance of domestic and foreign affairs in shaping American politics in the 1790s.

This question asks the student to deal with *both* domestic *and* foreign affairs. As the grading criteria for this question clearly state, if a student fails to deal with both parts of the question, it was not satisfactorily answered and could not receive more than a *4* on a 9-point scale. It may take only a few seconds to identify key terms and the parts of the essay question. If you take the trouble to do this, you will better understand the question and avoid the mistake of writing a perfectly good essay that receives a low score because it answers a question that was not asked.

Recommended Activity. As an initial skills-building activity, analyze the five essay questions at the end of each chapter. *Underline* the key word(s) that indicate what the writer should do and *circle* the words that indicate the specific parts or aspects of the content that need to be addressed.

Question: Evaluate the relative importance of domestic and foreign affairs in shaping American politics in the 1790s.

Domestic Affairs	Foreign Affairs	Politics
Hamilton's financial plan: national debt assumption; tariff, excise tax; Bank of the United States Constitution—loose vs. strict interpretation Whisky Rebellion Alien and Sedition acts	French Revolution British vs. French Proclamation of Neutrality Citizen Genêt Jay Treaty Pinckney Treaty Washington's Farewell Address XYZ Affair Convention of 1800	President Washington Jefferson vs. Hamilton Two-party system Election of 1796 Revolution of 1796

2. Organize the information. Many students start writing their answers to an essay question without first thinking through what they know, and they often write themselves into the proverbial corner. Directions for the AP history exam advise students to spend five minutes planning before starting to write each standard essay question. This fact indicates how critical it is first to identify what you know about the question and organize your information. A practice recommended by the AP directions is to make a brief outline of what you know about the question in the test booklet. A sample outline of the topics that could be treated in answering the essay question about domestic and foreign affairs in the 1790s is provided above. Listing facts pertaining to the question is to help you organize your thoughts, so you will want to use abbreviations and other memory aids.

The value of taking a few minutes to organize your knowledge becomes quickly apparent. First, you learn whether you have enough information to answer the question. Second, you can judge whether you have enough support for a potential thesis. It is obviously not very productive to select an essay or take a position that one cannot support. Based on this sample outline, an essay writer should have more than sufficient relevant information to support the importance of both domestic and foreign affairs in the politics of the 1790s. (In addition, of course, your analysis of the facts should be as good as your recall of them.)

Recommended Activity. Create a list of the kinds of relevant information that could be incorporated into the responses to the essays in the chapters. Try to organize the information under headings that reflect the major parts of the question. (*Note:* This activity parallels the lists developed by AP consultants before readers start scoring essays. It is a very useful prewriting activity.)

3. Develop a thesis. A strong thesis is an essential part of every AP history essay. A thesis is more than a restatement of the question or a description of relevant information. A thesis requires some judgment and interpretation of the evidence. The following thesis statement is from a student's essay written in response to the above question:

> During the 1790s, both domestic and foreign affairs contributed greatly to the shaping of American politics.

This statement is straightforward and simple, but it does take a position on the question. It affirms that both domestic and foreign affairs strongly influenced the political developments of the decade. An effective thesis does not have to be complex or sophisticated, but it must be focused on the question.

Surprisingly, many students seem to have difficulty taking a position. Some are afraid of making a mistake. Others seem afraid of offending anyone. A few students may not like controversy, complaining, "Why does everything have to become an issue!" Again, we need to go back to the nature of history. History does not offer the certitude of mathematics or the physical sciences. Disagreement over the interpretation of the historical evidence develops because of the limitations of both the evidence and the historians. AP readers are looking not for the "right answer" but for a writer's ability to interpret the evidence and marshal historical support for that interpretation.

For a thesis to be well developed it should have some power to explain the issues in question. For example, in the above question on politics in the 1790s, the student continued form the thesis statement with the following:

> The young nation was struggling with questions such as the interpretation of the Constitution's implied powers, which created domestic strife, while attempting to gain respect from foreign nations over issues such as British retention of northwest forts and the right of deposit at New Orleans, both of which were crucial to American morale and trade.

The thesis not only took a position but also offered an interpretation of events. This interpretation became the organizing principle that guided the development of the essay.

Recommended Activity. The "Guide to Writing an Essay" in Chapter 1 offers an exercise on identifying the strongest thesis statement. This exercise can help you identify the important elements of a strong, well-developed thesis. You can repeat this exercise by writing thesis statements for the essay questions at the end of the other chapters. Students could divide up into groups of four or five and discuss the relative strengths of the thesis statements from another group (without the names of students being revealed). Use the following questions to guide the discussion:

- Does the thesis take a position?

- Does the thesis offer an interpretation of the question?

- Does the thesis offer organizing or controlling ideas for an essay?

4. Write the introductory paragraph. AP readers are reluctant to recommend a specific structure for the introductory paragraph for a history essay, lest they limit a student's creativity. However, many more students suffer from poorly organized essays with no thesis statements or a thesis so embedded in the essay that it takes several readings to find it. Therefore, you can probably improve your essay by using some organizing principles for writing an introductory paragraph.

An effective introductory paragraph usually contains three elements: (1) the background to the question or your thesis, (2) the thesis statement, and (3) an introduction to the main ideas or points of the essay to be developed in the body or supporting paragraphs. This third element is sometimes called the essay's "blueprint" or "controlling ideas." By the end of the first paragraph, the reader should not only know your thesis but also have a clear idea of the main points to be developed in support of the thesis.

The model for an expository, five-paragraph essay on page xxiv illustrates how a well-organized essay relates back to an effective introductory paragraph. This model also emphasizes the importance of restating the thesis as the supporting paragraphs are developed. Do not conclude from the model that an essay should consist of five paragraphs, however. The total number of paragraphs and sentences is for the writer to determine. What the model does suggest is that the introductory paragraph is crucial because it should shape the full essay. An effective introduction tells the reader the view you will develop in the essay (your thesis), and then explains how you will develop that view, identifying the main points you will be making in the body of your essay. If your introductory paragraph is properly written, the rest of the paper will be relatively easy to write, especially if you have already organized your information.

Recommended Activity. Practice writing introductory paragraphs for the essay questions at the ends of the chapters, using the model for an expository

---

Model for an Expository History Essay

Introductory Paragraph: Background sentence 1: _____.
Background sentence 2: _____ Thesis statement: _____
_____. Development of thesis 1: _____.
Development of thesis 2: _____. Development of
thesis 3: _____.

    Development of thesis 1: Restate, add to, and thoroughly explain:
_____. Evidence: _____
_____. Evidence: _____
_____. Evidence: _____
_____ .

    Development of thesis 2: Restate, add to, and thoroughly explain:
_____. Evidence: _____
_____. Evidence: _____
_____. Evidence: _____
_____ .

    Development of thesis 3: Restate, add to, and thoroughly explain:
_____. Evidence: _____
_____. Evidence: _____
_____. Evidence: _____
_____

Conclusion: _____
_____
_____ .

---

history essay. Next, follow up the introductory paragraph with an outline of the supporting paragraphs. For each paragraph, list historical evidence that you would use. The exercise of writing an introductory paragraph and an outline of your supporting paragraphs helps you in two ways. First, it reinforces the connection of the main points in the introduction with the supporting paragraphs. Second, it requires you to think in terms of historical evidence before you start writing a complete essay.

    5. Write the supporting paragraphs and conclusion. The number and length of the supporting paragraphs forming the body of the essay should vary depending on the thesis, the main points to be supported, and the amount of historical evidence. Assuming a strong thesis and well-organized analysis to support it, the AP candidate also must remember to include specific historical evidence for support. Many students fail to achieve the full potential of an essay because they seem content to use a few historical references and assume the power of their logical arguments will carry the thesis. The amount of historical support is a key factor in AP grading. This does not mean providing "laundry lists" of information or detailed "stories." It does mean presenting relevant and analyzed historical information that supports the thesis. Remember the essay is also a measure of your knowledge of history, including proper names, people, places, events, laws, treaties, and movements. Do not hold back on the facts!

While length is no guarantee of a top grade, the longer essay often receives a higher grade because of its depth of analysis and factual support. However, the goal is not to fill up a specific number of pages, but to write an insightful and well-supported paper. A concise essay in which every word has a purpose is better than an essay bloated with fillers and flowery language in an attempt to impress the reader.

Other suggestions to keep in mind as you start practicing the writing of history essays for the AP exam are:

Write essays in the third person. Avoid use of the first person ("I," "we"). Essays in history are also usually written in the past tense, except when referring to documents or sources that currently exist (e.g., "the document implies"). The active voice is also preferred over the passive voice, because it is more effective in explaining cause and effect (e.g., "Edison created" is in the active voice; "was created by Edison" is in the passive voice).

Use specific words that clearly identify persons, factors, and judgment. Avoid vague verbs such as "felt" and "says," and vague references, such as "they" and "others." Avoid absolutes, such as "all" and "none." Rarely in history is in the evidence so absolutely conclusive that you can prove that there were no exceptions.

Define or explain key terms. If the question deals with terms (such as "liberal," "conservative," "sectionalism," or "manifest destiny"), an essential part of your analysis should include an explanation of these terms.

Communicate awareness of the complexity of history by distinguishing between primary and secondary causes and effects, between the significant and the less important. Use verbs that communicate judgment and analysis (e.g., "reveal," "exemplify," "demonstrate," "imply," "symbolize").

Anticipate counterarguments. Consider arguments that are against your thesis, not to prove them, but to show that you are aware of opposing points of view. The strongest essays confront conflicting evidence.

Remain objective. Avoid rhetoric, especially on social issues. The AP test is not the place to argue that one group were racists, or that one group were the "good guys" while another were the "bad guys." Do not use slang terms!

Communicate the organization and logical development of your argument. Each paragraph should develop a main point that is clearly stated in the topic sentence. Provide a few words or a phrase of transition to connect one paragraph to another.

The conclusion should focus on the thesis. Restate the thesis in a fresh and interesting manner or explain its significance. The conclusion should not try to summarize all the data or introduce new evidence. No conclusion is better than a meaningless effort. If you are running out of time, but have written a well-organized essay with a clear thesis that is restated in the supporting paragraphs, you should receive little or no penalty for not having a conclusion.

Recommended Activity. The first effort or two in writing a complete AP history essay will be a more positive experience for all involved if it is untimed and open book. After some confidence is gained in writing the standard essay, you should apply these skills in the context of a timed test, similar to that of the AP exam (e.g., 35 minutes for the standard essay). The purpose of this practice is to become familiar with the time restraints of the AP exam and to learn ways of (1) improving your writing and (2) gaining insight into the type of information needed. The feedback from these practice tests—whether from teachers, peers, or self-evaluation—is essential for making the practice produce progress.

6. Evaluate your AP essay. More essay writing does not necessarily produce better essays. Breaking down the process into manageable and sequential steps is one key for improvement. Peer evaluation of an essay as well as self-evaluation also help students to internalize the elements of an effective essay and learn ways to improve. The first evaluation activity (Activity 1) is a set of questions about how effectively an essay achieves the elements that the AP readers look for in their grading of essays. The second (Activity 2) is a generic practice scoring guide for the standard essay, similar to those developed for AP readers. The use of the essay-evaluation techniques can help AP candidates better understand the characteristics of a strong AP history essay.

Recommended Activity. Teacher evaluation and self-evaluation of essay work is initially less threatening than peer evaluation, but once a level of confidence is established, however, peer-evaluation will help students become better writers and is often the most useful form of feedback. The application of the standards of the AP graders by students to peer essays also helps them better understand the elements of a strong essay and apply them in their own work. Teachers can also supplement this activity by having students evaluate essays from prior AP history exams available from the College Board.

Activity 1: Evaluation of the Standard Essay

1. **Introductory Paragraph**   Underline the thesis and circle the structural elements identified in the introduction. How effectively does the introductory paragraph prepare the reader for the balance of the essay? How could the introductory paragraph be improved?

2. **Thesis**   Does the thesis address the question? How well does it deal with all parts of the question? Does the thesis acknowledge the complexity of the question? How could the thesis be improved?

3. **Analysis**   Does the body of the essay provide effective analysis of the question, or does it primarily describe? Does the essay deal with the full complexity of the question? Does it acknowledge opposing points of view on the question? How could the analysis be improved?

4. **Evidence**   Is the thesis supported with substantial, relevant information? What significant additional information could have been used for support?

5. **Errors**   What minor or major errors in fact or analysis were found in the essay?

6. **Presentation**   How well organized was the essay? Did paragraph composition, sentence structure, word choice, or spelling detract from the essays? Identify areas that need improvement.

Activity 2: Practice Scoring Guide for Standard Essays

Directions: Read through the full essay. circle the statements that reflect a fair evaluation of the specific elements of the essay, e.g., quality of thesis.

Grade	Comments
8–9	1. Clear, well-developed thesis 2. Understands complexity of question; deals with all parts of the question in depth 3. Provides effective analysis of the question; some imbalance permissible 4. Supports thesis with substantial, relevant information 5. May contain insignificant errors 6. Well organized and well written
5–7	1. Contains a clear thesis with limited development 2. Limited or lack of understanding of complexity; may deal with one part of the question in some depth, or all in a more general way 3. Limited analysis, mostly describes 4. Supports thesis with some factual information 5. May contain minor errors that do not detract from overall essay 6. Clearly organized and written, but not exceptional

2–4	1. Lacks a thesis, or thesis may be confused or underdeveloped
	2. Ignores complexity; may deal with one part of the question, or all elements of the question in a superficial way
	3. Weak or inappropriate analysis
	4. Lacks supporting information, or information given is minimal
	5. May contain major errors
	6. Weak organization and writing
0–1	1. No thesis
	2. May simply paraphrase or restate the question
	3. No analysis
	4. Incompetent, inappropriate response
	5. Contains many major and minor errors
	6. Disorganized and poorly written

Writing the Document-Based Question

The initial mystery of answering a DBQ largely disappears if you remember that it is an essay question. Your response needs the same elements as any other effective essay, including: (1) writing a thesis statement, (2) analyzing the main points of the question, (3) confronting the complexity of the question, and (4) drawing upon your knowledge of the era. The difference is that, for the DBQ, you must also use and interpret primary source documents in your argument.

To help students deal with the kinds of primary sources found on the AP history exam, every chapter of this text offers students a set of documents to interpret and analyze. The questions following the documents section ask students not only to deal with the content of the documents, but also relate them to one another and to historical issues. Starting with Chapter 4, you will find 10 document-based questions (at the end of Chapters 4, 8, 12, 13, 17, 19, 22, 25, and 28, and in the Practice Exam) that will allow you to develop your skills at organizing and writing the DBQ. The four-part "Guide to Writing the DBQ" feature, in Chapters 4, 8, 13, and 17, will also aid you in mastering each step of the process.

The greatest mistake a novice can make in answering a DBQ is to write little more than a description of the documents and try to explain how each document relates to the question. The focus on your DBQ essay should *not* be the documents, but a strong thesis that deals with the full complexity of the question. Use documents primarily for two purposes: (1) as an additional form of evidence (in addition to, but not as a substitute for, knowledge of events), and (2) as a way of demonstrating that you can handle conflicting evidence and points of view. The documents should not control the essay. You must learn to control the documents by understanding how they can be used to support your thesis.

Here are some specific suggestions for writing an effective DBQ:

1. Use the mandatory 15 minutes not only to read and make marginal notes on the documents in the free-response booklet but also to outline and organize the relevant "outside" knowledge you can bring to bear on the question. As in the standard essay, take time to formulate a thesis and its main points before you begin writing.

2. Brief references to the documents are enough. Because the readers probably know the documents almost word for word, there is no need to quote them at length. A reference to the document's author or letter (for example, document A) is enough. Study the examples in "Making Use of the Documents," page 350.

3. You can establish that you understand the era in question by setting the historical scene in the second paragraph using your "outside" information. The documents usually do not provide the historical context for the question. A solid, content-rich second paragraph clearly demonstrates that you have knowledge that goes beyond that found in the documents. Remember, *about 50 percent of the support for your essay should come from your "outside" knowledge.*

4. Use as many of the documents as you can, but you do not need to use all of them. Some may be irrelevant to your thesis and its defense. Keep in mind that some sources may be unreliable or contain biased views and questionable information. Part of your job is to demonstrate some judgment about the sources based on your knowledge of history. Do not treat all sources as equal. Some documents are more credible than others. Try to communicate your awareness of this fact to your reader.

5. Deal with the full complexity of the question. Most DBQs have two or three parts, as is evident in this question:

> To what extent did economic and political developments, as well as assumptions about the nature of women, affect the position of America during the period 1890–1925?

A superior essay will present an effective analysis of all three aspects of the question (economic and political developments, and assumptions about women). Use part of the 15 minutes to formulate a thesis that will address all parts of the question.

The DBQ allows you to demonstrate your sophistication as a student of history. The DBQ calls for judgment, not only about your knowledge of the past, but also documentary evidence from the past.

Recommended Activities. You should not start practicing the writing of DBQs until you have first developed the skills for writing a standard essay. You should, however, work on the skill of interpreting and identifying the point of view of a source, starting with the documents at the end of Chapter 1. For a prewriting activity, you could work in small groups to discuss the point of view of each document.

After writing a practice DBQ, evaluate it as you would a regular essay, using the generic DBQ scoring guide below, which is based on the 0–9-point scale used by AP readers for grading DBQs.

Practice Scoring Guide for Document-Based Questions

Directions: Read through the full essay. Circle the phrases that best evaluate this essay.

Grade	Comments
8–9	1. Contains a well-developed thesis that clearly addresses the question 2. Presents an effective analysis of all parts of the question, although treatment ma be uneven 3. Uses a substantial number of documents effectively 4. Makes substantial use of relevant outside information to support thesis 5. Clearly organized and well written 6. May have insignificant errors
5–7	1. Thesis addresses question, but not as focused or comprehensive as above 2. Analysis deals with part of the question in some depth, other parts in a more general way 3. Uses some of the documents effectively 4. Supports thesis with some outside information 5. Shows evidence of acceptable organization and writing 6. May contain errors that do not seriously detract from the quality of the essay
2–4	1. Presents a limited, confused, and/or poorly developed thesis 2. Deals with one aspect of the question in a general way or all parts in a superficial way simplistic explanation 3. Quotes or briefly cites documents 4. Contains little outside information or information that is inaccurate or irrelevant 5. Demonstrates weak organization and/or writing skills that interfere with comprehension 6. May contain major errors
0–1	1. Contains no thesis or a thesis that does not address the question 2. Inadequate or inaccurate understanding of the question 3. Contains little or no understanding of the documents or ignores them completely 4. Inappropriate or no use of outside information 5. Disorganized and poorly written 6. Numerous errors, both major and minor

Answering the Multiple-Choice Questions

The multiple-choice questions in the AP history exam are generally more difficult than those provided in a standard textbook. For one thing, the AP questions have five choices, which reduces the advantages of guessing. More important, the questions are difficult because there is less emphasis on recall and more emphasis on understanding, application, and analysis. Preparation for the multiple-choice section of the test is best achieved by developing a broad and detailed knowledge of U.S. history together with an analytical understanding of events.

Helping you prepare for the multiple-choice section are two end-of-chapter review and test features: Key Names, Events, and Terms and Multiple-Choice Questions. The questions in the latter are similar in both form and content to those appearing on past AP exams. The name and term review sections may be used in conjunction with a year-long course in U.S. history, as a final review before the AP exam, or both. In addition, the practice AP exam includes 80 multiple-choice questions.

Here are some suggestions for dealing successfully with the AP multiple-choice questions:

1. Read the question and the stem carefully and all five choices before you record your answer. A number of choices may appear to be correct, but you must select the BEST answer. Choices that reflect absolute positions, such as "always," "never," "exclusively," are seldom correct, for history itself can rarely offer such absolute certainty.

2. Should one guess on the AP exam? Wild guessing is discouraged, because in the grading of the multiple-choice section one-quarter of a point is taken off your score for each wrong answer, while a blank answer is not penalized. It does not pay to guess randomly. However, if you can eliminate two of the choices, it is to your advantage to answer the question, even with a guess.

3. Be prepared for EXCEPT, NOT, and LEAST questions, such as: "Which of the following was the LEAST important factor behind European exploration in the 16th century?" In these so-called reverse multiple-choice questions, the best answer is the *wrong* answer or the *least* correct. One approach is to cross out all the correct answers. The one that is left then becomes the best answer to a "reverse" question. The questions in the chapters provide frequent practice in this type of question.

4. Quotation questions based on a short selection from written sources can strike fear into the hearts of AP students. How can one know what all these historical figures wrote or said? You are not expected to be familiar with the specific quotation, but only with the *ideas* or *policies* they express. The purpose of most questions of this type is to evaluate whether you can recognize the most famous ideas of a person, groups, or movement in the quote. Like most AP questions, quotation questions do not require recall of documents—only analysis of the contents.

5. Questions using tables, charts, and graphs are ones that many students find the easiest on the exam, because often all the information needed to answer

the question is contained in the table or graphic. A careful reading of the title and of the two axes of a given chart or graph will help you understand the information. However, some data-based questions are actually cause-and-effect and chronology questions, such as the following graph question:

> Which of the following BEST accounts for the curve on the graph above depicting immigration to the United States from Asia, Africa, and the Americas between 1882 and 1900?

You would need to know something about the immigration restrictions placed on Asians starting in 1882 to answer this question correctly.

6. Chronology or "when" questions rarely require students to know a specific date, but rather the proper order of events. For example, the AP exam might test whether you know that the Declaration of Independence preceded the writing of the U.S. Constitution. Often, chronology questions ask which event occurred first or last, or in what presidential administration something happened.

7. The AP exam also expects some level of visual literacy. The multiple-choice exam will include a few examples of political cartoons, photographs, or artworks. The information provided in the visual will offer clues to the answer, but your ability to place the cartoon or photograph in the context of a particular era will help.

8. The AP history exam gives you 55 minutes to answer the 80 questions. Most students can answer two multiple-choice questions a minute. It is more sensible to follow a relaxed but reasonable pace than to rush through the exam and then go back and try to second-guess your decisions. However, 55 minutes does not allow enough time to spend two or three minutes on difficult questions. You need to mark them in your booklet (not on the answer sheet) and return to them after finishing the exam. Be careful when skipping questions and in making erasures.

Recommended Activity. Practicing sample multiple-choice questions is important before the exam, if for no reason than to reduce the number of surprises over the format of the questions. For most students, however, the review of content through multiple-choice questions is not the most efficient and useful way to prepare for the exam. It is the purpose of the chapter narrative in this text to provide a useful and meaningful review of the essential content of U.S. history. By reviewing essential facts in their historical content, you will better recall and understand the connections between events—so important for an analytical understanding of history.

EXPLORATION, DISCOVERY, AND SETTLEMENT, 1492–1700

*Thus out of small beginnings greater things have been produced by
His hand that made all things of nothing, and gives being to all
things that are; and, as one small candle may light a thousand, so
the light here kindled hath shone unto many, yea in some sort to
our whole nation.*

William Bradford, *Of Plymouth Plantation—1620–1647*

The original exploration, discovery, and settlement of North and South America occurred thousands of years before Christopher Columbus was born. In fact, many archeologists now believe that the first people to settle North America arrived as much as 40,000 years ago. At that time, waves of migrants from Asia may have crossed a land bridge that then connected Siberia and Alaska (a bridge now submerged under the Bering Sea). Over a long period of time, successive generations migrated southward from the Arctic Circle to the southern tip of South America. The first Americans—or Native Americans— adapted to the varied environments of the regions that they found. They divided into hundreds of tribes, spoke different languages, and practiced different cultures. Estimates of the Native population in the Americas in the 1490s vary from 50 to 75 million persons.

Cultures of North America

Estimates vary widely as to the population in the region north of Mexico (present-day United States and Canada) in the 1490s, when Columbus made his historic voyages. From under a million to over 10 million people may have been spread across this area.

Small settlements. Most of the Native Americans lived in semipermanent settlements, each with a small population seldom exceeding 300. The men spent their time making tools and hunting for game, while the women grew crops such as corn, beans, and tobacco. Some tribes were more nomadic than others. On the Great Plains, for example, the Sioux and the Pawnee followed the buffalo herds.

1

Larger societies. A few tribes had developed more complex cultures and societies in which thousands lived and worked together. The Pueblos in the Southwest lived in multistoried buildings and developed intricate irrigation systems for farming. East of the Mississippi River, the Woodland Native Americans prospered with a rich food supply. Mound-building cultures, including the Adena, Hopewell, and Mississippian, evolved in the Mississippi and Ohio River valleys and elsewhere. Supported by hunting, fishing, and agriculture, many permanent settlements developed. Cahokia (near present-day East St. Louis, Illinois), the largest, had as many as 30,000 inhabitants. For unknown reasons, Mississippian culture began to decline in the 15th century. In the Northeast (present-day New York), Iroquois tribes formed a political confederacy, the League of the Iroquois, which withstood attacks from opposing Native Americans and Europeans during much of the 17th and 18th centuries.

Cultures of Central and South America

While the exact population of Native Americans in this region in the 1490s is unknown, most historians agree that it was greater than that of North America. The great majority of Native Americans—estimates vary widely, to as many as 25 million people—lived in Central and South America. Three peoples in this region developed complex civilizations. Between A.D. 300 and 800, the Mayas built remarkable cities in the rain forests of the Yucatán Peninsula (present-day Guatemala, Belize, and southern Mexico). Centuries later, the Aztecs in central Mexico and the Incas in Peru ruled over vast empires. All three civilizations developed highly organized societies, carried on an extensive trade, and created calendars that were based on accurate scientific observations. The Aztecs' capital of Tenochtitlán was equivalent in size and population to the largest cities of Europe.

Europe Moves Toward Exploration

Until the late 1400s, Americans had no knowledge of the continents on the other side of the Atlantic Ocean. Neither did Europeans or Asians know of the existence of the two American continents (North and South America). Voyages and settlements such as those of the Vikings around the year 1000 to Greenland and North America had no lasting impact. As you know, Columbus' voyages of exploration finally brought Europe and the Americas into contact. But why was an oceanic crossing and exploration accomplished in the late 15th century and not before?

Improvements in Technology

In Europe, there occurred a rebirth of classical learning and an outburst of artistic and scientific activity known as the Renaissance. Columbus and other explorers lived when this era of creative vitality was at its height, in the late 1400s and early 1500s.

One aspect of the Renaissance was a gradual increase in scientific knowledge and technological change. Europeans made improvements in the inventions of others. For example, they began to use gunpowder (invented by the Chinese) and the sailing compass (adopted from the Chinese by Arab merchants). There were also major improvements in shipbuilding and mapmaking. The invention of the printing press in the 1450s also aided the spread of knowledge across Europe.

Religious Conflict

The later years of the Renaissance were a time of intense religious zeal and conflict. The Roman Catholic Church that had once dominated the culture of Western Europe was threatened from without by Ottoman Turks (followers of Islam) and from within by a Protestant revolt against the pope's authority.

Catholic victory in Spain. In the Middle Ages, Spain had been partly conquered by Muslim invaders. Only one Moorish stronghold remained in that country when Isabella, queen of Castile, and Ferdinand, king of Aragon, united their separate Christian kingdoms. In 1492, the very year that Christopher Columbus sailed on his historic first voyage, Isabella and Ferdinand succeeded in defeating the Moors of Granada. The uniting of Spain under Isabella and Ferdinand was a sign of new leadership, hope, and power for European believers in the Roman Catholic faith.

Protestant revolt in northern Europe. In the early 1500s, certain Christians in Germany, England, France, Holland, and other northern European countries revolted against the authority of the pope in Rome. Their revolt was known as the Protestant Reformation. Conflict between Catholics and Protestants led to a series of religious wars. It also caused the Catholics of Spain and Portugal and the Protestants of England and Holland to want their own versions of Christianity adopted by non-Christian peoples in Africa, Asia, and the Americas. Thus, a religious motive for exploration and colonization was added to political and economic motives.

Expanding Trade

Economic motives for exploration grew out of a fierce competition among European kingdoms for increased trade with Africa, India, and China. In the past, this trade had traveled from the Italian city-state of Venice and the Byzantine city of Constantinople on to an overland route that reached all the way to the capital of the Chinese empire. This land route to Asia had become blocked when, in 1453, the Ottoman Turks seized control of Constantinople.

Might a new way to the rich Asian trade be opened up by sailing either west across the Atlantic Ocean or south along the West African coast? At first, the latter possibility (sailing around Africa) seemed more promising. Voyages of exploration sponsored by Portugal's Prince Henry the Navigator eventually succeeded in opening up a long sea route around South Africa's Cape of Good Hope. In 1498, the Portuguese sea captain Vasco da Gama was the first European to reach India by this route. By this time, Columbus had attempted what he thought would be a shorter route to Asia. (He was wrong, of course. What he found was a sea route to the Americas.)

Developing Nation-States

Europe was also changing politically in the 15th century. Monarchs were gaining power and building nation-states in Spain, Portugal, France, England, and the Netherlands. (A nation-state is a country in which the majority of people share both a common culture and common political loyalties toward a central government.) The monarchs of the emerging nation-states depended on trade to bring in needed revenues and the Church to justify their right to rule. Among these monarchs were Isabella and Ferdinand of Spain and Prince Henry the Navigator of Portugal, who used their power to search for riches abroad and to spread the influence of the Roman Catholic Church to new overseas dominions.

Early Explorations

Changing economic, political, and social conditions in Europe shaped the ambitions of the Italian-born Christopher Columbus.

Columbus

Columbus spent eight years seeking financial support for his plan to sail west from Europe to the "Indies." Finally, in 1492, he succeeded in winning the backing of the two Spanish monarchs. Isabella and Ferdinand were then at the height of their power, having just defeated the Moors. They agreed to outfit three ships and to make Columbus governor, admiral, and viceroy of all the lands that he would claim for Spain.

After sailing from the Canary Islands on September 6, Columbus landed in the Bahamas on October 12. His success in discovering lands on the other side of the ocean brought him a burst of glory in Spain. But three subsequent voyages across the Atlantic were disappointing. Columbus died in 1506, still believing that he had found a western route to Asia.

Columbus' legacy. At the time of his death, many Spaniards viewed Columbus as a failure because they suspected that he had not found a route to the riches of China and the Indies, as he claimed, but a "New World." Today, some people scoff at Columbus for having erroneously given Native Americans the name "Indians." Even the land that he had explored was named for someone else, Amerigo Vespucci, another Italian sailor. Also Columbus' critics point out the many problems and injustices suffered by Native Americans after Europeans arrived and took over their land.

Nevertheless, no one can seriously dispute Columbus' importance. Modern scholars have recognized his great skills as a navigator and his daring and commitment in going forth where nobody else had ever dared to venture. Furthermore, there is no denying that Columbus' voyages brought about, for the first time in history, *permanent* interaction between Europeans and Native Americans.

Exchanges. Europeans and Native Americans had developed vastly different cultures over the millennia. The contact between the peoples of the Americas and the Europeans had both immediate and long-term effects. The Native Americans introduced Europeans to many new plants and foods, including beans, corn, sweet and white potatoes, tomatoes, and tobacco. They also infected Europeans with syphilis for the first time. Europeans brought sugar cane, bluegrasses, pigs, and horses, which all flourished in the new lands. They also introduced the wheel, iron implements, and guns to the Americas. Deadlier than all the guns was the European importation of germs and diseases, such as smallpox and measles, which within a century decimated the Native American population. Millions died (there was a mortality rate of over 90 percent), including entire tribal communities. These exchanges, biological and cultural, would permanently change the entire world.

Dividing the New World

Spain and Portugal were the first kingdoms to lay claim to territories in the New World. The Catholic monarchs of both countries turned to the pope in Rome to help settle their dispute over the ownership of newly discovered lands. In 1493, the pope drew a vertical, north-south line on a world map, giving Spain all lands to the west of the line and Portugal all lands to the east.

In 1494, the two disputing kingdoms signed the Treaty of Tordesillas, which moved the line a few degrees to the west. It was later discovered that the line passed through what is now the country of Brazil, and this, together with Portuguese explorations, established Portugal's claim to Brazil. Spain claimed the rest of the Americas. (Other European countries, however, were soon to challenge these claims.)

Spanish Exploration and Conquest

Spanish dominance in the Americas was based on more than a treaty and a papal line of demarcation. Spain owed its power in the New World to the efforts of explorers and conquerors (or conquistadores). Feats such as the journey across the Isthmus of Panama to the Pacific Ocean by Vasco Núñez de Balboa, the circumnavigation of the world by one of Ferdinand Magellan's ships, and the conquests of the Aztecs in Mexico by Hernan Cortés and of the Incas in Peru by Francisco Pizarro secured Spain's initial supremacy in the New World.

The conquistadores sent ships loaded with gold and silver back to Spain from the New World. They increased the gold supply by over 500 percent, making Spain the richest and most powerful nation in Europe. Other nations were encouraged to turn to the Americas in search of wealth and power. After seizing the wealth of the Indian empires, the Spanish turned to an *encomienda* system, with the king of Spain giving grants of land and Indians (Native

Americans) to individual Spaniards. These Indians had to farm or work in the mines. The fruits of their labors went to their Spanish masters, who in turn had to "care" for them. When Europeans' brutality and diseases reduced the Native American population, the Spanish brought slaves from West Africa under the *asiento* system. This required the Spanish to pay a tax to their king on each slave they imported to the Americas.

English Claims

England's earliest claims to territory in the New World rested on the voyages of John Cabot, an Italian sea captain who was under contract to England's King Henry VII. Cabot explored the coast of Newfoundland in 1497.

England, however, did not follow up Cabot's discoveries with other expeditions of exploration and settlement. England's monarchy in the 1500s was preoccupied with other matters, including Henry VIII's break with the Roman Catholic Church. In the 1570s and 1580s, under Queen Elizabeth I, England challenged Spanish shipping in both the Atlantic and Pacific oceans. Sir Francis Drake, for example, attacked Spanish ships, seized the gold and silver that they carried, and even attacked Spanish settlements on the coast of Peru. Another English adventurer, Sir Walter Raleigh, attempted to establish a settlement at Roanoke Island off the North Carolina coast in 1587, but the venture failed.

French Claims

The French monarchy first showed interest in exploration in 1524 when it sponsored a voyage by an Italian navigator, Giovanni da Verrazano. Hoping to find a northwest passage leading through the Americas to Asia, Verrazano explored part of North America's eastern coast, including New York harbor. French claims to American territory were also based on the voyages of Jacques Cartier (1534–1542), who explored the St. Lawrence River extensively.

Like the English, the French were slow to develop colonies in the New World. During the 1500s, the French monarchy was preoccupied with European wars as well as with internal religious conflict between Roman Catholics and Protestant Huguenots. Only in the next century did France develop a strong interest in following up its claims to North American land.

The first permanent French settlement in America was established by Samuel de Champlain in 1608 at Quebec, a fortified village on the St. Lawrence River. Champlain was later regarded as the "Father of New France" because of his strong leadership in establishing the colony. In time, other explorers extended French claims across a vast territory. In 1673, Louis Jolliet and Father Jacques Marquette explored the upper Mississippi River, and in 1682, Robert de La Salle explored the Mississippi basin, which he named Louisiana (after the French king, Louis XIV).

Dutch Claims

During the 1600s, the Netherlands also began to sponsor voyages of exploration. The Dutch government hired Henry Hudson, an experienced English seaman, to seek a northwest passage. In 1609, Hudson sailed up a broad river (later named for him as the Hudson River), an expedition that established Dutch claims to the surrounding area that would become New Amsterdam (and later New York). A private joint-stock company (see below), the Dutch West India Company, was given the privilege of taking control of the region for economic gain.

Early English Settlements

In the early 1600s, England was finally in a position to colonize the lands explored more than a century earlier by John Cabot. By defeating a large Spanish fleet—the Spanish Armada—in 1588, England had gained a reputation as a major naval power. Also in this period, England's population was growing rapidly while its economy was depressed. This condition gave rise to a large number of poor and landless people who were attracted by the idea of economic opportunities in the Americas. The English had also devised a practical method for financing the costly and risky enterprise of founding new colonies. Their *joint-stock companies* pooled the savings of people of moderate means and supported trading ventures that seemed potentially profitable. Thus, in the 1600s, various colonies on the North Atlantic Coast were able to attract large numbers of English settlers.

Jamestown

England's King James I chartered the Virginia Company, a joint-stock company that established the first permanent English colony in America at Jamestown in 1607.

Early problems. The first settlers of Jamestown suffered great hardships from Indian attacks, famine, and disease—and their own mistakes. The settlement's location in a swampy area along the James River resulted in outbreaks of dysentery and malaria, diseases that were fatal to many. Moreover, many of the settlers were gentlemen unaccustomed to physical work. Others were gold-seeking adventurers who refused to hunt or farm. Thus, food supplies dwindled to almost nothing, and the colonists nearly starved.

Tobacco prosperity. Through the forceful leadership of Captain John Smith and the establishment of a tobacco industry by John Rolfe, the Jamestown colony survived. Rolfe and his Indian wife, Pocahontas, developed a new variety of tobacco, which became very popular in Europe and brought financial prosperity to the colony.

EARLY SETTLEMENTS IN NORTH AMERICA
1600s

The growing of tobacco on Jamestown's plantations required a large labor force. At first, the Virginia Company hoped to meet the need for labor by sending indentured servants to the colony. An indentured servant was often a person (usually a young man) who, in exchange for free transportation to a colony, was obligated to work on a plantation for a certain number of years. After the arrival in Jamestown in 1619 of a few Africans who became indentured servants, the Virginia tobacco growers began to employ a combination of both forced labor (slavery) and free labor (indentured servitude).

Transition to a royal colony. Although it made profits from tobacco sales, the Virginia Company made unwise decisions that caused it to fall heavily into debt. The bankrupt company's charter was revoked in 1624, and the colony, now known as Virginia, came under the direct control of King James I. Thus, Virginia became England's first royal colony (a colony under the control of a king or queen).

Puritan Colonies

Religious motivation, not the search for wealth, was the principal force behind the settlement of two other English colonies on North America's Atlantic Coast. The first such colony was Plymouth, the second Massachusetts Bay. Both were settled by English Protestants who were influenced by John Calvin's teachings, including that of *predestination,* the belief that God guides those who are to be saved.

Founded by Henry VIII in the early 1500s, the Church of England, or Anglican Church, was Protestant in that it was under the control of the English monarch, not the pope in Rome. Its rituals, however, resembled those of the Roman Catholic Church. In the early 1600s, during the reign of James I, many people wanted to change both the ceremonies and the hierarchy (governing structure) of the Church of England. Because these religious reformers said they wanted to "purify" their church of Catholic influences, they became known as Puritans. James viewed the Puritans as a threat to both his religious and political authority and ordered some of them arrested and jailed.

The Plymouth Colony

One group of Puritans rejected the idea of simply reforming the Church of England. This group, known as the Separatists, wanted to organize a completely separate church, one that was independent of royal control. Several hundred Separatists left England in search of religious freedom. The Pilgrims, as they were called, first migrated to Holland. But economic hardship and cultural differences led many of the Pilgrims to seek another haven for their religion. They decided to settle in the new colony in America then operated by the Virginia Company of London. In 1620, a small group of Pilgrims set sail for Virginia aboard the *Mayflower.* Fewer than half of the 100 passengers on this ship were Separatists; the rest were people who had economic motives for making the voyage.

After a hard and stormy voyage of 65 days, the *Mayflower* dropped anchor off the Massachusetts coast, a few hundred miles to the north of the intended destination in Virginia. Rather than going on to Jamestown, the Pilgrims decided to establish a new colony at Plymouth.

Early hardships. After a first winter that saw half their number perish, the settlers at Plymouth were helped to adapt to the land by friendly Native Americans. They celebrated a good harvest at a thanksgiving feast (the first thanksgiving) in 1621. Under strong leaders, including Captain Miles Standish and Governor William Bradford, the Plymouth colony grew slowly. Fish, furs, and lumber became the mainstays of Plymouth's economy.

Massachusetts Bay Colony

In England, the persecution of Puritans increased as a result of the policies of a new king, Charles I. Seeking religious freedom, a group of Puritans (who were not Separatists) gained a royal charter for a new colonizing venture, the Massachusetts Bay Company (1629).

In 1630, about a thousand Puritans led by John Winthrop sailed for the Massachusetts shore and founded Boston and several other towns. A civil war in England in the 1630s drove some 15,000 more settlers to the Massachusetts Bay colony—a movement known as the *Great Migration.*

Early Political Institutions

From the very beginning, England allowed its American colonies a certain degree of self-rule.

Majority rule in Plymouth. Aboard the *Mayflower* in 1620, the Pilgrims drew up and signed a document that pledged them to make decisions by the will of the majority. This document, known as the Mayflower Compact, represented both an early form of colonial self-government and an early (though rudimentary) form of written constitution, establishing the powers and duties of the government.

Representative government at Jamestown. The Virginia Company sought to encourage settlement in Jamestown by guaranteeing colonists the same rights that they had had in England, including the right to be represented in the lawmaking process. In 1619, just 12 years after the founding of Jamestown, Virginia's colonists organized the first representative assembly in America, the House of Burgesses.

Representative government in Massachusetts. In the Massachusetts Bay Colony, there were limited but important democratic actions. All freemen—male members of the Puritan Church—had the right to participate in yearly elections of the colony's governor, his assistants, and a representative assembly.

Limited nature of colonial democracy. While some of the English colonies were partly democratic, a sizable part of the colonial population was excluded from the political process. Only male property owners could vote for representatives. Those who were either female or landless had few rights; slaves and indentured servants had practically none at all. Also, many colonial governors ruled with autocratic or unlimited powers, answering only to the king or others in England who provided the colonies' financial support. Thus, the gradual development of democratic ideas in the colonies coexisted with antidemocratic practices such as slavery and the widespread mistreatment of Native Americans.

Spanish Settlements in North America

Spanish settlements developed slowly, due to limited mineral resources and strong opposition from the Native Americans.

Florida. After a number of failed attempts and against the strong resistance of the Native Americans, the Spanish in 1565 established a permanent settlement at St. Augustine. Today, St. Augustine is the oldest city in North America.

New Mexico. Santa Fe was established as the capital of New Mexico in 1609. Harsh efforts to Christianize the Native Americans caused the Pueblo people to revolt in 1680. The Spanish were driven from the area until the early 1700s.

Texas. After they were driven from New Mexico, the Spanish established a few small settlements in Texas. These settlements grew in the early 1700s as Spain attempted to resist French efforts to explore the lower Mississippi River.

California. In response to Russian exploration from Alaska, the Spanish established permanent settlements at San Diego in 1769 and San Francisco in 1776. By 1784, a series of missions or settlements had been established along the California coast by members of the Franciscan order. Father Junípero Serra founded nine of these missions.

European Treatment of Native Americans

The various nations that colonized North and South America used a variety of approaches for controlling or subjugating Native Americans. The Spanish approach was to conquer, rule, and intermarry with the Aztecs, Mayas, and Incas. The English, on the other hand, occupied the land and forced the small, scattered tribes they encountered to move away from the coast to inland territories. The French, looking for furs and converts to Catholicism, tended to treat the Native Americans as economic and military allies.

In general, Europeans of all nationalities viewed Native Americans as inferiors who could be exploited for economic, political, and religious gain. Two long-term effects of European colonization were (1) the destruction by disease and war of large segments of the Native American population and (2) the establishment of a permanent legacy of subjugation.

Spanish Policy

In the American territories conquered and occupied by Spain, millions of Native Americans died as a result of both the conquistadores' methods of warfare, efforts at enslavement, and, even more, European diseases for which the Native Americans had no immunity. Spain incorporated the conquered peoples of Central and South America into a highly organized empire. Because few families came from Spain to settle the empire, the explorers and adventurers intermarried with Indians as well as with Africans. The latter group were captured in Africa and forced to travel across the ocean to provide slave labor for the Spanish colonists. A rigid class system developed that was dominated by pure-blooded Spaniards.

English Policy

Initially, at least in Massachusetts, the English and the Native Americans coexisted, traded, and shared ideas. The Native Americans taught the settlers how to grow new crops such as corn and showed them how to hunt in the forests. They traded various furs for an array of English manufactured goods, including iron tools and weapons. But peaceful relations soon gave way to conflict and open warfare. The English had no respect for Native American cultures, which they viewed as primitive or "savage." For their part, the Native Americans saw their way of life threatened as the English began to take more land to support their ever-increasing population.

French Policy

Unlike the Spaniards and the English, the French maintained relatively good relations with the Native American tribes who occupied the St. Lawrence Valley and the Great Lakes region. Seeking to control the fur trade, French soldiers assisted the Huron people in fighting their traditional enemy, the Iroquois. French traders built trading posts along the St. Lawrence River, the Great Lakes, and the Mississippi River, where they exchanged French goods for Indian furs. Because the French had few colonists, farms, or towns, they posed little threat to the native population.

HISTORICAL PERSPECTIVES: COLUMBUS

Over the centuries, Columbus has received both praise for his role as a "discoverer" and blame for his actions as a "conqueror." In the United States, he has traditionally been viewed as a hero. As early as 1828, Washington Irving wrote a popular biography extolling the explorer's virtues. The apex of Columbus' heroic reputation was reached in 1934 when President Franklin Roosevelt declared October 12 a national holiday.

In recent years, however, revisionist histories and biographies have been highly critical of Columbus, especially those written on the occasion of the 1992 quincentennial of Columbus' first voyage. His detractors argue that Columbus was simply at the right place at the right time. Europe at the end of the 15th century was ready to expand. If Columbus had not crossed the Atlantic in 1492, some other explorer—perhaps Vespucci or Cabot—would have done so a few years later. According to this interpretation, Columbus was little more than a good navigator and a self-promoter, who exploited an opportunity.

Some revisionists take a harsh view of Columbus and regard him not as the first discoverer of America but rather as its first conqueror. They portray him as a religious fanatic in the European

Christian tradition who sought to convert the Native Americans to Christianity and liquidated those who resisted.

The revisionist argument has not gone unanswered. The historian Arthur M. Schlesinger, Jr., for example, has argued that the chief motivation for Columbus' deeds was neither greed for gold nor ambition for conquest. What drove him, in Schlesinger's view, was the challenge of the unknown. Columbus' apologists admit that thousands of Native Americans died as a result of European exploration in the Americas, but they point out that thousands had also suffered horrible deaths from Aztec sacrifices. Moreover, the mistreatment of Native Americans was perhaps partially offset by such positive developments as the gradual development of democratic institutions in the colonies and later the United States.

The debate about the nature of Columbus' achievement is unresolved. As with other historical questions, it is sometimes difficult to distinguish between fact and fiction and to separate a writer's personal biases from objective reality. One conclusion is inescapable: As a result of Columbus' voyages, world history took a sharp turn in a new direction. His explorations established a permanent point of contact between Europe and the Americas, and we are still living with the consequences of that fact.

KEY NAMES, EVENTS, AND TERMS

Native Americans; land bridge

Sioux; Pawnee; Pueblo; Adena; Hopewell; Mississippian; Iroquois

Mayas; Incas; Aztecs

Renaissance

technology; compass; printing press

Spain; Moors

Ferdinand and Isabella

Protestant Reformation

trade

Portugal

Henry the Navigator

nation-states

Christopher Columbus

New World

Amerigo Vespucci

papal line of demarcation

Treaty of Tordesillas (1494)

Vasco Núñez de Balboa

Ferdinand Magellan

Hernan Cortés

Francisco Pizarro

conquistadores

encomienda system

asiento system

John Cabot

Giovanni de Verrazano

Jacques Cartier

Samuel de Champlain

Father Jacques Marquette

Robert de la Salle

Henry Hudson

joint-stock company

Father Junípero Serra

Virginia Company; Jamestown

Captain John Smith

John Rolfe; Pocahontas

royal colony

Puritans

Plymouth colony

Separatists

Pilgrims

Mayflower; Mayflower Compact

Massachusetts Bay Colony

John Winthrop

Great Migration

Virginia House of Burgesses

MULTIPLE-CHOICE QUESTIONS

1. "In the 1500s, Native Americans possessed a wide range of complex cultures." Each of the following gives evidence to support this statement EXCEPT
   (A) the Aztec capital of Tenochtitlán
   (B) the organization of Inca society
   (C) Native Americans' susceptibility to European diseases
   (D) the Mayas' agricultural system
   (E) the Maya calendar

2. Which of the following best describes the way Europeans treated Native Americans in the 1500s and 1600s?
   (A) Native Americans were regarded as inferior people subject to Christian domination.
   (B) Native American ways of life were respected.
   (C) Since nothing of value could be learned or obtained from the Native Americans, Europeans thought it was permissible to exterminate them.
   (D) Europeans cultivated good relations with Native Americans and sought to make them economic partners.
   (E) Only the English believed that Native Americans should be treated fairly.

3. Which of the following was the LEAST important factor behind European exploration and settlement in the 16th century?

   (A) increase in scientific knowledge and technological change
   (B) population increase
   (C) development of nation-states
   (D) competition for trade
   (E) religious commitment

4. By the end of the 16th century, all of the following were generally true about Spain's colonial empire EXCEPT
   (A) It was controlled by a bureaucracy in Madrid.
   (B) The Roman Catholic Church had great influence.
   (C) New universities were spreading education and culture.
   (D) Families continued to emigrate from Spain.
   (E) Great wealth was being sent back to Spain.

5. The delay in founding English settlements in the Americas was the result of
   (A) weak English monarchs
   (B) the lack of English territorial claims in the Americas
   (C) failure to develop trade with other nations
   (D) fear of Spain
   (E) religious upheavals in England

6. At the beginning of the 17th century, all of the following factors served to increase the English role in America EXCEPT
   (A) defeat of the Spanish Armada
   (B) population growth

(C) royal leadership

(D) development of joint-stock companies

(E) emigration for religious reasons

7. The survival of the Jamestown colony can be most directly attributed to the

(A) religious spirit of the settlers

(B) management of the Virginia Company

(C) development of a tobacco industry

(D) location of the settlement

(E) nobles' diligent search for gold

8. Which of the following sources would be most useful in studying the development of democratic institutions in the early colonial period?

(A) the Edict of Nantes

(B) the first charter of the Virginia Company

(C) Columbus' journals

(D) the Treaty of Tordesillas

(E) the Mayflower Compact

9. Which of the following statements is the most widely accepted description of Columbus' accomplishments?

(A) He discovered a New World.

(B) He bears much of the blame for oppressing Native American peoples in North America.

(C) He started a permanent relationship between Europe and the Americas.

(D) He is responsible for most of the problems in the Americas during the colonial period.

(E) His heroic deeds will always be respected by fair-minded American citizens.

10. The issue of religion figured most prominently in the consideration of which of the following?

(A) the settlement of Jamestown

(B) the establishment of Puritan colonies in Massachusetts

(C) France's Indian policy

(D) discoveries by the Spanish conquistadores

(E) Spain's support of Columbus' voyages

Guide to Writing an Essay

Stating Your Thesis

Teachers who will be grading the standard essay section of the AP U.S. History test are chiefly evaluating two aspects of a student's paper:

1. How clearly does the writer present a thesis (or organizing idea) in the essay's introductory paragraph?
2. How well does the writer support his or her thesis with relevant evidence from a historical period?

Writing an essay without a thesis statement would be like attempting to build a house without first laying the foundation. Thus, practicing the skill of writing the thesis statement is absolutely essential not only to doing well on an AP exam but also to writing a clear and convincing paper on *any* topic in *any* subject.

Let us look at three attempts to answer the first essay question in Chapter 1, on page 18 ("With the dawn of the 16th century . . ."). In your view, which of these introductory paragraphs contains the strongest thesis statement?

A. By the beginning of the 16th century, Columbus had already explored parts of Central and South America. Immediately following his four voyages, other explorers for Spain were strongly motivated to seek gold and glory in the New World. Explorers and conquistadores such as Cortés in Mexico, Balboa in Panama, and Pizarro in Peru were quick to establish Spanish claims to large parts of the Americas. An important reason for their being able to do this was the improved design of Spanish ships and such inventions as the compass and the astrolabe.

B. In the 16th century, Spain's success in conquering and colonizing American lands was based upon fundamental changes that had already occurred in the culture, economy, and technology of Europe in the preceding century. In religious terms, Spain in the late 1490s had unified itself as a Roman Catholic state by defeating the Moors (or Moslems). In economic terms, the desire for increased trade with Asia provided powerful motivation for voyages of exploration. In technological terms, improvements in navigation in the 1400s

16

made it possible for European ship captains to make the long transatlantic crossing in both directions.

C. Columbus' first voyage of discovery in 1492 was followed by other voyages by Spanish, Portuguese, and Italian navigators. Of course, Spanish explorers like Cortés, Pizarro, Coronado, de Soto, and others were the most successful in establishing claims to American land. Motivated by "God, gold, and glory," Cortés conquered the Aztecs of Mexico while Pizarro conquered the Incas of Peru. Cabral's voyage for Portugal helped to establish that nation-state's claim to Brazil. Henry Cabot's 1497 voyage for England was motivated by the desire to find a northwest passage to Asia. Cabot's voyage, however, did not really have important consequences until more than a 100 years later when England under Queen Elizabeth tried unsuccessfully to found colonies in North America.

Of course, there is more to an essay than the first paragraph. But if the AP graders had only these introductions to evaluate, then they would probably rank their effectiveness in the following order: (1) B; (2) A; (3) C.

Why is paragraph B the strongest of the three? Notice that it is the only paragraph that takes account of all aspects of the question. It mentions trade as a motivating force, technology as a means, and religious change as another factor in explaining Spain's success in the early 16th century. Thus, a foundation is laid for more detailed paragraphs that are sure to follow: one on religious change, a second on economic change, and a third on technological change. The writer has made sure that the sentences in the first paragraph address *everything that the question asks:* motivation, means, religion, trade, and technology.

Paragraphs A and C, on the other hand, fall short of the mark because they are not focused on a main idea. Notice that both consist of specific facts that are only loosely related to the question. Paragraph A ranks higher than C because it addresses *both* motivation *and* means, whereas C deals with motivation only. Also C's information about Cabot in the last sentence, while accurate, strays from the subject of the question. Avoid the temptation to overload your first paragraph with information. Concentrate instead on stating a general thesis, making sure that it ties directly to key phrases in question.

Practice

Learning to write a sharply focused opening paragraph with a thesis statement is not easy; but with practice, you too can create an impressive, high-scoring essay. Begin now by writing just the *first paragraph* and thesis statement for an essay chosen from questions 2–5 in Chapter 1 (below). Ask a partner to critique your first draft. Then revise it by (*a*) eliminating details that distract from your main idea and (*b*) adding phrases that connect to all parts of the question.

ESSAY QUESTIONS

1. "With the dawn of the 16th century, there came together in Europe both the motivation and the means to explore and colonize territory across the seas." Discuss this statement with reference to TWO of the following:
   religion
   trade
   technology

2. In what ways did the English colonies develop differently from the Spanish and the French colonies?

3. Assess the democratic characteristics in the English colonies in the context of TWO of the following:
   Massachusetts
   Plymouth
   Virginia

4. Analyze the extent to which early European colonists viewed the Native Americans as inferior people who could be exploited for the colonists' benefit.

5. Compare and contrast the English relationship and the French relationship with the Native Americans.

DOCUMENTS AND READINGS

How did Europeans view the people they encountered in the Americas? To what extent, if at all, were Spanish explorers and settlers able to understand the empathize with the culture of the Native Americans?

Probably the best way to gain insight into such questions is to read excerpts from the writings of Columbus and other explorers and conquistadores of the 15th and 16th centuries. Excerpts from three such primary sources are presented in Documents A, B, and C, below. The fourth reading, D, comes from a secondary source (a history written long after the events it describes). It is a modern historian's view of how Columbus reflected the European culture of his times. As you will see, this historian views past events with a strong bias *against* the European "conquest" and "genocide." Is the historian's interpretation supported by evidence in the primary source documents? Draw your own conclusion after completing your reading of all four sources.

DOCUMENT A. COLUMBUS' LOG

Upon his return to Spain in 1493, Columbus presented to Queen Isabella his captain's log—the daily account of what he had observed on his voyage. The following excerpts from that document describe his impressions of the Native Americans and also reveal his attitude toward them.

Friday, 12 October 1492:
I want the natives to develop a friendly attitude toward us because I know that they are a people who can be made free and converted to our Holy Faith more by love than by force. I therefore gave red caps to some and glass beads to others. They hung the beads around their necks, along with some other things of slight value that I gave them. And they took great pleasure in this and became so friendly that it was a marvel. They traded and gave everything they had with good will, but it seems to me that they have very little and are poor in everything. I warned my men to take nothing from the people without giving something in exchange.

Saturday, 13 October 1492:
I cannot get over the fact of how docile these people are. They have so little to give but will give it all for whatever we give them, if only broken pieces of glass and crockery. One seaman gave three Portuguese *ceitis* (not even worth a penny!) for about 25 pounds of spun cotton. I probably should have forbidden this exchange, but I wanted to take the cotton to Your Highnesses, and it seems to be in abundance. I think the cotton is grown on San Salvador, but I cannot say for sure because I have not been here that long. Also, the gold they wear hanging from their noses comes from here, but in order not to lose time I want to go to see if I can find the island of Japan.

Monday, 24 December 1492:
Your Highnesses may believe that in all the world there cannot be better or more gentle people. Your Highnesses must be greatly pleased because you will soon make them Christians and will teach them the good customs of your realms, for there cannot be a better people or country. The people are so numerous and the country so great that I do not yet know how to describe it.

Log of Christopher Columbus

DOCUMENT B. A SPANISH MISSIONARY IN HISPANIOLA

Bartolomé de Las Casas (1474–1566) was a Spanish priest and missionary who traveled to the island of Hispaniola in 1502 to convert the Native Americans there to Christianity. Las Casas found that the native people on the island were badly mistreated by Spanish officials and landowners. He did what he could to alleviate the Indians' sufferings and to stop the worst of the abuses. After living more than 40 years in the Americas, Las Casas returned to Spain, where he continued his campaign to prevent further mistreatment and enslavement of the Native Americans. In 1552, he wrote *In Defense of the Indian,* from which the following excerpts are taken.

Concerning the methods of Spanish soldiers after an attack:
Once the Indians were in the woods, the next step was to form squadrons and pursue them, and whenever the Spaniards found them, they pitilessly slaughtered everyone like sheep in a corral. It was a general rule among Spaniards to be cruel; not just cruel, but extraordinarily cruel so that harsh and bitter treatment would prevent Indians from daring to think of themselves as human beings or having a minute to think at all. So they would cut an Indian's hands and leave them dangling by a shred of skin and they would send him on saying "Go now, spread the news to your chiefs." They would test their swords and their manly strength on captured Indians and place bets on the slicing off of heads or the cutting of bodies in half with one blow. They burned or hanged captured chiefs.

Concerning the treatment of Native American workers:
When they were allowed to go home, they often found it deserted and had no other recourse than to go out into the woods to find food and to die. When they fell ill, which was very frequently because they are a delicate people unaccustomed to such work, the Spaniards did not believe them and pitilessly called them lazy dogs, and kicked and beat them; and when illness was apparent they sent them home as useless, giving them some cassava for the twenty- to eighty-league journey. They would go then, falling into the first stream and dying there in desperation; others would hold on longer, but very few ever made it home. I sometimes came upon dead bodies on my way, and upon others who were gasping and moaning in their death agony, repeating "Hungry, hungry."

Bartolomé de Las Casas,
In Defense of the Indian

DOCUMENT C.   CORONADO'S REPORT

Francisco Coronado (c. 1510–1554) was a Spanish soldier and commander who, in 1540, led an expedition north from Mexico into what is today Arizona, New Mexico, and Colorado. Seeking the legendary seven cities of gold, he was disappointed to find only adobe pueblos. The following is from Coronado's account of his travels in Quivira (northern New Mexico).

> The province of Quivira is 950 leagues from Mexico. Where I reached it, it is in the fortieth degree [of latitude]. . . . I have treated the natives of this province, and all the others whom I found wherever I went, as well as was possible, agreeably to what Your Majesty had commanded, and they have received no harm in any way from me or from those who went in my company. I remained twenty-five days in this province of Quivira, so as to see and explore the country and also to find out whether there was anything beyond which could be of service to Your Majesty, because the guides who had brought me had given me an account of other provinces beyond this. And what I am sure of is that there is not any gold nor any other metal in all that country, and the other things of which they had told me are nothing but little villages, and in many of these they do not plant anything and do not have any houses except of skins and sticks, and they wander around with the cows; so that the account they gave me was false, because they wanted to persuade me to go there with the whole force, believing that as the way was through such uninhabited deserts, and from the lack of water, they would get us where we and our horses would die of hunger. And the guides confessed this, and said they had done it by the advice and orders of the natives of these provinces.

> Francesco Coronado,
> *Travels in Quivira*

DOCUMENT D. *ONE HISTORIAN'S VIEW OF COLUMBUS*

In a controversial book, the historian David E. Stannard argues that Columbus and those explorers and settlers who came after him were responsible for the most destructive campaign of genocide in world history. (Genocide means the deliberate destruction of a group of people.) His history traces the violent treatment and even extermination of Indian peoples from 1492 into the 1890s. The following is Stannard's interpretation of Columbus.

> Apart from his navigational skills, what most set Columbus apart from other Europeans of his day were not the things that he believed, but the intensity with which he believed in them and the determination with which he acted upon those beliefs. . . .
> Columbus was, in most respects, merely an especially active and dramatic embodiment of the European—and especially the Mediterranean—mind and soul of his time: a religious fanatic obsessed

with the conversion, conquest, or liquidation of all non-Christians; a latter-day Crusader in search of personal wealth and fame, who expected the enormous and mysterious world he had found to be filled with monstrous races inhabiting wild forests, and with golden people living in Eden. He was also a man with sufficient intolerance and contempt for all who did not look or behave or believe as he did, that he thought nothing of enslaving or killing such people simply because they were not like him. He was, to repeat, a secular personification of what more than a thousand years of Christian culture had wrought. As such, the fact that he launched a campaign of horrific violence against the natives of Hispaniola is not something that should surprise anyone. Indeed, it would be surprising if he had *not* inaugurated such carnage.

David E. Stannard,
American Holocaust: Columbus and the Conquest of the New World (1992)

ANALYZING THE DOCUMENTS

David E. Stannard called Columbus "a religious fanatic obsessed with the conversion, conquest, or liquidation of all non-Christians."

1. To what extent is Stannard's view either supported or contradicted by Columbus' own words in reading A?

2. Which of the primary source documents do you think gives the strongest support for Stannard's thesis? Why?

3. Which of the primary source documents do you think offers the weakest support—or no support—for Stannard's thesis? Why?

THE THIRTEEN COLONIES AND THE BRITISH EMPIRE, 1607–1750

If they desire that Piety and godliness should prosper; accompanied with sobriety, justice and love, let them choose a Country such as this is; even like France, or England, which may yield sufficiency with hard labour and industry. . . .

Reverend John White, *The Planter's Plea,* 1630

Between the founding of Jamestown (Virginia) in 1607 and the founding of Georgia in 1733, a total of 13 distinctly different English colonies developed along the Atlantic Coast of North America. Every colony received its identity and its authority to operate by means of a *charter* (a document granting special privileges) from the English monarch. Each charter described in general terms the relationship that was supposed to exist between the colony and the crown. Over time, three types of charters—and three types of colonies—developed:

- Corporate colonies, such as Jamestown, were operated by joint-stock companies, at least during these colonies' early years.
- Royal colonies, such as Virginia after 1624, were to be under the direct authority and rule of the king's government.
- Proprietary colonies, such as Maryland and Pennsylvania, were under the authority of individuals granted charters of ownership by the king.

Unlike those who settled the French and Spanish colonies in the Americas, the English colonists brought with them a tradition of independence and representative government. They were accustomed, in other words, to holding elections for representatives who would speak for property owners and either approve or disapprove important measures, such as taxes, proposed by the king's government. While political and religious conflicts and civil war dominated England, feelings for independence grew in the colonies. Eventually, tensions developed between the king's purposes and those of his colonial subjects. This chapter summarizes the history of the English colonies as their separate political, economic, and social systems slowly took shape.

The Chesapeake Colonies

In 1632, King Charles I subdivided the vast area that had been the Virginia colony. He chartered a new colony located on either side of Chesapeake Bay and granted control of it to George Calvert (Lord Baltimore), as a reward for this Catholic nobleman's loyal service to the crown. The new colony of Maryland thus became the first of several proprietary colonies.

Maryland

The king decided to establish proprietorships rather than granting more colonial charters to joint-stock companies because he believed the new arrangement would give him almost total control. It was hoped that a loyal proprietor like Lord Baltimore could be trusted to faithfully carry out the king's policies and wishes.

The first Lord Baltimore died before he could fulfill his twin ambitions of achieving great wealth in his colony while also providing a haven for his fellow Catholics. Control of the Maryland proprietorship passed in 1632 to his son, Cecil Calvert—the second Lord Baltimore—who set about implementing his father's plan in 1634.

Act of Toleration. To avoid the intolerance and persecution of their Puritan enemies, a number of wealthy English Catholics emigrated to Maryland and established large colonial plantations. They were quickly outnumbered, however, by Protestant farmers. Protestants therefore held a majority in Maryland's representative assembly. In 1649, Calvert persuaded the assembly to adopt the Act of Toleration, the first colonial statute granting religious freedom to all Christians. However, the statute also called for the death of anyone who denied the divinity of Jesus.

Protestant revolt. In the late 1600s, Protestant resentment against a Catholic proprietor erupted into a brief civil war. The Protestants triumphed, and the Act of Toleration was repealed. Catholics lost their right to vote in elections for the Maryland assembly. In the 18th century, Maryland's economy and society was much like that of neighboring Virginia, except that in Maryland there was greater tolerance of religious diversity among different Protestant sects.

Virginia

Meanwhile, the first of England's colonies, Virginia, struggled with a number of problems in the late 17th century, including a rebellion against the colonial government.

Economic problems. Beginning in the 1660s, low tobacco prices, due largely to overproduction, brought hard times to the Chesapeake colonies, Maryland and Virginia. When Virginia's House of Burgesses attempted to raise tobacco prices, the merchants of London retaliated by raising their own prices on goods exported to Virginia.

Political problems and Bacon's Rebellion. Sir William Berkeley, the royal governor of Virginia (1641–1652; 1660–1677), adopted policies that favored the large planters and used dictatorial powers to govern on their behalf. He antagonized backwoods farmers on Virginia's western frontier because he failed to protect their settlements from Indian attacks.

Nathaniel Bacon, an impoverished gentleman farmer newly arrived from England, seized upon the grievances of the western farmers to lead a rebellion against Berkeley's government. Bacon and others resented the economic and political control exercised by a few large planters in the Chesapeake area. He raised an army of volunteers and, in 1676, conducted a series of raids and massacres against Indian villages on the Virginia frontier. Berkeley's government in Jamestown accused Bacon of rebelling against royal authority. Bacon's army succeeded in defeating the governor's forces and even burned the Jamestown settlement. Soon afterward, however, Bacon died of dysentery and the rebel army collapsed. Governor Berkeley brutally suppressed the remnants of the insurrection.

Lasting problems. Although it was short-lived, Bacon's Rebellion, or the Chesapeake Revolution, highlighted two long-lasting disputes in colonial Virginia: (1) sharp class differences between wealthy planters and landless or poor farmers and (2) colonial resistance to royal control. These problems would continue into the next century, even after the general conditions of life in the Chesapeake colonies became more stable and prosperous.

Labor Shortages

The Chesapeake colonies grew slowly. Retarding their growth in the early decades were an unhealthy climate and a high death rate due both to disease and Indian attacks. Another factor slowing the development of families was an imbalance between the number of men and women. Most of the early settlers were men brought from England and Scotland to work in the tobacco fields.

The tobacco industry required extensive labor which initially was not available. To solve the labor shortage, various methods were attempted. Chief among them were indentured servitude, the headright system, and slavery.

Indentured servants. Under contract with a master or landowner who paid for their passage, young people from the British Isles agreed to work for a specified period—usually between four to seven years—in return for room and board. In effect, indentured servants were under the absolute rule of their masters until the end of their work period. At the expiration of that period, they gained their freedom and either worked for wages or obtained land of their own to farm.

Headright system. As another method for attracting immigrants, Virginia offered 50 acres of land to (1) each immigrant who paid for his own passage and (2) any plantation owner who paid for an immigrant's passage.

Slavery. The first Africans to come to Virginia arrived in 1619 aboard a slave ship operated by a Dutch trader. At first, Africans were not held as slaves for life but had roughly the same status as white indentured servants. Moreover, the early colonists were struggling to survive and too poor to purchase the Africans who were being imported to provide slave labor for sugar plantations in the West Indies. By 1650, there were only about 400 African laborers in Virginia, and not all of them were held in permanent bondage. In the 1660s, however, the Virginia House of Burgesses enacted laws that discriminated between blacks and whites. Africans and their offspring were to be treated as lifelong slaves, whereas white laborers were to be set free after a certain period.

Development of New England

Strong religious convictions helped sustain the Puritans in their struggle to establish the Plymouth and Massachusetts Bay colonies. At the same time, Puritan leaders tended to be intolerant of anyone who questioned their religious teachings. A common method for dealing with dissidents was to banish them from the Bay colony. These dissidents formed the nucleus for the founding of

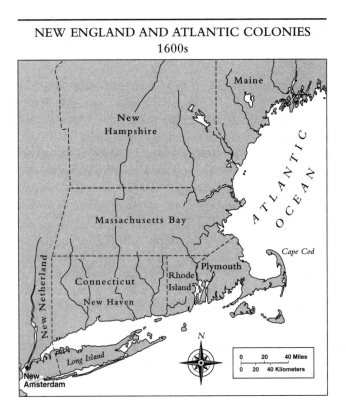

NEW ENGLAND AND ATLANTIC COLONIES
1600s

several colonies in New England, which would ultimately develop into Rhode Island and Connecticut.

Rhode Island. Roger Williams went to Boston in 1631 as a respected Puritan minister. He believed, however, that the individual's conscience was beyond the control of any civil or church authority. His teachings on this point placed him in conflict with other Puritan leaders, who ordered his banishment from the Bay colony. Leaving Boston, Williams fled southward to Narragansett Bay, where he and a few followers founded the settlement of Providence in 1636. The new colony was unique in two respects. First, it recognized the rights of the Native Americans and paid them for the use of their land. Second, Williams' government provided for complete religious toleration by allowing Catholics, Quakers, and Jews to worship freely. (In addition to founding Providence and later Rhode Island, Williams also founded one of the first Baptist churches in America.)

Another dissident who questioned the doctrines of the Puritan authorities was Anne Hutchinson. She believed in *antinomianism*—the idea that faith alone, not deeds, is necessary for salvation. Banished from the Bay colony, Hutchinson and a group of followers founded the colony of Portsmouth in 1638, not far from Williams' colony of Providence. A few years later, Hutchinson migrated to Long Island and was killed in an Indian uprising.

In 1644, Roger Williams was granted a charter from the English Parliament, which joined Providence and Portsmouth into a single colony, Rhode Island. Because this colony offered religious freedom for all, it served as a refuge for people of various faiths.

Connecticut. To the west of Rhode Island, the fertile Connecticut River Valley attracted other settlers who were unhappy with the Massachusetts authorities. The Reverend Thomas Hooker led a large group of Boston Puritans into the valley and founded the colony of Hartford in 1636. The Hartford settlers then drew up the first written constitution in American history, the *Fundamental Orders of Connecticut* (1639). It established a representative government consisting of a legislature elected by popular vote and a governor chosen by that legislature. South of Hartford, a second settlement in the Connecticut Valley was started by John Davenport in 1637 and given the name New Haven.

In 1665, New Haven joined with the more democratic Hartford settlers to form the colony of Connecticut. The royal charter for Connecticut granted it a limited degree of self-government, including election of the governor.

New Hampshire. The last colony to be founded in New England was New Hampshire. Originally part of Massachusetts Bay, it consisted of a few settlements north of Boston. Hoping to increase royal control over the colonies, King Charles II separated New Hampshire from the Bay colony in 1679 and made it a royal colony, subject to the authority of an appointed governor.

Halfway Covenant. In the 1660s, a generation had passed since the founding of the first Puritan colonies in New England. The new native-born generation showed signs of being less committed to religious faith and more interested in material success. How was the Puritan church to remain strong if younger people failed to become members? In an effort to maintain the church's influence and membership, a *halfway covenant* was offered by some clergymen to those who professed limited religious commitment. In other words, people could now take part in church services and activities without making a formal declaration of their total belief in Christ.

Other ministers rejected the halfway covenant and denounced it from the pulpit. Nevertheless, as the years passed, strict Puritan practices were weakened in most New England communities in order to maintain church membership.

New England Confederation. In the 1640s, the various New England colonies were constantly faced with the threat of attack from the Native Americans, the Dutch, and the French. Because of the civil war then being fought in England, the colonists could expect little assistance. Therefore in 1643, four New England colonies (Plymouth, Massachusetts Bay, Connecticut, and New Haven) formed a military alliance known as the New England Confederation. The confederation was directed by a board comprised of two representatives from each colony. It had limited powers to act on boundary disputes, the return of runaway servants, and dealings with the Native Americans.

The confederation lasted until 1684, when colonial rivalries and renewed control by the English monarch brought this first experiment in colonial cooperation to an end. It was important because it established a precedent for colonies taking unified action toward a common purpose.

King Philip's War. Only a few years before its demise, the confederation helped the New England colonists cope successfully with a dire threat. A chief of the Wampanoags named Metacom—known to the colonists as King Philip—united many tribes in southern New England against the English settlers, who were constantly encroaching on the Native Americans' lands. In a vicious war (1675–1676), thousands on both sides were killed, and dozens of towns and villages were burned. Eventually, the colonial forces managed to prevail, killing King Philip and virtually ending Native American resistance in New England.

Restoration Colonies

New American colonies were founded in the late 17th century during a period in English history known as the *Restoration.* (The name refers to the restoration to power of an English monarch, Charles II, in 1660 following a brief period of Puritan rule under Oliver Cromwell.)

The Carolinas

As a reward for helping him gain the throne, Charles II granted a huge tract of land between Virginia and Spanish Florida to eight nobles, who in 1663 became the lord proprietors of the Carolinas. Eventually, in 1729, two royal colonies, South Carolina and North Carolina, were formed from the original proprietorship.

South Carolina. In 1670, in the southern Carolinas, a few colonists from England and some planters from the island of Barbados founded a town named for their king. Initially, the southern economy was based on trading furs and providing food for the West Indies. By the middle of the 18th century, South Carolina's large rice-growing plantations worked by African slaves resembled the economy and culture of the West Indies.

North Carolina. The northern part of the Carolinas developed differently. There, farmers from Virginia and New England established small, self-sufficient tobacco farms. The region had few good harbors and poor transportation; therefore, compared to South Carolina, there were fewer large plantations and less reliance on slavery. North Carolina in the 18th century earned a reputation for democratic views and autonomy from British control.

New York

Charles II wished to consolidate the crown's holdings along the Atlantic Coast and close the gap between the New England and the Chesapeake colonies. This required compelling the Dutch to give up their colony of New Amsterdam centered on Manhattan Island and the Hudson River Valley.

In 1664, the king granted his brother, the Duke of York (the future James II), the lands lying between Connecticut and Delaware Bay. As the lord high admiral of the navy, James dispatched a force that easily took control of the Dutch colony from its governor, Peter Stuyvesant. James ordered his agents in the renamed colony of New York to treat the Dutch settlers well and to allow them freedom to worship as they pleased and speak their own language.

James also ordered new taxes, duties, and rents without seeking the consent of a representative assembly. In fact, he insisted that no assembly should be allowed to form in his colony. But taxation without representation met strong opposition from New York's English-speaking settlers, most of whom were Puritans from New England. Finally, in 1683, James yielded by allowing New York's governor to grant broad civil and political rights, including a representative assembly.

New Jersey

Believing that the territory of New York was too large to administer, James in 1664 gave to two friends, Lord John Berkeley and Sir George Carteret, that section of the colony located between the Hudson River and Delaware Bay. In 1674, one proprietor received West New Jersey and the other East New Jersey. To attract settlers, both proprietors made generous land offers and allowed religious freedom and an assembly. Eventually, they sold their proprietary interests to various groups of Quakers. Land titles in the Jerseys changed hands repeatedly, and inaccurate property lines added to the general confusion. To settle matters, the crown decided in 1702 to combine the two Jerseys into a single royal colony: New Jersey.

Pennsylvania and Delaware

To the west of New Jersey lay a broad expanse of forested land that was originally settled by a peace-loving Christian sect, the Quakers.

Quakers. Members of the Religious Society of Friends—popularly known as Quakers—believed in the equality of all men and women, nonviolence, and resistance to military service. They further believed that religious authority was found within each person's private soul and not in the Bible or any outside source. In the 17th century, such views seemed to pose a radical challenge to established authority. Therefore, the Quakers of England were widely persecuted and jailed for their beliefs.

William Penn. William Penn was a young convert to the Quaker faith. His father had been a victorious admiral in the service of the king. Although the elder Penn opposed his son's religious beliefs, he respected his sincerity and upon his death he left his son considerable wealth. In addition, the royal family owed the father a large debt, which was paid to William Penn in 1681 in the form of a grant of land in the Americas for a colony which he called Pennsylvania, or Penn's woods.

"The Holy Experiment." Penn wanted to test ideas he had developed based on his Quaker beliefs. He wanted his new colony to achieve three purposes: provide a religious refuge for Quakers and other persecuted people, enact liberal ideas in government, and generate income and profits for himself. He provided the colony with a Frame of Government (1682–1683), which guaranteed a representative assembly elected by landowners, and a written constitution, the Charter of Liberties (1701), which guaranteed freedom of worship for all and unrestricted immigration.

Unlike other colonial proprietors, who governed from afar in England, Penn crossed the ocean to supervise the founding of a new town on the Delaware River named Philadelphia. He brought with him a plan for a grid pattern of streets, which was later imitated by other American cities. Also unusual was Penn's attempt to treat the Native Americans fairly and not to cheat them when purchasing their land.

To attract settlers to his new land, Penn hired agents and published notices throughout Europe, which promised political and religious freedom and generous land terms. Penn's lands along the Delaware River had previously been settled by several thousand Dutch and Swedish colonists, who eased the arrival of the newcomers attracted by Penn's promotion.

Delaware. In 1702, Penn granted the lower three counties of Pennsylvania their own assembly. In effect, this act created Delaware as a separate colony, even though its governor was the same as Pennsylvania's until the American Revolution.

Georgia: The Last Colony

In 1732, a thirteenth colony, Georgia, was chartered. It was both the last of the British colonies and also the only one to receive direct financial support from the home government in London. There were two principal reasons for British interest in starting a new southern colony. First, Britain wanted to create a defensive buffer to protect the prosperous South Carolina plantations from the threat of invasion from Spanish Florida. Second, thousands of people in London and other cities were being imprisoned for debt. Wealthy philanthropists thought it would relieve the overcrowded jails and prison ships if debtors could be shipped to an American colony to start life over.

THE THIRTEEN ENGLISH COLONIES
AROUND 1750

Special regulations. Given a royal charter for a proprietary colony, a group of philanthropists led by James Oglethorpe founded Georgia's first settlement, Savannah, in 1733. Oglethorpe acted as the colony's first governor and put into effect an elaborate plan for making the colony thrive. There were strict regulations, including an absolute ban on drinking rum and the prohibition of slavery. Nevertheless, partly because of the constant threat of Spanish attack, the colony did not prosper.

Royal colony. By 1752, Oglethorpe and his group gave up their plan. Taken over by the British government, Georgia became a royal colony. Restrictions on rum and slavery were dropped. The colony grew slowly by adopting the plantation system of South Carolina. Even so, at the time of the American Revolution, Georgia was still the smallest and poorest of the 13 colonies.

Mercantilism and the Empire

Most European kingdoms in the 17th century adopted the economic policy of *mercantilism,* which looked upon trade, colonies, and the accumulation of wealth as the basis for a country's military and political strength. According to mercantilist doctrine, a government should regulate trade and production to enable it to become self-sufficient. Colonies were to provide raw materials to the parent country for the growth and profit of that country's industries. Colonies existed for one purpose only: to enrich the parent country.

Mercantilist policies had guided both the Spanish and the French colonies from their inception. Mercantilism began to be applied to the English colonies, however, only after the turmoil of England's civil war had subsided.

Acts of Trade and Navigation. England's government implemented a mercantilist policy with a series of Navigation Acts (1650 to 1673), which established three rules for colonial trade:

1. Trade to and from the colonies could be carried only by English or colonial-built ships, which could be operated only by English or colonial crews.
2. All goods imported into the colonies, except for some perishables, could pass only through ports in England.
3. Specified or "enumerated" goods from the colonies could be exported to England only. Tobacco was the original "enumerated" good, but over a period of years, the list was expanded to include most colonial products.

Impact on the colonies. The Navigation Acts had both positive and negative effects on the colonies.

Positive effects. (1) New England shipbuilding prospered. (2) Chesapeake tobacco had a monopoly in England. (3) English military forces protected the colonies from potential attacks by the French and Spanish.

Negative effects. (1) Colonial manufacturing was severely limited. (2) Chesapeake farmers received low prices for their crops. (3) Colonists had to pay high prices for manufactured goods from England.

In many respects, mercantilist regulations were unnecessary, since England would have been the colonies' primary trading partner in any case. Furthermore, whatever economic advantages were obtained from the Navigation Acts were more than offset by their negative political effects on British–colonial relations. Resentment slowly developed in the colonies against regulatory laws imposed by the distant government in London. Especially in New England, colonists would routinely defy the Navigation Acts by smuggling in French, Dutch, and other prohibited goods.

Enforcement of the acts. The British government was often lax in enforcing the acts, and its agents in the colonies were known for their corruption. Occasionally, however, the crown would attempt to overcome colonial resistance to its trade laws. In 1684, it revoked the charter of Massachusetts Bay because that colony had been the center of smuggling activity.

Brief experiment: the Dominion of New England. A new king, James II, succeeded to the throne in 1685. He was determined to increase royal control over the colonies by combining them into larger administrative units and doing away with their representative assemblies. In 1686, he combined New York, New Jersey, and the various New England colonies into a single unit called the Dominion of New England. Sir Edmund Andros was sent from England to serve as governor of the dominion. The new governor made himself instantly unpopular by levying taxes, limiting town meetings, and revoking land titles.

James II did not remain in power for long. His high-handed attempts at asserting his royal powers led to an uprising against him. The Glorious Revolution of 1688 succeeded in deposing James and replacing him with two new sovereigns, William and Mary. James' fall from power brought the Dominion of New England to an end. Massachusetts Bay, New York, and the other colonies again operated under separate charters.

Permanent restrictions. Despite the Glorious Revolution, mercantilist policies remained in force. In the 18th century, there were more English officials in the colonies than in any earlier era. Restrictions on colonial trade, though poorly enforced, were widely resented and resisted.

The Institution of Slavery

Of far greater importance than mercantilism was a colonial institution that became rooted in American society in the closing decades of the 17th century. That was the institution of slavery. The number of slaves grew rapidly, from only a few thousand in 1670 to tens of thousands in the early 18th century. By 1750, half of Virginia's population and two thirds of South Carolina's population were slaves.

Increased demand for slaves. The following factors explain why slavery became increasingly important, especially in the southern colonies:

1. *Reduced migration:* Increases in wages in England reduced the supply of immigrants to the colonies.
2. *Dependable work force:* Large-plantation owners were disturbed by the political demands of small farmers and indentured servants and by the disorders of Bacon's Rebellion (see page 25). They thought that slavery would provide a stable labor force totally under their control.
3. *Cheap labor:* As tobacco prices fell, rice and indigo became the most profitable crops. To grow such crops successfully required both a large land area and a large number of inexpensive, relatively unskilled field hands.

Slave laws. As the number of slaves increased, white colonists adopted laws to ensure that African Americans would be held in bondage for life and that their slave status would be inherited by their children. In 1641, Massachusetts became the first colony to recognize the slavery of "lawful" captives. Virginia in 1661 enacted legislation stating that children automatically inherited their mother's slave status for life. By 1664, Maryland further locked African slaves into perpetual bondage by declaring that baptism did not affect the slave's status, and that white women could not marry African American men. It became customary for whites to regard blacks (whether slave or free) as social inferiors. Thus, both racism and slavery became an integral part of American colonial society.

Triangular trade. In the 17th century, English trade in African slaves had been monopolized by a single company. But after the Royal African Company's monopoly expired, many New England merchants entered the lucrative slave trade. Merchant ships would regularly follow a triangular, or three-part, trade route. First, a ship loaded with barrels of rum would start out from a New England port like Boston and cross the Atlantic to West Africa; there the rum would be traded for hundreds of captive Africans. Second, the ship would set out on the horrendous Middle Passage (horrendous for the Africans who were forced to experience it). Those Africans who survived the frightful voyage would be traded as slaves in the West Indies for a cargo of sugarcane. Third, completing the last side of the triangle, the ship would return to a New England port where the sugar would be sold to be used in making rum. Every time that one type of cargo was traded for another, the slave-trading entrepreneur usually succeeded in making a substantial profit.

HISTORICAL PERSPECTIVES: THE PURITAN INFLUENCE

To what extent did the Puritan founders of Massachusetts shape the development of an American culture? Although some early historians such as James Truslow Adams have minimized the Puritan

COLONIAL TRIANGULAR TRADE ROUTES

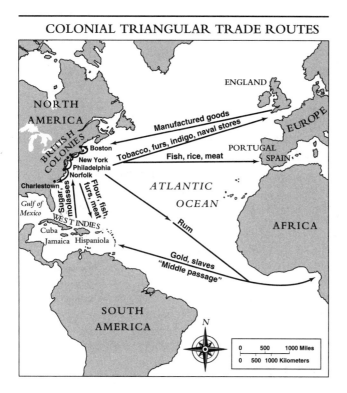

role, more recent scholars generally agree that the Puritans made significant cultural and intellectual contributions. There is continuing disagreement, however, about whether the Puritan influence encouraged an individualistic spirit or just the opposite.

Some historians have concentrated their study on the writings and sermons of the Puritan clergy and other leaders. They have concluded that the leaders stressed conformity to a strict moral code and exhorted people to sacrifice their individuality for the common good. According to these historians, in other words, the Puritan influence tended to suppress the individualism that later came to characterize American culture.

Other historians believe that the opposite is true. They raise objections to the method of studying only sermons and the journals of leading Puritans such as John Winthrop. If one examines the writings and actions of ordinary colonists in Massachusetts society, say these historians, then one observes many instances of independent thought and action by individuals in Puritan society. According to their argument, American individualism began with the Puritan colonists.

KEY NAMES, EVENTS, AND TERMS

corporate colonies
royal colonies
proprietary colonies
Chesapeake colonies
George Calvert, Lord Baltimore
Cecil Calvert, Lord Baltimore
Act of Toleration (1649)
Virginia
Sir William Berkeley
Bacon's Rebellion
indentured servant
headright system
slavery
Roger Williams
Providence
Anne Hutchinson
antinomianism

Rhode Island
Thomas Hooker
Fundamental Orders of Connecticut (1639)
John Davenport
Connecticut
New Hampshire
halfway covenant
New England Confederation
Wampanoags
Metacom; King Philip's War
Restoration colonies
the Carolinas
rice plantations
tobacco farms
New York
New Jersey
Pennsylvania

Quakers
William Penn
holy experiment
Frame of Government (1682–1683)
Charter of Liberties (1701)
Delaware
Georgia
James Oglethorpe
mercantilism
Navigation Acts
Dominion of New England
Sir Edmund Andros
Glorious Revolution
triangular trade
slave trade
Middle Passage

MULTIPLE-CHOICE QUESTIONS

1. The issue of religious toleration figured prominently in the founding of colonies by all of the following EXCEPT

(A) James Oglethorpe
(B) Cecil Calvert
(C) Anne Hutchinson
(D) William Penn
(E) Roger Williams

2. Which of the following accurately describes a problem faced by Virginia in the last decades of the 17th century?

(A) a decline in tobacco production
(B) frequent slave uprisings
(C) the lowering of wages caused by an influx of immigrants
(D) political control by small farmers in the House of Burgesses

(E) conflict between large plantation owners and settlers on Virginia's western frontier

3. Which of the following documents would be most useful in examining the origins of constitutional government in colonial America?

(A) the sermons of Puritan ministers
(B) newspaper commentary on the Halfway Covenant
(C) the Fundamental Orders of Connecticut
(D) political tracts concerning the Dominion of New England
(E) the correspondence of Sir Edmond Andros

4. "Puritan intolerance of dissent led to the founding of a number of new colonies." The founding of which of the following does NOT support this statement?
   (A) Providence
   (B) Portsmouth (Rhode Island)
   (C) Hartford
   (D) New Hampshire
   (E) New Haven

5. Roger Williams differed from other Puritan ministers in his emphasis on
   (A) the study of the Bible
   (B) the value of consensus in church meetings
   (C) nonviolence
   (D) the individual's private religious conscience
   (E) the supreme authority of church leaders

6. Which of the following was NOT a factor in the formation of the New England Confederation?
   (A) the problem of defending against Indian attacks
   (B) conflicts over colonial boundaries
   (C) concern about runaway servants
   (D) neglect by the English government
   (E) a desire to suppress religious dissent

7. The chief purpose of mercantilist policies was to
   (A) help colonies to be self-sufficient
   (B) strengthen the economy and power of the parent country
   (C) defend the colonies from rival powers
   (D) maintain tight control over the tobacco industry
   (E) foster stable relations between the Crown and the colonies

8. The acts of trade and navigation had all of the following consequences in the colonies EXCEPT
   (A) Colonial manufacturing was limited.
   (B) Colonial economies were regulated from London.
   (C) Low prices were charged for English imports.
   (D) Smuggling became a common practice.
   (E) New England shipbuilding prospered.

9. William Penn's "Holy Experiment" included all of the following ideas EXCEPT
   (A) nonviolence
   (B) the Bible as religious authority for all
   (C) fair treatment of Native Americans
   (D) a refuge for Quakers
   (E) religious toleration

10. In the mid-18th century, all of the following were generally true about slavery in the British colonies EXCEPT
    (A) Planters thought it provided a more dependable labor supply than other options.
    (B) There were more slaves than indentured servants in the southern colonies.

(C) It was strongly opposed in New England.

(D) Slaves accounted for about half the population of Virginia.

(E) Colonial laws gave slavery a permanent legal status.

ESSAY QUESTIONS

1. How do you account for the fact that while religious freedom was central to the development of some colonies, it was denied in other colonies?

2. To what extent did mercantilism affect the political and economic development of England's 13 American colonies?

3. "Beginning with the restoration of the monarchy in 1660, the English government made a continuous effort to exercise control over its American colonies."

   Give examples to prove this statement.

4. Compare and contrast William Penn's goals as Pennsylvania's founder with James Oglethorpe's goals as one of Georgia's founders.

5. Why did slavery in the colonies grow more rapidly in the last decades of the 17th century than in the earlier decades of that century?

DOCUMENTS AND READINGS

In the early 17th century, England's government in London, preoccupied with domestic troubles and civil war, could offer only minimal assistance to the American colonies. Furthermore, few of the joint-stock companies and proprietors who held charters to the colonies were able to offer much material assistance to the settlers. Left to their own resources, William Penn, Benjamin Franklin, and several other colonial leaders proposed that the various colonies form a common government and act together in common cause.

The three documents presented here represent early efforts at intercolonial cooperation and union. Only the first plan of government, the New England Confederation, was actually put into effect. The other two plans were never adopted. Even so, the different ideas for union might be viewed as preliminary steps toward the formation of the revolutionary colonial congress which, in 1776, decided upon united action against British rule.

DOCUMENT A.   THE NEW ENGLAND CONFEDERATION

In 1643, four New England colonies formed a confederation chiefly for the purpose of providing a common defense against attacks. (Rhode Island, with its differing religious views, was deliberately excluded from the union.) In the 1660s, attempts by Massachusetts to dominate the alliance caused the other members to end their participation. The confederation officially dissolved in 1684.

> The Articles of Confederation between the Plantations under the Government of the Massachusetts, the Plantations under the Government of New Plymouth, the Plantations under the Government of Connecticut, and the Government of New Haven with the Plantations in Combination therewith:
>
> . . . 2. The said United Colonies for themselves and their posterities do jointly and severally hereby enter into a firm and perpetual league of friendship and amity for offence and defence, mutual advice and succor upon all just occasions both for preserving and propagating the truth and liberties of the Gospel and for their own mutual safety and welfare. . . .
>
> 4. It is by these Confederates agreed that the charge of all just wars, whether offensive or defensive, upon what part or member of this Confederation soever they fall, shall both in men, provisions, and all other disbursements be borne by all the parts of this Confederation in different proportions according to their different ability. . . .
>
> 5. It is further agreed that if any of these Jurisdictions or any Plantation under or in combination with them, be invaded by any enemy whatsoever, upon notice and request of any three magistrates of that Jurisdiction so invaded, the rest of the Confederates without any further meeting or expostulation shall forthwith send aid to the Confederate in danger but in different proportions; namely, the Massachusetts an hundred men sufficiently armed and provided for such a service and journey, and each of the rest, forty-five so armed and provided, or any less number, if less be required according to this proportion . . .
>
> The New England Confederation,
May 19, 1643

DOCUMENT B.　PENN'S PLAN OF UNION

Seeing a need for military and economic cooperation among the colonies, William Penn proposed a plan of union in 1697. The plan was never implemented, but it nevertheless has significance as a forerunner of later efforts to unite the colonies. The following are excerpts from Penn's plan.

> A brief and plain scheme how the English colonies in the North parts of America—viz., Boston, Connecticut, Rhode Island, New York, New Jerseys, Pennsylvania, Maryland, Virginia, and Carolinas—may be made more useful to the crown and one another's peace and safety with an universal concurrence.

1. That the several colonies before mentioned do meet once a year, and oftener if need be during the war, and at least once in two years in times of peace, by their stated and appointed deputies, to debate and resolve of such measures as are most advisable for their better understanding and the public tranquillity and safety.

2. That, in order to it, two persons, well qualified for sense, sobriety, and substance, be appointed by each province as their representatives or deputies, which in the whole make the congress to consist of twenty persons. . . .

6. That their business shall be to hear and adjust all matters of complaint or difference between province and province. As, 1st, where persons quit their own province and go to another, that they may avoid their just debts, though they be able to pay them; 2d, where offenders fly justice, or justice cannot well be had upon such offenders in the provinces that entertain them; 3d, to prevent or cure injuries in point of commerce; 4th, to consider the ways and means to support the union and safety of these provinces against the public enemies. . . .

Penn's Plan of Union, 1697

DOCUMENT C.   THE ALBANY PLAN OF UNION

The historical context for this plan of union of 1754 is treated on pages 61–62. The plan is included here because it is the last of the colonial plans of union to be considered before the outbreak of the American Revolution. The chief author of the plan was the colonies' most famous citizen, Benjamin Franklin of Pennsylvania. Unwilling to give up control over their powers to tax, the various colonies rejected the plan, and it never went into effect.

It is proposed that humble application be made for an act of Parliament of Great Britain, by virtue of which one general government may be formed in America, including all the said colonies, within and under which government each colony may retain its present constitution, except in the particulars wherein a change may be directed by the said act, as hereafter follows:

1. That the said general government be administered by a President-General, to be appointed and supported by the crown; and a Grand Council, to be chosen by the representatives of the people of the several Colonies met in their respective assemblies. . . .

10. That the President-General, with the advice of the Grand Council, hold or direct all Indian treaties, in which the general interest of the Colonies may be concerned; and make peace or declare war with Indian nations.

11. That they make such laws as they judge necessary for regulating all Indian trade.

12. That they make all purchases from Indians, for the crown, of lands not now within the bounds of particular Colonies. . . .

13. That they make new settlements on such purchases, by granting lands in the King's name. . . .

14. That they make laws for regulating and governing such new settlements, till the crown shall think fit to form them into particular governments.

15. That they raise and pay soldiers and build forts for the defence of any of the Colonies, and equip vessels of force to guard the coasts and protect the trade on the ocean, lakes, or great rivers; but they shall not impress [coerce or draft] men in any Colony, without the consent of the Legislature.

16. That for these purposes they have power to make laws, and lay and levy such general duties, imposts, or taxes, as to them shall appear most equal and just (considering the ability and other circumstances of the inhabitants in the several Colonies), and such as may be collected with the least inconvenience to the people. . . .

The Albany Plan of Union, 1754

ANALYZING THE DOCUMENTS

1. What specific problems in colonial society and government are addressed in Documents A, B, and C?

2. Evaluate any evidence in Documents A, B, and C of a tradition of representative government in the early colonies.

3. "The history of colonial efforts to cooperate or unite demonstrates that the colonies had no strong or sustainable need for a common government."

Using the documents provided and your knowledge of colonial history, write an essay explaining why you either agree or disagree with the above statement.

COLONIAL SOCIETY IN THE EIGHTEENTH CENTURY

The American is a new man, who acts upon new principles; he must therefore entertain new ideas, and form new opinions. From involuntary idleness, servile dependence, and useless labor, he has passed to toils of a very different nature, rewarded by ample subsistence. This is an American.

J. Hector St. John Crèvecoeur, 1782

The Frenchman who wrote the above description of Americans in 1782 observed a very different society from the struggling and undeveloped colonial villages that had existed in the 1600s. Over the course of a century, the British colonies had grown and matured, and their inhabitants had slowly evolved a distinct culture different from any that existed in Europe. This chapter describes the colonies in their mature stage and poses the question: If Americans in the 1760s constituted a new kind of society, what were its characteristics and what forces went into shaping its "new people"?

Population Growth

At the start of the new century, in 1701, the English colonies on the Atlantic Coast had a population of barely 250,000 (not counting the Native Americans). By 1775, the figure had jumped to 2,500,000, a tenfold increase within the span of a single lifetime. (Among African Americans, the population increase was even more dramatic: from about 28,000 in 1701 to 500,000 in 1775.)

The spectacular gains in population during this period were the result of two factors: immigration of almost a million people and a sharp natural increase, caused chiefly by a high birthrate among colonial families. An abundance of fertile American land and a dependable food supply attracted thousands of European settlers each year and also encouraged the raising of large families.

European Immigrants

Newcomers to the British colonies came not only from Great Britain (England, Scotland, Wales, and Ireland) but also from other parts of Western and Central Europe, especially large numbers of Protestants from France and German-speaking people from various German kingdoms and principalities. Their motives for leaving Europe were many. Some came to escape religious persecution and wars. Others sought economic opportunity either by farming new land or setting up shop in a colonial town as an artisan or a merchant. Most immigrants settled in the middle colonies (Pennsylvania, New York, New Jersey, Maryland, and Delaware) and on the western frontier of the southern colonies (Virginia, the Carolinas, and Georgia). In the 18th century, fewer immigrants headed for New England because the lands in this region were both limited in extent and under Puritan control.

English. English settlers continued to come to the American colonies, but with fewer problems at home, their numbers were relatively small compared to others, especially the Germans and Scotch-Irish.

Germans. This group of non-English immigrants settled chiefly on the rich farmlands west of Philadelphia, an area that became known as Pennsylvania Dutch country. They maintained their German language, customs, and religion (Lutheran) and, while obeying colonial laws, showed little interest in English politics. By 1775, people of German stock comprised 6 percent of the colonial population.

Scotch-Irish. This group of English-speaking people emigrated from northern Ireland. Originally, their ancestors had moved to Ireland from Scotland, and they were thus commonly known as the Scotch-Irish. Scotch-Irish immigrants had little respect for the British government, which had pressured them into leaving Ireland. They settled along the frontier in the western parts of Pennsylvania, Virginia, the Carolinas, and Georgia. By 1775, they comprised 7 percent of the population.

Other Europeans. Other immigrant groups included French Protestants (called Huguenots), the Dutch, and the Swedes. These groups made up 5 percent of the population of all the colonies in 1775.

Africans

By far the largest single group of non-English immigrants did not come to America of their own free will. They were Africans—or the descendants of Africans—who had been taken captive, forced into the holds of European ships, and sold as slaves to southern plantation owners and other colonists. Some Africans were granted their freedom after years of forced labor. By 1775, the African American population (both slave and free) made up fully 20 percent of the colonial population. An overwhelming majority—90 percent—lived in the southern colonies in a state of lifelong bondage. African Americans formed a majority of the population in South Carolina and Georgia and significant minorities in North Carolina, Virginia, and Maryland. Outside the South, thousands of African Americans worked at a broad range of occupations, some as slaves and others as free wage earners and property owners. In every colony, from New Hampshire to Georgia, there were laws that discriminated against African Americans and placed limits on their rights and opportunities.

The Structure of Colonial Society

Each of the 13 British colonies developed along different lines and adopted its own unique institutions. However, the colonies also shared a number of characteristics in common.

General Characteristics

Dominance of English culture. The great majority of the population were English in origin, language, and tradition. At the same time, however, both Africans and European immigrants were creating a diversity of culture that would gradually modify the culture of the majority in significant ways.

Self-government. The government of each colony had a representative assembly that was elected by eligible voters (limited to white male property owners). Only in two colonies, Rhode Island and Connecticut, was the governor also elected by the people. The governors of the other colonies were either appointed by the crown (for example, New York and Virginia) or by a proprietor (Pennsylvania and Maryland).

Religious toleration. All of the colonies permitted the practice of different religions, but with varying degrees of freedom. Massachusetts, the least tolerant, excluded non-Christians and Catholics, although it accepted a number of Protestant denominations. Rhode Island and Pennsylvania were the most liberal.

No hereditary aristocracy. The social extremes of Europe, with a nobility that inherited special privileges and masses of hungry poor, were missing in the colonies. A narrower class system, based on economics, was developing. Wealthy landowners were at the top; craftspeople and small farmers made up the majority of the common people.

Social mobility. With the major exception of the African Americans, everybody in colonial society had an opportunity to improve their standard of living and social status by hard work.

The Family

The family was the economic and social center of colonial life. With an expanding economy and ample food supply, people were marrying at a young age and rearing more children. Over 90 percent of the people lived on farms. While life in the coastal communities and on the frontier was not easy, it did provide a higher standard of living than in Europe.

Men. While wealth was increasingly being concentrated in the hands of a few, most men did work. Landowning was primarily reserved to men, who also dominated politics. English law gave the husband almost unlimited power in the home, including the right to beat his wife.

Women. The average colonial wife bore eight children and performed a wide range of tasks. Household work included cooking, cleaning, clothes-making, and medical care. Women also educated the children. A woman usually worked next to her husband in the shop, on the plantation, or on the farm. Divorce was legal but rare, and women had limited legal and political rights. Yet the shared labors and mutual dependence with their husbands gave most women protection from abuse and an active role in decision-making.

The Economy

By the 1760s, almost half of England's world trade was with its American colonies. The government in England permitted limited kinds of colonial manufacturing, such as making flour or rum, but it restricted efforts that would compete with English industries, such as textiles. The richness of the American land and British mercantile policy produced a society almost entirely engaged in agriculture.

As the people prospered and communities grew, increasing numbers became ministers, lawyers, doctors, and teachers. The quickest route to wealth was through the land, although regional geography often provided distinct opportunities for the hardworking colonists.

New England. With rocky soil and long winters, farming was limited to subsistence levels that provided just enough for the farm family. Most farms were small—under 100 acres—and most work was done by family members and an occasional hired laborer. The industrious descendants of the Puritans profited from logging, shipbuilding, fishing, trading, and rum-distilling.

Middle colonies. Rich soil attracted farmers from Europe and produced an abundance of wheat and corn for export to Europe and the West Indies. Farms of up to 200 acres were common. Often, indentured servants and hired laborers worked with the farm family. A variety of small manufacturing efforts developed, including iron-making. Trading led to the growth of such cities as Philadelphia and New York.

Southern colonies. Because of the South's varied geography and climate, farming ranged from small subsistence family farms to large plantations of over 2,000 acres. Cash crops were mainly tobacco in the Chesapeake and North Carolina colonies, and rice and indigo in South Carolina and Georgia. On the plantations, a shortage of indentured servants led to the increased use of slaves. Most plantations were self-sufficient—they grew their own food and had their own slave craftspeople. The Carolinas also exported large quantities of timber and naval stores (tar and pitch). Most plantations were located on rivers so that their cash crops could be shipped directly to Europe.

Monetary system. A major English strategy in controlling the colonial economy was to limit the use of money. The growing colonies were forced to use much of the limited hard currency—gold and silver—to pay for the imports from England that increasingly exceeded colonial exports. To provide currency for domestic trade, many of the colonies issued paper money, but this often led to inflation. The government in England also vetoed colonial laws that might harm English merchants.

Transportation. Transporting goods by water was much easier than attempting to carry them overland on rough and narrow roads or trails. Therefore, trading centers like Boston, New York, Philadelphia, and Charleston were located on the sites of good harbors and navigable rivers. Despite the difficulty and expense of maintaining roads and bridges, overland travel by horse and stage became more common in the 18th century. Taverns not only provided food and lodging for travelers but also served as social centers where news was exchanged and politics discussed. A postal system using horses on overland routes and small ships on water routes was operating both within and between the colonies by the mid-18th century.

Religion

Although Maryland was founded by a Catholic proprietor, and many larger towns like New York and Boston attracted some Jewish settlers, the overwhelming majority of colonists belonged to different Protestant denominations. The Presbyterians were especially well represented in New England. People of Dutch descent in New York attended services of the Dutch Reformed Church. Lutherans, Mennonites, and Quakers were the most common Protestant sects in Pennsylvania.

Protestant Dominance

In the 17th century, certain colonial governments had taxed the people to support one of the Protestant denominations. Churches financed in this way were known as established churches. There were two such established churches in the early colonies: the Church of England (or Anglican Church) in Virginia and the Congregational Church in Massachusetts Bay and Connecticut. As various immigrant groups increased the religious diversity of the colonies, the governments gradually changed their policies on tax-supported churches. In Massachusetts and Connecticut, by the time of the Revolution, members of other established religions were exempt from supporting the Congregational Church. Some direct tax support remained until the 19th century. In Virginia, all tax support for the Anglican Church ended shortly after the Revolution.

Anglicans. Colonial members of the Church of England tended to be prosperous farmers and merchants in New York and plantation owners in Virginia and the Carolinas. There was no Anglican bishop in America to ordain ministers. The absence of such leadership hampered the church's development. Because the Church of England was headed by the king, it was viewed as a symbol of English control in the colonies.

Congregationalists. As successors to the Puritans, members of the Congregational Church were found mainly in New England. Protestant critics of this church thought its ministers were domineering and its doctrine overly complex.

The Great Awakening

In the first decades of the 18th century, sermons in Protestant churches tended to be long intellectual discourses and portrayed God as a benign creator of a perfectly ordered universe. There was less emphasis than in Puritan times on human sinfulness and the perils of damnation. In the 1730s, however, a dramatic change occurred that swept through the colonies with the force of a hurricane. This was the Great Awakening, a movement characterized by fervent expressions of religious feeling among masses of people. The movement was at its strongest during the 1730s and 1740s.

Jonathan Edwards. In a Congregational church at Northampton, Massachusetts, the Reverend Jonathan Edwards initiated the Great Awakening with a series of sermons, notably one called "Sinners in the Hands of an Angry God" (1741). Invoking the Old Testament Scriptures, Edwards argued that God was rightfully angry with human sinfulness. Each individual who expressed deep penitence could be saved by God's grace, but the souls who paid no heed to God's commandments would suffer eternal damnation.

George Whitefield. Edwards' influence was largely limited to the New England colonies. Another preacher, George Whitefield, came from England in 1739 and traveled from one end of colonial America to the other. More than any other figure, Whitefield ignited the Great Awakening with his rousing sermons on the hellish torments of the damned. He preached in barns, tents, and fields, sometimes attracting an audience of 10,000 people. He stressed that God was all-powerful and would save only those who openly professed belief in Jesus Christ; those who did not would be cast into hell. Whitefield taught that ordinary people who had faith and sincerity could understand the Christian Gospels without depending on ministers to lead them.

Religious impact. The Great Awakening had a profound effect on religious practice in the colonies. As sinners tearfully confessed their guilt and then joyously exulted in being "saved," emotionalism became a common part of Protestant services. Ministers lost some of their former authority among those who now studied the Bible in their own homes.

The Great Awakening also caused a major division within churches such as the Congregational and Presbyterian, between those supporting its teachings ("New Lights") and those condemning them ("Old Lights"). More evangelical sects such as the Baptists and Methodists attracted large numbers. As a result, there was greater competition to attract followers, increased religious diversity, and a call for separation of church and state.

Political influence. A movement as powerful as the Great Awakening was bound to affect all areas of life, including colonial politics. Unlike anything before it, the movement affected every social class in every section. For the first time, the colonists—regardless of their national origins—shared in a common experience as Americans. The Great Awakening may also have had a democratizing effect by changing the way people viewed authority. If the common people could make their own religious decisions without relying on the "higher" authority of ministers, then might they also make their own political decisions without deferring to the authority of the great landowners and merchants? This revolutionary idea was not expressed in the 1740s, but 30 years later, it would challenge the authority of a king and his royal governors.

Cultural Life

In the early 1600s, the chief concern of most colonists was economic survival. People had neither the time nor the resources to pursue leisure activities or create works of art and literature. One hundred years later, however, the colonial population had grown and matured to the point that the arts and other aspects of civilized living could flourish, at least among the well-to-do southern planters and the merchants of the northern cities.

Achievements in the Arts and Sciences

In the coastal areas, as fear of the Native Americans faded, people of means could display their prosperity and success by adopting architectural and decorative styles from England.

Architecture. In the 1740s and 1750s, the Georgian style of London was widely imitated in colonial houses, churches, and public buildings. Brick and stucco homes built in this style were characterized by a symmetrical placement of windows and dormers and a spacious center hall flanked by two fireplaces. Such homes were found only on or near the eastern seaboard. On the frontier, a one-room log cabin was the common shelter.

Painting. Many colonial painters were itinerant artists who wandered the countryside in search of families that wanted their portraits painted. Shortly before the Revolution, two American artists, Benjamin West and John Copley, went to England where they acquired the necessary training and financial support to establish themselves as prominent artists.

Literature. With limited resources available, most authors wrote on serious subjects, chiefly religion and politics. There were, for example, widely read religious tracts by two Massachusetts ministers, Cotton Mather and Jonathan Edwards. In the years preceding the American Revolution, a large number of political essays and treatises attempted to draw a line between American rights and English authority. Writers of this important literature included John Adams, James Otis, John Dickinson, Thomas Paine, and Thomas Jefferson.

By far the most popular and successful American writer of the 18th century was that remarkable jack-of-all-trades, Benjamin Franklin. His witty aphorisms and advice were collected in *Poor Richard's Almanack,* a best-selling book that was annually revised from 1732 to 1757.

The lack of support for literature did not stop everyone. The poetry of Phillis Wheatley is noteworthy both for her triumph over slavery and the quality of her verse.

Science. Most scientists, such as the botanist John Bartram of Philadelphia, were self-taught. Benjamin Franklin's pioneering work with electricity and his more practical developments of bifocal eyeglasses and the Franklin stove brought him international fame.

Education

Basic education was limited and varied greatly among the colonies. Formal efforts were directed to males, since females were to be trained only for household work.

New England. The Puritans' emphasis on learning the Bible led them to create the first tax-supported schools. A Massachusetts law in 1647 required towns with over fifty families to establish primary schools for boys, and towns with over a hundred families to establish grammar schools to prepare boys for college.

Middle colonies. Schools were either church-sponsored or private. Often, teachers lived with the families of their students.

Southern colonies. Parents gave their children whatever education they could. On plantations, tutors provided instruction for the owners' children.

Higher education. Harvard, the first colonial college, was founded at Cambridge, Massachusetts, in 1636 in order to give candidates for the ministry a proper theological and scholarly education. Two other early colleges were William and Mary in Virginia (opened in 1694) and Yale in Connecticut (1701). Like Harvard, both were sectarian, meaning that they existed to promote the doctrines of a particular religious sect. William and Mary was founded by Anglicans and Yale by Congregationalists.

The Great Awakening prompted the creation of five new colleges between 1746 and 1769:

- College of New Jersey (Princeton), 1746, Presbyterian
- King's College (Columbia), 1754, Anglican

- Rhode Island College (Brown), 1764, Baptist
- Queens College (Rutgers), 1766, Dutch Reformed
- Dartmouth College, 1769, Congregationalist

Only one nonsectarian college was founded during this period. The College of Philadelphia, the future University of Pennsylvania, had no religious sponsors. On hand for the opening ceremonies in 1765 were the college's civic-minded founders, chief among them Philadelphia's leading citizen, Benjamin Franklin.

Professions : Religion, Medicine, Law

For perhaps the first hundred years of colonial life (1607–1707), Christian ministry was the only profession to enjoy widespread respect among the common people. In the course of the 18th century, however, other professions gradually acquired respectability and social prominence.

Physicians. The thousands of colonists who fell prey to epidemics of smallpox and diphtheria were treated by a cure that only made matters worse. The common practice then was to bleed the sick, often by employing leeches or bloodsuckers. For a beginning doctor, there was little to no formal medical training other than acting as an apprentice to an experienced physician. The first medical college in the colonies was begun in 1765 as part of Franklin's idea for the College of Philadelphia.

Lawyers. Often viewed as talkative troublemakers, lawyers were not commonly seen in the colonial courts of the 1600s. In that period, individuals would argue their own cases before a colonial magistrate. During the 1700s, however, as trade expanded and legal problems became more complex, the need for expert assistance in court became apparent. The most able lawyers formed a bar (committee or board), which set rules and standards for aspiring young lawyers. Lawyers gained further respect in the 1760s and 1770s when they argued for colonial rights. John Adams, James Otis, and Patrick Henry were three such lawyers whose legal arguments would ultimately provide the intellectual underpinnings of the American Revolution.

The Press

News and ideas circulated in the colonies principally by means of a postal system and local printing presses.

Newspapers. In 1725 only five newspapers existed in the colonies, but by 1776 the number had grown to more than 40. Issued weekly, each newspaper consisted of a single sheet folded once to make four pages. It contained such items as month-old news from Europe, ads for goods and services and for the return of runaway indentured servants and slaves, and pious essays giving advice for better living. Illustrations were few or nonexistent. The first cartoon appeared in the Philadelphia *Gazette*, placed there by (you guessed it) Ben Franklin.

The Zenger case. Newspaper printers in colonial days ran the risk of being jailed for libel if any article offended the political authorities. In 1735, John Peter Zenger, a New York editor and publisher, was brought to trial on a charge of libelously criticizing New York's royal governor. Zenger's lawyer, Andrew Hamilton, argued that his client had printed the truth about the governor. According to English common law at the time, injuring a governor's reputation was considered a criminal act, no matter whether a printed statement was true or false. Ignoring the English law, the jury voted to acquit Zenger. While this case did not guarantee complete freedom of the press, it encouraged newspapers to take greater risks in criticizing a colony's government.

Rural Folkways

The majority of colonists rarely saw a newspaper or read any book other than the Bible. As farmers on the frontier or even within a few miles of the coast, they worked from first daylight to sundown. The farmer's year was divided into four ever-recurring seasons: spring planting, summer growing, fall harvesting, and winter preparations for the next cycle. Food was usually plentiful, but light and heat in the colonial farmhouse were limited to the kitchen fireplace and a few well-placed candles. Entertainment for the well-to-do consisted chiefly of cardplaying and horse-racing in the South, theatergoing in the middle colonies, and attending religious lectures in Puritan New England.

Emergence of a National Character

The colonists' motivations for leaving Europe, the political heritage of the English majority, and the influence of the American natural environment combined to bring about a distinctly American viewpoint and way of life. Especially among white male property owners, the colonists exercised the rights of free speech and a free press, became accustomed to electing representatives to colonial assemblies, and tolerated a variety of religions. English travelers in the colonies remarked that Americans were restless, enterprising, practical, and forever seeking to improve their circumstances.

Politics

By 1750, the 13 colonies had similar systems of government, with a governor acting as chief executive and a separate legislature voting either to adopt or reject the governor's proposed laws.

Structure of Government

There were eight royal colonies with governors appointed by the king (New Hampshire, Massachusetts, New York, New Jersey, Virginia, North Carolina, South Carolina, and Georgia). In the three proprietary colonies (Maryland, Pennsylvania, and Delaware), governors were appointed by the proprietors. The governors in only two of the colonies, Connecticut and Rhode Island, were elected by popular vote.

In every colony, the legislature consisted of two houses. The lower house, or assembly, elected by the eligible voters, voted for or against new taxes. Colonists thus became accustomed to paying taxes only if their chosen representatives approved. (Their unwillingness to surrender any part of this privilege would become a cause for revolt in the 1770s.) In the royal and proprietary colonies, members of the legislature's upper house—or council—were appointed by the king or the proprietor. In the two self-governing colonies, both the upper and lower houses were elective bodies.

Local government. From the earliest period of settlement, colonists in New England established towns and villages, clustering their small homes around an open space known as a green. In the southern colonies, on the other hand, towns were much less common, and farms and plantations were widely separated. Thus, the dominant form of local government in New England was the town meeting, in which people of the town would regularly come together, often in a church, to vote directly on public issues. In the southern colonies, local government was carried on by a law-enforcing sheriff and other officials who served a large territorial unit called a county.

Voting

If democracy is defined as the participation of all the people in the making of government policy, then colonial democracy was at best limited and partial. Those barred from voting—white women, poor white men, slaves of both sexes, and most free blacks—constituted a sizable majority of the colonial population. Nevertheless, the barriers to voting that existed in the 17th century were beginning to be removed in the 18th. Religious restrictions, for example, were removed in Massachusetts and other colonies. On the other hand, voters in all colonies were still required to own at least a small amount of property.

Another factor to consider is the degree to which members of the colonial assemblies and governors' councils represented either a privileged elite or the larger society of plain citizens. The situation varied from one colony to the next. In Virginia, membership in the House of Burgesses was tightly restricted to certain families of wealthy landowners. In Massachusetts, the legislature was more open to small farmers, although here, too, an educated, propertied elite held power for generations. The common people in every colony tended to defer to their "betters" and to depend upon the privileged few to make decisions for them.

Without question, colonial politics was restricted to participation by white males only. Even so, compared with other parts of the world, the English colonies showed tendencies toward democracy and self-government that made their political system unusual for the time.

HISTORICAL PERSPECTIVES: WAS COLONIAL SOCIETY DEMOCRATIC?

Shall we conclude that colonial America was or was not "democratic"? The question is important for its own sake and also because it affects our perspective on the American Revolution and on the subsequent evolution of democratic politics in the United States. In an effort to answer this question, a number of historians have studied the politics of colonial Massachusetts. They wanted to determine to what degree democracy had developed in Massachusetts before 1775 and whether or not the government in that colony was dominated by an elite.

Some historians have concluded that colonial Massachusetts was indeed democratic, at least for the times. By studying voting records and statistics, they determined that the vast majority of white male citizens could vote and were not restricted by property qualifications. According to these historians, class differences between an elite and the masses of people did not prevent the latter from participating fully in colonial politics.

Other historians question whether broad voting rights by themselves demonstrate the existence of real democracy. The true test of democratic practice, they argue, would be whether or not different groups in a colonial town felt free to debate political questions in a town meeting. In the records of such meetings, they found little evidence of true political conflict and debate. Instead, they found that the purpose of town meetings in colonial days was to reach a consensus and to avoid conflict and real choices. These historians believe that the nature of consensus-forming limited the degree of democracy.

A third historical perspective is based on studies of economic change in colonial Boston. According to this view, a fundamental shift from an agrarian to a maritime economy occurred in the 18th century. In the process, a new elite emerged to dominate Boston's finances, society, and politics. The power of this elite prevented colonial Massachusetts from being considered a true democracy.

The question remains: To what extent were Massachusetts and the other colonies democratic? Anyone attempting to answer the question must study voting patterns, social and economic patterns, and other relevant information. After surveying this information, we must determine whether or not it satisfies our own definition of democracy.

KEY NAMES, EVENTS, AND TERMS

J. Hector St. John Crèvecoeur	Great Awakening	sectarian; nonsectarian
immigrants	Jonathan Edwards	professions: religion, medicine, law
English cultural domination	George Whitefield	John Peter Zenger; libel case
self-government	Georgian style	Andrew Hamilton
religious toleration	Benjamin West	colonial governors
hereditary aristocracy	John Copley	colonial legislatures
social mobility	Cotton Mather	town meetings
colonial families	Benjamin Franklin	county government
subsistence farming	*Poor Richard's Almanack*	limited democracy
established church	Phillis Wheatley	
	John Bartram	

MULTIPLE-CHOICE QUESTIONS

1. The Great Awakening was a reaction to
   (A) the flood of immigrants
   (B) established churches in many of the colonies
   (C) churches' earlier failure to take account of people's emotional needs
   (D) guilt over the evils of slavery
   (E) the overly strict teachings of the Church of England

2. Preachers of the Great Awakening focused on the importance of
   (A) the consequences of leading a sinful life
   (B) the sovereignty and power of God
   (C) repenting of one's sins in order to be saved from eternal damnation
   (D) looking to the Bible as the final source of authority
   (E) all of the above.

3. The Great Awakening had all of the following consequences EXCEPT

   (A) reduced competition among Protestant sects
   (B) decline in the authority of Protestant ministers
   (C) a belief that common people could make their own decisions
   (D) increased emotionalism in church services
   (E) a feeling of shared experience among colonists in different regions and of different national origins.

4. Which of the following is true of immigration to the colonies during the first half of the 18th century?
   (A) Most immigrants settled in New England.
   (B) Most immigrants came from continental Europe.
   (C) A sizable minority of immigrants had no freedom of choice in coming to the colonies.
   (D) The English government tried to discourage immigration.

(E) Most immigrants worked for low wages in cities along the eastern seaboard.

5. In the 18th century, all of the following were generally true about colonial society in America EXCEPT

(A) The English language and English traditions were dominant.

(B) There were few poor people and no real aristocrats.

(C) Voters played an active role in government.

(D) It was impossible for individuals to better themselves economically or socially.

(E) A degree of religious toleration could be found in each colony.

6. At his trial, John Peter Zenger won acquittal on the grounds that

(A) the king had less authority in the colonies than in England

(B) English law permitted the press almost total freedom

(C) libel laws did not apply to government officials

(D) New York's governor deserved to be criticized

(E) truth could not be libel.

7. Which of the following did the colonies lack?

(A) an adequate monetary system

(B) good harbors and rivers for transportation

(C) the ability to import goods from England

(D) an adequate supply of slave labor

(E) sufficient markets for colonial timber and naval stores

8. Which of the following statements accurately describes the governments of *all* 13 colonies in the mid-18th century?

(A) The governor was appointed by the king.

(B) Members of the governor's council were elected.

(C) The government assisted an established church.

(D) One house of the legislature was elected by eligible voters.

(E) The governor had nearly dictatorial power.

9. "Benjamin Franklin was the epitome of the multitalented colonial American." Each of the following could be used to support this statement EXCEPT

(A) experiments with electricity

(B) *Poor Richard's Almanack*

(C) military leadership

(D) invention of bifocal lenses

(E) founding of a nonsectarian college

10. Which of the following best represents the "new man" described by Crèvecoeur?

(A) an indentured servant recently arrived from France

(B) a native-born Pennsylvania merchant

(C) an adult slave on a South Carolina plantation

(D) a German-speaking farmer on the frontier

(E) a royal governor of Virginia

ESSAY QUESTIONS

1. Analyze the ways in which colonial life and society changed from 1700 to 1775.

2. Compare and contrast the culture and economy of the southern colonies with that of the New England colonies.

3. Comment on the extent to which each of the following contributed to a more democratic society in the American colonies: (a) the Great Awakening (b) immigration (c) the Zenger case.

4. "The American colonists of the 18th century were slow to develop academic and artistic pursuits." Assess the validity of this statement by commenting on TWO of the following:

   architecture   literature

   painting   science

5. To what extent were economic opportunities in the colonies available to the white majority largely because such opportunities were denied to the black minority?

DOCUMENTS AND READINGS

With the English government and king 3,000 miles away, the question of authority was with the American colonists from the outset. In the Mayflower Compact, the first Pilgrims had clarified their independence from the Virginia Company. In the compact, they made it clear that they recognized the higher authority of both God and sovereign, and that they, the colonists, would decide what laws were needed for the general good.

Since many early settlers came to America because they disliked the authority that had sought to control them in Europe, the question of forming new governments became a primary concern. The settlers often looked beyond the political to more philosophical reasons. It was common to call on God and religion to provide the rationale for deciding questions of authority and government. Initially, arguments centered on God's delegation of authority to the king, and about the role of the people. A challenge to this view came from those who believed that it was the natural right of humanity to decide who should have authority. A close look at these early arguments over authority provides insights into what has been a continuous question in American history.

DOCUMENT A.   A SERMON ON LOYALTY AND FREEDOM

This reading comes from a sermon delivered by Jonathan Mayhew in 1750. He provides a rationale for the people redressing their grievances against the authority of the king and discusses circumstances when a popular revolt is justified. Mayhew was speaking on the one hundred and first anniversary of the execution of Charles I, and his ideas would have a profound effect on the colonies.

. . . A *people,* really oppressed to a great degree by their sovereign, cannot well be insensible when they are so oppressed. . . . For a nation thus abused to arise unanimously and to resist their prince, even to dethroning him, is not criminal but a reasonable way of vindicating their liberties and just rights; it is making use of the means, and the only means, which God has put into their power for mutual and self-defense. And it would be highly criminal in them not to make use of this means. It would be stupid tameness and unaccountable folly for whole nations to suffer *one* unreasonable, ambitious, and cruel man to wanton and riot in their misery. And, in such a case, it would, of the two, be more rational to suppose that they did *not resist* than that they who did would *receive to themselves damnation.* . . .

To conclude, let us all learn to be *free* and to be *loyal.* Let us not profess ourselves vassals to the lawless pleasure of any man on earth. But let us remember, at the same time, government is *sacred* and not to be trifled with. It is our happiness to live under the government of a prince who is satisfied with ruling according to law, as every other good prince will. We enjoy under his administration all the liberty that is proper and expedient for us. It becomes us, therefore, to be contented and dutiful subjects. Let us prize our freedom but not *use our liberty for a cloak of maliciousness.* There are men who strike at liberty under the term licentiousness. There are others who aim at popularity under the disguise of patriotism. Be aware of both. *Extremes* are dangerous.

Jonathan Mayhew,
sermon, Boston, 1750

DOCUMENT B.   *A SERMON ON SUBMISSION*

Jonathan Boucher was an Anglican minister who had come from England in 1759 to preach in the colonies. He was a strong supporter of the king and Parliament and opposed the growing revolutionary spirit in America. Boucher speaks of obedience to both God and his agent, the government. His call to Americans to submit peaceably to the divine authority of the government was ultimately rejected and he fled to England in 1775.

To your question, therefore, I hesitate not to answer that I wish and advise you to act the part of reasonable men and of Christians. You will be pleased to observe, however, that I am far from thinking that your virtue will ever be brought to so severe a test and trial. The question, I am aware, was an ensnaring one, suggested to you by those who are as little solicitous about your peace as they are for my safety; the answer which, in condescension to your wishes,

I have given to it is direct and plain and not more applicable to you than it is to all the people of America. . . .

I affirm with great authority that "there can be no better way of asserting the people's lawful rights than the disowning [of] unlawful commands, by thus patiently suffering." When this doctrine was more generally embraced, our holy religion gained as much by submission as it is now in a fair way of losing for want of it.

Having, then, my brethren, thus long been tossed to and fro in a wearisome circle of uncertain traditions or in speculations and projects still more uncertain concerning government, what better advice can you do than, following the Apostle's advice, to submit yourselves to every ordinance of man, for the Lord's sake; whether it be the King as supreme, or unto *governors,* as unto them that are *sent* by Him for the punishment of evildoers and for praise of them that do well? For, so is the will of God, that with well-doing you may put to silence the ignorance of foolish men; as free and not using your liberty for a cloak of maliciousness but as servants of God.

Jonathan Boucher,
sermon, Anglican Church, Maryland, 1775

DOCUMENT C.   *THE CONSENT OF THE PEOPLE*

For many Americans educated in the first half of the 18th century, the ideas of the English philosopher John Locke provided a foundation for ideas on authority and government that they would use to challenge the British claims of sovereignty. John Adams and Thomas Jefferson were among many who borrowed both the spirit and words of Locke in their arguments to free Americans from the control of both king and Parliament. The following selection presents some of Locke's ideas, which inspired so many.

To understand political power aright, and derive it from its original, we must consider what estate all men are naturally in, and that it is a state of perfect freedom to order their actions and dispose of their possessions and persons as they think fit, within the bounds of the law of nature, without asking leave, or depending upon the will of any other man. . . .

Whosoever therefore out of a state of nature unite into a community must be understood to give up all the power necessary to the ends for which they unite into society, to the majority of the community, unless they expressly agreed in any number greater than the majority. And this is done by barely agreeing to unite into one political society, which is all the compact that is, or needs be between the individuals that enter into or make up a commonwealth. And thus that which begins and actually constitutes any political society is nothing but the consent of any number of freemen capable of a majority to unite and incorporate into such a society. And this is that, and that only, which did or could give beginning to any lawful government in the world.

John Locke,
Second Treatise of Government, 1690

ANALYZING THE DOCUMENTS

1. Compare and contrast the views of Mayhew and Boucher on the uses of liberty.

2. According to John Locke, what is the primary force guiding man, or humankind?

3. "During the colonial period, religion provided the primary rationale for the authority of the king."

Evaluate this statement in an essay based on the documents provided and your own knowledge of this period.

IMPERIAL WARS AND COLONIAL PROTEST, 1754–1774

*The people, even to the lowest ranks, have become more attentive to
their liberties, more inquisitive about them, and more determined
to defend them than they were ever before
known or had occasion to be.*

John Adams, 1765

What caused American colonists in the 1760s to become, as John Adams expressed it, "more attentive to their liberties"? The chief reason for their discontent in these years was a dramatic change in Britain's colonial policy. Britain began to assert its power in the colonies and to collect taxes and enforce trade laws much more boldly and aggressively than in the past. To explain why Britain took this fateful step, we must study the effects of its various wars for empire.

Empires at War

Late in the 17th century, a war broke out involving Great Britain, France, and Spain. This was the first of a series of four wars that were worldwide in scope, being fought not only in Europe but also in India and North America. These wars occurred intermittently over a 74-year period from 1689 to 1763. The stakes were high, since the winner of the struggle stood to gain supremacy in the West Indies and Canada and to dominate the lucrative colonial trade.

The First Three Wars

The first three wars were named after the king or queen under whose reign they occurred. In both King William's War (1689–1697) and Queen Anne's War (1702–1713), the English launched expeditions to capture Quebec, but their efforts failed. Native Americans supported by the French burned English frontier settlements. Ultimately, the English forces prevailed in Queen Anne's War and gained both Nova Scotia from France and trading rights in Spanish America.

A third war was fought during the reign of George II: King George's War (1744–1748). Once again, the British colonies were under attack from their perennial rivals, the French and the Spanish. In Georgia, James Oglethorpe led a colonial army that managed to repulse Spanish attacks. To the north, a force of New Englanders captured Louisbourg, a major French fortress, on Cape Breton Island, controlling access to the St. Lawrence River. In the peace treaty ending the war, however, Britain agreed to give Louisbourg back to the French in exchange for political and economic gains in India. New Englanders were furious about the loss of a fort that they had fought so hard to win.

The French and Indian War

The first three wars between England and France focused primarily on battles in Europe and only secondarily on conflict in the colonies. The European powers saw little value in committing regular troops to America. In the fourth and final war in the series, however, the fighting actually began in the colonies and then spread to Europe. Moreover, England and France now recognized the full importance of their colonies and shipped large numbers of troops overseas to North America rather than rely on "amateur" colonial forces. This fourth and most decisive war was known in the colonies as the French and Indian War (in Europe, it was called the Seven Years' War).

Beginning of the war. From the British point of view, the French provoked the war by building a chain of forts in the Ohio River Valley. One of the reasons the French did so was to halt the westward growth of the British colonies. Hoping to stop the French from completing work on Fort Duquesne (Pittsburgh) and thereby win control of the Ohio River Valley, the governor of Virginia sent a small militia (armed force) under the command of a young colonel named George Washington. After gaining a small initial victory, Washington's troops surrendered to a superior force of Frenchmen and their Native American allies on July 3, 1754. With this military encounter in the wilderness, the final war for empire began.

At first the war went badly for the British. In 1755, another expedition from Virginia, led by General Edward Braddock, ended in a disastrous defeat, as more than 2,000 British regulars and colonial troops were routed by a smaller force of French and Native Americans near Ft. Duquesne. The Algonquin allies of the French ravaged the frontier from western Pennsylvania to North Carolina. A British invasion of French Canada in 1756 and 1757 was repulsed.

The Albany Plan of Union. Recognizing the need for coordinating colonial defense, the British government called for representatives from several colonies to meet in a congress at Albany, New York, in 1754. The delegates from seven colonies adopted a plan—the Albany Plan of Union—developed by Benjamin Franklin that provided for an intercolonial government and a system for recruiting troops and collecting taxes from the various colonies for their common defense. (For an excerpt from the Albany Plan of Union, see pages 40–41.) Each colony was too jealous of its own taxation powers to accept the plan, however, and it never took effect. The Albany congress was significant, however, because it set a precedent for later, more revolutionary congresses in the 1770s.

British victory. In London, William Pitt, the new British prime minister, concentrated the government's military strategy on conquering Canada. This objective was accomplished with the retaking of Louisbourg in 1758, the surrender of Quebec to General James Wolfe in 1759, and the taking of Montreal in 1760. With these victories and the signing of a peace treaty in 1763, the British extended their control of North America, and French power on the continent virtually ended.

Through the peace treaty (the Peace of Paris), Great Britain acquired both French Canada and Spanish Florida. France ceded (gave up) to Spain its huge western territory, Louisiana, and claims west of the Mississippi River in compensation for Spain's loss of Florida.

Immediate effects of the war. Its victory in the French and Indian War gave Great Britain unchallenged supremacy in North America and also established that country as the dominant naval power in the world. No longer did the American colonies face the threat of concerted attacks from the French, the Spanish, and their Native American allies.

From the American point of view, no consequence of the war was more momentous than a fundamental change in the relationship between the colonies and the British government. Foremost was the change in how the British viewed the colonies and how the colonists viewed the home government.

The British view. The British came away from the war with a generally low opinion of the colonial military effort. They held the American militia in contempt as a poorly trained, disorderly rabble. Furthermore, they noted that some of the colonies had refused to contribute either troops or money to the war effort. The British who took this view were convinced that the colonists were both unable and unwilling to defend the new frontiers of the vastly expanded British empire.

The colonial view. The colonists took an opposite view of their military performance. They were proud of their record in all four wars and developed confidence that they could successfully provide for their own defense. They were not impressed with British troops or their leadership, whose methods of warfare seemed badly suited to America's densely wooded terrain.

Reorganization of the British Empire

Even more serious than the resentful feelings stirred by the war experience was the British government's decision to change its colonial policies. Previously,

Britain had exercised little direct control over the colonies and had generally allowed its navigation laws regulating colonial trade to go unenforced. This earlier policy of *salutary neglect* was now abandoned as the British saw a need to adopt more forceful policies for taking control of their expanded North American dominions.

All four wars—and the last one in particular—had been extremely costly. In addition, Britain now felt the need to maintain a large British military force to guard its American frontiers. Among British landowners, pressure was building to reduce the heavy taxes that the colonial wars had laid upon them.

King George III and the dominant political party in Parliament (the Whigs) pursued a colonial policy aimed at solving Britain's domestic financial problems. Making the American colonies bear more of the cost of maintaining the British empire was a popular policy with the various factions of Whigs that vied for the king's favor.

Pontiac's rebellion. The first major test of the new British imperial policy came in 1763 when Chief Pontiac led a major attack against colonial settlements on the western frontier. The Native Americans were angered by the growing westward movement of European settlers and by the British refusal to offer gifts as the French had done. Pontiac's alliance of Native Americans in the Ohio Valley destroyed forts and settlements from New York to Virginia. Rather than relying on colonial forces to retaliate, the British sent regular troops to deal with the "rebellion."

Proclamation of 1763. As a further measure for stabilizing the western frontier, the British government issued a proclamation that prohibited colonists from settling west of the Appalachian Mountains. Such a measure, it was hoped, would help to prevent future hostilities between colonists and Native Americans. But the colonists reacted to the proclamation with anger and defiance. After their victory in the French and Indian War, Americans hoped to reap benefits in the form of access to western lands. For the British to deny such benefits was infuriating. Defying the prohibition, thousands streamed westward beyond the imaginary boundary line drawn by the British. (See map, page 68.)

British Actions and Colonial Reactions

The Proclamation of 1763 was the first of a series of acts by the British government that were met with anger and resistance in the colonies. From the British point of view, each act was justified as a proper method for protecting its colonial empire and making the colonies pay their share of costs for such protection. From the colonists' point of view, each act represented an alarming threat to their cherished liberties and long-established practice of representative government.

New Revenues and Regulations

In the first two years of peace, Parliament adopted three measures that aroused colonial suspicions of a British plot to subvert their liberties. These were the Sugar Act of 1764, the Quartering Act of 1765, and the Stamp Act of 1765. Each measure expressed the imperial policies of King George III's chancellor of the exchequer (treasury) and prime minister, Lord George Grenville.

Sugar Act. This act (also known as the Revenue Act of 1764) placed duties on foreign sugar and certain luxuries. Its chief purpose was to raise money for the crown, and a companion law also provided for stricter enforcement of the Navigation Acts to stop smuggling. Those accused of smuggling were to be tried in admiralty courts by crown-appointed judges without juries.

Quartering Act. This act required the colonists to provide food and living quarters for British soldiers stationed in the colonies.

Stamp Act. In an effort to raise funds to support British military forces in the colonies, Lord Grenville turned to a tax long in use in England. The Stamp Act, enacted by Parliament in 1765, required that revenue stamps be placed on most printed paper in the colonies, including all legal documents, newspapers, pamphlets, and advertisements. This was the first direct tax—collected from those who used the goods—paid by the people in the colonies, as opposed to the taxes on goods that were imported into the colonies, which were paid by merchants.

Protesting the Stamp Act. People in every colony reacted with fury and indignation to news of the Stamp Act. A young Virginia lawyer named Patrick Henry expressed the sentiments of many when he stood up in the House of Burgesses to demand that the king's government recognize the rights of all citizens—including no taxation without representation. In Massachusetts, James Otis initiated a call for cooperative action among the colonies to protest the Stamp Act. Representatives from nine colonies met in New York in 1765 to form the so-called Stamp Act Congress. They resolved that only their own elected representatives had the legal authority to approve taxes.

The protest against the stamp tax took a violent turn with the formation of the Sons and Daughters of Liberty, a secret society organized for the purpose of intimidating tax agents. Members of this society sometimes tarred and feathered revenue officials and destroyed revenue stamps.

Boycotts against British imports were the most effective form of protest. It became fashionable in the colonies in 1765 and 1766 for people not to purchase any article of British origin. Faced with a sharp drop in trade, London merchants put pressure on Parliament to repeal the controversial Stamp Act.

Declaratory Act. In 1766, Grenville was replaced by another prime minister, and Parliament voted to repeal the Stamp Act. When news of the repeal reached the colonies, there was widespread rejoicing. Few colonists at the time were aware that Parliament had also enacted a face-saving measure known as the Declaratory Act (1766). This act asserted that Parliament had the right to tax and make laws for the colonies "in all cases whatsoever." This declaration of policy would soon lead to renewed misunderstanding and conflict between the American colonists and the British government.

Second Phase of the Crisis, 1767–1773

Because the British government still needed new revenues, the newly appointed chancellor of the exchequer, Charles Townshend, proposed another tax measure.

The Townshend Acts. Adopting Townshend's program in 1767, Parliament enacted new duties to be collected on colonial imports of tea, glass, and paper. The law required that the revenues raised be used to pay crown officials in the colonies, thus making them independent of the colonial assemblies that had previously paid their salaries. The Townshend Acts also provided for the search of private homes for smuggled goods. All that an official needed to conduct such a search would be a *writ of assistance* (a general license to search anywhere) rather than a judge's warrant permitting a search only of a specifically named property. Another of the Townshend Acts suspended New York's assembly for that colony's defiance of the Quartering Act.

Colonial reaction. At first, the colonists did not strongly protest the taxes under the Townshend Acts because they were indirect taxes paid by merchants at the ports (not direct taxes on consumer goods). Eventually, however, a few colonial leaders such as John Dickinson of Pennsylvania and Samuel Adams and James Otis of Massachusetts argued forcefully against the new duties. In his *Letters From a Farmer in Pennsylvania*, Dickinson agreed that Parliament could regulate commerce but argued that because duties were a form of taxation, they could not be levied on the colonies without the consent of their representative assemblies. Dickinson argued that the principle of no taxation without representation was an essential principle of English law.

In 1768, James Otis and Samuel Adams jointly wrote the Massachusetts Circular Letter and sent copies to every colonial legislature. It urged the various colonies to petition Parliament to repeal the Townshend Acts. British officials in Boston ordered the letter retracted, threatened to dissolve the legislature, and increased the number of British troops in Boston.

Responding to the circular letter, the colonists again conducted boycotts of British goods. Merchants increased their smuggling activities to avoid the offensive Townshend duties.

Repeal of the Townshend Acts. Meanwhile, in London, there was another change in the king's ministers. Lord Frederick North as the new prime minister urged Parliament to repeal the Townshend Acts because their effect was to damage trade and to generate only a disappointing amount of revenue.

A small tax on tea was retained as a symbol of Parliament's right to tax the colonies. The repeal of the Townshend Acts in 1770 ended the colonial boycott and, except for an incident in Boston (the "massacre" described below), there was a three-year respite from political troubles as the colonies entered into a period of economic prosperity.

Boston Massacre. The people of Boston generally resented the British troops who had been quartered in their city to protect customs officials from being attacked by the Sons of Liberty. On a snowy day in March 1770, a crowd of colonists harassed the guards near the customs house. The guards fired into the crowd, killing five people including an African American, Crispus Attucks. At their trial for murder, the soldiers were defended by colonial lawyer John Adams and acquitted. Adams' more radical cousin, Samuel Adams, angrily denounced the shooting incident as a "massacre." Later, the episode was often used by colonial leaders to inflame anti-British feeling.

Renewal of the Conflict

Even during the years of comparative peace, 1770–1772, Samuel Adams and a few other Americans kept alive the view that British officials were deliberately conspiring against colonial liberties. A principal device for spreading this idea was by means of the Committees of Correspondence initiated by Samuel Adams in 1772. In Boston and other Massachusetts towns, Adams began the practice of organizing committees that would regularly exchange letters about suspicious or potentially threatening British activities. The Virginia House of Burgesses took the concept a step further when it organized intercolonial committees in 1773.

The *Gaspee*. One incident frequently discussed in the committees' letters was that of the *Gaspee*. This British customs ship had been successful in catching a number of smugglers. In 1772, the ship ran aground off the shore of Rhode Island. Seizing their opportunity to destroy the hated vessel, a group of colonists disguised as Native Americans ordered the British crew ashore and then set fire to the ship. The British ordered a commission to investigate and bring guilty individuals to Britain for trial.

Boston Tea Party. The colonists continued their refusal to buy British tea because the British insisted on their right to collect the tax. Hoping to help the British East India Company out of its financial problems, Parliament passed the Tea Act in 1773, which made the price of the company's tea—even with the tax included—cheaper than that of smuggled Dutch tea.

Many Americans refused to buy the cheaper tea because to do so would, in effect, recognize Parliament's right to tax the colonies. A shipment of the East India Company's tea arrived in Boston harbor, but there were no buyers. Before the royal governor could arrange to bring the tea ashore, a group of Bostonians disguised themselves as Native Americans, boarded the British ships, and dumped 342 chests of tea into the harbor. Colonial reaction to this incident (December 1773) was mixed. While many applauded the Boston Tea Party as a justifiable defense of liberty, others thought the destruction of private property was far too radical.

Intolerable Acts

In England, news of the Boston Tea Party angered the king, Lord North, and members of Parliament. In retaliation, the British government enacted a series of punitive acts (the *Coercive Acts*), together with a separate act dealing with French Canada (the Quebec Act). The colonists were outraged by these various laws, which were given the epithet "Intolerable Acts."

The Coercive Acts (1774). There were four Coercive Acts, directed mainly at punishing the people of Boston and Massachusetts and bringing the dissidents under control.

1. The Port Act closed the port of Boston, prohibiting trade in and out of the harbor until the destroyed tea was paid for.
2. The Massachusetts Government Act reduced the power of the Massachusetts legislature while increasing the power of the royal governor.
3. The Administration of Justice Act allowed royal officials accused of crimes to be tried in England instead of in the colonies.
4. A fourth law expanded the Quartering Act to enable British troops to be quartered in private homes. It applied to all colonies.

Quebec Act (1774). When it passed the Coercive Acts, the British government also passed a law organizing the Canadian lands gained from France. This plan was accepted by most French Canadians, but it was resented by many in the 13 colonies.

Provisions. The Quebec Act established Roman Catholicism as the official religion of Quebec, set up a government without a representative assembly, and extended Quebec's boundary to the Ohio River.

American Anger. The colonists viewed the Quebec Act as a direct attack on the American colonies because it took away lands that they claimed along the Ohio River. They also feared that the British would attempt to enact similar laws in America to take away their representative government. The predominantly Protestant Americans also resented the recognition given to Catholicism.

Philosophical Foundations of the American Revolution

For Americans, especially those who were in positions of leadership, there was a long tradition of loyalty to the king and England. As the differences between them grew, many Americans searched for an explanation and justification for this changing relationship.

BRITISH COLONIES: PROCLAMATION LINE OF 1763 AND QUEBEC ACT OF 1774

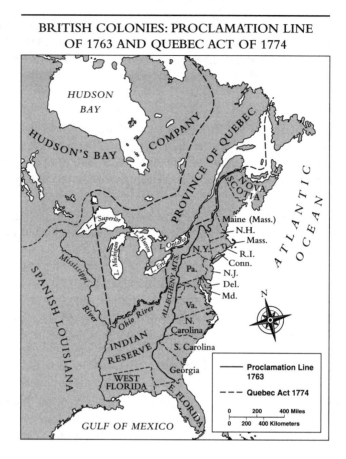

The Enlightenment

In the 18th century, some educated Americans were attracted to a European movement in literature and philosophy that is known as the Enlightenment. The leaders of this movement believed that the "darkness" of past ages could be corrected by the use of human reason in solving most of humanity's problems.

A major influence on the Enlightenment and on American thinking was the work of John Locke, a 17th-century English philosopher and political theorist. Locke, in his *Two Treatises of Government*, reasoned that while the state (the government) is supreme, it is bound to follow "natural laws" based on the rights that people have simply because they are human. He argued that sovereignty ultimately resides with the people rather than with the state. Furthermore, said Locke, citizens had a right and an obligation to revolt against whatever government failed to protect their rights.

Other Enlightenment philosophers adopted and expounded on Locke's ideas. His stress on natural rights would provide a rationale for the American Revolution and later for the basic principles of the U.S. Constitution.

Other ideas of the Enlightenment. The era of the Enlightenment was at its peak in the mid-18th century—the very years that future leaders of the American Revolution (Washington, Jefferson, Franklin, and Adams) were coming to maturity. Many of these Enlightenment thinkers in Europe and America were Deists, who believed that God had established natural laws in creating the universe, but that the role of divine intervention in human affairs was minimal. They believed in rationalism and trusted human reason to solve the many problems of life and society, and emphasized reason, science, and respect for humanity. Their political philosophy, derived from Locke and developed further by the French philosopher Jean-Jacques Rousseau, had a profound influence on educated Americans in the 1760s and 1770s—the decades of revolutionary thought and action that finally culminated in the American Revolution.

HISTORICAL PERSPECTIVES: REVOLUTION OR EVOLUTION?

Did America's break with Great Britain in the 18th century signify a true revolution with radical change, or was it simply the culmination of evolutionary changes in American life? For many years, the traditional view of the founding of America was that a revolution based on the ideas of the Enlightenment had fundamentally altered society.

During the 20th century, historians continued to debate whether American independence from Great Britain was revolutionary or evolutionary. At the start of the century, Progressive historians believed that the movement to end British dominance had provided an opportunity to radically change American society. A new nation was formed with a republican government based on federalism and stressing equality and the rights of the individual. The revolution was social as well as political.

During the second half of the 20th century, a different interpretation argued that American society had been more democratic and changed long before the war with Great Britain. Historian Bernard Bailyn has suggested that the changes that are viewed as revolutionary—representative government, expansion of the right to vote, and written constitutions—had all developed earlier, during the colonial period. According to this perspective, what was revolutionary or significant about the break from Great Britain was the recognition of an American philosophy based on liberty and democracy that would guide the nation.

KEY NAMES, EVENTS, AND TERMS

French and Indian War	Albany Plan of Union (1754)	George III; crown
George Washington	Peace of Paris (1763)	Whigs
Edward Braddock	salutary neglect	Parliament

Pontiac's Rebellion (1763)	*a Farmer in Pennsylvania*	Coercive Acts (1774)
Proclamation of 1763	Samuel Adams	Port Act
Sugar Act (1764)	James Otis	Massachusetts Government
Quartering Act (1765)	Massachusetts Circular Letter	Act
Stamp Act (1765)	Lord Frederick North	Administration of Justice Act
Patrick Henry	Boston Massacre (1770)	Quartering Act
Stamp Act Congress	Crispus Attucks	Quebec Act (1774)
Sons and Daughters of	Committees of	Enlightenment
Liberty	Correspondence	Deism
Declaratory Act (1766)	*Gaspee* incident	rationalism
Townshend Acts (1767)	Tea Act (1773)	John Locke
writs of assistance	Boston Tea Party (1773)	Jean-Jacques Rousseau
John Dickinson; *Letters From*	Intolerable Acts	

MULTIPLE-CHOICE QUESTIONS

1. Which of the following does NOT express a British criticism of the colonies in 1763?

    (A) Samuel Adams and other colonial leaders organized opposition to British authority.

    (B) Many colonists showed disloyalty by failing to support the war effort.

    (C) The colonial militia was badly trained.

    (D) Although the colonies benefited from the British victory, they failed to pay their fair share of war costs.

    (E) The Virginians under George Washington disobeyed orders in attacking a French fort.

2. "After the French and Indian War, the British government tried to make Americans pay for British protection in the colonies." Each of the following supports this statement EXCEPT the

    (A) Stamp Act

    (B) Sugar Act

    (C) Quartering Act

    (D) Townshend Acts

    (E) Quebec Act

3. Pontiac's Rebellion was a reaction to

    (A) the building of Fort Duquesne

    (B) the westward movement of English settlers

    (C) French control of the fur trade

    (D) the Proclamation of 1763

    (E) the outbreak of the French and Indian War

4. Which of the following was NOT a consequence of the Stamp Act?

    (A) Delegates from different colonies held a protest meeting in New York.

    (B) The Sons of Liberty threatened tax officials.

    (C) Colonial war debts were paid.

    (D) Colonists boycotted British goods.

    (E) London merchants suffered from a reduction in trade.

5. John Dickinson defended the idea of no taxation without representation by arguing that

(A) colonists owed no loyalty to the king

(B) Parliament could not regulate trade

(C) colonists were too poor to be taxed

(D) to tax people without their consent violated English law

(E) colonists did not have to submit to British authority

6. The Townshend Acts provoked all of the following colonial reactions EXCEPT

   (A) the Massachusetts Circular Letter

   (B) John Dickinson's *Letters From a Farmer in Pennsylvania*

   (C) the Stamp Act Congress

   (D) colonial boycotts of British goods

   (E) the *Gaspee* incident

7. The Boston Tea Party had which of the following causes?

   (A) the Boston Massacre

   (B) Parliament's efforts to improve the profits of the British East India Company

   (C) the Intolerable Acts

   (D) the arguments of the committees of correspondence

   (E) the imperial policies of Lord Grenville

8. Which of the following sources would be most useful in studying the philosophical foundations of the American Revolution?

   (A) John Dickinson's *Letters From a Farmer in Pennsylvania*

(B) Benjamin Franklin's *Poor Richard's Almanack*

(C) John Locke's *Two Treatises of Government*

(D) Jonathan Edwards' "Sinners in the Hands of an Angry God"

(E) the Albany Plan of Union

9. Enlightenment philosophers believed in all of the following ideas EXCEPT

   (A) People have the right to revolt against tyranny.

   (B) People have rights simply because they are human.

   (C) Sovereignty resides with the people.

   (D) A fundamental purpose of government is to protect people's rights.

   (E) God is the primary authority for government.

10. Which of the following is a correct statement about the American colonies in the 1770s before the outbreak of the Revolutionary War?

   (A) Except for a few radicals, Americans generally accepted the policies of George III's ministers.

   (B) Most Americans resisted the British government's efforts to impose new taxes.

   (C) France encouraged the British colonies to revolt.

   (D) Colonial boycotts failed to have an effect on British policy.

   (E) The 13 colonies had developed a single policy for dealing with Parliament.

Guide to Writing the DBQ

Deciding What Position to Argue

As with all essays, the crucial first step *before* writing is to take time to organize your thoughts. No matter what the question, decide first of all on the general idea—or thesis—you wish to prove or demonstrate.

Many students make an understandable but nevertheless serious mistake when approaching a question as long and complicated as the document-based question (DBQ). They assume that their essays must be based entirely on repeated references to the given documents. Often, therefore, they neglect to carry out the other part of the DBQ directions: "and your knowledge of the period." There is one good way to ensure that you incorporate into your essay both general and specific knowledge of a period—knowledge acquired from past study.

Try this: Before reading any of the documents, analyze the question carefully and decide how you would answer it *if there were no documents to deal with.* Consider the DBQ on page 74. Does the information about the American Revolution in the text lead you to agree or disagree with the statement? Why? On a piece of paper, jot down facts that support your *tentative* conclusion, or hypothesis. If several facts support your position, make that your thesis. If not, think of facts on the other side of the question and change your original response ("agree" or "disagree") to its opposite.

The next step is to look in the documents for additional support for your chosen position. (Historians generally work the other way around, from documentary evidence to conclusions, but time pressure on an exam compels you to work backward, from conclusions to evidence.) Read each document. Decide whether it can be used to support your thesis. If so, put a check next to the document. If not, move on to the next document. The exam writers are careful to include evidence on both sides of a question, and therefore you can be certain that at least three of the documents will give strong support to your case.

72

Practice

Divide a piece of paper into two vertical columns with these headings:

| *Agree With Statement* | | *Disagree With Statement* | |
| Facts | Documents | Facts | Documents |

For each position, list supporting and contradicting facts and documents in the appropriate columns. Compare your work with that of another student, adding to (or subtracting from) your lists to strengthen the arguments on both sides.

ESSAY QUESTIONS

1. "It is inseparably essential to the freedom of a People, and the undoubted Right of Englishmen, that no taxes be imposed on them, but with their own Consent, given personally, or by their representatives." (Resolutions of the Stamp Act Congress, 1765)

   Explain how TWO of the following incidents or activities demonstrated American support for this statement.

   Boston Tea Party
   colonial boycotts
   Gaspee incident
   Stamp Act Congress

2. Compare and contrast the American and the British views regarding the results of the French and Indian War.

3. "The passage of the Coercive Acts and the Quebec Act in 1774 was a direct assault against the rights of Americans." Assess this statement from the point of view of (a) Samuel Adams (b) Lord North.

4. Explain the connection between the ideas of the Enlightenment and the protest movement in the colonies against British imperial policy.

5. Compare and contrast the Townshend Acts of 1767 and the Intolerable Acts of 1774 in terms of (a) the British reason for enacting the laws (b) the nature of the laws.

DOCUMENT-BASED QUESTION

The following question is an example of a Document-Based Question (DBQ), which appears on each Advanced Placement examination. Write an essay that integrates your understanding of the documents that follow and your knowledge of the period.

> To what extent was the demand for no taxation without representation both the primary force motivating the American revolutionary movement and a symbol for democracy?

DOCUMENT A.

Resolved, That a most humble and dutiful Address be presented to his Majesty, imploring his Royal Protection of his faithful Subjects, the People of this Colony, in the Enjoyment of all their natural and civil Rights, as Men, and as Descendents of Britons; which rights must be violated, if Laws respecting the internal Government, and Taxation of themselves, are imposed upon them by any other Power than that derived from their own Consent, by and with the Approbation of their Sovereign, or his Substitute.

Resolution of the Virginia House of Burgesses, 1764

DOCUMENT B.

Section IV. That the people of these colonies are not, and from their local circumstances cannot be, represented in the House of Commons in Great-Britain.

Section V. That the only representatives of the people of these colonies, are persons chosen therein by themselves, and that no taxes ever have been, or can be constitutionally imposed on them, but by their respective legislatures.

Resolutions of the Stamp Act Congress, 1765

DOCUMENT C.

A right to impose an internal tax on the colonies, without their consent *for the single purpose of revenue,* is denied, a right to regulate their trade without their consent is admitted.

Daniel Dulany,
Considerations on the Propriety of
Imposing Taxes in the British Colonies, 1765

DOCUMENT D.

... and as it was soon found that this taxation could not be supported by reason and argument, it seemed necessary that one act of oppression should be enforced by another, and therefore, contrary to our just rights as possessing, or at least having a just title to possess, all the liberties and immunities of British subjects, a standing army was established among us in time of peace; and evidently for the purpose of effecting that which it was one principal design of the founders of the constitution to prevent (when they declared a standing army in a time of peace to be against law), namely, for the enforcement of obedience to acts which, upon fair examination, appeared to be unjust and unconstitutional.

Joseph Warren,
"Oration Delivered at Boston,"
March 5, 1772

DOCUMENT E.

To remind him [His Majesty] that our ancestors, before their emigration to America, were the free inhabitants of the British dominions in Europe, and possessed a right, which nature has given to all men, of departing from the country in which chance, not choice has placed them; of going in quest of new habitations, and of there establishing new societies, under such laws and regulations as in them shall seem most likely to promote public happiness.

Thomas Jefferson,
A Summary View of the Rights of British America, 1774

DOCUMENT F.

They [Parliament] have undertaken to give and grant our money without our consent, though we have ever exercised an exclusive right to dispose of our own property; statutes have been passed for extending the jurisdiction of courts of Admiralty and Vice-Admiralty beyond their ancient limits; for depriving us of the accustomed and inestimable privilege of trial by jury, in cases affecting both life and property; for suspending the legislature of one of the colonies; for interdicting all commerce to the capital of another; and for altering fundamentally the form of government established by charter, and secured by acts of its own legislature solemnly confirmed by the crown; for exempting the "murderers" of colonists from legal trial. . . .

Second Continental Congress,
Declaration of the Causes and Necessity
of Taking Up Arms, July 6, 1775

DOCUMENT G.

Small islands not capable of protecting themselves are the proper objects for kingdoms to take under their care; but there is something very absurd in supposing a continent to be perpetually governed by an island. In no instance hath nature made the satellite larger than its primary planet; and as England and America, with respect to each other, reverse the common order of nature, it is evident that they belong to different systems. England to Europe: America to itself. . . .

Thomas Paine,
Common Sense (1776)

DOCUMENT H.

Petitioners farther sheweth that we apprehand ourselves to be Aggreeved, in that while we are not allowed the Privilage of freemen of the State having no vote or influence in the Election of those that Tax us yet many of our Colour (as is well known) have cheerfully Entered the field of Battle in the defence of the Common Cause and that (as we conceive) against a similar Exertion of Power (in Regard to taxation). . . .

Petition of Seven Free Negroes to the
Massachusetts Legislature in Protest of Taxation
Without the Right to Vote,
February 10, 1780.
(Massachusetts Historical Society)

THE AMERICAN REVOLUTION AND CONFEDERATION, 1774–1787

O! ye that love mankind! Ye that dare oppose not only the tyranny but the tyrant, stand forth! Every spot of the Old World is overrun with oppression. Freedom hath been hunted round the globe. . . . O! receive the fugitive and prepare in time an asylum for mankind.

Thomas Paine, *Common Sense*, 1776

Parliament's passage of the Intolerable Acts in 1774 intensified the conflict between the colonies and Great Britain. In the next two years, many Americans reached the conclusion—unthinkable only a few years earlier—that the only solution to their quarrel with the British government was to sever all ties with it. How did events from 1774 to 1776 lead ultimately to this revolutionary outcome?

The First Continental Congress

The harsh and punitive nature of the Intolerable Acts drove all the colonies except Georgia to send delegates to a convention in Philadelphia in September 1774. The purpose of the convention—later known as the First Continental Congress—was to determine how the colonies should react to what, from their viewpoint, seemed to pose an alarming threat to their rights and liberties. At this time, most Americans had no desire for independence. They simply wanted to protest parliamentary intrusions on their rights and restore the relationship with the crown that had existed before the French and Indian War.

The Delegates

The delegates were a diverse group, whose views about the crisis ranged from radical to conservative. Leading the radical faction—those demanding the greatest concessions from Britain—were Patrick Henry of Virginia and Samuel Adams and John Adams of Massachusetts. The moderates included George Washington of Virginia and John Dickinson of Pennsylvania. The conservative delegates—those who favored a mild statement of protest—included John Jay of New York and Joseph Galloway of Pennsylvania. Unrepresented was the viewpoint of loyal colonists, who would not challenge the king's government in any way.

Actions of the Congress

The delegates voted on a series of proposed measures, each of which was intended to change British policy without offending moderate and conservative opinion in the colonies. Joseph Galloway proposed a plan, similar to the Albany Plan of 1754, that would have reordered relations with Parliament and formed a union of the colonies within the British empire. By only one vote, Galloway's plan failed to pass.

The following measures were adopted:

1. Originally enacted in Massachusetts, the *Suffolk Resolves* rejected the Intolerable Acts and called for their immediate repeal. The measure urged the various colonies to resist the Intolerable Acts by making military preparations and applying economic sanctions (boycott) against Great Britain.
2. Backed by moderate delegates, the Declaration of Rights and Grievances was a petition to the king urging him to redress (make right) colonial grievances and restore colonial rights. In a conciliatory gesture, the document recognized Parliament's authority to regulate commerce.
3. A third measure, the Association, urged the creation of committees in every town to enforce the economic sanctions of the Suffolk Resolves.
4. If colonial rights were not recognized, a final measure called for the meeting of a second congress in May 1775.

Fighting Begins

Angrily dismissing the petition of the First Continental Congress, the king's government declared Massachusetts to be in a state of rebellion and sent additional troops to that colony to deal with any further disorders there. The combination of colonial defiance and British determination to suppress it led to violent clashes in Massachusetts—what would prove to be the first battles of the American Revolution.

Lexington and Concord

On April 18, 1775, General Thomas Gage, the commander of British troops in Boston, sent a large force to seize colonial military supplies in the town of Concord. Warned of the British march by two riders, Paul Revere and William Dawes, the militia (or Minutemen) of Lexington assembled on the village green to face the British. The Americans were forced to retreat under heavy British fire; eight of their number were killed in the brief encounter. Who fired the first shot of this first skirmish of the American Revolution? The evidence is ambiguous, and the answer will probably never be known.

Continuing their march, the British entered Concord, where they destroyed some military supplies. On the return march to Boston, the long column of British soldiers was attacked by hundreds of militiamen firing at them from behind stone walls. The British suffered 250 casualties—and also considerable humiliation at being so badly mauled by "amateur" fighters.

Bunker Hill

Two months later, on June 17, 1775, a true battle was fought between opposing armies on the outskirts of Boston. A colonial militia of Massachusetts farmers fortified Breed's Hill, next to Bunker Hill, for which the ensuing battle was wrongly named. A British force attacked the colonists' position and managed to take the hill, suffering over a thousand casualties. Americans claimed a victory of sorts, having succeeded in inflicting heavy losses on the attacking British army.

The Second Continental Congress

Soon after the fighting broke out in Massachusetts, delegates to the Second Continental Congress met in Philadelphia in May 1775. The congress was divided between one group of delegates, mainly from New England, who thought the colonies should declare their independence, and another group, mainly from the middle colonies, who hoped the conflict could be resolved by negotiating a new relationship with Great Britain.

Military Actions

The congress adopted a Declaration of the Causes and Necessities for Taking Up Arms and called on the colonies to provide troops. George Washington was appointed the commander-in-chief of a new colonial army and sent to Boston to lead the Massachusetts militia and volunteer units from other colonies. Congress also authorized a force under Benedict Arnold to raid Quebec in order to draw Canada away from the British empire. An American navy and marine corps was organized in the fall of 1775 for the purpose of attacking British shipping.

Peace Efforts

At first the congress adopted a contradictory policy of waging war while at the same time seeking a peaceful settlement. Many in the colonies did not want independence, for they valued their heritage and Britain's protection, but they did want a change in their relationship with Britain. In July 1775, the delegates voted to send an "Olive Branch Petition" to King George III, in which they pledged their loyalty and asked the king to intercede with Parliament to secure peace and the protection of colonial rights.

King George angrily dismissed the congress' plea and agreed instead to Parliament's Prohibitory Act (August 1775), which declared the colonies in rebellion. A few months later, Parliament forbade all trade and shipping between England and the colonies.

Thomas Paine's Argument for Independence

In January 1776, a pamphlet was published that soon would have a profound impact on public opinion and the future course of events. The pamphlet, written by Thomas Paine, a recent English immigrant to the colonies, argued strongly for what until then had been considered a radical idea. Entitled *Common Sense,* Paine's essay argued in clear and forceful language for the colonies becoming independent states and breaking all political ties with the British monarchy. Paine argued that it was contrary to common sense for a large continent to be ruled by a small and distant island and for people to pledge allegiance to a king whose government was corrupt and whose laws were unreasonable.

The Declaration of Independence

After meeting for more than a year, the congress gradually and somewhat reluctantly began to favor independence rather than reconciliation. On June 7, 1776, Richard Henry Lee of Virginia introduced a resolution declaring the colonies to be independent. Five delegates including Thomas Jefferson formed a committee to write a statement in support of Lee's resolution. The declaration drafted by Jefferson listed specific grievances against George III's government and also expressed the basic principles that justified revolution:

> We hold these truths to be self-evident: That all men are created equal; that they are endowed by their Creator with certain unalienable rights; that among these are life, liberty, and the pursuit of happiness.

The congress adopted Lee's resolution calling for independence on July 2; Jefferson's work, the Declaration of Independence, was adopted on July 4, 1776.

The War

From the first shots fired on Lexington green in 1775 to the final signing of a peace treaty in 1783, the American War for Independence, or Revolutionary War, was a long and bitter struggle. Americans not only fought a war during this period but also forged a new national identity, as the former colonies became the United States of America.

Some 2.6 million people lived in the 13 colonies or states during the war. An estimated 40 percent of the population joined actively in the struggle against Britain. They called themselves American Patriots. A smaller number, 20–30 percent, sided with the British as Loyalists, while the rest tried to remain neutral and uninvolved.

Patriots

The largest number of Patriots were from the New England states and Virginia. Most of the soldiers were reluctant to travel outside their own region. They would serve in local militia units for short periods, leave to work their farms, and then return to duty. Thus, even though several hundred thousand people fought on the Patriot side in the war, General Washington never had more than 20,000 regular troops under his command at one time. His army was chronically short of supplies, poorly equipped, and rarely paid.

African Americans. Initially, George Washington rejected the idea of African Americans serving in the Patriot army. But when the British promised freedom to slaves who joined their side, Washington and the congress quickly made the same offer. Approximately 5,000 African Americans fought as Patriots. Most of them were freemen from the North, who fought in mixed racial forces, although there were some all-African American units. African Americans took part in most of the military actions of the war, and a number, including Peter Salem, were recognized for their bravery.

Loyalists

Tories. The Revolutionary War was in some respects a civil war in which anti-British Patriots fought pro-British Loyalists. Those who maintained their allegiance to the king were also called Tories (after the majority party in Parliament). Almost 60,000 American Tories fought and died next to British soldiers, supplied them with arms and food, and joined in raiding parties that pillaged Patriot homes and farms. Members of the same family sometimes joined opposite sides. While Benjamin Franklin was a leading patriot, for example, his son William Franklin joined the Tories and served during the war as the last royal governor of New Jersey.

How many American Tories were there? Estimates range from 520,000–780,000 people. In New York, New Jersey, and Georgia, they were probably in the majority. Toward the end of the war, about 80,000 Loyalists emigrated from the states to settle in Canada or Britain rather than face persecution at the hands of the victorious Patriots.

Social background. Although Loyalists came from all groups and classes, the majority tended to be wealthier and more conservative than the Patriots. Most government officials and Anglican clergymen in America remained loyal to the crown.

Native Americans. At first, the Native Americans tried to stay out of the war. Eventually, however, attacks by Americans moved many Native Americans to support the British, who promised to limit colonial settlements in the west.

Initial American Losses and Hardships

The first three years of the war, 1775 to 1777, went badly for Washington's poorly trained and equipped revolutionary army. It barely escaped complete disaster in a battle for New York City in 1776, in which Washington's forces were routed by the British. By the end of 1777, the British occupied both New York and Philadelphia. After losing Philadelphia, Washington's demoralized troops suffered through the severe winter of 1777–1778 camped at Valley Forge in Pennsylvania.

Economic troubles added to the Patriots' bleak prospects. British occupation of American ports resulted in a 95 percent decline in trade between 1775 and 1777. Goods were scarce, and inflation was rampant. The paper money issued by Congress, known as Continentals, became almost worthless.

Alliance With France

The few American military achievements early in the war had little impact on other nations. The turning point for the American revolutionaries came with a victory at Saratoga in upstate New York in October 1777. British forces under General John Burgoyne had marched from Canada in an ambitious effort to link up with other forces marching from the west and south. Their objective was to cut off New England from the rest of the colonies (or states). But Burgoyne's troops were attacked at Saratoga by troops commanded by American generals Horatio Gates and Benedict Arnold. The British army was forced to surrender.

The diplomatic outcome of the Battle of Saratoga was even more important than the military result. News of the surprising American victory persuaded France to join in the war against Britain. An absolute monarch, with all political power, Louis XVI had no interest in aiding a revolutionary movement. Nevertheless, the French king believed that he could weaken his country's traditional foe, Great Britain, by helping to undermine its colonial empire. France had secretly extended aid to the American revolutionaries as early as 1775, giving both money and supplies. After Saratoga, in 1778, France openly allied itself with the Americans. (A year later, Spain and Holland also entered the war against Britain.) The French alliance proved a decisive factor in the American struggle for independence because it widened the war and forced the British to divert military resources away from America.

Victory

Faced with a larger war, Britain decided to consolidate its forces in America. British troops were pulled out of Philadelphia, and New York became the chief base of British operations. In a campaign through 1778–1779, the Patriots, led by George Rogers Clark, captured a series of British forts in the Illinois country to gain control of parts of the vast Ohio territory. In 1780, the

British army adopted a southern strategy, concentrating its military campaigns in Virginia and the Carolinas where Loyalists were especially numerous and active.

Yorktown. In 1781, the last major battle of the Revolutionary War was fought near Yorktown, Virginia, on the shores of Chesapeake Bay. Strongly supported by French naval and military forces, Washington's army forced the surrender of a large British army commanded by General Charles Cornwallis.

Treaty of Paris. In London, news of Cornwallis' defeat at Yorktown came as a heavy blow to the Tory party in Parliament that was responsible for conducting the war. The war had become increasingly unpopular in England, partly because it placed a heavy strain on the British economy and the government's finances. Lord North and other Tory ministers resigned and were replaced by leaders of the Whig party who wanted to end the war.

In Paris, in 1783, a treaty of peace was finally signed by the various belligerents. The Treaty of Paris provided for the following: (1) Britain would recognize the existence of the United States as an independent nation. (2) The Mississippi River would be the western boundary of that nation. (3) Americans would have fishing rights off the coast of Canada. (4) Americans would pay debts owed to British merchants and honor Loyalist claims for property confiscated during the war.

Organization of New Governments

While the Revolutionary War was being fought, leaders of the 13 colonies worked to change them into independently governed states, each with its own constitution (written plan of government). At the same time, the revolutionary Congress that originally met in Philadelphia tried to define the powers of a new central government for the nation that was coming into being.

State Governments

By 1777, ten of the former colonies had written new constitutions. Most of these documents were both written and adopted by the states' legislatures. In a few of the states (Maryland, Pennsylvania, and North Carolina), a proposed constitution was submitted to a vote of the people for ratification (approval).

Each state constitution was the subject of heated debate between conservatives, who stressed the need for law and order, and liberals, who were most concerned about protecting individual rights and preventing future tyrannies. Although the various constitutions differed on specific points, they had the following features in common:

List of rights. Each state constitution began with a "bill" or "declaration" listing the basic rights and freedoms, such as a jury trial and freedom of religion, that belonged to all citizens by right and that state officials could not infringe (encroach on).

THE UNITED STATES IN 1783

Separation of powers. With a few exceptions, the powers of state government were given to three separate branches: (1) legislative powers to an elected two-house legislature, (2) executive powers to an elected governor, and (3) judicial powers to a system of courts. The principle of separation of powers was intended to be a safeguard against tyranny—especially against the tyranny of an overpowerful executive.

Voting. The right to vote was extended to all white males who owned some property. The property requirement, usually for a minimal amount of land or money, was based on the assumption that property-owners had a larger stake in government than did the poor and propertyless.

Office-holding. Those seeking elected office were usually held to a higher property qualification than the voters.

The Articles of Confederation

At Philadelphia in 1776, at the same time that Jefferson was writing the Declaration of Independence, John Dickinson drafted the first constitution for the United States as a nation. Congress modified Dickinson's plan to protect the powers of the individual states. The Articles of Confederation, as the document was called, was adopted by Congress in 1777 and submitted to the states for ratification.

Ratification. Ratification of the Articles was delayed by a dispute over the vast stretches of wilderness extending westward beyond the Alleghenies. Seaboard states like Rhode Island and Maryland insisted that such lands be placed under the jurisdiction of the new central government. When Virginia and New York finally agreed to give up their claims to western lands, the Articles were at last ratified in March 1781.

Structure of government. The Articles established a central government that consisted of just one body, a congress. In this unicameral (one-house) legislature, each state was given one vote, with at least nine votes out of 13 required to pass important laws. To amend the Articles, a unanimous vote was required. A Committee of States, with one representative from each state, could make minor decisions when the full congress was not in session.

Powers. The Articles gave the congress the power to wage war, make treaties, send diplomatic representatives, and borrow money. Certain important powers *not* given to the Congress were the power to regulate commerce or to collect taxes. (To finance any of its decisions, the congress had to rely upon taxes voted by each state.) Neither did the congress have any executive power to enforce its own laws.

Accomplishments. Despite its weaknesses, the congress under the Articles did succeed in accomplishing the following:

1. *Winning the war.* The U.S. government could claim some credit for the ultimate victory of Washington's army and for negotiating favorable terms in the treaty of peace with Britain.
2. *Land Ordinance of 1785.* Congress established a policy for surveying and selling the western lands. The policy provided for setting aside one section of land in each township for public education.
3. *Northwest Ordinance of 1787.* For the large territory lying between the Great Lakes and the Ohio River, the congress passed an ordinance (law) that set the rules for creating new states. The Northwest Ordinance granted limited self-government to the developing territory and prohibited slavery in the region.

Problems with the articles. The 13 states intended the central government to be weak—and it was. Making such a government work presented three kinds of problems:

1. Financial. Most war debts were unpaid. Individual states as well as the congress issued worthless paper money. The underlying problem was that the congress had no taxing power and could only request that the states donate money for national needs.

2. Foreign. European nations had little respect for a new nation that could neither pay its debts nor take effective and united action in a crisis. Britain and Spain threatened to take advantage of U.S. weakness by expanding their interests in the western lands soon after the war ended.

3. Domestic. In the summer of 1786, Captain Daniel Shays, a Massachusetts farmer and Revolutionary War veteran, led other farmers in an uprising against high state taxes, imprisonment for debt, and lack of paper money. The rebel farmers stopped the collection of taxes and forced the closing of debtors' courts. In January 1787, when Shays and his followers attempted to seize weapons from the Springfield armory, the state militia of Massachusetts broke Shays' Rebellion.

Social Change

In addition to revolutionizing the politics of the 13 states, the War for Independence also had a profound effect on American society. Some changes occurred immediately before the war ended, while others evolved gradually as the ideas of the Revolution began to filter into the thoughts and attitudes of the common people.

Abolition of Aristocratic Titles

State constitutions and laws abolished old institutions that had originated in medieval Europe. No legislature could grant titles of nobility, nor could any court recognize the feudal practice of primogeniture (the first born son's right to inherit his parents' property).

Whatever aristocracy existed in colonial America was further weakened by the confiscation of large estates owned by Loyalists. Many such estates were subdivided and sold to raise money for the war.

Separation of Church and State

Most states adopted the principle of separation of church and state; in other words, they refused to give financial support to any religious group. The Anglican Church, which formerly had been closely tied to the king's government, was disestablished in the South (lost state support). Only in three New England states—New Hampshire, Connecticut, and Massachusetts—did the Congregational Church continue to receive state support in the form of a religious tax. This practice was finally discontinued in New England early in the 19th century.

Women

During the war, both the Patriots and Loyalists depended on the active support of women. Some women followed their men into the armed camps and worked as cooks and nurses. In a few instances, women actually fought in battle, either taking their husband's place, as Mary McCauley (Molly Pitcher) did at the Battle of Monmouth, or passing as a man and serving as a soldier, as Deborah Sampson did for a year.

The most important contribution of women during the war was in maintaining the colonial economy. While fathers, husbands, and sons were away fighting, women ran the family farms and businesses. They provided much of the food and clothing necessary for the war effort.

Despite their contributions, women remained in a second-class status. Unanswered went pleas such of those of Abigail Adams to her husband, John Adams: "I desire you would remember the ladies and be more generous and favorable to them than your ancestors."

Slavery

The institution of slavery contradicted the spirit of the Revolution and the idea that "all men are created equal." For a time, the leaders of the Revolution recognized this fact and took some steps toward corrective action. The Continental Congress voted to abolish the importation of slaves, and most states went along with the prohibition. Most northern states ended slavery, while in the South, some owners voluntarily freed their slaves.

Soon after the Revolutionary War, however, a majority of southern slaveowners came to believe that slave labor was essential to their economy. As we shall see in later chapters, they developed a rationale for slavery that gave religious and political justification for continuing to hold human beings in lifelong bondage.

HISTORICAL PERSPECTIVES: THE REVOLUTION—RADICAL OR CONSERVATIVE?

Should we view the American Revolution as (1) a radical break with the past or (2) a conservative attempt simply to safeguard traditional British liberties? One approach to this question is to compare the American Revolution with other revolutions in world history.

In his *Anatomy of a Revolution* (1965), the historian Crane Brinton found striking similarities between the American Revolution and two later revolutions—the French Revolution (1789–1794) and the Russian Revolution (1917–1922). He observed that each revolution passed through similar stages and became increasingly radical from one year to the next.

Other historians have been more impressed with the differences between the American experience and the revolutions in Europe. They argue that the French and Russian revolutionaries reacted to conditions of feudalism and aristocratic privilege that did not exist in the American colonies. In their view, Americans did not revolt against outmoded institutions but, in their quest for independence, merely carried to maturity a liberal, democratic movement that had been gaining force for years.

In comparing the three revolutions, a few historians have concentrated on the actions of revolutionary mobs, such as the American Sons of Liberty. Again there are two divergent interpretations: (1) the mobs in all three countries engaged in the same radical activities, and (2) the American mobs had a much easier time of it than the French and Russian mobs, who encountered ruthless repression by military authorities.

Another interpretation of the American Revolution likens it to the colonial rebellions that erupted in Africa and Asia after World War II. According to this view, the colonial experience in America caused a gradual movement away from Britain that culminated in demands for independence. Other studies of the military aspects of the Revolution have pointed out similarities between American guerrilla forces in the 1770s and the guerrilla bands that fought in such countries as Cuba in the 1950s and Vietnam in the 1960s. Recall that the British controlled the cities while the American revolutionaries controlled the countryside—a pattern that in the 20th century was often repeated in revolutionary struggles throughout the world. Typically, as in the case of the American Revolution, insurgent forces were weak in the cities, but strong in the surrounding territory.

By going beyond the American Revolution, to view it relative to other revolutions, we gain valuable insights that enable us to understand it better.

KEY NAMES, EVENTS, AND TERMS

First Continental Congress (1774)	economic sanctions	Declaration of the Causes and Necessities for Taking Up Arms
Patrick Henry	Declaration of Rights and Grievances	
Samuel Adams	Paul Revere	Olive Branch Petition
John Adams	William Dawes	Prohibitory Act (1775)
George Washington	Minutemen	Thomas Paine; *Common Sense*
John Dickinson	Lexington	
John Jay	Concord	Declaration of Independence
Joseph Galloway	Battle of Bunker Hill	Thomas Jefferson
Suffolk Resolves	Second Continental Congress (1775)	Patriots
		Loyalists (Tories)

Valley Forge	Treaty of Paris (1783)	Shays' Rebellion
Continentals	Articles of Confederation	Mary McCauley (Molly
George Rogers Clark	unicameral legislature	Pitcher)
Battle of Saratoga	Land Ordinance of 1785	Deborah Sampson
absolute monarch	Northwest Ordinance of	Abigail Adams
Battle of Yorktown	1787	

MULTIPLE-CHOICE QUESTIONS

1. Which of the following sources would be most useful in researching a paper entitled "Arguments for Independence, 1776"?
   (A) John Dickinson's *Letters From a Farmer in Pennsylvania*
   (B) the Olive Branch Petition
   (C) John Locke's *Two Treatises of Government*
   (D) Treaty of Paris (1783)
   (E) Thomas Paine's *Common Sense*

2. The Battle of Saratoga had all of the following consequences EXCEPT
   (A) encouraged the British to grant most of the American demands
   (B) persuaded the French to form an alliance with the United States
   (C) defeated a British attempt to isolate New England from the other colonies
   (D) gave a boost to American morale
   (E) caused the British to adopt a different military strategy

3. The First Continental Congress was a reaction to
   (A) the Declaratory Act
   (B) fighting at Lexington and Concord
   (C) passage of the Intolerable Acts
   (D) the Boston Massacre
   (E) the British tax on tea

4. In his pamphlet *Common Sense,* Thomas Paine defended the idea of American independence on the grounds that
   (A) all men are created equal
   (B) Parliament was dictatorial
   (C) people should not pledge allegiance to a king and a corrupt government
   (D) democratic government of, by, and for the people was the only type based on natural law and reason
   (E) liberty belongs to those who fight for it.

5. As a result of the Treaty of Paris, the United States gained all of the following EXCEPT
   (A) fishing rights off the coast of Canada
   (B) British recognition of U.S. independence
   (C) a western boundary on the Mississippi River
   (D) the territory of Florida
   (E) a peaceful settlement of the Revolutionary War.

6. Which of the following most accurately describes those Americans who fought on the

British side in the American Revolution?

(A) They came from all groups and classes.

(B) They were a majority of the population.

(C) They were most numerous in New England.

(D) They were generally identified with the Whig party in England.

(E) They were motivated by a desire for financial gain.

7. Which of the following most accurately describes the change in American public opinion between January 1774 and July 1776?

(A) It changed from a desire for reconciliation to a decision for independence.

(B) Most people favored independence in 1774 but were willing to fight for it only after the Declaration of Independence.

(C) Loyalists were in the majority both in 1774 and 1776.

(D) By the summer of 1776, only a relatively small number of Americans expressed support for the king's government.

(E) Military support from France encouraged American Patriots.

8. Statement: "The Articles of Confederation succeeded in guiding the United States through its first decade." Each of the following actions supports this statement EXCEPT

(A) Congress regulated interstate trade.

(B) Congress enacted the Land Ordinance of 1785.

(C) Congress enacted the Northwest Ordinance.

(D) The U.S. government signed a favorable treaty of peace.

(E) The U.S. government conducted the war effort that resulted in American independence.

9. Statement: "The new state constitutions enacted during the Revolutionary War reflect the Patriots' emphasis on individual liberty." Each of the following actions supports this statement EXCEPT

(A) starting each constitution with a bill of rights

(B) providing for separation of powers to limit abuses

(C) submitting proposed constitutions to the people for ratification

(D) the absence of any provision for the abolition of slavery

(E) providing for separation of church and state

10. Which of the following is a correct statement about the United States at the end of the Revolutionary War?

(A) The central government was stronger than any state government.

(B) Women received greater political rights.

(C) Aristocratic privileges were reduced or eliminated.

(D) Slavery was unchallenged.

(E) Every state adopted the idea of separation of church and state.

ESSAY QUESTIONS

1. "The work of both the First and Second Continental Congresses was marked by disputes between moderates and radicals." Give detailed support for this statement by comparing and contrasting two documents: (a) Galloway's Plan and (b) the Declaration of the Causes and Necessities for Taking Up Arms.

2. Compare and contrast the background of two groups of Americans: those who became Loyalists and those who became Patriots.

3. "The writings of Thomas Paine had a greater impact on the winning of American independence than any other single event, including the Battle of Saratoga." Explain why you either agree or disagree with this statement.

4. To what extent is it accurate to call the American Revolution a civil war?

5. To what extent was the central government under the Articles of Confederation successful in governing the United States?

DOCUMENTS AND READINGS

Was it inevitable that the 13 colonies decided to seek their independence from the British empire? Or might there have been other, less drastic solutions to the problems that the colonies faced in the early 1770s?

As you know, moderates at the First and Second Continental Congresses proposed that the colonies and Great Britain work out a new and looser association between them. This plan, put forward by Joseph Galloway and others, suggested that the colonies have complete control over their own domestic affairs while Great Britain regulated such external affairs as transatlantic trade, diplomacy, and war.

In the documents that follow, you will read the arguments of two Americans (Richard Bland and James Wilson) supporting the idea of a federal empire and the arguments of two British leaders (Lord Mansfield and King George III) condemning the colonies for their "rebellious" acts.

DOCUMENT A. A NEW POLITICAL SOCIETY

Richard Bland, a member of the House of Burgesses for over 30 years, was one of the first American colonists to propose a federated British empire. After the Stamp Act crisis, he wrote the following essay (1766) in which he argued that the colonies had their own sovereignty distinct from that of Britain.

Now when Men exercise this Right, and withdraw themselves from their Country, they recover their natural Freedom and Independence: The Jurisdiction and Sovereignty of the State they have quitted ceases; and if they unite, and by common Consent take Possession of a new Country, and form themselves into a political Society, they become a sovereign State, independent of the State from which they separated. If then the Subjects of England have a natural Right to relinquish their Country, and by retiring from it, and associating together, to form a new political Society and independent State, they must have a Right, by Compact with the Sovereign of the Nation, to remove into a new Country, and to form a civil Establishment upon the Terms of the Compact. . . .

From this Detail of the Charters, and other Acts of the Crown, under which the first Colony in North America was established, it is evident that "the Colonists were not a few unhappy fugitives who had wandered into a distant Part of the World to enjoy their civil and religious liberties, which they were deprived of at home," but had a regular Government long before the first Act of Navigation, and were respected as a distinct State, independent, as to their *internal* Government, of the original Kingdom, but united with her, as to their *external* Polity, in the closest and most intimate LEAGUE and AMITY, under the same Allegiance, and enjoying the Benefits of a reciprocal Intercourse.

Richard Bland,
"An Inquiry Into the Rights of the British Colonies," 1766

DOCUMENT B.   *ALLEGIANCE TO THE KING—BUT NOT TO PARLIAMENT*

Responding to the Intolerable Acts of 1774, several American leaders, including Samuel Adams of Massachusetts, Thomas Jefferson of Virginia, and James Wilson of Pennsylvania, drew a distinction between Parliament's authority to make laws for the colonies and the king's authority in making foreign policy. They denied Parliament's claim to power while accepting the king's. Wilson's argument for this position follows.

What has already advanced will suffice to show, that it is repugnant to the essential maxims of jurisprudence, to the ultimate end of all governments, to the genius of the British constitution, and to the liberty and happiness of the Colonies, that they should be bound by the legislative authority of the parliament of Great Britain. . . .

I am sufficiently aware of an objection, that will be made to what I have said concerning the legislative authority of the British parliament. It will be alleged, that I throw off all dependence on Great Britain. . . . I shall take some pains to obviate the objection, and to show that a denial of the legislative authority of the British parliament over America is by no means inconsistent with that connection, which ought to subsist between the mother country and her Colonies, and which, at the first settlement of those Colonies, it was intended to maintain between them; but that, on the contrary, that connection would be entirely destroyed by the extension of the power of parliament over the American plantations. . . .

From this dependence, abstracted from every other source, arises a strict connection between the inhabitants of Great Britain and those of America. They are fellow-subjects; they are under allegiance to the same prince; and this union of allegiance naturally produces a union of hearts. It is also productive of a union of measures through the whole British dominions. To the King is intrusted the direction and management of the great machine of government. He therefore is fittest to adjust the different wheels, and to regulate their motions in such a manner as to co-operate in the same general designs. He makes war; he concludes peace: he forms alliances: he regulates domestic trade by his prerogative, and directs foreign commerce by his treaties with those nations with whom it is carried on. He names the officers of government; so that he can check every jarring movement in the administration. He has a negative [veto] on the different legislatures throughout his dominions, so that he can prevent any repugnancy in their different laws. . . .

James Wilson,
*Considerations on the Nature and Extent of the
Legislative Authority of the British Parliament,* 1774

DOCUMENT C. *THE BRITISH VIEW: PARLIAMENT'S RIGHT TO RULE*

Tory members of Parliament had an entirely different view of that body's authority as it applied to the American colonies. In a speech before the House of Lords in 1766, Lord Mansfield argued that Parliament had the ultimate legislative power for the entire empire.

What has been wrote by those who have treated on the laws of nature, or of other nations, in my opinion, is not at all applicable to the present question. . . .

. . . I shall therefore use my endeavors, in what I have to offer your lordships on this occasion, to quiet men's minds upon this subject.

In order to do this, I shall first lay down two propositions:

1st, That the British legislature, as to the power of making laws, represents the whole British empire, and has authority to bind every part and every subject without the least distinction, whether such subjects have a right to vote or not, or whether the law binds places within the realm or without.

2nd, That the colonists, by the condition on which they migrated, settled, and now exist, are more emphatically subjects of Great

Britain than those within the realm; and that the British legislature have in every instance exercised their right of legislation over them without any dispute or question til the 14th of January last.

As to the 1st proposition:

In every government the legislative power must be lodged somewhere, and the executive must likewise be lodged somewhere.

In Great Britain the legislative is in parliament, the executive in the crown. . . .

No distinction ought to be taken between the authority of parliament, over parts within or without the realm; but it is an established rule of construction, that no parts without the realm are bound unless named in the act. And this rule establishes the right of parliament; for unless they had a right to bind parts out of the realm, this distinction would have been made. . . .

As to the second proposition I laid out,

It must be granted that they migrated with leave as colonies, and therefore from the very meaning of the word were, are, and must be subjects, and owe allegiance and subjection to their mother country.

Lord Mansfield,
Debate on the Repeal of the Stamp Act,
House of Lords, 1766

DOCUMENT D.   *THE KING'S VIEW*

King George III expressed his view of the British–colonial relationship in a speech to Parliament in late 1775—after fighting had broken out at Lexington and Concord. Both the king and the majority party in Parliament viewed any compromise with the colonies as a threat to the continued existence of the British empire.

The authors and promoters of this desperate conspiracy have, in the conduct of it, derived great advantage from the difference of our intention and theirs. They meant only to amuse, by vague expressions of attachment to the parent state, and the strongest protestations of loyalty to me, whilst they were preparing for a general revolt. On our part, though it was declared in your last session that a rebellion existed within the province of the Massachusetts Bay, yet even that province we wished rather to reclaim than to subdue. The resolutions of parliament breathed a spirit of moderation and forbearance; conciliatory propositions accompanied the measures taken to enforce authority, and the coercive acts were adapted to cases of criminal combinations amongst subjects not then in arms. I have acted with the same temper, anxious to prevent, if it had been possible, the effusion of the blood of my subjects, and the calamities which are inseparable from a state of war; still hoping that my people in America would have discerned the traitorous views of their leaders, and have been convinced, that to be a subject of Great Britain, with all its consequences, is to be the freest member of any civil society in the known world.

The rebellious war now levied is become more general, and is manifestly carried on for the purpose of establishing an independent empire. I need not dwell upon the fatal effects of the success of such a plan. The object is too important, the spirit of the British nation too high, the resources with which God hath blessed her too numerous, to give up so many colonies which she has planted with great industry, nursed with great tenderness, encouraged with many commercial advantages, and protected and defended at much expense of blood and treasure. . . .

King George III,
Speech to Parliament,
October 1775

ANALYZING THE DOCUMENTS

1. Explain the differences between Mansfield's view of the colonial relationship and the views expressed by Bland and Wilson.

2. "By 1775, it was obvious to both the British government and American colonial leaders that there was no workable compromise between their differing views of empire."

Assess this statement in an essay based on the documents provided and your own knowledge of the period.

THE CONSTITUTION AND THE NEW REPUBLIC, 1787–1800

Thus I consent, sir, to this Constitution, because I expect no better, and because I am not sure that it is not the best. The opinions I have had of its errors I sacrifice to the public good. . . .

Benjamin Franklin, 1787

With these words, Franklin, the oldest delegate at the Constitutional Convention in Philadelphia, attempted to overcome the skepticism of other delegates about the document that they had created. Would the new document, the Constitution, establish a central government strong enough to hold 13 states together in a union that could prosper and endure?

In September 1787, when Franklin, Washington, and other delegates signed the Constitution that they had drafted, their young country was in a troubled state. This chapter will summarize the problems leading to the Constitutional Convention, the debates in the various states on whether to ratify the new plan of government, and the struggles of two presidents, Washington and Adams, to meet the domestic and international challenges of the 1790s.

The United States Under the Articles, 1781–1787

Between the signing of the Treaty of Paris of 1783 and the meeting of the Constitutional Convention in Philadelphia was a period of only four years. As you recall, the original U.S. government under the Articles of Confederation consisted of a one-house congress, no separate executive, and no separate judiciary (court system). Let us review some of the major problems the United States faced immediately after winning its independence.

Foreign Problems

Relations between the United States and the major powers of Europe were troubled from the start. The states failed to adhere to the Treaty of Paris, which required that Loyalists' property be restored and debts to foreigners be repaid. Also, a weak U.S. government under the Articles could do nothing to stop Britain from placing restrictions on trade and maintaining military outposts on the western frontier.

Economic Weakness and Interstate Quarrels

Reduced foreign trade and limited credit due to nonpayment of war debts contributed to widespread economic depression. The inability to levy national taxes and the printing of worthless paper money by many states added to the problems. In addition, the 13 states treated one another with suspicion and competed for economic advantage. They placed tariffs and other restrictions on the movement of goods across state lines. A number of states also entered into boundary disputes that increased interstate rivalry and tension.

The Annapolis Convention

To review what could be done about the country's inability to overcome critical problems, George Washington hosted a conference at his home in Mt. Vernon, Virginia (1785). Representatives from four states (Virginia, Maryland, Delaware, and Pennsylvania) agreed that the problems were serious enough to hold further discussions at a later meeting at Annapolis, Maryland, at which all the states might be represented.

In fact, only five states sent delegates to the Annapolis Convention in 1786. After discussing ways to improve commercial relations among the states, James Madison and Alexander Hamilton persuaded the others that another convention should be held in Philadelphia for the purpose of revising the Articles of Confederation.

Drafting the Constitution at Philadelphia

After a number of states elected delegates to the proposed Philadelphia convention, congress consented to give its approval to the meeting. It called upon all 13 states to send delegates to Philadelphia "for the sole and express purpose of revising the Articles of Confederation." Only Rhode Island, not trusting the other states, refused to send delegates.

The Delegates

Of the 55 white male delegates who went to Philadelphia for the convention in the summer of 1787, most were college-educated and relatively young (averaging in their early forties). With few exceptions, they were far wealthier than the average American of their day. They were well acquainted with issues of law and politics. A number of them were practicing lawyers, and many had helped to write their state constitutions.

The first order of business was to elect a presiding officer and decide whether or not to communicate with the public at large. The delegates voted to conduct their meetings in secret and say nothing to the public about their discussions until their work was completed. George Washington was unanimously elected chairperson. Benjamin Franklin, the elder statesman at age 81, provided a calming and unifying influence. The work in fashioning specific articles of the Constitution was directed by James Madison (who came to be known as the father of the Constitution), Alexander Hamilton, Gouverneur Morris, and John Dickinson. While they represented different states, these convention leaders shared the common goal of wanting to strengthen the young nation.

By no means were all the major leaders of the American Revolution represented at the convention. John Jay, Thomas Jefferson, John Adams, and Thomas Paine were on diplomatic business abroad. Samuel Adams and John Hancock were not chosen as delegates. Patrick Henry, who opposed any growth in federal power, refused to take part in the convention.

The Issues

At first the delegates disagreed sharply on the fundamental issue of whether they should simply make changes in the Articles or draft an entirely new document. Those committed to the latter alternative were strong nationalists like Madison and Hamilton, who quickly took control of the convention.

Americans in the 1780s generally distrusted government and feared that officials would seize every opportunity to abuse their powers, even if they were elected democratically. Therefore, James Madison and other convention delegates wanted to make sure that the new constitution would be based on a system of checks and balances (one branch of government having sufficient power to check the others).

Representation. Especially divisive was the issue of whether the larger states such as Virginia and Pennsylvania should have proportionally more representatives in Congress than the smaller states such as New Jersey and Delaware. Madison's proposal—the Virginia Plan—favored the large states; it was countered by the New Jersey Plan, which favored the small states. The issue was finally resolved by a compromise solution. The Connecticut Plan, or *Great Compromise,* provided for a two-house Congress. Each state would be given equal representation in the Senate; but in the larger body, the House of Representatives, each state would be represented according to the size of its population.

Slavery. How were slaves to be counted in the populations of the states? Were the slave trade and slavery itself to be allowed under the Constitution? Disagreement on these questions between northern and southern states was finally resolved by:

- the so-called *Three-fifths Compromise,* which counted each slave as three-fifths of a person for the purposes of determining a state's level of taxation and representation

- a guarantee that slaves could be imported for at least 20 years longer (until 1808), at which time Congress could vote to abolish the practice.

Trade. The northern states wanted the central government to regulate interstate commerce and foreign trade. The South was afraid that export taxes would be placed on its agricultural products such as tobacco and rice. The *Commercial Compromise* allowed Congress to regulate interstate and foreign commerce, including placing *tariffs* (taxes) on foreign imports, but it prohibited placing taxes on any exports.

Powers and election of the president. The delegates disagreed over the president's term of office (some arguing that the chief executive should hold office for life) and also over the method for electing a president. It was finally decided to grant the president considerable power, including the power to veto acts of Congress. The delegates limited the president's term of office to four years but set no limit to the number of terms to which a president could be reelected. Rather than having the people elect a president directly, the delegates decided to assign to each state a number of electors equal to the total of that state's representatives and senators. This electoral college system was instituted because the delegates at Philadelphia feared that too much democracy might lead to mob rule.

Ratification. On September 17, 1787, after 17 weeks of debate, the Philadelphia convention approved a draft of the Constitution to submit to the states for ratification. Anticipating opposition to the document, the Framers (delegates) specified that a favorable vote of only nine states out of 13 would be required for ratification. Each state would hold popularly elected conventions to debate and vote on the proposed Constitution.

Federalists and Anti-Federalists

Ratification was fiercely debated for almost a year, from September 1787 until June 1788. Those who supported the Constitution and a strong federal government were known as Federalists. Opponents were known as Anti-Federalists. Those on either side of the question could be found in all regions and classes, although Federalists tended to be most numerous along the Atlantic Coast and in the large cities while Anti-Federalists tended to be small farmers and settlers on the western frontier. The table on page 100 summarizes the arguments, advantages, and disadvantages of the opposing forces.

	Federalists	Anti-Federalists
Leaders	George Washington, Benjamin Franklin, James Madison, Alexander Hamilton	From Virginia: George Mason and Patrick Henry. From Massachusetts: James Winthrop and John Hancock. From New York: George Clinton
Arguments	Stronger central government was needed to maintain order and preserve the Union	Stronger central government would destroy the work of the Revolution, limit democracy, and restrict states' rights
Strategy	Emphasized the weaknesses of the Articles of Confederation; showed their opponents as merely negative opponents with no solutions	Argued that the proposed Constitution contained no protection of individual rights, that it gave the central government more power than the British ever had
Advantages	Strong leaders; well organized	Appealed to popular distrust of government based on colonial experience
Disadvantages	Constitution was new and untried; as originally written, it lacked a bill of rights	Poorly organized; slow to respond to Federalist challenge

The Federalist Papers

A key element in the Federalist campaign for the Constitution was a series of highly persuasive essays written for a New York newspaper by James Madison, Alexander Hamilton, and John Jay. The 85 essays, later published in book form as *The Federalist Papers,* presented cogent reasons for believing in the practicality of each major provision of the Constitution.

Outcome

The Federalists won early victories in the state conventions in Delaware, New Jersey, and Pennsylvania—the first three states to ratify. By promising to add a bill of rights to the Constitution, they successfully addressed the Anti-Federalists' most telling objection. With New Hampshire voting yes in June 1788, the Federalists won the necessary nine states to achieve ratification of the Constitution. Even so, the larger states of Virginia and New York had not yet acted. If they failed to ratify, any chance for national unity and strength would be in dire jeopardy.

Virginia. In 1788, Virginia was by far the most populous of the original 13 states. There, the Anti-Federalists rallied behind two strong leaders, George Mason and Patrick Henry, who viewed the Constitution and a strong central government as threats to Americans' hard-won liberty. Virginia's Federalists, led by Washington, Madison, and John Marshall, managed to prevail by a close vote only after promising a bill of rights.

Other states. News of Virginia's vote had enough influence on New York's ratifying convention (combined with Alexander Hamilton's efforts) to win the day for the Constitution in that state. North Carolina in November 1789 and Rhode Island in May 1790 reversed their earlier rejections and thus became the last two states to ratify the Constitution as the new "supreme law of the land."

Adding the Bill of Rights

Was it necessary for people's rights to be listed in the Constitution? In the early months of the ratification debates, Anti-Federalists argued vehemently in favor of a bill of rights, while Federalists argued against it.

Arguments for a Bill of Rights

Anti-Federalists argued as follows: Americans had fought the Revolutionary War to escape the tyranny of a central government in Britain. What was to stop a strong central government under the Constitution from acting in a tyrannical manner? Only by adding a bill of rights could Americans be protected against such a possibility.

Arguments Against a Bill of Rights

Federalists argued as follows: Since members of Congress would be elected by the people, they did not need to be protected against themselves. Furthermore, it was better to assume that all rights were protected than to create a limited list of rights, since unscrupulous officials could then assert that unlisted rights could be violated at will.

In order to win adoption of the Constitution in the ratifying conventions, the Federalists finally backed off their original argument and promised to add a bill of rights to the Constitution as the first order of business of a newly elected Congress.

The First Ten Amendments

In 1789, the first Congress elected under the Constitution acted quickly to adopt a number of amendments listing people's rights. Drafted largely by James Madison, the amendments were submitted to the states for ratification. The ten that were adopted in 1791 have been known ever since as the U.S. Bill of Rights. Together they provided the guarantees that Anti-Federalists wanted against possible abuses of power by the central (or federal) government.

Here is a summary of the rights guaranteed in each amendment:

First Amendment. Congress may make no laws that infringe a citizen's right to freedom of religion, speech, press, assembly, and petition. Congress may not favor one religion over another (separation of church and state).

Second Amendment. The people have the right to keep and bear arms in a state militia.

Third Amendment. The people cannot be required to quarter (house) soldiers during peacetime.

Fourth Amendment. The government may not carry out unreasonable searches or seizures of the people's property.

Fifth Amendment. No individual may be deprived of life, liberty, or property without due process of law. No defendant in a criminal case may be forced to give evidence against himself or herself or to stand trial twice for the same crime (double jeopardy).

Sixth Amendment. Anyone accused of a crime has the right to a speedy and public trial and the right to call and question witnesses.

Seventh Amendment. In most civil cases (one person suing another in court), citizens have the right to trial by jury.

Eighth Amendment. Persons accused or convicted of crimes are protected against excessive bail and fines and cruel and unusual punishments.

Ninth Amendment. Any rights not specifically mentioned in the Constitution are also guaranteed against government infringement.

Tenth Amendment. All powers not delegated to the federal government belong to the states or to the people.

Washington's Presidency

Members of the first Congress under the Constitution were elected in 1788 and began their first session in March 1789 in New York City (then the nation's temporary capital). It was widely assumed that George Washington would be the electoral college's unanimous choice for president, and indeed that is exactly what happened. Washington took the oath of office as the first U.S. president on April 30, 1789. From this point on, what the Constitution and its system of checks and balances actually meant in practice would be determined from day to day by the decisions of Congress as the legislative branch, the president as the head of the executive branch, and the Supreme Court as the top federal court in the judicial branch.

Organizing the Federal Government

Executive departments. As chief executive, Washington's principal task upon entering office was to organize new departments of the executive (law-enforcing) branch. In fact, the Constitution specifically authorizes the president to appoint chiefs of departments, provided that the president's nominees are confirmed, or approved, by the Senate. Washington appointed four heads of departments: Thomas Jefferson as secretary of state, Alexander Hamilton as secretary of the treasury, Henry Knox as secretary of war, and Edmund Randolph as attorney general. These four men formed a cabinet of advisers with whom President Washington met regularly to discuss major policy issues. Thus began the practice, continued to this day, of a president calling cabinet meetings as a basis for obtaining advice and information from key leaders in the administration.

Federal court system. The only federal court mentioned in the Constitution is the Supreme Court. Congress, however, was given the power to create other federal courts with lesser powers and to determine the number of justices making up the Supreme Court. One of Congress' first laws was the Judiciary Act of 1789, which established a Supreme Court with one chief justice and five associate justices. This highest court was empowered to rule on the constitutionality of decisions made by *state* courts. The act also provided for a system of 13 district courts and three circuit courts of appeals.

Hamilton's Financial Program

One of the most pressing problems faced by Congress under the Articles had been the government's financial difficulties. Alexander Hamilton, now secretary of the treasury, presented to the new Congress a comprehensive plan for putting U.S. finances on a firm and stable foundation. Hamilton proposed the following remedies for the government's financial plight: (1) Pay off the national debt at face value and have the federal government assume the war debts of the states. (2) Protect the young nation's "infant" (new and developing) industries and collect adequate revenues at the same time by imposing high tariffs on imported goods. (3) Create a national bank for depositing government funds and for printing banknotes that would provide the basis for a stable U.S. currency. Support for this program came chiefly from northern merchants, who would gain directly from high tariffs and a stabilized currency.

Opponents of Hamilton's financial plan included the Anti-Federalists, who feared that the states would lose power to the extent that the central government gained it. Thomas Jefferson led a faction of southern Anti-Federalists who viewed Hamilton's program as benefiting only the rich at the expense of indebted farmers.

After much political wrangling and bargaining, Congress finally adopted the three major parts of Hamilton's plan in slightly modified form.

Debt. Jefferson and his supporters agreed to Hamilton's urgent insistence that the U.S. government pay off the national debt at face value and also assume payment of the war debts of the states. In return for Jefferson's support on this vital aspect of his plan, Hamilton agreed to Jefferson's idea to establish the nation's capital in the South along the Potomac River (an area that, after Washington's death, would be named Washington, D.C.).

Tariffs and excise taxes. The tariff rates set by Congress were lower than Hamilton had wanted. To raise enough revenue to pay the government's debts, Hamilton persuaded Congress to pass excise taxes, particularly on the sale of whisky.

National bank. Jefferson argued that the Constitution did not give Congress the power to create a bank. But Hamilton took a broader view of the Constitution, arguing that the document's "necessary and proper" clause authorized Congress to do whatever was necessary to carry out its enumerated powers. Washington supported Hamilton on the issue, and the proposed bank was voted into law. Although chartered by the federal government, the Bank of the United States was privately owned. As a major shareholder of the bank, the federal government could print paper currency and use federal deposits to stimulate business.

Foreign Affairs

Washington's first term as president (1789–1793) coincided with the outbreak of revolution in France, a cataclysmic event that was to touch off a series of wars between the new French Republic and the monarchies of Europe. Washington's entire eight years as president, as well as the four years of his successor, John Adams, were taken up with the question of whether to give U.S. support to (a) France, (b) France's enemies, or (c) neither side.

The French Revolution. Americans generally supported the French people's aspiration to establish a republic, but many were also horrified by reports of mob hysteria and mass executions. To complicate matters, the U.S.–French alliance remained in effect, although it was an alliance with the French monarchy, not with the revolutionary republic. Jefferson and his supporters sympathized with the revolutionary cause. They also argued that, because Britain was seizing American merchant ships bound for French ports, the United States should join France in its defensive war against Britain.

Proclamation of neutrality (1793). President Washington, however, believed that the young nation was not strong enough to engage in a European war. Resisting the popular clamor, in 1793 he issued a proclamation of U.S.

neutrality in the conflict. Thomas Jefferson resigned from the cabinet in disagreement with Washington's order.

"Citizen" Genêt. Objecting to Washington's policy, "Citizen" Edmond Genêt, the French minister to the United States, broke all the normal rules of diplomacy by appealing directly to the American people to support the French cause. So outrageous was his conduct that even Jefferson approved of Washington's request to the French government that they remove the offending diplomat. Recalled by his government, Genêt chose to remain in the United States, where he married and became a U.S. citizen.

The Jay Treaty (1794). Washington sent Chief Justice John Jay on a special mission to Britain to talk that country out of its offensive practice of searching and seizing American ships and impressing seamen into the British navy. After a year of negotiations, Jay brought back a treaty in which Britain agreed to evacuate its posts on the U.S. western frontier. But the treaty said nothing about British seizures of American merchant ships. Narrowly ratified by the Senate, the unpopular Jay Treaty angered American supporters of France, but it did maintain Washington's policy of neutrality which kept the United States at peace.

The Pinckney Treaty (1795). Totally unexpected was the effect that the Jay Treaty had on Spain's policy toward its territories in the Americas. Seeing the treaty as a sign that the United States might be drawing closer to Britain (a longtime foe), Spain decided to consolidate its holdings in North America.

PINCKNEY'S TREATY, 1795

Thomas Pinckney, the U.S. minister to Spain, negotiated a treaty in which Spain agreed to open the lower Mississippi River and New Orleans to American trade. The right of deposit was granted to Americans so that they could transfer cargoes in New Orleans without paying duties to the Spanish government. Spain further agreed to accept the U.S. claim that Florida's northern boundary should be at the 31st parallel (not north of that line, as Spain had formerly insisted).

Domestic Concerns

In addition to coping with foreign challenges, stabilizing the nation's credit, and organizing the new government, Washington faced a number of domestic problems and crises.

Native Americans. Through the final decades of the 18th century, settlers crossed the Alleghenies and moved the frontier steadily westward into the Ohio Valley and beyond. The settlers encroached on the lands of Native Americans, who resisted the westward movement as a threat to their existence. Americans on the frontier were incensed by evidence that the British were supplying the Native Americans with arms and encouraging them to attack the "intruding" Americans. In 1794 the U.S. army led by General Anthony Wayne defeated the Shawnee, Wyandot, and other Native American peoples at the Battle of Fallen Timbers in northwestern Ohio. The next year, the chiefs of the defeated

THE TREATY OF GREENVILLE, 1795

peoples agreed to the Treaty of Greenville, in which they surrendered claims to the Ohio Territory and promised to open it up to settlement.

The Whisky Rebellion (1794). Was the new federal government strong enough to deal successfully with rebellion against its own laws? In western Pennsylvania, the refusal of a group of farmers to pay the federal excise tax on whisky seemed to pose a major challenge to the viability of the U.S. government under the Constitution. The rebelling farmers could ill afford to pay a tax on the whisky that they distilled from surplus corn. Rather than pay the tax, they defended their "liberties" by attacking the revenue collectors.

Washington responded to this crisis by federalizing 15,000 state militiamen and placing them under the command of Alexander Hamilton. The show of force had its intended effect, causing the Whisky Rebellion to collapse without any bloodshed on either side. Some Americans applauded Washington's action, contrasting it with the previous government's helplessness to do anything about Shays' Rebellion. Among westerners, however, the military action was widely resented and condemned as an unwarranted use of force against the common people. The government's chief critic, Thomas Jefferson, gained in popularity as a champion of the western farmer.

Western lands. In the 1790s, with the Jay Treaty and the victory at the Battle of Fallen Timbers, the federal government gained control of vast tracts of land. Congress encouraged the rapid settlement of these lands by passing

NEW STATES IN THE UNION, 1791–1796

the Public Land Act in 1796, which established orderly procedures for dividing and selling federal lands at reasonable prices.

The process for adding new states to the Union, as set forth in the Constitution, also went smoothly. In 1791 Vermont became the first new state, followed by Kentucky in 1792 and Tennessee in 1796.

Political Parties

Washington's election by unanimous vote of the Electoral College in 1789 underscored the popular belief that political parties were not needed. The Constitution itself did not mention political parties, and it was assumed by the Framers that none would arise. They were soon proven wrong. The debates between Federalists and Anti-Federalists in 1787 and 1788 were the first indication that a two-party system would emerge as an integral and permanent feature of American politics.

Origins

In colonial times, it was common enough for groups of legislators to form temporary factions and vote together either for or against a specific policy. When an issue was settled, the factions would dissolve. The dispute between Federalists and Anti-Federalists over the ratification of the Constitution resembled closely the factional disputes of an earlier period. What was unusual about this conflict was that it was organized—at least by the Federalists—across state lines and in that sense prefigured the national parties that emerged soon afterward.

In the 1790s, sometimes called the *Federalist era* because it was dominated by two Federalist presidents, political parties began to form around two leading figures, Hamilton and Jefferson. The Federalist party supported Hamilton and his financial program. An opposition party known as the Democratic-Republican party supported Jefferson and tried to elect candidates in different states who opposed Hamilton's program. The French Revolution further solidified the formation of national political parties. Americans divided sharply over whether or not to support France. A large number of them followed Jefferson's lead in openly challenging President Washington's neutrality policy.

Differences Between the Parties

The Federalists were the party whose strength was greatest in the northeastern states and whose political philosophy favored the growth of federal power. The Democratic-Republicans were the party whose supporters were chiefly in the southern states and on the western frontier and whose political philosophy favored the protection of states' rights and strict containment of federal power. For other major differences between the Federalists and the Democratic-Republicans, see the table on page 109.

Comparison of Federalist and Democratic-Republican Parties		
	Federalists	**Democratic-Republicans**
Leaders	John Adams Alexander Hamilton	Thomas Jefferson James Madison
View of the Constitution	Loose interpretation Strong central government	Strict interpretation Weak central government
Foreign Policy	Pro-British	Pro-French
Military Policy	Large peacetime army and navy	Small peacetime army and navy
Domestic Policy	Aid business National bank Tariffs	Favor agriculture No national bank Opposed tariffs
Chief Supporters	Northern businessmen Large landowners	Skilled workers Small farmers Plantation owners

By 1796, the two major political parties were already taking shape and becoming better organized. In that year, President Washington announced that he intended to retire to private life at the end of his second term.

Washington's Farewell Address

Assisted by Alexander Hamilton, the retiring president wrote a farewell address for publication in the newspapers in late 1796. In this message, which had enormous influence because of Washington's prestige, the president spoke about policies and practices that he considered unwise. He warned Americans:

- not to get involved in European affairs
- against the United States making "permanent alliances" in foreign affairs
- not to form political parties
- to avoid sectionalism

Future presidents would heed as gospel Washington's warning against "permanent alliances." In the case of political parties, however, Washington was already behind the times, since political parties were well on their way to becoming a vital part of the American political system.

One long-range consequence of Washington's decision to leave office after two terms was that later presidents followed his example. In the 19th century, presidents elected to two terms (including Jefferson, Madison, Monroe, and Jackson) would voluntarily retire even though the original Constitution placed no limit on a president's tenure in office. (The two-term tradition continued unbroken until 1940 when Franklin Roosevelt won election to a third term.)

John Adams' Presidency

Even as Washington was writing his Farewell Address, political parties were active in every state to gain majorities in the two houses of Congress and to line up enough electors from the various states to elect the next president. The vice president, John Adams, was the Federalists' candidate, while former secretary of state Thomas Jefferson was the choice of the Democratic-Republicans.

Adams won by just three electoral votes. Jefferson became vice president, since the Constitution as originally written provided that the candidate receiving the second highest number of electoral votes would become the vice president. (The method for selecting a vice president was changed by the Twelfth Amendment in 1804.)

The XYZ Affair

Troubles abroad related to the French Revolution presented Adams with the first major challenge of his presidency. Americans were angered by reports that U.S. merchant ships were being seized by French warships and privateers. Seeking a peaceful settlement, Adams sent a delegation to Paris to negotiate with the French government. Certain French ministers, known only as X, Y, and Z because their names were never revealed, requested bribes as the basis for entering into negotiations. The American delegates indignantly refused. Newspaper reports of the demands made by X, Y, and Z infuriated many Americans, who now clamored for war against France. "Millions for defense, but not one cent for tribute" became the slogan of the hour. One faction of the Federalist party, led by Alexander Hamilton, hoped that by going to war the United States could gain French and Spanish lands in North America.

President Adams, on the other hand, resisted the popular sentiment for war. Recognizing that the U.S. Army and Navy were not yet strong enough to fight a major power, the president avoided war and sent new ministers to Paris.

The Alien and Sedition Acts

Public anger against France strengthened the Federalists in the congressional elections of 1798. Winning a majority of seats in both houses, they hoped to take advantage of their victory by enacting laws that would restrict their political opponents, the Democratic-Republicans. Toward this end, the

Federalists adopted these laws: (1) the *Naturalization Act,* which increased from five to 14 the number of years required for immigrants to qualify for U.S. citizenship because most immigrants voted Democratic-Republican, (2) the *Alien Acts,* which authorized the president to deport any aliens considered dangerous and to detain any enemy aliens in time of war, and (3) the *Sedition Act,* which made it illegal for newspaper editors to criticize either the president or Congress and imposed heavy penalties (fines or imprisonment) for editors who violated the law.

The Kentucky and Virginia Resolutions

Republicans argued that the Alien and Sedition Acts violated rights guaranteed by the First Amendment of the Constitution. In 1799, however, the Supreme Court had not yet established the principle of judicial review (see Chapter 7). Republican leaders challenged the legislation of the Federalist Congress by enacting nullifying laws of their own in the state legislatures. The Kentucky legislature adopted a resolution that had been written by Thomas Jefferson, and the Virginia legislature adopted a resolution introduced by James Madison. Both resolutions declared that the states had entered into a "compact" in forming the national government, and, therefore, if any act of the federal government broke the compact, a state could nullify the federal law. Although only Kentucky and Virginia adopted nullifying resolutions in 1799, they set forth an argument and rationale that would be widely used in the nullification controversy of the 1830s (see Chapter 10).

The immediate crisis over the Alien and Sedition Acts faded because of two developments:

1. The Federalists lost their majority in Congress after the election of 1800, and the new Republican majority either allowed the acts to expire or repealed them.
2. The Supreme Court under John Marshall asserted its power as the court of last resort in deciding whether or not a certain federal law was constitutional.

The Election of 1800

During Adams' presidency, the Federalists rapidly lost popularity. People disliked the Alien and Sedition Acts and complained about the new taxes imposed by the Federalists to pay the costs of preparing for a war against France. (Adams avoided war but persuaded Congress that building up the U.S. Navy was necessary for the nation's defense.)

Election Results

The election of 1800 swept the Federalists from power in both the executive and legislative branches of the U.S. government. A majority of the presidential electors cast their ballots for two Republicans: Thomas Jefferson and Aaron Burr. Because *both* these Republican candidates received the same number of electoral ballots, it was necessary (according to the rules in the Constitution) to hold a special election in the House of Representatives to break the tie. In December 1800 the Federalists still controlled the House. They debated and voted for days before they finally gave a majority to Jefferson. (Alexander Hamilton had urged his followers to vote for Jefferson, whom he considered less dangerous and of higher character than Burr.)

Republican lawmakers elected in 1800 took control of both the House and the Senate when a new Congress met in March 1801.

A Peaceful Revolution

The passing of power in 1801 from one political party to another was accomplished without violence. This in itself was a rare event for the times and a major indication that the U.S. constitutional system would endure the various strains that were placed upon it. The Federalists quietly accepted their defeat in the election of 1800 and peacefully relinquished control of the federal government to Jefferson's party, the Democratic-Republicans. The change from Federalist control to Democratic-Republican control is sometimes known as the *Revolution of 1800.*

HISTORICAL PERSPECTIVES: VIEWS OF THE CONSTITUTION

From the moment it was drafted in 1787, the U.S. Constitution has been a continuing subject of controversy. As political issues changed from one era to the next, Americans changed their views of how the Constitution should be interpreted. The dispute between the Federalists and the Anti-Federalists over the proper powers of the central government has never been completely resolved and, to a certain extent, continues to be debated by modern-day Republicans and Democrats.

In the decades preceding the Civil War (1790–1860), the chief constitutional issue concerned the nature of the federal union and whether the states could or could not nullify acts of the federal government. The North's triumph in the Civil War settled the issue in favor of centralized power and against southern champions of states' rights. In the post-Civil War era, northerners regarded Hamilton and other Federalist Framers of the Constitution as heroes. At the same time, states'-rights advocates were portrayed as demagogues and traitors.

In the early 20th century, a change in politics again brought a change in scholars' views toward the Framers of the Constitution. Reacting to the excesses of big business, certain historians identified economic factors and class conflict as the primary force behind the Constitutional Convention of 1787. Published in 1913, at the height of the Progressive era, Charles Beard's *An Economic Interpretation of the Constitution* argued that, in writing the Constitution, the Framers were chiefly motivated by their own economic interests in preserving their wealth and property. Beard's controversial thesis dominated historical scholarship on the Constitution for almost 50 years. Expanding on Beard's thesis, some historians have argued that even the sectional differences between northern Framers and southern Framers were chiefly economic in nature.

In recent years, many historians have concluded that the economic interpretation of the Framers' motives, while valid up to a point, oversimplifies the issues of the 1780s. Historians place greater stress on the philosophical and intellectual backgrounds of the delegates at Philadelphia and explain how they shared similar 18th-century views of liberty, government, and society.

KEY NAMES, EVENTS, AND TERMS

Mt. Vernon Conference
Annapolis Convention
Constitutional Convention
Framers of Constitution
James Madison
Alexander Hamilton
Gouverneur Morris
John Dickinson
checks and balances
Virginia Plan
New Jersey Plan
Connecticut Plan; Great Compromise
House of Representatives
Senate
Three-fifths Compromise; slave trade
Commercial Compromise
electoral college system
Federalists

Anti-Federalists
The Federalist Papers
Bill of Rights; amendments
legislative branch
Congress
executive departments; cabinet
Henry Knox
Edmund Randolph
Judiciary Act (1789)
federal courts
Supreme Court
national debt
infant industries
national bank
tariffs; excise taxes
French Revolution
Proclamation of Neutrality (1793)
"Citizen" Edmond Genêt

Jay Treaty (1794)
Pinckney Treaty (1795)
right of deposit
Battle of Fallen Timbers
Whisky Rebellion (1794)
Public Land Act (1796)
Federalist era
Democratic-Republican party
political parties
Washington's farewell address
"permanent alliances"
two-term tradition
John Adams
XYZ Affair
Alien and Sedition Acts
Kentucky and Virginia Resolutions
Revolution of 1800

MULTIPLE-CHOICE QUESTIONS

1. In the 1780s, all of the following contributed to dissatisfaction with the Articles of Confederation EXCEPT
   (A) high taxes levied by the national government
   (B) a farmers' revolt in Massachusetts against the collection of state taxes
   (C) states refusing to honor the Treaty of Paris
   (D) worthless paper money printed by many states
   (E) states restricting trade with one another

2. Which of the following statements accurately describes an argument of the Anti-Federalists?
   (A) The Constitution failed to provide for a Supreme Court.
   (B) The Constitution lacked a Bill of Rights.
   (C) States' rights were strong enough to limit the central government.
   (D) The president's powers were too limited.
   (E) The small states had to be protected from the large ones.

3. "The U.S. Constitution is a bundle of compromises." Which of the following provisions of the Constitution does NOT reflect support for this statement?
   (A) representation in the U.S. House of Representatives
   (B) representation in the U.S. Senate

   (C) counting a slave as three-fifths of a person
   (D) Congress' power to tax imports but not exports
   (E) a national court system separate from the legislature

4. In his interpretation of the Constitutional Convention, the historian Charles Beard focused on the importance of
   (A) sectional differences
   (B) conflict over slavery
   (C) economic interests of a wealthy elite
   (D) political factions from colonial times
   (E) the genius and wisdom of the framers

5. In 1788, the Federalists promised to add a bill of rights to the Constitution in order to
   (A) protect their own liberties from possible abuse by the U.S. government
   (B) persuade state conventions to ratify the Constitution
   (C) ensure that government would be democratic
   (D) establish a popular platform for the election of George Washington
   (E) expand the rights of women

6. Alexander Hamilton's financial program consisted of all of the following EXCEPT
   (A) the creation of a U.S. bank

(B) the collection of a federal excise tax on whisky

(C) payment of state debts by the federal government

(D) payment of subsidies to farmers

(E) tariffs to protect infant U.S. industries

7. Which of the following was the underlying cause of the other four?

(A) the Jay Treaty

(B) the French Revolution

(C) the XYZ Affair

(D) Citizen Genêt controversy

(E) Washington's Proclamation of Neutrality

8. The Virginia and Kentucky Resolutions presented the argument that

(A) states had the power to organize political parties

(B) Congress had no power to legislate on questions of immigration

(C) states could nullify acts of Congress

(D) Congress should consult the states before declaring war

(E) the Constitution should be amended

9. The decline in support for the Federalist party can be traced most directly to its handling of the issue of

(A) the Bill of Rights

(B) the XYZ Affair

(C) Citizen Genêt

(D) the Alien and Sedition acts

(E) *Marbury v. Madison*

10. Which of the following was NOT a significant consequence of the election of 1800?

(A) Thomas Jefferson became president.

(B) The Democratic-Republicans took control of Congress.

(C) The Twelfth Amendment was added to the Constitution.

(D) The U.S. government gave less attention to foreign affairs.

(E) The party in power left office peacefully.

ESSAY QUESTIONS

1. Assess the Constitution in terms of the compromises developed by the delegates in the context of TWO of the following:

presidency

representation

slavery

2. Analyze the role and influence of TWO of the following in the debate over the ratification of the Constitution:

Anti-Federalists

The Federalist Papers

Bill of Rights compromise

3. Compare and contrast the views and actions of Thomas Jefferson and Alexander Hamilton while they were members of President Washington's cabinet.

4. Discuss, with respect to TWO of the following, America's first foreign policy, formulated by Presidents Washington and Adams, which had as its

primary goal the avoidance of war.
Citizen Genêt controversy
Jay Treaty
Proclamation of Neutrality
XYZ Affair

5. What factors contributed to the development of political parties in the United States during the 1790s?

DOCUMENTS AND READINGS

The ratification of the Constitution in 1788 did not end the debate over the nature and functions of government. In fact, the disagreement between Anti-Federalists and Federalists (and in later years between Democrats and Whigs) continued for decades until it was more or less resolved by the outcome of the Civil War in the 1860s.

The documents presented here represent two major concerns that were expressed in the years immediately following ratification. One concern of the white majority was the scope of federal power under the Constitution. A second concern chiefly felt by the black minority was that the Constitution protected the rights of whites only and permitted the institution of slavery.

DOCUMENT A.   HAMILTON'S VIEW OF THE CONSTITUTION

As Washington's secretary of the treasury, Alexander Hamilton argued that the federal government could exercise "implied" powers in addition to the "express," or delegated, powers listed in the Constitution. The following excerpt is from a written argument Hamilton presented to Washington on the question of whether or not Congress could establish a bank.

It is not denied that there are *implied* as well as *express powers,* and that the *former* are as effectually delegated as the *latter.* And for the sake of accuracy it shall be mentioned, that there is another class of powers, which may be properly denominated *resulting powers.* It will not be doubted, that if the United States should make a conquest of any of the territories of its neighbours, they would possess sovereign jurisdiction over the conquered territory. This would be rather a result from the whole mass of the powers of the government, and from the nature of political society, than a consequence of either of the powers specially enumerated. . . .

It is conceded that *implied powers* are to be considered as delegated equally with *express ones.* Then it follows, that as a power of erecting a corporation [such as a bank] may as well be *implied* as any other thing, it may as well be employed as an *instrument* or *means* of carrying into execution any of the specified powers, as any other *instrument* or *means* whatever. The only question must be, in this, as in every other case, whether the means to be employed, or, in this instance, the corporation to be erected, has a natural relation to any of the acknowledged object or lawful ends of the government. Thus a corporation may not be erected by Congress for superintending the police of the city of Philadelphia, because they are not authorized to *regulate* the *police* of that city. But one may be erected in relation to the trade with foreign countries, or to the trade between the States, or with the Indian tribes; because it is the province of the federal government to *regulate* those objects, and because it is incident to a general *sovereign* or *legislative* power to *regulate* a thing, to employ all the means which relate to its regulation to the best and greatest advantage.

Alexander Hamilton,
Opinion on the constitutionality of an act
to establish a bank, 1791

DOCUMENT B. JEFFERSON'S VIEW OF THE CONSTITUTION

As vice president from 1797 to 1801, Thomas Jefferson opposed the Alien and Sedition Acts but did so secretly by writing the Kentucky Resolutions anonymously. (He could not speak out openly without coming into direct conflict with President Adams' Federalist government.) Jefferson's arguments in the Kentucky Resolutions provided a rationale for those who believed that states could overrule decisions of the federal government. In later years, believers in states' rights would make repeated use of the document quoted here:

Resolved, that the several States composing the United States of America are not united on the principle of unlimited submission to their general government; but that by compact under the style and title of a Constitution for the United States and of amendments thereto, they constituted a general government for specific purposes, delegated to that government certain definite powers, reserving, each State to itself, the residuary mass of right to their own self-government; and that whensoever the general government assumes undelegated powers, its acts are unauthoritative, void, and of no force: That to this compact each State acceded as a State, and is an integral party, its co-States forming, as to itself, the other party: That the government created by this compact was not made the exclusive or final judge of the extent of the powers delegated to itself; since that would have made its discretion, and not the Constitution, the measure of its powers; but that as in all other cases of compact among parties having no common judge, each party has an equal right to judge for itself, as well of infractions as of the mode and measure of redress. . . .

That they will view this as seizing the rights of the States, and consolidating them in the hands of the general government, with a power assumed to bind the States (not merely in cases made Federal) but in all cases whatsoever, by laws made, not with their consent, but by others against their consent: That this would be to surrender the form of government we have chosen, and to live under one deriving its powers from its own will, and not from our authority; and that the co-States, recurring to their natural right in cases not made Federal, will concur in declaring these acts void and of no force. . . .

Kentucky Resolutions,
November 16, 1798

DOCUMENT C.   A LETTER CONCERNING SLAVERY

Benjamin Banneker was a free (nonslave) African American from Maryland who made a number of contributions to 18th-century science. He is best known as one of the planners of Washington, D.C., the nation's new capital along the Potomac River. He also wrote extensively on a wide range of topics, including political issues and individual rights. His stature as an intellectual is reflected in his correspondence with Thomas Jefferson. The following excerpt from a letter to Jefferson (then secretary of state) points out the contradictions between the republican ideals of the U.S. government and the existence of slavery.

Sir, suffer me to recall to your mind that time, in which the arms and tyranny of the British crown were exerted, with every powerful effort, in order to reduce you to a state of servitude. . . .

This, Sir, was a time when you clearly saw into the injustice of a State of slavery, and in which you had just apprehensions of the horror of its condition. It was now that your abhorrence thereof was so excited, that you publicly held forth this true and invaluable doctrine, which is worthy to be recorded and remembered in all succeeding ages: "We hold these truths to be self-evident, that all men are created equal; that they are endowed by their Creator with certain inalienable rights. . . ."

Here was a time, in which your tender feelings for yourselves had engaged you thus to declare, you were then impressed with the proper ideas of the great violation of liberty, and the free possession of those blessings, to which you were entitled by nature; but, Sir, how pitiable is it to reflect, that although you were so fully convinced of the benevolence of the Father of Mankind, and of his equal and impartial distribution of these rights and privileges, which he hath conferred upon them, that you should at the same time counteract his mercies, in detaining by fraud and violence so numerous a part of my brethren, under groaning captivity, and cruel oppression, that you should at the same time be found guilty of that most criminal act, which you professedly detested in others, with respect to yourselves.

I suppose that your knowledge of the situation of my brethren is too extensive to need a recital here; neither shall I presume to prescribe methods by which they may be relieved, otherwise than by recommending to you and all others, to wean yourselves from those narrow prejudices which you have imbibed with respect to them. . . .

Letter of Benjamin Banneker to
Secretary of State Thomas Jefferson,
Philadelphia, 1792

DOCUMENT D.   DISCRIMINATION AGAINST FREE BLACKS

In every state of the Union in the 1790s, a number of African Americans lived as free citizens. Yet, as the following document indicates, they were not treated as citizens with rights equal to those of the white majority. In Charleston, South Carolina, in 1791, a group of free blacks wrote the following petition to the South Carolina legislature asking for an end to discriminatory laws.

The memorial of Thomas Cole, bricklayer, P. B. Mathews and Mathew Webbe, butchers, on behalf of themselves and others, free men of color, humbly shows:

That in the enumeration of free citizens by the Constitution of the United States for the purpose of representation of the Southern states in Congress your memorialists have been considered under that description as part of the citizens of this state.

Although by the fourteenth and twenty-ninth clauses in an Act of Assembly made in the year 1740 and entitled an Act for the Better Ordering and Governing Negroes and Other Slaves in this Province, commonly called the Negro Act, now in force, your memorialists are deprived of the rights and privileges of citizens by not having it in their power to give testimony in prosecutions on behalf of the state; from which cause many culprits have escaped the punishment due to their atrocious crimes, nor can they give their testimony in recovering debts due to them. . . .

That by the said clauses in the said Act, they are debarred of the rights of free citizens by being subject to a trial without the benefit of a jury and subject to prosecution by testimony of slaves without oath by which they are placed on the same footing.

Your memorialists show that they have at all times since the independence of the United States contributed and do now contribute to the support of the government by cheerfully paying their taxes proportionable to their property with others who have been during such period, and now are, in full enjoyment of the rights and immunities of citizens, inhabitants of a free independent state.

That as your memorialists have been and are considered as free citizens of this state, they hope to be treated as such; they are ready and willing to take and subscribe to such oath of allegiance to the states as shall be prescribed by this honorable House, and are also willing to take upon them any duty for the preservation of the peace in the city or any other occasion if called on. . . .

May it therefore please Your Honors to take your memorialists' case into tender consideration, and make such Acts or insert such clauses for the purpose of relieving your memorialists from the unremitted grievance they now labor under as in your wisdom shall seem meet.

Historical Commission of South Carolina,
Columbia, S.C., 1791

ANALYZING THE DOCUMENTS

1. How does Alexander Hamilton's view of the Constitution, in Document A, differ from Thomas Jefferson's view, in Document B?

2. What connection is Benjamin Banneker making between Jefferson's professed beliefs during the American Revolution and the continued existence of slavery?

3. The U.S. Constitution had many critics. Using Documents A–D and your knowledge of politics in the 1790s, write an essay supporting either of two positions: (a) the Constitution was fundamentally sound although in need of minor adjustments, or (b) the Constitution had fatal flaws with respect to both the rights of states and the rights of African Americans.

THE AGE OF JEFFERSON, 1800–1816

Let us then, fellow-citizens, unite with one heart and one mind. Let us restore to social intercourse that harmony and affection without which liberty and even life itself are but dreary things. . . . But every difference of opinion is not a difference of principle. We have called by different names brethren of the same principle. We are all Republicans, we are all Federalists.

Thomas Jefferson, First Inaugural Address, 1801

In the election of 1800, there had been much animosity and bitter partisan feeling between the two national political parties. Following this Revolution of 1800, Thomas Jefferson, the new president, recognized the need for a smooth and peaceful transition of power from the Federalists to the Republicans. That is why, in his inaugural address of 1801, Jefferson stressed the popular acceptance of the basic principles of constitutional government when he stated: "We are all Republicans, we are all Federalists."

By the end of the period covered in this chapter, it may be argued that the people were "all Republicans," for the Federalists were no longer a political power. We shall see how, under the leadership of Jefferson and his close friend James Madison, the nation experienced peaceful political change, expanded territorially, survived another war, and strengthened its democratic and nationalistic spirit. This new nation had its problems—including slavery, the treatment of Native Americans, and loyalty to local interests—but it was also a new nation that was surviving and growing.

Jefferson's Presidency

During his first term, the Democratic-Republican president attempted to win the allegiance and trust of Federalist opponents by maintaining the national bank and debt-repayment plan of Hamilton. In foreign policy, he carried on the neutrality policies of Washington and Adams. At the same time, Jefferson retained the loyalty of Republican supporters by adhering to his party's guiding principle of limited central government. He reduced the size of the military, eliminated a number of federal jobs, repealed the excise taxes—including those on whisky, and lowered the national debt. Only Republicans were named to his cabinet, as he sought to avoid the internal divisions that had distracted Washington.

Compared to Adams' troubled administration, Jefferson's first four years in office were relatively free of discord. The single most important achievement of these years was the acquisition by purchase of vast western lands known as the Louisiana Territory.

The Louisiana Purchase

The Louisiana Territory encompassed a vast, largely unexplored tract of western land through which the Mississippi and Missouri rivers flowed. At the mouth of the Mississippi lay the territory's most valuable property in terms of commerce—the port of New Orleans. For many years, Louisiana and New Orleans had been claimed by Spain. But in 1800, the French military and political leader Napoleon Bonaparte secretly forced Spain to give the Louisiana Territory back to its former owner, France. Napoleon hoped to restore the French empire in the Americas. By 1803, however, Napoleon had lost interest in this plan for two reasons: (1) he needed to concentrate French resources on fighting England and (2) a rebellion led by Toussaint l'Ouverture against French rule on the island of Santo Domingo had resulted in heavy French losses.

U.S. interest in the Mississippi River. During Jefferson's presidency, the western frontier extended beyond Ohio and Kentucky into the Indiana Territory. Settlers in this region depended for their economic existence on transporting goods on rivers that flowed westward into the Mississippi and southward as far as New Orleans. They were greatly alarmed therefore when in 1802 Spanish officials, who were still in charge of New Orleans, closed the port to Americans. They revoked the *right of deposit* granted in the Pinckney Treaty of 1795, which had allowed American farmers tax-free use of the port. People on the frontier clamored for government action. In addition to being concerned about the economic impact of the closing of New Orleans, President Jefferson was troubled by its consequences on foreign policy. He feared that, so long as a foreign power controlled the river at New Orleans, the United States risked entanglement in European affairs.

Negotiations. Jefferson sent ministers to France with instructions to offer up to $10 million for both New Orleans and a strip of land extending from that port eastward to Florida. If the American ministers failed in their negotiations with the French, they were instructed to begin discussions with Britain for a U.S.-British alliance. Napoleon's ministers, seeking funds for a war against Britain, offered to sell not only New Orleans but also the entire Louisiana Territory for $15 million. The surprised American ministers quickly went beyond their instructions and accepted.

Constitutional predicament. Jefferson and most Americans strongly approved of the Louisiana Purchase. Nevertheless, a constitutional problem troubled the president. Jefferson was committed to a strict interpretation of the Constitution and rejected Hamilton's argument that certain powers were implied. No clause in the Constitution explicitly stated that a president could purchase foreign land. In this case, Jefferson determined to set aside his idealism for the country's good. He submitted the purchase agreement to the Senate, arguing that lands could be added to the United States as an application of the president's power to make treaties. Casting aside the criticisms of Federalist senators, the Republican majority in the Senate quickly ratified the purchase.

Consequences. The Louisiana Purchase more than doubled the size of the United States, removed a foreign presence from the nation's borders, and guaranteed the extension of the western frontier to lands beyond the Mississippi. Furthermore, the acquisition of millions of acres of land strengthened Jefferson's hopes that his country's future would be based on an agrarian society of independent farmers rather than Hamilton's vision of an urban and industrial

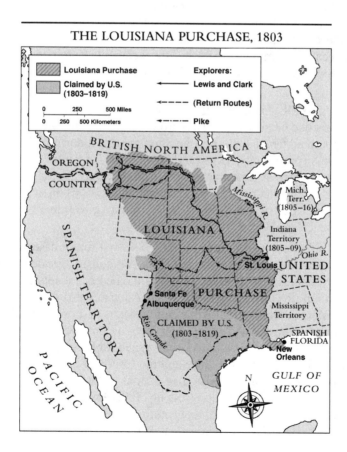

THE LOUISIANA PURCHASE, 1803

society. In political terms, the Louisiana Purchase increased Jefferson's popularity and showed the Federalists to be a weak, sectionalist (New England-based) party that could do little more than complain about Republican policies.

Lewis and Clark expedition. Even before Louisiana was purchased, Jefferson had persuaded Congress to fund a scientific exploration of the trans-Mississippi West to be led by Captain Meriwether Lewis and Lieutenant William Clark. The Louisiana Purchase greatly increased the importance of the expedition. Lewis and Clark set out from St. Louis in 1804, crossed the Rockies, reached the Oregon coast on the Pacific Ocean, then turned back and completed the return journey in 1806. The benefits of the expedition were many: increased geographic and scientific knowledge of previously unexplored country, strengthened U.S. claims to the Oregon Territory, improved relations with Native American tribes, and developed maps and land routes for fur trappers and future settlers.

John Marshall and the Supreme Court

After the sweeping Republican victory of 1800, the only power remaining to the Federalists was their control of the federal courts. The Federalist appointments to the courts, previously made by Washington and Adams, were not subject to recall or removal except by impeachment. Federalist judges therefore continued in office, much to the annoyance of the Republican president, Jefferson.

John Marshall. Ironically, the Federalist judge who caused Jefferson the most grief was one of his own cousins from Virginia, John Marshall. Marshall had been appointed Chief Justice of the Supreme Court during the final months of John Adams' presidency. He would serve in this position for 34 years, in which time he exerted as strong an influence on the Supreme Court as Washington had exerted on the presidency. Marshall's decisions in many landmark cases had the effect of strengthening the central government, often at the expense of states' rights.

Case of *Marbury v. Madison* (1803). The first major case to be decided by Marshall put him in direct conflict with his cousin, President Jefferson. Upon taking office, Jefferson wanted to block the Federalist appointments made at the last minute by his predecessor, John Adams. He ordered Secretary of State James Madison *not* to deliver the commissions to those Federalists judges whom Adams had appointed in his last days as president. One of Adams' "midnight appointments," William Marbury, sued for his commission. The case of *Marbury v. Madison* went to the Supreme Court for review in 1803. Chief Justice Marshall ruled that Marbury had a right to his commission according to the Judiciary Act passed by Congress in 1789. However, Marshall said, the Judiciary Act of 1789 was itself unconstitutional. The law passed by Congress had given to the Court greater power and jurisdiction than the Constitution allowed. Therefore, the law was unconstitutional, and Marbury could not be given his commission.

In effect, Marshall sacrificed what would have been a small Federalist gain (the appointment of Marbury) for a much larger, long-term judicial victory. By ruling a law of Congress to be unconstitutional, Marshall established the doctrine of *judicial review*. From this point on, the Supreme Court would exercise the power to decide whether an act of Congress or of the president was or was not allowed by the Constitution. In effect, the Supreme Court could now overrule actions of the other two branches of the federal government.

Judicial impeachments. Jefferson tried other methods for overturning past Federalist measures and appointments. Soon after entering office, he suspended the Alien and Sedition Acts and released those jailed under them. Hoping to remove partisan Federalist judges, Jefferson supported a campaign of impeachment. The judge of one federal district was found to be mentally unbalanced. The House voted his impeachment and the Senate then voted to remove him. The House also impeached a Supreme Court justice, Samuel Chase, but the Senate acquitted him after finding no evidence of "high crimes." Except for these two cases, the impeachment campaign was largely a failure, as almost all the Federalist judges remained in office. Even so, the threat of impeachment caused the judges to be more cautious and less partisan in their decisions.

Jefferson's Reelection

In 1804 Jefferson was reelected president by an overwhelming margin, receiving all but 14 of the 176 electoral votes. His second term was marked by growing difficulties. There were plots by his former vice president, Aaron Burr; opposition by a faction of his own party (the "Quids"), who accused him of abandoning Republican principles; and foreign troubles from the Napoleonic wars in Europe.

Aaron Burr

A Republican caucus (closed meeting) in 1804 decided not to nominate Aaron Burr for a second term as vice president. Burr then embarked on a series of ventures, one of which threatened to break up the Union and another of which resulted in the death of Alexander Hamilton.

Federalist conspiracy. Secretly forming a political pact with some radical New England Federalists, Burr planned to win the governorship of New York in 1804, unite that state with the New England states, and then lead this group of states to secede from the nation. Most Federalists followed Alexander Hamilton in opposing Burr, who was defeated in the New York election. The conspiracy then disintegrated.

Duel with Hamilton. Angered by an insulting remark attributed to Hamilton, Burr challenged the Federalist leader to a duel and fatally shot him. Hamilton's death in 1804 deprived the Federalists of their last great leader and earned Burr the enmity of many.

Trial for treason. By 1806, Burr's intrigues had turned westward with a plan to take Mexico from Spain and possibly unite it with Louisiana under his rule. Learning of the conspiracy, Jefferson ordered Burr's arrest and trial for treason. Presiding at the trial was Chief Justice John Marshall, an adversary of Jefferson. A jury acquitted Burr, basing its decision on Marshall's narrow definition of treason and the lack of witnesses to any "overt act" by Burr.

Difficulties Abroad

As a matter of policy and principle, Jefferson tried to avoid war with a foreign power. Rejecting the idea of permanent alliances, he sought to maintain U.S. neutrality in the face of increasing provocation from both France and Britain during the Napoleonic wars.

Barbary pirates. The first major challenge to Jefferson's foreign policy came, not from a major European power, but from the piracy practiced by the Barbary states on the North African coast. To protect U.S. merchant ships from being seized by Barbary pirates, Presidents Washington and Adams had reluctantly agreed to pay tribute to the Barbary governments. The ruler of one state, the Pasha of Tripoli, demanded a higher sum in tribute when Jefferson took office. Rather than pay this sum, Jefferson decided to send a small fleet of U.S. naval vessels to the Mediterranean. Sporadic fighting with Tripoli lasted for four years (1801–1805). The American navy did not achieve a decisive victory but gained some respect and also offered a measure of protection to U.S. vessels trading in Mediterranean waters.

Challenges to U.S. neutrality. Meanwhile, the Napoleonic wars continued to dominate the politics of Europe—and to a lesser extent the commercial economy of the United States. The two principal belligerents, France and Britain, attempted naval blockades of enemy ports. They regularly seized the ships of neutral nations and confiscated their cargoes. The chief offender from the U.S. point of view was Britain, since its navy dominated the Atlantic. Most infuriating was the British practice of capturing U.S. sailors and impressing (forcing) them to serve in the British navy.

Chesapeake-Leopard **affair.** One incident at sea especially aroused American anger and almost led to war. In 1807, only a few miles off the coast of Virginia, the British warship *Leopard* fired on the U.S. warship *Chesapeake*. Three Americans were killed and four others were taken captive and impressed into the British navy. Anti-British feeling ran high, and many Americans demanded war. Jefferson, however, resorted to diplomacy and economic pressure as his response to the crisis.

Embargo Act (1807). As an alternative to war, Jefferson persuaded the Republican majority in Congress to pass the Embargo Act in 1807. This measure prohibited American merchant ships from sailing to any foreign port. Since the United States was Britain's largest trading partner, Jefferson hoped that the British would stop violating the rights of neutral nations rather than lose U.S. trade. The embargo, however, backfired and brought much greater economic hardship to the United States than to Britain. The British were determined to control the seas at all costs, and they had little difficulty substituting supplies from South America for U.S. goods. The embargo's effect on the U.S. economy, however, was devastating, especially for the merchant marine and shipbuilders of New England. So bad was the depression that a movement developed in the New England states to secede from the Union.

Recognizing that the Embargo Act had failed, Jefferson called for its repeal in 1809 during the final days of his presidency. Even after repeal, however, U.S. ships could trade legally with all nations *except* Britain and France.

Madison's Presidency

Jefferson believed strongly in the tradition established by Washington of voluntarily retiring from the presidency after a second term. For his party's nomination for president, he supported his close friend, Secretary of State James Madison.

The Election of 1808

Ever since leading the effort to write and ratify the Constitution, Madison was widely viewed as a brilliant thinker and statesman. He had worked tirelessly with Jefferson in developing the Democratic-Republican party. On the other hand, he was a weak public speaker, possessed a stubborn temperament, and lacked Jefferson's political skills. With Jefferson's backing, Madison was nominated for president by a caucus of congressional Republicans. Other factions of the Republican party nominated two other candidates. Even so, Madison was able to win a majority of electoral votes and to defeat both his Republican opponents and the Federalist candidate, Charles Pinckney. The Federalists nevertheless managed to gain seats in Congress due to widespread unhappiness with the effects of the embargo.

Commercial Warfare

Madison's presidency was dominated by the same European problems that had plagued Jefferson's second term. Like Jefferson, he attempted a combination of diplomacy and economic pressure to deal with the Napoleonic wars. Unlike Jefferson, he finally consented to take the United States to war.

Nonintercourse Act of 1809. After the repeal of Jefferson's disastrous embargo act, Madison hoped to end economic hardship while maintaining his country's rights as a neutral nation. The Nonintercourse Act of 1809 provided that Americans could now trade with all nations except Britain and France.

Macon's Bill No. 2 (1810). Economic hardships continued into 1810. Nathaniel Macon, a member of Congress, introduced a bill that restored U.S. trade with Britain and France. Macon's Bill No. 2 provided, however, that if either Britain or France formally agreed to respect U.S. neutral rights at sea, then the United States would prohibit trade with that nation's foe.

Napoleon's deception. Upon hearing of Congress' action, Napoleon announced his intention of revoking the decrees that had violated U.S. neutral rights. Taking Napoleon at his word, Madison carried out the terms of Macon's Bill No. 2 by embargoing U.S. trade with Britain in 1811. It soon became apparent, however, that Napoleon had no intention of fulfilling his promise. The French continued to seize American merchant ships despite their emperor's deceitful pledge to the United States.

The War of 1812

Neither Britain nor the United States wanted their dispute to end in war. And yet war between them did break out in 1812.

Causes of the War

From the U.S. point of view, the pressures leading to war came from two directions: the continued violation of U.S. neutral rights at sea and troubles with the British on the western frontier.

Free seas and trade. As a trading nation, the United States depended upon the free flow of shipping across the Atlantic. Yet the chief belligerents in Europe, Britain and France, had no interest in respecting neutral rights so long as they were locked in a life-and-death struggle with each other. Since the French Revolution in the 1790s, the majority of Americans had tended to sympathize with France against Britain. They well remembered that Britain had seemed a cruel enemy during the American Revolution. And Jeffersonian Republicans applauded the French for having overthrown their monarchy in their Revolution. Moreover, even though both the French and the British violated U.S. neutral rights, the British violations appeared to be more blatant because of the British navy's practice of impressing American seamen.

Frontier pressures. Added to long-standing grievances over British actions at sea were the ambitions of western Americans for more open land. Americans on the frontier longed for the lands of British Canada and Spanish Florida. Standing in the way of their ambitions were the British and their Indian and Spanish allies.

Conflict with the Native Americans was a perennial problem for the restless westerners. For decades, settlers had been gradually pushing the Native Americans farther and farther westward. In an effort to defend their lands from further encroachment, Shawnee twin brothers—Tecumseh, a warrior, and Prophet, a religious leader—attempted to unite all of the tribes east of the Mississippi River. White settlers became suspicious of Tecumseh and persuaded the governor of the Indiana Territory, General William Henry Harrison, to take aggressive action. In the Battle of Tippecanoe, in 1811, Harrison destroyed the Shawnee headquarters and put an end to Tecumseh's efforts to form an Indian confederacy. The British had provided only limited aid to Tecumseh. Nevertheless, Americans on the frontier blamed the British for instigating the rebellion.

War hawks. A congressional election in 1810 had brought a group of new, young Republicans to Congress, many of them from frontier states (Kentucky, Tennessee, and Ohio). Known as war hawks because of their eagerness for war with Britain, they quickly gained significant influence in the House of Representatives. Led by Henry Clay of Kentucky and John C. Calhoun of South Carolina, the war-hawk Congressmen argued that war with Britain would be the only way to defend American honor, gain Canada, and destroy Native American resistance on the frontier.

Declaration of war. British delays in meeting U.S. demands over neutral rights combined with political pressures from the war-hawk Congress finally persuaded Madison to seek a declaration of war against Britain. Ironically, the British government had by this time (June 1812) agreed to suspend its naval blockade. News of its decision reached the White House after Congress had declared war.

A Divided Nation

Neither Congress nor the American people were united in support of the war. In Congress, Pennsylvania and Vermont joined the southern and western states to provide a slight majority for the war declaration. Voting against the war were most of the northern states: New York, New Jersey, and the rest of the states in New England.

Election of 1812. A similar division of opinion was seen in the presidential election of 1812, in which Republican strength in the South and West overcame Federalist and antiwar Republican opposition to war in the North. Madison won reelection, defeating De Witt Clinton of New York, the candidate of the Federalists and antiwar Republicans.

Opposition to the war. Those Americans who opposed the war viewed it as "Mr. Madison's War" and the work of the war hawks in Congress. Most outspoken in their criticism of the war were three groups: New England merchants, Federalist politicians, and "Quids," or "Old" Republicans. New England merchants were opposed because, after the repeal of the Embargo

Act, they were making sizable profits from the European war and viewed impressment as merely a minor inconvenience. Both commercial interests and religious ties to Protestantism made them more sympathetic to the Protestant British than to the Catholic French. Opposed as a matter of principle to anything Madison did, Federalist politicians viewed the war as a Republican scheme to conquer Canada and Florida, with the ultimate aim of increasing Republican voting strength. For their part, the "Quids" or "Old" Republicans criticized the war because it violated the classic Republican commitment to limited federal power and to the maintenance of peace.

Military Defeats and Naval Victories

Facing Britain's overwhelming naval power, Madison's military strategists based their hope for victory on (1) Napoleon's continued success in Europe and (2) a U.S. land campaign against Canada.

Invasion of Canada. A poorly equipped American army initiated military action in 1812 by launching a three-part invasion of Canada, one force starting out from Detroit, another from Niagara, and a third from Lake Champlain. These and later forays into Canada were easily repulsed by the British defenders. An American raid and burning of government buildings in York (Toronto) in 1813 only served to encourage retaliation by the British.

Naval battles. The U.S. navy achieved some notable victories, due largely to superior shipbuilding and the valorous deeds of American seamen, including many free African Americans. In late 1812, the U.S. warship *Constitution* (nicknamed "Old Ironsides") raised American morale by defeating and sinking a British ship off the coast of Nova Scotia. Also effective were the attacks of American privateers who, motivated by both patriotism and profit, captured numerous British merchant ships. Offsetting these gains was the success of the British navy in establishing a blockade of the U.S. coast, which crippled trading and fishing.

Probably the most important naval battle of the war was fought in 1813 on Lake Erie. At the end of an unrelenting and murderous three-hour engagement, a 28-year-old American, Captain Oliver Hazard Perry, declared proudly, "We have met the enemy and they are ours." Perry's naval victory prepared the way for General William Henry Harrison's military victory at the Battle of Thames River (near Detroit), in which Tecumseh was killed. The next year, 1814, another young naval captain, Thomas Macdonough, defeated a British fleet on Lake Champlain. As a result, the British were forced to retreat and to abandon their plan to invade New York and New England.

Chesapeake campaign. By the spring of 1814, the defeat of Napoleon in Europe enabled the British to increase their forces in North America. In the summer of that year, a British army marched through the nation's capital, Washington, D.C., and set fire to the White House, the Capitol, and other government buildings. The British also attempted to take Baltimore, but Fort McHenry held out after a night's bombardment—an event immortalized by Francis Scott Key in the words of "The Star-Spangled Banner."

Southern campaign. Meanwhile, U.S. troops in the South were ably commanded by General Andrew Jackson. In March 1814, at the Battle of Horseshoe Bend in present-day Alabama, Jackson ended the power of an important British ally, the Creek nation. The victory not only eliminated the Native American ally but also opened new lands to white settlers. A major British effort to control the Mississippi River was halted at New Orleans by Jackson leading a force of frontiersmen, free blacks, and Creoles. The victory was impressive—but also meaningless. The Battle of New Orleans was fought on January 8, 1815, two weeks *after* a treaty ending the war had been signed in Ghent, Belgium.

The Treaty of Ghent

By 1814, the British were weary of war. Having fought Napoleon for more than a decade, they now faced the prospect of maintaining the peace in Europe. At the same time, Madison's government recognized that the Americans would be unable to win a decisive victory. American peace commissioners traveled to Ghent, Belgium, to discuss terms of peace with British diplomats. On Christmas Eve, 1814, an agreement was reached. The terms were:

- a halt to the fighting

- the return of all conquered territory to the prewar claimant

- recognition of the prewar boundary between Canada and the United States.

The Treaty of Ghent, promptly ratified by the Senate in 1815, said nothing at all about the grievances that led to war. Britain made no concessions concerning impressment, blockades, or other maritime differences. Thus, the war ended in stalemate with no gain for either side.

The Hartford Convention

Before the war ended, the New England states came close to seceding from the Union. Bitterly opposed to both the war and the Republican government in Washington, radical Federalists in New England urged that the Constitution be amended and that, as a last resort, secession be voted upon. To consider these matters, a special convention was held at Hartford, Connecticut, in December 1814. Delegates from the New England states rejected the radical calls for secession. But to limit the growing power of the Republicans in the South and West, they adopted a number of proposals. One of them called for a two-thirds vote of both houses for any future declaration of war.

Shortly after the convention dissolved, news came of both Jackson's victory at New Orleans and the Treaty of Ghent. These events ended criticism of the war and further weakened the Federalists by stamping them as unpatriotic.

The War's Legacy

From Madison's point of view, the war achieved none of its original aims. Nevertheless, it had a number of important consequences for the future development of the American republic. They may be listed as follows:

1. Having now survived two wars with Britain, a great power, the United States gained the respect of other nations.
2. The United States came to accept Canada as a neighbor and a part of the British Empire.
3. Widely denounced for its talk of secession and disunion in New England, the Federalist party came to an end as a national force and declined even in New England.
4. Talk of nullification and secession in New England set a precedent that would later be used by the South.
5. Abandoned by their British allies, Native Americans in the West were forced to surrender large areas of land to white settlement.
6. As European goods became unavailable due to the British naval blockade, more U.S. factories were built, and Americans took a big step toward industrial self-sufficiency.
7. War heroes such as Andrew Jackson and William Henry Harrison would soon be in the forefront of a new generation of political leaders.
8. As a result of the war, there was a strong feeling of American nationalism and also a growing belief that the future for the United States lay in the West and away from Europe.

HISTORICAL PERSPECTIVES: POLITICAL PARTIES

Thomas Jefferson's election to the presidency was popularly known as the Revolution of 1800. It is true that the first Republican administration brought about significant changes in policy, but Jefferson made sure that there would be a large measure of continuity as well. The real revolution in 1800 was the complete *absence* of violence and disorder in the transition of power. While the Framers of the Constitution had opposed political parties, now they were accepted as an essential element of the U.S. political system.

Historians have traced the development of the two-party system and have identified various stages in the emergence of two major parties. In the first stage (1787–1789), Federalist and Anti-Federalist factions arose in the various state ratifying conventions as people debated the merits and pitfalls of the proposed Constitution. The first years of the new federal government (1789–1800) marked a second stage. Especially during Adams' controversial presidency, the Anti-Federalists became a true political party—Jefferson's Republican party. In 1800, for the first time, a party actively recruited members (both voters and candidates for office) and forged alliances with politicians in every state. Largely as a result of their organized efforts, the Republicans were able to accomplish their peaceful revolution.

From one era to the next, historians' interpretations of the early parties have changed. Historians of the Progressive era (early 20th century) described the partisan struggles of the 1790s as a conflict between the undemocratic, elitist Hamiltonian Federalists and the democratic, egalitarian Jeffersonian Republicans. Charles Beard's *Economic Origins of Jeffersonian Democracy* interpreted the struggle as one between Hamilton's capitalist class and Jefferson's agrarian (farmer) class. More recently, historians have looked at the importance of personalities in defining the two parties. Finding general agreement in the practices and even the ideologies of the opposing parties, these historians emphasize the differing characters of Jefferson and Hamilton and the significance of Washington's friendship with Hamilton and of Jefferson's friendship with Madison.

Richard Hofstadter, a leading historian of the 1950s and 1960s, observed both the differences *and* the shared ideas of the Republicans and Federalists. He saw the parties maturing in 1800, moving past excessive rhetoric to accommodation, as both came to terms with the same political realities.

KEY NAMES, EVENTS, AND TERMS

Thomas Jefferson	impressment	Battle of Lake Erie
Louisiana Purchase	*Chesapeake-Leopard* affair	Oliver Hazard Perry
Napoleon Bonaparte	Embargo Act (1807)	Battle of the Thames River
Toussaint l'Ouverture	James Madison	Thomas Macdonough
strict interpretation, of Constitution	Nonintercourse Act (1809)	Battle of Lake Champlain
Lewis and Clark expedition	Macon's Bill No. 2 (1810)	Francis Scott Key, "The Star-Spangled Banner"
John Marshall	Tecumseh; Prophet	Andrew Jackson
judicial review	William Henry Harrison	Battle of Horseshoe Bend
Marbury v. Madison	Battle of Tippecanoe	Creek nation
Aaron Burr	war hawks	Battle of New Orleans
"Quids"	Henry Clay	Treaty of Ghent (1814)
Barbary pirates	John C. Calhoun	Hartford Convention (1814)
neutrality	War of 1812	
	"Old Ironsides"	

MULTIPLE-CHOICE QUESTIONS

1. Which of the following leaders is INCORRECTLY paired with a notable event or deed?
   (A) Thomas Jefferson—Louisiana Purchase
   (B) Andrew Jackson—Battle of New Orleans
   (C) Tecumseh—Battle of Tippecanoe
   (D) Henry Clay—declaration of war in 1812
   (E) Alexander Hamilton—Embargo Act of 1807

2. Thomas Jefferson's revolution of 1800 changed the Federalist policies of Washington and Adams in all of the following areas EXCEPT
   (A) size of the military
   (B) number of federal employees
   (C) amount of national debt
   (D) foreign affairs
   (E) Alien and Sedition Acts

3. Which of the following accurately characterizes the foreign policy goals of Jefferson and Madison before 1812?
   (A) strengthen U.S. trade relations with Britain and France
   (B) maintain U.S. neutral rights without going to war
   (C) seek an alliance with either Britain or France
   (D) explore various means for acquiring Canada
   (E) provide aid to independence movements in Latin America

4. John Marshall's Supreme Court decision in the case of *Marbury v. Madison* established
   (A) a means for installing Federalist judges in office
   (B) rules for impeachment trials
   (C) the principle of judicial review
   (D) the federal government's authority over the states
   (E) a procedure for reviewing treaties

5. Native Americans in the West allied themselves with the British in the War of 1812 because they
   (A) wanted to stop American settlers from taking their lands
   (B) were persuaded to do so by Aaron Burr
   (C) had ambitions to establish an Indian confederacy
   (D) had always been friendly with the British
   (E) had signed a binding treaty with Britain during the American Revolution

6. Thomas Jefferson's chief reason for purchasing Louisiana was to
   (A) challenge Hamilton's loose interpretation of the Constitution
   (B) challenge Napoleon's bid for world empire
   (C) give the United States control of the Mississippi River
   (D) provide a rationale for the Lewis and Clark Expedition
   (E) strengthen the Republican party in the trans-Mississippi West

7. All of the following contributed to the U.S. decision to go to war in 1812 EXCEPT

   (A) the election of war hawks to Congress in 1810

   (B) a desire to acquire parts of Canada

   (C) British impressment of American seamen

   (D) efforts to protect the land of Native Americans

   (E) American sympathy with France against Britain

8. Which of the following documents or sources would be *most* useful for analyzing the effects of the Embargo of 1807 on the U.S. economy?

   (A) Jefferson's instructions to Lewis and Clark

   (B) resolutions of the Hartford Convention

   (C) records of shipbuilding activity in a New England state from 1805 to 1810

   (D) financial accounts of Georgia plantations from 1805 to 1807

   (E) speeches of Henry Clay (1810–1812)

9. The War of 1812 had all of the following consequences in the United States EXCEPT

   (A) acquisition of new land

   (B) Native Americans' loss of Britain as an ally

   (C) the demise of the Federalist party

   (D) an increase in U.S. manufacturing

   (E) an increase in American nationalism

10. The Hartford Convention had long-term significance because it

    (A) encouraged Britain to sign the Treaty of Ghent

    (B) presented a major challenge to Madison's domestic policies

    (C) forced repeal of the Embargo Act of 1807

    (D) marked the end of the Federalists as a national party

    (E) organized national opposition to the War of 1812

ESSAY QUESTIONS

1. Analyze, with respect to his domestic and foreign policies, the statement by President Jefferson, "We are all Republicans, we are all Federalists."

2. Assess the pressures in the early part of the 19th century to force Native Americans from their lands along the western frontier of the United States in the context of TWO of the following:

   Andrew Jackson
   Tecumseh
   Lewis and Clark expedition
   William Henry Harrison

3. Explain the influence of TWO of the following on the U.S. decision to go to war in 1812:

   embargo policies of Jefferson and Madison

British impressment of American seamen

settlers' conflicts with the Native Americans

expansionist goals of the war hawks

4. To what extent did Jefferson violate his avowed constitutional principles when he accepted the Louisiana Purchase?

5. Analyze the consequences of the War of 1812 in the context of TWO of the following:

foreign relations

industry

nationalism

Native Americans

DOCUMENTS AND READINGS

For 22 years (1790–1812), the foreign policy of two Federalist presidents (Washington and Adams) and two Republican presidents (Jefferson and Madison) had consistently focused on a single aim: avoiding war with a European power while at the same time defending U.S. neutral rights at sea. Finally, however, as you have read, a majority of Republicans including the president decided in 1812 to abandon a policy of peace and neutrality in order to fight a war against Great Britain. What were the reasons for this change in policy from peace to war? The following documents from the congressional debate of December 1811 and the presidential war message of June 1812 provide some of the historical evidence.

DOCUMENT A.   A WAR HAWK'S ARGUMENTS FOR WAR

Felix Grundy, a war-hawk representative from Tennessee, argued for war with Britain. The following is an excerpt from his speech in the House in December 1811.

> What, Mr. Speaker, are we now called on to decide? It is, whether we will resist by force the attempt, made by that Government [Britain], to subject our maritime rights to the arbitrary and capricious rule of her will; for my part I am not prepared to say that this country shall submit to have her commerce interdicted or regulated, by any foreign nation. Sir, I prefer war to submission.
>
> Over and above these unjust pretensions of the British Government, for many years past they have been in the practice of impressing our seamen, from merchant vessels; this unjust and lawless invasion of personal liberty, calls loudly for the interposition of this Government. To those better acquainted with the facts in relation to it, I

leave it to fill up the picture. My mind is irresistibly drawn to the West.

Although others may not strongly feel the bearing which the late transactions in that quarter [war with Tecumseh] have on this subject, upon my mind they have great influence. It cannot be believed by any man who will reflect, that the savage tribes, uninfluenced by other Powers, would think of making war on the United States. They understand too well their own weakness, and our strength. They have already felt the weight of our arms; they know they hold the very soil on which they live as tenants at sufferance. How, then, sir, are we to account for their late conduct? In one way only; some powerful nation must have intrigued with them, and turned their peaceful disposition toward us into hostilities. Great Britain alone has intercourse with those Northern tribes; I therefore infer, that if British gold has not been employed, their baubles and trinkets, and the promise of support and a place of refuge if necessary, have had their effect.

Felix Grundy,
Speech in the U.S. House of Representatives,
December 9, 1811

DOCUMENT B. *ANTIWAR VIEWS OF AN "OLD REPUBLICAN"*

John Randolph, a Republican Congressman from Virginia, led the faction of "Old Republicans" that opposed Jefferson's and Madison's leadership. He attempted to rebut the war hawks' arguments by pointing out their "true" motives for wanting war.

Sir, if you go to war it will not be for the protection of, or defence of your maritime rights. Gentlemen from the North have been taken up to some high mountain and shown all the kingdoms of the earth; and Canada seems tempting in their sight. That rich vein of Genesee land, which is said to be even better on the other side of the lake than on this. Agrarian cupidity, not maritime right, urges the war. Ever since the report of the Committee on Foreign Relations came into the House, we have heard but one word— like the whip-poor-will, but one eternal monotonous tone—Canada! Canada! Canada! . . . It is to acquire a preponding northern influence, that you are to launch into war.

John Randolph,
Speech in the House of Representatives,
December 16, 1811

DOCUMENT C.   MADISON'S WAR MESSAGE TO CONGRESS

President Madison's arguments for going to war with Britain in 1812 were summarized in the following written message to both houses of Congress.

> British cruisers have been in the continued practice of violating the American flag on the great highway of nations, and of seizing and carrying off persons sailing under it, not in the exercise of a belligerent right founded on the law of nations against an enemy. . . . British jurisdiction is thus extended to neutral vessels in a situation where no laws can operate but the law of nations and the laws of the country to which the vessels belong. . . .
>
> Against this crying enormity, which Great Britain would be so prompt to avenge if committed against herself, the United States have in vain exhausted remonstrances and expostulations. . . . The communication passed without effect.
>
> British cruisers have been in the practice also of violating the rights and the peace of our coasts. They hover over and harass our entering and departing commerce. To the most insulting pretensions they have added the most lawless proceedings in our very harbors, and have wantonly spilt American blood within the sanctuary of our territorial jurisdiction. . . .
>
> In reviewing the conduct of Great Britain toward the United States, our attention is necessarily drawn to the warfare just renewed by the savages on one of our extensive frontiers—a warfare which is known to spare neither age nor sex and to be distinguished by features peculiarly shocking to humanity. It is difficult to account for the activity and combinations [alliances] which have for some time been developing themselves among tribes in constant inter-course with British traders and garrisons without connecting their hostility with that influence and without recollecting the authenticated examples of such interpositions heretofore furnished by the officers and agents of that Government.
>
> Such is the spectacle of injuries and indignities which have been heaped on our country, and such the crisis which its unexampled forbearance and conciliatory efforts have not been able to avert.

James Madison,
War Message to Congress,
June 1, 1812

DOCUMENT D.   UNPREPARED FOR WAR

Arguing against the war on the floor of the Senate, Obadiah German stressed that the nation was militarily unprepared to fight Britain.

Before we take the step proposed by the bill before us [war], I think we ought also to make some calculation on the general state of the nation. Except some trifling Indian war, it will be recollected we have been twenty-nine years at peace, and have become a nation, in a great degree, of active moneymakers. We have lost much of the spirit of war and chivalry possessed by our Revolutionary fathers; and we are a people, also, not overfond of paying taxes to the extent of our ability; and this because our purses have been sweated down by our restrictive system till they have become light. . . .

I do not, Mr. President, draw all these discouraging pictures, or relate these lamentable facts, because I would shrink from the conflicts or terrors of war, for the defense of the rights of my injured country, sooner than any gentleman of this Senate, nor with a wish that all these evils may be realized; my object is to avert them from my country. I do it, sir, to check the precipitate step of plunging my country prematurely into a war without any of the means of making the war terrible to our enemy, and with the certainty that it will be terrible to ourselves, or at least to our merchants, our seaports, and cities.

Obadiah German,
Speech, U.S. Senate,
June 13, 1812

ANALYZING THE DOCUMENTS

1. According to John Randolph, in Document B, what was the real reason the war hawks wanted war with Britain?

2. In your opinion, did Senator German, in Document D, have a valid point that the United States was unprepared for war? Should the degree of preparedness be a major consideration when debating whether a nation should go to war?

3. "Although President Madison stressed U.S. neutral rights as the principal reason for war, other reasons were probably far more important."

   Based on the documents you have read and your knowledge of the historical period 1800–1812, write an essay that takes a position either for or against the above interpretation.

NATIONALISM AND ECONOMIC DEVELOPMENT

A high and honorable feeling generally prevails, and the people begin to assume, more and more, a national character; *and to look at home for the only means, under divine goodness, of preserving their religion and liberty.*

Hezekiah Niles, *Niles' Weekly Register,* September 2, 1815

The election of James Monroe as president in 1816 (less than two years after the last battle of the War of 1812) inaugurated what one newspaper editorial characterized as an "Era of Good Feelings." The term gained wide currency and was later adopted by historians to describe Monroe's two terms in office.

The Era of Good Feelings

According to the traditional view of the period, the Monroe years were marked by a spirit of nationalism, optimism, and goodwill, chiefly as a result of one party, the Federalists, fading into oblivion and Monroe's party, the Republicans, dominating politics in every section: North, South, and West.

This perception of unity and harmony, however, was probably misleading and certainly oversimplified. Throughout the era there were heated debates over tariffs, the national bank, internal improvements, and public land sales. Sectionalist tensions over slavery were becoming ever more apparent. Moreover, a sense of political unity was illusory, since antagonistic factions within the Republican party would soon split that party in two. The actual period of "good feelings" may have lasted only from the election of 1816 to the Panic of 1819.

James Monroe

As a young man, James Monroe had fought in the Revolutionary War and suffered through the Valley Forge winter. He had become prominent in Virginia's Republican party and had served in high-level diplomatic roles as President Jefferson's minister to Great Britain and as Madison's secretary of state. His choice as Madison's successor continued what appeared to be a Virginia dynasty of presidents. (Of the first five presidents, four were from Virginia; the exception, John Adams, was from Massachusetts.)

In the election of 1816, Monroe defeated his Federalist opponent, Rufus King, by an overwhelming margin—183 electoral votes to King's 34. Four years later, the Federalist party had practically ceased to exist, and Monroe achieved an easy victory in 1820, receiving every electoral vote except one. With no organized political opposition to stand in his way, President Monroe supported the growing nationalism of the American people. His eight-year presidency is noted for the acquisition of Florida, the Missouri Compromise, and of course the Monroe Doctrine.

Cultural Nationalism

The popular votes for James Monroe were cast by a younger generation of Americans whose concerns were different from those of the nation's founders. The young were excited about the prospects of the new nation expanding westward and had little interest in European politics now that the Napoleonic wars (as well as the War of 1812) were in the past. As fervent nationalists, they believed their young country was entering an era of unlimited prosperity.

Patriotic themes infused every aspect of American society, from paintings to schoolbooks. Heroes of the Revolution were enshrined in the paintings of Gilbert Stuart, Charles Willson Peale, and John Trumball. Parson Mason Weems' fictionalized biography extolling the virtues of George Washington was widely read. The expanding public schools embraced Noah Webster's blue-backed speller, which promoted patriotism long before his famous dictionary was published. Clearly evident were the basic ideas and ideals of nationalism and patriotism, which would dominate most of the 19th century.

Economic Nationalism

Running parallel with cultural nationalism was a political movement to support the growth of the nation's economy. Subsidizing internal improvements (the building of roads and canals) was one aspect of the movement. Protecting budding U.S. industries from European competition was a second aspect.

Tariff of 1816. Before the War of 1812, Congress had levied low tariffs on imports as a method for raising government revenue. After the war, in 1816, Congress raised the tariff rates on certain goods for the express purpose of protecting U.S. manufacturers from ruin. A number of factories had been erected during the war to supply goods that previously had been imported from Britain. Now in peacetime, American manufacturers feared that British goods would be dumped on American markets and take away much of their business. Congress' tariff of 1816 was the first *protective tariff* in U.S. history—the first of many to come.

New England, which had little manufacturing at the time, was the only section to oppose the higher tariffs. Even the South and West, which had opposed tariffs in the past and would oppose them in the future, generally supported the 1816 tariff, believing that it was needed for national prosperity.

Henry Clay's American System. Henry Clay of Kentucky, a leader in the House of Representatives, proposed a comprehensive method for advancing the nation's economic growth. His plan, which he called the American System, consisted of three parts: (1) protective tariffs, (2) a national bank, and (3) internal improvements. Clay argued that protective tariffs would promote American manufacturing and also raise revenue with which to build a national transportation system of federally constructed roads and canals. A national bank would keep the system running smoothly by providing a national currency. The tariffs would chiefly benefit the East, internal improvements would promote growth in the West and the South, and the bank would aid the economies of all sections.

Two parts of Clay's system were already in place in 1816, the last year of James Madison's presidency. Congress in that year adopted a protective tariff and also chartered the Second Bank of the United States. (The charter of the First Bank—Hamilton's brainchild—had been allowed to expire in 1811.)

On the matter of internal improvements, however, both Madison and Monroe objected that the Constitution did not explicitly provide for the spending of federal money on roads and canals. Throughout his presidency, Monroe consistently vetoed acts of Congress providing funds for road-building and canal-building projects. Thus, the individual states were left to make internal improvements on their own.

The Panic of 1819

The Era of Good Feelings was fractured in 1819 by the first major financial panic since the Constitution had been ratified. The economic disaster was largely the fault of the Second Bank of the United States, which had tightened credit in a belated effort to control inflation. Many state banks closed, the value of money became deflated (fell), and there were large increases in unemployment, bankruptcies, and imprisonment for debt. Although every section was hurt, the depression was most severe in the West. In this region, land speculation based on postwar euphoria had placed many people in debt, and in 1819, the Bank of the United States foreclosed on large amounts of western farmland.

As a result of the bank panic and depression, nationalistic beliefs were shaken. In the West, the economic crisis changed many voters' political outlook. Westerners began calling for land reform and expressing strong opposition to both the national bank and debtors' prisons.

Political Changes

A principal reason for the rapid decline of the Federalist party was its failure to adapt to the changing needs of a growing nation. Having opposed the War of 1812 and presided over a secessionist convention at Hartford, the party seemed completely out of step with the nationalistic temper of the times. After its crushing defeat in the election of 1816, it ceased to be a national party and failed to nominate a presidential candidate in 1820.

Changes in the Republican party. Meanwhile, the Republican party, as the only remaining national party, underwent serious internal strains as it adjusted to changing times. Certain members of the party, such as John Randolph, clung to the old Republican ideals of limited government and strict interpretation of the Constitution. The majority of Republicans, however, adopted what had once been a Federalist program. Even after the War of 1812, a Republican Congress authorized the maintaining of a large army and navy. In chartering a Second Bank of the United States in 1816, the majority faction of Republicans adopted an institution originally championed by the Federalist leader Alexander Hamilton.

On several issues, the political principles of many Republicans were sorely tested during Monroe's presidency, and some even reversed their views from one decade to the next. Daniel Webster of Massachusetts, for example, strongly opposed both the tariffs of 1816 and 1824; he then did an about-face by supporting even higher tariff rates in 1828. John C. Calhoun of South Carolina was another Republican leader who reversed his position. An outspoken war hawk and nationalist in 1812, Calhoun became a leading champion of states' rights after 1828.

Political factions and sectional differences became more intense during Monroe's second term. When Monroe, honoring the two-term tradition, declined to be a candidate again, four other Republicans sought election as president in 1824. How this election resulted in the splitting of the Republican party and the emergence of two rival parties is explained in Chapter 10.

Marshall's Supreme Court and Central Government Powers

One Federalist official continued to have major influence throughout the years of Republican ascendancy. John Marshall, who had been appointed to the Supreme Court in 1800 by Federalist President John Adams, was still leading the Court as its chief justice. His decisions in many landmark cases consistently favored the central government and the rights of property against the advocates of states' rights. Even when Republican justices formed a majority on the Court, they sided with Marshall because they too were persuaded that the U.S. Constitution had created a Union of states, whose government had strong and flexible powers.

Marshall's first landmark decision establishing the principle of judicial review (*Marbury v. Madison,* 1803) was described in Chapter 7. Here are other decisions that went a long way toward defining the relationship between the central government and the states.

Fletcher v. Peck (1810). In a case involving land fraud in Georgia, Marshall concluded that a state could not pass legislation invalidating a contract. This was the first time that the Supreme Court declared a state law to be unconstitutional and invalid. (Remember that in *Marbury v. Madison* it was a federal law that had been ruled unconstitutional.)

Martin v. Hunter's Lease (1816). In this case, the Supreme Court established the principle that it had jurisdiction over state courts in cases involving constitutional rights.

Dartmouth College v. Woodward (1819). This case involved a law of New Hampshire that changed Dartmouth College from a privately chartered college into a public institution. The Marshall Court struck down the state law as unconstitutional, arguing that a contract for a private corporation could not be altered by the state.

McCulloch v. Maryland (1819). Did Congress have the power to create a bank even if no clause in the Constitution mentioned a bank? Could a state place a tax on a federally created bank? These were the two questions involved in a case concerning a tax that the state of Maryland tried to collect from the Second Bank of the United States. Using a loose interpretation of the Constitution, Marshall ruled that the federal government had the *implied power* to create the bank. Furthermore, a state could *not* tax a federal institution because "the power to tax is the power to destroy," and federal laws are supreme over state laws.

Cohens v. Virginia (1821). In Virginia, the Cohens were convicted of selling Washington, D.C., lottery tickets authorized by Congress. Marshall and the Court upheld the conviction. More important, this case established the principle that the Supreme Court could review a state court's decision involving any of the powers of the federal government.

Gibbons v. Ogden (1821). Could the state of New York grant a monopoly to a steamboat company if that action conflicted with a charter authorized by Congress? In ruling that the New York monopoly was unconstitutional, Marshall established the federal government's broad control of interstate commerce.

Western Settlement and the Missouri Compromise

Less than ten years after the start of the War of 1812, the population west of the Appalachian Mountains had doubled. Much of the nationalistic and economic interest in the country was centered on the West, which presented both opportunities and new questions.

Reasons for Westward Movement

A number of factors combined to stimulate rapid growth along the western frontier during the presidencies of Madison and Monroe.

Acquisition of Native Americans' lands. Large areas were open for settlement after Native Americans were driven from their lands by the victories of Generals William Henry Harrison in the Indiana Territory and Andrew Jackson in Florida and the South.

Economic pressures. The economic difficulties in the Northeast from the embargo and the war caused people from this region to seek a new future across the Appalachians. In the South, tobacco planters needed new land to replace the soil exhausted by years of poor farming methods. They found good land for planting cotton in Alabama, Mississippi, and Arkansas.

Improved transportation. Pioneering families had an easier time reaching the frontier as a result of the building of roads and canals, steamboats and railroads.

Immigrants. More Europeans were being attracted to America by speculators offering cheap land in the Great Lakes region and the Ohio, the Cumberland, and the Mississippi River valleys.

New Questions and Issues

Despite their rapid growth, the new states of the West had small populations relative to those of the other two sections. To enhance their limited political influence in Congress, western representatives bargained with politicians from other sections to obtain their objectives. Of greatest importance to the western states were: (1) "cheap money" (easy credit) from state banks rather than from the Bank of the United States, (2) land made available at low prices by the government, and (3) improved transportation.

On another issue, slavery, westerners could not agree whether to permit it or to exclude it. Those settling territory to the south wanted slavery for economic reasons (labor for the cotton fields), while those settling to the north had no use for slavery. In 1819, when the Missouri Territory applied to Congress for statehood, the slavery issue became a subject of angry debate.

The Missouri Compromise

Ever since 1791–1792, when Vermont entered the Union as a free state and Kentucky entered as a slave state, politicians in Congress had attempted to preserve a sectional balance between the North and the South. Population in the North grew more rapidly than in the South, so that by 1818 the northern states held a majority of 105 to 81 in the House of Representatives. In the Senate, however, the votes were divided evenly, since in 1819 there was an even balance of 11 slave and 11 free states. So long as this balance was preserved, southern senators could block legislation that threatened the interests of their section.

Missouri's bid for statehood alarmed the North because slavery was well established there. If Missouri came in as a slave state, it would tip the political balance in the South's favor. Furthermore, Missouri was the first part of the Louisiana Purchase to apply for statehood. Southerners and northerners alike worried about the future status of other new territories applying for statehood from the rest of the vast Louisiana Purchase.

Tallmadge amendment. Representative James Tallmadge from New York ignited the debate about the Missouri question by proposing an amendment to the bill for Missouri's admission. The amendment called for (1) prohibiting the further introduction of slaves into Missouri and (2) requiring the children of Missouri slaves to be emancipated at the age of 25. If adopted, the Tallmadge Amendment would have led to the gradual elimination of slavery in Missouri. The amendment was defeated in the Senate as enraged southerners saw it as the first step in a northern effort to abolish slavery in all states.

Clay's proposals. After months of heated debate in Congress and throughout the nation, Henry Clay won majority support for three bills that, taken together, represented a compromise:

1. Missouri was to be admitted as a slaveholding state.
2. Maine was to be admitted as a free state.
3. In the rest of the Louisiana Territory north of latitude 36° 30', slavery was prohibited.

Both houses passed the compromise plan, and President Monroe added his signature in March 1820 (one full year after the Tallmadge Amendment had touched off the controversy).

Aftermath. Sectional feelings on the slavery issue subsided after 1820. The Missouri Compromise preserved sectional balance for over 30 years and provided time for the nation to mature. Nevertheless, if an era of good feelings existed, it was badly damaged by the storm of sectional controversy over Missouri. After this political crisis, Americans were torn between feelings of nationalism (loyalty to the Union) on the one hand and feelings of sectionalism (loyalty to one's own region) on the other.

Foreign Affairs

Following the War of 1812, the United States adopted a more aggressive, nationalistic approach it its relations with other nations. During Madison's presidency, when problems with the Barbary pirates again developed, a fleet under Stephen Decatur was sent in 1815 to force the rulers of North Africa to allow American shipping the free use of the Mediterranean. President Monroe and Secretary of State John Quincy Adams continued to follow a nationalistic policy that actively advanced American interests while maintaining peace.

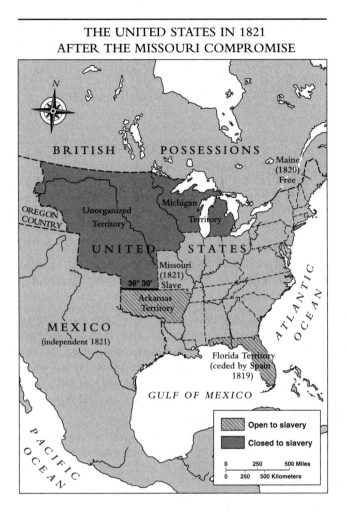

THE UNITED STATES IN 1821
AFTER THE MISSOURI COMPROMISE

Canada

Although the Treaty of Ghent of 1814 had ended the war between Britain and the United States, it left unresolved most of their diplomatic differences, including many involving Canada.

Rush-Bagot Agreement (1817). During Monroe's first year as president, British and American negotiators agreed to a major disarmament pact. The Rush-Bagot Agreement strictly limited naval armament on the Great Lakes. In time the agreement was extended to place limits on border fortifications as well. Ultimately, the border between the United States and Canada was to become the longest unfortified boundary in the world.

Treaty of 1818. Improved relations between the United States and Britain continued in a treaty that provided for (1) shared fishing rights off the coast of Newfoundland; (2) joint occupation of the Oregon Territory for ten years; and (3) the setting of the northern limits of the Louisiana Territory at the 49th parallel, thus establishing the western U.S.-Canada boundary line.

Florida

During the War of 1812, U.S. troops had occupied western Florida, a strip of land on the Gulf extending all the way to the Mississippi delta. Previously, this land had been held by Spain, Britain's ally. After the war, Spain had difficulty governing the rest of Florida (the peninsula itself) because its troops had been removed from Florida to battle revolts in the South American colonies. The chaotic conditions permitted groups of Seminoles, runaway slaves, and white outlaws to conduct raids into U.S. territory and retreat to safety across the Florida border. These disorders gave Monroe and General Andrew Jackson an opportunity to take military action in Spanish Florida, a territory long coveted by American expansionists.

Jackson's military campaign. In late 1817, the president commissioned General Jackson to stop the raiders and, if necessary, pursue them across the border into Spanish west Florida. Jackson carried out his orders with a vengeance and probably went beyond his instructions. In 1818, he led a force of militia into Florida, destroyed Seminole villages, and hanged two Seminole chiefs. Capturing Pensacola, Jackson drove out the Spanish governor, and even hanged two British traders accused of aiding the Seminoles.

Many members of Congress feared that Jackson's overzealousness would precipitate a war with both Spain and Britain. However, Secretary of State John Quincy Adams persuaded Monroe to support Jackson, and the British decided not to intervene.

Florida Purchase Treaty (1819). Spain worried that the United States would seize Florida by force. Preoccupied with troubles in Latin America, the Spanish government decided to get the best possible terms for Florida. By treaty in 1819, Spain turned over the rest of western Florida along with all of the east and its own claims in the Oregon Territory to the United States. In exchange, the United States agreed to assume $5 million in claims against Spain and give up any U.S. territorial claims to the Spanish province of Texas.

The Monroe Doctrine

Although focused on its own growth, the United States could not ignore the ambitions of Europe as they affected the future of the Western Hemisphere. The restoration of a number of monarchies in Europe after the fall of Napoleon produced a backlash against republican and democratic movements. The restored monarchies (France, Austria, and Prussia), together with Russia, cooperated with one another in suppressing liberal elements in Italy and Spain. They also considered helping Spain to return to power in South America, where a number of republics had recently declared their independence. Russia's presence in Alaska posed a special problem that worried British and Americans alike. Using their trading posts in Alaska as a base, Russian seal hunters had spread southward and established a trading post at San Francisco Bay. British and U.S. leaders decided they had a common interest in protecting North and South America from the possible aggression of a European power.

British initiative. The power of the British navy was most important in deterring the Spanish monarchy from attempting a comeback in Latin America. Also important was the diplomacy of British Foreign Secretary George Canning, who wanted to maintain British trade with the Latin American republics. Canning suggested to Richard Rush, the U.S. minister in London, the idea of issuing a joint Anglo-American warning to the European powers not to intervene in South America.

American response. Monroe and most of his advisers thought Canning's idea of a joint declaration made sense. Secretary of State John Quincy Adams, however, argued against such a move. Adams believed that joint action with Britain would restrict U.S. opportunities for further expansion in the hemisphere. He reasoned as follows: (1) If the United States acted alone, Britain could be counted upon to stand behind the U.S. policy. (2) No European power would risk going to war in South America, and if it did, the British navy would surely defeat the aggressor. Changing his mind, the president decided to act as Adams advised—in short, to issue a statement to the world that did not have Britain as a coauthor.

The doctrine. On December 2, 1823, President Monroe inserted into his annual message to Congress a declaration of U.S. policy toward Europe and Latin America. The Monroe Doctrine, as it came to be called, asserted

> as a principle in which the rights and interests of the United States are involved, that the American continents, by the free and independent condition which they have assumed and maintain, are henceforth not to be considered as subjects for future colonization by any European powers.

Monroe declared further that the United States was opposed to attempts by a European power to interfere in the affairs of any republic in the Western Hemisphere.

Impact. Monroe's bold words of nationalistic purpose were applauded by the American public but soon forgotten, as most citizens were more concerned with domestic issues. In Britain, Canning was annoyed by the doctrine because he recognized that it applied, not just to the other European powers, but to his country as well. In effect, the British too were warned not to intervene and not to seek new territory in the Western Hemisphere. The European monarchs reacted angrily to the president's message; but they recognized full well that their purposes were thwarted, not by a few high-sounding words, but by the might of the British navy.

The Monroe Doctrine had less significance at the time than in later decades, when it would be hailed by politicians and citizens alike as the cornerstone of U.S. foreign policy toward Latin America. In the 1840s, President James Polk was the first of many presidents to justify his foreign policy by referring to Monroe's warning words.

A National Economy

In the early 1800s, the Jeffersonian dream of a nation of independent farmers remained strong in rural areas. As the century progressed, however, an increasing percentage of the American people were swept up in the dynamic economic changes of the Industrial Revolution. Political conflicts over tariffs, internal improvements, and the Bank of the United States reflected the importance to people's lives of a national economy that was rapidly growing and changing.

Population Growth

Population growth was vital if the nation was to have both the laborers and the consumers required for industrial development. Between 1800 and 1825, the U.S. population doubled; in the next 25 years it doubled again. A high birthrate accounted for most of this growth, but it was strongly supplemented after 1830 by immigrants arriving from Europe, particularly from Great Britain and Germany. The nonwhite population—African Americans and Native Americans—grew despite the ban on the importation of slaves after 1808. As a percentage of the total population, however, nonwhites declined from almost 20 percent in 1790 to 15 percent in the 1850s.

By the 1830s, almost one-third of the population lived west of the Alleghenies. At the same time, both old and new urban areas were growing rapidly.

Transportation

Vital to the development of both a national and an industrial economy was an efficient network of interconnecting roads and canals for moving people, raw materials, and manufactured goods.

Roads. Pennsylvania's Lancaster Turnpike, built in the 1790s, connected Philadelphia with the rich farmlands around Lancaster. Its success stimulated the construction of other privately built and relatively short toll roads that, by the mid-1820s, connected most of the country's major cities.

Despite the need for interstate roads, states' righters blocked the spending of federal funds on internal improvements. Construction of highways that

United States Population, 1790–1860

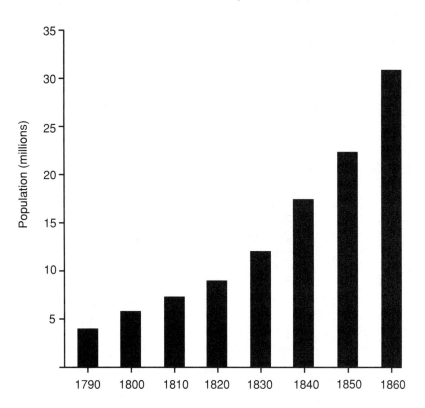

crossed state lines was therefore unusual. One notable exception was the National, or Cumberland Road, a paved highway and major route to the west extending more than a thousand miles from Maryland to Illinois. It was begun in 1811 and completed in the 1850s, using both federal and state money, with the different states receiving ownership of segments of the highway.

Canals. The completion of the Erie Canal in New York State in 1825 was an event of major importance in linking the economies of western farms and eastern cities. The success of this canal in stimulating economic growth touched off a frenzy of canal-building in other states. In little more than a decade, canals joined together all of the major lakes and rivers east of the Mississippi. Improved transportation meant lower food prices in the East, more immigrants settling in the West, and stronger economic ties between the two sections.

Steamboats. The age of mechanized, steam-powered travel began in 1807 with the successful voyage up the Hudson River of the *Clermont,* a steamboat

MAJOR CANALS, ROADS, AND RAILROADS 1820–1850

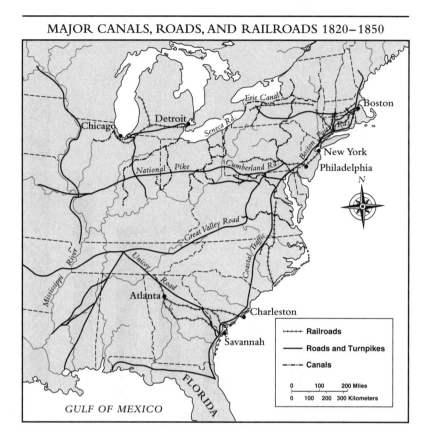

developed by Robert Fulton. Commercially operated steamboat lines soon made round-trip shipping on the nation's great rivers both faster and cheaper.

Railroads. Even more rapid and reliable links between cities became possible with the building of the first U.S. railroad lines in the late 1820s. The early railroads were hampered at first by safety problems, but by the 1830s they were competing directly with canals as an alternative method for carrying passengers and freight. Combined with the other major improvements in transportation (especially steamboats and canals), the railroad swiftly changed small western towns such as Cleveland, Cincinnati, Detroit, and Chicago into booming commercial centers of the expanding national economy.

Growth of Industry

At the start of the 19th century, a manufacturing economy had barely begun in the United States. By midcentury, however, U.S. manufacturing surpassed agriculture in value, and by century's end, it was the world's leader. This rapid industrial growth was the result of a unique combination of factors.

Mechanical inventions. Protected by patent laws, inventors looked forward to handsome rewards if their ideas for new tools or machines proved practical. Eli Whitney was only the most famous of hundreds of Americans whose long hours of tinkering in their workshops resulted in improved technology. Besides inventing the cotton gin in 1793, Whitney devised a system for making rifles out of interchangeable parts during the War of 1812. Interchangeable parts then became the basis for mass production methods in the new northern factories.

Corporations for raising capital. In 1811, New York passed a law that made it easier for a business to incorporate and raise capital (money) by selling shares of stock. Other states soon imitated New York's example. Owners of a corporation risked only the amount of money that they invested in a venture. Changes in state corporation laws facilitated the raising of the large sums of capital necessary for building factories, canals, and railroads.

Factory system. When Samuel Slater emigrated from Britain, he took with him the British secrets for building cotton-spinning machines, and he put this knowledge to work by helping establish the first U.S. factory in 1791. Early in the next century, the embargo and the War of 1812 stimulated domestic manufacturing, and the tariffs enacted by Republican congresses allowed the new factories to prosper.

In the 1820s, New England emerged as the country's leading manufacturing center due to the region's abundant waterpower for driving the new machinery and good seaports for shipping goods. Also, the decline of New England's maritime industry made capital available for manufacturing, while the decline of farming in the region yielded a ready labor supply. Other northern states with similar resources and problems—New York, New Jersey, and Pennsylvania—followed New England's lead. As the factory system expanded, it encouraged the growth of financial businesses such as banking and insurance.

Labor. At first, finding workers for the mills and factories was a major problem, because factories had to compete with the lure of cheap land in the West. Textile mills in Lowell, Massachusetts, recruited young farm women and housed them in company dormitories. In the 1830s, the Lowell System was widely imitated. Many factories also made extensive use of child labor. (Children as young as seven left home to work in the new factories.) Only toward the middle of the century did northern manufacturers begin to employ immigrants in large numbers.

Unions. Trade (or craft) unions were organized in major cities as early as the 1790s and increased in number as the factory system took hold. Many skilled workers (shoemakers and weavers, for example) had to seek employment in factories because their earlier practice of working in their own shops (the crafts system) could no longer compete with lower-priced, mass-produced goods. Long hours, low pay, and poor working conditions led to widespread discontent among factory workers. A prime goal of the early unions was to reduce the workday to ten hours. The obstacles to union success, however, were many: (1) immigrant replacement workers, (2) state laws outlawing unions, and (3) frequent economic depressions with high unemployment.

Commercial Agriculture

In the early 1800s, farming became more of a commercial enterprise and less a means of providing subsistence for the family. This change to cash crops was brought about by a blend of factors.

Cheap land and easy credit. Large areas of western land were made available at low prices by the federal government. State banks also made it easy to acquire land by providing farmers with loans at low interest rates.

Markets. Initially, western farmers were limited to sending their products down the Ohio and Mississippi rivers to southern markets. The advent of canals and railroads opened new markets in the growing factory cities in the East.

Cotton and the South

Throughout the 19th century, the principal cash crop in the South was cotton. Eli Whitney's invention of the cotton gin in 1793 transformed the agriculture of an entire region. Now that they could easily separate the cotton fiber from the seeds, southern planters found cotton more profitable than tobacco and indigo, the leading crops of the colonial period. They invested their capital in the purchase of slaves and new land in Alabama and Mississippi and shipped most of their cotton crop overseas for sale to British textile factories.

Effects of the Market Revolution

Specialization on the farm, the growth of cities, industrialization, and the development of modern capitalism meant the end of self-sufficient households and a growing interdependence among people. All combined to bring about a revolution in the marketplace. The farmers fed the workers in the cities, who in turn provided farm families with an array of mass-produced goods. For most Americans, the standard of living increased. At the same time, however, adapting to an impersonal, fast-changing economy presented challenges and problems.

Women. As American society became more urban and industrialized, the nature of work and family life changed for women, many of whom no longer worked next to their husbands on family farms. Women seeking employment in a city were usually limited to two choices: domestic service or teaching. Factory jobs, as in the Lowell System, were not common. The overwhelming majority of working women were single. If they married, they left their jobs and took up duties in the home.

In both urban and rural settings, women were gaining relatively more control over their lives. Marriages arranged by one's parents were less common, and some women elected to have fewer children. Nevertheless, legal and political restrictions on women (not being able to vote, for example) remained.

Economic and social mobility. Real wages improved for most urban workers in the early 1800s, but the gap between the very wealthy and the very poor increased. Social mobility (moving upward in income level and social status) did occur from one generation to the next, and economic opportunities in the United States were greater than in Europe. Extreme examples of poor, hard-working people becoming millionaires, however, were rare.

Slavery. At the outset of the 19th century, there were many people throughout the nation who felt that slavery would gradually disappear. Economically, it was becoming unfeasible due to both the exhausted soil of the coastal lands of Virginia and the Carolinas and the constitutional ban on the importation of slaves after 1808. Hopes for a quiet end to slavery were ended by the rapid growth of the cotton industry. As the arguments over the Missouri Compromise suggested, slavery was an issue that defied clear answers.

HISTORICAL PERSPECTIVES: THE MONROE DOCTRINE

At times, the facts surrounding an event in history are open to question, while in other instances, the facts are accepted but historians reach different conclusions or interpretations concerning the event. The Monroe Doctrine is an example of the latter. There can be no question about the language of the doctrine itself nor about the sequence of events leading up to it. Working from the same sources, however, historians disagree in their interpretation of: (1) who was chiefly responsible for the Monroe Doctrine, (2) what its primary purpose was, and (3) the extent to which it was influenced by British diplomacy.

There are some who argue that the original inspiration for the doctrine came, not from Monroe, but from either the past policies of his fellow Virginians, George Washington and Thomas Jefferson, or the astute thinking of Secretary of State John Quincy Adams. Those crediting Jefferson with the policy of nonintervention in the Western Hemisphere point to his idea of the political world falling into "two spheres," one European and the other American. Those stressing the key role played by John Quincy Adams argue that Adams (1) had consistently opposed further colonization by a European power and (2) had written the original draft of Monroe's message to Congress containing the doctrine. Other historians say that Monroe himself deserves all credit for having made the policy choice and issued the doctrine.

A second area of contention concerns the real purpose behind the doctrine. Was it aimed primarily, as some historians argue, at stopping the territorial ambitions of Spain, France, and Russia? In the early 1820s, France was threatening to reconquer Spanish colonies in South America, and Russia was advancing southward from Alaska toward the California coast. A contrary view argued by revisionist historians is that Monroe and Adams were chiefly concerned about sending a message to Great Britain. Not only was Britain the dominant seapower in 1823, but it was also regarded with suspicion as a traditional foe of American liberty.

A third question revolves around the role of British Foreign Secretary George Canning, whose suggestion for a joint Anglo-U.S. communiqué against the restoration of the Spanish colonies precipitated President Monroe's declaration. Historians disagree about Canning's motivation for suggesting the communiqué. Was he more concerned with protecting British political interests by attempting to block a European alliance? Or was he chiefly concerned with cultivating U.S.-British economic cooperation so as to lower U.S. tariff barriers and promote British trading interests?

These are by no means the only questions concerning the Monroe Doctrine. Historians also take different positions about Latin Americans' perception of U.S. policy and also about the extent to which the doctrine continued to influence U.S. policy in the second half of the 20th century. We see from these examples of historians' disagreements that understanding a historical event involves far more than simply amassing relevant facts; just as important is applying critical thought and analysis.

KEY NAMES, EVENTS, AND TERMS

Era of Good Feelings
sectionalism
James Monroe
nationalism: cultural, economic
Tariff of 1816
protective tariff
Henry Clay; American System
Second Bank of the United States
Panic of 1819
John Marshall
Fletcher v. Peck
McCulloch v. Maryland

Dartmouth College v. Woodward
Gibbons v. Ogden
implied powers
Tallmadge Amendment
Missouri Compromise (1820)
Stephen Decatur
Rush-Bagot Agreement (1817)
Treaty of 1818
Andrew Jackson
Florida Purchase Treaty (1819)
Monroe Doctrine (1823)
Lancaster Turnpike

National (Cumberland) Road
Erie Canal
Robert Fulton; steamboats
railroads
Eli Whitney; interchangeable parts
corporations
Samuel Slater
factory system
Lowell System; textile mills
industrialization
specialization
unions
cotton gin
market revolution

MULTIPLE-CHOICE QUESTIONS

1. Which of the following statements accurately describes the Monroe Doctrine?

   (A) It caused an immediate change in the U.S. role in world affairs.

   (B) It asserted the U.S. right to send troops into the countries of Latin America to provide political stability.

   (C) It declared U.S. opposition to European intervention in the affairs of independent countries of the Western Hemisphere.

   (D) It was fully supported by the British government.

   (E) It established the U.S. claim to being a world power.

2. The map shows the United States directly after the

   (A) Louisiana Purchase

   (B) War of 1812

   (C) Rush-Bagot Treaty

   (D) Florida Purchase

   (E) Missouri Compromise

3. Which of the following increased southern planters' reliance on slaves?

   (A) Missouri Compromise

   (B) invention of the steamboat

   (C) invention of the cotton gin

   (D) Lowell System

   (E) Louisiana Purchase

4. The Erie Canal was significant because it

   (A) challenged railroads as the primary transportation system of the early 1800s

   (B) tied the manufacturing of the East to the farming of the West

(C) was the first federally funded internal improvement

(D) stimulated subsistence farming and manufacturing in the West

(E) increased trade with Great Britain

5. A major effect of John Marshall's Supreme Court decisions was to

(A) expand federal power and limit the states' power

(B) expand the states' power and limit federal power

(C) declare federal laws to be unconstitutional

(D) protect and enlarge the jurisdiction of state courts

(E) legitimize a strict interpretation of the U.S. Constitution

6. Henry Clay's idea of an American System included all of the following EXCEPT

(A) protective tariffs

(B) internal improvements

(C) state banks

(D) increased trade between all sections of the country

(E) federal funds for a national transportation system

7. Which of the following is a correct statement about the United States at the beginning of the Era of Good Feelings?

(A) Sectionalism had become the dominant force in the nation.

(B) There were no more divisions within the ranks of the Republican party.

(C) Federalists and Republicans united on an economic program of internal improvements and protective tariffs.

(D) Friendliness and cooperation with Britain replaced earlier policies of hostility.

(E) Nationalism strongly influenced American culture and politics.

8. Which pair of issues aroused the most controversy in 1819 and 1820?

(A) internal improvements and Latin American independence

(B) slavery in Missouri and Latin American independence

(C) slavery in Missouri and a financial crisis

(D) Monroe's prospects for reelection and a financial crisis

(E) Monroe's prospects for reelection and the protective tariff

9. Which of the following best describes changes in the American economy in the 1820s?

(A) improved transportation in the West, depressed conditions in the South

(B) industrialization in the Northeast, diversified farming in the South

(C) improved transportation in the West, industrialization in the North

(D) cotton farming in the South, depressed conditions in the North

(E) railroads in all sections providing the primary stimulus for economic growth

10. In the first decades of the 19th century, the Industrial Revolution in the United States was supported by developments in all

of the following areas EXCEPT

(A) the factory system

(B) transportation

(C) corporations

(D) mechanical inventions

(E) crafts unions

ESSAY QUESTIONS

1. Discuss how the administration of James Monroe, in the years immediately following the War of 1812, pursued a nationalistic foreign policy while maintaining peace.

2. Analyze the ways TWO of the following helped bring about a shift from an agricultural to an industrial economy in the United States in the early 1800s:

   commercial farming

   factory system

   labor

   transportation

3. How do you account for a sectional dispute over slavery being touched off in 1819 by the settlement of western territories? Explain, using Thomas Jefferson's comment on the Missouri crisis: "[T]his momentous question, like a firebell in the night, awakened and filled me with terror. I considered it at once as the knell of the nation."

4. What factors contributed to the formulation of the Monroe Doctrine?

5. To what extent did industrialization from 1800 onward have an impact on women, labor unions, and sectional differences?

Guide to Writing the DBQ

Organizing the Historical Evidence

Think of the question posed by the DBQ as if it were an intellectual crossroads—or a fork in the road—presenting you with a choice of turning either left toward one conclusion or right toward a different conclusion. The DBQ on page 163 is a good example. In effect, the question is asking you to decide whether (a) nationalism or (b) sectionalism was more important in the Era of Good Feelings.

Suppose that your choice is nationalism. Then your essay would emphasize such facts and ideas as these:

Increased expression of patriotism in popular culture as well as politics after the War of 1812

Internal improvements (canal-building, the National Road) linking western territories and markets to eastern cities

Political unity as represented by dominance of a single party and nearly unanimous election of Monroe in 1820

Henry Clay's American System

Population growth in all sections, especially in the most nationalistic of the three sections, the West

But suppose that you chose the other option and wished to demonstrate that sectionalism was a more powerful force than nationalism. You would then emphasize the following:

Crisis over the admission of Missouri as a slave state in 1819–1820

Westerners' interest in national funding of internal improvements blocked by proponents of states' rights

Controversy over Second Bank of the United States, intensified by Panic of 1819

Whitney's cotton gin made the South more dependent on slavery, while the North became increasingly industrialized

Factions in the Republican party divided over sectional issues, resulting in the breakup of that party in election of 1824

Whichever direction you take, it is important to list the historical evidence you intend to be using *before* reading the given documents. Since organizing your ideas is such a critical first step, the proctor of the

AP exam will instruct you to spend 15 minutes sketching, or blocking out, your approach before writing a single word of the essay itself. You should first outline your essay by doing the following: (a) review the documents and reflect on your own knowledge of the period, (b) decide what position to argue, and (c) list historical evidence. Select the documents that, together with your own knowledge, will be most useful in developing your argument. Remember that it is not absolutely necessary to use all of the documents.

Listing facts and ideas is one thing; arranging them into logical groupings is another. Going into the exam, it helps if you have a workable structure, or blueprint, for shaping your DBQ essay, so that you know in advance how to give it coherent form. The model five-paragraph outline below provides you with such a blueprint. Study it closely. Notice the function of each paragraph:

First paragraph: Introduces your thesis, touching in a general way on a few main points that connect directly with the question.

Second paragraph: Focuses on a historical event or trend that supports your thesis and also cites one or more of the documents relating to that event or trend.

Third paragraph: Discusses another historical event or trend and, if possible, refers to one or more of the documents.

Fourth paragraph: Discusses another topic, while blending in reference to a document.

Fifth and concluding paragraph: Ties everything together by summarizing the evidence presented in the body of the essay and restating the thesis—a position that you have now "proven" to be well grounded in the facts of history.

Practice

The five-paragraph blueprint below argues for sectionalism as a more important force than nationalism. Create a blueprint for a DBQ essay that takes the opposite position, arguing that nationalism was more important to the period than sectionalism. After completing this task, evaluate the blueprint. Does it help you deal successfully with the complexities of answering a DBQ? Would you use it on the exam?

Organizational Blueprint and Model

An Era of Sectional Bad Feelings, 1815–1830

1. Thesis paragraph

Despite its reputation as an Era of Good Feelings and widespread nationalism, the period following the War of 1812 was in fact marked by intense sectional rivalry. Sectionalism, not nationalism, was the basis for the bitter dispute over Missouri's admission to the Union in 1820 and economic and states' rights issues.

2. Historical evidence: Topic A

Missouri Compromise. Explain the historical background and sectional causes of this controversy in some detail. Cite Jefferson's letter and famous comment about a "firebell in the night" (Document G) and the note in John Quincy Adams' diary (Document F). Argue that drawing a line between slave and free states would prove only a temporary solution to the deepening sectional rift between North and South.

3. Historical evidence: Topic B

Growing economic differences between North and South. Explain the impact of Eli Whitney's cotton gin in enlarging the South's dependence on slavery. Contrast single-crop agrarianism in the South with industrial development in the North. Point to the fact that while all other sections voted for the protective Tariff of 1816, a majority of southerners voted against it (Document H).

4. Historical evidence: Topic C

Factional disputes in the so-called Era of Good Feelings. Argue that sectional divisions were only masked, not eliminated, by the appearance of party unity during Monroe's presidency. In fact, opposition by eastern Republicans prevented passage of national support for internal improvements—a key component of Henry Clay's American System. Mention that, while John C. Calhoun supported internal improvements in 1817 (Document D), he would soon become a leading champion of states' rights. Clinch argument with your strongest point—that tensions between southern and northern factions of the Republican party shattered even the appearance of national harmony in the bitterly contested election of 1824.

5. Concluding paragraph

Restate evidence that you have used to prove your thesis. Example: Although Monroe's presidency has been termed an Era of Good Feelings, sectionalist conflicts were more important than nationalism in explaining such events as the controversy over Missouri and the breakup of the Republican party in the election of 1824. The spread of slavery in the South and industrialism in the North increased the economic basis for sectional troubles in future decades.

DOCUMENT-BASED QUESTION

Write an essay that integrates your understanding of the documents that follow and your knowledge of the period.

Both nationalism and sectionalism increased during the Era of Good Feelings.

How did both of these beliefs develop concurrently, and did one become of greater importance in the economics and politics of the period?

DOCUMENT A.

Our Country! In her intercourse with foreign nations may she always be in the right; but our country, right or wrong!

Stephen Decatur,
Toast given at Norfolk, Virginia, April, 1816

DOCUMENT B.

Flag of the free heart's hope and home,
    By angel hands to valor given;
Thy stars have lit the welkin dome
    And all the hues were born in heaven!
Forever float that standard sheet!
    Where breathes the foe but falls before us?
With freedom's soil beneath our feet,
    And freedom's banner streaming o'er us?

Joseph Rodman Drake,
"The American Flag," early 19th-century poem

DOCUMENT C.

But where is that wise and heroic country which has considered that our rights [as women] are sacred, though we cannot defend them? History shows not that country. Yet though history lifts not her finger to such a one, anticipation does. She points to a nation which, having thrown off the shackles of authority and precedent, shrinks not from schemes of improvement because other nations have never attempted them; but which, in its pride of independence, would rather lead than follow in the march of human improvement: a nation, wise and magnanimous to plan, enterprising to undertake, and rich in resources to execute. Does not every American exult that this country is his own?

Emma Hart Willard,
Address to the New York State Legislature, 1819

DOCUMENT D.

Let it not be said that internal improvements may be wholly left to the enterprise of the states and of individuals. In a country so new and so extensive as ours, there is room enough for all the general and state governments and individuals in which to exert their resources. But many of the improvements contemplated are on too great a scale for the resources of the states or individuals; and many of such a nature that the rival jealousy of the states, if left alone, might prevent. They require the resources and the general superintendence of this government to effect and complete them.

John C. Calhoun,
Speech to the U.S. House of Representatives,
February 4, 1817

DOCUMENT E.

Are we doomed to behold our industry languish and decay yet more and more? But there is a remedy, and that remedy consists in modifying our foreign policy, and in adopting a genuine *American system*. We must naturalize the arts in our country; and we must naturalize them by the only means which the wisdom of nations has yet discovered to be effectual—by adequate protection against the otherwise overwhelming influence of foreigners. This is only to be accomplished by the establishment of a tariff, to the consideration of which I am now brought. . . . The sole object of the tariff is to tax the produce of foreign industry with the view of promoting American industry. The tax is exclusively leveled at foreign industry.

Henry Clay,
Speech in Congress, March 31, 1824

DOCUMENT F.

I have favored this Missouri Compromise, believing it to be all that could be effected under the present Constitution, and from extreme unwillingness to put the Union at hazard. But perhaps it would have been wiser as well as a bolder course to have persisted in the restriction upon Missouri, till it should have terminated in a convention of states to revise and amend the Constitution. This would have produced a new Union of thirteen or fourteen States, unpolluted with slavery, with a great and glorious object to effect; namely that of rallying to their standard the other states by the universal emancipation of their slaves. If the Union must be dissolved, slavery is precisely the question upon which it ought to break. For the present, however, this contest is laid asleep.

John Quincy Adams,
Diary, March 3, 1820

DOCUMENT G.

I thank you, dear sir, for the copy you have been so kind to send me of the letter to your constituents on the Missouri question. It is perfect justification to them. I had for a long time ceased to read newspapers, or pay any attention to public affairs, confident they were in good hands. . . . But this momentous question, like a firebell in the night, awakened and filled me with terror. I considered it at once as the knell of the union. It is hushed, indeed, for the moment. But this is a reprieve only, not a final sentence. A geographical line, coinciding with a marked principle, moral and political, once conceived and held up to the angry passions of men, will never be obliterated; and every new irritation will mark it deeper and deeper.

Thomas Jefferson,
Letter to Congressman John Holmes of Massachusetts,
April 22, 1820

DOCUMENT H.

Vote in the U.S. House of Representatives on the Tariff of 1816		
	For	**Against**
South	23	34
Middle States	44	10
West (Ohio)	4	0
New England	17	10
Total	88	54

Congressional Record,
April 27, 1816

SECTIONALISM

The East, the West, the North, and the stormy South all combine to throw the whole ocean into commotion, to toss its billows to the skies, and to disclose its profoundest depths.

Daniel Webster, March 7, 1850

In 1826, Americans took great pride in celebrating 50 years of independence. A unique political system based on a written Constitution had proven practical and flexible enough to permit territorial growth and industrial change. It should be remembered, however, that the United States was both a nation with a central government and a collection of semiautonomous, self-governing states. Recall, too, that the original 13 states had resisted giving up any of their powers to a national government and that two political parties, the Federalists in New England and the Democratic-Republicans in the South, had expressed strong sectional differences. In short, although the American nation was young and vibrant in the 1820s, it was still a fragile union, with sectionalism an ever-present and growing concern.

The previous chapter treated the nation as a whole in the early 1800s; this chapter looks at the differences among the three sections—North, South, and West. Daniel Webster, in the opening quote of this chapter, rhetorically refers to these three sections in terms of the four main points of the compass as he attempts to portray the dangers these divisions hold for the nation. By examining sectional differences, we can better understand the *sectionalism* (loyalty to a particular region) that ultimately led to the Union's worst crisis: civil war between the North and the South in the early 1860s.

The North

The northern section of the country in the early 19th century contained two parts: (1) the Northeast, which included both New England and the Middle Atlantic states, and (2) the Old Northwest, which stretched from Ohio to Minnesota. The northern states were bound together by improved transportation and a high rate of economic growth based on both commercial farming and industrial innovation. While manufacturing was rapidly expanding, the vast majority of northerners were still involved in agriculture. The North was the most populous section in the country as a result of both a high birthrate and increased immigration.

The Industrial Northeast

Originally, the Industrial Revolution centered in the textile industry, but by the 1830s, northern factories were producing a wide range of goods—everything from farm implements to clocks and shoes.

U.S. Manufacturing by Region, 1860			
	Number of Establishments	Number of Employees	Value of Product
North Atlantic states	69,831	900,107	$1,213,897,518
Old Northwest states	33,335	188,651	346,675,290
Southern states	27,779	166,803	248,090,580
Western states	8,777	50,204	71,229,989

Census of the U.S., *Manufactures of the United States in 1860*

Organized Labor. Industrial development meant that large numbers of people who had once earned their living as independent farmers and artisans became dependent on wages paid by factory owners. With the common problems of low pay, long hours, and unsafe working conditions, urban workers in different cities organized both unions and local political parties to protect their interests. The first U.S. labor party, founded in Philadelphia in 1828, succeeded in electing a few members of the city council. For a brief period in the 1830s, an increasing number of urban workers joined unions and participated in strikes.

Organized labor achieved one notable victory in 1842 when the Massachusetts Supreme Court ruled in *Commonwealth v. Hunt* that "peaceful unions" had the right to negotiate labor contracts with employers. During the 1840s and 1850s, most state legislatures in the North passed laws establishing a ten-hour day for industrial workers. Improvement for workers, however, continued to be limited by (1) periodic depressions, (2) employers and courts that were hostile to unions, and (3) an abundant supply of cheap immigrant labor.

Urban life. The North's urban population grew from approximately 5 percent of the population in 1800 to 15 percent by 1850. As a result of such rapid growth in cities from Boston to Baltimore, slums also expanded so that crowded housing, poor sanitation, infectious diseases, and high rates of crime soon became characteristic of large working-class neighborhoods. Nevertheless, the new opportunities offered by the Industrial Revolution continued to attract both native-born Americans from the farms and immigrants from Europe.

African Americans. The 250,000 African Americans who lived in the North in 1860 constituted only a small minority (1 percent) of northerners, but as free citizens, they represented 50 percent of all free African Americans. Freedom may have meant they could maintain a family and in some instances own land, but it did not mean economic or political equality, since strong racial prejudices kept them from voting and holding jobs in most skilled professions and crafts. In the mid-1800s, immigrants displaced them from occupations and jobs that they had held since the time of the Revolution. Denied membership in unions, African Americans were often hired as strikebreakers—and often dismissed after the strike ended.

The Agricultural Northwest

The Old Northwest consisted of six states west of the Alleghenies that were admitted to the Union before 1860: Ohio (1803), Indiana (1816), Illinois (1818), Michigan (1837), Wisconsin (1848), and Minnesota (1858). These states came from territories formed by land ceded to the national government in the 1780s by several of the original 13 states. The procedure for turning territories of the Old Northwest into states was set forth in the Northwest Ordinance, passed by Congress in 1787.

In the early years of the 19th century, much of the Old Northwest was unsettled frontier, and the part of it that was settled relied upon the Mississippi to transport grain to southern markets via New Orleans. By midcentury, however, this region became closely tied to the other northern states by two factors: (1) military campaigns by federal troops that drove Native Americans from the land and (2) the building of canals and railroads that established common markets between the Great Lakes and the East Coast.

Agriculture. In the states of the Old Northwest, large grain crops of corn and wheat were very profitable. Using the newly invented steel plow (by John Deere) and mechanical reaper (by Cyrus McCormick), a farm family was more efficient and could plant many more acres, needing only to supplement its labor with a few hired workers at harvesttime. The grain could spoil quickly and, immediately after the harvest, had to be shipped to urban centers for sale. Part of the crop was used to feed cattle and hogs and to supply distillers and brewers with grain for making whiskey and beer.

New cities. At key transportation points, what had once been small villages and towns grew into thriving cities after 1820: Buffalo, Cleveland, Detroit, and Chicago on the Great Lakes, Cincinnati and St. Louis on major rivers. The new cities served as transfer points, processing farm products for shipment to the East, and also distributing manufactured goods from the East to different parts of the region.

Immigration

In 1820, some 8,000 immigrants arrived from Europe, but beginning in 1832, there was a sudden increase. After that year, the number of new arrivals never fell below 50,000 a year and in one year, 1854, climbed as high as 428,000. From the 1830s through the 1850s, nearly 4 million people from northern Europe crossed the Atlantic to seek a new life in the United States. Arriving by ship in the northern seacoast cities of Boston, New York, and Philadelphia, many immigrants remained where they landed, while others traveled to farms and cities of the Old Northwest. Few journeyed to the South, where the plantation economy and slavery limited the opportunities for free labor.

The surge in immigration from 1830–1860 was chiefly the result of: (1) the development of inexpensive and relatively rapid ocean transportation, (2) famines and revolutions in Europe that drove people from their homelands, and (3) the growing reputation of the United States as a country offering economic opportunities and political freedom. The immigrants strengthened the U.S. economy by providing both a steady stream of cheap labor and an increased demand for mass-produced consumer goods.

Irish. During this period, half of all the immigrants—almost 2 million— came from Ireland. These Irish immigrants were mostly tenant farmers driven from their homeland by potato crop failures and a devastating famine in the 1840s, and they now had limited interest in farming, few other skills, and little money. They faced strong discrimination because of their Roman Catholic religion. The Irish worked hard at whatever employment they could find, usually competing with African Americans for domestic work and unskilled laborer jobs. Faced with limited opportunities, they congregated for mutual support in the northern cities (Boston, Philadelphia, and New York) where they had first landed. Many Irish entered local politics. They organized their fellow immigrants and joined the Democratic party, which had long traditions of anti-British feelings and support for the common people and workers. Their progress was difficult but steady. For example, the Irish were initially excluded from joining New York City's Democratic organization, Tammany Hall. But by the 1850s they had secured jobs and influence, and by the 1880s they controlled this party organization.

Germans. Both economic hardships and the failure of democratic revolutions in 1848 caused over 1 million Germans to seek refuge in the United States in the late 1840s and the 1850s. Most German immigrants had at least modest means as well as considerable skills as farmers and artisans. Moving westward in search of cheap, fertile farmland, they established homesteads throughout the Old Northwest and generally prospered. At first their political influence was limited, but as they became more active in public life, they were both strong supporters of public education and staunch opponents of slavery.

Nativists. A large number of native-born Americans were alarmed by the influx of immigrants, fearing that the newcomers would take their jobs and also subvert (weaken) the culture of the Anglo majority. The *nativists* (those reacting most strongly against the foreigners) were Protestants who distrusted the Roman Catholicism practiced by the Irish and many of the Germans. In the 1840s, opposition to immigrants led to sporadic rioting in the big cities and the organization of a secret antiforeign society, the Supreme Order of the Star-Spangled Banner. This society turned to politics in the early 1850s, nominating candidates for office as the American party, or Know-Nothing party (see Chapter 13).

The antiforeign movement faded in importance as North and South divided over slavery in the years immediately before the Civil War. Nativism would periodically return, however, whenever a sudden increase in immigration seemed to threaten the native-born majority.

The South

Defined in economic, political, and social terms, the South as a distinct region included those states that permitted slavery, including certain border states (Delaware, Maryland, Kentucky, and Missouri) that did not join the Confederacy in 1961.

Agriculture and King Cotton

Agriculture was the foundation of the South's economy, even though by the 1850s small factories in the region were producing approximately 15 percent of the nation's manufactured goods. Tobacco, rice, and sugarcane were important cash crops, but these were far exceeded by the South's chief economic activity: the production and sale of cotton.

The development of mechanized textile mills in England, coupled with Eli Whitney's cotton gin, made cotton cloth affordable, not just in Europe and the United States, but throughout the world. Before 1860, the world depended chiefly on Britain's mills for its supply of cloth, and Britain in turn depended chiefly on the American South for its supply of cotton fiber. Originally, the cotton was grown almost entirely in two states, South Carolina and Georgia, but as demand and profits increased, planters moved westward into Alabama, Mississippi, Louisiana, and Texas. New land was constantly needed, for the high cotton yields required for profits quickly depleted the soil. By the 1850s, cotton provided two-thirds of all U.S. exports and tied the South's economy to its best customer, Britain. "Cotton is king," said one southerner of his region's greatest asset.

AGRICULTURE, MINING, AND MANUFACTURING BEFORE THE CIVIL WAR

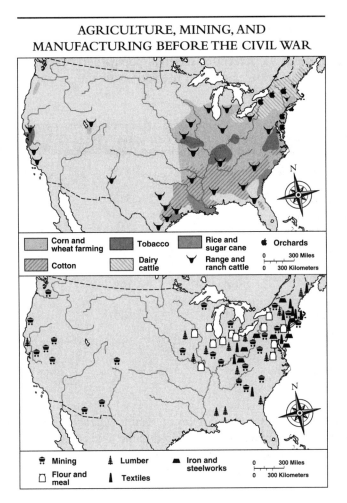

Slavery, the "Peculiar Institution"

Wealth in the South was measured in terms of land and slaves. The latter were treated as a form of property, subject to being bought and sold. Southern whites were sensitive to the fact that slaves were human beings, however. Their uneasiness with this fact and the need continually to defend slavery caused them to refer to it as "that peculiar institution." In colonial times, it had been justified as an economic necessity, but in the 19th century, apologists for slavery used historical and religious arguments to support their claim that it was good for both slave and master.

Population. The cotton boom was largely responsible for a fourfold increase in the number of slaves, from 1 million in 1800 to nearly 4 million in 1860. Most of the increase came from natural reproduction, although thousands of Africans were also smuggled into the South in defiance of Congress' prohibition in 1808 against importing slaves. In many parts of the Deep South, slaves made up as much as 75 percent of the total population. Fearing slave revolts, southern legislatures added increased restrictions on movement and education to their slave codes.

United States Labor Force, 1800–1860 (in thousands)			
Year	Free	Slave	Total
1800	1,330	530	1,860
1810	1,590	740	2,330
1820	2,185	950	3,135
1830	3,020	1,180	4,200
1840	4,180	1,480	5,660
1850	6,280	1,970	8,250
1860	8,770	2,340	11,110

Economics. Slaves were employed doing whatever their owners demanded of them. The great majority labored in the fields, but many also became expert in a variety of skilled crafts, while others worked as house servants, in factories, and on construction gangs. Because of the greater profits to be made on the new cotton plantations in the West, many slaves were sold from the Upper South to the cotton-rich Deep South of the lower Mississippi Valley. By 1860, the value of a field slave had risen to almost $2,000. One result of the heavy capital investment in slaves was that the South had much less capital than the North to undertake industrialization.

Slave life. Conditions of slavery varied from one plantation to the next. Some slaves were humanely treated, while others were routinely beaten. All suffered alike from being deprived of their freedom. Families could be separated at any time by an owner's decision to sell a wife, a husband, or a child. Women were vulnerable to sexual exploitation. Despite the hard, nearly hopeless circumstances of their lives, African Americans managed to maintain a strong sense of family and of religious faith.

Resistance. Slaves contested their status through a range of actions, including work slowdowns, sabotage, escape, and revolt. There were a few major slave uprisings. One was led by Denmark Vesey in 1822 and another by Nat

Turner in 1831. The revolts were quickly and violently suppressed, but even so, they had a lasting impact. They gave hope to enslaved African Americans, drove southern states to tighten already strict slave codes, and demonstrated to many, especially in the North, the evils of slavery.

Free African Americans

By 1860, as many as 250,000 African Americans in the South were not slaves. They were free citizens (even though, as in the North, racial prejudice restricted their liberties). A number of slaves had been emancipated during the American Revolution. Some were mulatto children whose white fathers had decided to liberate them. Others achieved freedom on their own, when permitted, through self-purchase—if they were fortunate enough to have been paid wages for extra work, usually as skilled craftspeople.

Most of the free southern blacks lived in cities where they could own property. By state law, they were not equal with whites, were not permitted to vote, and were barred from entering certain occupations. Constantly in danger of being kidnapped by slave traders, they had to show legal papers proving their free status. They remained in the South for various reasons. Some wanted to be near family members who were still in bondage; others believed the South to be home and the North to offer no greater opportunities.

White Society

Southern whites observed a rigid hierarchy among themselves, with aristocratic planters at the top and poor whites and mountain people at the bottom of the social pyramid.

Aristocracy. To be a member of the South's small elite of wealthy planters, a person usually had to own at least 100 slaves and farm at least 1,000 acres. The planter aristocracy maintained its power politically by dominating the state legislatures of the South and enacting laws that favored the large landholders' economic interests.

Farmers. The vast majority of slaveholders had fewer than 20 slaves working several hundred acres. Southern white farmers produced the bulk of the cotton crop, worked in the fields with their slaves, and lived as modestly as farmers of the North.

Poor whites. Three-fourths of the South's white population owned no slaves. They could not afford the rich river-bottom farmland controlled by the planters, and many lived in the hills as subsistence farmers. These "hillbillies" or "poor white trash," as they were derisively called by the planters, defended the slave system, thinking that some day they too could own slaves and that at least they were superior on the social scale to someone (slaves).

Mountain people. A number of small farmers lived in frontier conditions in isolation from the rest of the South, along the slopes and valleys of the Appalachian and Ozark mountains. The mountain people disliked the planters and their slaves. During the Civil War, many (including a future president, Andrew Johnson of Tennessee) would remain loyal to the Union.

Cities. Because the South was primarily an agricultural region, there was only a limited need for major cities. Only New Orleans among the southern cities could be counted among the nation's 15 largest in 1860 (it was fifth, after New York, Philadelphia, Baltimore, and Boston). Cities such as Atlanta, Charleston, Chattanooga, and Richmond were important southern trading centers, but had relatively small populations in comparison to those of the North.

Southern Thought

The South developed a culture and outlook on life that was uniquely its own. As cotton became the basis of its economy, slavery became the focus of its political thought. White southerners felt increasingly isolated and defensive about slavery, as northerners grew hostile toward it, and as England, France, and other European nations outlawed it altogether.

Code of chivalry. Dominated by the aristocratic planter class, the agricultural South was largely a feudal society. The southern gentleman ascribed to a code of chivalrous conduct, which included a strong sense of personal honor, the defense of womanhood, and paternalistic treatment of all who were deemed inferior, especially slaves.

Education. The upper class valued a college education for their children, more so than in the North. Acceptable professions for a southern gentleman were limited to farming, law, the ministry, and the military. For the lower classes, schooling beyond the early elementary grades was generally not available. To reduce the risk of slave revolts, slaves were strictly prohibited by law from receiving any instruction in reading and writing.

Religion. The slavery question affected church membership. Partly because they preached biblical support for slavery, both Methodist and Baptist churches gained in membership in the South while splitting in the 1840s with their northern brethren. The Unitarians, who challenged slavery, faced declining membership and hostility. Catholics and Episcopalians took a neutral stand on slavery, and their numbers declined in the South.

The West

From one era to another, as the United States expanded westward, the definition of the "West" kept changing. In the 1600s, the West referred to all the lands not along the Atlantic Coast. In the 1700s, the West meant lands on the other side of the Appalachian Mountains. By the mid-1800s, the West lay beyond the Mississippi River and reached as far as California and the Oregon Territory on the Pacific Coast.

Native Americans

The original settlers of the West—and, in fact, of the entire North American continent—were of course various groups of Native Americans. From the time of Columbus, Native Americans did not move west voluntarily as pioneers. They were cajoled, pushed, or driven westward as white settlers encroached on their original homelands.

Exodus. By 1850, the vast majority of Native Americans were living west of the Mississippi River. Those to the east had either been killed off, emigrated reluctantly, or been forced to leave their land by treaty or military action. The Great Plains, however, would provide only a temporary respite from conflict with white settlers.

Life on the plains. Horses, brought to America by the Spanish in the 1500s, proved to be a revolutionary benefit for many Native Americans. On the Great Plains, some Native Americans still lived in villages and grew crops as farmers, but the horse allowed many other tribal groups, such as the Cheyenne and the Sioux, to become nomadic hunters following the buffalo. Those living a nomadic way of life could more easily move away from advancing settlers or oppose their encroachments by force.

The Frontier

Although the location of the western frontier constantly shifted, the *concept* of the frontier remained the same from generation to generation. The same forces that had brought the original colonists to the New World motivated their descendants and new immigrants to move westward. In the public imagination, the West represented the possibility of a fresh start and new opportunities for those willing to venture there. If not in fact, at least in theory and myth, the West beckoned as a place promising greater freedom for all ethnic groups: Native Americans, African Americans, European Americans, and eventually Asian Americans as well.

Mountain men. From the point of view of native-born white Americans, the Rocky Mountains in the 1820s were a far-distant frontier—a total wilderness except for the villages of Native Americans. The earliest whites in the area had followed Lewis and Clark and explored Native American trails as they trapped for furs. These mountain men, as they were called, would serve as the guides and pathfinders for settlers crossing the mountains into California and Oregon in the 1840s. (See Chapter 12, page 228.)

White Settlers on the Western Frontier

Whether the frontier lay in Minnesota or Oregon or California in the 1840s and 1850s, daily life for white settlers was similar to that of the early colonists. They worked hard from sunrise to sunset and lived in log cabins or other improvised shelters. More of them died at an early age from disease and malnutrition than from Indian raids.

Women. Often living many miles from the nearest neighbor, pioneer women performed a myriad of daily tasks, including those of doctor, teacher, seamstress, and cook—as well as chief assistant in the fields to their farmer-husbands. The isolation, endless work, and rigors of childbirth meant a limited lifespan for women on the frontier.

Environmental damage. European Americans had little understanding of the fragile nature of land and wildlife. As settlers moved into an area, they would clear entire forests and after only two generations exhaust the soil with poor farming methods. At the same time, trappers and hunters decimated the beaver and the buffalo to the brink of extinction.

HISTORICAL PERSPECTIVES: THE NATURE OF SLAVERY

Slavery was of fundamental importance in defining both the character of the South and its differences with the North. Beyond its historical importance in the 19th century, we need to understand the nature of slavery in order to assess its impact on U.S. society in general and African Americans in particular in our own times. Historians have viewed slavery from different perspectives. It is each student's task to decide which of several interpretations seems the most convincing and enlightening.

Until about 1950, the prevailing scholarship on slavery followed Ulrich Phillips' *American Negro Slavery* (1918). Phillips portrayed slavery as an economically failing institution in which the paternalistic owners were civilizing the inferior but contented African Americans. The civil rights movement of the 1950s and 1960s stimulated new studies and interpretations. Chief among them was Kenneth Stampp's *The Peculiar Institution: Slavery in the Ante-Bellum South* (1956), which challenged Phillips' thesis by showing slaves and owners to be in continual conflict. Today the older view of slavery as a paternalistic and even benign institution has been largely discredited.

There is still much debate, however, about how destructive slavery was. At one extreme is the view that the oppressive and racist nature of slavery destroyed the culture and self-respect of the slaves and their descendants. A contrary view holds that slaves managed to adapt and to overcome their hardships by developing a unique African American culture. Historians arguing for this position point to African American churches and two-parent families as part of an enduring heritage from the era of slavery.

Economics has also provided a focus for viewing the nature of slavery. Historians have debated the question of whether or not slave labor was profitable to southern planters, as compared to using free labor. Contrary to earlier interpretations, computer-assisted studies have demonstrated that, for the most part, slavery was profitable. A more complex analysis of the economics, social, and cultural nature of slavery is found in Eugene Genovese's *Roll, Jordan, Roll: The World the Slaves Made.* In this work, southern society is shown centered on a paternalism that gave rise to a unique social system with a clear hierarchy, in which people were classified according to their ability or their economic and social standing. For whites this paternalism meant control, while for slaves it provided the opportunity to develop and maintain their own culture, including family life, tradition, and religion.

Recently, some historians have argued that slavery differed from place to place and that more study should be made of regional variations. For example, slaves in the tobacco-growing Upper South lived under circumstances that were quite different from slaves in the cotton fields of the Deep South.

As we can see, historians have developed numerous interpretations of the nature of slavery in the United States, providing us with a rich *historiography*—the writing of history based on a critical examination of sources. If the purpose of history is to help us better understand the present, then, as Kenneth Stampp says in *The Peculiar Institution,* "there is a strange paradox in the historian's involvement with both present and past, for his knowledge of the present is clearly a key to his understanding of the past."

The many varied interpretations of slavery and of history can be explained pragmatically as the natural result of the changing times in which they were written. While some historical interpretations may have greater merit than others, most provide us with an improved perspective with which to develop our own views.

KEY NAMES, EVENTS, AND TERMS

sectionalism	Old Northwest	planters; poor whites;
Daniel Webster	immigration	mountain men
Industrial Revolution	Nativists	the West
unions	American party	the frontier
urbanization; urban life	King Cotton	Native American removal
Cyrpus McCormick; John Deere	Eli Whitney	Great Plains
	"peculiar institution"	white settlers
new cities	Denmark Vesey; Nat Turner	environmental damage
Irish; potato famine	slave codes	
Germans	free African Americans	

MULTIPLE-CHOICE QUESTIONS

1. In the 1830s and 1840s, all of the following were generally true about immigration EXCEPT

(A) Most immigrants came from the British Isles and northern Europe.

(B) Improvements in ship technology made the ocean voyage relatively cheap and fast.

(C) The South attracted the least number of immigrants.

(D) An overwhelming majority of native-born Americans welcomed the immigrants as a cheap source of labor.

(E) Poorer immigrants lived in the cities while those with some money farmed in the West.

2. During the 1840s, large numbers of Irish immigrated to the United States mainly because of

(A) British persecutions in Ireland

(B) U.S. policies offering free land

(C) support from the Irish-American Aid Society

(D) the development of textile mills in New England

(E) famine resulting from the failure of the potato crop

3. Nativist reaction to immigration resulted in

(A) the formation of the Know-Nothing party

(B) the splitting of the Democratic-Republican party

(C) major changes in the immigration laws

(D) increased immigration from southern Europe

(E) greater sectional differences between North and South

4. All of the following restricted the growth of labor unions before the Civil War EXCEPT

(A) increased numbers of immigrant workers

(B) economic depressions

(C) opposition by factory employers

(D) opposition by southern plantation owners

(E) judicial decisions

5. Twenty years after the ratification of the U.S. Constitution, Congress prohibited
   (A) slavery in all U.S. territories
   (B) slave ownership by federal employees
   (C) immigration
   (D) importation of slaves into the United States
   (E) efforts to change naturalization laws

6. Which of the following activities was most commonly practiced by African Americans as a means of resisting slavery in the early 1800s?
   (A) sitdown strike
   (B) legal action
   (C) political action
   (D) armed revolt
   (E) work slowdown

7. Before the Civil War, which of the following groups of southern whites did NOT defend slavery?
   (A) Methodist congregations
   (B) farmers
   (C) poor whites
   (D) large landowners
   (E) mountain people

8. Before 1860, the change that most influenced the lives of Native Americans on the Great Plains was
   (A) the introduction of the horse
   (B) the building of a transcontinental railroad
   (C) sectional tensions between North and South
   (D) immigration
   (E) the establishment of reservations

9. Which of the following regions is INCORRECTLY paired with an economic or social characteristic?
   (A) Old Northwest—agriculture
   (B) New England—factory system
   (C) western frontier in 1850— tobacco farming
   (D) Deep South—cotton farming
   (E) border states—slavery

10. Which of the following is a CORRECT statement about the United States in 1850?
   (A) The vast majority of Native Americans lived west of the Mississippi River.
   (B) A majority of Americans lived in cities.
   (C) All free African Americans lived in the North.
   (D) Most industrial workers were protected by laws providing for an eight-hour day.
   (E) The Mississippi River defined the western frontier.

ESSAY QUESTIONS

1. Assess the discrimination against people different from the white Protestant majority in the United States during the early 19th century in the context of TWO of the following:

free African Americans

Native Americans

Irish immigrants

German immigrants

2. Compare and contrast the experiences of two immigrant groups, the Irish and the Germans, in the 1840s and 1850s.

3. How did people in TWO of the following sections reflect the belief in 1826 that there were good reasons to expect continued growth and prosperity in America?

    North   West
    South

4. Compare and contrast the North and the South in terms of both economic and cultural characteristics in the pre-Civil War era.

5. Analyze the extent to which southern society in the mid-1800s was hierarchical.

DOCUMENTS AND READINGS

To what extent were economic and social differences in the North and the South increasing in the first half of the 19th century? As evidence of sectional differences in this period, you will read four documents (A–D), written by southerners and northerners.

DOCUMENT A. AN ARGUMENT AGAINST A SINGLE-CROP ECONOMY

Thoughtful southerners realized that there was an economic danger in dependence on a single crop, cotton. The anonymous author of the following newspaper editorial was one of a number of southerners who urged, largely unsuccessfully, economic diversification as a means of strengthening the South.

> . . . . Let us manufacture, because it is our best policy. Let us go more on provision crops and less on cotton, because we have had everything about us poor and impoverished long enough. This we can do without manifesting any ill nature to any of the members of the same great family, all whose earnings go to swell the general prosperity and happiness.
>
> Much of our chagrin and ill nature on this subject may be justly, because truly, ascribed to a sense of shame which we of the Southern states feel, that we have been so long behind our Northern neighbors in the production of everything that substantially administers to the elegance or the comforts of life. It has been our own fault—not theirs. If we have followed a ruinous policy and bought all the articles of subsistence instead of raising them, who is to blame?
>
> Let us change our policy, but without that spirit and those expressions which leave a festering sore in the hearts of those who should be brothers. . . . We have good land, unlimited waterpower, capital in plenty, and a patriotism which is running over in some places.

Georgia Courier, June 21, 1827

DOCUMENT B. RACIAL PREJUDICE IN THE NORTH

Just as some southerners could be critical of their own section, some northerners called attention to faults within their region. The novelist Lydia M. Child was a northern white who pointed out that African Americans faced racial prejudice in northern cities no less than on southern plantations.

While we bestow our earnest disapprobation on the system of slavery, let us not flatter ourselves that we are in reality any better than our brethren in the South. Thanks to our soil and climate and the early exertions of the Quakers, the *form* of slavery does not exist among us; but the very spirit of the hateful and mischievous thing is here in all its strength. The manner in which we use what power we have gives us ample reason to be grateful that the nature of our institutions does not entrust us with more. Our prejudice against colored people is even more inveterate than it is at the South. The planter is often attached to his Negroes, and lavishes caresses and kind words upon them, as he would on a favorite hound; but our coldhearted, ignoble prejudice admits of no exceptions—no intermission.

The Southerners have long-continued habit, apparent interest and dreaded danger to palliate the wrong they do; but we stand without excuse. The intelligent and well-informed have the least share of this prejudice; and when our minds can reflect upon it, I have generally observed that they soon cease to have any at all. But such a general apathy prevails, and the subject is so seldom brought into view, that few are really aware how oppressively the influence of society is made to bear upon this injured class of the community.

Lydia M. Child,
An Appeal in Favor of That Class of Americans Called Africans, 1833

DOCUMENT C. A NORTHERN POET'S VIEW OF SLAVERY

Sectional views were voiced in every available medium: in literature and art as well as in political speeches and debates. The poet John Greenleaf Whittier wrote the following poem in response to southern demands for the return of a fugitive slave, George Latimer.

The blast from Freedom's northern hills, upon its Southern way,
Bears greeting to Virginia from Massachusetts Bay:
No word of haughty challenging, nor battle bugle's peal,
Nor steady tread of marching files, nor clang of horseman's steel.

We hear thy threats, Virginia! thy stormy words and high
Swell harshly on the Southern winds which melt along our sky;
Yet, not one brown, hard hand forgoes it honest labor here,
No hewer of our mountain oaks suspends his axe in fear.

What asks the Old Dominion? If now her sons have proved
False to their fathers' memory, false to the faith they love;
If she can scoff at Freedom, and its great charter spurn,
Must we of Massachusetts from truth and duty turn?

All that a sister State should do, all that a free State may,
Heart, hand, and purse we proffer, as in our day;
But that one dark loathsome burden ye must stagger alone,
And reap the bitter harvest which ye yourselves have sown!

We wage no war, we lift no arm, we fling no torch within
The fire-damps of the quaking mine beneath your soil of sin;
We leave ye with your bondmen, to wrestle, while ye can,
With the strong upward tendencies and godlike soul of man!

But for us and for our children, the vow which we have given
For freedom and humanity, is registered in heaven;
No slave-hunt in our borders—no prate on our strand!
No fetters in the Bay State—no slave upon our land!

John Greenleaf Whittier,
"Massachusetts to Virginia," 1843

DOCUMENT D.   *IN DEFENSE OF SLAVERY*

After the slave revolt in Virginia led by Nat Turner, Virginia's legislature conducted a lengthy debate (1831–1832) on the morality of slavery. Commenting on the debate, Thomas Dew, a professor at the College of William and Mary, wrote a defense of slavery that was to have widespread influence on public opinion in the South. Following is an excerpt from Dew's essay.

It is said slavery is wrong, in the *abstract* at least, and contrary to the spirit of Christianity. . . . With regard to the assertion that slavery is against the spirit of Christianity, we are ready to admit the general assertion, but deny most positively, that there is any thing in the Old or New Testament [of the Bible], which would go to show that slavery, when once introduced, ought at all events to be abrogated, or that the master commits any offence in holding slaves. The children of Israel themselves were slaveholders, and were not condemned for it. All the patriarchs themselves were slaveholders; Abraham had more than three hundred; Isaac had a "great store" of them; and even the patient and meek Job himself had "*a very great household.*" . . . When we turn to the New Testament, we find not one single passage at all calculated to disturb the conscience of an honest slaveholder. No one can read it without seeing and admiring that the meek and humble Saviour of the world in no instance meddled with the established institutions of mankind; he came to save a fallen world, and not to excite the black passions of men, and array them in deadly hostility against each other. . . . He was born in the Roman world—a world in which the most galling slavery existed, a thousand times more cruel than the slavery in our own country; and yet he no where encourages insurrection; he no where fosters discontent; but exhorts *always* to implicit obedience and fidelity.

Thomas R. Dew,
*Review of the Debate in the Virginia Legislature
of 1831 and 1832,* 1832

ANALYZING THE DOCUMENTS

1. Based on the documents presented, how do you think Lydia Child or John Greenleaf Whittier would respond to Thomas Dew's defense of slavery?

2. "Although there were differences between the North and the South, the racial attitudes of both sections were not far apart, nor is it correct to call the northern economy 'industrial' and the southern economy 'agrarian.' "

Referring to the documents, tell how you would either defend or refute the position taken by the above statement.

3. "Growing sectional differences in the United States during the first half of the 19th century made a breakup of the Union inevitable."

Referring to the documents, take a position either supporting or criticizing this statement.

THE AGE OF JACKSON, 1824–1844

The political activity that pervades the United States must be seen in order to be understood. No sooner do you set foot upon American ground than you are stunned by a kind of tumult.

Alexis de Tocqueville, *Democracy in America*, 1835

The era that saw the emergence of popular politics in the 1820s and the presidency of Andrew Jackson (1829–1837) is often called the Age of the Common Man, or the Era of Jacksonian Democracy. Historians debate whether Jackson was a major molder of events, a political opportunist exploiting the democratic ferment of the times, or merely a symbol of the era. Nevertheless, the era and Jackson's name seem permanently linked. (Of course, to attach a name to an age does not explain either what it was or why it happened.)

Jacksonian Democracy

The changing politics of the Jacksonian years paralleled complex social and economic changes.

The Rise of a Democratic Society

Visitors to the United States in the 1830s, such as Alexis de Tocqueville, a young French aristocrat, were amazed by the informal manners and democratic attitudes of Americans. In hotels, under the American Plan, men and women from all classes ate together at common tables. On stagecoaches, steamboats, and later in railroad cars, there was also only one class for passengers, so that the rich and poor alike sat together in the same compartments. It was also difficult for European visitors to distinguish between classes in the United States. Men of all backgrounds wore simple dark trousers and jackets, while less well-to-do women emulated the fanciful and confining styles illustrated in wide-circulation women's magazines like *Godey's Lady's Book.* Equality was becoming the governing principle of American society.

Among the white majority in American society, there was widespread belief in the principle of equality—or more precisely, equality of opportunity for

184

white males. (At the same time, the oppression of black slaves and discrimination against free blacks coexisted with and contradicted whites' ideal of equality.) Equality of opportunity would, at least in theory, allow the young man of humble origins to rise as far as his native talent and industry would take him. The hero of the age was the "self-made man."

There was no equivalent belief in the "self-made woman," but feminists in a later period would take up the theme of equal rights and insist that it should be applied to both women and men (see Chapter 11).

Politics of the Common Man

Between 1824 and 1840, politics moved out of the fine homes of rich southern planters and northern merchants who had dominated government in past eras. These were the years when white males of the lower and middle classes began to vote in large numbers. The number of votes cast for president rose from about 350,000 in 1824 to over 2.4 million in 1840, a nearly sevenfold increase in just 16 years. The new state suffrage laws that enabled more citizens to vote were a significant cause of the change. But there were other reasons as well. Changes in political parties and campaign methods, improved education, and increases in newspaper circulation also contributed to the democratic trend.

The most important political changes and reforms during the Jacksonian years were the following:

Universal male suffrage. Western states recently admitted to the Union— Indiana (1816), Illinois (1818), and Missouri (1821)—adopted state constitutions that allowed all white males to vote and hold office. Absent from these newer constitutions were any religious or property qualifications for voting. Most eastern states soon followed suit, eliminating such restrictions from their constitutions. As a result, from one end of the country to the other, all white males could vote regardless of their social class or religion. Also, political offices could now be held by people in the lower and middle ranks of society.

Party nominating conventions. In the past, it had been common for candidates for office to be nominated either by state legislatures or by "King Caucus"—a closed-door meeting of a political party's leaders in Congress. The common people had no opportunity to participate. In the 1830s, however, caucuses were replaced by nominating conventions. Party politicians and voters would gather in a large meeting hall to nominate the party's candidates. The Anti-Masons were the first to hold such a nominating convention. This method was more open to popular participation, hence more democratic.

Popular election of the president. In the presidential election of 1832, only South Carolina used the old system whereby its electors for president were chosen by the state legislature. All other states in the Union had adopted a new and more democratic method of allowing the voters to choose a state's slate of presidential electors.

Two-party system. The popular election of presidential electors—and, in effect, of the president as well—had important consequences for the two-party system. Campaigns for president now had to be conducted on a national scale. To organize these campaigns, large political parties were needed.

Rise of third parties. While only the large national parties (the Democrats and the Whigs in Jackson's day) could hope to win the presidency, other political parties also emerged. The Anti-Masonic party and the Workingmen's party, for example, reached out to groups of people who previously had shown little interest in politics. The Anti-Masons attacked the secret societies of Masons and accused them of belonging to a privileged, antidemocratic elite.

More elected offices. During the Jacksonian era, a much larger number of state and local officials were elected to office, instead of being appointed, as in the past. This change gave the voters more voice in their government and also tended to increase their interest in participating in elections.

Popular campaigning. Candidates for office directed their campaigns to the interests and prejudices of the common people. Politics also became a form of local entertainment. Campaigns of the 1830s and 1840s featured parades of floats and marching bands and large rallies in which voters were treated to free food and drink. To be sure, there was also a negative side to the new campaign techniques. In trying to appeal to the masses, the candidates would often resort to personal attacks and downplay the issues. A politician, for example, might attack an opponent's "aristocratic airs" and make him seem unfriendly to "the common man."

Spoils system and rotation of officeholders. Winning government jobs became the lifeblood of party organizations. At the national level, President Jackson believed in appointing people to federal jobs (as postmasters, for example) strictly according to whether they had actively campaigned for the Democratic party. Any previous holder of the office who was not a Democrat was fired and replaced with a loyal Democrat. This practice of dispensing government jobs in return for party loyalty was called the spoils system by critics because it promoted government corruption.

In addition, Jackson believed in a system of rotation in office. To make it possible for a maximum number of Democrats to hold office, he would limit a person's tenure in office to just one term and appoint some other deserving Democrat in his place. Jackson defended the replacement and rotation of officeholders by the new administration as a democratic reform. "No man," he said, "has any more intrinsic claim to office than another." Jacksonians had contempt for experts and believed that ordinary Americans were capable of holding any government office. Both the spoils system and the rotation of officeholders affirmed the democratic ideal that one man was as good as another. They also helped build a strong two-party system.

Jackson Versus Adams

Political change in the Jacksonian era began several years *before* Jackson moved into the White House as president. In the controversial election in 1824, Jackson won more popular and electoral votes than any other candidate, but he ended up losing the election.

The Election of 1824

Recall the brief Era of Good Feelings that characterized U.S. politics during the two-term presidency of James Monroe. The era ended in political bad feelings in 1824, the year of a bitterly contested and divisive presidential election. By then, the old congressional caucus system for choosing presidential candidates had broken down. As a result, four candidates of the same party (the Republican party founded by Jefferson) campaigned for the presidency. The candidates were John Quincy Adams, Henry Clay, William Crawford, and Andrew Jackson.

Jackson won the greatest number of popular votes. But because the vote was split four ways, he lacked a majority in the electoral college as required by the Constitution. Therefore, the House of Representatives had to choose a president from among the top three candidates. Henry Clay used his influence in the House to provide John Quincy Adams of Massachusetts with enough votes to win the election. When President Adams appointed Clay his secretary of state, Jackson and his followers were certain that the popular choice of most voters had been foiled by secret political maneuvers. Angry Jackson supporters accused Adams and Clay of making a "corrupt bargain."

President John Quincy Adams

Adams further alienated the followers of Jackson when he asked Congress for money for internal improvements, aid to manufacturing, and even a national university and an astronomical observatory. Jacksonians viewed all these measures as a waste of money and a violation of the Constitution.

In 1828, toward the end of Adams' presidency, Congress patched together a new tariff law, which generally satisfied northern manufacturers but alienated southern planters. Southerners denounced it as a "tariff of abominations."

The Revolution of 1828

Adams sought reelection in 1828. But the Jacksonians were now ready to use the discontent of southerners and westerners and the new campaign tactics of party organization to sweep "Old Hickory" (Jackson) into office. Going beyond parades and barbecues, Jackson's party resorted to smearing the president and accusing Adams' wife of being born out of wedlock. Adams' supporters retaliated in kind, accusing Jackson's wife of adultery. The mudslinging campaign attracted a lot of interest. Three times the number of voters participated in the election of 1828 as in the previous election.

Jackson won handily, carrying every state west of the Appalachians. His reputation as a war hero and man of the western frontier accounted for his victory more than the positions he took on issues of the day.

The Presidency of Andrew Jackson

Jackson was a different kind of president from any of his predecessors. A strong leader, he not only dominated politics for eight years but also became a symbol of the emerging working class and middle class (the so-called common man). Born in a frontier cabin, Jackson gained fame as an Indian fighter and as hero of the Battle of New Orleans, and came to live in a fine mansion in Tennessee as a wealthy planter and slaveowner. But he never lost the rough manners of the frontier. He chewed tobacco, fought several duels, and displayed a violent temper. Jackson was the first president since Washington to be without a college education. In a phrase, he could be described as an extraordinary ordinary man. This self-made man and living legend drew support from every social group and every section of the country.

Role of the president. Jackson presented himself as the representative of all the people and the protector of the common man against abuses of power by the rich and the privileged. He was a frugal Jeffersonian, who opposed increasing federal spending and the national debt. Jackson interpreted the powers of Congress narrowly and therefore vetoed more bills (12) than the total vetoes cast by all six preceding presidents. For example, he vetoed the use of federal money to construct the Maysville Road, because it was wholly within one state, Kentucky, the home state of Jackson's rival, Henry Clay.

Advising Jackson was a group of politicians who did not belong to his official cabinet. This group became known as the "kitchen cabinet." Thus, members of the appointed cabinet had less influence on policy than under earlier presidents.

Peggy Eaton affair. The champion of the common man also went to the aid of the common woman, at least in the case of Peggy O'Neale Eaton. The wife of Jackson's secretary of war, she was the target of malicious gossip by other cabinet wives, much as Jackson's recently deceased wife had been in the 1828 campaign. They refused to invite her to their private parties because they suspected her of being an adulteress. When Jackson tried to force the cabinet wives to accept Peggy Eaton socially, most of the cabinet resigned. This controversy also contributed to the resignation of Jackson's vice president, John C. Calhoun, a year later. For remaining loyal to Jackson through this crisis, Martin Van Buren of New York was chosen to be the new vice president.

Indian removal act (1830). Jackson's concept of democracy did not extend to Native Americans. Like most whites of the time, Jackson sympathized with land-hungry citizens who were impatient to take over lands previously held by Native Americans. Jackson thought the most humane solution was to compel the Native Americans to leave their traditional homelands and resettle west of the Mississippi. In 1830, he signed into law the Indian Removal Act, which forced the resettlement of many thousands of Native Americans. By 1835 most eastern tribes had reluctantly complied and moved west. The Bureau of Indian Affairs was created in 1836 to assist the resettled tribes.

A majority of politicians in various states also believed in a policy of Indian removal. Georgia and other states passed laws requiring the Cherokees to migrate to the West. When the Cherokees challenged Georgia in the courts, the Supreme Court ruled in *Cherokee Nation v. Georgia* (1831) that Cherokees were not a foreign nation with the right to sue in a federal court. But in a second case, *Worcester v. Georgia* (1832), the high court ruled that the laws of Georgia had no force within the boundaries of the Cherokee territory. In this clash between a state's laws and the federal courts, Jackson sided with the states. He said defiantly, "John Marshall has made his decision, now let him enforce it."

Most Cherokees repudiated the settlement of 1835, which provided land in the Indian territory. It was not until 1838, after Jackson had left office, that the U.S. Army forced 15,000 Cherokees to leave Georgia. The hardships on the "trail of tears" were so great that 4,000 Cherokees died on their tragic westward trek.

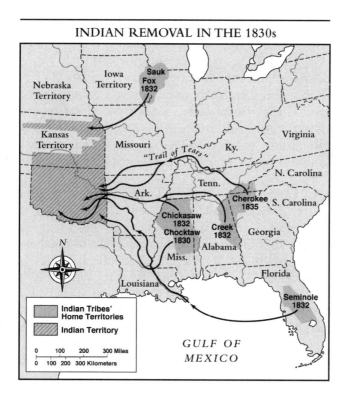

INDIAN REMOVAL IN THE 1830s

Nullification crisis. Jackson favored states' rights—but not if it would lead to disunion. In 1828, the South Carolina legislature declared the increased tariff of 1828, the so-called Tariff of Abominations, to be unconstitutional. In doing so, it affirmed a theory advanced by Jackson's first vice president, John C. Calhoun. According to this *nullification theory,* each state had the right to decide whether to obey a federal law or to declare it null and void (of no effect).

In 1830, Daniel Webster of Massachusetts debated Robert Hayne of South Carolina on the nature of the federal Union under the Constitution. Webster attacked the idea that any state could defy or leave the Union. Following this famous Webster-Hayne debate, President Jackson declared his own position in a toast he presented at a political dinner. "Our federal Union," he declared, "it must be preserved." Calhoun responded immediately with another toast: "The Union, next to our liberties, most dear!"

In 1832, Calhoun's South Carolina turned up the war of words by holding a special convention to nullify not only the hated tariff of 1828 but also a new tariff law of 1832. The convention passed a resolution forbidding the collection of tariffs within the state. Jackson's reaction was decisive. He told the secretary of war to prepare for military action. He persuaded Congress to pass a Force bill giving the president the authority to take military action in South Carolina. The president also issued a Proclamation to the People of South Carolina, stating that nullification and disunion were treason.

But federal troops did not march in this crisis. Jackson opened the door for compromise by suggesting that Congress lower the tariff. South Carolina postponed nullification and later formally rescinded it after Congress enacted a new tariff along the lines suggested by the president.

Jackson's strong defense of federal authority forced the militant advocates of states' rights to retreat. On another issue, however, militant southerners won Jackson's support. The president shared southerners' alarm about the growing antislavery movement in the North. He used his executive power to stop antislavery literature from being sent through the U.S. mails. Jacksonians in the South could trust the president *not* to extend the benefits of democracy to African Americans.

Bank veto. Another major issue of Jackson's presidency concerned the rechartering of the Bank of the United States. This bank and its branches, although privately owned, received federal deposits and attempted to serve a public purpose by cushioning the ups and downs of the national economy. The bank's president, Nicholas Biddle, managed it effectively. Biddle's arrogance, however, contributed to the suspicion that the bank abused its powers and served the interests of the wealthy. Jackson shared this suspicion. He believed that the Bank of the United States was unconstitutional.

Henry Clay, Jackson's chief political opponent, favored the bank. In 1832, an election year, Clay decided to challenge Jackson on the bank issue by persuading a majority in Congress to pass a bank-recharter bill. Jackson promptly vetoed this bill, denouncing it as a private monopoly that enriched the wealthy and foreigners at the expense of the common people. The issue backfired for Clay in the 1832 election. An overwhelming majority of voters approved Jackson's attack on the "hydra of corruption." Jackson won reelection with more than three-fourths of the electoral vote.

The Two-Party System

The one-party system that had characterized Monroe's presidency (the Era of Good Feelings) gave way to a two-party system under Jackson. Supporters of Jackson were now known as Democrats, while supporters of his leading rival, Henry Clay, were called Whigs. The Democratic party harked back to the old Republican party of Jefferson, and the Whig party resembled the defunct Federalist party of Hamilton. At the same time, the new parties reflected the changed conditions of the Jacksonian era. Democrats and Whigs alike were challenged to respond to the relentless westward expansion of the nation and the emergence of an industrial economy.

For the differences between Democrats and Whigs, refer to the table below.

Democrats and Whigs in the Age of Jackson		
	Democrats	**Whigs**
Positions on issues	*Favored* local rule, limited government, free trade, equal economic opportunity (for white males). *Opposed* monopolies, a national bank, high tariffs, high land prices.	*Favored* Clay's American System (a national bank, federal funding of internal improvements, a protective tariff). *Opposed* immorality, vice, and crime, which some blamed on immigrants.
Base of voter support	Southerners, westerners, small farmers, urban workers	New Englanders and residents of mid-Atlantic and upper-Middle-Western states; Protestants of old English stock; middle-class urban professionals.

Jackson's Second Term

After winning reelection in 1832, Jackson had to deal with the economic consequences of his decision to oppose the Bank of the United States.

Pet banks. Jackson "killed" the national bank not only by vetoing its recharter but also by withdrawing all federal funds. Aided by Secretary of the

Treasury Roger Taney, he transferred the funds to various state banks, which Jackson's critics called "pet banks."

Specie Circular. As a result of both Jackson's financial policies and feverish speculation in western lands, prices for land and various goods became badly inflated. Jackson hoped to check the inflationary trend by issuing a presidential order known as the *Specie Circular*. It required that all future purchases of federal lands be made in gold and silver rather than in paper banknotes. Soon afterward, as banknotes lost their value and land sales plummeted, a financial crisis—the Panic of 1837—plunged the nation's economy into a depression.

The Election of 1836

Following the two-term tradition set by his predecessors, Jackson decided not to seek a third term. To make sure his policies were carried out even in his retirement, Jackson persuaded the Democratic party to nominate his loyal vice president, Martin Van Buren, who was a master of practical politics.

Fearing defeat, the Whig party adopted the unusual strategy of nominating three candidates from three different regions. In doing so, the Whigs hoped to throw the election into the House of Representatives, where each state had one vote in the selection of the president. The Whig strategy failed, however, as Van Buren took 58 percent of the electoral vote.

President Van Buren and the Panic of 1837

Just as Van Buren took office, the country suffered a financial panic as one bank after another closed its doors. Jackson's opposition to the rechartering of the Bank of the United States was only one of many causes of the panic and resulting economic depression. But the Whigs were quick to blame the Democrats for their laissez-faire economics, which allowed for little federal involvement in the economy.

The "Log Cabin and Hard Cider" Campaign of 1840

In the election of 1840, the Whigs were in a strong position to defeat Van Buren and the Jacksonian Democrats. Voters were unhappy with the bad state of the economy. In addition, the Whigs were better organized than the Democrats, and also had a popular war hero, William Henry "Tippecanoe" Harrison, as their presidential candidate. The Whigs took campaign hoopla to new heights. To symbolize Harrison's humble origins, they put log cabins on wheels and paraded them down the streets of cities and towns. They also passed out hard cider for voters to drink and buttons and hats to wear. Name-calling as a propaganda device also marked the 1840 campaign. The Whigs attacked "Martin Van Ruin" as an aristocrat with a taste for foreign wines.

A remarkable 78 percent of eligible voters (white males) turned out on election day to cast their ballots. Old "Tippecanoe" and John Tyler of Virginia, a former states' rights Democrat who joined the Whigs, took 53 percent of the popular vote and swept most of the electoral votes in all three sections: North, South, and West. This election established the Whigs as a national party.

Unfortunately for the Whigs, Harrison died of pneumonia less than a month after taking office, and "His Accidency," John Tyler, became the first vice-president to succeed to the presidency. President Tyler proved to be not much of a Whig. He vetoed the Whigs' national bank bills and other legislation, and favored southern and expansionist Democrats during the balance of his term (1841–1845). The Jacksonian era was in its last stage, and came to an end with the Mexican War and the increased focus on the issue of slavery. (See Chapter 12.)

HISTORICAL PERSPECTIVES: JACKSONIAN DEMOCRACY

Historians still debate whether or not the election of Jackson in 1828 marked a revolutionary new turn in American politics or was merely an extension of an ongoing trend. The traditional view is that Jackson's election began the era of the common man, when the masses of newly enfranchised voters drove out the entrenched ruling class and elected one of their own. The Revolution of 1828 has also been characterized as a victory of the democratic West against the aristocratic East.

Nineteenth-century Whig historians, on the other hand, viewed Jackson as a despot whose appeal to the uneducated masses and "corrupt" spoils system threatened the republic.

In the 1940s, the historian Arthur M. Schlesinger, Jr. argued that Jacksonian democracy relied as much on the support of eastern urban workers as on western farmers. Jackson's coalition of farmers and workers foreshadowed a similar coalition that brought another Democratic president, Franklin D. Roosevelt, to power in the depression decade of the 1930s.

Contemporary historians have used quantitative analysis of voting returns to compare elections before, during, and after Jackson's presidency. This analysis showed that increased voter participation was evident in local elections years before 1828 and did not reach a peak until the election of 1840, an election that the Whig party won. Strong links were discovered between voting behavior and the voters' religious and ethnic backgrounds. For example, Catholic immigrants objected to the imposition of the Puritan moral code (e.g., temperance) by the native Protestants. Much of the increased participation in the election process had little to do with the election of 1828 or Jackson's politics.

Other contemporary historians see Jackson's popularity in the 1830s as a reaction of subsistence farmers and urban workers *against* powerful and threatening forces of economic change. A capitalist, or market, economy was rapidly taking shape in the early years of the 19th century. This market revolution divided the electorate. Some people (chiefly Whigs) welcomed the changes as the hope for enterprising and disciplined men. Others (chiefly Jacksonian Democrats) viewed the wealth of successful capitalists and entrepreneurs as a threat to Jefferson's vision of a nation of independent farmers. Those who were most uncomfortable with economic change rallied around Jackson. Why was Jackson's veto of the bank such a key event? Some contemporary historians, such as Charles Seller (*The Market Revolution: Jacksonian America,* 1992), see Jackson's popularity as expressing people's unspoken fears about the rise of capitalism.

KEY NAMES, EVENTS, AND TERMS

common man	popular campaigning	Proclamation to the People of South Carolina
universal male suffrage	Revolution of 1828	Bank of the United States
party nominating convention	role of the president	Nicholas Biddle
"King Caucus"	rotation in office	two-party system: Democrats; Whigs
popular election of president	Peggy Eaton affair	
Anti-Masonic party	Indian Removal Act (1830)	Roger Taney
Workingmen's party	*Cherokee Nation v. Georgia*	"pet banks"
spoils system	*Worchester v. Georgia*	Specie Circular
John Quincy Adams	trail of tears	Panic of 1837
"corrupt bargain"	states' rights	Martin van Buren
Henry Clay	nullification crisis	"log cabin and hard cider" campaign
Tariff of 1828; "tariff of abominations"	Webster-Hayne debate	
Andrew Jackson	John C. Calhoun	

MULTIPLE-CHOICE QUESTIONS

1. Jacksonian Democrats favored all of the following EXCEPT
   (A) rotation in office
   (B) universal suffrage for white males
   (C) the caucus system of nominating candidates
   (D) rewarding political supporters with government jobs
   (E) presidential electors being chosen by popular vote

2. After the election of 1824, the president's choice of Henry Clay as secretary of state resulted in
   (A) the end of political bitterness between the major parties
   (B) the revival of the Federalist party
   (C) widespread criticism of the spoils system
   (D) charges of a corrupt bargain with John Q. Adams

(E) a political alliance between Clay and Andrew Jackson

3. An important effect of the tariff of abominations of 1828 was

 (A) increased prices for cotton overseas

 (B) South Carolina's adoption of the theory of nullification

 (C) the election of a Democratic president, Andrew Jackson

 (D) an alliance of northeastern workers and western farmers

 (E) the growth of manufacturing in the South

4. The Revolution of 1828 revealed that political power was

 (A) shifting to the western states

 (B) shifting to the southern states

 (C) entrenched on the eastern seaboard

 (D) gravitating toward conservative elements

 (E) evenly divided between Whigs and Democrats

5. Which of the following documents would be most useful in evaluating President Jackson's commitment to democratic values?

 (A) the Specie Circular

 (B) veto message on the rechartering of the Second Bank of the United States

 (C) congressional hearings on the "corrupt bargain"

 (D) Supreme Court cases on the Indian-removal issue

 (E) Calhoun's writings on nullification

6. In the 1830s, the factor that most directly promoted the development of a two-party system was

 (A) the growth of the immigrant population

 (B) increased interest in foreign affairs

 (C) changes in methods of nominating and electing the president

 (D) increasing sectional conflict between northern and southern states over the tariff issue

 (E) the dropping of constitutional limitations on the party system

7. "The duties of all public officers are, or at least admit of being made, so plain and simple that more is lost by the long continuance of men in office than is generally to be gained by their experience."

This statement best reflects the views of

 (A) John C. Calhoun

 (B) Daniel Webster

 (C) John Q. Adams

 (D) Andrew Jackson

 (E) Henry Clay

8. The main issue in the presidential campaign of 1832 was

 (A) the recharter of the Bank of the United States

 (B) the removal of Native Americans from eastern states

 (C) the use of federal funds for internal improvements

 (D) the cost of western lands sold by the government

 (E) the nullification of the "tariff of abominations"

9. President Jackson's response to Supreme Court decisions on the treaty rights of Native Americans resulted in which of the following?
    (A) Jackson's loss of popularity among working-class voters
    (B) Indian uprisings in the eastern states
    (C) the division of tribal lands into family units
    (D) impeachment of the president for not enforcing the law
    (E) the forced removal of Cherokees from their lands in Georgia

10. Supporters of the Whig party included all of the following groups EXCEPT
    (A) supporters of Clay's American System
    (B) new immigrants, such as the Germans and the Irish
    (C) westerners who wanted federal funds for internal improvements
    (D) reformers concerned about immorality and vice
    (E) advocates of a national bank

ESSAY QUESTIONS

1. How did TWO of the following contribute to changes in the political process during the Jacksonian era?

    universal white male suffrage

    popular election of the president

    spoils system

2. Analyze the ways in which the politics of the common man were evident in TWO of the presidential elections of the 1824–1840 era.

3. To what extent was President Andrew Jackson one of the nation's most effective presidents?

4. Analyze the degree to which Jacksonian Democrats promoted TWO of the following from 1824 to 1844:

    political democracy

    equal opportunity

    personal liberty

5. Compare and contrast the policies of the Jacksonian Democrat and Whig parties of the 1830s with the Democratic Republican and Federalist parties of the early 1800s.

DOCUMENTS AND READINGS

Today it is easy to identify the limitations of American democracy in the 1830s. Political and basic human rights were denied to women, African Americans, and Native Americans. Despite these failures, Jacksonian democracy was a powerful, sometimes radical, egalitarian movement that transformed American politics and provided the foundation of later reforms.

The first principle of Jacksonian democracy was majority rule, which at the time included only white male voters. If it had a second principle, it was that a popularly elected president was the only true representative of the people of the United States. The following readings illustrate both the strengths and weaknesses of majority rule and a strong popular presidency. Is majority rule the ultimate value of the democratic process?

DOCUMENT A.   *DEMOCRACY IN AMERICA*

Alexis de Tocqueville toured the United States extensively in 1831–1832 to study American prison reform for the French government, but his subject ultimately became the new democratic political and social order that was developing in the United States. Once back in France, this reflective and curious young aristocrat published what turned out to be a masterful analysis of democracy and the United States, *Democracy in America.* Tocqueville found the United States during the Jacksonian era an excellent laboratory in which to study both the strengths and weaknesses of democracy.

It is incontestable that the people frequently conduct the public business very badly; but it is impossible that the lower orders should take a part in public business without extending the circle of their ideas and quitting the ordinary routine of their thought. The humblest individual who co-operates in the government of society acquires a certain degree of self-respect.

When the opponents of democracy assert that a single man performs what he undertakes better than the government of all, it appears to me that they are right. . . . Democratic liberty is far from accomplishing all it projects with the skill of an adroit despotism. It frequently abandons them before they have borne their fruits, or risks them when the consequences may be dangerous; but in the end it produces more than any absolute government; if it does fewer things well, it does a greater number of things. . . . Democracy does not give people the most skillful government, but it produces what the ablest governments are frequently unable to create: namely, an all-pervading and restless activity.

We must first understand what is wanted of society and its government. Is it your object to refine the habits, embellish the manners, and cultivate the arts, to promote the love of poetry, beauty, and glory? Would you constitute a people fitted to act powerfully upon all other nations, and prepared for those high enterprises which, whatever be their results, will leave a name forever famous in history? If you believe such to be the principal object of society, avoid democracy, for it would not lead you with certainty to the goal.

But if you hold it expedient to divert the moral and intellectual activity of man to production of comfort and promotion of general well-being; if a clear understanding be more profitable to man than genius, if your object is not to stimulate the virtues of heroism, but the habits of peace, if you had rather witness vices than crimes . . . if, instead of living in the midst of a brilliant society, you are contented to have prosperity around you; if, in short, you are of the opinion that the principal object of a government is not to confer the greatest possible powers and glory upon the body of the nation, but to ensure the greatest enjoyment and to avoid the misery to each of the individuals who compose it—if such be your desire, then equalize the conditions of men and establish democratic institutions.

Alexis de Tocqueville,
Democracy in America, 1835

### DOCUMENT B.	THE NULLIFICATION ISSUE

Was democratic government, as understood by Andrew Jackson, compatible with southerners' ideas about the nature of the federal Union? In 1828 and 1832, South Carolina answered that question in the negative when it declared the tariffs voted by Congress to be null and void. Jackson's vice president, John C. Calhoun of South Carolina, presented the theory that the United States was nothing more or less than a loose compact of states and that a state could decide to nullify, or ignore, any federal law that wrongly injured the state's interests and rights. In 1832, a South Carolina convention adopted Calhoun's ideas and defended the doctrine of nullification in the following terms:

We hold, then, that on their separation from the Crown of Great Britain, the several colonies became free and independent States, each enjoying the separate and independent right of self-government; and that no authority can be exercised over them or within their limits, but by their consent, respectively given as States. It is equally true, that the Constitution of the United States is a compact formed between the several States, acting as sovereign communities; that the government created by it is a joint agency of the States, appointed to execute the powers enumerated and granted by that instrument; that all its acts not intentionally authorized are of themselves essentially null and void, and that the States have the right, in the same sovereign capacity in which they adopted the Federal Constitution, to pronounce, in the last resort, authoritative judgment on the usurpations of the Federal Government, and to adopt such measures as they may deem necessary and expedient to arrest the operation of the unconstitutional acts of the Government, within their respective limits. Such we deem to be inherent rights of the States; rights, in the very nature of things, absolutely inseparable from sovereignty.

—"Address to the People of the United States"
(November 1832), in *Statutes at Large of South Carolina*

DOCUMENT C.   *JACKSON'S VETO MESSAGE*

Andrew Jackson presented his view of the U.S. system of government when he vetoed the recharter of the Bank of the United States. The following is an excerpt from his veto message of 1832.

It is to be regretted that the rich and powerful too often bend the acts of government to their selfish purposes. Distinctions in society will always exist under every just government. Equality of talents, of education, or of wealth cannot be produced by human institutions. In the full enjoyment of the gifts of heaven and the fruits of superior industry, economy, and virtue, every man is equally entitled to protection by law.

But when the laws undertake to add to these natural and just advantages artificial distinctions, to grant titles, gratuities, and exclusive privileges, to make the rich richer and the potent more powerful, the humble members of society—the farmers, mechanics, and laborers—who have neither the time nor the means of securing like favors to themselves, have a right to complain of the injustices of their government.

There are no necessary evils in government. Its evils exist only in its abuses. If it would confine itself to equal protection, and, as heaven does its rains, shower its favors alike on the high and the low, the rich and the poor, it would be an unqualified blessing. In the act before me there seems to be a wide and unnecessary departure from these just principles.

Messages and Papers of the Presidents, 1896

DOCUMENT D.   *REMOVAL OF NATIVE AMERICANS FROM TREATY LANDS*

In 1831, Edward Everett, a young representative from Massachusetts (later to become president of Harvard College), delivered a speech in the House attacking Jackson's policy on the removal of Native Americans. The following is an excerpt from Everett's speech.

I cannot disguise my impression that it [the annulment of the Indian treaties] is the greatest question which ever came before Congress, short of the question of peace and war. It concerns not an individual, but entire communities of men, whose fate is wholly in our hands. . . .

Sir, the Secretary [of War] says a new era has arisen in Indian affairs. This is true. Up to the year 1828, the course of proceeding in our Indian affairs is well known, at least in reference to all the tribes whose rights are now in controversy. The United States had negotiated treaties with all the Southwestern tribes. Our relations with them, and the boundary between them and us, were regulated by treaty; . . . No State had pretended to extend her laws over either of these tribes till the year 1828. . . .

Georgia led the way. In 1828, she passed a summary law, to take effect prospectively [at some later time], extending her jurisdiction . . . over the Indian tribes within her limits. In 1829, this law, with more specific provisions, was re-enacted, to take effect on the 1st day of June, 1830. This example of Georgia was imitated by Alabama and Mississippi. By these State laws, the organization previously existing in the Indian tribes was declared unlawful, and was annulled. . . . The political existence of these communities was accordingly dissolved, and their members declared citizens or subjects of the States. . . .

The Indians, as was natural, looked to the Government of the United States for protection. It was the quarter whence they had a right to expect it—where, as I think, they ought to have found it. They asked to be protected in the rights and possessions guaranteed to them by numerous treaties, and demanded the execution, in their favor, of the laws of the United States governing the intercourse of our citizens with the Indian tribes. They came first to the President, deeming, and rightly, that it was his duty to afford them this protection. They knew . . . he had but one constitutional duty to perform toward the treaties and laws—the duty of executing them. The President refused to afford the protection demanded. He informed them that he had no power, in his view of the rights of the States, to prevent their extending their laws over the Indians. . . .

Congressional Debates,
21st Congress, 2nd Session
(February 14, 1831)

ANALYZING THE DOCUMENTS

1. What did Tocqueville consider the advantages and the disadvantages of American democracy?

2. According to the compact theory of John Calhoun, why was it legitimate for a state to nullify a federal law?

3. Why did President Jackson oppose the recharter of the Bank of the United States?

4. Why did Everett think that three states and President Jackson violated the rights of the Native American tribes?

5. Andrew Jackson and his supporters have been criticized for upholding the principles of majority rule and the supremacy of the federal government inconsistently and unfairly. Assess the validity of this criticism in the cases of the recharter of the Bank, the nullification controversy, and the removal of Native Americans.

SOCIETY, CULTURE, AND REFORM, 1820–1860

We would have every path laid open to Woman as freely as to Man
. . . . As the friend of the Negro assumes that one man cannot by right
hold another in bondage, so should the friend of Woman assume
that Man cannot by right lay even well-meant restrictions on Woman.

Margaret Fuller, 1845

Many of the significant reform movements in American history began during the Jacksonian era and in the following decades. The period before the Civil War is also known as the *antebellum period*. During this time, a diverse mix of reformers dedicated themselves to such causes as establishing free (tax-supported) public schools, improving the treatment of the mentally ill, controlling or abolishing the sale of liquors and beers, winning equal legal and political rights for women, and abolishing slavery. The enthusiasm for reform had many historic sources: the Puritan sense of mission, the Enlightenment belief in human goodness and perfectability, the politics of Jacksonian democracy, and changing relationships among men and women and among social classes and ethnic groups. Perhaps most important of all were the powerful religious motives behind the reformers' zeal.

Religion: The Second Great Awakening

Religious revivals swept through the United States during the early decades of the 19th century. They were partly a reaction against the rationalism (belief in human reason) that had been the fashion during the Enlightenment and the American Revolution. Calvinist (Puritan) teachings of original sin and predestination had been rejected by believers in more liberal and forgiving doctrines, such as those of the Unitarian Church.

Calvinism began a counterattack against these liberal views in the 1790s. The Second Great Awakening began among educated people such as Reverend Timothy Dwight, president of Yale College in Connecticut. Dwight's campus revivals motivated a generation of young men to become evangelical preachers.

However, in revivals of the early 1800s, successful preachers were audience-centered and easily understood by the uneducated; they offered the opportunity for salvation to all. These populist movements seemed attuned to the democratization of American society.

Revivalism in New York. In 1823, a Presbyterian minister named Charles G. Finney started a series of revivals in upstate New York, where many New Englanders had settled. Instead of delivering sermons based on rational argument, Finney appealed to people's emotions and fear of damnation and persuaded thousands to publicly declare their revived faith. He preached that all were free to be saved through faith and hard work—ideas that strongly appealed to the rising middle class. Because of Finney's influence, western New York became known as the "burned-over district" for its frequent "hell-and-brimstone" revivals.

Baptists and Methodists. In the South and on the advancing western frontier, Baptist and Methodist circuit preachers, such as Peter Cartwright, would travel from one location to another and attract thousands to hear their dramatic preaching at outdoor revival, or camp meetings. They converted many of the unchurched into respectable members of the community. By 1850, the Baptists and the Methodists had become the largest Protestant denominations in the country.

Millennialism. Much of the religious enthusiasm of the time was based on the widespread belief that the world was about to end with the second coming of Christ. The preacher William Miller gained tens of thousands of followers by predicting a specific date (October 21, 1844) when the second coming would occur. There were obvious disappointments when nothing happened on the appointed day, but the Millerites would continue as a new religion, the Seventh-Day Adventists.

Mormons. Another religious group, the Church of the Latter-Day Saints, or Mormons, was founded by Joseph Smith in 1830. Smith based his religious thinking on a book of Scripture—the Book of Mormon—which traced a connection between the Native Americans and the lost tribes of Israel. Smith gathered a following and moved from New York State to Ohio, Missouri, and, finally, Illinois. There, the Mormon founder was murdered by a local mob. To escape persecution, the Mormons under the leadership of Brigham Young migrated to the far western frontier, where they established the New Zion (as they called their religious community) on the banks of the Great Salt Lake in Utah. Their cooperative social organization helped the Mormons to prosper in the wilderness. Their practice of polygamy (allowing a man to have more than one wife), however, aroused the hostility of the U.S. government.

The Second Great Awakening, like the first, caused new divisions in society between the newer, evangelical sects and the older Protestant churches. It affected all sections of the country. But it was only in the northern states from Massachusetts westward to Ohio that the Great Awakening played a significant role in social reform. Activist religious groups provided both the leadership and the well-organized voluntary societies that drove the reform movements of the antebellum era.

Culture: Ideas, the Arts, and Literature

In Europe, during the early years of the 19th century, a romantic movement in art and literature stressed intuition and feelings, individual acts of heroism, and the study of nature. At the same time, in the United States from 1820 to 1860, these romantic and idealistic themes were best expressed by the transcendentalists, a small group of New England writers and reformers.

The Transcendentalists

Writers like Ralph Waldo Emerson and Henry David Thoreau questioned the doctrines of established churches and the capitalistic habits of the merchant class. They argued for a mystical and intuitive way of thinking as a means for discovering one's inner self and looking for the essence of God in nature. Their views challenged the materialism of American society by suggesting that artistic expression was more important than the pursuit of wealth.

Although the transcendentalists were highly individualistic and viewed organized institutions as unimportant, they supported a variety of reforms, especially the antislavery movement.

Ralph Waldo Emerson (1803–1882). The best-known transcendentalist, Ralph Waldo Emerson, was among the most popular American lecturers of the 19th century. His essays and lectures expressed the individualistic mood of the period. In an 1837 address at Harvard College ("The American Scholar"), Emerson evoked the nationalistic spirit of Americans by urging them not to imitate European culture but to create an entirely new and original *American* culture. His essays and poems argued for self-reliance, independent thinking, and the primacy of spiritual matters over material ones. As a northerner, Emerson became a leading critic of slavery in the 1850s and then an ardent supporter of the Union during the Civil War.

Henry David Thoreau (1817–1862). Living in the same town as Emerson (Concord, Mass.) was one of his close friends, Henry David Thoreau. To test his transcendentalist philosophy, Thoreau conducted a two-year experiment of living by himself in the woods outside town. There he used observations of nature to discover essential truths about life and the universe. His writings from these years were published in the book for which he is best known, *Walden* (1854). Because of this book, Thoreau is remembered today as a pioneer ecologist and conservationist.

Through his essay "On Civil Disobedience," Thoreau established himself as an early advocate of nonviolent protest. The essay presented Thoreau's argument for not obeying unjust laws. The philosopher's own act of civil disobedience was to refuse to pay a tax that might be used in an "immoral" war—the U.S. war with Mexico (1846–1848). For breaking the tax law, Thoreau was forced to spend one night in the Concord jail. In the next century, Thoreau's essay and actions would inspire the nonviolent movements of both Mohandas Gandhi in India and Martin Luther King, Jr., in the United States.

Brook Farm. Could a community of people live out the transcendentalist ideal? In 1841, George Ripley, a Protestant minister, launched a communal experiment at Brook Farm in Massachusetts. His goal was to achieve "a more natural union between intellectual and manual labor." Living at Brook Farm at different times were some of the leading intellectuals of the period. Emerson went, as did Margaret Fuller, a feminist (advocate of women's rights) writer and editor; Theodore Parker, a theologian and radical reformer; and Nathaniel Hawthorne, the novelist. A bad fire and heavy debts forced the end of the experiment in 1849. But Brook Farm was remembered for its atmosphere of artistic creativity and an innovative school that attracted the sons and daughters of New England's intellectual elite.

Communal Experiments

The idea of withdrawing from conventional society to create an ideal community, or utopia, in a fresh setting was not a new idea. But never before were the social experiments so numerous as during the middle decades of the 19th century. The open lands of the United States before the Civil War proved fertile ground for over a hundred experimental communities. The early Mormons may be considered an example of a religious communal effort and Brook Farm an example of a humanistic or secular experiment. Although many of the communities were shortlived, these "backwoods utopias" reflect the diversity of the reform ideas of the time.

Shakers. One of the earliest religious communal movements, the Shakers had about 6,000 members in various communities by the 1840s. Shakers held property in common and kept women and men strictly separate (forbidding marriage and sexual relations). For lack of new recruits, the Shaker communities virtually died out by the mid-1900s. The Amana settlements founded in Iowa by German Pietists were also dedicated to an ascetic life, but allowed for marriage, which helped to ensure the survival of their communities.

New Harmony. The secular (nonreligious) experiment in New Harmony, Indiana, was the work of the Welsh industrialist and reformer Robert Owen. Owen hoped his utopian socialist community would provide an answer to the problems of inequity and alienation caused by the Industrial Revolution. The experiment failed, however, as a result of both financial problems and disagreements among members of the community.

Oneida community. After undergoing a religious conversion, John Humphrey Noyes in 1848 started a cooperative community in Oneida, New York, that became highly controversial. Dedicated to an ideal of perfect social and economic equality, members of the community shared property—and later even shared marriage partners. Critics attacked the Oneida system of planned reproduction and communal child-rearing as a sinful experiment in "free love." Even so, the community managed to prosper economically by producing and selling silverware of excellent quality.

Fourier Phalanxes. In the 1840s, many Americans, including the newspaper editor Horace Greeley, became interested in the theories of the French socialist Charles Fourier. To solve the problems of a fiercely competitive society, Fourier advocated that people share work and living arrangements in communities popularly known as Fourier Phalanxes. This movement died out, however, almost as quickly as it appeared. Americans proved too individualistic to adapt to communal living.

Arts and Literature

The democratic and reforming impulses of the Age of Jackson expressed themselves in painting, architecture, and literature.

Painting. Genre painting—portraying the everyday life of ordinary people—became the vogue of artists in the 1830s. George Caleb Bingham, for example, depicted the common people in various settings: riding riverboats, voting on election day, and carrying out domestic chores. William S. Mount won fame and popularity for his lively rural compositions. Both Thomas Cole and Frederick Church emphasized the heroic beauty of American landscapes, especially in uplifting dramatic scenes along the Hudson River in New York State and the western frontier wilderness. The Hudson River school, as it was called, expressed the romantic age's fascination with the natural world.

Architecture. Reflecting upon the democracy of ancient Athens, American architects adapted classical Greek styles during the Jacksonian era to glorify the democratic spirit of the republic. Columned facades like those of ancient Greek temples graced the entryways to public buildings, banks, hotels, and even some private homes.

Literature. In addition to the transcendentalist authors (notably Emerson and Thoreau), other writers helped to create a literature that was distinctively American. Partly as a result of the War of 1812, the American people became more nationalistic and eager to read the works of American writers about American themes. Washington Irving and James Fenimore Cooper, for example, wrote fiction using American settings. Cooper's *Leatherstocking Tales* were a series of novels written from 1824 to 1841, that included *The Last of the Mohicans, The Pathfinder,* and *The Deerslayer,* which glorified the frontiersman as nature's nobleman. *The Scarlet Letter* (1850) and other novels by Nathaniel Hawthorne questioned the intolerance and conformity in American life. Herman Melville's innovative novel *Moby-Dick* (1855) reflected the theological and cultural conflicts of the era, as it told the story of Captain Ahab's pursuit of the white whale.

Reforming Society

Reform during the antebellum era went through several stages. At first, the leaders of reform hoped to improve people's behavior through moral persuasion. After they tried sermons and pamphlets, however, reformers often moved on to political action and to ideas for creating new institutions to replace the old.

Temperance

It is easy to understand, given the high rate of alcohol consumption (five gallons of hard liquor per person in 1820), why reformers targeted alcohol as the cause of social ills, and why temperance became the most popular of the reform movements.

The temperance movement was an excellent example of the shift from moral exhortation to political action. In 1826, Protestant ministers and others, concerned with the high rate of alcohol consumption and the effects of such excessive drinking, founded the American Temperance Society. Using moral arguments, the society tried to persuade drinkers not just to moderate their drinking but to take a pledge of total abstinence. Another society, the Washingtonians, was begun in 1840 by recovering alcoholics, who argued that alcoholism was a disease that needed practical, helpful treatment. By the 1840s, the various temperance societies had more than a million members, and it was becoming respectable in middle-class households to drink only cold water. Temperance had become a path to middle-class respectability.

German and Irish immigrants were largely opposed to the temperance reformers' campaign. But they did not have the political power to prevent state and city governments from siding with the reformers. Factory owners and politicians joined with the reformers when it became clear that temperance measures could reduce crime and poverty and increase workers' output on the job. In 1851, the state of Maine went beyond earlier measures that had simply placed taxes on the sale of liquor. Maine became the first of 13 states to prohibit the manufacture and sale of intoxicating liquors before the Civil War. In the late 1850s, the issue of slavery came to overshadow the temperance movement. However, the movement would gain strength again in the late 1870s (with strong support from the Women's Christian Temperance Union) and achieve national success with the passage of the Eighteenth Amendment in 1919.

Movement for Public Asylums

Humanitarian reformers of the 1820s and 1830s called attention to the increasing numbers of criminals, emotionally disturbed persons, and paupers. Often these people were forced to live in wretched conditions and were regularly either abused or neglected by their caretakers. To alleviate the lot of these unfortunates, reformers proposed setting up new public institutions—state-supported prisons, mental hospitals, and poorhouses. They hoped that the inmates of these institutions would be cured of their antisocial behavior as a result of being withdrawn from squalid surroundings and treated to a disciplined pattern of life in some rural setting.

Mental hospitals. Dorothea Dix, a former schoolteacher from Massachusetts, was horrified to find mentally ill persons locked up with convicted criminals in unsanitary cells. She dedicated the rest of her adult life to improving conditions for emotionally disturbed persons. In the 1840s, her travels across the country and reports of awful treatment caused one state legislature after another to build new mental hospitals or improve existing institutions. As a result of Dix's crusade, mental patients began receiving professional treatment at state expense.

Schools for blind and deaf persons. Two other reformers founded special institutions to help people with physical disabilities. Thomas Gallaudet founded a school for the deaf, and Dr. Samuel Gridley Howe founded a school for the blind. By the 1850s, special schools modeled after the work of these reformers had been established in many states of the Union.

Prisons. Taking the place of crude jails and lock-ups were new prisons erected in Pennsylvania. These penitentiaries, as they were called, experimented with the technique of placing prisoners in solitary confinement to force them to reflect on their sins and repent. The experiment was dropped because of the high rate of prisoner suicides. These prison reforms reflected a major doctrine of the asylum movement: structure and discipline would bring about moral reform. Another penal experiment, the Auburn system in New York, enforced rigid rules of discipline while also providing moral instruction and work programs.

Public Education

Another reform movement started in the Jacksonian era focused on the need for establishing free public schools for children of all classes. Middle-class reformers were motivated in part by their fears for the future of the republic posed by growing numbers of the uneducated poor—both immigrant and native-born. Workers' groups in the cities generally supported the reformers' campaign for free (tax-supported) schools.

Free common schools. Horace Mann (1796–1859) was the leading advocate of the common (public) school movement. As secretary of the newly founded Massachusetts Board of Education, Mann worked for improved schools, compulsory attendance for all children, a longer school year, and increased teacher preparation. In the 1840s, the movement for tax-supported schools spread rapidly to other states.

Moral education. Besides the teaching of basic literacy, Mann and other educational reformers wanted children to be instructed in principles of morality. Toward this end, William Holmes McGuffey, a Pennsylvania teacher, created a series of elementary textbooks that became widely accepted as the basis of reading and moral instruction in hundreds of schools. The McGuffey readers extolled the virtues of hard work, punctuality, and sobriety—the kind of behaviors needed in an emerging industrial society.

Objecting to the evangelical Protestant tone of the public schools, Roman Catholic groups founded private schools for the instruction of Catholic and foreign-born children.

Higher education. The religious enthusiasm of the Second Great Awakening helped fuel the growth of private colleges. Beginning in the 1830s, various Protestant denominations founded small denominational colleges, especially in the newer western states (Ohio, Indiana, Illinois, and Iowa). At the same time, several new colleges, including Mt. Holyoke College in Massachusetts (founded by Mary Lyon in 1837) and Oberlin College in Ohio, began to admit women. Adult education was furthered by lyceum lecture societies, which provided speakers like Ralph Waldo Emerson to small-town audiences.

The Changing American Family and Women's Rights Movement

American society was still overwhelmingly rural in the mid-19th century. Even so, the growing part of society that was urban and industrial underwent fundamental changes that would be felt for decades to come. In cities, as a result of office and factory jobs created by the Industrial Revolution, the roles of men and women, husbands and wives were redefined. Men left home to work for salaries or wages six days a week in the office or factory; middle-class women typically remained at home to take charge of the household and children.

Industrialization also had the effect of reducing the economic value of children. In middle-class families, birth control was used to reduce average family size, which declined from 7.04 family members in 1800 to 5.42 in 1830. More affluent women now had the leisure time to devote to religious and moral uplift organizations. The New York Female Moral Reform Society, for example, worked to prevent impoverished young women from being forced into lives of prostitution.

Cult of domesticity. The new definitions of men's and women's roles soon became an established norm in urban, middle-class households. Those holding this view of gender roles expected men to be responsible for economic and political affairs while women concentrated on the care of home and children. The idealized view of women as moral leaders in the home and educators of children has been labeled the cult of domesticity.

Origins of the women's rights movement. Women reformers, especially those involved in the antislavery movement, resented the way men relegated them to secondary roles in the movement and prevented them from taking part fully in policy discussions. Two sisters, Sarah and Angelina Grimke, objected to male opposition to their antislavery activities. In protest, Sarah Grimke wrote her *Letter on the Condition of Women and the Equality of the Sexes* (1837). Another pair of reformers, Lucretia Mott and Elizabeth Cady Stanton, began campaigning for women's rights after they had been barred from speaking at an antislavery convention.

Seneca Falls Convention (1848). The leading feminists met at Seneca Falls, New York, in 1848. At the conclusion of their convention—the first women's rights convention in American history—they issued a document closely modeled after the Declaration of Independence. Their "Declaration of Sentiments" declared that "all men and women are created equal" and listed women's grievances against laws and customs that discriminated against them.

Following the Seneca Falls Convention, Elizabeth Cady Stanton and Susan B. Anthony led the campaign for equal voting, legal, and property rights for women. In the 1850s, however, the issue of women's rights was overshadowed by the crisis over slavery.

Antislavery Movement

Opponents of slavery ranged from moderates who proposed gradual abolition to radicals who urged immediate abolition and freeing slaves without compensating their owners. The Second Great Awakening encouraged many northerners to view slavery as a sin. This view limited the possibilities for compromise and promoted radical abolitionism.

American Colonization Society. The idea of transporting freed slaves to an African colony originated in 1817 with the founding of the American Colonization Society. The idea appealed to antislavery reformers with moderate views and especially to politicians, in part because large numbers of whites with racist attitudes hoped to remove, or banish, free blacks from U.S. society. In 1822, the American Colonization Society established an African American settlement in Monrovia, Liberia. Colonization never proved a practical option, since between 1820 and 1860, the slave population grew from 1.5 to nearly 4 million, while only about 12,000 African Americans were settled in Africa during the same decades.

American Antislavery Society. In 1831, William Lloyd Garrison began publication of an abolitionist newspaper, *The Liberator,* an event that marks the beginning of the radical abolitionist movement. The uncompromising Garrison advocated immediate abolition of slavery in every state and territory without compensating the slaveowners. In 1833, Garrison and other abolitionists founded the American Antislavery Society. Garrison stepped up his attacks by condemning and burning the Constitution as a proslavery document. He argued for "no Union with slaveholders" until they repented for their sins by freeing their slaves.

Liberty party. Garrison's radicalism soon led to a split in the abolitionist movement. Believing that political action was a more practical route to reform than Garrison's moral crusade, a group of northerners formed the Liberty party in 1840. They ran James Birney as their candidate for president in 1840 and 1844. The party's one campaign pledge was to bring about the end of slavery by political and legal means.

Black abolitionists. Escaped slaves and free blacks were among the most outspoken and convincing critics of slavery. A former slave like Frederick Douglass could speak about the brutality and degradation of slavery from firsthand experience. An early follower of Garrison, Douglass later advocated both political and direct action to end slavery and racial prejudice. In 1847, he started the antislavery journal *The North Star.* Other black leaders, such as Harriet Tubman, David Ruggles, Sojourner Truth, and William Still, helped organize the effort to assist fugitive slaves escape to free territory in the North or to Canada, where slavery was prohibited.

Violent abolitionism. David Walker and Henry Highland Garnet were two northern blacks who advocated the most radical solution to the slavery question. They argued that slaves should take action themselves by rising up in revolt against their "masters." In 1831, a Virginia slave named Nat Turner led a revolt in which 55 whites were killed. In retaliation, whites killed hundreds of blacks in brutal fashion and managed to put down the revolt. Before this event, there had been some antislavery sentiment and discussion in the South. After the revolt, fear of future uprisings as well as Garrison's inflamed rhetoric put an end to antislavery talk in the South.

Other Reforms

Efforts to reform individuals and society were not limited to movements for temperance, asylums, free public education, women's rights, and abolition of slavery. Other reforms of the antebellum era included:

- the American Peace Society, founded in 1828 with the objective of abolishing war. It influenced some New England reformers to oppose the later Mexican War.

- laws to protect seamen from being flogged

- dietary reforms (eating whole wheat bread and Sylvester Graham's crackers) to promote good digestion

- dress reform for women (wearing Amelia Bloomer's pantalettes instead of long skirts)

- a new pseudoscience called phrenology (the study of the skull's shape to assess a person's character and ability)

Southern Reaction to Reform

The antebellum reform movement was largely a regional phenomenon. It succeeded at the state level in the northern and western states but had little impact on many areas of the South. While "modernizers" worked to perfect society in the North, southerners were more committed to tradition and slow to support public education and humanitarian reforms. They were alarmed to see northern reformers join forces to support the antislavery movement. Increasingly, they viewed social reform as a northern conspiracy against the southern way of life.

HISTORICAL PERSPECTIVES: MOTIVES FOR REFORM

In her history of antebellum reform, *Freedom's Ferment* (1944), Alice Tyler portrayed the reformers as idealistic humanitarians whose chief goal was to create a just and equitable society for all. Other historians generally accepted Tyler's interpretation.

In recent years, however, historians have questioned whether the reforms were truly motivated by humanitarian concerns. They view such reforms as temperance, asylums, and public education as attempts by the upper and middle classes to control the masses. According to their argument, the temperance movement was designed to control the drinking of the poor and recent immigrants. The chief purpose of penitentiaries was to control crime, of poorhouses to motivate the lower classes to pursue work, and of public schools to "Americanize" the immigrant population. Schools were supported by the wealthy, because they would teach the working class hard work, punctuality, and obedience. Revisionist historians also have discovered that most of the reformers were Whigs, not Jacksonian Democrats.

Some historians have argued that the reformers had multiple motivations for their work. They point out that, although some reasons for reform may have been self-serving and bigoted, most reformers sincerely thought that their ideas for improving society would truly help people. Dorothea Dix, for example, gave two reasons for increased spending for treatment of the mentally ill. Appealing to people's self-interest, she said that the reform would save the public money in the long run. Appealing to their religious and social ideals, she also argued that the reform was humane and morally right. Historians point out further that the most successful reforms were ones that had broad support across society—often for a mix of reasons.

KEY NAMES, EVENTS, AND TERMS

antebellum period	millennialism	New Zion
Second Great Awakening	Church of Latter-Day Saints; Mormons	romantic movement
Timothy Dwight		transcendentalists
revivalism; revival (camp) meetings	Joseph Smith; Brigham Young	Ralph Waldo Emerson, "The American Scholar"

Henry David Thoreau, *Walden,* "On Civil Disobedience"

Brook Farm; George Ripley

feminists

Margaret Fuller

Theodore Parker

utopian communities

Shakers

Robert Owen; New Harmony

Joseph Henry Noyes; Oneida community

Charles Fourier; phalanxes

Horace Greeley

George Caleb Bingham

William S. Mount

Thomas Cole

Frederick Church

Hudson River school

Washington Irving

James Fenimore Cooper

Nathaniel Hawthorne

temperance

American Temperance Society

Washingtonians

Women's Christian Temperance Union

asylum movement

Dorothea Dix

Thomas Gallaudet

Samuel Gridley Howe

penitentiaries

Auburn system

Horace Mann

public school movement

McGuffey readers

women's rights movement

Sarah Grimke, Angelina Grimke

Letter on the Condition of Women and the Equality of the Sexes

Lucretia Mott

Elizabeth Cady Stanton

Seneca Falls Convention (1848)

Susan B. Anthony

American Colonization Society

American Antislavery Society

abolitionism

William Lloyd Garrison; *The Liberator*

Liberty party

Frederick Douglass; *The North Star*

Harriet Tubman

David Ruggles

Sojourner Truth

William Still

David Walker

Henry Highland Garnet

Nat Turner

American Peace Society

Sylvester Graham

Amelia Bloomer

MULTIPLE-CHOICE QUESTIONS

1. The Second Great Awakening was characterized by all of the following EXCEPT

   (A) efforts to counter the rationalism and disbelief of the Revolutionary era

   (B) opportunity for salvation offered to all

   (C) efforts to appeal to people's emotions

   (D) growing unity among Protestant churches

   (E) widespread belief that the second coming of Christ was near

2. Which of the following is true of the American transcendentalists?

   (A) supported government actions and regulations as the solution to social problems

   (B) argued for the importance of human intuition and individualism

   (C) persecuted for their radical religious views

   (D) belonged to an experimental commune that practiced plural marriage

   (E) played a leading role in the Second Great Awakening

3. According to the cult of domesticity, a woman's proper role was

   (A) teaching in the growing number of free public schools

   (B) balancing the obligations of family and career

   (C) striving toward social and economic equality with men

   (D) leading the movement for political and social reform

   (E) acting as moral leader and educator of the family

4. The leading spokesperson for the tax-supported public school movement was

   (A) Neal Dow

   (B) Joseph Smith

   (C) Charles Finney

   (D) Horace Mann

   (E) Timothy Dwight

5. All of the following were true of the temperance movement EXCEPT

   (A) It was largely restricted to the southern states.

   (B) German and Irish immigrants often opposed the movement.

   (C) By the 1850s, the movement advocated the legal prohibition of alcohol.

   (D) The early leaders of the movement were Protestant clergymen.

   (E) It was the most popular of the Jacksonian era reform movements.

6. Dorothea Dix was inspired to dedicate her life to a humanitarian crusade by

   (A) the mistreatment of women factory workers

   (B) conditions in the poorly funded public schools

   (C) discovery of the confinement of the mentally ill in local jails

   (D) the lack of schools for the blind and deaf

   (E) the increased suicide rate in Pennsylvania and New York prisons

7. The abolitionist movement had the effect of

   (A) weakening white southerners' attachment to slavery

   (B) converting most Americans to the abolitionist position

   (C) increasing the chances for compromise between North and South

   (D) proving moral persuasion was more effective than political action

   (E) bringing the issue of slavery to the forefront of the reform movement

8. William Lloyd Garrison and the American Antislavery Society supported

   (A) gradual emancipation of slaves without compensation to owners

   (B) immediate emancipation of slaves without compensation or emigration

   (C) gradual emancipation of slaves with emigration to Asia

(D) immediate emancipation of slaves with compensation to owners

(E) violent overthrow of slavery in the South

9. The Seneca Falls Convention was significant because it

(A) initiated the religious revivals in the "burned-over district"

(B) demanded the immediate abolition of slavery

(C) issued a historic declaration of women's rights

(D) addressed concerns for the education of children

(E) concluded that the Auburn system was a failure

10. Perfectionist aspirations to create a utopian society are best reflected in

(A) the Hudson River School

(B) Thoreau's experiment at Walden Pond

(C) American Colonization Society

(D) the organizing of revivalist camp meetings

(E) the founding of New Harmony, Brook Farm, and Fourier Phalanxes

ESSAY QUESTIONS

1. In what ways did the Second Great Awakening and religion influence the reform movements of the period 1820 to 1860?

2. Explain the popularity and failure of the communal experiments of the 1820-to-1860 period.

3. Assess the extent to which economic changes in American society encouraged TWO of the following reform movements:
public education
temperance
women's rights

4. To what extent were the Transcendentalists and other writers of the era critical of the changes in American society during the period 1820 to 1860?

5. How and why did the antislavery movement become more radical over the period 1815 to 1860?

DOCUMENTS AND READINGS

Nineteenth-century reformers had a deep faith in progress and the perfectibility of the individual and society. As a result, the reform movements of the antebellum era were remarkable for their diversity. The following readings reflect some of the wide range of opinions about goals and the tactics needed to achieve them.

DOCUMENT A.   *THE ARGUMENT FOR FREE PUBLIC SCHOOLS*

As the first secretary of the Massachusetts State Board of Education (1837–1848), Horace Mann developed the Massachusetts public school system into a model for the nation.

> [S]ince the achievement of American independence, the universal and ever-repeated argument in favor of free schools has been that the general intelligence which they are capable of diffusing, and which can be imparted by no other human instrumentality, is indispensable to the continuance of a republic government.
>
> Again, the expediency of free schools is sometimes advocated on grounds of political economy. An educated people is always a more industrious and productive people. Intelligence is a primary ingredient in the wealth of nations. . . .
>
> And yet . . . there is not at the present time, with the exception of the States of New England and a few small communities elsewhere, a country or state in Christendom which maintains a system of free schools for the education of its children. . . .
>
> I believe that this amazing dereliction from duty, especially in our own country, originates more in the false notions which men entertain *respecting the nature of their right to property* than in anything else. . . . The rich man who has not children declares that the exaction of a contribution from him to educate the children of his neighbor is an invasion of his rights of property. The man who has reared and educated a family of children denounces it as a double tax when he is called upon to assist in educating the children of others also. . . .
>
> I believe in the existence of a great immortal, immutable principle of natural law, or natural ethics . . . which proves the *absolute right* to an education of every human being that comes into the world, and which, of course, proves the correlative duty of every government to see the means of that education are provided for all.
>
> The claim of a child, then, to a portion of pre-existent property, begins with the first breath he draws. The new-born infant must have sustenance and shelter and care. If the natural parents are removed or parental ability fails, in a word, if parents either cannot or will not supply the infant's wants, then society at large—the government having assumed to itself the ultimate control of all property—is bound to step in and fill the parent's place. To deny this to any child would be equivalent to a sentence of death. . . .

Horace Mann,
Tenth Annual Report as Secretary of the
Massachusetts State Board of Education, 1848

DOCUMENT B.   A DECLARATION OF WOMEN'S RIGHTS

The delegates to the Seneca Falls Convention of 1848 modified the familiar phrases of the Declaration of Independence to their purposes as champions of women's rights. Their "Declaration of Sentiments" began by asserting: "We hold these truths to be self-evident: that all men and women are created equal." It then went on to enumerate what "he" (men in general) had done to deny women their rights.

The history of mankind is a history of repeated injuries and usurpations on the part of man toward woman, having in direct object the establishment of an absolute tyranny over her. To prove this, let facts be submitted to a candid world.

He has never permitted her to exercise her inalienable right to the elective franchise.

He has compelled her to submit to laws, in the formation of which she had no voice.

He has withheld from her rights which are given to the most ignorant and degraded men—both native and foreigners.

He has made her, if married, in the eye of the law, civilly dead.

He has taken from her all right in property, even to the wages she earns. . . .

He has monopolized nearly all the profitable employments, and from those she is permitted to follow, she receives but a scanty remuneration. He closes against her all the avenues to wealth and distinction which he considers most honorable to himself. As a teacher of theology, medicine, or law she is not known.

He has denied her the facilities for obtaining a thorough education, all colleges being closed against her.

He has created a false public sentiment by giving to the world a different code of morals for men and women, by which moral delinquencies which exclude women from society, are not only tolerated, but deemed of little account in man.

He has endeavored, in every way that he could, to destroy her confidence in her own powers, to lessen her self-respect, and to make her willing to lead a dependent and abject life.

Now, in view of this entire disfranchisement of one-half the people of this country, their social and religious degradation—in view of the unjust laws above mentioned, and because women do feel themselves aggrieved, oppressed, and fraudulently deprived of their most sacred rights, we insist that they have immediate admission to all the rights and privileges which belong to them as citizens of the United States.

Report of the Woman's Rights Convention
Held at Seneca Falls, N.Y., 1848

DOCUMENT C.   *A RADICAL PROPOSAL*

Born into slavery in 1816, Henry Highland Garnet escaped to New York and freedom when he was 11 years old. He graduated from the Oneida Institute in 1840, and three years later, at the age of 27, attended a convention of free blacks at Buffalo, New York. Garnet urged the convention to adopt a resolution calling upon all slaves to rise up in armed revolt. The convention turned down Garnet's proposal by just one vote.

> Brethren, the time has come when you must act for yourselves. It is an old and true saying that, "if hereditary bondsmen would be free, they must themselves strike the blow." You can plead your own cause, and do the work of emancipation better than any others. . . . Think of the undying glory that hangs around the ancient name of Africa—and forget not that you are native-born American citizens, and as such, you are justly entitled to all the rights that are granted to the freest. Think how many tears you have poured out upon the soil which you have cultivated with unrequited toil and enriched with your blood; and then go to your lordly enslavers and tell them plainly, that you *are determined to be free.* Appeal to their sense of justice, and tell them that they have no more right to oppress you than you have to enslave them. . . . Inform them that all you desire is FREEDOM and that nothing else will suffice. Do this, and forever after cease to toil for the heartless tyrants, who give you no other reward but stripes and abuse. If they then commence work of death, they, and not you, will be responsible for the consequences. You had far better all die—*die immediately,* than live slaves, and entail your wretchedness upon your posterity. If you would be free in this generation, here is your only hope. However much you and all of us may desire it, there is not much hope of redemption without the shedding of blood. If you must bleed, let it all come at once— rather *die freemen than to live to be slaves.* . . .

> *A Memorial Discourse,*
> by Henry Highland Garnet, 1843

DOCUMENT D.   *INDIVIDUAL CHANGE VERSUS INSTITUTIONAL REFORM*

Orestes Brownson was one of the more complex reform voices of the pre-Civil War era in United States. In the following selection, he discusses the best means to achieve reform, particularly justice for the growing class of poor working people.

This is our work. There must be no class of our fellow men doomed to toil through life as mere workmen at wages. If wages are tolerated it must be . . . only under such conditions that by the time he is of a proper age to settle in life, he shall have accumulated enough to be an independent laborer on his own capital—on his own farm, or in his own shop. Here is our work. How is it to be done?

Reformers in general answer this question, or what they deem its equivalent, in a manner which we cannot but regard as very unsatisfactory. They would have all men wise, good and happy; but in order to make them so, they tell us that we want not external changes, but internal; and therefore instead of declaiming against society and seeking to disturb existing social arrangements, we should confine ourselves to the individual reason and conscience; seek merely to lead the individual to repentance, and to reformation of life. . . .

This is doubtless a capital theory, and has the advantage that kings, hierarchies, nobilities,—in a word, all who fatten on the toil and blood of their fellows, will feel no difficulty in supporting it. . . . [B]ut we confess that we look not for the regeneration of the race from priests and pedagogues. They have had a fair trial. They cannot construct the temple of God. . . . They merely cry peace, peace, and that too when there is no peace, and can be none.

Now the evils of which we have complained are of a social nature. That is, they have their root in the constitution of society as it is, and they have attained to their present growth by means of social influences, the action of government, of laws, and of systems and institutions upheld by society, and of which individuals are slaves. This being the case, it is evident that they are to be removed only by the action of society, that is, by government, for the action of society *is* government.

We have no faith in those systems of elevating the working classes which propose to elevate them without calling in the aid of government. We must have government, and legislation expressly directed to this end. . . . Following the destruction of the Banks, must come that of all monopolies, of all PRIVILEGE. There are many of these. We cannot specify them all; we therefore select only one, the greatest of them all, the privilege which some have of being born rich and others are born poor. . . . [W]e have abolished hereditary monarchy and hereditary nobility, we must complete the work by abolishing hereditary property.

Orestes Brownson,
"Laboring Classes," 1840

ANALYZING THE DOCUMENTS

1. What were the benefits of free public schools to the individual and society, according to Mann?

2. Identify the political, legal, and economic rights of women, which, according to the Seneca Falls document, were repeatedly abused.

3. How did Garnet's position compare to that of the abolitionists William Lloyd Garrison and Frederick Douglass?

4. Why was Brownson critical of contemporary reformers who advocated only individual or "internal" change?

5. "During the reform era of 1820–1860, reforms that depended on moral changes of the individual were generally accepted and successful, but those that called for institutional change were resisted and unsuccessful."

Assess this statement, using the documents and your knowledge of the various reform movements.

TERRITORIAL AND ECONOMIC EXPANSION, 1830–1860

Away, away with all these cobweb tissues of the rights of discovery, exploration, settlement, . . . [The American claim] is by the right of our manifest destiny to overspread and to possess the whole of the continent which Providence has given us for the development of the great experiment of liberty. . . .

John L. O'Sullivan, *Democratic Review*, 1845

The theme of America's manifest destiny was used by a host of supporters of territorial expansion after the term was penned by O'Sullivan. It spread across the land as the rallying cry for westward expansion. At first, in the 1840s and 1850s, expansionists wanted to see the United States extend westward all the way to the Pacific and southward into Mexico, Cuba, and even Central America. In a later decade, the 1890s, expansionists fixed their sights on acquiring islands in the Pacific and the Caribbean.

The phrase *manifest destiny* expressed the popular belief that the United States had a divine mission to extend its power and civilization across the breadth of North America. Enthusiasm for expansion reached a fever pitch in the 1840s. It was driven by a number of forces: nationalism, population increase, rapid economic development, technological advances, and reform ideals. But by no means were all Americans united behind the idea of manifest destiny and expansionism. Northern critics argued vehemently that at the root of the expansionist drive was the southern ambition to spread slavery into western lands.

Conflicts Over Texas, Maine, and Oregon

U.S. interest in pushing its borders southward into Texas (a Mexican province) and westward into the Oregon Territory (claimed by Britain) was largely the result of American pioneers migrating into these lands during the 1820s–1830s.

221

Texas

In 1823, after having won its national independence from Spain, Mexico hoped to attract settlers—even Anglo settlers—to farm its sparsely populated northern frontier province of Texas. Moses Austin, a Missouri banker, had obtained a large land grant in Texas but died before he could carry out his plan to recruit American settlers for the land. His son, Stephen Austin, succeeded in bringing 300 families into Texas and thereby beginning a steady migration of American settlers into the vast frontier territory. By 1830, Americans (both white farmers and black slaves) outnumbered the Mexicans in Texas by three to one.

Friction developed between the Americans and the Mexicans when, in 1829, Mexico outlawed slavery and required all immigrants to convert to Roman Catholicism. When many settlers refused to obey these laws, Mexico closed Texas to additional American immigrants. Land-hungry Americans from the southern states ignored the Mexican prohibition and streamed into Texas by the thousands.

Revolt and independence. A change in Mexico's government intensified the conflict. In 1834, General Antonio López de Santa Anna made himself dictator of Mexico and abolished that nation's federal system of government. When Santa Anna insisted on enforcing Mexico's laws in Texas, a group of American settlers led by Sam Houston revolted and declared Texas to be an independent republic (March 1836).

A Mexican army led by Santa Anna captured the town of Goliad and attacked the Alamo in San Antonio, killing every one of its American defenders. Shortly afterward, however, at the Battle of the San Jacinto River, an army under Sam Houston caught the Mexicans by surprise and captured their general, Santa Anna. Under the threat of death, the Mexican leader was forced to sign a treaty that recognized Texas' independence and granted the new republic all territory north of the Rio Grande. When the news of San Jacinto reached Mexico City, however, the Mexican legislature rejected the treaty and insisted that Texas was still part of Mexico.

Annexation denied. As the first president of the Republic of Texas (or Lone Star Republic), Houston applied to the U.S. government for his country to be annexed, or added to, the United States as a new state. Both presidents Jackson and Van Buren, however, put off Texas' request for annexation primarily because of political opposition among northerners to the expansion of slavery and the potential addition of up to five new slave states created out of the Texas territories. The threat of a costly war with Mexico also dampened expansionist zeal. The next president, John Tyler (1841–1845), was a southern Whig, who was worried about the growing influence of the British in Texas. He worked to annex Texas, but the U.S. Senate rejected his treaty of annexation in 1844.

Boundary Dispute in Maine

Another diplomatic issue arose in the 1840s over the ill-defined boundary between Maine and the Canadian province of New Brunswick. At this time, Canada was still under British rule, and many Americans regarded Britain as their country's worst enemy—an attitude carried over from two previous wars (the Revolution and the War of 1812). A conflict between rival groups of lumbermen on the Maine-Canadian border erupted into open fighting. Known as the Aroostook War, or "battle of the maps," the conflict was soon resolved in a treaty negotiated by U.S. Secretary of State Daniel Webster and the British ambassador, Lord Alexander Ashburton. In the Webster-Ashburton Treaty of 1842, the disputed territory was split between Maine and British Canada. The treaty also settled the boundary of the Minnesota territory, leaving what proved to be the iron-rich Mesabi range on the U.S. side of the border.

Boundary Dispute in Oregon

A far more serious British-American dispute involved Oregon, a vast territory on the Pacific Coast that originally stretched as far north as the Alaskan border. At one time, this territory was claimed by four different nations: Spain, Russia, Great Britain, and the United States. Spain gave up its claim to Oregon in a treaty with the United States (the Adams-Onis Treaty of 1819).

Britain based its claim to Oregon on the Hudson Fur Company's profitable fur trade with the Native Americans of the Pacific Northwest. By 1846, however, there were fewer than a thousand Britishers living north of the Columbia River.

The United States based its claim on (1) the discovery of the Columbia River by Captain Robert Gray in 1792, (2) the overland expedition to the Pacific Coast by Meriwether Lewis and William Clark in 1805, and (3) the fur trading post and fort in Astoria, Oregon, established by John Jacob Astor in 1811. Protestant missionaries and farmers from the United States settled the Willamette Valley in the 1840s. Their success in farming this fertile valley caused 5,000 Americans to catch "Oregon fever" and travel 2,000 miles over the Oregon Trail to settle in the area south of the Columbia River.

By the time of the election of 1844, many Americans believed it to be their country's manifest destiny to take undisputed possession of all of Oregon and to annex the Republic of Texas as well. In addition, expansionists hoped to persuade Mexico to give up its province on the West Coast—the huge land of California. By 1845, Mexican California had a small Spanish-Mexican population of some 7,000 along with a much larger number of Native Americans, but American emigrants were arriving in sufficient numbers "to play the Texas game."

The Election of 1844

Because slavery was allowed in Texas, many northerners were opposed to its annexation. Leading the northern wing of the Democratic party, former president Martin Van Buren opposed immediate annexation. Challenging him for the Democratic nomination in 1844 was the proslavery, proannexation southerner, John C. Calhoun. The dispute between these candidates caused the Democratic convention to deadlock and, after hours of wrangling, the Democrats finally nominated a *dark horse* (lesser known candidate). The man they chose, James K. Polk of Tennessee, had been a protegé of Andrew Jackson. Firmly committed to expansion and manifest destiny, Polk favored the annexation of Texas, the "reoccupation" of all of Oregon, and the acquisition of California. The Democratic slogan "Fifty-four Forty or Fight!" appealed strongly to American westerners and southerners who in 1844 were in an expansionist mood. ("Fifty-four forty" referred to the line of latitude that marked the border between the Oregon Territory and Russian Alaska.)

Henry Clay of Kentucky, the Whig nominee, attempted to straddle the controversial issue of Texas annexation, saying at first that he was against it and later that he was for it. This strategy alienated a group of voters in New York State, who abandoned the Whig party to support the antislavery Liberty party (see Chapter 11). In a close election, the Whigs' loss of New York's electoral votes proved decisive, and Polk, the Democratic dark horse, was the victor. The Democrats interpreted the election as a mandate to add Texas to the Union.

Annexing Texas and Dividing Oregon

Outgoing president John Tyler took the election of Polk as a signal to push the annexation of Texas through Congress. Instead of seeking Senate approval of a treaty, Tyler persuaded both houses of Congress to pass a joint resolution for annexation. This procedure had the advantage of requiring only a simple majority of each house. To Polk was left the problem of dealing with Mexico's reaction to annexation.

On the Oregon question, Polk decided to compromise with Britain and back down from his party's bellicose campaign slogan, "Fifty-four Forty or Fight!" Rather than fighting for all of Oregon, the president was willing to settle for just the southern half of it. British and American negotiators agreed to divide the Oregon territory at the 49th parallel (the parallel that had been established in 1818 for the Louisiana territory). Final settlement of the issue was delayed until the United States agreed to grant Vancouver Island to Britain and guarantee its right to navigate the Columbia River. In June 1846, the treaty was submitted to the Senate for ratification. Some northerners viewed the treaty as a sellout to southern interests because it removed British Columbia as a source of potential free states. Nevertheless, by this time war had broken out between the United States and Mexico. Not wanting to fight both Britain and Mexico, Senate opponents of the treaty reluctantly voted for the compromise settlement.

War With Mexico

The U.S. annexation of Texas led quickly to diplomatic trouble with Mexico. Shortly after taking office in 1845, President Polk dispatched John Slidell as his special envoy to the government in Mexico City. Polk wanted Slidell to (1) persuade Mexico to sell the California and New Mexico territories to the United States and (2) settle a dispute concerning the Mexico-Texas border. Slidell's mission failed on both counts. The Mexican government refused to sell California and insisted that Texas' southern border was on the Nueces River. Polk and Slidell asserted that the border lay farther to the south, along the Rio Grande.

Immediate Causes of the War

While Slidell waited for Mexico City's response to the U.S. offer, Polk ordered General Zachary Taylor to move his army toward the Rio Grande across territory claimed by Mexico. On April 24, 1846, a Mexican army crossed the Rio Grande and captured an American army patrol, killing 11. Polk used the incident to send his already prepared war message to Congress. Northern Whigs (among them, a freshman Illinois Congressman named Abraham Lincoln) opposed going to war over the incident and doubted that American blood had been shed on American soil, as the president claimed. Nevertheless, Whig protests were in vain; a large majority in both houses approved the war resolution.

Military Campaigns

Most of the war was fought in Mexican territory by relatively small armies of Americans. Leading a force that never exceeded 1,500, General Stephen Kearney succeeded in taking Santa Fe, the New Mexico territory, and southern California. Backed by only several dozen soldiers, a few navy officers, and American civilians who had recently settled in California, John C. Frémont quickly overthrew Mexican rule in northern California (June 1846) and proclaimed California to be an independent republic with a bear on its flag—the so-called Bear Flag Republic.

Meanwhile, Zachary Taylor's force of 6,000 men drove the Mexican army from Texas, crossed the Rio Grande into northern Mexico, and won a major victory at Buena Vista (February 1847). President Polk then selected General Winfield Scott to invade central Mexico. The army of 14,000 under Scott's command succeeded in taking the coastal city of Vera Cruz and then captured Mexico City in September 1847.

Consequences of the War

For Mexico, the war was a military disaster from the start, but the Mexican government was unwilling to sue for peace and concede the loss of its northern lands. Finally, after the fall of Mexico City, the government had little choice but to agree to U.S. terms.

Treaty of Guadalupe Hidalgo—Mexican Cession (1848). The treaty negotiated in Mexico by American diplomat Nicholas Trist provided for the following:

1. Mexico would recognize the Rio Grande as the southern border of Texas.

2. The United States would take possession of the former Mexican provinces of California and New Mexico—the Mexican Cession. For these territories, the United States would pay $15 million and assume the claims of American citizens against Mexico.

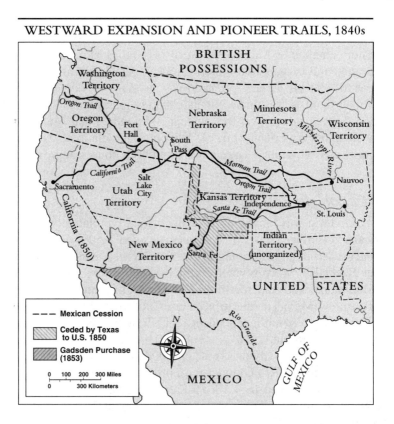

WESTWARD EXPANSION AND PIONEER TRAILS, 1840s

In the Senate, some Whigs opposed the treaty because they saw the war as an immoral effort to expand slavery. A few southern Democrats disliked the treaty for opposite reasons; as expansionists, they wanted the United States to take all of Mexico. Nevertheless, the treaty was finally ratified in the Senate by the required two-thirds vote.

Wilmot Proviso. U.S. entry into a war with Mexico provoked controversy from start to finish. In 1846, the first year of war, Pennsylvania Congressman David Wilmot proposed that an appropriations bill be amended to forbid slavery in any of the new territories acquired from Mexico. The Wilmot Proviso, as it was called, passed the House twice but was defeated in the Senate.

Prelude to civil war? By increasing tensions between the North and the South, did the war to acquire territories from Mexico lead inevitably to the American Civil War? Without question, the acquisition of vast western lands did renew the sectional debate over the extension of slavery. Many northerners viewed the war with Mexico as part of a southern plot to extend the "slave power." Some historians see the Wilmot Proviso as the first round in an escalating political conflict that led ultimately to civil war.

Manifest Destiny to the South

Many southerners were dissatisfied with the territorial gains from the Mexican War. In the early 1850s, they hoped to acquire new territories, especially in areas of Latin America where plantations worked by slaves were thought to be economically feasible. The most tempting, eagerly sought possibility in the eyes of southern expansionists was the acquisition of Cuba.

Ostend Manifesto. President Polk offered to purchase Cuba from Spain for $100 million, but Spain refused to sell the last major remnant of its once glorious empire. Several southern adventurers led small expeditions to Cuba in an effort to take the island by force of arms. These forays, however, were easily defeated, and those who participated were executed by Spanish firing squads.

Elected to the presidency in 1852, Franklin Pierce adopted prosouthern policies and dispatched three American diplomats to Ostend, Belgium, where they secretly negotiated to buy Cuba from Spain. The Ostend Manifesto that the diplomats drew up was leaked to the press in the United States and provoked an angry reaction from antislavery members of Congress. President Pierce was forced to drop the scheme.

Walker Expedition. Expansionists continued to seek new empires with or without the federal government's support. Southern adventurer William Walker had tried unsuccessfully to take Baja California from Mexico in 1853. Finally, leading a force mostly of southerners, he took over Nicaragua in 1855. Walker's regime even gained temporary recognition from the United States in 1856. His grandiose scheme to develop a proslavery Central American empire collapsed, however, when a coalition of Central American countries invaded and defeated him. Walker was executed by Honduran authorities in 1860.

Clayton-Bulwer Treaty (1850). Another American ambition concerned the building of a canal through Central America. Wanting to check each other from seizing this opportunity, Great Britain and the United States agreed to a treaty in 1850 (the Clayton-Bulwer Treaty). It provided that neither nation would attempt to take exclusive control of any future canal route in Central America. This treaty continued in force until the end of the century. A new treaty signed in 1901 (the Hay-Pauncefote Treaty) gave the United States a free hand to build a canal without British participation.

Gadsden Purchase. Although he failed to acquire Cuba, President Pierce succeeded in adding a strip of land to the American Southwest for a railroad. In 1853, Mexico agreed to sell thousands of acres of semidesert land to the United States for $10 million. Known as the Gadsden Purchase, the land forms the southern sections of present-day New Mexico and Arizona.

Expansion After the Civil War

From 1855 until 1870, the issues of union, slavery, civil war, and postwar reconstruction would overshadow the drive to acquire new territory. Even so, manifest destiny continued to be an important force for shaping U.S. policy. In 1867, for example, Secretary of State William Seward succeeded in purchasing Alaska at a time when the nation was just recovering from the Civil War.

Settlement of the Western Territories

Following the peaceful acquisition of Oregon and the more violent acquisition of California, the migration of Americans into these lands began in earnest. The arid area between the Mississippi Valley and the Pacific Coast was popularly known in the 1850s and 1860s as the Great American Desert. Emigrants passed quickly over this vast, dry region to reach the more inviting lands on the West Coast. Therefore, California and Oregon were settled several decades before people attempted to farm the Great Plains.

Fur Traders' Frontier

Fur traders known as mountain men were the earliest nonnative group to open the Far West. In the 1820s, they held yearly rendezvous in the Rockies with Native Americans to trade for animal skins. James Beckwourth, Jim Bridger, Kit Carson, and Jedediah Smith were among the hardy band of explorers and trappers who provided much of the early information about trails and frontier conditions.

Overland Trails

The next and much larger group of pioneers took the hazardous journey west in hopes of clearing the forests and farming the fertile valleys of California and Oregon. By 1860, hundreds of thousands had reached their westward goal by following the Oregon, California, Santa Fe, and Mormon trails. The long and arduous trek usually began in St. Joseph or Independence, Missouri, or in Council Bluffs, Iowa, and followed the river valleys through the Great Plains. Months later, the wagon trains would finally reach the foothills of the Rockies or face the hardships of the southwestern deserts. The final life-or-death challenge was to get through the mountain passes of the Sierras and Cascades before the first heavy snow. A wagon train inched westward at an average rate of only 15 miles a day. Far more serious than any threat of attack by Indians were the daily experience of disease and depression from harsh conditions on the trail.

Mining Frontier

The discovery of gold in California in 1848 set off the first of many migrations to the mineral-rich mountains of the West. The gold rush to California (1848–1850) was followed by gold or silver rushes in Colorado, Nevada, the Black Hills of the Dakotas, and other western territories. The mining boom brought tens of thousands of men (and afterward women as well) into the western mountains. Mining camps and towns—many of them short-lived— sprang up wherever a strike (discovery) was reported. Largely as a result of the gold rush, California's population soared from a mere 14,000 in 1848 to 380,000 by 1860.

What is often forgotten is that the discoveries of gold and silver attracted miners from around the world. By the 1860s, almost one-third of the miners in the West were Chinese.

Farming Frontier

Most pioneer families moved west to start homesteads and begin farming. Congress' Preemption Acts of the 1830s and 1840s gave squatters the right to settle public lands and purchase them for low prices once the government put them up for sale. In addition, the government made it easier for settlers by offering parcels of land as small as 40 acres for sale.

However, the move to western lands was not for the penniless. A family needed at least $200 to $300 to make the overland trip, which eliminated many of the poor and made the trek to California and Oregon largely a middle-class movement.

The isolation of the frontier made life for pioneers especially difficult during the first years, but rural communities soon developed. The institutions that the people established (schools, churches, clubs, and political parties) were modeled after those that they had known in the East or, for immigrants from abroad, in their native lands.

Urban Frontier

Western cities that arose as a result of railroads (see below), mineral wealth, and farming attracted a number of professionals and businesspersons. San Francisco and Denver are examples of instant cities created by the gold and silver rushes. Salt Lake City grew because it offered fresh supplies to travelers on overland trails for the balance of their westward journey.

The Expanding Economy

The era of territorial expansion coincided with a period of remarkable economic growth from the 1840s to 1857.

Industrial Technology

Before 1840, factory production had mainly been concentrated in the textile mills of New England. After 1840, industrialization spread rapidly to the other states of the Northeast. The new factories produced shoes, sewing machines, ready-to-wear clothing, firearms, precision tools, and iron products for railroads and other new technologies. The invention of the sewing machine by Elias Howe took much of the production of clothing out of the home into the factory. An electric telegraph successfully demonstrated in 1844 by its inventor, Samuel F. B. Morse, went hand in hand with the growth of railroads in enormously speeding up communication and transportation across the country.

Railroads

The canal-building era of the 1820s and 1830s was replaced in the next two decades with the rapid expansion of rail lines, especially across the Northeast and Midwest. The railroads soon emerged as America's largest industry. As such, they required immense amounts of capital and labor and gave rise to complex business organizations. Local merchants and farmers would often buy stocks in the new railroad companies in order to connect their area to the outside world. Local and state governments also helped the railroads grow by granting special loans and tax breaks. In 1850, the U.S. government granted 2.6 million acres of federal land to build the Illinois Central Railroad from Lake Michigan to the Gulf of Mexico, the first such federal land grant.

Cheap and rapid transportation particularly promoted western agriculture. Farmers in Illinois and Iowa were now more closely linked to the Northeast by rail than by the river routes to the South. The railroads not only united the common commercial interests of the Northeast and Midwest, but would also give the North strategic advantages in the Civil War.

Foreign Commerce

The growth in manufactured goods as well as in agricultural products (both western grains and southern cotton) caused a significant growth of exports and imports. Other factors also played a role in the expansion of U.S. trade in the mid-1800s:

1. Shipping firms encouraged trade and travel across the Atlantic by having their sailing packets depart on a regular schedule (instead of the unscheduled departures that had been customary in the 18th century).

2. The demand for whale oil to light the homes of middle-class Americans caused a whaling boom between 1830 and 1860, in which New England merchants took the lead.

3. Improvements in the design of ships came just in time to speed gold-seekers on their journey to the California gold fields. The development of the American clipper ship cut the five- or six-month trip from New York around the Horn to San Francisco to as little as 89 days.

4. Steamships took the place of clipper ships in the mid-1850s because they had greater storage capacity, could be maintained at lower cost, and could more easily follow a regular schedule.

5. The federal government played a role in expanding U.S. trade by sending Commodore Matthew C. Perry to Japan to persuade that country to open up its ports to trade with Americans. In 1854, Perry convinced Japan's government to agree to a treaty that opened two Japanese ports to U.S. trading vessels.

Panic of 1857. The midcentury economic boom ended in 1857 with a financial panic. There was a serious drop in prices, especially for midwestern farmers, and increased unemployment in northern cities. The South was less affected, for cotton prices remained high. This fact gave some southerners the idea that their plantation economy was superior and that continued union with the northern economy was not needed.

HISTORICAL PERSPECTIVES: MANIFEST DESTINY

Traditional historians stressed the accomplishments of westward expansion in bringing civilization and democratic institutions to a wilderness area. The heroic efforts of mountain men and pioneering families to overcome a hostile environment have long been celebrated by both historians and the popular media.

In recent years, a number of historians have taken a different and more critical view of manifest destiny and U.S. actions in the war with Mexico. They suggest that there were strong racist motives behind U.S. foreign policy in the 1840s and quote extensively from minority voices of the period who had condemned the Mexican War as a plot to expand slavery. These historians argue that there may have been racist motives even behind the decision to withdraw U.S. troops from Mexico instead of attempting to conquer and occupy that country. They point out that Americans who opposed the idea of keeping Mexico had resorted to racist arguments, asserting that it would be undesirable to incorporate large non-Anglo populations into the republic.

As a result of the civil rights movement of the 1950s and 1960s, historians today are more sensitive than earlier historians to racist language and beliefs. They see the racial undercurrents in the political speeches of the 1840s that argued for expansion into Native American, Mexican, and Central American territories. Rather than concentrating on the achievements of Anglo pioneers, recent histories of the westward movement tend to focus on the following: (a) the impact on Native Americans, who were dispossessed from their lands, (b) the influence of Mexican culture on U.S. culture, (c) the contributions of African American and Asian American pioneers on the frontier, and (d) the role of women in the development of western family and community life.

In addition, we should consider how Mexican historians view the events of the 1840s. As they point out, the Treaty of Guadalupe Hidalgo took half of its territory from Mexico. From the Mexican point of view, the war of 1846 gave rise to a number of long-standing economic and political problems, which have impeded Mexico's development as a modern nation.

From another perspective, the war with Mexico and especially the taking of California were motivated by imperialism rather than by racism. Historians taking this position argue that the United States was chiefly interested in trade with China and Japan and needed California as a base for U.S. commercial ambitions in the Pacific. U.S. policy makers were afraid that California would fall into the hands of Great Britain or some other European power if the United States did not move in first.

KEY NAMES, EVENTS, AND TERMS

manifest destiny	Webster-Ashburton Treaty (1842)	Stephen Kearney
Texas		Winfield Scott
Stephen Austin	Oregon territory	John C. Frémont
Antonio López de Santa Anna	"Fifty-four Forty or Fight!"	California; Bear Flag Republic
Sam Houston	James K. Polk	Treaty of Guadalupe Hidalgo (1848)
Alamo	Rio Grande; Nueces River	
John Tyler	Mexican War (1846–1847)	Mexican Cession
Aroostook War	Zachary Taylor	Wilmot Proviso

Franklin Pierce	Far West	Elias Howe
Ostend Manifesto (1852)	overland trails	Samuel F. B. Morse
Walker Expedition	mining frontier	railroads; federal land grants
Clayton-Bulwer Treaty (1850)	gold rush; silver rush	foreign commerce; exports
Gadsden Purchase (1853)	farming frontier	and imports
Great American Desert	urban frontier	Matthew C. Perry; Japan
mountain men	industrial technology	Panic of 1857

MULTIPLE-CHOICE QUESTIONS

1. Which of the following BEST reflected the idea of manifest destiny?
   - (A) the signing of the Webster-Ashburton Treaty
   - (B) Henry Clay's position on Texas in the election of 1844
   - (C) the establishment of Texas as an independent republic
   - (D) the campaign platform of James Polk in 1844
   - (E) northern Whigs during the Mexican War

2. All of the following contributed to the conflict between Mexico's government and settlers in Texas in the early 1830s EXCEPT
   - (A) the collection of import duties
   - (B) the support for annexation by John Tyler and James Polk
   - (C) Mexico's decision to abolish slavery in its territory
   - (D) Mexico's law requiring acceptance of the Catholic faith
   - (E) the coming to power of General Santa Anna

3. The main reason for the U.S. delay in annexing Texas was the
   - (A) controversy over the boundary of Texas and Mexico

   - (B) opposition of Great Britain and France
   - (C) independent spirit of the settlers in Texas
   - (D) opposition in Congress to adding slave states
   - (E) opposition of the Mexican government

4. Which of the following was the LEAST important issue in the election of 1844?
   - (A) settlement of the Oregon border
   - (B) acquisition of California
   - (C) rechartering the Bank of the United States
   - (D) reduction of the tariff
   - (E) annexation of Texas

5. Which of the following was NOT a major consequence of the U.S. war with Mexico?
   - (A) U.S. annexation of Texas
   - (B) long-term Mexican resentment against the United States
   - (C) securing Texas' southern border on the Rio Grande
   - (D) increased sectional tensions over slavery
   - (E) cession of California and New Mexico to the United States

6. Which of the following is a correct statement about the Wilmot Proviso?

(A) It forbade the introduction of slavery into territory acquired from Mexico.

(B) It denied President Polk additional funds to conduct the war with Mexico.

(C) It compromised differences between the North and the South.

(D) It passed both houses of Congress but was vetoed by the president.

(E) It was proposed by the Whigs to embarrass the Democrats.

7. Which of the following is LEAST useful in arguing that territorial expansion was motivated by a desire to spread slavery?

(A) William Walker's campaign in Nicaragua

(B) the Ostend Manifesto

(C) the slogan "Fifty-four Forty or Fight"

(D) the annexation of Texas

(E) opposition to the Wilmot Proviso

8. During the settlement of the West, all of the following were true EXCEPT

(A) the overland trails were used primarily by the very poor

(B) a large percentage of the western miners were foreign-born

(C) the mountain men provided much of the early information about the West

(D) in the 1830s and 1840s, the U.S. government gave squatters the right to buy federal lands

(E) the chief interest of most pioneering families who moved West was to engage in agriculture

9. Which of the following had the greatest impact on transportation in the 1850s?

(A) canal building

(B) improvements in the steamboat

(C) the expansion of railroads

(D) the development of clipper ships

(E) changes in design of the overland wagon

10. In what way did the Panic of 1857 have an effect on sectional conflict?

(A) Unemployment increased in the eastern manufacturing centers.

(B) Prices for farm products fell, especially in midwestern states.

(C) The South blamed the North for falling cotton prices.

(D) Southerners concluded that their economic system was superior to the North's.

(E) The North gained the necessary economic advantages to defeat the South when civil war broke out.

ESSAY QUESTIONS

1. Analyze the use of diplomacy by the United States in TWO of the following territorial disputes:

   annexation of Texas

   boundary of Maine

   boundary of Oregon

2. How did the belief in manifest destiny influence U.S. politics and policies in the 1840s?

3. Analyze the causes and results of the Mexican War.

4. Assess the role of TWO of the following in the development of the territories west of the Mississippi River between 1820 and 1860:

   fur traders

   overland trails

   mining

   farming

5. Compare and contrast the expansionist policies of President Jefferson and President Polk.

DOCUMENT-BASED QUESTION

To what extent did manifest destiny and territorial expansion unite or divide the United States from 1830 to 1860?

Use the documents and your knowledge of the period 1830 to 1860 to construct your response.

DOCUMENT A.

After twenty-five years, the American population has begun to extend itself to the Oregon. Some hundreds went a few years ago; a thousand went last year; two thousand are now setting out from the frontier of Missouri; tens of thousands are meditating the adventure. I say to them all, Go on! the Government will follow you, and will give protection and land. . . .

Let the emigrants go on, and carry their rifles. We want thirty thousand rifles in the valley of the Oregon; they will make all quiet there, in the event of a war with Great Britain for the domination of that country. Thirty thousand rifles on the Oregon will annihilate the Hudson Bay Company, drive them off our continent, quiet their Indians, and protect the American interests in all the vast region of the Rocky Mountains. Besides . . . the settlers in Oregon will also recover and open for us the North American road to India!

Thomas Hart Benton of Missouri,
Speech in the U.S. Senate, 1844

DOCUMENT B.

I proceed now to a consideration of what is to me the strongest argument against annexing Texas to the United States. This measure will extend and perpetuate slavery. . . .

As far back as the year 1829, the annexation of Texas was agitated in the Southern and Western States; and it was urged on the ground of the strength and extension it would give to the slaveholding interest. . . . The great argument for annexing Texas is, that it will strengthen "the peculiar institution" of the South, and open a new and vast field for slavery. . . .

By this act, slavery will be perpetuated in the old States as well as spread over new. It is well known, that the soil of some of the old states has become exhausted by slave cultivation. . . . It is by slave breeding and slave selling that these states subsist. . . . By annexing Texas, we shall not only create [slavery] where it does not exist, but breathe new life into it, where its end seemed to be near. States, which might and ought to throw it off, will make the multiplication of slaves their great aim and chief resource.

Reverend William Ellery Channing,
A Letter to Hon. Henry Clay, 1837

DOCUMENT C.

[The slave] population of the United States cannot be diminished, but must be increased. Now, if we shall annex Texas, it will operate as a safety-valve to let off the superabundant slave population from among us; and will, at the same time, improve their condition. They will be more happy, and we all shall be more secure . . .

Senator George McDuffie of South Carolina,
Congressional Globe, 1844

DOCUMENT D.

California will, probably, next fall away from [Mexico]. . . . The Anglo-Saxon foot is already on its borders. Already the advance guard of the irresistible army of Anglo-Saxon emigration has begun to pour down upon it, armed with the plough and the rifle, and marking its trail with schools and colleges, courts and representative halls, mills and meeting-houses. A population will soon be in actual occupation of California, over which it be idle for Mexico to dream of dominion. They will necessarily become independent. All this without ... responsibility of our people—in the natural flow of events.

John L. O'Sullivan,
Democratic Review, 1845

DOCUMENT E.

Why, says the chairman of this Committee on Foreign Relations, it is the most reasonable thing in the world! We ought to have the Bay of San Francisco. Why? Because it is the best harbor on the Pacific! It has been my fortune, Mr. President, to have practiced a good deal in criminal courts in the course of my life, but I have never yet heard a thief, arraigned for stealing a horse, plead that it was the best horse that he could find in the country! We want California. What for? Why, says the Senator from Michigan, we will have it; and the Senator from South Carolina, with a very mistaken view, I think, of policy, says you can't keep our people from going there. I don't desire to prevent them. Let them go and seek their happiness in whatever country or clime it pleases them.

Senator Thomas Corwin of Ohio,
Congressional Globe, 1845

DOCUMENT F.

None can fail to see the danger to our safety and future peace if Texas remains an independent state, or becomes an ally or dependency of some foreign nation more powerful than herself. Is there one among our citizens who would not prefer perpetual peace with Texas to occasional wars, which often occur between bordering independent nations? Is there one who would not prefer free intercourse with her, to high duties on all our products and manufactures which enter her ports or cross her frontiers? Is there one who would not prefer an unrestricted communication with her citizens, to the frontier obstructions which must occur if she remains out of the Union?

President James Polk,
Inaugural Address, 1845

DOCUMENT G.

Resolved, That the present war with Mexico has its primary origin in the unconstitutional annexation to the United States of the foreign state of Texas while the same was still at war with Mexico; that it was unconstitutionally commenced by the order of the President, to General Taylor, to take military possession of territory in dispute between the United States and Mexico, and in the occupation of Mexico; and that it is now waged ingloriously—by a powerful nation against a weak neighbor—unnecessarily and without just cause, at immense cost of a portion of her territory, from which slavery has already been excluded, with the triple object of extending slavery, of strengthening "Slave Power," and of obtaining the control of the Free States, under the Constitution of the United States.

Resolved, That our attention is directed anew to the the wrong and "enormity" of slavery, and to the tyranny and usurpation of the "Slave Power," as displayed in the history of our country, particularly in the annexation of Texas and the present war with Mexico. . . .

Charles Sumner,
Legislature of Massachusetts, 1847

DOCUMENT H.

The [Mexican] race is perfectly accustomed to being conquered, and the only new lesson we shall teach is that our victories will give liberty, safety, and prosperity to the vanquished. To *liberate* and *ennoble*—not to *enslave* and *debase*—is our mission. Well may the Mexican nation, whose great masses have never yet tasted liberty, prattle over their lost phantom of nationality. . . . [T]here is no excuse for the man educated under our institutions, who talks of our "wronging the Mexicans" when we offer them a position infinitely above any they have occupied, since their history began, and in which, for the first time, they may aim at the greatness and dignity of a truly republican and self-governing people.

Editor, New York *Sun,*
November 20, 1847

GUIDE TO ORGANIZING A DBQ ESSAY

The document-based question (DBQ) challenges you to create an essay that demonstrates both your understanding of the documents *and* your knowledge of the period. To get an idea of how such an essay is constructed, study the Building Blocks table, below.

As an exercise in organizing the DBQ essay, you might develop a different thesis—one in which you argue that slavery was only a secondary issue, not a "root cause," of expansionism. Study the Building Blocks table to see how you might organize your evidence and line of argument.

Building Blocks for a DBQ on Expansionism

Thesis statement: Although slavery was not the sole underlying cause for expansionism in the mid-19th century, it was a primary motivating force behind U.S. dealings with Texas and Mexico.

Knowledge of events and issues	Documents
1 *Expansionist policies that were unrelated to slavery*	
Dispute over Oregon	A. Benton's speech on Oregon
Ambition to acquire California (imperialist rivalry with other nations)	D. Sullivan on California
Gadsden Purchase and railroad interests	F. Corwin on California
2 *Slavery as a key issue in case of Texas and the Mexican War*	
Change in Mexico's law on slavery as cause of Texas revolt	B. Channing letter
Slavery as major issue in annexation debate: support of southerners, opposition of northerners	C. McDuffie
	G. Sumner on Mexican War
3 *Slavery as a key issue in southern ambition to acquire Cuba and Nicaragua*	
Pierce's policy and Ostend Manifesto	
Walker expedition to Nicaragua	

An **evaluation** of the available evidence in the form of documents and key historical events reveals that slavery was a critical issue with respect to Texas and Cuba, less critical with respect to Oregon and California.

Summarize and **restate** thesis

THE UNION IN PERIL, 1848–1861

The real issue in this controversy—the one pressing upon every mind—is the sentiment on the part of one class that looks upon the institution of slavery as a wrong, and of another class that does not look upon it as a wrong.

Abraham Lincoln, 1858

Nobody disagrees about the sequence of major events from 1848 to 1861 that led ultimately to the outbreak of the Civil War between the northern and southern states. Facts in themselves, however, do not automatically assemble themselves into a convincing interpretation of *why* war occurred when it did. Historians have identified at least four main causes of the conflict between the North and the South: (1) *slavery,* as a growing moral issue in the North, versus its defense and expansion in the South; (2) *constitutional disputes* over the nature of the federal Union and states' rights; (3) *economic differences* between the industrializing North and the agricultural South over such issues as tariffs, banking, and internal improvements; (4) *political blunders and extremism* on both sides, which some historians conclude resulted in an unnecessary war. This chapter summarizes the events leading up to Lincoln's election and the secession of the southern states from the Union. In attempting to understand the events and issues, it remains your task to decide the relative importance of the causes of this national tragedy.

Conflict Over Status of Territories

The issue of slavery in the territories gained in the Mexican War became the focus of sectional differences in the late 1840s. The Wilmot Proviso, which excluded slavery from the new territories, would have upset the Compromise of 1820 and the delicate balance of 15 free and 15 slave states. Its defeat only intensified sectional feelings. On the issue of how to deal with these new western territories, there were essentially three conflicting positions.

Free-Soil Movement

Northern Democrats and Whigs supported the Wilmot Proviso and the position that all blacks—slave and free—should be excluded from the Mexican

Cession (territory ceded to the U.S. by Mexico in 1848). In the North, antislavery forces and racists alike could find common ground in their support for the free-soil position. Unlike the abolitionists, who insisted on eliminating slavery everywhere, the Free-Soilers did not demand the end of slavery. Instead, they sought to keep the West a land of opportunity for whites only so that the white majority would not have to compete with the labor of slaves or free blacks. In 1848, northerners favoring this approach to the territories organized the Free-Soil party, which adopted the slogan "free soil, free labor, and free men." In addition to its chief objective—preventing the extension of slavery—the new party also advocated free homesteads (public land grants to small farmers) and internal improvements.

Southern Position

Most southern whites viewed any attempts to restrict the expansion of slavery as a violation of their constitutional right to take and use their property as they wished. They saw both the abolitionists and the Free-Soilers as intent on the ultimate destruction of slavery. More moderate southerners favored extending the Missouri Compromise line of 36°30' westward to the Pacific Ocean and permitting territories north of that line to be nonslave.

Popular Sovereignty

Lewis Cass, a Democratic senator from Michigan, proposed a compromise solution that soon won considerable support from both moderate northerners and moderate southerners. Instead of Congress determining whether to allow slavery in a new western territory or state, Cass suggested that the matter be determined by a vote of the people who settled the territory. Cass' approach to the problem was known as "squatter," or "popular sovereignty."

The Election of 1848

In 1848, the Democrats nominated Senator Cass and adopted a platform pledged to popular sovereignty. The Whigs nominated Mexican War hero General Zachary Taylor, who had never been involved in politics and took no position on slavery in the territories. A third party, the Free-Soil party, nominated former president Martin Van Buren. It consisted of "conscience" Whigs (who opposed slavery) and antislavery Democrats; the latter group were ridiculed as "barnburners" because their defection threatened to destroy the Democratic party. Taylor narrowly defeated Cass, in part because of the vote given the Free-Soil party in such key northern states as New York and Pennsylvania.

The Compromise of 1850

The gold rush of 1849 and the influx of about 100,000 settlers into California created the need for law and order in the West. In 1849, Californians drafted a constitution for their new state—a constitution that banned slavery. Even though President Taylor was a southern slaveholder himself, he supported the immediate admission of both California and New Mexico as free states. (At this time, however, the Mexican population of the New Mexico territory had little interest in applying for statehood.)

Taylor's plan sparked talk of secession among the "fire-eaters" (radicals) in the South. Some southern extremists even met in Nashville in 1850 to discuss secession. By this time, however, the astute Henry Clay had proposed yet another compromise for solving the political crisis:

- Admit California to the Union as a free state

- Divide the remainder of the Mexican Cession into two territories— Utah and New Mexico—and allow the settlers in these territories to decide the slavery issue by majority vote, or popular sovereignty

- Give the land in dispute between Texas and the New Mexico territory to the new territories in return for the federal government assuming Texas' public debt of $10 million

- Ban the slave trade in the District of Columbia but permit whites to hold slaves as before

- Adopt a new Fugitive Slave Law and enforce it rigorously

In the ensuing Senate debate over the compromise proposal, the three congressional giants of their age—Henry Clay of Kentucky, Daniel Webster of Massachusetts, and John C. Calhoun of South Carolina—delivered the last great speeches of their lives. (Born in the same year, 1782, Webster and Calhoun would also die in the same year, 1850; Clay died two years later.) Webster courageously argued for compromise in order to save the Union, and in so doing alienated the Massachusetts abolitionists who had supported him. Calhoun argued against compromise and insisted that the South be given equal rights in the acquired territory.

Northern opposition to compromise came from younger antislavery law-makers, such as Senator William H. Seward of New York, who argued that there was a higher law than the Constitution. The opponents managed to prevail until the sudden death in 1850 of President Taylor, who had also opposed Clay's plan. Succeeding him was a strong supporter of compromise, Vice President Millard Fillmore. Stephen A. Douglas, a politically astute young senator from Illinois, engineered different coalitions to pass each part of the compromise separately. President Fillmore readily signed the bills into law.

The passage of the Compromise of 1850 bought time for the nation. Because California was admitted as a free state, the compromise added to the North's political power, and the political debate deepened the commitment of many northerners to saving the Union from secession. On the other hand, parts of the compromise became sources of controversy, especially the new Fugitive Slave Law and the provision for popular sovereignty.

Agitation Over Slavery

For a brief period—the four years between the Compromise of 1850 and the passage of the Kansas-Nebraska Act in 1854—sectional tensions abated slightly. Even during these years, however, the enforcement of the Fugitive Slave Act and the publication of a best-selling antislavery novel kept the slavery question in the forefront of public attention in both the North and South.

Fugitive Slave Law

It was the passage of a strict Fugitive Slave Law that persuaded many southerners to accept the loss of California to the abolitionists and Free-Soilers. Yet the enforcement of the new law in the North was bitterly and sometimes forcibly resisted by antislavery northerners. In effect, therefore, enforcement of the new law added to the aggrieved feelings on both sides.

Enforcement and opposition. The law's chief purpose was to track down runaway (fugitive) slaves who had escaped to a northern state, capture them, and return them to their southern owners. The law placed fugitive slave cases under the exclusive jurisdiction of the federal government. Special U.S. commissioners were authorized to issue warrants for the arrest of fugitives. Any captured person who claimed to be a free black and not a runaway slave (a common occurrence) was denied the right of trial by jury. Citizens who attempted to hide a runaway or obstruct enforcement of the law were subject to heavy penalties.

Underground Railroad

The Underground Railroad, the fabled network of "conductors" and "stations" to help escaped slaves reach freedom in the North or in Canada, was neither well organized nor dominated by white abolitionists as is sometimes believed. Both northern free blacks and courageous ex-slaves led other blacks to freedom. The escaped slave Harriet Tubman made at least 19 trips into the South to help some 300 slaves escape. Free blacks in the North and abolitionists also organized vigilance committees to protect fugitive slaves from the slave catchers. Once the Civil War broke out, black leaders such as Frederick Douglass, Harriet Tubman, and Sojourner Truth continued to take an active role in the emancipation of slaves and supported black soldiers in the Union cause.

Literature on Slavery—Pro and Con

Popular books as well as unpopular laws stirred the emotions of the people of all regions.

Uncle Tom's Cabin. The most influential book of its day was a novel about the conflict between a slave named Tom and the brutal white slave owner Simon Legree. The publication of *Uncle Tom's Cabin* in 1852 by the northern writer Harriet Beecher Stowe moved a generation of northerners as well as many Europeans to regard all slave owners as monstrously cruel and inhuman. Southerners condemned the "untruths" in the novel and looked upon it as one more proof of the North's incurable prejudice against the southern way of life. Later, when President Lincoln met Mrs. Stowe, he is reported to have said, "So you're the little woman who wrote the book that made this great war."

Impending Crisis of the South. Although it did not appear until 1857, Hinton R. Helper's book of nonfiction, *Impending Crisis of the South,* attacked slavery from another angle. The author, a native of North Carolina, used statistics to demonstrate to fellow southerners that slavery had a negative impact on the South's economy. Southern states acted quickly to ban the book, but it was widely distributed in the North by antislavery and Free-Soil leaders.

Southern reaction. Responding to the northern literature that condemned slavery as evil, proslavery southern whites counterattacked by arguing that slavery was just the opposite—a positive good for slave and master alike. They argued that slavery was sanctioned by the Bible and was firmly grounded in philosophy and history. Southern authors contrasted the conditions of northern wage workers—"wage slaves" forced to work long hours in factories and mines—with the familial bonds that often developed on plantations between slaves and master. George Fitzhugh, the boldest and best known of the proslavery authors, questioned the principle of equal rights for "unequal men" and attacked the capitalist wage system as worse than slavery. Among his works were *Sociology for the South* (1854) and *Cannibals All!* (1857).

Effect of Law and Literature

The effect of the Fugitive Slave Law and the antislavery and proslavery literature was to polarize the nation even more. Northerners who had earlier scorned the abolitionist cause now became concerned about the moral issues posed by slavery. At the same time, a growing number of southerners became convinced that the North's goal was to destroy the institution of slavery and the way of life based upon it.

National Parties in Crisis

Occurring simultaneously in the mid-1850s were two tendencies that caused further political instability: (1) the weakening of the two major parties—the Democrats and the Whigs—and (2) a disastrous application of popular sovereignty in the western territory of Kansas.

The Election of 1852

Signs of trouble for the Whig party were apparent in the 1852 election for president. The Whigs nominated another military hero of the Mexican

War, General Winfield Scott. Ignoring the slavery issue, the Whig campaign concentrated on the party's innocuous plans for improving roads and harbors. But Scott soon discovered that sectional issues could not be held in check, as the antislavery and southern factions of the party fell to quarreling.

The Democrats nominated a safe compromise candidate, Franklin Pierce of New Hampshire. This northerner was acceptable to southern Democrats because of his support for the Fugitive Slave Law. In the electoral college vote, Pierce and the Democrats won all but four states in a sweep that proved the days of the Whig party were numbered.

The Kansas-Nebraska Act (1854)

With the Democrats firmly in control of national policy both in the White House and in Congress, a new law was passed that was to have disastrous consequences. Senator Stephen A. Douglas of Illinois devised a plan for building a railroad and promoting western settlement (while at the same time increasing the value of his own real estate holdings in Chicago). Douglas needed to win southern approval for his plan to build a transcontinental railroad through the central United States, with a major terminus in Chicago. (Southern Democrats preferred a more southerly route for the railroad.) The senator obtained southern approval for his railroad route by introducing a bill on another matter. This bill proposed that the Nebraska Territory be divided into the Kansas Territory and Nebraska Territory, and the settlers there be free to decide whether or not to allow slavery. Since these territories were located *north* of the 36°30' line, Douglas's bill gave southern slave owners an opportunity that previously had been closed to them by the Missouri Compromise.

After three months of bitter debate, both houses of Congress passed Douglas' bill as the Kansas-Nebraska Act of 1854, and President Pierce signed it into law.

Passage of the Kansas-Nebraska Act renewed the sectional controversy that had been at least partly resolved by the Compromise of 1850. In effect, it repealed the Compromise of 1820. Northern Democrats condemned the law as a surrender to the "slave power." Furthermore, a new political party emerged whose membership was entirely northern and western. Its overriding purpose was to express opposition to the spread of slavery in the territories. This new antislavery party called itself the Republican party.

New Parties

In hindsight, it is clear that the breakup of truly national political parties in the mid-1850s paralleled the breakup of the Union. The new parties came into being at this time—one temporary, the other permanent. Both played a role in bringing about the demise of a major national party, the Whigs.

Know-Nothing party. In addition to sectional divisions between North and South, there was also in the mid-1850s growing ethnic tension in the North

THE UNITED STATES AFTER
THE KANSAS–NEBRASKA ACT OF 1854

between native-born Protestant Americans and immigrant Germans and Irish Catholics. Nativist hostility to these newcomers led to the formation of the American party—or the Know-Nothing party, as it was more commonly known (because party members commonly responded "I know nothing" to political questions). The Know-Nothings drew support away from the Whigs at a time when that party was reeling from its defeat in the 1852 election. Their one burning issue was opposition to Catholics and immigrants who, in the 1840s and 1850s, were entering northern cities in large numbers.

Although the Know-Nothings won a few local and state elections in the mid-1850s and helped to weaken the Whigs, they quickly lost influence, as sectional issues again became paramount.

Birth of the Republican party. The Republican party was founded in Wisconsin in 1854 as a direct reaction to the passage of the Kansas-Nebraska Act. A coalition of Free-Soilers and antislavery Whigs and Democrats made up the new party. Its first platform of 1854 called for the repeal of both the Kansas-Nebraska Act and the Fugitive Slave Law. Although abolitionists were later to join the party, its leaders were chiefly northern and western moderates who were united in their opposition to slavery in the territories. They were content to see slavery continue so long as it was confined to the old slave states of the South. From 1854 to 1860, the Republican party grew rapidly in the North and soon established itself as the second largest party. But because it remained in these years strictly a northern or sectional party, its success could only alienate and threaten the South.

The Election of 1856

The Republicans' first major test of strength came in the presidential election of 1856. Their nominee for president was the young explorer and "Pathfinder," John C. Frémont, then a senator from the new state of California. The Republican platform called for no expansion of slavery, free homesteads, and a probusiness protective tariff. The Know-Nothings also competed strongly in this election, winning 20 percent of the popular vote for their candidate, former President Millard Fillmore. As the one major national party, the Democrats were expected to win. They nominated James Buchanan of Pennsylvania, rejecting both President Pierce and Stephen Douglas because they were too closely identified with the controversial Kansas-Nebraska Act. As expected, the Democratic ticket won a majority of both the popular and electoral vote. But the Republicans made a remarkably strong showing for a sectional party. In the electoral college, Frémont carried 11 of the 16 free states. It was becoming evident that the antislavery Republicans could win the White House without a single vote from the South.

The election of 1856 foreshadowed the emergence of a powerful political party that would win all but four presidential elections between 1860 and 1932.

Extremists and Violence

The conflicts between antislavery and proslavery forces were not confined to politics and public debate. By the mid-1850s, both sides resorted to violence.

"Bleeding Kansas"

Well before the 1856 election, the tragic and bloody consequences of the Kansas-Nebraska Act had become obvious to all. Stephen Douglas, the sponsor of the measure, expected the slavery issue in the territory to be settled peacefully by the antislavery farmers from the Midwest who migrated to Kansas. These settlers did in fact constitute a majority of the population. But slaveholders from the neighboring state of Missouri also set up homesteads in Kansas chiefly as a means of winning control of the territory for the South. Northern abolitionists and Free-Soilers responded by organizing the New England Emigrant Aid Company (1855), which paid for the transportation of antislavery settlers to Kansas. Fighting soon broke out between the proslavery and the antislavery groups, and the territory became known as "bleeding Kansas."

Proslavery Missourians, mockingly called "border ruffians" by their enemies, crossed the border to create a proslavery legislature in Lecompton, Kansas. Antislavery settlers refused to recognize this government and created their own legislature in Topeka. In 1856, proslavery forces attacked the free-soil town of Lawrence, killing two and destroying homes and businesses. Two days later, John Brown, a stern abolitionist from Connecticut, retaliated for the Lawrence incident by leading his sons on an attack of a proslavery farm settlement at Pottawatomie Creek. The Browns brutally killed five settlers.

In Washington, the Pierce administration kept aloof from the turmoil in Kansas. It did nothing to keep order in the territory and failed to support honest elections there. As "bleeding Kansas" became bloodier, the Democratic party became ever more divided between its northern and southern factions.

Caning of Senator Sumner. The violence in Kansas spilled over into the halls of the U.S. Congress. In 1856 Massachusetts Senator Charles Sumner verbally attacked the Democratic administration in a vitriolic speech, "The Crime Against Kansas." His intemperate remarks included personal charges against South Carolina Senator Andrew Butler. Butler's nephew, Congressman Preston Brooks, defended his absent uncle's honor by walking into the Senate chamber and beating Sumner over the head with a cane. (Brooks explained that dueling was too good for Sumner, but a cane was fit for a dog.)

Brooks' action outraged the North, and the House voted to censure him. Southerners, however, applauded Brooks' deed and sent him numerous canes to replace the one he broke beating Sumner. The Sumner-Brooks incident was another sign of growing passions on both sides.

Constitutional Issues

Both the Democrats' position of popular sovereignty and the Republicans' stand against the expansion of slavery received serious blows during the Buchanan administration (1857–1861). Republicans attacked Buchanan as a weak president under southern control.

Lecompton Constitution

One of Buchanan's first challenges as president in 1857 was deciding whether to accept or reject a proslavery state constitution for Kansas submitted by the southern legislature at Lecompton. It was obvious that the Lecompton constitution, as it was called, did not have the support of the majority of settlers. Even so, President Buchanan asked Congress to accept the document and admit Kansas as a slave state. Congress did not do so, because many Democrats, including Stephen Douglas, joined with the Republicans in rejecting the Lecompton constitution. The next year, 1858, the proslavery document was overwhelmingly defeated by the majority of Kansas settlers, most of whom were antislavery Republicans.

Dred Scott v. Sandford (1857)

Congressional folly and presidential ineptitude contributed to the sectional crisis of the 1850s. Then the Supreme Court, far from calming the situation, infuriated the North with its controversial proslavery decision in the Dred Scott case.

Dred Scott had been held as a slave in Missouri and then taken to the free territory of Wisconsin where he lived for two years before returning to Missouri. Arguing that his period of residence on free soil made him a free citizen, Scott went to a Missouri court and sued for his freedom. The case was appealed to the Supreme Court, which rendered its decision in March 1857 only two days after Buchanan was sworn in as president. Presiding over the Court was Chief Justice Roger Taney, a southern Democrat.

A majority of the Court decided against Scott and gave the following reasons:

1. Dred Scott had no right to sue in a federal court because the Framers of the Constitution did not intend people of African descent to be U.S. citizens.

2. Congress did not have the power to deprive any person of property without due process of law; and, if slaves were a form of property, then Congress could not exclude slavery from any federal territory.

3. Because Congress' law of 1820 (the Missouri Compromise) excluded slavery from Wisconsin and other northern territories, that law was unconstitutional.

Southern Democrats were delighted with the Court's ruling, while northern Republicans were shocked and indignant. In effect, the Supreme Court declared that all parts of the western territories were open to slavery. Republicans denounced the Dred Scott decision of "the greatest crime in the annals of the republic." Because of the timing of the decision, right after Buchanan's inauguration, many northerners suspected that the Democratic president and the Democratic majority on the Supreme Court, including Taney, had secretly planned the Dred Scott decision, hoping that it would settle the slavery question once and for all. The decision increased northerners' suspicions of a slave power conspiracy and induced thousands of former Democrats to vote Republican.

Northern Democrats like Senator Douglas were left with the almost impossible task of supporting popular sovereignty without repudiating the Dred Scott decision. Douglas' hopes for a sectional compromise and his ambitions for the presidency were both in jeopardy.

Lincoln-Douglas Debates

In 1858 the focus of the nation was on Stephen Douglas' campaign for reelection as senator from Illinois. Challenging him for the Senate seat was a successful trial lawyer and former member of the Illinois legislature, Abraham

Lincoln. The Republican candidate had served only one two-year term in Congress in the 1840s as a Whig. Nationally, he was an unknown compared to Douglas (the Little Giant), the champion of popular sovereignty and possibly the last hope for holding the North and South together if elected president in 1860.

Lincoln was not an abolitionist. Even so, as a moderate who was against the expansion of slavery, he could effectively speak of slavery as a moral issue. ("If slavery is not wrong, nothing is wrong.") Accepting the Illinois Republicans' nomination, the candidate delivered the celebrated "house-divided" speech that was reported in the nation's press. "This government," said Lincoln, "cannot endure permanently half slave and half free," a statement that made southerners view Lincoln as a radical. In seven campaign debates held in different Illinois towns, Lincoln shared the platform with his famous opponent, Douglas. The Republican challenger attacked Douglas' seeming indifference to slavery as a moral issue.

In a debate in Freeport, Illinois, Lincoln questioned how Douglas could reconcile popular sovereignty with the Dred Scott decision. In what became known as the Freeport Doctrine, Douglas responded that slavery could not exist in a community if the local citizens did not pass and enforce laws (slave codes) for maintaining it. This doctrine angered southern Democrats because, from their point of view, Douglas did not go far enough in supporting the implications of the Dred Scott decision.

Douglas ended up winning his campaign for reelection to the U.S. Senate. In the long run, however, he lost ground in his own party by alienating southern Democrats. Lincoln, on the other hand, emerged from the debates as a national figure and a leading contender for the Republican nomination for president in 1860.

The Road to Secession

Outside Illinois, the Republicans did well in the congressional elections of 1858, a fact that alarmed many southerners. They worried not only about the antislavery plank in the Republicans' program but also about that party's economic program, which favored the interests of northern industrialists at the expense of the South. The higher tariffs pledged in the Republican platform could only help northern business and hurt the South's dependence on the export of cotton. Southerners feared therefore that a Republican victory in 1860 would spell disaster for their economic interests and also threaten their "constitutional right," as affirmed by the Supreme Court, to hold slaves as property. As if this were not enough cause for alarm, northern radicals provided money to John Brown, the man who had massacred five farmers in Kansas in 1856.

John Brown's Raid at Harpers Ferry

The fanatical and violent John Brown confirmed the South's worst fears of radical abolitionism when he tried to start a slave uprising in Virginia. In October 1859 he led a small band of followers, including his four sons and some former slaves, in an attack on the federal arsenal at Harpers Ferry. His impractical plan was to use guns from the arsenal to arm Virginia's slaves, whom he expected to rise up in general revolt. Federal troops under the command of Robert E. Lee captured Brown and his band after a two-day siege. Brown and six of his followers were tried for treason, convicted, and hanged by the state of Virginia.

Moderates in the North, including Republican leaders, condemned Brown's use of violence, but southerners were not convinced by their words. Southern whites saw the raid as final proof of the North's true intentions—to use slave revolts to destroy the South. Because John Brown spoke with simple eloquence at his trial of his humanitarian motives in wanting to free the slaves, he was hailed as a martyr by many antislavery northerners. (A few years later, when civil war broke out, John Brown was celebrated by advancing northern armies singing: "Glory, glory, hallelujah! His soul is marching on.")

The Election of 1860

The final event that triggered the South's decision to leave the Union was the election of Abraham Lincoln, the Republican candidate, as president in 1860.

Breakup of the Democratic party. After John Brown's raid, most Americans understood that their country was moving to the brink of disunion. As 1860 began, the Democratic party represented the last practical hope for coalition and compromise. The Democrats held their national nominating convention in Charleston, South Carolina. Stephen Douglas was clearly the party's leading candidate and the person most capable of winning election to the presidency. However, his nomination was blocked by a combination of angry southerners and supporters of President Buchanan.

After deadlocking at Charleston, the Democrats held a second convention in Baltimore. Many delegates from the slave states walked out, enabling the remaining delegates to nominate Douglas on a platform of popular sovereignty and enforcement of the Fugitive Slave Law. Southern Democrats then held their own convention in Baltimore and nominated Vice President John C. Breckinridge of Kentucky as their candidate. The southern Democratic platform called for the unrestricted extension of slavery in the territories and the annexation of Cuba as another land where slavery could flourish.

Republican nomination of Lincoln. When the Republicans met in Chicago, they enjoyed the prospect of an easy win over the divided Democrats. They made the most of their advantage by drafting a platform that appealed strongly to the economic self-interest of northerners and westerners. In addition to calling for the exclusion of slavery from the territories, the Republican platform promised a protective tariff for industry, free land for homesteaders, and internal improvements to encourage western settlement, including a railroad to the Pacific. To ensure victory, the Republicans turned away from the better known but more radical Senator William H. Seward to the strong debater from Illinois, Abraham Lincoln—a candidate who could carry the key midwestern states of Illinois, Indiana, and Ohio.

One cloud on the horizon darkened the Republicans' otherwise bright future. In the South, secessionists warned that if Lincoln was elected president, their states would leave the Union.

A fourth political party. Fearing the consequences of a Republican victory, a group of former Whigs, Know-Nothings, and moderate Democrats formed a new party: the Constitutional Union party. For president, they nominated John Bell of Tennessee. The party's platform pledged enforcement of the laws and the Constitution and, above all, preserving the Union.

Election results. While Douglas campaigned across the country, Lincoln confidently remained at home in Springfield, Illinois, meeting with Republican leaders and giving statements to the press. The election results were predictable. Lincoln carried every one of the free states of the North, which represented a solid majority of 59 percent of the electoral votes. He won only 39.8 percent of the popular vote, however, and would therefore be a minority president. Breckinridge, the southern Democrat, carried the Deep South, leaving Douglas and Bell with just a few electoral votes in the border states.

Together, Douglas as a northern Democrat and Breckinridge as a southern Democrat received many more *popular* votes than Lincoln, the Republican. Nevertheless, the new political reality was that the populous free states had enough electoral votes to select a president without the need for a single electoral vote from the South.

Secession of the Deep South

The Republicans controlled neither the Congress nor the Supreme Court. Even so, the election of Lincoln was all that southern secessionists needed to call for immediate disunion. In December 1860 a special convention in South Carolina voted unanimously to secede. Within the next six weeks, other state conventions in Florida, Georgia, Alabama, Mississippi, Louisiana, and Texas did the same. In February 1861, representatives of the seven states of the Deep South met in Montgomery, Alabama, and created the Confederate States of America. The constitution of this would-be southern nation was similar to the U.S. Constitution, except that the Confederacy placed limits on the government's power to impose tariffs and restrict slavery. Elected president and vice president of the Confederacy were Senator Jefferson Davis of Mississippi and Alexander Stephens of Georgia.

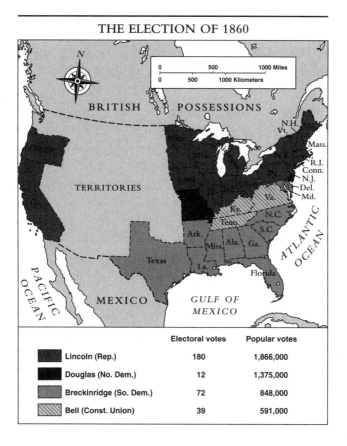

THE ELECTION OF 1860

	Electoral votes	Popular votes
Lincoln (Rep.)	180	1,866,000
Douglas (No. Dem.)	12	1,375,000
Breckinridge (So. Dem.)	72	848,000
Bell (Const. Union)	39	591,000

Crittenden compromise. A lame-duck president (a leader facing immi-nent retirement), Buchanan had five months in office before President-elect Lincoln was due to succeed him. Buchanan was a conservative who did nothing to prevent the secession of the seven states. Congress was more active. In a last-ditch effort to appease the South, Senator John Crittenden of Kentucky proposed a constitutional amendment that would guarantee the right to hold slaves in all territories south of 36°30′. Lincoln, however, said that he could not accept this compromise because it violated the Republican position against extension of slavery into the territories.

Southern whites who voted for secession believed they were acting in the tradition of the Revolution of 1776. They argued that they had a right to national independence and to dissolve a constitutional compact that no longer protected them from "tyranny" (the tyranny of northern rule). Many of them also thought that Lincoln, like Buchanan, might permit secession without a fight. As we shall see, those who thought this had badly miscalculated.

HISTORICAL PERSPECTIVES: CAUSES OF THE CIVIL WAR

Was slavery the primary cause of the Civil War? In the decades after the war, northern historians argued emphatically that the South's attachment to slavery was the principal, if not the only, cause. They blamed the war on a conspiracy of slave owners—a small minority of southerners—who wanted only to expand slavery at the expense of whites and blacks alike.

Southern historians, on the other hand, viewed the conflict between the two sections, North and South, as a dispute over the nature of the Constitution. They argued that northern abolitionists and Free-Soil politicians attempted to overturn the original compact of the states, and that the southern states seceded to defend the constitutional rights threatened by northern aggression.

By the early 20th century, passions had cooled on both sides, and scholars of the Progressive era (1900–1917) thought economic interests were the foundation of all political conflict. Thus, Charles Beard, a leading historian of this era, viewed the sectional conflict of the 1850s as a clash of two opposing economic systems: the industrial North versus the agricultural South. His economic interpretation of the Civil War stressed the importance of the Republicans' commitment to the economic ambitions of northern industrialists for high tariffs and of western farmers for free land.

American disillusionment with World War I led historians to question whether the Civil War was any more necessary or inevitable than the world war had been. Previously, people had assumed that the Civil War was, in William Seward's words, an "irrepressible conflict between opposing forces." Now, in the 1920s and 1930s, that assumption was challenged by revisionist historians who argued that it was only the blundering of politicians and the rash acts of a few extremists such as John Brown that were chiefly responsible for secession and war. In an essay in 1940, James G. Randall summarized the thinking of the revisionist school: "If one word or phrase were selected to account for the war, that word would not be slavery, or states' rights, or diverse civilizations. It would have to be such a word as fanaticism (on both sides), or misunderstanding, or perhaps politics." Politicians of the 1850s who worked for compromise (Clay, Douglas, and Crittenden) were treated as the revisionists' heroes, whereas Lincoln was criticized for fomenting sectional passions with his house-divided and other speeches.

In the 1950s and 1960s, the civil rights movement provided the backdrop for rethinking the causes of the Civil War. Historians who were sympathetic with African Americans' struggles for civil rights returned to the view that slavery was the chief cause of disunion after all. They argued that moral issues such as slavery are impossible to compromise. Arthur Schlesinger, Jr., a leading historian of the 1950s, wrote: "A society closed in the defense of evil institutions thus creates moral differences far too profound to be solved by compromise." In this view, slavery as an inherently evil institution was at the root of a conflict that was indeed "irrepressible."

KEY NAMES, EVENTS, AND TERMS

free-soil movement; Free-Soil party	Harriet Beecher Stowe, *Uncle Tom's Cabin*	John Brown; Pottawatomie Creek
conscience Whigs	Hinton R. Helper, *Impending Crisis of the South*	Sumner-Brooks incident
"barnburners"		Lecompton constitution
popular sovereignty	George Fitzhugh, *Sociology of the South*	*Dred Scott v. Sandford*
Lewis Cass	Franklin Pierce	Roger Taney
Henry Clay	Kansas-Nebraska Act (1854)	Abraham Lincoln
Zachary Taylor	Know-Nothing party	Lincoln-Douglas debates
Compromise of 1850	Republican party	house-divided speech
Stephen A. Douglas	John C. Frémont	Freeport Doctrine
Millard Fillmore	James Buchanan	Harpers Ferry raid
Fugitive Slave Law	New England Emigrant Aid Company	election of 1860
Underground Railroad		secession
Harriet Tubman	"bleeding Kansas"	Crittenden compromise

MULTIPLE-CHOICE QUESTIONS

1. Which of the following most accurately describes Stephen Douglas' idea of popular sovereignty?

   (A) A section of western land would be given free to anyone who would homestead it for a certain number of years.

   (B) Only citizens of the United States would be permitted to settle territories acquired from Mexico.

   (C) Public lands in the new territories would be open on a first-come first-served basis.

   (D) The status of slavery in a territory would be determined by the voters in the territory.

   (E) New territories would be closed to both slaves and free blacks.

2. All of the following figured prominently in debates over the Compromise of 1850 EXCEPT the

   (A) provision for a new Fugitive Slave Law

   (B) slave trade in the District of Columbia

(C) admission of California into the Union as a free state

(D) future of slavery in the Mexican Cession territories

(E) extension of slavery into Kansas and Nebraska territories

3. Which of the following was a major factor in the decline of the Whig party in the 1850s?

(A) death of John Calhoun

(B) election of Zachary Taylor

(C) Lincoln-Douglas debates

(D) Know-Nothing movement

(E) "bleeding Kansas"

4. A political effect of the fighting in Kansas in 1855 and 1856 was to

(A) further divide the Democratic party

(B) cause the founding of the Republican party

(C) gain increased congressional support for proslavery forces in Kansas

(D) unite northern and southern Democrats against Republicans

(E) elect a Republican president in 1856

5. The Supreme Court's decision in the Dred Scott case outraged public opinion in the North chiefly because it

(A) declared the Fugitive Slave Law unconstitutional

(B) guaranteed citizenship to free blacks

(C) removed restrictions against the spread of slavery into the western territories

(D) failed to abolish slavery in the South

(E) challenged California's status as a free state

6. The Kansas-Nebraska Act of 1854 increased sectional tension because it

(A) enriched northern railroad investors at the expense of the South

(B) reopened the issue of slavery in a territory north of 36°30′

(C) supported proslavery state constitutions in Kansas and Nebraska

(D) repealed the Compromise of 1850

(E) persuaded the Whig party to side with the South

7. The Lincoln-Douglas debates resulted in all of the following EXCEPT

(A) Lincoln's emergence as a national political figure

(B) increased support for Douglas in the South

(C) Douglas' reelection to the Senate

(D) Douglas' attempt to reconcile popular sovereignty with the Dred Scott decision

(E) increased public awareness of slavery as a moral issue

8. John Brown's primary purpose in attacking Harpers Ferry was to

(A) gain contributions from northern abolitionists

(B) take revenge for the death of antislavery settlers in Kansas

(C) start a slave rebellion in Virginia

(D) open up a new path for the underground railroad

(E) destroy the federal arsenal in Virginia

9. In the 1860 election, what was the position of Lincoln and the Republican party on slavery?

(A) Slavery was immoral and should be abolished immediately.

(B) Slavery should not be allowed to expand into the territories.

(C) Popular sovereignty would be allowed in the new territories north of 36°30′.

(D) The Dred Scott decision should be supported in the territories but not in the states.

(E) The federal government should act to bring about the gradual emancipation of slaves in the South.

10. All of the following statements about the election of 1860 are accurate EXCEPT:

(A) The Republicans won control of the presidency but not Congress.

(B) No candidate received a majority of the popular vote.

(C) The popular and electoral votes were divided among four candidates.

(D) Lincoln won election because of the split in the Democratic party.

(E) A major consequence of the election was that several southern states seceded from the Union.

ESSAY QUESTIONS

1. To what degree did the Compromise of 1850 delay the breakup of the Union?

2. Analyze the ways that the Free-Soil movement influenced U.S. politics from 1848 to 1860.

3. What factors account for the remarkable success of a new party—the Republican—in the elections of 1856 and 1860?

4. How did TWO of the following contribute to the events that led to disunion?

passage of the Kansas-Nebraska Act

decision in the *Dred Scott* case

raid on Harpers Ferry

5. Assess the extent to which slavery was the main cause of disunion and the Civil War.

Guide to Writing the DB2

Writing the Introduction and the Conclusion

Probably the most difficult sentence to write in any composition is the first sentence of the opening paragraph. Not knowing how to start and struggling to find those first words may consume many precious minutes of the 45 minutes allotted for writing the DBQ essay. Here are some ideas for successfully clearing that first high hurdle. A strong introduction shows your sophistication and skill at framing a historical issue while leading into your thesis statement.

For each of the suggested approaches, you will first read an example of a lead sentence for the DBQ on page 260 and then consider how that sentence could be applied to any topic (X).

Approach A: Neutral statement about the historical debate

Example: Whether or not the Civil War was inevitable or "irrepressible" has long been debated by historians.

Application to other DBQs: Whether or not X was true has long been debated by historians.

Approach B: General survey of relevant facts

Example: Without doubt, sectional conflict over slavery was the leading issue of the 1850s from the controversy over the Fugitive Slave Law of 1850 to the intense public reaction to John Brown's raid at Harpers Ferry in 1859.

Application: Without doubt, X (general trend or condition) occurred starting with Y (event) and continuing to Z (event).

Approach C: Bold declaration of revisionist thesis

Example: Despite what is popularly believed and traditionally taught, slavery was not the chief cause of the Civil War. Moreover, the South's decision to secede in 1860 was by no means inevitable.

258

Application: Despite what is popularly believed and traditionally taught, the conclusion that X happened is not supported by the relevant evidence.

Approach D: Generalization about history

Example: Rarely does a single cause explain such a complex event as the outbreak of a major war. The Civil War is no exception.

Application: Rarely does a single cause explain a complex event. X is no exception.

Approach E: Acknowledgment of the opposing argument

Example: There are those who argue that the slavery issue led inevitably to secession and civil war. On the other hand, a stronger argument can be made that secession was not at all inevitable and could have been avoided by adopting the compromises proposed by a number of moderates.

Application: There are those who argue that X led inevitably to Y. On the other hand, a stronger argument can be made that the real reason for Y was Z (*or* that Y could have been avoided if only Z had happened).

Thinking of a strong concluding statement is usually less difficult since, by now, you have built up sufficient intellectual energy and momentum to carry you to the end. An excellent technique for creating an impressive conclusion is to build your last sentence around a phrase quoted from one of the documents.

Example: That secession and Civil War were indeed inevitable was best expressed by Abraham Lincoln himself when he declared: "A house divided against itself cannot stand."

Application: That X was true was best expressed by Y when he or she stated "Z."

Practice

Write a complete five-paragraph essay in response to the DBQ on page 260. Begin with one of the approaches (A–E) suggested above and conclude with a phrase quoted from one of the documents.

DOCUMENT-BASED QUESTION (DBQ)

"The Civil War was not inevitable; it was the result of extremism and failures of leadership on both sides."

Assess the validity of this statement, using the following documents *and* your knowledge of the period from 1830 to 1861.

DOCUMENT A.

I do not, then, hesitate to avow before this House and the country, and in the presence of the living God, that if by your legislation you [northerners] seek to drive us from the territories of California and New Mexico, purchased by the common blood and treasure of the whole people, and to abolish slavery in this District [Washington, D.C.] thereby attempting to fix national degradation upon half the states of this Confederacy, I am for disunion. And if my physical courage be equal to the maintenance of my convictions or right and duty, I will devote all I am and all I have on earth to its consummation.

> Congressman Robert Toombs of Georgia,
> Response on the floor of the House to northern efforts
> to keep slavery out of the territories, December 13, 1849

DOCUMENT B.

Sir, there are those abolition societies, of which I am unwilling to speak, but in regard to which I have very clear notions and opinions. I do not think them useful. I think their operations of the last twenty years have produced nothing good or valuable.

I do not mean to impute gross motives even to the leaders of these societies, but I am not blind to the consequences. I cannot but see what mischiefs their interference with the South has produced. . . .

These abolition societies commenced their course of action in 1835. It is said—I do not know how true it may be—that they sent incendiary publications into the slave states. At any event, they attempted to arouse, and did arouse, a very strong feeling. In other words, they created great agitation in the North against Southern slavery.

> Daniel Webster,
> Speech in the Senate supporting the
> Compromise of 1850, March 7, 1850

DOCUMENT C.

Tom spoke in a mild voice, but with a decision that could not be mistaken. Legree shook with anger; his greenish eyes glared fiercely, and his very whiskers seemed to curl with passion. But, like some ferocious beast, that plays with its victim before he devours it, he kept back his strong impulse to proceed to immediate violence, and broke into bitter raillery.

"Well, here's a pious dog, at last, let down among us sinners!— a saint, a gentleman, and no less, to talk to us sinners about our sins! Powerful holy crittur, he must be! Here, you rascal, you make to believe to be so pious—didn't you never hear, out of yer Bible, 'Servants, obey yer masters'? An't I yer master? Didn't I pay down twelve hundred dollars, cash, for all there is inside yer old cussed black shell? An't yer mine now body and soul?" he said, giving Tom a violent kick with his heavy boot; "tell me!"

In the very depth of physical suffering, bowed by brutal oppression, this question shot a gleam of joy and triumph through Tom's soul. He suddenly stretched himself up, and looking earnestly to heaven, while the tears and blood that flowed down his face mingled, he exclaimed,

"No! no! no! my soul an't yours, Mas'r! You haven't bought it—ye can't buy it! It's been bought and paid for by One that is able to keep it. No matter, no matter, you can't harm me!"

"I can't!" said Legree, with a sneer, "we'll see—we'll see! Here, Sambo, Qimbo, give this dog such a breakin' in as he won't get over this month!"

Harriet Beecher Stowe,
Uncle Tom's Cabin, 1852

DOCUMENT D.

Why . . . can we not withdraw this vexed question from politics? Why can we not adopt the principle of this bill as a rule of action in all new territorial organizations? Why can we not deprive these agitators of their vocation, and render it impossible for senators to come here upon bargains on the slavery question? . . . leave the people, under the Constitution, to do as they may see proper in respect to their own internal affairs. . . . The bill does equal and exact justice to the whole Union, and every part of it; it violates the rights of no state or territory . . . and leaves the people thereof to the free enjoyment of all their rights.

Speech of Stephen Douglas
defending the Kansas-Nebraska Act, 1854

DOCUMENT E.

Party Strength in Congress, 1849–1861					
	Senate			**House**	
	Majority Party	Principal Minority Party	Other	Majority Party	Principal Minority Party	Other
1849–1851	D 35	W 25	2	D 112	W 109	9
1851–1853	D 35	W 24	3	D 140	W 88	5
1853–1855	D 38	W 22	2	D 159	W 71	4
1855–1857	D 40	R 15	5	R 108	D 83	43
1857–1859	D 36	R 20	8	D 118	R 92	26
1859–1861	D 36	R 26	4	R 114	D 92	31

D   Democrat   W   Whig   R   Republican

U.S. Government Printing Office,
Historical Statistics of the United States, 1973

DOCUMENT F.

"A house divided against itself can not stand." I believe this Government can not endure permanently half slave and half free. I do not expect the Union to be dissolved—I do not expect the house to fall—but I do expect it will cease to be divided. It will become all one thing, or all the other. Either the opponents of slavery will arrest the further spread of it, and place it where the public mind shall rest in the belief that it is in the course of ultimate extinction; or its advocates will push it forward till it shall become alike lawful in all the States, old as well as new, North as well as South.

Abraham Lincoln,
Speech at the Republican state convention,
Springfield, Illinois, June 17, 1858

DOCUMENT G.

In my opinion our government can endure forever, divided into free and slave States as our fathers made it,—each State having the right to prohibit, abolish, or sustain slavery, just as it pleases. This government was made upon the great basis of the sovereignty of the states, the right of each State to regulate its own domestic institutions to suit itself; and that right was conferred with the understanding and expectation that, inasmuch as each locality had separate interests, each locality must have different and distinct local and domestic institutions, corresponding to its wants and interests. Our fathers knew, when they made the government, that the laws and institutions which were well adapted to the green mountains of Vermont, were unsuited to the rice plantations of South Carolina.

Stephen Douglas,
Speech at Alton, Illinois, October 15, 1858

DOCUMENT H.

If John Brown did not end the war that ended slavery, he did, at least, begin the war that ended slavery. . . .

The irrepressible conflict was one of words, votes, and compromises. When John Brown stretched forth his arm the sky was cleared . . . and the clash of arms was at hand.

Frederick Douglass,
Speech at Storer College,
Harpers Ferry, Virginia, May, 1882

DOCUMENT I.

We affirm that these ends for which this government was instituted have been defeated and the Government itself has been destructive of them by the action of the nonslaveholding States. Those states have assumed the right of deciding upon the propriety of our domestic institutions; and have denied the rights of property established in fifteen of the states and recognized by the Constitution; they have denounced as sinful the institution of slavery; they have permitted the open establishment among them of societies, whose avowed object is to disturb the peace of and eloign [take away] the property of the citizens of other States. They have encouraged and assisted thousands of our slaves to leave their homes; and those who remain, have been incited by emissaries, books, and pictures, to servile insurrection.

For twenty-five years this agitation has been steadily increasing, until it has now secured to its aid the power of the common Government. Observing the *forms* of the Constitution, a sectional party has found within that article establishing the Executive Department, the means of subverting the Constitution itself. A geographical line has been drawn across the Union, and all the States north of that line have united in the election of a man to the high office of President of the United States whose opinions and purposes are hostile to slavery. He is to be entrusted with the administration of the common Government, because he has declared that that "Government can not endure permanently half slave [and] half free," and that the public mind must rest in the belief that slavery is in the course of ultimate extinction.

A Declaration of the Causes Which Induced
the Secession of South Carolina,
Charleston, South Carolina, December 24, 1860

THE CIVIL WAR, 1861–1865

It is enough to make the whole world start to see the awful amount of death and destruction that now stalks abroad. Daily for the past two months has the work progressed and I see no signs of a remission till one or both the armies are destroyed. . . . I begin to regard the death and mangling of a couple of thousand men as a small affair, a kind of morning dash—and it may be well that we become so hardened.

General William T. Sherman, June 30, 1864

The Civil War between the North and the South (1861–1865) was the most costly of all American wars in terms of the loss of human life—and also the most destructive war ever fought in the Western Hemisphere. The deaths of 620,000 men was a true national tragedy, but constituted only part of the impact of the war years on American society. As a result of the Civil War, 4 million people were freed from slavery, which gave the nation, as President Lincoln said at Gettysburg, a "new birth of freedom." The war also transformed American society by accelerating industrialization and modernization in the North and largely destroying the plantation system in the South. These changes were so fundamental and profound that some historians refer to the Civil War as the Second American Revolution. While this chapter summarizes the major military aspects of the Civil War, students should also place at least equal emphasis on understanding the social, economic, and political changes that took place during the war.

The War Begins

When Lincoln was inaugurated as the first Republican president in March 1861, it was not at all clear that he would employ military means to challenge the secession of South Carolina and other states. In his inaugural address, Lincoln assured southerners that he had no intention of interfering with slavery or any other southern institution. At the same time, he warned, no state had the right to break up the Union. Lincoln concluded by appealing for restraint:

> In *your* hands, my dissatisfied fellow-countrymen, and not in *mine,* is the momentous issue of civil war. The government will not assail *you.* You can have no conflict without being yourselves the aggressors.

Fort Sumter

Despite the president's message of both conciliation and warning, the danger of a war breaking out was acute. Most critical was the status of two forts in the South that were held by federal troops but claimed by a seceded state. One of these, Fort Sumter, in the harbor of Charleston, South Carolina, was cut off from vital supplies and reinforcements by southern control of the harbor. Rather than either giving up Fort Sumter or attempting to defend it, Lincoln announced that he was sending provisions of food to the small federal garrison. He thus gave South Carolina the choice of either permitting the fort to hold out or opening fire with its shore batteries. Southern guns thundered their reply and thus, on April 12, 1861, the war began. The attack on Fort Sumter and its capture after two days of incessant pounding united most northerners behind a patriotic fight to save the Union.

Use of executive power. More than any previous president, Lincoln acted in unprecedented ways, drawing upon his powers as both chief executive and commander in chief, often without the authorization or approval of Congress. He did so for the first time in the Fort Sumter crisis by (1) calling for 75,000 volunteers to put down the "insurrection" in the South, (2) authorizing spending for the war, and (3) suspending the privilege of the writ of habeas corpus. Since Congress was not in session, the president acted completely on his own authority. Lincoln later explained that he had to take strong measures without congressional approval "as indispensable to the public safety."

Secession of the Upper South

Before the attack on Fort Sumter, only seven states of the Deep South had seceded. After it had become clear that Lincoln would use troops in the crisis, four states of the Upper South—Virginia, North Carolina, Tennessee, and Arkansas—also seceded and joined the Confederacy. The capital of the Confederacy was then moved to Richmond, Virginia. The people of western Virginia remained loyal to the Union, and the region became a separate state in 1863.

Keeping the Border States in the Union

Four other slaveholding states might have seceded, but instead remained in the Union. The decision of Delaware, Maryland, Missouri, and Kentucky *not* to join the Confederacy was partly due to Union sentiment in those states and partly the result of shrewd federal policies. In Maryland, prosecessionists attacked Union troops and threatened the railroad to Washington. The Union army resorted to martial law to keep the state under federal control. In Missouri, the presence of U.S. troops prevented the pro-South elements in the state from gaining control, although guerrilla forces sympathetic to the Confederacy were active throughout the war. In Kentucky, the state legislature voted to remain neutral in the conflict. Lincoln initially respected its neutrality and waited for the South to violate it before moving in federal troops.

Keeping the border states in the Union was a primary military as well as political goal for Lincoln. Their loss would have increased the Confederate population by more than 50 percent and also would have severely weakened the North's strategic position for conducting the war. Not wanting to alienate Unionists in the border states, Lincoln was reluctant to push for early emancipation of slaves.

Wartime Advantages

Military. The South entered the war with the advantage of having to fight only a defensive war to win, while the North had to conquer an area as large as Western Europe. The South had to move troops and supplies shorter distances than the North. It had a long, indented coastline that was difficult to blockade and, most importantly, experienced military leaders and high troop morale. The North's hope was that its population of 22 million against the South's free population of only $5\frac{1}{2}$ million free whites would work to its favor in a war of attrition. The North's advantage was enhanced during the war by 800,000 immigrants who in large numbers enlisted in the Union cause. Emancipation also brought over 180,000 African Americans into the Union army in the critical final years of the war. The North could also count on a loyal U.S. Navy, which ultimately gave it command of the rivers and territorial waters.

Economic. The North's great strength was an economy that controlled most of the banking and capital of the country, over 85 percent of the factories and manufactured goods, over 70 percent of the railroads, and even 65 percent of the farmlands. The skills of northern clerks and bookkeepers also proved valuable in the logistical support of large military operations. The hope of the southern economy was that overseas demand for its cotton would bring recognition and financial aid. History supports the belief that outside help is essential if wars for independence are to be successful.

Political. Its struggle for independence may seem to have given the South more motivation than the North's task of preserving the Union. However, the South's ideology of states' rights proved a serious liability for the new Confederate government. The irony was that in order to win the war, the South needed a strong central government with strong public support. The South had neither, while the North had a well-established central government, and in Abraham Lincoln and in the Republican and Democratic parties it had experienced politicians with a strong popular base. The ultimate hope of the South was that the people of the North would turn against Lincoln and the Republicans and quit the war because it was too costly.

The Confederate States of America

The constitution of the Confederacy was modeled after the U.S. Constitution, but it provided a nonsuccessive six-year term for the president and vice president and presidential item veto. Its constitution denied the Confederate congress the powers to levy a protective tariff and to appropriate funds for internal improvements, but it did prohibit the foreign slave trade. President Jefferson Davis tried to increase his executive powers during the war, but southern governors resisted attempts at centralization, some holding back men and resources to protect their own states. At one point, Vice President Alexander H. Stephens, in defense of states' rights, even urged the secession of Georgia in response to the "despotic" actions of the Confederate government.

The Confederacy always faced a serious shortage of money. It tried loans, income taxes (including a 10 percent tax in-kind on farm produce), and even impressment of private property, but these revenues paid for only a small percentage of the war's costs. The government was forced to issue more than $1 billion in inflationary paper money, which reduced the value of a Confederate dollar to less than two cents by the closing days of the war. The Confederate congress nationalized the railroads and encouraged industrial development. The Confederacy sustained nearly 1 million troops at its peak, but a war of attrition doomed its efforts. The real surprise is that the South was able to persist for four years.

First Years of a Long War: 1861–1862

Northerners at first expected the war to last no more than a few weeks. Lincoln called up the first volunteers for an enlistment period of only 90 days. "On to Richmond!" was the optimistic cry, but as Americans soon learned, it would take almost four years of ferocious fighting before northern troops finally did march into the Confederate capital.

First Battle of Bull Run. In the first major battle of the war (July 1861) 30,000 federal troops marched from Washington, D.C., to attack Confederate forces positioned near Bull Run Creek at Manassas Junction, Virginia. Just as the Union forces seemed close to victory, Confederate reinforcements under General Thomas (Stonewall) Jackson counterattacked and sent the inexperienced Union troops in disorderly and panicky flight back to Washington (together with civilian curiosity-seekers and picnickers). The battle ended the illusion of a short war and also promoted the myth that the Rebels were invincible in battle.

Union strategy. General-in-Chief Winfield Scott, veteran of the 1812 and Mexican wars, devised a three-part strategy for winning a long war:

- Use the U.S. navy to blockade southern ports (the Anaconda Plan, as it was called) and thereby cut off essential supplies from reaching the South
- Divide the Confederacy in two by taking control of the Mississippi River
- Raise and train an army 500,000 strong to take Richmond

As it happened, the first two parts of the strategy were easier to achieve than the third, but ultimately all three aspects of Scott's plan were important in achieving northern victory.

After the Union's defeat at Bull Run, federal armies experienced a succession of crushing defeats as they attempted various campaigns in Virginia, each less successful than the one before.

Peninsula campaign. General George B. McClellan, the new commander of the Union army in the East, insisted that his troops be given a long period of training and discipline before going into battle. Finally, after many delays that sorely tested Lincoln's patience, McClellan's army invaded Virginia in March 1862. The Union army was stopped as a result of brilliant tactical moves by Confederate General Robert E. Lee, who emerged as the commander of the South's eastern forces. After five months, McClellan was forced to retreat and was ordered back to the Potomac, where he was replaced by General John Pope.

Second Battle of Bull Run. Lee took advantage of the change in Union generals to strike quickly at Pope's army in northern Virginia. He drew Pope into a trap, then struck the enemy's flank, and sent the Union army backward to Bull Run. Pope withdrew to the defenses of Washington.

Antietam. Following up his victory at Bull Run, Lee led his army across the Potomac into enemy territory in Maryland. In doing so, he hoped that a major Confederate victory in the North would convince Britain to give official recognition and support to the Confederacy. By this time (September 1862), Lincoln had restored McClellan to command of the Union army. McClellan had the advantage of knowing Lee's battle plan, because a copy of it had been dropped accidentally by a Confederate officer. The Union army intercepted the invading Confederates at Antietam Creek in the Maryland town of Sharpsburg. Here the bloodiest single day of combat in the entire war took place, a day in which over 22,000 men were either killed or wounded.

Unable to break through Union lines, Lee's army retreated to Virginia. Disappointed with McClellan for failing to pursue Lee's weakened and retreating army, Lincoln removed him for a final time as commander of the Union army. The president complained that his general had a "bad case of the slows." While technically a draw, Antietam in the long run proved to be a decisive battle, because it stopped the Confederates from getting what they so urgently needed—open recognition and aid from a foreign power. Lincoln too found enough encouragement in the results of Antietam to claim it as a Union victory. Grasping at a rare opportunity to make a bold change in policy, Lincoln used the partial triumph of Union arms to announce plans for the Emancipation Proclamation (see below, page 272).

Fredericksburg. Replacing McClellan with the more aggressive General Ambrose Burnside, Lincoln discovered that a strategy of reckless attack could have even worse consequences than McClellan's strategy of caution and inaction. In December 1862, a large Union army under Burnside attacked Lee's army at Fredericksburg, Virginia, and suffered immense losses: 12,000 dead or wounded compared to 5,000 Confederate casualties. Both Union and Confederate generals were slow to learn that improved weaponry, especially the deadly fire from enemy artillery, took the romance out of heroic charges against entrenched positions. By the end of 1862, the awful magnitude of the war was all too clear—with no prospect of military victory for either side.

The second year of war, 1862, was a disastrous one for the North except for two engagements, one at sea and the other on the rivers of the West.

***Monitor* vs. *Merrimac*.** The North's hopes for winning the war depended upon its ability to maximize its economic and naval advantages by shutting down the South's sources of supply. Establishing an effective blockade of southern ports (the Anaconda Plan) was crucial to this objective. During McClellan's Peninsula campaign, the North's blockade strategy was placed in jeopardy by the Confederate ironclad ship the *Merrimac* (a former Union ship, rebuilt and renamed the *Virginia*) that could attack and sink the Union's wooden ships almost at will. The Union navy countered with an ironclad of its own, the *Monitor*, which fought a five-hour duel with the southern ironclad near Hampton Roads, Virginia, in March 1862. Although the battle ended in a draw, the *Monitor* prevented the South's formidable new weapon, an ironclad ship, from seriously challenging the U.S. naval blockade.

The *Monitor-Merrimac* duel was also important for another reason. The ease with which these two ironclads destroyed wooden sailing ships was to revolutionize the future of naval warfare.

Grant in the West. The battle of the ironclads occurred at about the same time as a far bloodier encounter in western Tennessee, a Confederate state. The North's campaign for control of the Mississippi River was partly under the command of a West Point graduate, Ulysses S. Grant, who had joined up for the war after an unsuccessful civilian career. Striking south from Illinois in early 1862, Grant used a combination of gunboats and army maneuvers to capture Fort Henry and Fort Donelson on the Cumberland River (a branch of the Mississippi). These stunning victories, in which 14,000 Confederates were taken prisoner, opened up the state of Mississippi to Union attack. A few weeks later, a Confederate army under Albert Johnston surprised Grant at Shiloh, Tennessee, but the Union army held its ground and finally forced the Confederates to retreat after terrible losses on both sides (over 23,000 dead and wounded). Grant's drive down the Mississippi was complemented in April 1862 by the capture of New Orleans by the Union navy under David Farragut.

Foreign Affairs and Diplomacy

The South's hopes for securing its independence hinged as much on its diplomats as on its soldiers. Confederate leaders fully expected that cotton would indeed prove to be "king" and induce Britain or France, or both, to give direct aid to the South's war effort. Besides depending on southern cotton for their textile mills, wealthy British industrialists and members of the British aristocracy looked forward with pleasure to the breakup of the American democratic experiment. From the North's point of view, it was critically important to prevent the Confederacy from gaining the foreign support and recognition that it so desperately needed.

Trent Affair

Britain came close to siding with the Confederacy in late 1861 over an incident at sea. Confederate diplomats James Mason and John Slidell were traveling to England on a British steamer, the *Trent,* on a mission to gain recognition for their government. A Union warship stopped the British ship, removed Mason and Slidell, and brought them to the United States as prisoners of war. Britain threatened war over the incident unless the two diplomats were released. Although he faced severe public criticism for doing so, Lincoln gave in to British demands. Mason and Slidell were duly set free, but after again sailing for Europe, they failed to obtain full recognition of the Confederacy from either Britain or France.

Confederate Raiders

The South was able to gain enough recognition as a belligerent to purchase warships from British shipyards. Confederate commerce-raiders did serious harm to U.S. merchant ships. One of them, the *Alabama,* captured over 60 vessels before being sunk off the coast of France by a Union warship. After the war, Great Britain eventually agreed to pay the United States $15.5 million for damages caused by the South's commerce-raiders.

The U.S. minister to Britain, Charles Francis Adams, prevented a potentially much more serious threat. Learning that the Confederacy had arranged to purchase Laird rams (ships with iron rams) from Britain for use against the North's naval blockade, Adams persuaded the British government to cancel the sale rather than risk war with the United States.

Failure of Cotton Diplomacy

In the end, the South's hopes for European intervention were disappointed. "King Cotton" did not have the power to dictate another nation's foreign policy, since Europe quickly found ways of obtaining cotton from other sources. By the time shortages of southern cotton hit the British textile industry, adequate shipments of cotton began arriving from Egypt and India. Also, materials other than cotton could be used for textiles, and the woolen and linen industries were not slow to take advantage of their opportunity.

Two other factors went into Britain's decision not to recognize the Confederacy. First, as mentioned, General Lee's setback at Antietam played a role; without a decisive Confederate military victory, the British government would not risk recognition. Second, Lincoln's Emancipation Proclamation (January 1863) made the end of slavery an objective of the North, a fact that appealed strongly to Britain's working class. While conservative leaders of Britain were sympathetic to the South, they could not defy the pronorthern, antislavery feelings of the British majority.

The End of Slavery

Even though Lincoln in the 1850s spoke out against slavery as "an unqualified evil," as president he seemed hesitant to take action against slavery as advocated by many of his Republican supporters. Lincoln's concerns included (1) keeping the support of the border states, (2) the constitutional protections of slavery, (3) the prejudices of many northerners, and (4) the fear that premature action could be overturned in the next election. All these concerns made the timing and method of freeing the slaves fateful decisions. Slaves were freed during the Civil War as a result of military events, governmental policy, and their own actions.

Confiscation Acts

Early in the war (May 1861), Union General Benjamin Butler refused to return captured slaves to their Confederate owners, arguing that they were "contraband of war." The power to seize enemy property used to wage war against the United States was the legal basis for the first Confiscation Act passed by Congress in August 1861. Soon after the passage of this act, thousands of "contrabands" were using their feet to escape slavery by finding their way into Union camps. In July 1862 a second Confiscation Act was passed that freed the slaves of persons engaged in rebellion against the United States. The law also empowered the president to use freed slaves in the Union army in any capacity, including battle.

Emancipation Proclamation

By July 1862 Lincoln had already decided to use his powers as commander in chief of the armed forces to free all slaves in the states then at war with the

United States. He would justify his policy by calling it a "military necessity." Lincoln delayed announcement of the policy, however, until he could win the support of conservative northerners. At the same time, he encouraged the border states to come up with plans for emancipating slaves, with compensation to the owners.

After the Battle of Antietam, on September 22, 1862, Lincoln issued a warning that slaves in all states still in rebellion on January 1, 1863 would be "then, thenceforward, and forever free." As promised, on the first day of the new year, 1863, the president issued his Emancipation Proclamation. After listing states from Arkansas to Virginia that were in rebellion, the proclamation stated:

> . . . I do order and declare that all persons held as slaves within said designated States and parts of States are, and henceforward shall be, free; and that the Executive Government of the United States, including the military and naval authorities thereof, shall recognize and maintain the freedom of said persons.

Consequences. Since the president's proclamation applied only to slaves residing in Confederate states *outside* Union control, it did not immediately free a single slave. Slavery in the border states was allowed to continue. Even so, the proclamation was of major importance. Not only did it commit the U.S. government to a policy of abolition in the South, but it also enlarged the purpose of the war. Now, for the first time, Union armies were fighting against slavery, not merely against secession and rebellion. The proclamation gave added weight to the Confiscation acts, increasing the number of slaves who sought freedom by fleeing to Union lines. Thus, with each advance of northern troops into the South, more slaves were liberated. As an added blow to the South, the proclamation also authorized the recruitment of freed slaves as Union soldiers.

Thirteenth Amendment

Standing in the way of full emancipation were phrases in the U.S. Constitution that seemed to legitimize slavery. To free the slaves in the border states, a constitutional amendment was needed. Even the abolitionists gave Lincoln credit for playing an active role in the political struggle to secure enough votes in Congress to pass the Thirteenth Amendment. By December 1865 (months after Lincoln's death), this amendment abolishing slavery was ratified by the required number of states. The language of the amendment could not be simpler or clearer:

> Neither slavery nor involuntary servitude, except as a punishment for crime whereof the party shall have been duly convicted, shall exist within the United States, or any place subject to their jurisdiction.

Freedmen in the War

After the Emancipation Proclamation (January 1863), hundreds of thousands of southern blacks—approximately one-quarter of the slave population—walked away from slavery to seek the protection of the approaching Union armies. Almost 200,000 African Americans, most of whom were newly freed slaves, served in the Union army and navy. Segregated into all-black units, such as the Massachusetts 54th Regiment, black troops performed courageously under fire and won the respect of northern white soldiers. Over 37,000 African American soldiers died in what became known as the Army of Freedom.

The Union Triumphs, 1863–1865

By the beginning of 1863, the fortunes of war had turned against the South. Although General Robert E. Lee started the year with another major victory at Chancellorsville, Virginia, the Confederate economy was in desperate shape, southern planters and farmers were losing control of their slave-labor force, and an increasing number of poorly provisioned soldiers were deserting from the Confederate army.

Turning Point

The decisive turning point in the war came in the first week of July when the Confederacy suffered two crushing defeats in the West and the East.

Vicksburg. In the West, by the spring of 1863, Union forces controlled New Orleans and most of the Mississippi River and surrounding valley. Thus, the Union objective of securing complete control of the Mississippi River was close to an accomplished fact when General Grant began his siege of the heavily fortified city of Vicksburg, Mississippi. Union artillery bombarded Vicksburg for seven weeks before the Confederates finally surrendered the city (and nearly 29,000 soldiers) on July 4. Federal warships now controlled the full length of the Mississippi and cut off Texas, Louisiana, and Arkansas from the rest of the Confederacy.

Gettysburg. Meanwhile, in the East, Lee again took the offensive by leading an army into enemy territory: the Union states of Maryland and Pennsylvania. If he could either destroy the Union army or capture a major northern city, Lee hoped to force the North to call for peace—or at least to gain foreign intervention for the South. On July 1, 1863, the invading southern army surprised Union units at Gettysburg in southern Pennsylvania. What followed was the most crucial battle of the war and the bloodiest, with over 50,000 casualties. Lee's assault on Union lines on the second and third days, including Pickett's charge, proved futile, and destroyed a good part of the Confederate army. What was left of Lee's forces retreated to Virginia, never to regain the offensive.

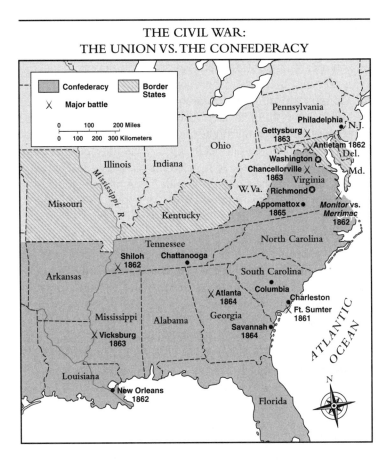

THE CIVIL WAR:
THE UNION VS. THE CONFEDERACY

Grant in Command

Lincoln finally found a general who could fight and win. In early 1864 he brought Grant east to Virginia and made him commander of all the Union armies. Grant's approach to ending the war was simply to outlast Lee by fighting a war of attrition. Recognizing that the South's resources were dwindling, he aimed to wear down the southern armies and systematically destroy their vital lines of supply. Fighting doggedly for months, Grant's Army of the Potomac suffered heavier casualties than Lee's forces in the battles of the Wilderness, Spotsylvania, and Cold Harbor. But by never letting up, Grant succeeded in reducing Lee's army in each battle and forcing it into a defensive line around Richmond. In this final stage of the Civil War, the fighting foreshadowed the trench warfare that would later characterize World War I. No longer was this a war "between gentlemen" but a modern "total" war against civilians as well as soldiers.

Sherman's March. The chief instrument of Grant's aggressive tactics for subduing the South was a hardened veteran, General William Tecumseh Sherman. Leading a force of 100,000 men, Sherman set out from Chattanooga, Tennessee, on a campaign of deliberate destruction that went clear across the state of Georgia and then swept north into South Carolina. Sherman was a pioneer of the tactics of total war. Marching relentlessly through Georgia, his troops destroyed everything in their path, burning cotton fields, barns, and houses—everything the enemy might use to survive. Sherman took Atlanta in September 1864 in time to help Lincoln's prospects for reelection. He marched into Savannah in December and completed his campaign in February 1865 by setting fire to Columbia, the capital of South Carolina and cradle of secession.

Sherman's march had its intended effects: helping to break the will of the Confederacy and destroying its will to fight on.

The election of 1864. The Democrat's nominee for president was the popular General George McClellan. The Democrats' platform calling for peace had wide appeal among millions of voters who had grown weary of war. The Republicans renamed their party the Unionist party as a way of attracting the votes of "War Democrats" (those who disagreed with the Democratic platform). A brief "ditch-Lincoln" movement fizzled out, and the Republican (Unionist) convention again chose Lincoln as its presidential candidate and a loyal War Democrat from Tennessee, Senator Andrew Johnson, as his running mate. The Lincoln-Johnson ticket won 212 electoral votes to the Democrats' 21. The popular vote, however, was much closer, for McClellan took 45 percent of the total votes cast.

The End of the War

The effects of the Union blockade, combined with Sherman's march of destruction, spread hunger through much of the South in the winter of 1864–1865. On the battlefront in Virginia, Grant continued to outflank Lee's lines until they collapsed around Petersburg, resulting in the fall of Richmond (April 3, 1865). By now, everyone knew that the end was near.

Surrender at Appomattox. The Confederate government tried to negotiate for peace, but Lincoln would accept nothing short of restoration of the Union and Jefferson Davis nothing less than independence. Lee retreated from Richmond with an army of less than 30,000 men. He tried to escape to the mountains only to be cut off and forced to surrender to Grant at Appomattox Court House on April 9, 1865. The Union general treated his longtime enemy with respect and allowed Lee's men to return to their homes with their horses.

Assassination of Lincoln. Only a month before Lee's surrender, Lincoln delivered one of his greatest speeches—the second inaugural address. He urged that the defeated South be treated benevolently, "with malice toward none; with charity for all."

On April 14, John Wilkes Booth, an embittered actor and southern sympathizer, shot and killed the president while he was attending a performance in Ford's Theater in Washington. On the same night, a coconspirator attacked but only wounded Secretary of State William Seward. These shocking events aroused the fury of northerners at the very time that the South most needed a sympathetic hearing. The loss of Lincoln's leadership was widely mourned, but the extent of the loss was not fully appreciated until the two sections of a reunited country had to cope with the overwhelming problems of postwar Reconstruction.

Effects of the War on Civilian Life

Both during the war and in the years that followed, American society underwent deep and wrenching changes.

Political Change

The electoral process continued during the war with surprisingly few restrictions. Secession of the southern states had created Republican majorities in both houses of Congress. Within Republican ranks, however, there were sharp differences between the radical faction (those who championed the cause of immediate abolition of slavery) and the moderate faction (Free-Soilers who were chiefly concerned about economic opportunities for whites). Most Democrats supported the war but criticized Lincoln's conduct of it. Peace Democrats and Copperheads opposed the war and wanted a negotiated peace. The most notorious Copperhead, Congressman Clement L. Vallandigham of Ohio, was briefly banished from the United States to Canada for his "treasonable," pro-Confederacy speeches against the war.

Civil liberties. In wartime, governments tend to be more concerned with prosecuting the war than with protecting citizens' constitutional rights. Lincoln's government was no exception. Early in the war, Lincoln suspended the writ of habeas corpus in Maryland and other states where there was much pro-Confederate sentiment. Suspension of this constitutional right meant that persons could be arrested without being informed of the charges against them. During the war, an estimated 13,000 people were arrested on suspicion of aiding the enemy; without a right to habeas corpus, many of them were held without trial.

How flagrant was Lincoln's abuse of civil liberties? At the time, Democrats said that Lincoln acted no better than a tyrant, but few historians today would go that far in their judgment of the habeas corpus issue. Especially in the border states, it was often hard to distinguish between combatants and noncombatants. Moreover, the Constitution does state that the writ of habeas corpus "shall not be suspended, unless when in cases of rebellion or invasion the public safety may require it." After the war, in the case of *Ex Parte Milligan* (1866), the

Supreme Court ruled that the government had acted improperly in Indiana where, during the war, certain civilians had been subject to a military trial. The Court declared that such procedures could be used only when regular civilian courts were unavailable.

The draft. At first, those who fought in the Civil War were volunteers, but as the need for replacements became acute, both the North and the South resorted to laws for conscripting, or drafting, men into service. The Congress' first Conscription Act, adopted in March 1863, made all men between the ages of 20 and 45 liable for military service but allowed a draftee to avoid service by either finding a substitute to serve or paying a $300 exemption fee. The law provoked fierce opposition among poorer laborers, who feared that—if and when they returned to civilian life—their jobs would be taken by freed African Americans. In July 1863, riots against the draft erupted in New York City, in which a mostly Irish American mob attacked blacks and wealthy whites. Some 117 people were killed before federal troops and a temporary suspension of the draft restored order.

Political dominance of the North. The suspension of habeas corpus and the operation of the draft were only temporary. Far more important were the long-term effects of the war on the balance of power between two sectional rivals, the North and the South. With the military triumph of the North came a new definition of the nature of the federal union. Southern arguments for nullification and secession ceased to be issues. After the Civil War, the supremacy of the federal government over the states was treated as an established fact.

Furthermore, the abolition of slavery—in addition to its importance to freed African Americans—gave new meaning and legitimacy to the concept of American democracy. In his famous Gettysburg Address of November 19, 1863, Lincoln rallied Americans to the idea that their nation was "dedicated to the proposition that all men are created equal." Lincoln was probably alluding to the Emancipation Proclamation when he spoke of the war bringing "a new birth of freedom." His words—and even more, the fact of slavery being abolished—advanced the cause of democratic government in the United States and inspired champions of democracy around the world.

Economic Change

The costs of the war in both money and men were staggering and called for extraordinary measures by both the Union and Confederate legislatures.

Financing the war. The North financed the war chiefly by borrowing $2.6 billion, obtained through the sale of government bonds. Even this amount was not enough, so Congress was forced to resort to raising tariffs (Morrill Tariff of 1861), adding excise taxes, and instituting the first income tax. The U.S. Treasury also issued over $430 million in a paper currency known as

Greenbacks. This paper money could not be redeemed in gold, a fact that contributed to creeping inflation; prices in the North rose by about 80 percent from 1861–1865. To manage all the added revenue moving in and out of the Treasury, Congress created a National Banking System in 1863. This was the first unified banking network since Andrew Jackson vetoed the recharter of the Bank of the United States in the 1830s.

Modernizing northern society. The war's impact on the northern economy was no less significant. Economic historians differ on the question of whether, in the short run, the war promoted or retarded the growth of the northern economy. On the negative side, workers' wages did not keep pace with inflation. On the other hand, there is little doubt that many aspects of a modern industrial economy were accelerated by the war. Because the war placed a premium on mass production and complex organization, it speeded up the consolidation of the North's manufacturing businesses. War profiteers took advantage of the government's urgent needs for military supplies to sell shoddy goods at high prices. Fortunes made during the war (whether honestly or dishonestly) produced a concentration of capital in the hands of a new class of millionaires, who would finance the North's industrialization in the postwar years.

Republican politics also played a major role in stimulating the economic growth of the North and the West. Taking advantage of their wartime majority in Congress, the Republicans passed an ambitious economic program that included not only a national banking system, but also the following:

- *The Morrill Tariff Act* (1861) raised tariff rates to increase revenue and protect American manufacturers. Its passage initiated a Republican program of high protective tariffs to help industrialists.

- The *Homestead Act* (1862) promoted settlement of the Great Plains by offering parcels of 160 acres of public land free to whatever person or family would farm that land for at least five years.

- The *Morrill Land Grant Act* (1862) encouraged states to use the sale of federal land grants to maintain agricultural and technical colleges.

- The *Pacific Railway Act* (1862) authorized the building of a transcontinental railroad over a northern route in order to link the economies of California and the western territories with the eastern states.

Social Change

Although no part of American society away from the battlefield was untouched by the war, those most directly affected were women of all ages, whose labors became more burdensome, and African Americans, who were emancipated from slavery.

Women at work. The absence of millions of men from their normal occupations in fields and factories added to the labors and responsibilities of women at home. Southern and northern women alike stepped into the labor vacuum created by the war. They operated farms and plantations by themselves or, in the cities, took factory jobs normally held by men. In addition, women played a critical role as military nurses and as volunteers in soldiers' aid societies.

When the war ended and the war veterans returned home, most urban women vacated their jobs in government and industry, while rural women gladly accepted male assistance on the farm. Of course, for the women whose men never returned—or returned disabled—the economic struggle continued for a lifetime.

The Civil War had at least two permanent effects on American women. First, the field of nursing was now open to women for the first time; previously, hospitals employed only men as doctors and nurses. Second, the enormous responsibilities undertaken by women during the war gave impetus to the movement to obtain equal voting rights for women. (The suffragists' goal would not be achieved until women's efforts in another war—World War I— finally convinced male conservatives to adopt the Nineteenth Amendment.)

End of slavery. Both in the short run and the long run, the group in American society whose lives were most profoundly changed by the Civil War were those African Americans who had been born into slavery. After the adoption of the Thirteenth Amendment in 1865, 4 million people (3.5 million in the Confederate states, 500,000 in the border states) were "freed men" and "freed women." For these people and their descendants, economic hardship and political oppression would continue for generations, but even so, the end of slavery represented a momentous step. Suddenly, slaves with no rights were protected by the U.S. Constitution, with open-ended possibilities of freedom.

While four years of nearly total war, the tragic human loss of 620,000 men, and an estimated $15 billion in war costs and property losses had enormous effects on the nation, far greater changes were set in motion. The Civil War destroyed slavery and devastated the southern economy, and it also acted as a catalyst to transform America into a complex modern industrial society of capital, technology, national organizations, and large corporations. During the war, the Republicans were able to enact the probusiness Whig program that was designed to stimulate the industrial and commercial growth of the United States. The characteristics of American democracy and its capitalist economy were strengthened by this *second American Revolution.*

HISTORICAL PERSPECTIVES: WHY THE NORTH WON

The North's victory in the Civil War was by no means inevitable. Why did the North win and the South lose? To be sure, the North had the advantage of a larger population and superior wealth, industry, and transportation. On the other hand, the South's advantages were also formidable. The Confederacy needed merely to fight to a stalemate and hold out long enough to secure foreign recognition or intervention. The North faced the more daunting challenge of having to conquer an area comparable in size to Western Europe.

Some historians blame the South's defeat on the overly aggressive military strategy of its generals. For example, Lee's two invasions of the North leading to Antietam and Gettysburg resulted in a much higher loss of his own men, in percentage terms, than of his opponent's forces. If the Confederates had used more defensive and conservative tactics, they may have secured a military stalemate—and political victory (independence).

Other historians blame the South's loss on its political leadership. They argue that, compared to the Lincoln administration, Jefferson Davis and his cabinet were ineffective. Another weakness was the lack of a strong political party system in the South. Its absence meant that Davis had trouble developing a base of popular support. Southerners' traditional emphasis on states' rights also worked against a unified war effort. Governors of Confederate states would withhold troops rather than yield to the central government's urgent requests for cooperation. Vital supplies were also held back in state warehouses, where they remained until war's end.

Historian Henry S. Commager argued that slavery may have been responsible for the South's defeat. For one thing, slavery played a role in deterring European powers from intervening in support of the South and its backward institution. Beyond this, Commager also believed that slavery undermined the South's ability to adapt to new challenges. It fostered an intolerant society, which lacked the "habit of independent inquiry and criticism." Thus, according to Commager, the failure of the Confederacy was not a "failure of resolution or courage or will but of intelligence and morality." If so, then the South's attachment to an outdated institution, slavery, was what ultimately meant the difference between victory and defeat.

KEY NAMES, EVENTS, AND TERMS

Fort Sumter	Jefferson Davis	George McClellan
executive power	Alexander H. Stephens	Robert E. Lee
habeas corpus	Bull Run	Antietam
insurrection	Thomas (Stonewall) Jackson	Fredericksburg
border states		*Monitor* and *Merrimac*
Confederate States of America	Winfield Scott	Ulysses S. Grant
	Anaconda Plan	Shiloh

David Farragut	Vicksburg	greenbacks
Trent Affair	Sherman's March	Morrill Tariff Act (1861)
Alabama	election of 1864	Homestead Act (1862)
laird rams	Appomattox Court House	Morrill Land Grant Act
Confiscation acts	John Wilkes Booth	(1862)
Emancipation Proclamation	Copperheads	Pacific Railway Act (1862)
Thirteenth Amendment	*Ex Parte Milligan*	second American Revolution
Gettysburg	draft riots	

MULTIPLE-CHOICE QUESTIONS

1. Northern advantages in the Civil War included all of the following EXCEPT
   (A) a superior navy
   (B) a political party system that could marshal support for the war
   (C) a superior railroad network
   (D) general agreement over war aims
   (E) greater capacity to produce military equipment

2. All of the following were part of the initial Union strategy to win the Civil War EXCEPT
   (A) a naval blockade of southern ports
   (B) control of the Mississippi River
   (C) the capture of Richmond
   (D) keeping the border states in the Union
   (E) emancipation of slaves in the seceded states

3. The Confederate government was able to achieve which of the following goals?

   (A) recognition by a foreign power
   (B) frequent victories over Union armies
   (C) a stable monetary system
   (D) a strong central government
   (E) control of the southern river system

4. President Lincoln was reluctant to emancipate the slaves in the first year of the Civil War because
   (A) he feared that freeing the slaves would bring England and France into the war
   (B) Congress was opposed to emancipation
   (C) he knew that a proclamation about slavery would only further alienate the South
   (D) he feared that emancipation would drive the border states out of the Union
   (E) he had always been opposed to the abolitionists in his party

5. Which of the following best describes an immediate effect of the Emancipation Proclamation?

(A) Slaves in the border states became free.

(B) Slaves in the Deep South became free.

(C) The abolition of slavery in Confederate territory became one of the North's war goals.

(D) Lincoln's reelection was assured.

(E) Draft riots erupted in New York City.

6. Lee's major reason for invading northern territory in 1863 was to

(A) win foreign recognition for the Confederacy

(B) obtain military supplies

(C) seek revenge for northern attacks in Virginia

(D) break the Union blockade

(E) destroy the North's industrial capacity

7. The economic impact of the Civil War included all of the following EXCEPT

(A) an increasing number of women in the labor force

(B) widespread destruction of property in the South

(C) creation of a national banking system in the North

(D) reduced rate of industrial production in the North

(E) runaway inflation in the South

8. Which of the following accurately describes northern politics during the Civil War?

(A) Democrats challenged Republicans for control of national and state offices.

(B) Republicans were united behind Lincoln's leadership.

(C) The suspension of habeas corpus discouraged many Democrats from voting.

(D) Lincoln had no trouble winning reelection in 1864.

(E) Copperhead candidates campaigned for equal rights for women.

9. All of the following were factors in the defeat of the South in 1865 EXCEPT

(A) shortages caused by the Union's naval blockade

(B) slave uprisings against southern plantations

(C) Grant's war of attrition in Virginia

(D) Sherman's march through Georgia

(E) the Confederacy's failure to obtain foreign intervention

10. One of the long-term political consequences of northern victory was

(A) an end of threats of nullification and secession

(B) dominance of the Republican party in the South

(C) continuing sectional conflict over the issue of slavery

(D) a balance of power in Congress between the North and the South

(E) suspension of the writ of habeas corpus

ESSAY QUESTIONS

1. How did economic and political factors help cause the South to lose the Civil War?

2. "Lincoln was one of the most democratic and also one of the most autocratic of presidents." Explain what is meant by this statement and then give reasons for either agreeing or disagreeing with it.

3. Assess the effectiveness of the military leadership, strategies, and tactics of the North and the South during the Civil War.

4. Analyze the impact of any TWO of the following on the ending of slavery during the Civil War:
   President Lincoln
   U.S. Congress
   slaves and former slaves

5. To what extent is it correct to say that the Civil War represented a second American Revolution?

DOCUMENTS AND READINGS

The documents section opens and closes with examples of important and influential statements of President Lincoln. However, diaries, letters, and interviews of lesser known participants, including women and slaves, can also provide powerful insights into the events of the Civil War.

DOCUMENT A. THE NATURE OF THE UNION

President Lincoln's message to a special session of Congress on July 4, 1861, included a carefully worded argument against secession and states' rights. In the process he explained the basis for the supremacy of the Union over the states, which it ultimately took victory on the battlefield to establish.

> It might seem, at first thought, to be of little difference whether the present movement at the South be called "secession" or "rebellion" . . . they [South] commenced by an insidious debauching of the public mind. They invented an ingenious sophism which, if conceded, was followed by perfectly logical steps, through all the incidents, to the complete destruction of the Union. The sophism itself is that any State of the Union may *consistently* with the national Constitution, and therefore lawfully and peacefully, withdraw from the Union without the consent of the Union or of any other State. . . .
>
> Our States have neither more nor less power than that reserved to them in the Union by the Constitution—no one of them have been a State out of the Union . . . excepting Texas. . . . Having never

been States either in substance or in name outside of the Union, whence this magical omnipotence of "State rights," asserting a claim of power to lawfully destroy the Union itself? The States have their status in the Union, and they have no other legal status. If they break from this, they can only do so against law and by revolution. The Union and not themselves separately, procured their independence and their liberty. By conquest or purchase the Union gave each of them whatever of independence or liberty it has. The Union is older than any of the States and, in fact, it created them as States. . . . Not one of them ever had a State constitution independent of the Union.

Our popular government has often been called an experiment. It is now for [our people] to demonstrate to the world that those who can fairly carry an election can also suppress a rebellion; that ballots are the rightful and peaceful successors of bullets; and that when ballots have fairly and constitutionally decided, there can be no successful appeal back to bullets; that there can be no successful appeal, except to ballots themselves, at succeeding elections. Such will be a great lesson of peace: teaching men that what they cannot take by an election, neither can they take it by war; teaching all the folly of being the beginners of a war. . . .

Abraham Lincoln,
Message to Congress,
July 4, 1861

DOCUMENT B.   *LAST YEAR OF THE CONFEDERACY*

As the wife of a U.S. senator from South Carolina and the daughter of a governor of that state, Mary Chesnut viewed the events of 1861–1865 from the vantage point of a member of the governing elite. She kept a diary, faithfully recording her impression of events as they unfolded. The following excerpts from her Columbia, South Carolina diary are from the Confederacy's last full year, 1864.

March 24—Yesterday, we went to the capitol grounds to see our returned prisoners. We walked slowly up and down until Jeff Davis was called to speak. There I stood, almost touching the bayonets when he left me. I looked straight into the prisoners' faces, poor fellows. They cheered with all their might, and I wept for sympathy and enthusiasm. I was deeply moved. These men were so forlorn, so dried up and shrunken, with such a strange look in some of their eyes, others so restless and wild looking; others, again, placidly vacant, as if they had been dead to the world for years. A poor woman was too much for me. She was searching for her son. He had been expected back. She said he was taken prisoner at Gettysburg. She kept going in and out among them with a basket of provisions she had brought for him to eat. It was too pitiful. She was utterly unconscious of the crowd. The anxious dread, expectation, hurry, and hope which led her on showed in her face.

September 21—Went with Mrs. Rhett to hear Dr. Palmer [Protestant minister]. Despair was his word, and martyrdom. He offered us nothing more in this world than the martyr's crown. He is not for slavery, he says, he is for freedom, and freedom to govern our own country as we see fit. . . . Every day shows slavery is doomed the world over; for that he thanked God. He spoke of our agony, and then came the cry, "Help us, O God! Vain is the help of man." And so we came away shaken to the depths.

September 24—These stories of our defeats in the valley fall like blows upon a dead body. Since Atlanta fell, I felt as if all were dead within me forever. . . . The reserves, as somebody said, have been secured only by robbing the cradle and the grave—the men too old, the boys too young.

Isabella D. Martin and Mytra L. Avary, eds.,
A Diary From Dixie, 1905

DOCUMENT C.   *ESCAPING FROM SLAVERY*

A northern newspaper reporter interviewed an escaped slave named John Parker, who explained how he had used the presence of Union troops at the Battle of Bull Run in July 1861 to flee to freedom. Parker had actually been made to participate in the battle by his master before he saw his opportunity to escape into Union ranks.

There were officers prowling round the neighborhood in search of all the Negroes, but we dodged round so smartly, they didn't catch us. . . . I was afraid to stay long in the neighborhood for fear of the officers, so I left and came nearer the American lines. I found the U.S. soldiers at Alexandria, who gave two papers, one for myself and one for my wife; they asked me whether I could get my wife, I said I would try. . . . I fixed another plan to get my wife over, I was to meet her in a canoe and ferry her across, but I missed her though, and I think she must have gone too high up the river. When I had given her up I went along up the river and came up with some of the pickets in Gen. Banks' division, near Frederick, Md. I was afraid, but they welcomed me and shouted; "Come on! don't hurt him!" Some of the pickets were on horseback, they gave me a suit of clothes and plenty to eat, and treated me well. They wanted me to stay and go down into Virginia and tell them all about where the batteries were, but I was afraid to try that country again, and said that I was bound for the North, I told them all I knew about the position of the other army, about the powder mill on the Rappahannock river, etc. They let me go. . . . I left at night and travelled for the [North] star, I was afraid of the Secessionists in Maryland, and I only walked at night. I came to Gettysburg in a week, and I thought when I saw the big barns, that I was in another country. . . . I am going from here to New York where I hope to meet my wife; she has two girls with her; one of my boys is with my master, and the other, who is 14 years old, I think was taken to Louisiana. My wife and I are going to travel from New York to Canada.

Quoted in James M. McPherson, *Marching Toward Freedom*
(Alfred A. Knopf, 1965)

DOCUMENT D.   BLACK TROOPS IN SOUTH CAROLINA

Freed slaves in the South Carolina Sea Islands volunteered for military service in late 1862 to form the first regiment of black troops in the Union army. Thomas Wentworth Higginson, their commanding officer, was a white abolitionist from Massachusetts. After the regiment's first battle, Higginson wrote the following report:

> No officer in this regiment now doubts that the key to the successful prosecution of this war lies in the unlimited employment of black troops. Their superiority lies simply in the fact that they know the country, while white troops do not, and, moreover, that they have peculiarities of temperament, position, and motive which belong to them alone. Instead of leaving their homes and families to fight they are fighting for their homes and families. . . . It would have been madness to attempt, with the bravest white troops, what I have successfully accomplished with black ones. Everything, even to the piloting of the vessels and the selection of the proper points for cannonading, was done by my own soldiers.

Thomas Wentworth Higginson,
Army Life in a Black Regiment, 1869

DOCUMENT E. DEDICATING A NATIONAL CEMETERY

Historians like Gary Wills (*Lincoln at Gettysburg: Words That Remade America*) suggest that, in dedicating a cemetery at Gettysburg, Lincoln helped to redefine the purpose of the nation.

> Four score and seven years ago our fathers brought forth on this continent, a new nation, conceived in Liberty, and dedicated to the proposition that all men are created equal.
>
> Now we are engaged in a great civil war, testing whether that nation, or any nation so conceived and so dedicated, can long endure. We are met on a great battle-field of that war. We have come to dedicate a portion of that field, as a final resting place for those who here gave their lives that that nation might live. It is altogether fitting and proper that we should do this.
>
> But, in a larger sense, we can not dedicate—we can not consecrate—we can not hallow—this ground. The brave men, living and dead, who struggled here, have consecrated it, far above our poor power to add or detract. The world will little note, nor long remember what we say here, but it can never forget what they did here. It is for us the living, rather, to be dedicated here to the unfinished work which they who fought here have thus far so nobly advanced. It is rather for us to be here dedicated to the great task remaining before us—that from these honored dead we take increased devotion to that cause for which they gave the last full measure of devotion— that we here highly resolve that these dead shall not have died in vain—that this nation, under God, shall have a new birth of freedom—and that government of the people, by the people, for the people, shall not perish from the earth.

Abraham Lincoln, Gettysburg Address,
November 19, 1863

ANALYZING THE DOCUMENTS

1. Compare and contrast Lincoln's views on the federal Union with nullification theory found in Document B, Chapter 10, page 198.

2. How do the events detailed in Mary Chesnut's diary reflect the growing difficulties of the Confederacy in 1864?

3. What evidence could one draw from Documents C and D to support the statement that both slaves and free blacks played an active role in bringing slavery to an end?

4. Explain the ways that Lincoln in Document E used the words "dedicate" or "dedicated" and their significance in the Gettysburg Address.

RECONSTRUCTION, 1863–1877

Though slavery was abolished, the wrongs of my people were not ended. Though they were not slaves, they were not yet quite free. No man can be truly free whose liberty is dependent upon the thought, feeling, and action of others, and who has no means in his own hands for guarding, protecting, defending, and maintaining his liberty.

Frederick Douglass, 1882

The silencing of the cannons of war left the victorious United States with a new set of problems no less challenging than the war itself. How would the South rebuild its shattered society and economy after the damage inflicted by four years of war? What would be the place in that society of 4 million freed blacks, and to what extent, if at all, was the federal government responsible for helping them to adjust to freedom? Should the former states of the Confederacy be treated as states that had never really left the Union (Lincoln's position) or as conquered territory subject to continued military occupation? Under what conditions would the southern states be fully accepted as coequal partners in the restored Union? Finally, who had the authority to decide these questions of Reconstruction: the president or the Congress?

The conflicts that existed before and during the Civil War—between regional sections, political parties, and economic interests—continued after the war. Republicans in the North wanted to continue the economic progress begun during the war. The southern aristocracy still needed a cheap labor force to work its plantations. The freedmen and women hoped to achieve independence and equal rights. However, traditional beliefs limited the actions of the federal government. Constitutional concepts of limited government and states' rights discouraged national leaders from taking bold action. Little economic help was given to either whites or blacks in the South, because most Americans believed that free people in a free society had both an opportunity and a responsibility to provide for themselves. The physical rebuilding of the South was largely left up to the states and individuals, while the federal government concentrated on political issues.

Reconstruction Plans of Lincoln and Johnson

Throughout his presidency, Abraham Lincoln held firmly to the belief that the southern states could not constitutionally leave the Union and therefore never did leave. The Confederates in his view represented only a disloyal minority. After Lincoln's assassination, Andrew Johnson attempted to carry out Lincoln's plan for the political Reconstruction of the 11 former states of the Confederacy.

Lincoln's Policies

During the war years, Lincoln hoped that the southern states could be reestablished (though technically, in his view, they had never left) by meeting a minimum test of political loyalty.

Proclamation of Amnesty and Reconstruction (1863). As early as December 1863, Lincoln set up an apparently simple process for political Reconstruction—that is, for reconstructing the state governments in the South so that Unionists were in charge rather than secessionists. The president's Proclamation of Amnesty and Reconstruction provided for the following:

- Full presidential pardons would be granted to most southerners who (1) took an oath of allegiance to the Union and the U.S. Constitution and (2) accepted the emancipation of slaves.

- A state government could be reestablished and accepted as legitimate by the U.S. president as soon as at least 10 percent of the voters in that state took the loyalty oath.

In practice, Lincoln's proclamation meant that each southern state would be required to rewrite its state constitution to eliminate the existence of slavery. Lincoln's seemingly lenient policy was designed both to shorten the war and to give added weight to his Emancipation Proclamation. (At that time, late 1863, Lincoln feared that if the Democrats won the 1864 election, they would overturn the proclamation.)

Wade-Davis Bill (1864). Many Republicans in Congress objected to Lincoln's 10 percent plan, arguing that it would allow a supposedly reconstructed state government to fall under the domination of disloyal secessionists. In 1864 Congress passed the Wade-Davis Bill, which proposed far more demanding and stringent terms for Reconstruction. The bill required 50 percent of the voters of a state to take a loyalty oath and permitted only non-Confederates to vote for a new state constitution. Lincoln refused to sign the bill, pocket-vetoing it after Congress adjourned. How serious was the conflict between President Lincoln and the Republican Congress over Reconstruction policy? Historians still debate this question. In any case, Congress was no doubt ready to reassert its powers in 1865, as Congresses traditionally do after a war.

Freedmen's Bureau. In March 1865, Congress created an important new agency: the Bureau of Refugees, Freedmen, and Abandoned Lands, better known simply as the Freedmen's Bureau. The bureau acted as a kind of early welfare agency, providing food, shelter, and medical aid for those made destitute by the war—both blacks (chiefly freed slaves) and homeless whites. At first, the Freedmen's Bureau had authority to resettle freed blacks on confiscated farmlands in the South. Its efforts at resettlement, however, were later frustrated when President Johnson pardoned Confederate owners of the confiscated lands, and courts then restored most of the lands to their original owners.

The bureau's greatest success was in education. Under the able leadership of General Oliver O. Howard, it helped to establish nearly 3,000 schools for freed blacks, including several black colleges. Before federal funding was stopped in 1870, the bureau's schools taught an estimated 200,000 African Americans how to read.

Lincoln's last speech. In his last public address, on April 11, 1865, Lincoln encouraged northerners to accept Louisiana as a reconstructed state. (Louisiana had already drawn up a new constitution that abolished slavery in the state and provided for African Americans' education.) The president also addressed the question—highly controversial at the time—of whether freedmen should be granted the right to vote. Lincoln said: "I myself prefer that it were *now* conferred on the very intelligent, and on those who serve our cause as soldiers." Three days later, Lincoln's evolving plans for Reconstruction were ended with his assassination. His last speech suggested that, had he lived, he probably would have moved closer to the position taken by the progressive, or Radical Republicans. In any event, hope for lasting reform was dealt a devastating blow by the sudden removal of Lincoln's intelligent and flexible leadership.

Johnson and Reconstruction

Andrew Johnson's origins were as humble as Lincoln's. A self-taught tailor, he rose in Tennessee politics by championing the interests of poor whites in their economic conflict with rich planters. Johnson was the only senator from a Confederate state who remained loyal to the Union. After Tennessee was occupied by Union troops, he was appointed that state's war governor. Johnson was a southern Democrat, but Republicans picked him to be Lincoln's running mate in 1864 in order to encourage pro-Union Democrats to vote for the Union (Republican) party. In one of the accidents of history, Johnson became the wrong man for the job. As a white supremacist, the new president was bound to clash with Republicans in Congress who believed that the war was fought not just to preserve the Union but also to liberate blacks from slavery.

Johnson's Reconstruction policy. At first, many Republicans in Congress welcomed Johnson's presidency because of his apparent hatred for the southern aristocrats who had led the Confederacy. In May 1865, Johnson issued his own Reconstruction proclamation that was very similar to Lincoln's 10 percent plan. In addition to Lincoln's terms, it provided for the disfranchisement (loss of the right to vote and hold office) of (1) all former leaders and officeholders of the Confederacy and (2) Confederates with more than $20,000 in taxable property. However, the president retained the power to grant individual pardons to "disloyal" southerners. This was an escape clause for the wealthy planters, and Johnson made frequent use of it. As a result of the president's pardons, many former Confederate leaders were back in office by the fall of 1865.

Southern governments of 1865. Just eight months after Johnson took office, all 11 of the ex-Confederate states qualified under the president's Reconstruction plan to become functioning parts of the Union. The southern states drew up constitutions that repudiated secession, negated the debts of the Confederate government, and ratified the Thirteenth Amendment abolishing slavery. On the other hand, none of the new constitutions extended voting rights to blacks. Furthermore, to the dismay of Republicans, former leaders of the Confederacy were elected to seats in Congress. For example, Alexander Stephens, the former Confederate vice president, was elected U.S. senator from Georgia.

Black Codes. The Republicans became further disillusioned with Johnson when the southern state legislatures adopted Black Codes that restricted the rights and movements of the newly freed African Americans. The codes (1) prohibited blacks from either renting land or borrowing money to buy land; (2) placed freedmen into a form of semibondage by forcing them, as "vagrants" and "apprentices," to sign work contracts; and (3) prohibited blacks from testifying against whites in court. The contract-labor system, in which blacks worked the cotton fields under white supervision for deferred wages, seemed little different from slavery.

Appalled by reports of what was happening in the South, Republicans began to ask, "Who won the war?" In early 1866, Congress' unhappiness with Johnson developed into an open rift when the northern Republicans in Congress challenged the results of elections in the South. They refused to seat Alexander Stephens and other duly elected representatives and senators from ex-Confederate states.

Johnson's vetoes. Johnson alienated even moderate Republicans when, in early 1866, he vetoed two important bills: (1) a bill increasing the services and protection offered by the Freedmen's Bureau and (2) a civil rights bill that nullified the Black Codes and guaranteed full citizenship and equal rights to blacks.

The Election of 1866. Unable to work with Congress, Johnson took to the road in the fall of 1866 in his infamous "swing around the circle" to attack his congressional opponents. His speeches appealed to the racial prejudices of whites by arguing that equal rights for blacks would result in an "Africanized" society. Republicans counterattacked by accusing Johnson of being a drunkard and a traitor. They appealed to antisouthern prejudices by employing a campaign tactic known as "waving the bloody shirt"—inflaming the hatreds of northern voters by reminding them of the hardships of war. Republican propaganda made much of the fact that southerners were Democrats and, by a gross jump in logic, branded the entire Democratic party as a party of rebellion and treason.

Election results gave the Republicans an overwhelming victory. After 1866, Johnson's political enemies—both moderate and radical Republicans— would have commanding control of Congress with more than a two-thirds majority in both the House and the Senate.

Congressional Reconstruction

Reconstruction can be confusing unless we recognize that there were *three* rounds of Reconstruction, not just one. The first round (1863–spring 1866) was directed by presidents Lincoln and Johnson who, through executive powers, restored the 11 ex-Confederate states to their former position in the Union. Then came the congressional reaction against the Reconstruction achieved by the presidents. The return of ex-Confederates to high offices and the passage of the Black Codes by southern legislatures angered the Republicans in Congress. Thus began a second phase, or second round, in which Congress imposed upon the South its own version of Reconstruction. Rejecting presidential Reconstruction, Congress adopted a plan that was harsher on southern whites and more protective of freed blacks.

Radical Republicans

There had long been a division in Republican ranks between (1) moderates, who were chiefly concerned with economic gains for the white middle class, and (2) radicals, who championed civil rights for blacks. Although most Republicans were moderates, they shifted toward the radical position in 1866 partly out of fear that a reunified Democratic party might again become dominant. After all, now that the federal census counted blacks as equal to whites (no longer applying the old three-fifths rule for slaves), the South would have more representatives in Congress than before the war and more strength in the electoral college in future presidential elections.

The leading Radical Republican in the Senate was Charles Sumner of Massachusetts (now fully recovered from his earlier caning by Brooks). In the House, Thaddeus Stevens of Pennsylvania hoped to revolutionize southern society through an extended period of military rule in which blacks would be free to exercise their civil rights, would be educated in schools operated by the federal government, and would receive lands confiscated from the planter class. A number of Radical Republicans, including Benjamin Wade of Ohio, endorsed other liberal causes: women's suffrage, rights for labor unions, and civil rights for northern blacks. Although their program was never fully implemented, the Radical Republicans struggled for about four years, 1866 to 1870, to extend equal rights to all Americans.

Enacting the Radical Program

Presidential Reconstruction began to shift toward round two, congressional Reconstruction, in the spring of 1866. It was then that Congress prevailed in a struggle to enact two pieces of legislation vetoed by President Johnson.

Civil Rights Act of 1866. With some modifications, Republicans were able to override Johnson's vetoes of both the Freedmen's Bureau Act and the first Civil Rights Act. The Civil Rights Act pronounced all African Americans to be U.S. citizens (thereby repudiating the decision in the Dred Scott case) and also attempted to provide a legal shield against the operation of the southern states' Black Codes. Republicans feared, however, that the law could be repealed if the Democrats ever won control of Congress. They therefore looked for a more permanent solution in the form of a constitutional amendment.

Fourteenth Amendment. Late in 1866, Congress passed and sent to the states an amendment that, when ratified in 1868, was to have both immediate and long-term significance for all segments of American society. The Fourteenth Amendment

- Declared that all persons born or naturalized in the United States were citizens

- Obligated the states to respect the rights of U.S. citizens and provide them with "equal protection of the laws" and "due process of law" (clauses full of meaning for future generations)

For the first time, in other words, the *states* (not just the U.S. government) were required by the U.S. Constitution to uphold the rights of citizens. The amendment's key clauses concerning citizenship and rights produced mixed results in 19th-century courtrooms. In the 1950s and thereafter, however, the Supreme Court would make "equal protection of the laws" and the "due process" clause the keystone of civil rights for minorities, women, children, disabled persons, and those accused of crimes.

Other parts of the Fourteenth Amendment applied specifically to Congress' plan of Reconstruction. These clauses

- Disqualified former Confederate political leaders from holding either state or federal offices

- Repudiated the debts of the defeated governments of the Confederacy

- Penalized a state if it kept any eligible person from voting by reducing that state's proportional representation in Congress and the electoral college

Report of the joint committee. In June 1866, a joint committee of the House and the Senate issued a report recommending that the reorganized former states of the Confederacy were not entitled to representation in Congress. Therefore, those elected from the South as senators and representatives should not be permitted to take their seats. The report further asserted that Congress, not the president, had the authority to determine the conditions for allowing reconstructed states to rejoin the Union. By this report, Congress officially rejected the presidential plan of Reconstruction and promised to substitute its own plan, part of which was embodied in the Fourteenth Amendment.

Reconstruction acts of 1867. Over Johnson's vetoes, Congress passed three Reconstruction acts in early 1867, which took the drastic step of placing the South under military occupation. The acts divided the former Confederate states into five military districts, each under the control of the Union army. In addition, the Reconstruction acts increased the requirements for gaining readmission to the Union. To win such readmission, an ex-Confederate state had to ratify the Fourteenth Amendment and place guarantees in its constitution for granting the franchise (right to vote) to all adult males, regardless of race.

Impeachment of Andrew Johnson

Also in 1867, over Johnson's veto, Congress passed the Tenure of Office Act. This unusual (and probably unconstitutional) law prohibited the president from removing a federal official or military commander without the approval of the Senate. The purpose of the law was strictly political. Congress wanted to protect the Radical Republicans in Johnson's cabinet, such as Secretary of War Edwin Stanton, who was in charge of the military governments in the South.

Believing the new law to be unconstitutional, Johnson challenged it by dismissing Stanton on his own authority. The House responded by impeaching Johnson, charging him with 11 "high crimes and misdemeanors." Johnson thus became the first president to be impeached. (Bill Clinton was impeached in 1998.) In 1868, after a three-month trial in the Senate, Johnson's political enemies fell one vote short of the necessary two-thirds vote required to remove a president from office. Seven moderate Republicans joined the Democrats against conviction, because they thought it was a bad precedent to remove a president for political reasons.

Reforms After Grant's Election

The impeachment and trial of Andrew Johnson occurred in 1868, a presidential election year. At their convention, the Democrats nominated another candidate, Horatio Seymour, so that Johnson's presidency would have ended soon in any case, with or without impeachment by the Republicans.

The election of 1868. At their convention, the Republicans turned to a war hero, giving their presidential nomination to General Ulysses S. Grant, even though Grant had no political experience. Despite Grant's popularity in the North, he managed to win only 300,000 more popular votes than his Democratic opponent. The votes of 500,000 blacks gave the Republican ticket its margin of victory. Even the most moderate Republicans began to realize that the voting rights of the freedmen needed federal protection, if their party hoped to keep control of the White House in future elections.

Fifteenth Amendment. Republican majorities in Congress acted quickly in 1869 to secure the vote for African Americans. Adding one more Reconstruction amendment to those already adopted (the Thirteenth Amendment in 1865, and the Fourteenth Amendment in 1868), Congress passed the Fifteenth Amendment, which prohibited any state from denying or abridging a citizen's right to vote "on account of race, color, or previous condition of servitude."

Civil Rights Act of 1875. The last of many civil rights reforms enacted by Congress in the Reconstruction era was the Civil Rights Act of 1875. This law guaranteed equal accommodations in public places (hotels, railroads, and theaters) and prohibited courts from excluding African Americans from juries. The law was poorly enforced, however, because by this time, moderate and conservative Republicans had become frustrated with trying to reform an unwilling South—and also were afraid of losing white votes in the North. As we shall see, the abandonment of Reconstruction was only two years away.

Reconstruction in the South

During the second round of Reconstruction, dictated by Congress, the Republican party in the South reorganized and dominated the governments of the ex-Confederate states. Beginning in 1867, each Republican-controlled government was under the military protection of the U.S. Army until such time as Congress was satisfied that a state had met its Reconstruction requirements. Then the troops were withdrawn. The period of Republican rule in a southern state lasted from as little as one year (Tennessee) to as much as nine years (Florida), depending on how long it took conservative Democrats to regain control.

Composition of the Reconstruction Governments

In every radical, or Republican, state government in the South except one, whites were in the majority in both houses of the legislature. The exception was South Carolina, where the freedmen controlled the lower house in 1873. Republican legislators included native-born white southerners, freemen, and recently arrived northerners.

"Scalawags" and "carpetbaggers." Democratic opponents gave nicknames to their hated Republican rivals. They called southern Republicans "scalawags" and northern newcomers "carpetbaggers." Southern whites who supported the Republican governments were usually former Whigs who were interested in economic development for their state and peace between the sections. Northerners went South after the war for various reasons. Some were investors interested in setting up new businesses, while others were missionaries and teachers who went with humanitarian goals. In an age of greed and graft, no doubt some also went to plunder.

African American legislators. Most of the blacks who held elective office in the reconstructed state governments were educated property holders who took moderate positions on most issues. During the Reconstruction era, Republicans in the South sent two black senators (Blanche K. Bruce and Hiram Revels) and more than a dozen black representatives to Congress. Revels was elected in 1870 to take the Senate seat from Mississippi once held by Jefferson Davis. The fact that blacks and former slaves were in positions of power in the South caused bitter resentment among disfranchised ex-Confederates.

Evaluating the Republican Record

Much controversy still surrounds the legislative record of the Republicans during their brief control of southern state politics. Did they abuse their power for selfish ends (plunder and corruption), or did they govern responsibly in the public interest? The judgment of history is that they did some of both.

Accomplishments. On the positive side of the ledger, Republican legislators liberalized state constitutions in the South by providing for universal male suffrage, property rights for women, debt relief, and modernized penal codes. They also promoted the building of roads, bridges, railroads, and other internal improvements. They established such needed state institutions as hospitals and asylums for the care of the handicapped. The reformers established state-supported public school systems in the South, which benefited whites and blacks alike. To pay for these measures, tax systems were overhauled and bonds were issued.

Failures. After Reconstruction ended, it was long popular in the South (and even among some northern historians) to depict Republican rule as utterly wasteful and corrupt. To be sure, instances of graft and wasteful spending did occur, as Republican politicians took advantage of their power to take kickbacks and bribes from contractors who did business with the state. It is also clear that such corrupt practices in the South were no worse than the corruption practiced in the Grant administration in Washington; nor were they worse than the graft that was rife in the northern states and cities. No geographic section, political party, or ethnic group was immune to the general decline in ethics in government that marked the postwar era.

African Americans Adjusting to Freedom

Undoubtedly, the group of southerners who had the greatest adjustment to make during the Reconstruction era were the freedmen and freedwomen.

Having been so recently emancipated from slavery, they were faced with the challenge of securing their economic survival as well as their political rights as citizens.

Building black communities. Freedom meant many things to southern blacks: reuniting families, learning to read and write, migrating to cities where "freedom was free-er"—but most of all, emancipation was viewed as an opportunity for achieving independence from white control. This drive for autonomy was most evident in the founding of hundreds of independent black churches after the war. By the hundreds of thousands, African Americans left white-dominated churches for the Negro Baptist and African Methodist Episcopal churches. It was during Reconstruction that black ministers became leading figures in the black community.

The desire for education induced large numbers of African Americans to use their scarce resources to establish independent schools for their children and to pay educated blacks to become their teachers. Black colleges such as Howard, Atlanta, Fisk, and Morehouse were established during Reconstruction to train black ministers and teachers.

Another aspect of blacks' search for independence and self-sufficiency was the decision of many freedmen to migrate from the South and establish new black communities in frontier states such as Kansas.

Sharecropping. The South's agricultural economy was in turmoil after the war, in part because a compulsory labor force was gone. At first, white landowners attempted to force freed blacks into signing contracts to work the fields. These contracts set terms that nearly bound the signer to permanent and unrestricted labor—in effect, slavery by a different name. Black insistence on autonomy, however, combined with changes in the postwar economy, led white landowners to adopt a system based on tenancy and sharecropping. Under sharecropping, the landlord provided the seed and other needed farm supplies in return for a share (usually half) of the harvest. While this system gave poor people of the rural South (whites as well as blacks) the opportunity to work a piece of land for themselves, sharecroppers usually remained either dependent on the landowners or in debt to local merchants. By 1880, no more than 5 percent of southern blacks had managed to realize their dreams of becoming independent landowners. In a sense, sharecropping had evolved into a new form of servitude.

The North During Reconstruction

The North's economy in the postwar years continued to be driven by the Industrial Revolution and the probusiness policies of the Republicans. As the South struggled to reorganize its house, the main concern of northerners seemed to be railroads, steel, labor problems, and money.

Greed and Corruption

During the Grant administration, as the material interests of the age (see Chapter 19) took center stage, the idealism of Lincoln's generation and the radical Republicans' crusade for civil rights were pushed aside.

Rise of the spoilsmen. In the early 1870s, leadership of the Republican party passed from the reformers (Thaddeus Stevens, Charles Sumner, and Benjamin Wade) to political manipulators such as Senators Roscoe Conklin of New York and James Blaine of Maine. These politicians were masters of the game of patronage—giving jobs and government favors (spoils) to their supporters.

Corruption in business and government. The postwar years were notorious for the number of corrupt schemes devised by business bosses and political bosses to enrich themselves at the public's expense. In 1869, for example, two Wall Street financiers, Jay Gould and James Fisk, obtained the help of President Grant's brother-in-law in a scheme to corner the gold market. The Treasury Department broke the scheme but not before Gould had made a huge profit.

In the Crédit Mobilier affair, insiders gave stock to influential members of Congress to avoid investigation of the profits they were making—as high as 348 percent—from government subsidies for building the transcontinental railroad. In the case of the Whiskey Ring, federal revenue agents conspired with the liquor industry to defraud the government of millions in taxes. While Grant himself did not personally profit from the corruption, his loyalty to dishonest men around him badly tarnished his presidency.

Local politics in the Grant years was equally scandalous. In New York City, William Tweed, the boss of the local Democratic party, masterminded dozens of schemes for helping himself and cronies to large chunks of graft. The Tweed Ring virtually stole about $200 million from New York's taxpayers before *The New York Times* and the cartoonist Thomas Nast exposed "Boss" Tweed and brought about his arrest and imprisonment in 1871.

The Election of 1872

The scandals of the Grant administration drove reform-minded Republicans to break with the party in 1872 and select Horace Greeley, editor of the New York *Tribune,* as their presidential candidate. The Liberal Republicans advocated civil service reform, an end of railroad subsidies, withdrawal of troops from the South, reduced tariffs, and free trade. Surprisingly, the Democrats joined them and also nominated Greeley.

The regular Republicans countered by merely "waving the bloody shirt" again—and it worked. Grant was reelected in a landslide. Weeks after his overwhelming defeat, the luckless Horace Greeley died.

The Panic of 1873

Grant's second term began with an economic disaster that rendered thousands of northern laborers both jobless and homeless. In 1873 overspeculation by financiers and overbuilding by industry and railroads led to widespread business failures and depression. Debtors on the farms and in the cities sought an inflationary, easy-money solution by demanding Greenback paper money that was not supported by gold. In 1874, Grant finally decided to side with the hard-money bankers and creditors who wanted a stable money supply backed by gold and vetoed a bill calling for the release of additional Greenbacks.

The End of Reconstruction

During Grant's second term, it was apparent that Reconstruction had entered another phase, which proved to be its third and final round. With Radical Republicanism on the wane, southern conservatives—known as redeemers—took control of one state government after another. This process was completed by 1877. The redeemers had different social and economic backgrounds, but they agreed on their political program: states' rights, reduced taxes, reduced spending on social programs, and white supremacy.

White Supremacy and the Ku Klux Klan

During the period that Republicans controlled state governments in the South, groups of southern whites organized various secret societies to intimidate blacks and white reformers. The most prominent of these was the Ku Klux Klan, founded in 1867 by an ex-Confederate general, Nathaniel Bedford Forrest. The "invisible empire" burned black-owned buildings and flogged and murdered freedmen to keep them from exercising their voting rights. In 1870, Congress in the Force Acts of 1870 and 1871 gave power to federal authorities to stop Ku Klux Klan violence and to protect the civil rights of citizens in the South.

The Amnesty Act of 1872

Seven years after Lee's surrender at Appomattox, many northerners were ready to put hatred of the Confederacy behind them. As a sign of the changing times, Congress in 1872 passed a general amnesty act that removed the last of the restrictions on ex-Confederates, except for the top leaders. The chief political consequence of the Amnesty Act was that it allowed southern conservatives to vote for Democrats to retake control of state governments.

The Election of 1876

By 1876, federal troops had been withdrawn from all but three southern states—South Carolina, Florida, and Louisiana. The Democrats had returned to power in all ex-Confederate states except these. This fact was to play a critical role in the presidential election.

CONGRESSIONAL RECONSTRUCTION 1865–1877

Dates refer to year when a state was readmitted to the Union and ( ) to reestablishment of conservative government.

0   100   200   300 Miles

0 100 200 300 Kilometers

Delaware free 1865

Maryland free 1864

W.Va. 1863 free 1865

Virginia 1870 (1869)

Missouri free 1865

Kentucky free 1865

N. Carolina 1868 (1870)

Tennessee 1866 (1869)

S. Carolina 1868 (1876)

Arkansas 1868 (1874)

Miss. 1870

Alabama 1868 (1874)

Georgia 1870 (1872)

ATLANTIC OCEAN

Louisiana 1868 (1877)

Texas 1870 (1873)

Florida 1868 (1877)

N

GULF OF MEXICO

At their convention, the Republicans looked for someone untouched by the corruption of the Grant administration and nominated the governor of Ohio, Rutherford B. Hayes. The Democrats chose New York's reform governor, Samuel J. Tilden, who had made a name for himself fighting the corrupt Tweed Ring. When the popular votes were counted, the Democrats had won a clear majority and expected to put Tilden in the White House. In three southern states, however, the returns were contested. To win the election, Tilden needed only one *electoral* vote from the contested returns of South Carolina, Florida, and Louisiana.

A special electoral commission was created to determine who was entitled to the disputed votes of the three states. In a straight party vote of 8–7, the commission gave all the electoral votes to Hayes, the Republican. Outraged Democrats threatened to filibuster the results and send the election to the House of Representatives, which they controlled.

The Compromise of 1877

An informal deal was finally worked out between the two parties. Hayes would become president on the condition that he would (1) immediately end federal support for the Republicans in the South and also (2) support the building of a southern transcontinental railroad. Shortly after his inauguration, President Hayes fulfilled his part in the Compromise of 1877. He promptly withdrew the last of the federal troops protecting blacks and other Republicans.

The end of federal military presence in the South was not the only thing that brought Reconstruction to an end. In a series of decisions in the 1880s and 1890s, the Supreme Court struck down one Reconstruction law after another that protected blacks from discrimination. Supporters of the New South promised a future of industrial development, but most southern blacks and whites in the decades after the Civil War remained poor farmers, and they fell further behind the rest of the nation.

HISTORICAL PERSPECTIVES: WAS RECONSTRUCTION A FAILURE?

Reconstruction is probably the most controversial period in U.S. history. Generations of both northern and southern historians, starting with William Dunning in the early 1900s, portrayed Reconstruction as a failure. According to this traditional interpretation, illiterate blacks and corrupt northern carpetbaggers abused the rights of southern whites and stole vast sums from the state governments. The Radical Republicans brought on these conditions when, in an effort to punish the South, they gave the former slaves too many rights too soon. The Dunning school of historical thought provided a rationale for policies of racial segregation in the early 20th century. It was given popular expression in a 1915 movie, D. W. Griffith's *The Birth of a Nation,* which pictured the Ku Klux Klanmen as the heroes coming to the rescue of southern whites oppressed by vindictive northern radicals and blacks.

Black historians such as W. E. B. Du Bois and John Hope Franklin countered this interpretation by highlighting the positive achievements of the Reconstruction governments and black leaders. Their view was supported and expanded upon in 1965 with the publication of Kenneth Stampp's *Era of Reconstruction.* Other historians of the 1960s and 1970s followed Stampp's lead in stressing the significance of the civil rights legislation passed by the Radical Republicans and pointing out the humanitarian work performed by northern reformers.

By the 1980s, some historians criticized Congress' approach to Reconstruction, not for being too radical, but for not being radical enough. They argued that the Radical Republicans neglected to provide land for African Americans, which would have enabled them to achieve economic independence. Furthermore, according to these liberal critics, the military occupation of the South should have lasted longer to protect the freedmen's political rights. Eric Foner's comprehensive *Reconstruction: America's Unfinished Revolution* (1988) acknowledged the limitations of Reconstruction in achieving lasting reforms but also pointed out that, in the post-Civil War years, the freedmen established many of the institutions in the black community upon which later progress depended. According to Foner, it took a "second Reconstruction" after World War II (the civil rights movement of the 1950s and 1960s) to achieve the promise of the "first Reconstruction."

KEY NAMES, EVENTS, AND TERMS

presidential Reconstruction	due process of law	Crédit Mobilier
Proclamation of Amnesty and Reconstruction (1863)	Reconstruction Acts (1867)	William (Boss) Tweed; Tweed Ring
Wade-Davis Bill (1864)	Tenure of Office Act (1867)	Thomas Nast
Andrew Johnson	Edwin Stanton	Liberal Republicans
Freedmen's Bureau	impeachment	Horace Greeley
Black Codes	Fifteenth Amendment	Panic of 1873
congressional Reconstruction	Civil Rights Act of 1875	Greenbacks
Radical Republicans	scalawags	redeemers
Charles Sumner	carpetbaggers	Ku Klux Klan
Thaddeus Stephens	Blanche K. Bruce	Force Acts (1870, 1871)
Benjamin Wade	Hiram Revels	Amnesty Act of 1872
Civil Rights Act of 1866	sharecropping	Rutherford B. Hayes
Fourteenth Amendment	spoilsmen	Samuel J. Tilden
equal protection of the laws	patronage	Compromise of 1877
	Jay Gould	

MULTIPLE-CHOICE QUESTIONS

1. The purpose of Lincoln's and Johnson's plan for Reconstruction was to
   (A) punish the South for causing the Civil War
   (B) give Congress the final authority in the process of Reconstruction
   (C) give equal voting rights for both white and black males in the South
   (D) provide financial aid to rebuild the South
   (E) encourage rapid readmission of ex-Confederate states into the Union

2. In 1865, a number of southern states passed Black Codes in order to
   (A) control movement and provide a stable workforce for the plantations
   (B) keep the two races segregated in public places
   (C) limit the educational opportunities of recently freed slaves

(D) embarrass President Johnson's administration

(E) convince the North that the South could handle its own problems

3. The Freedmen's Bureau provided all of the following EXCEPT

(A) food, shelter, and medical aid for the victims of the war

(B) resettlement of some freed slaves on confiscated lands

(C) protection from sharecropping agreements

(D) schools to promote literacy among blacks

(E) colleges for blacks

4. Which of the following was NOT provided for African Americans by congressional Reconstruction?

(A) guarantee of U.S. citizenship

(B) equal protection of the laws

(C) distribution of confiscated Confederate farmlands

(D) protection for voting rights

(E) equal access to public accommodations

5. President Andrew Johnson was impeached for

(A) vetoing the Civil Rights Act of 1866

(B) refusing to support the Thirteenth Amendment

(C) taking a controversial position on states' rights

(D) removing a Radical Republican from his cabinet

(E) attempting to break up the Republican party

6. An analysis of the election of 1868 best supports the conclusion that

(A) the Republicans had given up on gaining the black vote

(B) the weakened Democratic party had little chance to elect a president

(C) northerners overwhelmingly approved the policies of the Radical Republicans

(D) voters approved the impeachment of Andrew Johnson

(E) Republican victory depended on the votes of African Americans

7. The Republican Reconstruction governments in the South accomplished all of the following EXCEPT

(A) developing state-supported public school systems for whites and blacks

(B) reducing waste and corruption in local and state governments

(C) founding state institutions to care for the sick and handicapped

(D) building of roads, bridges, harbors, and railroads

(E) adopting liberalized state constitutions

8. By the end of Reconstruction, most blacks in the South

(A) had migrated to lands in the West

(B) owned small family farms

(C) earned wages as factory workers in the new industries

(D) worked on farms as renters and sharecroppers

(E) operated independent businesses in the black community

9. The "redeemers" in the South supported

(A) integrated schools and public places

(B) states' rights and white supremacy

(C) increased state spending for internal improvements

(D) continued cooperation with the military to protect the freedmen

(E) redemption of Greenback dollars with gold

10. Congressional Reconstruction ended in 1877 because

(A) it was part of a compromise to resolve the disputed election of 1876

(B) African Americans in the South no longer needed federal protection of their civil rights

(C) the Supreme Court ignored the requirements of the Fourteenth Amendment

(D) the newly elected president was a moderate Republican

(E) the Union army had succeeded in suppressing the Ku Klux Klan

ESSAY QUESTIONS

1. Analyze the goals and strategies of Reconstruction of TWO of the following:

   President Lincoln

   President Johnson

   Congressional Republicans

2. In what ways and to what extent did the Fourteenth and Fifteenth amendments change the relationship between the federal government and the state governments?

3. What political, economic, and social changes were implemented by Republican governments in the southern states between 1865 and 1877?

4. How were politics and business affected by corruption and scandals in the era from 1865 to 1880?

5. What were the long-term political and economic effects of Reconstruction and southern reaction on African Americans?

DOCUMENTS AND READINGS

As the following documents reveal, the policies of Reconstruction expressed the complex interaction of politics, economics, reform, race, and sectionalism.

DOCUMENT A.   *THE REPORT OF A NORTHERN OBSERVER*

Carl Schurz, a liberal Republican and German-American reformer, sent the following report of postwar attitudes in the South to a Boston newspaper in July 1865. His friendship with reform-minded Republicans may have shaped what he thought worthy of reporting.

> But there is another class of people here [in Savannah], mostly younger men, who are still in the swearing mood. You can overhear their conversations as you pass them on the streets or even sit near them on the stoop of a hotel. They are "not conquered but only overpowered." They are only smothered for a time. They want to fight the war over again, and they are sure in five years they are going to have a war bigger than any we have seen yet. They are meaning to get rid of this d----d military despotism. . . . They have a rope ready for this and that Union man when the Yankee bayonets are gone. They will show the northern interlopers that have settled down here to live on their substance the way home. They will deal largely in tar and feathers. They have been in the country and visited this and that place where a fine business is done in the way of killing Negroes. They will let the Negro know what freedom is, only let the Yankee soldiers be withdrawn.
>
> Unfortunately, this spirit receives much encouragement from the fair sex. We have heard so much of the bitter resentment of the southern ladies that the tale becomes stale by frequent repetition, but when inquiring into the feelings of the people, this element must not be omitted. . . . But there is a large number of southern women who are as vindictive and defiant as ever, and whose temper does not permit them to lay their tongues under any restraint. . . . A day or two ago a Union officer yielding to an impulse of politeness, handed a dish of pickles to a southern lady at the dinner-table of a hotel in this city. A look of unspeakable scorn and indignation met him. "So you think," said the lady, "a southern woman will take a dish of pickles from a hand that is dripping with the blood of her countrymen?"

Carl Schurz,
Boston Advertiser, July 31, 1865

DOCUMENT B.　BLACK CODES

The following are examples of the Black Codes enacted by two southern state governments in 1865 and early 1866.

Sec. 2. All freedmen, free negroes and mulattoes . . . over the age of eighteen years found on the second Monday in January, 1866, or there after, with no lawful employment or business . . . shall be deemed vagrants, and on conviction thereof shall be fined . . . fifty dollars . . . and imprisoned at the discretion of the court.

Sec. 7. If any freedman, free negro or mulatto shall fail . . . to pay any tax . . . it shall be the duty of the sheriff to arrest such freedman, free negro or mulatto . . . and proceed at once to hire for the shortest time such delinquent tax-payers to any one who will pay the said tax. . . .

Laws of Mississippi, 1865

Sec. 2 . . . Every laborer . . . shall not be allowed to leave his place of employment until the fulfillment of his contract. . . .

Sec. 8 . . . in case of sickness of the laborer, wages for the time lost shall be deducted, and where the sickness is feigned . . . double the amount of wages shall be deducted for the time lost . . . and should the refusal to work continue beyond three days, the offender . . . shall be forced to labor on roads, levees, and other public works, without pay, until the offender consents to return to his labor.

Acts of the General Assembly of Louisiana, 1865

DOCUMENT C.　THE ARGUMENT OF A RADICAL REPUBLICAN

The Joint Committee on Reconstruction drafted the Fourteenth Amendment in part to protect the freedmen against the Black Codes. In a speech to the House, Thaddeus Stevens argued for the amendment in the following terms:

The first section [of the amendment] prohibits the States from abridging the privileges and immunities of citizens of the United States, or unlawfully depriving them of life, liberty, or property, or denying to any person within their jurisdiction the "equal" protection of the laws.

I can hardly believe that any person can be found who will not admit that every one of these provisions is just. They are all asserted, in some form or other, in our DECLARATION or organic law. But the Constitution limits only the action of Congress, and is not a limitation on the States. This amendment supplies that defect, and allows Congress to correct the unjust legislation of the States, so far that the law operated upon one man shall operate *equally* upon all. Whatever law punishes a white man for a crime shall punish the black man precisely in the same way and to the same degree. Whatever law protects the white man shall afford "equal" protection to the black man. Whatever means to redress is afforded to one shall be afforded to all. Whatever law allows the white man to testify in court shall allow the man of color to do the same. These are great advantages over the present codes. Now different degrees of punishment are inflicted, not on account of the magnitude of the crime, but according to the color of the skin. I need not enumerate these partial and oppressive laws. Unless the Constitution should restrain them those States will all, I fear, keep up this discrimination, and crush to death the hated freedmen. Some answer, "Your civil rights bill secures the same things." That is partly true, but a law is repealable by a majority. And I need hardly say that the first time that the South and their copperhead allies obtain the command of Congress it will be repealed. The veto of the President and their votes on the bill are conclusive evidence of that.

Thaddeus Stevens,
Speech in Congress, May 8, 1866

DOCUMENT D.　FREDERICK DOUGLASS LOOKS BACK ON RECONSTRUCTION

In this 1883 speech, Douglass challenged black Americans to have "sufficient spirit and wisdom to organize and combine to defend themselves from outrage, discrimination, and oppression," and not to depend on the Republican party. "Parties were made for men, not men for parties." He also looked back with both regret and hope to the Reconstruction Era.

Though we have had war, reconstruction, and abolition as a nation, we still linger in the shadow and blight of an extinct institution. Though the colored man is no longer subject to be bought and sold, he is still surrounded by an adverse sentiment which fetters all his movements. In his downward course he meets no resistance, but his course upward is resented and resisted at every step of his progress. . . . The color line meets him everywhere, and in a measure shuts him out from all respectable and profitable trades and callings. . . .

If liberty, with us, is yet but a name, our citizenship is but a sham, and our suffrage thus far only a cruel mockery, we may yet congratulate ourselves upon the fact that the laws and institutions of the country are sound, just, and liberal. There is hope for a people when their laws are righteous, whether for the moment they conform to their requirements or not. But until this nation shall make its practice accord with its Constitution and its righteous laws, it will not do to reproach the colored people of this country. . . .

Frederick Douglass,
Speech of September 24, 1883

ANALYZING THE DOCUMENTS

1. How could the report of Carl Schurz be related to the later problems of Reconstruction?

2. From the point of view of southern landowners, what were the primary purposes for enacting the Black Codes?

3. According to Stevens, why was the Fourteenth amendment constitutionally and politically necessary?

4. To what was Douglass referring when he said that "the laws and the institutions of the country are sound, just, and liberal"?

5. Do the above documents support or refute the view that Reconstruction was a failure?

THE LAST WEST
AND THE NEW SOUTH,
1865–1900

American social development has been continually beginning over again on the frontier. This perennial rebirth, this fluidity of American life, this expansion westward with its new opportunities, its continuous touch with the simplicity of primitive society, furnish the forces dominating American character. The true point of view in the history of this nation is not the Atlantic coast, it is the Great West.

Frederick Jackson Turner, 1893

As the last federal troops were withdrawn from the South in 1877, the U.S. Army had a few more battles to fight in the West on behalf of the miners and farmers who settled the last frontier. This chapter describes how two regions, the West and the South, underwent profound changes after the Civil War.

The West: Settlement of the Last Frontier

After the Civil War, many Americans turned their energies to the daunting task of settling the final western frontier: the vast arid territory that included the Great Plains, the Rocky Mountains, and the Western Plateau. Before 1860, these lands between the Mississippi River and the Pacific Coast were known as "the Great American Desert" by pioneers passing through on the way to the green valleys of Oregon and the goldfields of California. The plains west of the 100th meridian had few trees and usually less than 15 inches of rainfall a year, which was not considered enough moisture to support farming. While the winter blizzards and hot dry summers discouraged settlement, the open grasslands of the plains supported an estimated 15 million bison, or buffalo. The buffalo in turn provided food, clothing, shelter, and even tools for many of the 250,000 Native Americans living in the West in 1865.

In only 35 years, conditions on the Great Plains changed to such an extent that there was virtually no more frontier. By 1900, the great buffalo herds had been wiped out. The open western lands were now fenced in by homesteads

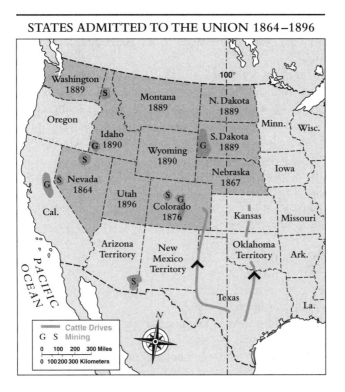

STATES ADMITTED TO THE UNION 1864–1896

and ranches, crisscrossed by steel rails, and modernized by new towns. By the turn of the century, ten new western states had already been carved out of the last frontier, leaving only Arizona, New Mexico, and Oklahoma as territories awaiting statehood. Progress came at a cost. The frenzied rush for the West's natural resources caused the near extermination of the buffalo and serious damage to the environment. The Native Americans who happened to be in the way of development also paid a high human and cultural price.

The settlement of the last frontier was achieved by three groups of pioneers: miners, cattlemen and cowboys, and farmers.

The Mining Frontier

The discovery of gold in California in 1848 caused the first flood of newcomers to the West. The California gold rush was only the beginning of a feverish quest for gold and silver that would extend well into the 1890s and would help to settle much of the West. A series of gold strikes and silver strikes in what became the states of Colorado, Nevada, Idaho, Montana, Arizona, and South Dakota kept a steady flow of hopeful young prospectors pushing into the western mountains. The discovery of gold near Pike's Peak in 1859 brought nearly 100,000 miners to Colorado. In the same year, the discovery of the fabulous Comstock Lode (which produced over $340 million in gold and silver by 1890) was responsible for Nevada entering the Union in 1864. Idaho and Montana were also granted early statehood, largely because of the mining boom.

California's great gold rush of 1849 set the pattern for what happened elsewhere. First, individual prospectors would look for traces of gold in the mountain streams by a method called placer mining, using simple tools such as shovels and washing pans. Eventually, however, such methods gave way to deep-shaft mining that required expensive equipment and the resources of wealthy investors and corporations.

Rich strikes would create boomtowns almost overnight—towns that became infamous for their saloons, dance-hall girls, and vigilante justice. A few towns, such as Nevada's Virginia City (created by the Comstock Lode), added theaters, churches, newspapers, schools, libraries, railroads, and organized law enforcement. Mark Twain started his career as a writer working on a Virginia City newspaper in the early 1860s. Many mining towns, however, became lonely ghost towns within a few years after the gold and silver ran out. Other towns that served the mines, such as San Francisco, Sacramento, and Denver, became important commercial centers.

Most of the mining towns that endured and grew were more like industrial cities than the frontier towns depicted in western films. As the mines developed, mining companies employed experienced miners from Europe, Latin America, and China. It was not unusual for half the population of a mining town to be foreign-born. About one-third of the western miners in the 1860s were Chinese immigrants. Native-born Americans resented the competition. In California, hostility to foreigners took the form of a Miner's Tax of $20 a month on all foreign-born miners. Political pressure from western states moved Congress to pass the Chinese Exclusion Act in 1882, which prohibited further immigration to the United States by Chinese laborers. Renewed ten years later, this law was the first major act of Congress to restrict immigration on the basis of race and nationality.

Mining not only stimulated the settlement of the West but also had an impact on the economics and politics of the nation. First of all, a vast increase in the supply of silver created a crisis over the relative value of gold- and silver-backed currency, which became a leading political issue for both westerners and the nation in the 1880s and 1890s. The mining boom also left environmental scars that are still visible today. It had a disastrous effect on Native Americans, who lost their lands to the miners' pursuit of instant riches.

The Cattle Frontier

The economic potential of the vast open grasslands that reached from Texas to Canada was realized by cattlemen and ranchers in the decades after the Civil War. Earlier, cattle had been raised and rounded up in Texas on a smaller scale by Mexican cowboys, or *vaqueros.* The traditions and techniques of the cattle business in the late 1800s were borrowed from the Mexicans, just as the cattle themselves, the hardy "Texas" longhorns, came originally from Mexico. During the Civil War, after the Union army cut off Texas from the rest of the Confederacy, wild herds of about 5 million head of cattle roamed freely over the Texas grasslands. When the war ended, the Texas cattle business was easy to get into because both the cattle and the grass were free.

The construction of railroads into Kansas after the war opened up eastern markets for the Texas cattle. Joseph G. McCoy realized the huge profits to be made at the end of the line in Chicago where cattle could be sold for $30 to $50 a head. At the rail stop in Abilene, Kansas, McCoy built the first stockyards to ship out cattle to Chicago. Dodge City and other cow towns were soon established along the railroads to handle the millions of cattle driven up the Chisholm, Goodnight-Loving, and other trails out of Texas during the 1860s and 1870s. The cowboys, many of whom were blacks and Mexicans, received about a dollar a day for their dangerous work.

The long cattle drives began to come to an end in the 1880s when overgrazing destroyed the grass and a winter blizzard and drought of 1885–1886 killed off 90 percent of the cattle. Another factor that closed down the cattle frontier was the arrival of homesteaders, who used barbed wire fencing to cut off access to the formerly open range. Wealthy cattlemen turned to developing huge ranches and using scientific ranching techniques to raise more tender breeds of cattle by feeding them hay and grains. The Wild West was largely tamed by the 1890s, but not before the era changed America's eating habits from pork to beef and created the legend of the rugged, self-reliant American cowboy.

The Farming Frontier

The Homestead Act of 1862 encouraged farming on the Great Plains by offering 160 acres of public land free to any family that settled on it for a period of five years. The promise of free land combined with the promotions of railroads and land speculators induced hundreds of thousands of native-born and immigrant families to attempt to farm the Great Plains between 1870 and 1900. About 500,000 families took advantage of the Homestead Act, but five times that number had to purchase their land, because the best public lands often ended up in the hands of railroad companies and speculators.

Problems and solutions. The first "sodbusters" on the dry and treeless plains often built their homes of sod bricks. Extremes of hot and cold weather, plagues of grasshoppers, and the lonesome life on the plains challenged even the most resourceful of the pioneer families. Water was scarce, and wood for fences was almost nonexistent. The invention of barbed wire by Joseph Glidden in 1874 helped farmers to fence in their lands on the lumber-scarce plains. Using mail-order windmills to drill deep wells provided some water. Even so, many homesteaders discovered too late that 160 acres was not adequate for

NATIVE AMERICANS IN THE WEST

farming the Great Plains. Long spells of severe weather, together with falling prices for their crops and the cost of new machinery, caused the failure of two-thirds of the homesteaders' farms on the Great Plains by 1900. Western Kansas alone lost half of its population between 1888 and 1892.

Those who managed to survive adopted "dry farming" and deep-plowing techniques to use the moisture available. They also learned to plant hardy strains of Russian wheat that withstood the extreme weather. Ultimately, dams and irrigation saved many western farmers, as humans reshaped the rivers and physical environment of the West to provide water for agriculture.

Turner's frontier thesis. The Oklahoma Territory, once set aside for the use of Native Americans, was thrown open for settlement in 1889, and hundreds of prospective homesteaders took part in the last great land rush in the West. The next year, 1890, the U.S. Census Bureau declared that the entire frontier—except for a few isolated pockets—had been settled.

Reacting to this announcement of the close of the frontier, the historian Frederick Jackson Turner wrote an influential essay, "The Significance of the Frontier in American History" (1893). Turner argued that 300 years of frontier experience had played a fundamental role in shaping the unique character of American society. According to Turner's thesis, the frontier experience had promoted a habit of independence and individualism. The frontier had also acted as a powerful social leveler, breaking down class distinctions and thus fostering social and political democracy. Furthermore, the challenges of frontier life caused Americans to be inventive and practical-minded—but also wasteful in their attitude toward natural resources.

The closing of the frontier troubled Turner. He saw the availability of free land on the frontier as a safety valve for harmlessly releasing discontent in American society. The frontier had always held out the promise of a fresh start. Once the frontier was gone, would the United States be condemned to follow the patterns of class division and social conflict that troubled the nations of Europe?

While many debate the Turner thesis, historians acknowledge that by the 1890s the largest movement of Americans was to the cities and industrialized areas. Not only was the era of the western frontier coming to a close, but the dominance of rural farming America was also on a decline.

The Removal of Native Americans

From the point of view of Native Americans, the frontier was nothing less than their own homeland and the source of their livelihood. As that frontier was progressively taken over by white settlers, the Native Americans lost both their land and the freedom to live according to their traditions.

The Native Americans who occupied the West in 1865 belonged to dozens of different cultural and tribal groups. In New Mexico and Arizona, Pueblo groups such as the Hopi and Zuni lived in permanent settlements as farmers raising corn and livestock. The Navajo and Apache peoples of the Southwest were nomadic hunter-gatherers who adapted a more settled way of life, not only raising crops and livestock but also producing arts and crafts. In the Pacific Northwest (Washington and Oregon), such tribes as the Chinook and Shasta developed complex communities based on abundant fish and game.

About two-thirds of the western tribal groups lived on the Great Plains. These nomadic tribes, such as the Sioux, Blackfoot, Cheyenne, Crow, and Comanche, had given up farming in colonial times after the introduction of the horse by the Spanish. By the 1700s, they had become skillful horsemen and developed a way of life centered on the hunting of buffalo. Although they belonged to tribes of several thousand, they lived in smaller bands of 300–500 members. In the late 19th century, their conflicts with the U.S. government were partly the result of white Americans having little understanding of the Plains people's loose tribal organization and nomadic lifestyle.

Reservation policy. In the 1830s, President Andrew Jackson's policy of removing eastern Native Americans to the West was based on the belief that lands west of the Mississippi would permanently remain "Indian country." This expectation soon proved false, as wagon trains rolled westward on the Oregon Trail, and plans were made for building a transcontinental railroad. In 1851, in councils (negotiations) at Fort Laramie and Fort Atkinson, the federal government began to assign the plains tribes large tracts of land—or reservations—with definite boundaries. Most Plains tribes, however, refused to restrict their movements to the reservations and continued to follow the migrating buffalo wherever they roamed.

Indian wars. As thousands of miners, cattlemen, and homesteaders began to settle on Native American lands, warfare became inevitable. Sporadic outbursts of fighting between U.S. troops and Plains people were characterized by brutal episodes. In 1864, the Colorado militia massacred an encampment of Cheyenne women, children, and men at Sand Creek, Colorado. In 1866, during the Sioux War, the tables were turned when an army column under Captain William Fetterman was wiped out by Sioux warriors. Following these wars, another round of treaties attempted to isolate the Native Americans of the Plains on smaller reservations with promises of government support to be provided by federal agents. However, gold miners refused to stay off Native Americans' lands if gold was to be found on them, as indeed it was in the Dakota's Black Hills. Soon, minor chiefs not involved in the treaty-making and younger warriors denounced the treaties and tried to return to ancestral lands.

The 1870s witnessed a new round of conflicts in the West. There was the Red River War against the Comanche and a second Sioux War led by Sitting Bull and Crazy Horse. Before the Sioux went down to defeat, they ambushed and destroyed Colonel George Custer's command at Little Big Horn in 1876. Chief Joseph's courageous effort to lead a band of the Nez Percé into Canada ended in defeat and surrender in 1877. The constant pressure of the U.S. Army forced tribe after tribe to comply with Washington's terms. In addition, the slaughter of most of the buffalo by the early 1880s doomed the way of life of the Plains people.

Assimilationists. The injustices done to Native Americans were chronicled in a best-selling book by Helen Hunt Jackson, *A Century of Dishonor* (1881). Although this book created sympathy for Native Americans, especially in the eastern part of the United States, most of those motivated to help Native Americans proposed assimilation as the solution. These humanitarians emphasized formal education and training and conversion to Christianity. Boarding schools such as the Carlisle School in Pennsylvania were set up to segregate Native American children from their people and teach them white culture and farming and industrial skills.

Dawes Severalty Act (1887). Reformers persuaded Congress to abandon the practice of dealing with Native American tribes as separate nations. A new approach incorporated in the Dawes Act of 1887 was designed to break up tribal organizations, which many felt kept Native Americans from becoming "civilized" and law-abiding citizens. The Dawes Act divided the tribal lands into plots of 160 acres or less, depending on family size. U.S. citizenship was granted to those who stayed on the land for 25 years and "adopted the habits of civilized life."

Under the Dawes Act, as intended, 47 million acres of land were distributed to Native Americans. What reformers did not anticipate, however, was that 90 million acres of former reservation land—often the best land—would be sold over the years to white settlers by the government, speculators, or Native Americans themselves. The new policy proved a failure. By the turn of the century, disease and poverty had reduced the Native American population to just 200,000 persons, most of whom lived as wards of the federal government.

Ghost Dance movement. The last effort of Native Americans to resist U.S. domination and drive whites from their ancestral lands came through a religious movement known as the Ghost Dance. In the government's campaign to suppress the movement, the famous Sioux medicine man Sitting Bull was killed during his arrest. Then in December 1890, over 200 Native American men, women, and children were gunned down by the U.S. Army in the "battle" (massacre) of Wounded Knee in the Dakotas. This final tragedy marked the end of the Indian Wars on the crimsoned prairie.

Aftermath: U.S. policy in the 20th century. In 1924, in partial recognition of the failure of its policy of forced assimilation, the federal government granted U.S. citizenship to all Native Americans, whether or not they had complied with the Dawes Act. As part of President Franklin Roosevelt's New Deal in the 1930s, Congress adopted the Indian Reorganization Act (1934), which promoted the reestablishment of tribal organization and culture. Today, over 1.8 million Native Americans, living both on and off reservations, belong to 116 tribes within the United States, each consisting of 1,000 or more members.

The New South

While the West was being "won" by settlers and the U.S. Army, the South was still recovering from the devastation of the Civil War. Even before Reconstruction ended in 1877, some southerners promoted a new vision for a self-sufficient southern economy built on modern capitalist values, industrial growth, and improved transportation. Chief among them was Henry Grady, the editor of the Atlanta *Constitution*. Grady spread the gospel of the *New South* with editorials that argued for economic diversity and laissez-faire capitalism. Local governments helped spur growth by offering tax exemptions to attract investors to start new industries. Cheap (low-wage) labor was another incentive for businesses to locate in the New South.

Economic Progress

A number of southern cities prospered in the late 19th century. Birmingham, Alabama, became a symbol of the New South by developing into one of the nation's leading steel centers. Memphis, Tennessee, prospered as a center for the South's growing lumber industry. Richmond, the former capital of the Confederacy, recovered from being burned down at the end of the Civil War to become the capital of the nation's tobacco industry.

Cheaper labor rates enabled the states of Georgia, North Carolina, and South Carolina to overtake the New England states as the chief producers of textiles. By 1900, the South had 400 cotton mills employing almost 100,000 white workers.

Railroads also gave a boost to the emergence of the New South. During the postwar years, the southern railroad companies rapidly converted to the standard-gauge rails used in the North and West. As a result, by 1890, an integrated rail network was established throughout the South. The South's rate of postwar growth from 1865 to 1900 equalled or surpassed that of the other regions of the country in terms of population, industry, and railroads.

Continued Poverty

Despite progress and growth, the South remained a largely agricultural section—and also the poorest region in the country. To a greater extent than before the war, northern financing dominated much of the southern economy. Northern investors controlled three-quarters of the southern railroads and by 1900 had control of the South's steel industry as well. A large share of the profits from the new industries went to northern banks and financiers. Industrial workers in the South (94 percent of whom were white) earned half of the national average and worked longer hours than elsewhere. Most southerners of both races remained in traditional roles and barely got by from year to year as sharecroppers and farmers.

The poverty of the majority of southerners was not caused by northern capitalists. Two other factors were chiefly responsible: (1) the South's late start at industrialization and (2) a poorly educated workforce. Only a small number of southerners had the technological skills needed for industrial development. The South failed to invest in technical and engineering schools as did the North. Furthermore, in the late 1800s, political leadership in the South provided little support for the education of either poor whites or poor African Americans. Without adequate education, the southern workforce was cut off from economic opportunities in the fast-changing world of the late 19th century.

Agriculture

The South's postwar economy remained tied mainly to growing cotton. Between 1870 and 1900, the number of acres planted in cotton more than doubled. Increased productivity, however, only added to the cotton farmer's problems, as a glut of cotton on world markets caused cotton prices to decline by more than 50 percent by the 1890s. Per capita income in the South actually declined, and many farmers lost their farms. By 1900, over half the region's white farmers and three-quarters of the black farmers were tenants (or sharecroppers), most of them straining to make a living from small plots of 15 to 20 acres. A shortage of credit forced farmers to borrow supplies from local merchants in the spring with a lien, or mortgage, on their crops to be paid at harvest. The combination of sharecropping and crop liens forced poor farmers to remain tenants, virtual serfs tied to the land by debt.

Some southern farmers sought to diversify their farming to escape the trap of depending entirely on cotton. George Washington Carver, an African American scientist at Tuskegee Institute in Alabama, promoted the growing of such crops as peanuts, sweet potatoes, and soybeans. His work played an important role in shifting southern agriculture toward a more diversified base.

Even so, most small farmers in the South remained in the cycle of debt and poverty. As in the North and the West, the hard times produced a harvest of discontent. By 1890, the Farmers' Southern Alliance claimed more than 1 million members. A separate organization for African Americans, the Colored Farmers' National Alliance, had about 250,000 members. Both organizations rallied behind political reforms to solve the farmers' economic problems. If poor black and poor white farmers in the South could have united, they would have been a potent political force, but the upper class' economic interests as well as powerful racial attitudes stood in their way.

Segregation

With the end of Reconstruction in 1877, the North withdrew its protection of the freedmen and left southerners to work out solutions to their own social and economic problems. As we have seen, the redeemers were Democratic politicians who came to power in the southern states after Reconstruction. They won support from two groups: the business community and the white supremacists. The latter group favored policies of separating, or segregating, public facilities for blacks and whites as a means of treating African Americans as social inferiors. The redeemers often used race as a rallying cry to deflect attention away from the real concerns of tenant farmers and the working poor. They discovered that they could gain and keep political power by playing on the racial fears of whites.

Discrimination and the Supreme Court. During Reconstruction, federal laws protected southern blacks from discriminatory acts by local and state governments. Starting in the late 1870s, however, the U.S. Supreme Court struck down one Reconstruction act after another applying to civil rights. In the *Civil Rights Cases* of 1883, the Court ruled that Congress could not legislate against the racial discrimination practiced by private citizens, which included railroads, hotels, and other businesses used by the public.

Then, in 1896, in the landmark case of *Plessy v. Ferguson,* the Supreme Court upheld a Louisiana law requiring "separate but equal accommodations" for white and black passengers on railroads. The Court ruled that the Louisiana law did not violate the Fourteenth Amendment's guarantee of "equal protection of the laws." Soon after this decision, a wave of segregation laws, commonly known as *Jim Crow laws,* were adopted by southern states. These laws required segregated washrooms, drinking fountains, park benches, and other facilities in virtually all public places. Only the use of streets and most stores was not restricted according to a person's race.

Loss of civil rights. Other discriminatory laws resulted in the wholesale disfranchisement of black voters by 1900. In Louisiana, for example, 130,334 black voters were registered in 1896 but only 1,342 in 1904—a 99 percent decline. Various political and legal devices were invented to prevent southern blacks from voting. Among the most common obstacles were literacy tests, poll taxes, and political party primaries for whites only. Many southern states adopted so-called grandfather clauses, which allowed a man to vote only if his grandfather had cast ballots in elections before Reconstruction. The Supreme Court again gave its sanction to such laws in a case of 1898, in which it upheld a state's right to use literacy tests to determine citizens' qualifications for voting.

Discrimination took many forms. In southern courts, African Americans were barred from serving on juries. If convicted of crimes, they were often given stiffer penalties than whites. In some cases, African Americans accused of crimes were not even given the benefit of a court-ordered sentence. Lynch mobs killed over 1,400 men during the 1890s. Economic discrimination was also widely practiced, keeping most southern African Americans out of skilled trades and even factory jobs. Thus, while poor whites and immigrants learned the industrial skills that would help them rise into the middle class, African Americans remained engaged in dead-end farming and low-paying domestic work.

Responding to segregation. Disenfranchisement, segregation, and lynching left African Americans in the South in a nearly powerless condition. Some black leaders advocated leaving the oppression behind by migrating to Kansas, Oklahoma, or even to Africa. Bishop Henry Turner formed the International Migration Society in 1894 to help American blacks emigrate to Africa. Ida B. Wells, editor of the Memphis *Free Speech,* a black newspaper, devoted her efforts to campaigning against lynching and the Jim Crow laws. Death threats and the destruction of her printing press forced Wells to carry on her work in the North.

One response to discrimination that was widely accepted by whites and African Americans in the hostile racial climate of the 1880s and 1890s was proposed by Booker T. Washington, a former slave who had graduated from Hampton Institute. In 1881, Washington established an industrial and agricultural school at Tuskegee, Alabama, which he built into the largest and best-known industrial school in the nation. Washington's mission became to teach southern African Americans skilled trades, the virtues of hard work, moderation, and economic self-help. Earning money, he said, was like having "a little green ballot" that would empower African Americans more effectively than a political ballot. Speaking at an exposition in Atlanta in 1895, Washington argued that "the agitation of the questions of social equality is the extremest folly." In 1900, he organized the National Negro Business League, which established 320 chapters across the country to support businesses owned and operated by African Americans. Largely because Washington preached racial harmony and economic cooperation, his leadership was praised by industrialist Andrew Carnegie and by President Theodore Roosevelt.

In a later era, many civil rights leaders would consider Booker T. Washington's approach (especially his Atlanta speech) to be a sellout to segregation and discrimination. After 1900, the younger African American leader W. E. B. Du Bois would demand an end to segregation and the granting of equal civil rights to all Americans. (See Chapter 21.)

Farm Problems: North, South, and West

In the late 1800s, all farmers faced similar problems, whether they were westerners or southerners, whether they were white or African American. For one thing, farmers were becoming a minority within American society. While the number of U.S. farms more than doubled between 1865 and 1900, people working as farmers declined from 60 percent of the working population in 1860 to less than 37 percent in 1900.

Changes in Agriculture

With every passing decade, farming became increasingly commercialized—and also more specialized. Northern and western farmers of the late 19th century concentrated on raising single cash crops, such as corn or wheat, for both national and international markets. As consumers, farmers began to procure their food from the stores in town and their manufactured goods from the mail-order catalogs sent to them by Montgomery Ward and Sears, Roebuck. As producers, farmers became more dependent on large and expensive machines, such as steam engines, seeders, and reaper-thresher combines. Larger farms of thousands of acres were run like factories. Unable to afford the new equipment, small, marginal farms could not compete and, in many cases, were driven out of business.

Falling prices. Increased American production as well as global competition from farms in Argentina, Russia, and Canada drove prices down for wheat, cotton, and other crops. The static money supply in the United States in the

1870s and 1880s also had a deflationary impact on prices. These figures tell the depressing story:

Wheat and Corn Prices, per bushel, 1867 and 1889		
Year	Wheat	Corn
1867	$2.00	$.78
1889	.70	.23

As prices fell, farmers with mortgages faced both high interest rates and the need to grow two or three times as much to pay off old debts. Of course, overproduction only lowered prices. The predictable results of this vicious circle were more debts, foreclosures by banks, and more independent farmers forced to become tenants and sharecroppers.

Rising costs. Farmers felt victimized by impersonal forces of the larger national economy. Industrial corporations were able to keep prices high on manufactured goods by forming monopolistic trusts. Middlemen (wholesalers and retailers) took their cut before selling to farmers. Railroads, warehouses, and elevators took what little profit remained by charging high or discriminatory rates for the shipment and storage of grain. Railroads would often charge more for short hauls on lines with no competition than for long hauls on lines with competition.

Taxes too seemed unfair to farmers. Local and state governments placed heavy taxes on property and land but did not tax income from stocks and bonds. The tariffs protecting various American industries were viewed as just another unfair tax paid by farmers and consumers for the benefit of the industrialists.

Fighting Back

A long tradition of independence and individualism restrained farmers from taking collective action. Finally, however, they began to organize for their common interests and protection.

National Grange Movement. The National Grange of Patrons of Husbandry was organized in 1868 by Oliver H. Kelley primarily as a social and educational organization for farmers and their families. By the 1870s, however, the Grange organized economic ventures and took political action to defend members against the middlemen, trusts, and railroads. The organization's greatest strength was in the region formerly known as the Old Northwest, now more commonly called the Middle West, or simply Midwest. By 1873, there were Granges in almost every state, including the South and the Pacific Coast. Grangers in every part of the country established *cooperatives*—businesses owned and run by the farmers to save the costs charged by middlemen.

Storage fees assessed by grain elevators and freight rates charged by railroads became the next targets of the Grange movement. In the midwestern states of Illinois, Iowa, Minnesota, and Wisconsin, the Grangers, with help from local businesses, successfully lobbied their state legislatures to pass laws regulating the rates charged by railroads and elevators. Other Granger laws made it illegal for railroads to fix prices by means of pools and to give rebates to privileged customers. In the landmark case of *Munn v. Illinois* (1877), the Supreme Court upheld the right of a state to regulate businesses of a public nature, such as railroads.

Interstate Commerce Act (1886). The state laws regulating railroad rates ran into numerous legal problems, especially with railroads that crossed state lines. States could only regulate local or short-haul rates. Interstate commerce, on the other hand, was a federal matter, and railroad companies adapted to the Granger laws by simply raising their long-haul (interstate) rates. The Supreme Court ruled in the case of *Wabash v. Illinois* (1886) that individual states could not regulate interstate commerce. In effect, the Court's decision nullified many of the state regulations achieved by the Grangers.

Congress responded to the outcry of farmers and shippers by passing the first federal effort to regulate the railroads. The Interstate Commerce Act of 1886 required railroad rates to be "reasonable and just." It also set up the first federal regulatory agency, the Interstate Commerce Commission (ICC), which had the power to investigate and prosecute pools, rebates, and other discriminatory practices. Ironically, the first U.S. regulatory commission helped the railroads more than the farmers. The new commission lost most of its cases in the federal courts in the 1890s. On the other hand, railroads found the ICC useful in helping to stabilize rates and curtail destructive competition.

Farmers' alliances. The discontent of rural America was on the rise again in the late 1880s as prices for crops fell to new lows. By 1890, about 1 million farmers had joined farmers' alliances for much the same reasons that they had earlier joined the Grange. Separate alliances were formed in different states and regions to serve farmers' needs for education in the latest scientific methods as well as for organized economic and political action. In alliances in the South, both poor white and black farmers joined the movement. Unlike the Grange, the alliance movement had serious potential for turning into an independent political party on the national level.

Ocala platform. Potential nearly became reality in 1890 when a national organization of farmers—the National Alliance—met in Ocala, Florida, to address the problems of rural America. The alliance attacked both major parties as subservient to Wall Street bankers and big business. Delegates at Ocala created a platform that would have significant impact in later years. They supported (1) direct election of U.S. senators, (2) lower tariff rates, (3) a graduated income tax, and (4) a new banking system regulated by the federal government.

In addition, the alliance platform demanded that Treasury notes and silver be used to increase the amount of money in circulation, which farmers hoped would create inflation and raise crop prices. The platform also proposed federal storage for farmers' crops and federal loans, which would free farmers from dependency on middlemen and creditors.

The alliances stopped short of forming a political party. Even so, their backing of local and state candidates who pledged support for alliance goals often proved decisive in the elections of 1890. Many of the reform ideas of the Grange and the Farmers' alliances would become part of the Populist movement, which would shake the foundations of the two-party system in the elections of 1892 and 1896. (The story of the Populist crusade is told in Chapter 19.)

HISTORICAL PERSPECTIVES: STAGES OF FRONTIER DEVELOPMENT

Frederick Jackson Turner set the agenda for generations of historians with his frontier thesis. One aspect of his thesis presented the settling of the frontier as an evolutionary process. At first, according to Turner, the frontier was an open and isolated wilderness and then slowly passed through different stages of development. The hunting frontier came first, which was followed by either the mining or the cattle frontier, and then the farming frontier. Finally, the founding of towns and cities completed the process.

Later historians challenged Turner's evolutionary view by arguing that frontier cities played an early and primary role in the development of the trans-Mississippi West. The historian Charles Glaab, for example, documented the role of town "boosters," who tried to create settlements on the frontier overnight in the middle of nowhere. After laying out town plots on paper, boosters of different western towns would strive to establish their own town as a territory's central hub of development by competing to capture the county seat or state capital, a state asylum, a railroad depot, or a college. Many would-be towns, promoted as the next "Athens of the West," proved a booster's false prophecy and died as ghost towns.

How central were cities to the development of the West? In his analysis of the growth of Chicago in the 19th century (*Nature's Metropolis,* 1991), the historian William Cronon argued that the "frontier and the metropolis turn out to be two sides of the same coin. . . . The history of the Great West is a long dialogue between the place we call city and the place we call country." Cronon used the early history of Chicago to show that the commerce between a city and the surrounding hinterland was the motor of frontier development. Urban markets made rural development possible. The cattlemen's frontier developed because it was linked by the railroads to Chicago and eastern markets. By "reading Turner backward," Cronon demonstrated how Chicago helped to create the mining, cattle, lumber, and farming frontiers as it developed into the great city of the West, or "nature's metropolis."

By integrating the history of city and frontier, Cronon avoids the traditional American dualism between cities and countryside. Not only frontier history but also environmental and rural issues are clarified when we understand that, as Cronon states, "every city is nature's metropolis and every countryside its rural hinterland."

KEY NAMES, EVENTS, AND TERMS

Great American desert

mining frontier

Comstock Lode

Chinese Exclusion Act (1882)

cattle drives

cowboys; *vaqueros*

barbed wire

farming frontier

Great Plains

Oklahoma Territory

Frederick Jackson Turner; frontier thesis

reservations

Indian wars

Sitting Bull

Crazy Horse

George Custer; Little Big Horn

Chief Joseph

Helen Hunt Jackson, *A Century of Dishonor*

assimilationists

Dawes Severalty Act (1887)

Ghost Dance movement

Wounded Knee

Indian Reorganization Act (1934)

New South

crop lien system

George Washington Carver

Tuskegee Institute

Farmers' Southern Alliance

Colored Farmers' National Alliance

segregation laws

Civil Rights Cases of 1883

Plessy v. Ferguson

Jim Crow laws

grandfather clause; poll tax; literacy test

Henry Turner

Ida B. Wells, Memphis *Free Speech*

Booker T. Washington

National Negro Business League

commercial farming

crop-price deflation

National Grange movement

cooperatives

Granger laws

Munn v. Illinois

Wabash v. Illinois

Interstate Commerce Act (1886)

farmers' alliances

National Alliance

Ocala Platform

MULTIPLE-CHOICE QUESTIONS

1. Which of the following characterized agriculture in BOTH the West and the South in the period 1870–1900?

   (A) use of dry-farming techniques

   (B) increased production

   (C) introduction of sharecropping

   (D) raising crops for subsistence, not commerce

   (E) rising prices for farm products

2. The outbreak of the Indian Wars of the 1870s was caused by all of the following EXCEPT

(A) the U.S. government's effort to isolate Indian tribes on smaller reservations

(B) the rejection of earlier treaties by young Sioux warriors

(C) the rush of gold miners into Indian lands

(D) perceived failure of the U.S. government to honor past treaty commitments

(E) the division of tribal lands into individual farms for tribal members

3. The goals of the assimilationists were most in conflict with which of the following?

(A) founders of the Carlisle School

(B) proponents of farming and industrial training

(C) terms of the Dawes Act of 1887

(D) terms of the Indian Reorganization Act of 1934

(E) the granting of citizenship to Native Americans

4. The chief cause of farm protest in the late 19th century was

(A) the closing of the open range

(B) overproduction of crops on the Great Plains

(C) middlemen, trusts, and railroads

(D) the increased money supply and prices

(E) increased competition from international sources

5. The Chinese Exclusion Act of 1882 is most closely associated with

(A) the expensive technologies involved in deep-shaft mining

(B) hostility to foreigners in western states

(C) competition of a transcontinental railroad

(D) farmers' grievances

(E) segregation and racial tensions in the South

6. According to the Turner thesis, the frontier encouraged all of the following EXCEPT

(A) social and political democracy

(B) inventive and practical approaches to problems

(C) a safety valve for discontent

(D) growth of class divisions

(E) a wasteful attitude toward natural resources

7. After the Granger laws ran into legal problems and were overturned in the case of *Wabash v. Illinois,* Congress attempted to provide relief through the

(A) Sherman Antitrust Act

(B) Interstate Commerce Act

(C) graduated income tax

(D) Homestead Act

(E) Atlanta Compromise

8. The main result of the crop lien system in the South in the late 19th century was

(A) a fairer distribution of land ownership among whites and blacks

(B) a decrease in the number of acres planted in cotton

(C) a cycle of debt for tenant farmers

(D) increased credit from northern bankers

(E) greater diversification of crops

9. The New South movement promoted all of the following EXCEPT

(A) tax exemptions to attract new industries

(B) southern railroad systems integrated with the North

(C) a more self-sufficient southern economy

(D) social integration of the races

(E) investment in manufacturing

10. The Supreme Court upheld "separate but equal" accommodations for public transportation in the case of

(A) *Plessy v. Ferguson*

(B) *Munn v. Illinois*

(C) *Wabash v. Illinois*

(D) *Dred Scott v. Sandford*

(E) *Brown v. Topeka*

ESSAY QUESTIONS

1. Discuss the shifts in the federal government's policy toward Native Americans from the 1830s to the 1930s.

2. Explain how TWO of the following influenced the development of the last West from the 1850s to 1900.

   miners

   cattlemen

   farmers

3. Analyze the ways that the federal government contributed to the economic development of the West.

4. To what extent were the problems of American farmers in the period 1865–1900 caused (a) by big business and government policy and (b) by farmers' own decisions?

5. To what extent did changes in the South from 1877 to 1900 reflect (a) the vision of the New South and (b) traditional attitudes and policies?

DOCUMENTS AND READINGS

For various minorities in the American population, neither the states nor the federal government offered any protection from the racial prejudice of the majority or from economic exploitation by the "money power" (railroads, banks, and corporate monopolies). The first two documents present the viewpoints of a Sioux chief (Document A) and a midwestern journalist (Document B), who expressed both bewilderment and resentment at the forces of change. On the issue of racial segregation, two documents (C and D) present opposing opinions in the landmark Supreme Court case of *Plessy v. Ferguson.*

DOCUMENT A.   *SPEECH BY CHIEF RED CLOUD*

Red Cloud, chief of the Teton Sioux Nation, traveled to Washington and New York City in 1870 to present the case for his people to the president and the public press. The following is an excerpt from his speech given at the Cooper Union in New York.

When you first came we were many, and you were few; now you are many, and we are getting very few, and we are poor. You do not know who appears before you today to speak. I am representative of the original American race, the first people of this continent. We are good and not bad. The reports that you hear concerning us are all on one side. . . . We are driven into a very little land, and we want you now, as our dear friends to help us with the government of the United States.

At the mouth of the Horse Creek in 1852, the Great Father made a treaty with us by which we agreed to let all that country open for fifty-five years for the transit of those who were going through. We kept this treaty; we never treated any man wrong; we never committed any murder or depredation until afterward the troops were sent into that country, and the troops killed our people and ill-treated them, and thus war and trouble arose; but before the troops were sent there we were quiet and peaceable, and there was no disturbance. . . .

Colonel Fitzpatrick of the government said we must go to farm, and some of the people went to Fort Laramie and were badly treated. I only want to do that which is peaceful, and the Great Fathers know it, and also the Great Father who made us both. I came to Washington to see the Great Father [President] in order to have peace and in order to have peace continue. That is all we want, and that is the reason we are here now.

In 1868 men came out and brought papers. We are ignorant and do not read papers, and they did not tell us right what was in these papers. We wanted them to take away their forts, leave our country, not make war, and give our traders something. They said we had bound ourselves to trade on the Missouri, and we said, no, we did not want that. The interpreters deceived us. . . .

Look at me, I am poor and naked, but I am the Chief of the Nation. We do not want riches, we do not ask for riches, but we want our children properly trained and brought up. We look to you for your sympathy. Our riches will . . . do us no good; we cannot take away into the other world anything we have—we want to have love and peace. . . . We would like to know why commissioners are sent out there to do nothing but rob [us] and get the riches of this world away from us.

And I am going to leave you today, and I am going back to my home. I want to tell the people that we cannot trust [President Grant's] agents. I don't want strange people that we know nothing about. . . . I don't want any more such men sent out there, who are so poor that when they come out their first thoughts are how they can fill their own pockets. . . .

Speech by Red Cloud, reported in
The New York Times, July 17, 1870

DOCUMENT B.   CAUSES OF FARM PROTEST

In the following selection, an Iowa journalist explained why bankers, trusts, and especially railroads became the target for farm protests in the 1880s and 1890s.

Nothing has done more to injure the [western] region than these freight rates. The railroads have retarded its growth as much as they first hastened it. The rates are often four times as large as eastern rates. . . . The extortionate character of the freight rates has been recognized by all parties, and all have pledged themselves to lower them, but no state west of the Missouri has been able to do so.

Railways have often acquired mines and other properties by placing such high freight rates upon their products that the owner was compelled to sell at the railroad companies' own terms. These freight rates have been especially burdensome to the farmers, who are far from their selling and buying markets, thus robbing them in both directions.

Another fact which has incited the farmer against corporations is the bold and unblushing participation of the railways in politics. At every political convention their emissaries are present with blandishments and passes and other practical arguments to secure the nomination of their friends. The sessions of these legislatures are disgusting scenes of bribery and debauchery. There is not an attorney of prominence in western towns who does not carry passes [free tickets for unlimited trips] or has had the opportunity to do so. . . . By these means, the railroads have secured an iron grip upon legislatures and officers, while no redress has been given to the farmer.

The land question also is a source of righteous complaint. Much of the land of the West, instead of being held for actual settlers, has been bought up by speculators and eastern syndicates in large tracts. They have done nothing to improve the land and have simply waited for the inevitable settler who bought a small "patch" and proceeded to cultivate it. While he had prospered so that he needed more land, he found that his own labor had increased tremendously the value of the adjacent land. . . .

Closely connected with the land abuse are the money grievances. As his pecuniary condition grew more serious, the farmer could not make payments on his land. Or he found that, with ruling prices, he could not sell his produce at a profit. In either case he needed money, to make the payment or maintain himself until prices should rise. When he went to the moneylenders, these men, often dishonest usurers, told him the money was very scarce, that the rate of interest was rapidly rising, etc., so that in the end the farmer paid as much interest a month as the moneylender was paying a year for the same money. In this transaction, the farmer obtained his first glimpse of the idea of "the contraction of the currency at the hands of eastern money sharks."

F. B. Tracy,
The Forum, October 1893

DOCUMENT C. *MAJORITY OPINION IN* **PLESSY V. FERGUSON**

By a vote of 7 to 1, the U.S. Supreme Court upheld the constitutionality of a Louisiana statute providing for "equal but separate accommodations for the white and colored races" on railroads within the state. The Court's decision rested on its interpretation of the Fourteenth Amendment.

The object of the [Fourteenth] amendment was undoubtedly to enforce the absolute equality of the two races before the law, but, in the nature of things, it could not have been intended to abolish distinctions based upon color, or to enforce social, as distinguished from political, equality, or a commingling of the two races upon terms unsatisfactory to either. Laws permitting, and even requiring, their separation, in places where they are liable to be brought into contact, do not necessarily imply the inferiority of either race to the other, and have been generally, if not universally, recognized as within the competency of the state legislatures in the exercise of their police power. . . .

So far, then, as a conflict with the Fourteenth amendment is concerned, the case reduces itself to the question whether the statute of Louisiana is a reasonable regulation, and with respect to this there must necessarily be a large discretion on the part of the legislature. In determining the question of reasonableness, it is at liberty to act with reference to the established usages, customs, and traditions of the people, and with a view to the promotion of their comfort, and the preservation of the public peace and good order. . . .

We consider the underlying fallacy in the plaintiff's argument to consist in the assumption that the enforced separation of the two races stamps the colored race with a badge of inferiority. If this be so, it is not by reason of anything found in the act, but solely because the colored race chooses to put that construction upon it.

U.S. Supreme Court,
Plessy v. Ferguson, 1896

DOCUMENT D.   *DISSENTING OPINION IN* PLESSY V. FERGUSON

The lone dissenter in *Plessy v. Ferguson* was a former slaveholder from Kentucky, Justice John Marshall Harlan. The following excerpt from his dissenting opinion was partly the basis for the Supreme Court decision in 1954 (*Brown v. Board of Education of Topeka*) that would overturn *Plessy.*

It was said in argument that the statute of Louisiana does not discriminate against either race, but prescribes a rule applicable to white and colored citizens. But this argument does not meet the difficulty. Everyone knows that the statute in question had its origin in the purpose, not so much to exclude white persons from railroad cars occupied by blacks as to exclude colored people from coaches occupied by or assigned to white persons.

The fundamental objection, therefore, to the statute is that it interferes with personal freedom of citizens. . . . If a white man and a black man choose to occupy the same public conveyance on a public highway, it is their right to do so, and no government proceeding alone on grounds of race can prevent it without infringing the personal liberty of each. . . . Further, if this statute of Louisiana is consistent with the personal liberty of citizens, why may not the state require the separation in railroad coaches of native and naturalized citizens of the United States, or of Protestants and Catholics?

The white race deems itself to be the dominant race in this country. And so it is, in prestige, in achievements, in education, in wealth, and in power. So, I doubt not, it will continue to be for all time, if it remains true to its great heritage and holds fast to the principles of constitutional liberty. But in the view of the Constitution, in the eye of the law, there is in this country no superior, dominant, ruling class of citizens. Our Constitution is color-blind and neither knows nor tolerates classes among citizens.

In respect of civil rights, all citizens are equal before the law. The humblest is the peer of the most powerful. The law regards man as man and take no account of his surroundings or his color when his civil rights as guaranteed by the supreme law of the land are involved. It is therefore to be regretted that this high tribunal, the final expositor of the fundamental law of the land, has reached the conclusion that it is competent for a state to regulate the enjoyment by citizens of their civil right solely upon the basis of race.

John Marshall Harlan,
dissenting opinion in *Plessy v. Ferguson,* 1896

ANALYZING THE DOCUMENTS

1. What government abuses against his tribe does Red Cloud identify in his speech?
2. Some historians have argued that farmers did not understand the real causes of their economic problems. Contrast Tracy's complaints with other possible causes of declining farm profits.
3. In *Plessy v. Ferguson,* why did the majority opinion conclude that Louisiana's "separate but equal" statute was "a reasonable regulation"?
4. What did Justice Harlan find unreasonable about the "separate but equal" ruling?
5. Were the complaints of Native Americans, western farmers, and African Americans in the later 19th century that are expressed in these readings the result of too little or too much government action?

THE RISE OF INDUSTRIAL AMERICA, 1865–1900

As we view the achievements of aggregated capital, we discover the existence of trusts, combinations and monopolies, while the citizen is struggling far in the rear or is trampled to death beneath an iron heel. Corporations, which should be the carefully restrained creatures of the law and servants of the people, are fast becoming the people's masters.

President Grover Cleveland, 1888

By 1900, the United States had emerged as the leading industrial power in the world. Its manufacturing output exceeded that of its three largest rivals, Great Britain, France, and Germany. The rapid growth of the U.S. economy, averaging 4 percent a year, was the result of a combination of factors:

- The country was a treasure-house of natural resources, including raw materials essential to industrialization—coal, iron ore, copper, lead, timber, and oil.

- An abundant labor supply was, between 1865 and 1900, supplemented yearly by the arrival of hundreds of thousands of immigrants.

- A growing population, combined with an advanced transportation network, made the United States the largest market in the world for industrial goods.

- Capital was plentiful, as Europeans with surplus wealth recognized a good investment and joined well-to-do Americans in funding the economic expansion.

- The development of laborsaving technologies increased productivity. Over 440,000 new patents were granted by the federal government from 1860 to 1890.

- Businesses benefited from friendly government policies that protected private property, subsidized railroads with land grants and loans, supported U.S. manufacturers with protective tariffs, and refrained from either regulating business operations or heavily taxing corporate profits.

■ Talented entrepreneurs emerged during this era who were able to build and manage vast industrial and commercial enterprises.

The Business of Railroads

The dynamic combination of business leadership, capital, technology, markets, labor, and government support is especially evident in the development of the nation's first big business—railroads. After the Civil War, railroad mileage increased more than fivefold in a 35-year period (from 35,000 miles in 1865 to 193,000 in 1900).

More than any other technological innovation or industrial achievement of the 19th century, the development of a nationwide railroad network had the greatest impact on American economic life. Railroads created a market for goods that was national in scale, and by so doing encouraged mass production, mass consumption, and economic specialization. The resources used in railroad-building promoted the growth of other industries, especially coal and steel. Railroads also affected the routines of daily life. Soon after the American Railroad Association divided the country into four time zones in 1883, railroad time became standard time for all Americans. Finally, the most important innovations of the railroads may have been the creation of the modern stockholder corporation and the development of complex structures in finance, business management, and the regulation of competition.

Eastern Trunk Lines

In the early decades of railroading (1830–1860), the building of dozens of separate local lines had resulted in different gauges (distance between tracks) and incompatible equipment. These inefficiencies were reduced after the Civil War through the consolidation of competing railroads into integrated trunk lines. (A trunk line was the major route between large cities; smaller branch lines connected the trunk line with outlying towns.) "Commodore" Cornelius Vanderbilt used his millions earned from a steamboat business to merge local railroads into the New York Central Railroad (1867), which ran from New York City to Chicago and operated more than 4,500 miles of track. Other trunk lines, such as the Baltimore and Ohio Railroad and the Pennsylvania Railroad, connected eastern seaports with Chicago and other midwestern cities and set standards of excellence and efficiency for the rest of the industry.

Western Railroads

The great age of railroad-building coincided with the settlement of the last frontier. In fact, railroads themselves played a critical role in the trans-Mississippi West by (1) promoting settlement on the Great Plains and (2) linking the West with the East and thereby creating one great national market.

Federal land grants. Recognizing that western railroads would lead the way to settlement, the federal government provided railroad companies with huge subsidies in the form of loans and land grants. Some 80 railroad companies received more than 170 million acres of public land, more than three times the acres given away under the Homestead Act. The land was given in alternate mile-square sections in a checkerboard pattern along the proposed route of the railroad. The government expected that the railroad would make every effort to sell the land to new settlers to finance construction. Furthermore, it was hoped that the completed railroad would both increase the value of government lands and provide preferred rates for carrying the mails and transporting troops.

There were also negative consequences to the subsidies. The land grants and cash loans (1) promoted hasty and poor construction and (2) led to widespread corruption in all levels of government. Insiders used construction companies, like the notorious Crédit Mobilier (see Chapter 15), to pocket huge profits, while bribing government officials and legislators. Protests against the land grants mounted in the 1880s when citizens discovered that the railroads controlled half of the land in some western states.

Transcontinental railroads. During the Civil War, Congress authorized land grants and loans for the building of the first transcontinental railroad to tie California to the rest of the Union. The task was divided between two newly incorporated railroad companies. The Union Pacific was to build westward across the Great Plains, starting from Omaha, Nebraska, while the Central Pacific took on the formidable challenge of laying track across mountain passes in the Sierras by pushing eastward from Sacramento, California. General Grenville Dodge directed construction of the Union Pacific using thousands of war veterans and Irish immigrants. Charles Crocker recruited 6,000 Chinese immigrants, who at enormous risk, blasted tunnels through the Sierras for the Central Pacific. Completing one of the great engineering feats of the 1800s, the two railroads came together on May 10, 1869, at Promontory Point, Utah, where a golden spike was ceremoniously driven into the ground to mark the linking of the Atlantic and the Pacific states.

Before 1900, four other transcontinental railroads were constructed across different sections of the West. Three of them were completed in the same year, 1883: the Southern Pacific, which tied New Orleans to Los Angeles; the Atchison, Topeka, and Santa Fe, which carried passengers and freight between Kansas City and Los Angeles; and the Northern Pacific, which connected Duluth, Minnesota, with Seattle, Washington. A fourth transcontinental railroad also connecting St. Paul, Minnesota, and Seattle was completed in 1893. James Hill's well-planned Great Northern was the only transcontinental railroad to be built without federal subsidies.

TRANSCONTINENTAL RAILROADS, 1865–1900

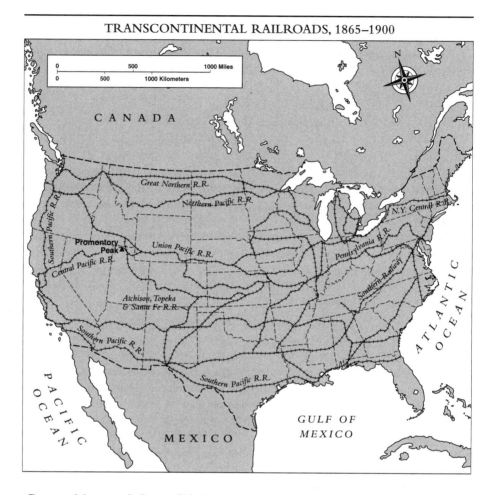

Competition and Consolidation

New technologies and industries tend to be overbuilt. Certainly this was the case with the railroads built in the 1870s and 1880s, many of which were unprofitable. In addition to overbuilding, the railroads frequently suffered from mismanagement and outright fraud. Speculators like Jay Gould went into the railroad business for quick profits and made their millions by selling off assets and watering stock (inflating the value of a corporation's assets and profits before selling its stock to the public). In a ruthless scramble to survive, railroads competed by offering rebates (discounts) and kickbacks to favored shippers while charging exorbitant freight rates to smaller customers such as farmers. They also attempted to increase profits by forming pools, in which competing companies agreed secretly and informally to fix rates and share traffic.

A financial panic in 1893 forced a quarter of all railroads into bankruptcy. J. Pierpont Morgan and other bankers quickly moved in to take control of the bankrupt railroads and consolidate them. With competition eliminated, they could stabilize rates and reduce debts. By 1900, seven giant systems controlled nearly two-thirds of the nation's railroads. A positive result was a more efficient rail system. On the negative side, however, the system was controlled by a few powerful men like Morgan, who dominated the boards of competing railroad corporations through interlocking directorates (the same directors ran competing companies). In effect, they created regional railroad monopolies.

Railroads captured the imagination of late-19th century America, as the public, local communities, states, and the federal government invested in their development. At the same time, however, customers and small investors often felt that they were the victims of slick financial schemes and ruthless practices. Railroad moguls seemed to affirm this ruthlessness. William Vanderbilt, who had inherited his father Cornelius Vanderbilt's transportation empire, reportedly responded to critics, "The public be damned." Early attempts to regulate the railroads by law did little good. The Granger laws passed by midwestern states in the 1870s were overturned by the courts, and the federal Interstate Commerce Act of 1886 was at first ineffective (see Chapter 16). It was not until the Progressive era in the early 20th century that the Interstate Commerce Commission was given expanded powers to protect the public interest.

Industrial Empires

The late 19th century witnessed a major shift in the nature of industrial production. Early factories had concentrated on producing textiles, clothing, and leather products. After the Civil War, in what some scholars have termed a "second Industrial Revolution," the growth was in heavy industry and the production of steel, petroleum, electric power, and the industrial machinery to produce other goods.

The Steel Industry

The technological breakthrough that launched the rise of heavy industry was the discovery of a new process for making large quantities of steel (a more durable metal than iron). In the 1850s, both Henry Bessemer in England and William Kelly in the United States discovered that blasting air through molten iron produced high-quality steel. The Great Lakes region, with its abundant coal reserves and access to the iron ore of Minnesota's Mesabi Range, soon emerged as the leading steel producer.

Andrew Carnegie. Leadership of the fast-growing steel industry passed to a shrewd business genius, Andrew Carnegie, who in the 1850s had worked his way up from being a poor Scottish immigrant to becoming the superintendent of a Pennsylvania railroad. In the 1870s, he started manufacturing steel in Pittsburgh and soon outdistanced his competitors by a combination of salesmanship and the use of the latest technology. Carnegie employed a business strategy known as vertical integration, by which a company would control every stage of the industrial process, from mining the raw materials to transporting the finished product. By 1900, Carnegie Steel had climbed to the top of the steel industry. It employed 20,000 workers and produced more steel than all the steel mills in Britain.

U.S. Steel Corporation. Deciding to retire from business to devote himself to philanthropy, Carnegie sold his company in 1900 for over $400 million to a new steel combination headed by J. P. Morgan. The new corporation, United States Steel, was the first billion-dollar company and also the largest enterprise in the world, employing 168,000 people and controlling over three-fifths of the nation's steel business.

The Oil Industry

The first U.S. oil well was drilled by Edwin Drake in 1859 in Pennsylvania. Only four years later, in 1863, a youthful businessman, John D. Rockefeller, founded a company that would come to control most of the nation's oil refineries by eliminating its competition.

Rockefeller and the Standard Oil Trust. Rockefeller took charge of the chaotic oil refinery business by applying the latest technologies and efficient practices. At the same time, as his company grew, he was able to extort rebates from railroad companies and temporarily cut prices for Standard Oil kerosene to force rival companies to sell out. By 1881 his company—now known as the Standard Oil Trust—controlled 90 percent of the oil refinery business. The trust that Rockefeller put together consisted of the various companies that he had acquired, all managed by a board of trustees that Rockefeller and Standard Oil controlled. Such a combination represented a horizontal integration of an industry, in which former competitors were brought under a single corporate umbrella. By controlling the supply and prices of oil products, Standard Oil's profits soared and so did Rockefeller's fortune, which at the time of his retirement amounted to $900 million. By eliminating waste in the production of kerosene, the Standard Oil monopoly was also able to keep prices low for consumers. Emulating Rockefeller's success, dominant companies in other industries (sugar, tobacco, leather, meat) also organized trusts.

Antitrust Movement

The trusts came under widespread scrutiny and attack in the 1880s. Middle-class citizens feared the trusts' unchecked power, and urban elites (old wealth) resented the increasing influence of the new rich. After failing to curb trusts on the state level, reformers finally moved Congress to pass the Sherman Antitrust Act in 1890, which prohibited any "contract, combination, in the form of trust or otherwise, or conspiracy in restraint of trade or commerce."

Although a federal law against monopolies was now on the books, it was too vaguely worded to stop the development of trusts in the 1890s. Furthermore, the Supreme Court in *United States v. E. C. Knight Co.* (1895) ruled that the Sherman Antitrust Act could be applied only to commerce, not to manufacturing. As a result, the U.S. Department of Justice secured few convictions until the law was strengthened during the Progressive era (see Chapter 21).

Laissez-Faire Capitalism

The idea of government regulation of business was alien to the prevailing economic, scientific, and religious beliefs of the late 19th century. The economic expression of these beliefs was summed up in the phrase "laissez-faire."

Conservative Economic Theories

As early as 1776, the economist Adam Smith had argued in *The Wealth of Nations* that business should be regulated, not by government, but by the "invisible hand" (impersonal economic forces) of the law of supply and demand. This was the origin of the concept of laissez-faire. If government kept hands off, so the theory went, businesses would be motivated by their own self-interest to offer improved goods and services at low prices. In the 19th century, American industrialists appealed to laissez-faire theory to justify their methods of doing business—even while they readily accepted the protection of high tariffs and federal subsidies. The rise of monopolistic trusts in the 1880s seemed to undercut the very competition needed for natural regulation. Even so, among conservatives and business leaders, laissez-faire theory was constantly invoked in legislative halls and lobbies to ward off any threat of government regulation.

Social Darwinism. Although it offended many, Charles Darwin's theory of natural selection in biology played a role in bolstering the views of economic conservatives. The English social philosopher Herbert Spencer was the most influential of the social Darwinists who thought that Darwin's ideas of natural selection and survival of the fittest should be applied to the marketplace. Spencer concluded that the concentration of wealth in the hands of the "fit" was a benefit to the future of the human race. An American social Darwinist, Professor William Graham Sumner of Yale University, argued that help for the poor was misguided because it interfered with the laws of nature and would only weaken the evolution of the species by preserving the unfit.

Gospel of wealth. A number of Americans found religion more convincing than social Darwinism in justifying the wealth of successful industrialists and bankers. Because he diligently applied the Protestant *work ethic* (that hard work and material success are signs of God's favor) to both his business and personal life, John D. Rockefeller concluded that "God gave me my riches." In a popular lecture, "Acres of Diamonds," the Reverend Russell Conwell preached that everyone had a duty to become rich. Andrew Carnegie's article "Wealth" argued that the wealthy had a God-given responsibility to carry out projects of civic philanthropy for the benefit of society. Practicing what he preached, Carnegie distributed over $350 million of his fortune to support the building of libraries, universities, and various public institutions.

Technology and Innovations

Vital to industrial progress were the inventions that led to greater productivity in the workplace and a larger variety of mass-produced goods in the home.

Inventions

The first radical change in the speed of communications was the invention of a workable telegraph by Samuel F. B. Morse, first successfully demonstrated in 1844. By the time of the Civil War, electronic communication by telegraph and rapid transportation by railroad were already becoming standard parts of modern living, especially in the northern states. After the war, Cyrus W. Field's invention of an improved transatlantic cable in 1866 suddenly made it possible to send messages across the seas in an instant's time. By 1900, cables linked all continents of the world in an electronic network of instantaneous, global communication. Another huge leap in communications technology was the invention of the telephone by Alexander Graham Bell in 1876.

Topping the list of hundreds of noteworthy inventions of the late 19th century were the typewriter (1867), the cash register (1879), the calculating machine (1887), and the adding machine (1888). Products for the consumer that were in widespread use by the end of the century were George Eastman's Kodak camera (1888), Lewis E. Waterman's fountain pen (1884), and King Gillette's safety razor and blade (1895).

Edison and Westinghouse

Possibly the greatest inventor of the 19th century, Thomas Edison started out as young telegraph operator and patented his first invention (a machine for recording votes) in 1869. The success of his early inventions gave Edison the resources to establish in 1876 a laboratory in Menlo Park, New Jersey, for the purpose of inventing new technologies. This was the world's first modern research laboratory. It may also have been Edison's single most important contribution to science and industry, because it introduced the concept of mechanics and engineers working on a project as a team rather than as lone inventors. Out of Edison's lab came more than a thousand patented inventions, including the phonograph, the incandescent lamp (the first practical electric lightbulb), the dynamo for generating electric power, the mimeograph machine, and the motion picture camera.

Another remarkable inventor, George Westinghouse, held more than 400 patents and was responsible for developing an air brake for railroads (1869) and a transformer for producing high-voltage alternating current (1885). The latter invention made possible the lighting of cities and the operation of electric streetcars, subways, and electrically powered machinery and appliances.

Marketing Consumer Goods

The increased output of U.S. factories as well as the invention of new consumer products created a need for businesses to find ways of selling their merchandise to a large public. R. H. Macy in New York and Marshall Field in Chicago made the large department store the place to shop in urban centers, while Frank Woolworth's Five and Ten Cent Store brought nationwide chain stores to the towns and urban neighborhoods. Two large mail-order companies, Sears, Roebuck and Montgomery Ward, used the improved rail system to ship to rural customers everything from hats to houses ordered from their thick catalogs, which were known to millions of Americans as the "wish book."

Packaged foods under such brand names as Kellogg and Post became a common item in the kitchen pantries of American homes. Refrigerated railroad cars and canning enabled Gustavus Swift and other packers to change the eating habits of Americans with mass-produced meat and vegetable products. Advertising and new marketing techniques not only promoted a consumer economy but also created a consumer culture in which "going shopping" became a favorite pastime.

Impact of Industrialization

The growth of American industry raised the standard of living for most people, but it also created sharper economic and class divisions among the rich, the middle class, and the poor.

The Concentration of Wealth

By the 1890s, the richest 10 percent of the U.S. population controlled nine-tenths of the nation's wealth. Industrialization created a new class of millionaires, most of whom flaunted their wealth by living in ostentatious mansions, sailing enormous yachts, and throwing lavish parties. The Vanderbilts graced the waterfront of Newport, Rhode Island, with summer homes that rivaled the villas of European royalty. Guests at one of their dinner parties were invited to hunt for their party favors by using small silver shovels to seek out the precious gems hidden in sand on long silver trays.

Horatio Alger myth. At first, Americans tended to ignore the widening gap between the rich and the poor by finding comfort in the highly publicized examples of "self-made men" in business (Andrew Carnegie, Thomas Edison, and others). They also thought there might be some truth in the popular novels by Horatio Alger, Jr., which sold more than a million copies. Every Alger novel portrayed a young man of modest means who became rich and successful through honesty, hard work, and a little luck. In reality, opportunities for upward mobility (movement into a higher economic bracket) did exist, but the rags-to-riches career of an Andrew Carnegie was unusual. Statistical studies demonstrate that the typical wealthy businessperson of the day was a white, Anglo-Saxon, Protestant male who came from an upper- or middle-class background and whose father was in business or banking.

The Expanding Middle Class

The growth of large corporations introduced the need for thousands of white-collar workers (salaried workers whose jobs generally do not involve manual labor) to fill the highly organized administrative structures. Middle management was needed to coordinate the operations between the chief executives and the factories. In addition, industrialization helped expand the middle class by creating jobs for accountants, clerical workers, and salespersons. In turn, these middle-class employees increased the demand for services from other middle-class workers: professionals (doctors and lawyers), public employees, and storekeepers. The increase in the number of good-paying occupations after the Civil War significantly increased the income of the middle class.

Wage Earners

By 1900, two-thirds of all working Americans worked for wages, usually at jobs that required them to work ten hours a day, six days a week. Wages were determined by the laws of supply and demand, and because there was usually a large supply of immigrants competing for factory jobs, wages were barely above the level needed for bare subsistence. Low wages were justified by David Ricardo (1772–1823), whose famous "iron law of wages" argued that raising wages arbitrarily would only increase the working population, and the availability of more workers would in turn cause wages to fall, thus creating a cycle of misery and starvation. Real wages (income adjusted for inflation) rose steadily in the late 19th century, but even so most wage earners could not support a family decently on one income. Therefore, working-class families depended on the additional income of women and children. In 1890, 11 million of the 12.5 million families in the United States averaged less than $380 a year in income.

Working Women

One adult woman out of every five in 1900 was in the labor force working for wages. Most were young and single, since only 5 percent of all married women worked outside the home. In 1900, men and women alike believed that, if it was economically feasible, a woman's proper role was in the home raising children. Factory work for women was often restricted to industries that were perceived as an extension of the home: the textile, garment, and food-processing industries, for example. As the demand for clerical workers increased, women moved into formerly male occupations as secretaries, book-keepers, typists, and telephone operators. Occupations or professions that became feminized (women becoming the majority) usually lost status and received lower wages and salaries.

Labor Discontent

Before the Industrial Revolution, workers had enjoyed a personal and relaxed workplace that valued an artisan's skills. They often had a sense of accomplishment in creating a product from start to finish. Factory work was radically different, since it was highly structured and regulated to increase productivity. Industrial workers were assigned just one step in the manufacturing of a product, performing semiskilled tasks that were repetitive and monotonous. Both immigrants from abroad and migrants from rural America had to learn to work under the tyranny of the clock. In many industries, such as railroads and mining, working conditions were dangerous. Many workers were exposed to chemicals and pollutants that only later were discovered to cause chronic illness and early death.

The workplace was also unstable and highly mobile. Industrial workers changed jobs on the average of every three years. Absenteeism and quitting, not strikes and labor unions, were the most common forms of protest against intolerable working conditions. An estimated 20 percent of those who worked in factories for a period of time eventually dropped out of the industrial workplace rather than continuing. This was a far higher percentage than those who protested by joining labor unions.

The Struggle of Organized Labor

The late 19th century witnessed the most violent labor conflicts in the nation's history. So common were the reports of striking workers battling police and state militia that many feared the country was heading toward open class warfare between capital and labor.

Industrial Warfare

With a surplus of cheap labor, management held most of the power in its struggles with organized labor. Strikers could easily be replaced by bringing in strikebreakers, or scabs—unemployed persons desperate for jobs. Employers also used all of the following tactics for defeating unions:

- the *lockout:* closing the factory to break a labor movement before it could get organized

- *blacklists:* names of prounion workers circulated among employers

■ *yellow-dog contracts:* workers being told, as a condition for employ-ment, that they must sign an agreement not to join a union

■ calling in *private guards* and *state militia* to put down strikes

■ obtaining *court injunctions* against strikes

Moreover, management fostered public fear of unions as anarchistic and un-American. Before 1900, it won most of its battles with organized labor because, if violence developed, employers could almost always count on the support of the federal and state governments.

Labor itself was often divided on the best methods for fighting manage-ment. Some union leaders advocated political action. Others favored direct confrontation: strikes, picketing, boycotts, and slowdowns to achieve union recognition and collective bargaining.

Great railroad strike of 1877. One of the worst outbreaks of labor violence in the century erupted in 1877, during an economic depression, when the railroad companies cut wages in order to reduce costs. A strike on the Baltimore and Ohio Railroad quickly spread across 11 states and shut down two-thirds of the country's rail trackage. Railroad workers were joined by an estimated 500,000 workers from other industries in an escalating strike that was quickly becoming national in scale. For the first time since the 1830s, a president (Rutherford B. Hayes) used federal troops to end labor violence. The strike and the violence finally ended, but not before more than a hundred people had been killed. After the strike, some employers addressed the workers' grievances by improving wages and working conditions, while others took a hard line by busting workers' organizations.

Attempts to Organize National Unions

Before the 1860s, unions had been organized as local associations of craft workers (a craft union of Philadelphia shoemakers, a craft union of New York printers, and so on).

National Labor Union. The first attempt to organize *all* workers in all states—both skilled and unskilled, both agricultural workers and industrial workers—was the National Labor Union. Founded in 1866, it had some 640,000 members by 1868. Besides championing the goals of higher wages and the eight-hour day, the first national union also had a broad social program: equal rights for women and blacks, monetary reform, and worker cooperatives. Its chief victory was winning the eight-hour day for workers employed by the federal government. It lost support, however, after a depression began in 1873 and after the unsuccessful strikes of 1877.

Knights of Labor. A second national labor union, the Knights of Labor, began in 1869 as a secret society in order to avoid detection by employers. Under the leadership of Terence V. Powderly, the union went public in 1881, opening its membership to all workers, including African Americans and women. Powderly advocated a variety of reforms: (1) worker cooperatives "to make each man his own employer," (2) abolition of child labor, and (3) abolition of trusts and monopolies. He favored settling labor disputes by means of arbitration rather than resorting to strikes. Because the Knights were loosely organized, however, he could not control local units that decided to strike.

The Knights of Labor grew rapidly in the early 1880s and attained a peak membership of 730,000 workers in 1886. It declined just as rapidly, however, after the violence of the Haymarket riot in Chicago in 1886 turned public opinion against the union.

Haymarket bombing. Chicago, with about 80,000 Knights in 1886, was the site of the first May Day labor movement. Also living in Chicago were about 200 anarchists who advocated the violent overthrow of all government. In response to the May Day movement calling for a general strike to achieve an eight-hour day, labor violence broke out at Chicago's McCormick Harvester plant. On May 4, workers held a public meeting in Haymarket Square, and as police attempted to break up the meeting, someone threw a bomb, which killed seven police officers. The bomb thrower was never found. Even so, eight anarchist leaders were tried for the crime and seven were sentenced to death. Horrified by the bomb incident, many Americans concluded that the union movement was radical and violent. The Knights of Labor, as the most visible union at the time, lost popularity and membership.

American Federation of Labor. Unlike the idealistic, reform-minded Knights of Labor, the American Federation of Labor (AF of L) concentrated on attaining practical economic goals. Founded in 1886 as an association of 25 craft unions, the AF of L did not advocate a reform program to remake American society. Samuel Gompers, who led the union from 1886 to 1924, went after the basics of higher wages and improved working conditions. He directed his local unions of skilled workers to walk out until the employer agreed to negotiate a new contract through collective bargaining. By 1901, the AF of L was by far the nation's largest union, with 1 million members. Even this union, however, would not achieve major successes until the early decades of the 20th century.

Strikebreaking in the 1890s

Two massive strikes in the last decade of the 19th century demonstrated both the growing discontent of labor and the continued power of management to prevail in industrial disputes.

Homestead strike. Henry Clay Frick, the manager of Andrew Carnegie's Homestead Steel plant near Pittsburgh, precipitated a strike in 1892 by cutting wages by nearly 20 percent. Frick used the weapons of the lockout, private guards, and strikebreakers to defeat the steelworkers' walkout after five months. The failure of the Homestead strike set back the union movement in the steel industry until the New Deal in the 1930s.

Pullman strike. Even more alarming to conservatives was a strike of workers living in George Pullman's model company town near Chicago. Pullman manufactured the famous railroad sleeping cars that bore his name (Pullman cars). In 1894, he announced a general cut in wages and fired the leaders of the workers' delegation that came to bargain with him. The workers at Pullman laid down their tools and appealed for help from the American Railroad Union whose leader, Eugene V. Debs, directed railroad workers not to handle any trains with Pullman cars. The union's boycott tied up rail transportation across the country.

Railroad owners supported Pullman by linking Pullman cars to mail trains. They then appealed to President Grover Cleveland, persuading him to use the army to keep the mail trains running. A federal court issued an injunction forbidding interference with the operation of the mails and ordering railroad workers to abandon the boycott and the strike. For failing to respond to this injunction, Debs and other union leaders were arrested and jailed. The jailing of Debs and others effectively ended the strike. In the case of *In re Debs* (1895), the Supreme Court approved the use of court injunctions against strikes, which gave employers a very powerful weapon to break unions. After serving a six-month jail sentence, Debs concluded that more radical solutions were needed to cure labor's problems. He turned to socialism and the American Socialist party, which he helped to found in 1900.

By 1900, only 3 percent of American workers belonged to unions. Management held the upper hand in labor disputes, with government generally taking its side. However, some of the public were beginning to recognize the need for a better balance between the demands of employers and employees to avoid the numerous strikes and violence that characterized the late 19th century.

HISTORICAL PERSPECTIVES: INDUSTRIAL STATESMEN OR ROBBER BARONS?

Middle-class Americans who enjoyed the benefits of increased industrial production, new consumer goods, and a higher standard of living generally admired the business leaders of the age, viewing them as great industrial statesmen. University professors gave intellectual respectability to this view by drawing upon social Darwinism to argue that business leaders' success was due to their superior intelligence and fitness. Did they not, after all, make the United States the leading economic power in the world?

In the early 20th century, however, a growing number of citizens and historians questioned the methods used by business leaders to build their industrial empires. Charles Beard and other Progressive historians called attention to the oppression of farmers and workers, the corruption of democratic institutions, and the plundering of the nation's resources. Their critical view of 19th-century business leaders received support from historians of the 1930s (the Depression decade). Matthew Josephson, for example, popularized the view that John D. Rockefeller and others like him were robber barons, who took from American workers and small businesses to build personal fortunes. The robber barons were presented as ruthless exploiters who used unethical means to destroy competition, create monopolies, and corrupt the free enterprise system. Any positive contributions that might have been made were merely unplanned by-products of the industrialists' ruthlessness and greed.

The prevailing wisdom of the 1930s shifted in the 1950s, as Allan Nevins urged other historians to right the injustice done to "our business history and our industrial leaders." Nevins and other revisionists argued that the mass production that helped win two world wars and that made the United States an economic superpower far outweighed in significance any self-serving actions by business leaders.

Another approach to the era was taken by historians who analyzed statistical data in an effort to judge the contributions of industrialists and big business. They asked: Were big corporations essential for the economic development of the United States? Did monopolies such as the Standard Oil Trust advance or retard the growth of the U.S. economy? Robert Fogel, for example, used statistical data to prove his startling thesis that railroads were *not* indispensable to the economic growth of the era. Despite these studies, critics of big business and the robber barons maintain that, in the final analysis, the *quantity* of economic growth was less important than the *quality* of life for the average American.

KEY NAMES, EVENTS, AND TERMS

Cornelius Vanderbilt	Panic of 1893	John D. Rockefeller
New York Central Railroad	J. Pierpont Morgan	Protestant work ethic
trunk line	interlocking directorates	Standard Oil Trust
federal land grants	William Vanderbilt	horizontal integration
transcontinental railroads	Second Industrial Revolution	antitrust movement
Union and Central Pacific	Bessemer process	Sherman Antitrust Act (1890)
Jay Gould	Andrew Carnegie	*United States v. E. C. Knight*
watered stock; pools	vertical integration	laissez-faire capitalism
rebates	U. S. Steel	Adam Smith

social Darwinism	consumer goods	railroad strike of 1877
Herbert Spencer	Sears, Roebuck; Montgomery Ward	National Labor Union
survival of the fittest		Knights of Labor
gospel of wealth	concentration of wealth	Terence V. Powderly
Russell Conwell	Horatio Alger	Haymarket bombing (1886)
Protestant work ethic	upward mobility	American Federation of Labor
Samuel F. B. Morse	white-collar workers	Samuel Gompers
transatlantic cable	middle class	Homestead strike (1892)
Alexander Graham Bell	David Ricardo; iron law of wages	Pullman strike (1894)
telephone		Eugene V. Debs
Thomas A. Edison; research laboratory	scab; lockout; blacklist; yellow-dog contract;	*In re Debs*
George Westinghouse	injunction	

MULTIPLE-CHOICE QUESTIONS

1. During the railroad expansion from 1860 to 1900, all of the following were true EXCEPT
   (A) Numerous short lines were consolidated into trunk lines.
   (B) Four transcontinental lines were built with government help.
   (C) Technical innovations made railroads the most popular form of transportation.
   (D) No laws were passed to regulate the railroads.
   (E) The building of railroads was used by speculators for quick profit.

2. In the 19th century, railroads formed pools in order to
   (A) share equipment and terminals for greater efficiency
   (B) fix prices and divide business for greater profit
   (C) inflate the value of assets and profits before selling the stock
   (D) better serve farmers in remote rural areas

   (E) increase competition by dividing up large companies into smaller ones

3. Which of the following was NOT considered a proper function of government in the late 19th century?
   (A) protection of private property with state or federal troops
   (B) distribution of public lands to private corporations
   (C) protection of American industry against foreign competition
   (D) use of court injunctions to stop workers' strikes
   (E) protection of workers from unfair labor practices

4. The U.S. economy in the late 19th century was characterized by all of the following EXCEPT
   (A) consolidation of businesses into trusts
   (B) technological innovations
   (C) acceptance of unions and collective bargaining

(D) growing concentration of wealth

(E) control of industries by bankers

5. The decisions of the Supreme Court in the late 19th century most often

(A) favored corporations

(B) favored labor unions

(C) avoided cases involving labor disputes

(D) protected consumers

(E) supported government regulation of business

6. Social Darwinists would most likely support which of the following?

(A) enforcement of the Sherman Antitrust Act

(B) relief for the unemployed

(C) nonregulation of business

(D) guarantee of a living wage for workers

(E) subsidies for farmers

7. The concept of the gospel of wealth is reflected in all of the following statements EXCEPT

(A) Each man had a duty to become rich.

(B) Money should be distributed to the poor and the homeless.

(C) The wealthy had a responsibility to use their wealth for the good of society.

(D) Wealth was God's reward for a life of virtue and hard work.

(E) Philanthropy should support educational, health, and religious institutions.

8. Which of the following accurately describes a trend in American society in the 1880s and 1890s?

(A) The middle class declined in numbers and influence.

(B) The percentage of women in the labor force decreased.

(C) Most married women worked to support their families.

(D) The workplace became more tightly organized and structured.

(E) The wealthy avoided signs of self-indulgence.

9. The most effective and enduring labor union in the post-Civil War era

(A) championed worker cooperatives

(B) supported a broad program of social reforms

(C) adopted socialist and anarchist ideas about government

(D) accepted both skilled and unskilled workers as members

(E) focused on such goals as higher wages and shorter hours for skilled workers

10. Which of the following was NOT true of the American labor movement in the late 19th century?

(A) Labor's rights were protected by laws of Congress.

(B) A number of major strikes were defeated by business and government.

(C) Some unions tried to organize both skilled and unskilled workers.

(D) Middle-class Americans often concluded that unions were radical and violent.

(E) Immigrants were often used as strikebreakers.

Guide to Writing the DBQ

Making Use of the Documents

To earn a high score on the DBQ, you must skillfully weave a substantial number of the documents into the body of your essay. In the College Board's own words, the writer of the DBQ should demonstrate "analytical and thematic use of most documents."

Here are three examples of paragraphs that refer to selected documents for the DBQ in this chapter. Which paragraph most skillfully integrates the writer's background knowledge with use of the documents?

Writer One: Most industrialists, like Carnegie and Rockefeller, were honest men, working for the good of American society. Russell Conwell in Document E supports this position: "Let me say here clearly, and say it briefly . . . that ninety-eight out of one hundred of the rich men in America are honest. That is why they are rich. That is why they are trusted with money." William Sumner in Document G expresses similar views: "The captains of industry and the capitalists . . . if they are successful, win, in these days, great fortunes in a short time. There are no earnings which are more legitimate or for which greater services are rendered to the whole industrial body." The steel king Andrew Carnegie himself, in Document C, cites "the law of competition between these, as being not only beneficial, but essential for the future progress of the race."

Writer Two: The concentration of business and wealth deeply divided the nation in the late 1800s. Business leaders such as Rockefeller and Carnegie believed that unrestrained competition produced more benefits for society than harm. Carnegie in his famous article, "Wealth," argued the advantages of competition: "For it is this law that we owe our wonderful material development which brings improved conditions. While the law may be sometimes hard for the individual, it is best for the race. . . ." Populist leader James Weaver, however, saw the consolidation of business into trusts as impoverishing workers, consumers, and especially farmers. The example of the downsizing of the Oat Meal Trust to increase profits proved that the "robber barons" were more interested in increased profits than benefits to society (Document D).

Writer Three: The admiration of business leaders as "industrial statesmen" was supported by the intellectual movements of the times. Social philosophers of the 19th century, such as Herbert Spencer, applied Charles Darwin's theories of natural selection and survival of the fittest to the marketplace. Social Darwinists, such as William Graham Sumner, argued that society and the economy benefited from unrestrained competition. While the "captains of industry" accumulated vast personal fortunes, they also enriched society with a higher standard of living, improved technology, and more jobs. The gospel of wealth popularized by Andrew Carnegie in "Wealth" and Russell Conwell in *Acres of Diamonds* made the accumulation of wealth not only respectable, but also a moral duty. Industrial leaders such as Carnegie and Rockefeller acted on these beliefs by returning hundreds of millions of dollars back to society in form of libraries, universities, and other public institutions.

Evaluation

Writer Three most effectively integrated his/her knowledge with the documents provided, for the following reasons:

Paragraph Three most effectively used the documents within a larger historical context. The writer does not refer to the documents simply for their own sake, but uses them to support the analysis of key concepts of the historical period, Social Darwinism and Gospel of Wealth, which are essential outside knowledge not found it the documents. Paragraph Three also provided a higher level of analysis that showed some awareness of "industrial statesmen" interpretation of historical events.

Paragraph One does little more than quote directly three documents. Outside of labeling Carnegie "steel king," there is no use of outside knowledge. Outside of organizing the quotes under an introductory sentence, there is also no analysis of the question or evidence of understanding conflicting interpretations.

The writers of paragraph One, and to a lesser extent paragraph Two, waste both words and valuable time simply copying long quotes from the documents. Long quotes do not impress AP readers. Instead, they are more likely to appear to be padding for a writer who has little to say. AP readers thoroughly know the documents and give no credit for simply copying the information. A better approach is found in paragraph Three, which simply referred to the author or the title of the document. Paragraph Two also used an acceptable approach by referencing the document in a parentheses, e.g. (Document D).

Paragraph Two does not provide the level of outside information and analysis as paragraph Three does. It has, however, one key essential to an effective DBQ essay: It acknowledges and explains to some extent the conflicting points of view found in the documents. The writer of an effective DBQ needs to deal with the full complexity of the question, including documents with opposing views.

The writers of paragraph Two and Three each also do a nice job of identifying at least one of the authors of the documents, e.g., William Sumner and James Weaver. Whenever you know something about the author of a document, or the context of the document itself, it's a good idea to state what you know briefly in an identifying phrase.

Practice

Review the previous features on answering a DBQ, on pages 72, 160, 235, and 258. Then organize and write a five-paragraph response to the DBQ on page 353. Spend 15 minutes planning the essay and 45 minutes writing it. Use the following checklist to guide your own evaluation of your composition:

1. Is your thesis clearly stated in the first paragraph?
2. Does your thesis statement address all aspects of the question?
3. Does each of the substantive historical paragraphs (2, 3, and 4) develop a different argument or topic in support of your thesis?
4. Does each substantive paragraph demonstrate knowledge of a historical period that goes beyond the given documents?
5. Are *most* of the given documents either referred to or briefly quoted (or both) in your essay?
6. Does your concluding paragraph (a) provide a summary of the most important historical evidence and (b) restate your thesis?

ESSAY QUESTIONS

1. Analyze to what extent TWO of the following promoted the industrial development of the United States from 1865 to 1900.

   natural resources

   capital and technology

   labor

   business management

2. How did consolidation of businesses affect the United States economy from 1865 to 1900?

3. Compare and contrast the roles of the federal government as both promoter and regulator of United States industrial development from 1865 to 1900.

4. Analyze the goals, methods, and achievements of TWO of the following organizations:

National Labor Union

Knights of Labor

American Federation of Labor

5. Assess the impact of industrialization from 1865 to 1900 on TWO of the following groups:

middle class

wage earners

working women

DOCUMENT-BASED QUESTION

Write a coherent essay that integrates your interpretation of Documents A–H *and* your knowledge of the period to answer the following question:

> To what extent is it justified to characterize the industrial leaders of the 1865–1900 era as either "robber barons" or "industrial statesmen"?

DOCUMENT A.

Q: How is the freight and passenger pool working?

W.V.: Very satisfactorily. I don't like that expression "pool," however, that's a common construction applied by the people to a combination which the leading roads have entered into to keep rates at a point where they will pay dividends to the stockholders. The railroads are not run for the benefit of the "dear public"—that cry is all nonsense—they are built by men who invest their money and expect to get a fair percentage on the same.

Q: Does your limited express pay?

W.V.: No; not a bit of it. We only run it because we are forced to do so by the action of the Pennsylvania road. It doesn't pay expenses. We would abandon it if it was not for our competitor keeping its train on.

Q: But don't you run it for the public benefit?

W.V. The public be damned. What does the public care for the railroads except to get as much out of them for as small consideration as possible? I don't take any stock in this silly nonsense about working for anybody's good but our own. . . .

Interview with William H. Vanderbilt,
Chicago *Daily News*, October 9, 1882

DOCUMENT B.

My laboratory will soon be completed. . . . I will have the best equipped and largest Laboratory extant, and the facilities incomparably superior to any other for rapid & cheap development of an invention, & working it up into Commercial shape with models, patterns & special machinery. In fact there is no similar institution in Existence. We do our own castings and forgings. Can build anything from a ladys watch to a Locomotive.

The Machine shop is sufficiently large to employ 50 men & 30 men can be worked in other parts of the works. Invention that formerly took months & cost a large sum can now be done in 2 or 3 days with very small expense, as I shall carry a stock of almost every conceivable material of every size, and with the latest machinery a man will produce 10 times as much as in a laboratory which has but little material, not of a size, delays of days waiting for castings and machinery not universal or modern. . . .

You are aware from your long acquaintance with me that I do not fly any financial Kites, or speculate, and that the works I control are well managed. In the early days of the shops it was necessary that I should largely manage them [alone], first because the art had to be created, 2nd, because I could get no men who were competent in such a new business. But as soon as it was possible I put other persons in charge. I am perfectly well aware of the fact that my place is in the Laboratory; but I think you will admit that I know how a shop should be managed & also know how to select men to manage them.

Letter from Thomas Alva Edison,
November 14, 1887, Edison Laboratory,
West Orange, New Jersey

DOCUMENT C.

The problem of our age is the proper administration of wealth so that the ties of brotherhood may still bind together the rich and poor in harmony. The conditions of human life have been revolutionized within the past few hundred years. The contrast between the palace of the millionaire and the cottage of the laborer with us today measures the change which has come with civilization.

This change, however, is not to be deplored, but welcomed as highly beneficial. It is essential for the progress of the race that the houses of some should be homes for all that is highest and best in literature and the arts, rather than none should be so. Much better this great inequity than universal squalor. . . .

The price which society pays for the law of competition, like the price it pays for cheap comforts and luxuries, is also great; but the advantages of this law are also greater still. For it is to this law that we owe out wonderful material development which brings improved conditions. While the law may be sometimes hard for the individual, it is best for the race, because it insures the survival of the fittest in every department. We welcome, therefore, as conditions to which we must accommodate ourselves, great inequality of environment, the concentration of business, industrial and commercial, in the hands of a few; and the law of competition between these, as being not only beneficial, but essential for the future progress of the race.

Andrew Carnegie,
"Wealth," *North American Review*, 1889

DOCUMENT D.

It is clear that trusts are contrary to public policy and hence in conflict with the common law. They are monopolies organized to destroy competition and restrain trade. . . .

It is contended by those interested in trusts that they tend to cheapen production and diminish the price of the article to the consumer. . . . Trusts are speculative in their purpose and formed to make money. Once they secure control of a given line of business, they are masters of the situation and can dictate to the two great classes with which they deal—the producer of the raw material and the consumer of the finished product. They limit the price of the raw material so as to impoverish the producer, drive him to a single market, reduce the price of every class of labor connected with the trade, throw out of employment large numbers of persons who had before been engaged in a meritorious calling and finally . . . they increase the price to the consumer. . . .

The main weapons of the trust are threats, intimidation, bribery, fraud, wreck, and pillage. Take one well-authenticated instance in the history of the Oat Meal Trust as an example. In 1887 this trust decided that part of their mills should stand idle. They were accordingly closed. This resulted in the discharge of a large number of laborers who had to suffer in consequence. The mills which continued in operation would produce seven million barrels of meal during the year. Shortly after shutting down, the trust advanced the price of meal one dollar per barrel, and the public was forced to stand the assessment. The mills were more profitable when idle than when in operation.

James B. Weaver,
A Call to Action, 1892

DOCUMENT E.

I say that you ought to get rich, and it is you duty to get rich. How many of my pious brethren say to me, "Do you, a Christian minister, spend your time going up and down the country advising young people to get rich, to get money?" "Yes, of course I do." They say, "Isn't that awful! Why don't you preach the gospel instead of preaching about man's making money?" "Because to make money honestly is to preach the gospel." The men who get rich may be the most honest men you find in the community. . . .

Let me say here clearly, and say it briefly . . . that ninety-eight out of one hundred of the rich men in America are honest. That is why they are rich. That is why they are trusted with money. That is why they carry on great enterprises and find plenty of people to work with them. It is because they are honest men. . . .

Russell H. Conwell,
Acres of Diamonds, 1900

DOCUMENT F.

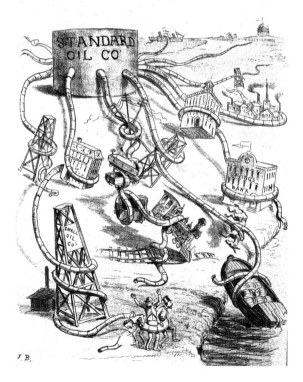

Culver Pictures

DOCUMENT G.

The captains of industry and the capitalists . . . if they are successful, win, in these days, great fortunes in a short time. There are no earnings which are more legitimate or for which greater services are rendered to the whole industrial body. The popular notions about this matter really assume that all the wealth accumulated by these classes of persons would be here just the same if they had not existed. They are supposed to have appropriated it out of the common stock. This is so far from being the true that, on the contrary, their own wealth would not be but for themselves; and besides that, millions more of wealth, manyfold greater than their own, scattered in the hands of thousands, would not exist but for them.

William Graham Sumner,
Forum, March 1894

DOCUMENT H.

List of major gifts given by John D. Rockefeller by the time of his death in 1937.

American Baptist Foreign Mission Society, New York City	$ 6,845,688.52
American Baptist Home Mission Society, New York City	6,994,831.62
American Baptist Missionary Society, Dayton, Ohio	1,902,132.58
General Education Board	129,209,167.10
Laura Spelmen Rockefeller Memorial, New York	73,985,313.77
Minister and Missionaries Benefit Board of Northern Baptist Convention	7,090,579.06
Rockefeller Foundation, New York	182,851,480.90
Rockefeller Institute for Medical Research	59,931,891.62
University of Chicago, Chicago, Illinois	34,708,375.28
Yale University, New Haven	1,001,000.00
Y.M.C.A., International Committee	2,295,580.73
[TOTAL:	$506,816,041.18]

The New York Times, May 24, 1937

THE GROWTH OF CITIES AND AMERICAN CULTURE, 1865–1900

Give me your tired, your poor,
Your huddled masses yearning to breathe free,
The wretched refuse of your teeming shore,
Send these, the homeless, tempest-tossed, to me:
*   I lift my lamp beside the golden door.*

Emma Lazarus, *The New Colossus,* 1883
(Inscription on the base of the Statue of Liberty)

In 1893, the city of Chicago hosted the World's Columbian Exposition. Over 12 million people traveled to the White City, as Chicago's fairgrounds and gleaming white buildings were popularly called. They went to see the progress of American civilization as represented by new industrial technologies and by the architects' grand visions of an ideal urban environment. Outside the fairgrounds, the real city of Chicago had its own attractions and interest. In little more than half a century, the population of this midwestern city had grown to over one million. Its central business district was a marvel of modern urban structures, consisting of steel-framed skyscrapers, department stores, and theaters. Around this central hub lay a sprawling gridiron of workers' housing near the city's factories and warehouses, and a few miles beyond were tree-lined suburban retreats for the wealthier class. The entire urban complex was connected by a network of hundreds of miles of streetcars and railroads.

Visitors to Chicago also experienced a "gray city" of pollution, poverty, crime, and vice. Some complained of the confusion of tongues, "worse than the tower of Babel," for in 1893 Chicago was a city of immigrants. More than three-fourths of its population were either foreign-born or the children of the foreign-born. Both the real Chicago and the idealized "White City" represented the complex ways in which three great forces of change—industrialization, immigration, and urbanization—were transforming the nature of American society in the late 19th century. The previous chapter described the impact of industrialization. This chapter now looks at the related forces of immigration and urbanization.

A Nation of Immigrants

In the last half of the 19th century, the U.S. population increased more than threefold, from about 23.2 million in 1850 to 76.2 million in 1900. A significant portion of the growth was fueled by the arrival in these years of some 16.2 million immigrants. An additional 8.8 million more arrived during the peak years of immigration, 1901–1910.

Growth of Immigration

In every era, the motives for emigrating from one country to another are a combination of "pushes" (negative factors from which people are fleeing) and "pulls" (positive attractions of the adopted country). The negative forces driving Europeans to emigrate in the late 19th century included (1) the poverty of displaced farmworkers driven from the land by the mechanization of farmwork, (2) overcrowding and joblessness in European cities as a result of a population boom, and (3) religious persecution, such as that of the Jews in Russia. Positive reasons for choosing to emigrate to the United States included this country's reputation for political and religious freedom and the economic opportunities afforded by the settling of the Great Plains and the abundance of industrial jobs in U.S. cities. Furthermore, the introduction of large steamships and the relatively inexpensive one-way passage in the ships' "steerage" made it possible for millions of poor Europeans to emigrate.

"Old" Immigrants and "New" Immigrants

Through the 1880s, the overwhelming majority of immigrants came from northern and western Europe: the British Isles, Germany, and Scandinavia. Most of these "old" immigrants were Protestants, although a sizable minority were Irish and German Catholics. Their language (mostly English-speaking) and high level of literacy and occupational skills made it relatively easy for these immigrants to blend into a mostly rural American society in the early decades of the 19th century.

New immigrants. Beginning in the 1890s and continuing to the outbreak of World War I in 1914, there was a notable change in the national origins of most immigrants. The "new" immigrants came from southern and eastern Europe. They were Italians, Greeks, Croats, Slovaks, Poles, and Russians. Many were poor and illiterate peasants, who had left autocratic countries and therefore were unaccustomed to democratic traditions. Unlike the earlier groups of Protestant immigrants, the newcomers were largely Roman Catholic, Greek Orthodox, Russian Orthodox, and Jewish. On arrival, most new immigrants crowded into poor ethnic neighborhoods in New York, Chicago, and other major U.S. cities.

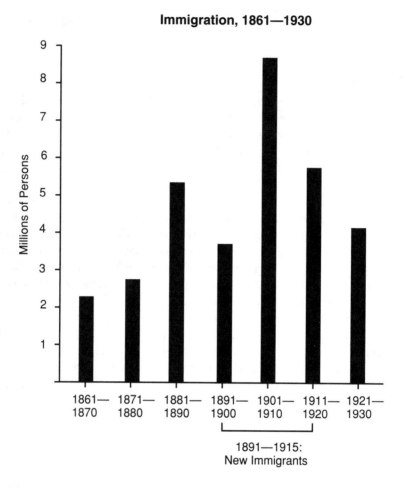

Immigration, 1861—1930

An estimated 25 percent of them were "birds of passage," young men contracted for unskilled factory, mining, and construction jobs, who would return to their native lands once they had saved a fair sum of money to bring back to their families.

Restricting Immigration

In the 1870s, when the French sculptor Frédéric-Auguste Bartholdi began work on the Statue of Liberty, there were few legal restrictions on immigration to the United States. By 1886, however—the year that the great welcoming statue was placed on its pedestal in New York harbor—Congress had passed a number of new laws restricting immigration. First came the Chinese Exclusion Act of 1882, placing a ban on all new immigrants from China. Then came restrictions on the immigration of "undesirable" persons (those convicted of criminal acts or diagnosed as mentally incompetent). Another law in 1885 prohibited contract labor in order to protect American workers. Soon after the opening of Ellis Island as an immigration center in 1892, the new arrivals had to pass more rigorous medical and document examinations and pay an entry tax before being allowed into the United States.

These efforts to restrict immigration were supported by diverse groups such as (1) labor unions, which feared that employers would use immigrants to depress wages and break strikes, (2) a nativist society called the American Protective Association, which was openly prejudiced against Roman Catholics, and (3) social Darwinists, who viewed the new immigrants as biologically inferior to English and Germanic stocks. During a severe depression in the 1890s, foreigners became a convenient scapegoat for jobless workers as well as for employers who blamed strikes and the labor movement on foreign agitators.

By no means, however, did the anti-immigrant feelings and early restrictions stop the flow of newcomers. At the turn of the century, almost 15 percent of the U.S. population were immigrants. The Statue of Liberty remained a beacon of hope for the poor and the oppressed of southern and eastern Europe until the 1920s, when the Quota Acts almost closed Liberty's golden door (see Chapter 23).

Urbanization

Urbanization and industrialization developed simultaneously as two sides of the same coin. Cities provided both a central supply of labor for factories and also a principal market for factorymade goods. The shift in population from rural to urban became more obvious with each passing decade. By 1900 almost 40 percent of Americans lived in towns or cities, and by 1920, for the first time, more Americans lived in urban communities than in rural areas.

Those moving into the cities were both immigrants and native-born Americans. In the late 19th century, millions of young Americans from rural areas decided to seek new economic opportunities in the cities. They left the farms for industrial and commercial jobs, and few of them returned. Among those who joined the inexorable movement from farms to cities were African Americans from the South. Between 1897 and 1930, nearly 1 million southern blacks settled in northern and western cities.

Changes in the Nature of Cities

Cities of the late 19th century underwent significant changes not only in their size but also in their internal structure and design.

Streetcar cities. A number of improvements in urban transportation made the growth of cities possible. In the walking cities of the pre-Civil War era, people had little choice but to live within walking distance of their shops or jobs. Such cities gave way to streetcar cities, in which people lived in residences many miles from their jobs and commuted to work on horse-drawn streetcars. By the 1890s, both horse-drawn cars and cable cars were being replaced by electric trolleys, elevated railroads, and subways, which could transport people to urban residences even farther from the city's commercial center. The building of massive steel suspension bridges such as the Brooklyn Bridge (completed in 1883) also made possible longer commutes between residential neighborhoods and the center city.

Mass transportation had the effect of segregating urban workers by income. The upper and middle classes moved to streetcar suburbs to escape the pollution, poverty, and crime of the city. The exodus of higher-income residents left older sections of the city to the working poor, many of whom were immigrants.

Skyscrapers. As cities expanded outward, they also soared upward, since increasing land values in the central business district dictated the construction of taller and taller buildings. In 1885, William Le Baron Jenny built the ten-story Home Insurance Company Building in Chicago—the first true skyscraper with a steel skeleton. Structures of this size were made possible by such innovations as the Otis elevator and the central steam-heating system with radiators in every room. By 1900 steel-framed skyscrapers for offices of industry and commerce had replaced church spires as the dominant feature of American urban skylines.

Ethnic neighborhoods. As the more affluent citizens deserted residences near the business district, the poor moved into them. To increase their profits, landlords divided up inner-city housing into small, windowless rooms. The resulting slums and tenement apartments could cram over 4,000 people into one city block. In an attempt to correct unlivable conditions, New York City passed a law in 1879 that required each bedroom to have a window. The cheapest way for landlords to respond to the law was to build the so-called dumbbell tenements, with ventilation shafts in the center of the building to provide windows for each room. However, overcrowding and filth in new tenements continued to promote the spread of deadly diseases, such as cholera, typhoid, and tuberculosis.

In their crowded tenement quarters, different immigrant groups created distinct ethnic neighborhoods where each group could maintain its own language, culture, church or temple, and social club. Many groups even supported their own newspapers and schools. While often crowded, unhealthy, and crime ridden, these neighborhoods (sometimes called "ghettos") often served as springboards for ambitious and hardworking immigrants and their children to achieve their version of the American dream.

Residential suburbs. In contrast to social and residential patterns in the United States, in Europe the wealthiest people today live, as in the past, near the business districts of modern cities, while lower-income people live in the outlying areas. There is a historical explanation for U.S. divergence from this pattern. During the 19th century, upper- and middle-class Americans decided that the best way to escape the problems of the city was to move out to the suburbs. The factors that promoted suburban growth included: (1) abundant land available at low cost, (2) inexpensive transportation by rail, (3) low-cost construction methods such as the wooden, balloon-frame house, (4) ethnic and racial prejudice, and (5) an American fondness for grass, privacy, and detached individual houses.

In the late 1860s, the landscape architect Frederick Law Olmsted designed a suburban community with graceful curved roads and open spaces—"a village in the park." By 1900, suburbs had grown up around every major U.S. city, and a single-family dwelling surrounded by an ornamental lawn soon became the American ideal of comfortable living. Thus began the world's first suburban nation.

Private city versus public city. At first, city residents tried to carry on life in large cities much as they had in small villages. They did not expect a lot of public services from municipal governments, and as a result, American cities could not deal effectively with the build-up of waste, pollution, disease, crime, and other hazards. Only slowly did advocates for healthier and more beautiful cities convince citizens and city governments of the need for water purification, sewerage systems, waste disposal, street lighting, police departments, and zoning laws to regulate urban development.

Boss and Machine Politics

The consolidation of power in business had its parallel in urban politics. Political parties in major cities came under the control of tightly organized groups of politicians, known as political machines. Each machine had its boss, the top politician who gave orders to the rank and file and doled out government jobs to loyal supporters. Several political machines, such as Tammany Hall in New York City, started as social clubs and later developed into power centers to coordinate the needs of businesses, immigrants, and the underprivileged. In return for performing these functions, they asked for people's votes on election day.

Successful party bosses knew how to manage the competing social, ethnic, and economic groups in the city. In many cases, the political machines that they ran brought modern services to the city, including a crude form of welfare for urban newcomers. The political organization would find jobs and apartments for recently arrived immigrants and show up at a poor family's door with baskets of food during hard times. But the political machine could be greedy as well as generous and often stole millions from the taxpayers in the form of graft and fraud. In New York City in the 1860s, for example, an estimated 65 percent of public building funds ended up in the pockets of Boss Tweed and his cronies.

Awakening of Reform

Urban problems, including the desperate poverty of working-class families, inspired a new social consciousness among members of the middle class. Reform movements begun in earlier decades gathered renewed strength in the 1880s and 1890s.

Books of social criticism. A San Francisco journalist, Henry George, published a provocative book in 1879 that became an instant best-seller and jolted readers to look more critically at the effects of laissez-faire economics. George's book, *Progress and Poverty,* proposed placing a single tax on land as the solution to poverty. More important, George succeeded in calling attention to the alarming inequalities in wealth caused by industrialization. Another popular book of social criticism, *Looking Backward, 2000–1887,* was written by Edward Bellamy in 1888. It envisioned a future era in which a cooperative society had eliminated poverty, greed, and crime. So enthusiastic were many of the readers of George's and Bellamy's books that they joined various reform movements and organizations to try to implement the authors' ideas. Both books encouraged a shift in American public opinion away from pure laissez-faire and toward greater government regulation.

Settlement houses. Concerned about the lives of the poor, a number of young, idealistic, and well-educated women and men of the middle class settled into immigrant neighborhoods to learn about the problems of immigrant families at first hand. Living and working in places called settlement houses, the young reformers hoped to relieve the effects of poverty by providing social services for people in the neighborhood. The most famous such experiment was Hull House in Chicago, which was started by Jane Addams and a college classmate in 1889. Settlement houses taught English to immigrants, pioneered early-childhood education, taught industrial arts, and established neighborhood theaters and music schools. By 1910 there were over 400 settlement houses in America's largest cities.

Settlement workers were civic-minded volunteers whose work provided the foundation in a later era for the professional social worker. They were also political activists who crusaded for child-labor laws, housing reform, and women's rights. Two settlement workers, Frances Perkins and Harry Hopkins, went on to leadership roles in President Franklin Roosevelt's reform program, the New Deal, in the 1930s.

Social Gospel. In the 1880s and 1890s, a number of Protestant clergymen espoused the cause of social justice for the poor—especially the urban poor. They preached what they called the Social Gospel, or the importance of applying Christian principles to social problems. Leading the Social Gospel movement in the late 19th and early 20th centuries was a New York minister, Walter Rauschenbusch, who worked in New York City's Hell's Kitchen and wrote several books urging organized religions to take up the cause of social justice. His Social Gospel preaching linked Christianity with the Progressive reform movement (see Chapter 21) and encouraged many middle-class Protestants to attack urban problems.

Religion and society. All religions found the need to adapt to the stresses and challenges of modern urban living. Roman Catholics gained enormous numbers from the influx of new immigrants. Catholic leaders such as Cardinal James Gibbons of Baltimore inspired the devoted support of old and new immigrants alike by defending the Knights of Labor and the cause of organized labor. Among Protestants, Dwight Moody and his Moody Bible Institute (founded in Chicago in 1889) would help generations of urban evangelists to adapt traditional Christianity to city life. The Salvation Army, imported from England in 1879, provided the basic necessities of life for the homeless and the poor, while also preaching the Christian gospel.

Members of the urban middle class were attracted to the religious message of Mary Baker Eddy, who taught that good health was the result of correct thinking about "Father Mother God." By the time of her death in 1910, hundreds of thousands had joined the church she had founded, the Church of Christ, Scientist—popularly known as Christian Science.

Families and women in urban society. Urban life placed severe strains on parents and their children by isolating them from the extended family (relatives beyond the family nucleus of parents and children) and village support. Divorce rates increased to one in 12 marriages by 1900, partly because a number of state legislatures had expanded the grounds for divorce to include cruelty and desertion. Another consequence of the shift from rural to urban living was a reduction in family size. Children were an economic asset on the farm, where their labor was needed at an early age. In the city, however, they were more of an economic liability. Therefore, in the last decades of the 19th century, the national average for birthrates and family size continued to drop.

The cause of woman's suffrage, launched at Seneca Falls in 1848, was vigorously carried forward by a number of middle-class women. In 1890, two of the pioneer feminists of the 1840s, Elizabeth Cady Stanton and Susan B. Anthony of New York, helped found the National American Women's Suffrage Association to secure the vote for women. A western state, Wyoming, was the first to grant full suffrage to women, in 1869. By 1900, some states allowed women to vote in local elections, and most allowed women to own and control property after marriage.

Temperance and morality. Another cause that attracted the attention of urban reformers was the temperance movement. Women especially were convinced that excessive drinking of alcohol by male factory workers was a principal cause of poverty for immigrant and working-class families. The Women's Christian Temperance Union (WCTU) was formed in 1874. Advocating total abstinence from alcohol, the WCTU under the leadership of Frances E. Willard of Illinois had 500,000 members by 1898. The Antisaloon League, founded in 1893, became a powerful political force and by 1916 had persuaded 21 states to close down all saloons and bars. Unwilling to wait for the laws to change, Carry A. Nation of Kansas created a sensation by raiding saloons and smashing barrels of beer with a hatchet.

Moralists thought of cities as a breeding ground for vice, obscenity, and prostitution. Anthony Comstock of New York formed the Society for the Suppression of Vice to be the watchdog of American morals. He and his followers persuaded Congress in 1873 to pass the "Comstock Law," which prohibited the mailing or transportation of obscene and lewd material and photographs.

Intellectual and Cultural Movements

The change from an agricultural to an industrial economy and from rural to urban living profoundly affected all areas of American life and culture: education, the arts, even sports.

Changes in Education

The growing complexity of modern life, along with the intellectual influence of Darwin's theory of evolution, raised challenging questions about what schools and universities should teach.

Public schools. Elementary schools after 1865 continued to teach the 3 R's (reading, writing, arithmetic) and the traditional values promoted in the standard texts, McGuffey's readers. New compulsory laws, however, dramatically increased the number of children enrolled in public schools. As a result, the literacy rate rose to 90 percent of the population by 1900. The practice of sending children to kindergarten (a concept borrowed from Germany) became popular and reflected the growing interest in early-childhood education in the United States.

Perhaps even more significant was the growing support for tax-supported public high schools. At first these schools followed the college preparatory curriculum of private academies, but soon the public high schools became more comprehensive and began to emphasize vocational and citizenship education for a changing urban society.

Higher education. The number of U.S. colleges increased in the late 1800s largely as a result of: (1) land grant colleges established under the Morrill acts of 1862 and 1890, (2) universities founded by wealthy philanthropists— the University of Chicago by John D. Rockefeller, for example, and (3) the founding of new colleges for women, such as Smith, Bryn Mawr, and Mount Holyoke. By 1900, 71 percent of the colleges admitted women, who represented more than one-third of the attending students.

There were also significant changes in the college curriculum. Soon after becoming president of Harvard in 1869, Charles W. Eliot reduced the number of required courses and introduced electives (courses chosen by students) to accommodate the teaching of modern languages and the sciences: physics, chemistry, biology, and geology. Johns Hopkins University was founded in Baltimore in 1876 as the first American institution to specialize in advanced graduate studies. Following the model of German universities, Johns Hopkins emphasized research and free inquiry. As a result of such innovations in curriculum, the United States produced its first generation of scholars who could compete with the intellectual achievements of Europeans. At the same time, however, there was a trend in another direction as life at many colleges became dominated by social activities, fraternities, and intercollegiate sports.

Social sciences and the professions. The application of the scientific method and the theory of evolution to human affairs revolutionized the social sciences in the late 19th century. The new social sciences included behavioral psychology, sociology, anthropology, and political science. Richard T. Ely of Johns Hopkins attacked laissez-faire economic thought as dogmatic and outdated and used economics to study labor unions, trusts, and other existing economic institutions not only to understand them but to suggest remedies for economic problems of the day. Evolutionary theory influenced leading sociologists (Lester F. Ward), political scientists (Woodrow Wilson), and historians (Frederick Jackson Turner) to study the dynamic process of actual human behavior instead of logical abstractions. In the legal profession, Oliver Wendell Holmes, Jr., taught that the law should evolve with the times in response to changing needs and not remain restricted by legal precedents and judicial decisions of the past. Clarence Darrow, a famous lawyer, argued that criminal behavior could be caused by a person's environment of poverty, neglect, and abuse. Other professions—doctors, educators, and social workers—also began applying scientific theory and methodology to their work.

The leading black intellectual of his day, W. E. B. Du Bois, was the first African American to receive a doctorate from Harvard. Du Bois used the new statistical methods of sociology to study crime in an urban neighborhood. As an activist, he advocated full equal rights for blacks, integrated schools, and equal access to higher education for the "talented tenth" of African American youth.

Although fewer than 5 percent of Americans attended college before 1900, the new trends in education and the professions would have a significant impact on progressive legislation and liberal reforms in the next century.

Literature and the Arts

American writers and artists responded in diverse ways to industrialization and urban problems. In general, the work of the best-known innovators of the era reflected a new realism and an attempt to express an authentic American style.

Realism and naturalism. Many of the popular works of literature of the post-Civil War years were romantic novels that depicted ideal heroes and heroines. The first break with this genteel literary tradition came with regionalist writers like Bret Harte, who depicted life in the rough mining camps of the West. Mark Twain (the pen name for Samuel L. Clemens) became the first great realist author. His classic work, *The Adventures of Huckleberry Finn* (1884), revealed the greed, violence, and racism in American society. Another leading realist, William Dean Howells, seriously considered the problems of industrialization and unequal wealth in the novels *The Rise of Silas Lapham* (1885) and *A Hazard of New Fortunes* (1890).

A younger generation of authors who emerged in the 1890s became known for their naturalism, which described how emotions and experience shaped human experience. In his naturalistic novel *Maggie: A Girl of the Streets* (1893), Stephen Crane told how a brutal urban environment could destroy the lives of young people. Crane also wrote the popular *Red Badge of Courage* about fear and human nature on the Civil War battlefield before dying himself of tuberculosis at only 29. Jack London, a young California writer and adventurer, portrayed the conflict between nature and civilization in novels like *The Call of the Wild* (1903). A naturalistic book that caused a sensation and shocked the moral sensibilities of the time was Theodore Dreiser's novel about a poor working girl in Chicago, *Sister Carrie* (1900).

Painting. Several American painters responded to the new emphasis on realism, while others continued to cater to the popular taste for romantic subjects. Winslow Homer, the foremost American painter of seascapes and watercolors, often rendered scenes of nature in a matter-of-fact way. Thomas Eakins specialized in painting the everyday lives of working-class men and women and used the new technology of serial-action photographs to study human anatomy and paint it more realistically.

Born in Massachusetts, James McNeill Whistler became an American expatriate when he sailed to Europe at the age of 21 and spent most of his life in Paris and London. His most famous painting, *Arrangement in Grey and Black* (popularly known as "Whistler's Mother"), hangs in the Louvre. This study of color, rather than subject matter, influenced the development of modern art. A distinguished portrait painter, Mary Cassatt, also spent much of her life in France where she learned the techniques of impressionism, especially in her use of pastel colors. As the 19th century drew to a close, a group of social realists known as the "Ashcan School" painted scenes of everyday life in poor urban neighborhoods. Upsetting to realists and romanticists alike were the abstract, nonrepresentational paintings exhibited in the Armory Show in New York City in 1913. Art of this kind would be rejected by most Americans until the 1950s when it finally achieved recognition and respect among collectors of fine art.

Architecture. In the 1870s, Henry Hobson Richardson changed the direction of American architecture. His designs, based on the Romanesque style of massive stone walls and rounded arches, gave a gravity and stateliness to functional commercial buildings. Louis Sullivan of Chicago went a step further by rejecting historic styles in his quest for a suitable style for the tall, steel-framed office buildings of the 1880s and 1890s. Sullivan's buildings achieved a much-admired aesthetic unity, in which the form of a building flowed from its function—a hallmark of the Chicago School of architecture. Frank Lloyd Wright, an employee of Sullivan's in the 1890s, developed an "organic" style of architecture that was in harmony with its natural surroundings. Wright's vision is exemplified in his prairie houses. Wright became the most famous American architect of the 20th century. Other architects, such as Daniel H. Burnham, who revived classical Greek and Roman architecture in his designs for the World's Columbian Exposition of 1893, continued to explore both historical and modern styles in their buildings.

One of the most influential urbanists, Frederick Law Olmsted specialized in the planning of city parks and scenic boulevards, including Central Park in New York City and the grounds of the U.S. Capitol in Washington. As the originator of landscape architecture, Olmsted not only designed parks, parkways, campuses, and suburbs but also established the basis for all later efforts at urban landscaping.

Music. With the growth of cities came increasing demand for musical performances and entertainment appealing to a variety of tastes. By 1900, most large cities had either a symphony orchestra, an opera house, or both. In smaller towns, outdoor bandstands were the setting for the playing of popular marches by John Philip Sousa.

Probably the greatest innovators of the era were African American musicians in New Orleans. Jelly Roll Morton and Buddy Bolden introduced the general American public to jazz, a form of music that combined African rhythms with western-style instruments and mixed improvisation with a structured band format. The remarkable black composer and performer Scott Joplin sold nearly a million copies of sheet music of his "Maple Leaf Rag" (1899). Also from the South came blues music that expressed the pain of the black experience. Jazz, ragtime, and blues music gained popularity during the early 20th century as New Orleans performers headed north into the urban centers of Memphis, St. Louis, Kansas City, and Chicago.

Popular Culture

Entertaining the urban masses became a major business in the late 19th century. Even newspapers became less a medium of objective information and more of a mass medium for amusing millions of readers.

Popular press. Mass-circulation newspapers had been around since the 1830s, but the first newspaper to exceed a million in circulation was Joseph Pulitzer's New York *World*. Pulitzer achieved this success by filling his daily paper with both sensational stories of crimes and disasters and crusading feature stories about political and economic corruption. Another New York publisher, William Randolph Hearst, pushed scandal and sensationalism to new heights (or lows).

Mass-circulation magazines also became increasingly popular and numerous in the 1880s and 1890s. Advertising revenues and new printing technologies made it possible for the *Ladies' Home Journal* and other popular magazines to sell for as little as 10 cents a copy.

Amusements. In addition to urbanization, other factors also promoted the growth of leisure-time activities: (1) a gradual reduction in the hours people worked, (2) improved transportation, (3) promotional billboards and advertising, and (4) the decline of restrictive Puritan and Victorian values that discouraged "wasting" time on play. Based on numbers alone, the most popular form of recreation in the late 19th century (despite the temperance movement), was drinking and talking at the corner saloon. Legitimate theaters for the performance of comedies and dramas flourished in most large cities, but vaudeville with its variety of acts had more appeal for the urban masses. The circus became the "Greatest Show on Earth" in the 1880s through the showmanship of Phineas T. Barnum and James A. Bailey. Also immensely popular was the Wild West show brought to urban audiences by William F. Cody ("Buffalo Bill") and headlining such personalities as Sitting Bull and the markswoman Annie Oakley.

Commuter streetcar and railroad companies also promoted weekend recreation in order to keep their cars running on Sundays and holidays. They created parks in the countryside near the end of the line so that urban families could enjoy picnics and outdoor recreation.

Spectator sports. Enthusiasm for professionally organized spectator sports (baseball, football, basketball, and boxing) had its origins in the late 19th century. The most famous athlete of the era was the heavyweight boxer John L. Sullivan. Professional boxing bouts drew mostly male spectators from both the upper and lower classes to cheer and wager on their favorite pugilist. Baseball, while it recalled a rural past of green fields and fences, was very much an urban game that demanded the teamwork needed for an industrial age. Owners organized teams into leagues, much as trusts of the day were organized. In 1909, when President William Howard Taft started the tradition of throwing out the first ball of the season, the national pastime was already a well-established part of American popular culture. Basketball was invented in 1891 at Springfield College, in Massachusetts. In only a few years, high schools and colleges across the nation had teams. The first professional basketball league was organized in 1898. The first intercollegiate football game was played by two New Jersey colleges, Rutgers and Princeton, in 1869. Football remained a college sport for decades and did not become a commercial enterprise of professional league teams until the 1920s.

American spectator sports were played and attended by men. They were part of what historians have called the "bachelor subculture" for single men in their twenties and thirties, whose lives centered around saloons, horse races, and pool halls. It took years for some spectator sports, such as boxing and football, to gain middle-class respectability.

Amateur sports. The value of playing sports as healthy exercise for the body gained acceptance by the middle and upper classes in the late 19th century. Women were considered unfit for most competitive sports, but they too engaged in such recreational activities as croquet and bicycling. Participation in golf and tennis grew, but was often limited to members of athletic clubs, which kept out most of the working class. The very rich could separate themselves from lower-income people by pursuing the expensive sports of polo and yachting. While Jews and Catholics were kept out of some private clubs, the most severely discriminated against were African Americans, who were prevented by Jim Crow laws from joining whites-only clubs and from playing on all-white big-league baseball teams until the late 1940s.

HISTORICAL PERSPECTIVES: MELTING POT OR CULTURAL DIVERSITY?

To what extent did immigrants from different nationalities give up their original heritage to become Americanized, or fully assimilated into the mainstream culture? The prevailing view in the 19th and early 20th centuries was that the United States was a melting pot, in which immigrant groups quickly learned to shed old-world characteristics in order to become successful citizens of their adopted country. This view was expressed as early as 1782 by a naturalized Frenchman, J. Hector St. John Crèvecoeur. In his *Letters From an American Farmer,* Crèvecoeur described how the American experience "melted" European immigrants "into a new race of men." The term "melting pot" became firmly associated with immigration in a popular play by that name: Israel Zangwill's *The Melting Pot* (1908). One line of this drama described "how the great Alchemist melts and fuses them [immigrants] with purging flames!"

In recent decades, the melting pot concept has come under intense scrutiny and challenge by modern historians. Carl N. Degler, for example, has argued that a more accurate metaphor would be the salad bowl, in which each ingredient (ethnic culture) remains intact. To support this view, Degler points to the diversity of religions in the United States. Neither immigrants nor their descendants gave up their religions for the Protestantism of the American majority.

In his groundbreaking study of immigration, *The Uprooted* (1952), Oscar Handlin observed that newcomers to a strange land often became alienated from both their native culture and the culture of their new country. According to Handlin, first-generation immigrants remained alienated and did not lose their cultural identity in the melting pot. Only the immigrants' children and children's children became fully assimilated into mainstream culture.

Many historians agree with Handlin that, after two or three generations, the melting pot, or assimilation, process has effectively reduced the cultural differences among *most* ethnic groups. Certain groups, on the other hand, have had a different experience. Historian Richard C. Wade has observed that African Americans who migrated to northern cities faced the special problem of racism, which has created seemingly permanent ghettos with "a growingly alienated and embittered group."

Historians remain divided in their analysis of the melting pot. Those who accept the concept see people of diverse ethnic backgrounds coming together to build a common economy and culture. Others see American urban history characterized by intergroup hostility, alienation, crime, and corruption. The questions about past immigration are important because they shape our view of ethnic tensions in contemporary society. Is there a process, common to all groups, in which initial prejudice against the most recent immigrants fades after two or three generations? Is the cultural diversity that we observe in U.S. society today a permanent condition—or just unmelted bits of foreign ways that will ultimately fuse into a homogeneous culture?

KEY NAMES, EVENTS, AND TERMS

Columbian Exposition	ethnic neighborhoods	Social Gospel movement
"old" immigrants	ghettos	Walter Rauschenbusch
"new" immigrants	tenements	Dwight Moody
Statue of Liberty	suburbs	Salvation Army
Chinese Exclusion Act (1882)	Frederic Law Olmsted	Mary Baker Eddy
Ellis Island	political machine	National American Women's
contract labor law	party boss	Suffrage Association
American Protective Association	Henry George, *Progress and Poverty*	Women's Christian Temperance Union
urbanization	Edward Bellamy, *Looking Backward*	Frances E. Willard
streetcar cities		Antisaloon League
mass transportation	settlement house	Carry A. Nation
skyscrapers	Jane Addams	Anthony Comstock

Charles W. Eliot	Thomas Eakins	Buddy Bolden
Johns Hopkins University	James McNeill Whistler	jazz
Oliver Wendell Holmes	Mary Cassatt	Scott Joplin; ragtime
Lester F. Ward	Ashcan School	Joseph Pulitzer
Clarence Darrow	Armory Show of 1913	William Randolph Hearst
W. E. B. Du Bois	Henry Hobson Richardson	P. T. Barnum; James A.
Bret Harte	Louis Sullivan	Bailey
Mark Twain	Chicago School	Buffalo Bill; Annie Oakley
William Dean Howells	Frank Lloyd Wright	John L. Sullivan
Stephen Crane	Daniel Burnham	spectator sports; amateur
Jack London	Frederick Law Olmsted	sports; bachelor sports
Theodore Dreiser	John Philip Sousa	melting pot
Winslow Homer	Jelly Roll Morton	cultural diversity

MULTIPLE-CHOICE QUESTIONS

1. Which of the following is a correct statement about immigration from 1890–1914?

   (A) The number of immigrants declined because of restrictive quota laws.

   (B) Most of the immigrants came from southern and eastern Europe.

   (C) Most immigrants of this period were readily accepted because of their education and wealth.

   (D) Workers from Latin America were excluded from immigrating by federal laws.

   (E) Labor unions supported the rights of Chinese immigrants.

2. Which of the following groups were NOT included among the new immigrants of the late 19th century?

   (A) Russian Jews escaping religious persecution

   (B) Italian peasants

   (C) Greeks, Slovaks, and Poles

   (D) Scandinavian farmers

   (E) unemployed Europeans seeking factory jobs in U.S. cities

3. All of the following characterized America's large cities in the last decades of the 19th century EXCEPT

   (A) outbreaks of deadly diseases such as cholera and tuberculosis

   (B) transportation limited to the central business district

   (C) crowded tenements

   (D) increasing segregation of social groups by income

   (E) poor treatment of water, sewage, and waste

4. Which of the following were most likely to help immigrants adjust to city life in the late 19th century?

   (A) politicians from Tammany Hall

   (B) followers of social Darwinists

   (C) members of the American Protective Association

(D) lawmakers in Congress

(E) employers in major industries

5. Settlement houses were characterized by all of the following EXCEPT

(A) located in poor working-class and immigrant neighborhoods

(B) staffed by college-educated, middle-class men and women

(C) took little interest in legislative reforms

(D) taught English to immigrants

(E) helped to educate immigrant children

6. Which of the following did NOT contribute to the development of suburbs in the United States?

(A) European suburban development patterns

(B) low-cost and abundant land

(C) improved streetcar and railroad transportation

(D) ethnic and racial prejudices

(E) unhealthy living conditions in the cities

7. "This association of poverty with progress is the great enigma of our times. . . . So long as all the increased wealth which modern progress brings goes but to build up great fortunes . . . progress is not real and cannot be permanent." The above statement was written by

(A) Dwight Moody

(B) Anthony Comstock

(C) Henry George

(D) Charles W. Eliot

(E) Carry Nation

8. Changes in education between 1865 and 1900 included all of the following EXCEPT

(A) introduction of the elective system in some colleges

(B) establishment of land grant colleges and universities

(C) introduction of kindergartens

(D) increased educational opportunities for women

(E) increased emphasis on classical curriculum

9. Which of the following were *both* examples of realism in 19th-century literature and art?

(A) Jack London novel and Ashcan School

(B) James Fenimore Cooper novel and Winslow Homer painting

(C) Walt Whitman poem and Thomas Cole painting

(D) Mark Twain novel and Grant Wood painting

(E) Ralph Waldo Emerson essay and Armory Show of 1913

10. All of the following contributed to the growth of sports and entertainment in late-19th-century America EXCEPT

(A) Puritan ethic and Victorian values

(B) improvements in transportation

(C) gradual reduction of working hours

(D) bachelor subculture

(E) advertising in the popular press

ESSAY QUESTIONS

1. How did the characteristics and experiences of the "new" immigrants of the 1880–1914 period compare to those of the "old" immigrants who came before them?

2. Analyze how TWO of the following factors contributed to the development of American cities between 1865 and 1900:

   technology

   urban politics

   class divisions

3. Analyze the reform ideas and influence of TWO of the following:

   Jane Addams

   Henry George

   Walter Rauschenbush

4. Assess the contributions made to American culture in TWO of the following areas between 1865 and 1900:

   literature

   painting

   architecture

   music

5. To what extent did changes in popular culture, such as the growth of the popular press and increased leisure-time and sports activities, reflect the changes in American society from 1865 to 1900?

DOCUMENTS AND READINGS

Each of the following selections reflects the response of leading intellectuals and reformers of late-19th-century America to urbanization and industrialization. As you read each document, assess the extent to which the writer views the changes in urban America to be either positive or negative.

DOCUMENT A. TENEMENTS AND URBAN PROBLEMS

Jacob A. Riis was a Danish immigrant who arrived in the United States in 1870 and, after studying urban problems, wrote a best-selling book in 1890, *How the Other Half Lives,* which described conditions in immigrant ghettoes in New York City. The following is an excerpt from Riis's book, together with an illustration of the tenement life of the period.

Today three-fourths of its [New York's] people live in tenements, and the nineteenth century drift of the population to the cities is sending ever-increasing multitudes to crowd them. The fifteen thousand tenant houses that were the despair of the sanitarian in the past generation have swelled into thirty-seven thousand, and more than twelve hundred thousand persons call them home. . . .

If it shall appear that the sufferings and the sins of the "other half," and the evil they breed, are but as a just punishment upon the community that gave it no other choice, it will be because that is the truth. . . . [I]n the tenements all the influences make for evil; because they are the hotbeds of the epidemics that carry death to rich and poor alike; the nurseries of pauperism and crime that fill our jails and police courts; that throw off a scum of forty thousand human wreaks to the island asylums and workhouses year by year; that turned out in the last eight years a round half million beggars to prey upon our charities; that maintain a standing army of ten thousand tramps with all that that implies; because above all, they touch the family life with deadly moral contagion. . . .

Jacob A. Riis,
How the Other Half Lives, 1890

DOCUMENT B. *REFORM OF MUNICIPAL GOVERNMENT*

Richard T. Ely, a reform-minded economist, opposed traditional laissez-faire economics for reasons given in this passage.

> Government is the God-given agency through which we must work. To many, I am aware, this is not a welcome word, but it is a true word. We may twist and turn as long as we please, but we are bound to come back to recognition of this truth. . . .
>
> Societies [private and religious] have failed and will fail. They cannot, acting simply as societies, do the work. Their resources are inadequate. The territory they can cover is too small, and power is insufficient. . . . There is plenty of room for the individual and for individual activity. Not all the work can be done by government, although without government very little can be accomplished. . . .
>
> An objection may be raised here on account of the poor character of our government of cities. Of course our governments are poor. Why should they not be? We have done everything to make them so. We have been taught to turn away from government for the accomplishments of business purposes and for social improvement. We have been trying to reduce government to a contemptible insignificance, and in many cases have succeeded in reducing it to contemptible impotence. Lest men should do some wrong thing, we have made it impossible for them to do any good thing. We succeeded in turning the energy and talent of the community, for the most part, away from public life and diverted the great bulk of talent and energy into private life. We have reaped the legitimate fruits that might have been expected, one is tempted to say, which have been deserved.

Richard T. Ely,
The Needs of the City, 1889

DOCUMENT C. *CLASH OF CULTURES*

Jane Addams, settlement house founder and peace activist, was one of the most distinguished of the first generation of college-educated women who made a lifelong commitment to the poor and social reform. In the following selections from a speech before the National Education Association, Addams explained the challenges faced by teachers in urban schools, based on her experience working with Italian immigrants on the west side of Chicago.

> Italian parents count upon the fact that their children learn the English language and American customs before they themselves do, and act not only as interpreters of the language about them but as buffers between them and Chicago; and this results in a certain,

almost pathetic, dependence of the family upon the child. When a member of the family, therefore, first goes to school, the event is fraught with much significance to all the others. The family has no social life in any structural form and can supply none to the child. If he receives it in the school and gives it to his family, the school would thus become the connector with the organized society about them. . . .

Too often the teacher's conception of her duty is to transform him [son of immigrants] into an American of a somewhat smug and comfortable type, and she insists that the boy's powers must at once be developed in an abstract direction, quite ignoring the fact that his parents have had to do only with tangible things. She has little idea of the development of Italian life. Her outlook is national, and not racial; and she fails, therefore, not only in knowledge of but also in respect for the child and his parents. She quite honestly estimates the child upon an American basis. The contempt for the experiences and languages of their parents which foreign children sometimes exhibit, and which is most damaging to their moral as well as intellectual life, is doubtless due in part to the overestimation which the school places upon speaking and reading in English. This cutting into his family loyalty takes away one of the most conspicuous and valuable traits of the Italian child.

Jane Addams,
Addresses at the Thirty-sixth
Annual Meeting of the NEA, 1897

DOCUMENT D.   *EDUCATION FOR A SOCIETY OF SPECIALISTS*

Charles W. Eliot, in his inaugural address on becoming president of Harvard, recommended a fundamental shift in higher education from a uniform curriculum of classical studies to an elective system that allowed students to follow their particular talents.

Only a few years ago, all students who graduated at this college passed through one uniform curriculum. Every man studied the same subjects in the same proportions, without regard to his natural bent or preference. The individual student had no choice of either subjects or teachers. . . .

As a people, we do not apply to mental activities the principle of division of labor; and we have but a halting faith in special training for high professional employments. The vulgar conceit that a Yankee can turn his hand to anything we insensibly carry into high places, where it is preposterous and criminal. We are accustomed to seeing men leap from farm and shop to courtroom or pulpit, and we half believe that common men can safely use the seven-league boots of genius. . . .

The civilization of people may be inferred from the variety of its tools. There are thousands of years between the stone hatchet and the machine shop. As tools multiply, each is more ingeniously adapted to its own exclusive purpose. So with the men that make the state. For the individual, concentration and the highest development of his own peculiar faculty is the only prudence. But for the state, it is variety, not uniformity, of intellectual product which is needful.

These principles are the justification of the system of elective studies which had gradually developed in this college during the past forty years. At present the freshmen year is the only one in which there is a fixed course prescribed for all. In the other three years, more than half the time allotted to study is filled by subjects chosen by each student. . . .

Charles W. Eliot,
Inaugural Address, 1869

ANALYZING THE DOCUMENTS

1. Why were late-19th-century reformers like Jacob Riis more inclined than earlier reformers to trace the causes of poverty, crime, and vice to the environment?

2. Why did Richard Ely look to government as the solution for the urban problems of his day?

3. What is Jane Addams' criticism of the typical teacher of immigrant children?

4. What benefits does Charles Eliot envision from the elective system of education for both the individual and society?

5. What specific changes in American society after the Civil War most probably account for the observations and recommendations found in each of the four readings?

NATIONAL POLITICS IN THE GILDED AGE, 1877–1900

My country, 'is of thee, Once land of liberty, Of thee I sing.
Land of the Millionaire; Farmers with pockets bare;
Caused by the cursed snare—The Money Ring.

Alliance Songster, 1890

Congress had enacted an ambitious reform program during the 1860s and 1870s—the era of Civil War and Reconstruction. After the election of Rutherford B. Hayes and the Compromise of 1877, however, the national government settled into an era of stalemate and comparative inactivity. Americans at this time shifted their attention away from national politics to economic change: the development of the West (described in Chapter 16), industrialization and the labor movement (Chapter 17), and the growth of cities (Chapter 18).

Politics in the Gilded Age

The expression *Gilded Age,* first used by Mark Twain in 1873 as the title of a book, referred to the superficial glitter of the new wealth so prominently displayed in the last years of the 19th century. The politics of the era is often criticized as mostly show with little substance. It was the era of "forgettable" presidents, none of whom served two consecutive terms, and of politicians who largely ignored problems arising from the growth of industry and cities. The two major parties in these years avoided taking a stand on controversial issues.

Causes of Stalemate

Factors accounting for the complacency and conservatism of the era included (1) the prevailing political ideology of the time, (2) campaign tactics of the two parties, and (3) party patronage.

Belief in limited government. The idea of "do-little" government was in tune with two other popular ideas of the time: laissez-faire economics and social Darwinism. Furthermore, the federal courts narrowly interpreted the government's powers to regulate business, and this limited the impact of the few regulatory laws that Congress did pass.

Campaign strategy. The closeness of elections between 1876 and 1892 was one reason that Republicans and Democrats alike avoided taking strong positions on the issues. The Democrats won only two presidential contests in the electoral college (but four in the popular vote). They nevertheless controlled the House of Representatives after eight of the ten general elections. The result was divided government in Washington (except for two years of the Harrison administration, 1889–1891, when the Republicans were in control of both the presidency and the two houses of Congress). With elections so evenly matched, the objective was to get out the vote and not alienate voters on the issues.

Election campaigns of the time were characterized by brass bands, flags, campaign buttons, picnics, free beer, and crowd-pleasing oratory. Both parties had strong organization, the Republicans usually on the state level and the Democrats in the cities. The irony is that the issue-free campaigns brought out nearly 80 percent of the eligible voters for presidential elections, much higher than elections in the 20th century. The high turnout was a function of strong party identification and loyalty, often connected with the voters' regional, religious, and ethnic ties.

Republican politicians kept memories of the Civil War alive during the Gilded Age by figuratively waving the "bloody shirt" in every campaign and reminding the millions of veterans of the Union army that their wounds had been caused by (southern) Democrats and that Abraham Lincoln had been murdered by a Democrat. The party of Lincoln, because of its antislavery past, kept the votes of reformers and African Americans. The core of Republican strength came from men in business and from middle-class, Anglo-Saxon Protestants. Republicans remained rooted in their Whig past, supporting an economic program of high protective tariffs for business.

Democrats after 1877 could count upon winning every election in the former states of the Confederacy. The solid South was indeed solidly Democratic until the mid-20th century. In the North, Democratic strength came from big-city political machines and the immigrant vote. Democrats were often Catholics, Lutherans, and Jews who objected to temperance and prohibition crusades conducted by Protestant (and largely Republican) groups. Democrats of the Gilded Age continued to believe in states' rights and limited powers for the federal government.

Party patronage. Since neither party had an active legislative agenda, politics in this era was chiefly a game of gaining office, holding office, and providing government jobs to the party faithful. In New York, for example, Republican Senator Roscoe Conkling became a powerful leader of his party by dictating who in the Republican ranks would be appointed to lucrative jobs in the New York Customs House. Conkling and his supporters were known as the Stalwarts, while their rivals for patronage were the Halfbreeds, led by James G. Blaine. Who got the patronage jobs within the party became a more important issue than anything else. Republicans who did not play the patronage game were ridiculed as the Mugwumps for sitting on the fence—their "mugs" on one side of the fence and "wumps" on the other. Historians generally consider this era a low point in American politics.

Presidential Politics

The administrations of presidents Hayes, Garfield, and Arthur reflected the political stalemate and patronage problems of the Gilded Age.

Rutherford B. Hayes. After being declared the winner of the disputed election of 1876, Rutherford B. Hayes' most significant act was to end Reconstruction by withdrawing the last federal troops from the South. President Hayes also attempted to reestablish honest government after the corrupt Grant administration. As temperance reformers, Hayes and his wife, "Lemonade Lucy," cut off the flow of liquor in the White House. Hayes vetoed efforts to restrict Chinese immigration.

James Garfield. Republican politicians, more interested in spoils and patronage than reform, were happy to honor President Hayes' pledge in 1877 to serve only one term. In the election of 1880, the Republicans compromised on the nomination of "Halfbreed" James A. Garfield of Ohio (a key swing state of the times), and "Stalwart" Chester A. Arthur of New York as vice president. The Democrats nominated Winfield S. Hancock, a former Union general who had been wounded at Gettysburg. The Garfield-Arthur ticket defeated the Democratic war hero in a very close popular vote.

In his first weeks in office, Garfield was besieged in the White House by hordes of Republicans seeking some 100,000 federal jobs. Garfield's choice of Halfbreeds for most offices provoked a bitter contest with Senator Conkling and his Stalwarts. While the president was preparing to board a train for a summer vacation in 1881, a deranged office seeker who identified with the Stalwarts shot Garfield in the back. After an 11-week struggle, the gunshot wound proved fatal. Chester A. Arthur then became president.

Chester A. Arthur. Arthur proved a much better president than people expected. He distanced himself from the Stalwarts, supported a bill reforming the civil service, and approved the development of a modern American navy. He also began to question the high protective tariff. His reward was denial of renomination by the Republican party in 1884.

Congressional Leaders

Weak presidents do not necessarily mean strong Congresses. Lawmakers of the Gilded Age typically had long but undistinguished careers. John Sherman, brother of the famous Civil War general, was in Congress from 1855 to 1898 but did little other than allow his name to be attached to a number of bills, including the Sherman Antitrust Act of 1890. Thomas "Czar" Reed from Maine, a sharp-tongued bully, became Speaker of the House in 1890 and instituted an autocratic rule over the House that took years to break. Senator James G. Blaine, also from Maine, had the potential of being a great political leader and largely succeeded in reshaping the Republicans from an antislavery party into a well-organized, business-oriented party. Blaine's reputation as the Plumed Knight was tarnished, however, by evidence of his connection with railroad scandals and other corrupt dealings.

The Election of 1884

In 1884 the Republicans nominated Blaine for president, but suspicions about Blaine's honesty were enough for the reform-minded Mugwumps to switch allegiance and campaign for the Democratic nominee, Grover Cleveland. Unlike most Gilded Age politicians, Cleveland was honest, frugal, conscientious, and uncompromising. He had been an honest mayor of Buffalo and incorruptible governor of New York State. Republicans raised questions, however, about the honest New Yorker's private life, making much of the fact that Cleveland had fathered an illegitimate child. In one of the dirtiest election campaigns in history, the Democrats were labeled the party of "Rum, Romanism, and Rebellion." Catholic voters were offended by the phrase, and their votes in key states like New York may have been enough to ensure Cleveland's victory as the first Democrat to be elected president since Buchanan in 1856.

Cleveland's First Term

The Democratic president believed in frugal and limited government in the tradition of Jefferson. He implemented the new civil service system (see below) and vetoed hundreds of private pension bills for those falsely claiming to have served or been injured in the Civil War. He signed into law both (1) the Interstate Commerce Act of 1887, the federal government's first effort to regulate business, and (2) the Dawes Act, which reformers hoped would benefit Native Americans. Cleveland's administration also retrieved some 81 million acres of government land from cattle ranchers and the railroads.

Issues: Civil Service, Currency, and Tariffs

During the 1870s and 1880s, the Congresses in Washington were chiefly concerned with such issues as patronage, the money supply, and the tariff issue. They left the states and local governments to deal with the growing problems of the cities and industrialization.

Civil service reform. Public outrage over the assassination of President Garfield in 1881 pushed Congress to remove certain government jobs from the control of party patronage. The Pendleton Act of 1881 set up the Civil Service

Commission and created a system by which applicants for classified federal jobs would be selected on the basis of their scores on a competitive examination. The law also prohibited civil servants from making political contributions. At first, the law applied to only 10 percent of federal employees, but in later decades, the system was expanded until most federal jobs were classified (that is, taken out of the hands of politicians).

Politicians adapted to the reform by depending less on their armies of party workers and more on the rich to fund their campaigns. A hundred years later, social scientists still debate which approach is more harmful to democratic government.

Money question. One of the most hotly debated issues of the era was whether or not to expand the money supply. The money question reflected the growing tension during the industrial age between the "haves" and the "have-nots."

Debtors, farmers, and start-up businesses wanted more money in circulation, since this would enable them to (1) borrow money at lower interest rates and (2) pay off their loans more easily with inflated dollars. After the Panic of 1873, many Americans blamed the gold standard for restricting the money supply and causing the depression. To expand the supply of U.S. currency, easy- or "soft"-money advocates campaigned first for more paper money (greenbacks) and then for the unlimited minting of silver coins.

On the opposite side of the question, bankers, creditors, investors, and established businesses stood firm for sound, or hard, money—meaning currency backed by gold stored in government vaults. Dollars backed by gold would more likely hold their value against inflation. The big holders of money understood that as the U.S. economy and population grew, a limited number of gold-backed dollars would gain in value. In fact, as predicted, the dollar *did* increase in value by as much as 300 percent between 1865 and 1895.

Greenback party. Paper money not backed by specie (gold or silver) had been issued by the federal government in the 1860s as an emergency measure for financing the Civil War. Northern farmers, who received high prices during the war, associated the greenbacks with prosperity. On the other hand, creditors and investors attacked the use of paper money not backed by specie as a violation of natural law. Siding with the creditors, Congress in 1875 passed the Specie Resumption Act, which withdrew the last of the greenbacks from circulation.

Supporters of paper money formed a new political party, the Greenback party. In the congressional election of 1878, Greenback candidates received nearly 1 million votes, and 14 members were elected to Congress, including James B. Weaver of Iowa (a future leader of the Populist party). When the hard times of the 1870s ended, the Greenback party died out, but the goal of increasing the amount of money in circulation did not.

Demands for silver money. In addition to removing greenbacks, Congress in the 1870s also stopped the coining of silver (the Crime of 1873, as critics called it). Then silver discoveries in Nevada revived demands for the use of silver to expand the money supply. A compromise law, the Bland-Allison Act, was passed over Hayes' veto in 1878. It allowed only a limited coinage of between $2 million and $4 million in silver each month at the standard silver-to-gold ratio of 16 to 1. Not satisfied, farmers, debtors, and western miners continued to press for the *unlimited* coinage of silver.

Tariff issue. Western farmers and eastern capitalists also disagreed on the question of whether tariff rates on foreign imports should be high or low. During the Civil War, the Republican Congress had enacted a high tariff to protect U.S. industry and also fund the Union government. After the war, southern Democrats as well as some northern Democrats objected to high tariffs because these taxes raised the prices on consumer goods. Another result of the protective tariff was that other nations retaliated by placing taxes of their own on U.S. farm products. American farmers lost a share of the overseas market, creating surpluses of corn and wheat and resulting in lower farm prices and profits. From a farmer's point of view, industry seemed to be growing rich at the expense of rural America.

The Growth of Discontent, 1888–1896

The politics of stalemate and complacency would begin to lose their hold on the voters by the late 1880s. Discontent over government corruption, the money issue, tariffs, railroads, and trusts was growing. In response, politicians began to take small steps to respond to public concerns, but it would take a third party (the Populists) and a major depression in 1893 to shake the Democrats and the Republicans from their lethargy.

Harrison and the Billion-Dollar Congress

Toward the end of his first term, President Cleveland created a political storm by challenging the high protective tariff. He proposed that Congress set lower tariff rates, since there was a growing surplus in the federal treasury and the government did not need the added tax revenue.

The election of 1888. With the tariff question, Cleveland introduced a real issue, the first in years that truly divided Democrats and Republicans. In the election of 1888, Democrats campaigned for Cleveland and a lower tariff; Republicans campaigned for Benjamin Harrison (grandson of the former president, William Henry Harrison) and a high tariff. The Republicans argued that a lower tariff would wreck business prosperity. They played upon this fear to raise campaign funds from big business and to rally workers in the North, whose jobs depended on the success of U.S. industry. The Republicans also attacked Cleveland's vetoes of pension bills to bring out the veteran vote.

The election was extremely close. Cleveland received more popular votes than Harrison, but ended up losing the election because Harrison's sweep of the North gained the Republican ticket a majority of votes in the electoral college.

Billion-dollar Congress. For the next two years, Republicans controlled the presidency and both houses of Congress—unusual for this era of close elections. The new Congress was the most active in years, passing the first billion-dollar budget in U.S. history. It enacted the following:

- The *McKinley Tariff* of 1890, which raised the tax on foreign products to a peacetime high of over 48 percent

- *Increases in the monthly pensions* to Civil War veterans, widows, and children

- The *Sherman Antitrust Act,* outlawing "combinations in restraint of trade" (see Chapter 17)

- The *Sherman Silver Purchase Act of 1890,* which increased the coinage of silver, but in amounts too small to satisfy farmers and miners

- A *bill to protect the voting rights of African Americans,* passed by the House but defeated in the Senate

Return of the Democrats. In the congressional elections of 1890, the voters especially in the Midwest replaced many Republicans with Democrats. They were reacting in part to unpopular measures passed by Republican state legislatures: prohibition of alcohol and Sunday closing laws. Voters who were neither Anglo-Saxon nor Protestant rushed back to the Democrats, who had not tried to legislate public morality.

Rise of the Populists

Another factor in the Republican setbacks of 1890 was growing agrarian discontent in the South and West. Members of the Farmers' Alliances elected U.S. senators and representatives, the governors of several states, and majorities in four state legislatures in the West.

Omaha platform. The Alliance movement provided the foundation of a new political party—the People's, or Populist, party. Delegates from different states met in Omaha, Nebraska, in 1892 to draft a political platform and nominate candidates for president and vice president for the new party. Populists were determined to do something about the concentration of economic power in the hands of trusts and bankers. Their Omaha platform called for both political and economic reforms. Politically, it demanded the restoration of government to the people by means of (1) direct popular election of U.S. senators (instead of indirect election by state legislatures) and (2) enacting of state laws by voters themselves through initiatives and referendums placed on the ballot.

Economically, the Populist platform was even more ambitious. Populists advocated: (1) unlimited coinage of silver to increase the money supply, (2) a graduated income tax (the greater a person's income, the greater the tax), (3) public ownership of railroads by the U.S. government, (4) telegraph and telephone systems owned and operated by the government, (5) loans and federal warehouses for farmers to enable them to stabilize prices for their crops, and (6) an eight-hour day for industrial workers.

At the time, the Populist movement seemed revolutionary not only because of its attack on laissez-faire capitalism but also because of its attempt to form a political alliance between poor whites and poor blacks. In the South, Thomas Watson of Georgia appealed to poor farmers of both races to unite on their common economic grievances by joining the People's party.

The election of 1892. In 1892, James Weaver of Iowa, the Populist candidate for president, won more than 1 million votes and was also one of the few third-party candidates in U.S. history to win electoral votes (22). Nevertheless, the Populist ticket lost badly in the South and failed to attract urban workers in the North. The fear of Populists uniting poor blacks and whites drove conservative southern Democrats to use every technique to disfranchise African Americans (see Chapter 16).

In terms of the major parties, the election was a rematch between President Harrison and former president Cleveland. This time, Cleveland won a solid victory in both the popular and electoral vote. He won in part because of the unpopularity of the high-tax McKinley Tariff. Cleveland became the first and only former president thus far to return to the White House after having left it.

Depression Politics

No sooner did Cleveland take office than the country entered into one of its worst and longest depressions.

Panic of 1893. In the spring and summer of 1893, the stock market crashed as a result of overspeculation, and dozens of railroads went into bankruptcy as a result of overbuilding. The depression continued for almost four years. Farm foreclosures reached new highs, and the unemployed reached 20 percent of the workforce. Many people ended up relying on soup kitchens and riding the rails as hoboes. President Cleveland, more conservative than he had been in the 1880s, dealt with the crisis by championing the gold standard and otherwise adopting a hands-off policy toward the economy.

Gold reserve and tariff. A decline in silver prices encouraged investors to trade their silver dollars for gold dollars. The gold reserve (bars of gold bullion stored by the U.S. Treasury) fell to a dangerously low level, and President Cleveland saw no alternative but to repeal the Sherman Silver Purchase Act of 1890. This action, however, failed to stop the gold drain. The president then turned to the Wall Street banker J. P. Morgan to borrow $65 million in gold to support the dollar and the gold standard. This deal convinced many Americans that the government in Washington was only a tool of rich eastern bankers. Workers became further disenchanted with Cleveland when he used court injunctions and federal troops to crush the Pullman strike in 1894 (see Chapter 17).

The Democrats did enact one measure that was somewhat more popular. Congress passed the Wilson-Gorman Tariff in 1894, which (1) provided a moderate reduction in tariff rates and (2) included a 2 percent income tax on incomes of more than $2,000. Since the average American income at this time was less than $1,000, only those with higher incomes would be subject to the income tax. Within a year after the passage of the law, however, the conservative Supreme Court declared an income tax unconstitutional.

Jobless on the march. As the depression worsened and the numbers of jobless people grew, conservatives feared class war between capital and labor. They were especially alarmed by Coxey's Army—a march to Washington in 1894 by thousands of the unemployed led by Populist Jacob A. Coxey of Ohio. The "army" demanded that the federal government spend $500 million on public works programs to create jobs. Coxey and other protest leaders were arrested for trespassing, and the dejected "army" then left for home.

Also in 1894, a little book by William H. Harvey presenting lessons in economics seemed to offer easy answers for ending the depression. Illustrated with cartoons, *Coin's Financial School* taught millions of discontented Americans that their troubles were caused by a conspiracy of rich bankers, and that prosperity would return if only the government coined silver in unlimited quantities.

Turning Point in American Politics: 1896

National politics was in transition. The repeal of the Silver Purchase Act and Cleveland's handling of the depression thoroughly discredited the conservative leadership of the Democratic party. The Democrats were buried in the congressional elections of 1894 by the Republicans. At the same time, the Populists continued to gain both votes and legislative seats. The stage was set for a major reshaping of party politics in 1896.

The Election of 1896

The election of 1896 was one of the most emotional in U.S. history. It also would mark of the beginning of a new era in American politics.

Bryan, Democrats, and Populists. Democrats were divided in 1896 between "gold" Democrats loyal to Cleveland and prosilver Democrats looking for a leader. Their national convention in Chicago in the summer of 1896 was dominated by the prosilver forces. Addressing the convention, William Jennings Bryan of Nebraska captured the hearts of the delegates with a speech that ended with these words: "We will answer their demands for a gold standard by saying to them: 'You shall not press down upon the brow of labor this crown of thorns, you shall not crucify mankind upon a cross of gold.' " So powerful was Bryan's "Cross of Gold" speech that it made him, literally overnight, the Democratic nominee for president. The candidate was only 36 years old.

The Democratic platform favored the unlimited coinage of silver at the traditional, but inflationary, ratio of 16 ounces of silver to one ounce of gold. (The market price then was about 32 to 1.) Thus, the Democrats had taken over the leading issue of the Populist platform. Given little choice, the Populist convention in 1896 also nominated Bryan and conducted a "fused" campaign for "free silver."

Unhappy with Bryan and free silver, the conservative faction of "Gold Bug" Democrats, including Cleveland, either formed the separate National Democratic party or voted Republican.

McKinley, Hanna, and Republicans. For their presidential nominee, the Republicans nominated William McKinley of Ohio, best known for his support of a high protective tariff but also considered a friend of labor. Marcus Hanna, who had made a fortune in business, was the financial power behind McKinley's nomination as well as the subsequent campaign for president. After blaming the Democrats for the Panic of 1893, the Republicans offered the American people the promise of a strong and prosperous industrial nation. The Republican platform proposed a high tariff to protect industry and upheld the gold standard against unlimited coinage of silver.

Campaign. The defection of "Gold Bug" Democrats over the silver issue gave the Republicans an early advantage. Bryan countered by turning the Democratic-Populist campaign into a nationwide crusade. Traveling by train from one end of the country to the other, the young candidate covered 18,000 miles and gave more than 600 speeches. His energy, positive attitude, and rousing oratory convinced millions of farmers and debtors that the unlimited coinage of silver was their salvation.

Mark Hanna meanwhile did most of the work of campaigning for McKinley. He raised millions of dollars for the Republican ticket from business leaders who feared that "silver lunacy" would lead to runaway inflation. Hanna used the money to sell McKinley through the mass media (newspapers, magazines), while the Republican candidate stayed home and conducted a safe, front-porch campaign, greeting delegations of supporters.

In the last weeks of the campaign, Bryan was hurt by (1) a rise in wheat prices, which made farmers less desperate, and (2) employers telling their workers that factories would shut down if Bryan was elected. On election day, McKinley carried all of the Northeast and the upper Midwest in a decisive victory over Bryan in both the popular vote (7.1 million to 6.5 million) and the electoral vote (271 to 176).

McKinley's Presidency

McKinley was lucky to take office just as the economy began to revive. Gold discoveries in Alaska in 1897 increased the money supply under the gold standard, which resulted in the inflation that the silverites had wanted. Farm prices rose, factory production increased, and the stock market climbed. The Republicans honored their platform by enacting a higher tariff (the Dingley Tariff of 1897) and making gold the official standard of the U.S. currency (in 1900). McKinley was generally a well-liked, well-traveled president, who actively tried to bring conflicting interests together. As leader during the war with Spain in 1898, he helped to make the United States a world power.

Significance of the Election of 1896

The election of 1896 had a number of both short-term and long-term consequences on American politics. For one thing, it marked the end of the stalemate and stagnation that had characterized politics in the Gilded Age. For another, the defeat of Bryan and the Populist free-silver movement initiated an era of Republican dominance of the presidency (seven of the next nine elections) and of both houses of Congress (17 of the next 20 sessions). Once the party of "free soil, free labor, and free men," the Republicans were now the party of business, industry, and a strong national government. The Democrats carried on in defeat as the sectional party of the South and host of whatever Populist sentiment remained.

Populist demise. The Populist party declined after 1896 and soon ceased to be a national party. In the South, Thomas Watson and other Populist leaders gave up trying to unite poor whites and blacks, having discovered the hard lesson that racism was stronger than common economic interests. Ironically, in defeat, much of the Populist reform agenda, such as the graduated income tax and popular election of senators, was adopted by both the Democrats and Republicans during the reform-minded Progressive era (1900–1917).

Urban dominance. The election of 1896 was a clear victory for big business, urban centers, conservative economics, and moderate, middle-class values. It proved to be the last hope of rural America to reclaim its former dominance in American politics. Some historians see the election marking the triumph of the values of modern industrial and urban America over the rural ideals of the America of Jefferson and Jackson.

Beginning of modern politics. McKinley emerged as the first modern president, an active leader who took the United States from being relatively isolated to becoming a major player in international affairs. Mark Hanna, the master of high-finance politics, created a model for organizing and financing a successful campaign focused on winning favorable publicity in the mass media.

HISTORICAL PERSPECTIVES: WHO WERE THE POPULISTS?

Historians debate whether the Populist crusade was realistic or romantic. Was it a liberal response to the problems of the era or a reactionary effort to bring back a farmer-dominated society?

Early histories of the Populists depicted them as idealistic farmers and small producers who challenged the abuses of industrial America and the corruption of the political system. As reformers, they were seeking only economic fairness and an honest democratic process. The reforms that they advocated in the Omaha platform of 1892 had long-term significance in preparing the way for similar reforms in the Progressive era (1900–1917) and the New Deal (1933–1939).

An alternative view of the Populists sees them largely as reactionaries who dreamed up conspiracies by eastern bankers instead of seriously trying to understand the complex causes of the decline of farm income. Critics argue that Populists—rather than dealing with the world as it was—isolated themselves from the new urban and industrial age and became racists, nativists, anti-Semites, and anti-Catholics. Richard Hofstadter in *The Age of Reform* (1955) saw both positive and negative aspects in the Populist movement. He credited the Populists as being the first political party to insist on the federal government's responsibility to promote the common good and deal with problems of industrialization. At the same time, Hofstadter criticized the Populists' backward-looking and nostalgic ideology and their hopeless quest to restore an agrarian golden age that existed only in myth.

More recently, historians have returned to the view that the farmers' grievances were real and that American democracy was in fact in serious danger of being dominated by powerful economic groups. According to the latest scholarship, members of the National Farmers' Alliance and the Populist movement were *not* ignorant of complex economic changes; instead, farmers worked to educate themselves in the economics and politics of the day. Nor does the charge of racial bigotry fit the majority of Populists. Walter Nugent in *The Tolerant Populists* (1963) depicts them as democratic humanists who welcomed into their ranks people of all races, creeds, and ethnic backgrounds.

As a style of politics, populism is far from dead but continues to the present day. Michael Kazin in *The Populist Persuasion* (1995) analyzed populism as a political attitude and posture that combines antielitism with advocacy for the common people. According to Kazin, populism shifted to the right in the 1960s with the emergence of George Wallace and the presidency of Richard Nixon. The populist revolt of the late 20th century often appeared as a revolt of the silent majority of middle-class Americans against an intrusive big government. The study of the dynamics of the late-19th-century Populist movement has helped political scientists understand the workings and differences between reform politics and mainstream politics. The Populist appeal of the outsiders and antiestablishment reformers remains a relevant part of the American political process.

KEY NAMES, EVENTS, AND TERMS

Gilded Age	"Rum, Romanism, and Rebellion"	Omaha platform
solid South		Panic of 1893
Roscoe Conkling	Pendleton Act	gold drain
Stalwarts	Greenback party	Coxey's Army
Halfbreeds	James B. Weaver	William Harvey, *Coin's Financial School*
Mugwumps	Crime of 1873	
	Bland-Allison Act (1878)	William Jennings Bryan, "Cross of Gold"
Rutherford B. Hayes	Benjamin Harrison	
James Garfield	billion-dollar Congress	free silver
Chester A. Arthur	veterans' pensions	"Gold Bug" Democrats
Thomas Reid	McKinley Tariff (1890)	William McKinley
James G. Blaine	Sherman Silver Purchase Act (1890)	Mark Hanna
Grover Cleveland	Populist (People's) party	Dingley Tariff (1897)

MULTIPLE-CHOICE QUESTIONS

1. Which of the following is a correct statement about national politics in the Gilded Age?

   (A) Congress focused on the problems of industrialization and urbanization.

   (B) The presidents of the era expanded executive powers.

   (C) The two major parties avoided taking strong positions on the issues.

   (D) Republicans held firm control of both Congress and the presidency.

   (E) Lack of interest in national politics resulted in low voter turnout.

2. The issue of patronage was least involved in which of the following?

   (A) rivalry between the Stalwarts and Halfbreeds

   (B) the assassination of James A. Garfield

   (C) the passage of the Pendleton Act

(D) the nomination of James B. Weaver as a presidential candidate

(E) the control of New York politics by Roscoe Conkling

3. What two issues dominated national politics in the late 19th century?

(A) the money supply and the protective tariff

(B) wages and working conditions of factory workers

(C) overseas expansion and the growth of the military

(D) civil service reform and welfare of the poor

(E) pension reform and balancing the federal budget

4. In the late 19th century, inflationary monetary policies did NOT appeal to

(A) supporters of the Greenback party

(B) emerging businesses with large debts

(C) cotton farmers

(D) founders of the Populist party

(E) bankers

5. The Republican billion-dollar Congress did all of the following EXCEPT

(A) increase tariff rates

(B) increase pensions for Civil War veterans

(C) increase the coinage of silver

(D) enact an antitrust law

(E) enact a law regulating interstate commerce

6. "Transportation being a means of exchange and a public necessity, the government should own and operate the railroads in the interests of the people. The telegraph and telephone, like the post office system, being a necessity for the transmission of news, should be owned and operated by the government in the interests of the people."

The passage above is most likely from which of the following?

(A) the Interstate Commerce Act

(B) Grover Cleveland's annual message to Congress

(C) the platform of the Republican party

(D) the platform of the Populist party

(E) the Sherman Antitrust Act

7. In the election of 1896, the major issue was

(A) the lowering of tariff rates

(B) the free and unlimited coinage of silver

(C) the reduction of veterans' pensions

(D) Cleveland's handling of the Panic of 1893

(E) welfare for the unemployed

8. All of the following were reasons for the decline of the Populist party EXCEPT

(A) racism in the South

(B) failure of farmers and industrial workers to unite

(C) adoption of the silver issue by the Democrats

(D) waning popularity of Grover Cleveland

(E) decline of the political power of rural America

Political Party Affiliations in Congress, 1881–1901				
	House		Senate	
Year	Major Parties	Minor Parties	Major Parties	Minor Parties
1881–1883	R-147, D-135	11	R-37, D-37	1
1883–1885	D-197, R-118	10	R-38, D-36	2
1885–1887	D-183, R-140	2	R-43, D-34	0
1887–1889	D-169, R-152	4	R-39, D-37	0
1889–1891	R-166, D-159		R-39, D-37	0
1891–1893	D-235, R-88	9	R-47, D-39	2
1893–1895	D-218, R-127	11	D-44, R-38	3
1895–1897	R-244, D-105	7	R-43, D-39	6
1897–1899	R-204, D-113	40	R-47, D-34	7
1899–1901	R-185, D-163	9	R-53, D-26	8

R—Republican   D—Democrat

Source: *Historical Statistics of the United States*

Questions 9 and 10 refer to the table:

9. Which of the following conclusions is supported by data in the table?

(A) Democrats dominated both houses of Congress during Cleveland's two terms in office.

(B) The Republicans broke the divided control of Congress in elections of the late 1890s.

(C) Minor parties were best represented in Congress during 1880s and declined in the 1890s.

(D) Democrats and Republicans were stalemated by their divided control of Congress in the 1880s and 1890s.

(E) After the election of 1896, the Populists ceased to be represented in Congress.

10. The data in the table would be *most revelant* in an investigation of which of the following historical topics?

(A) origins of the Greenback party

(B) sectionalism after the Civil War

(C) influence of political machines on the Republican party

(D) impact of industrialization on the two-party system

(E) political dominance in Congress from Garfield to McKinley

ESSAY QUESTIONS

1. Analyze the reasons for relatively few congressional or presidential accomplishments during the Gilded Age, despite high voter participation in national politics.

2. Describe and account for the federal government's reactions to the Panic of 1893.

3. In what ways did the creation of the Greenback and Populist parties indicate that the two major parties had failed to deal with the critical problems of the period from 1877 to 1900?

4. To what extent were the supporters and the reforms of the Populists of the 1890s both ahead of their times and behind their times?

5. To what extent did the election of 1896 represent a turning point in the history of U.S. politics?

DOCUMENT-BASED QUESTION (DBQ)

Write an essay that integrates your understanding of the documents and your knowledge of the period.

"The politics of the Gilded Age failed to deal with the critical social and economic issues of the times."

Assess the validity of this statement. Use both the documents and your knowledge of the United States from 1865 to 1900.

DOCUMENT A.

To explain the causes which keep much of the finest intellect of the country away from national business is one thing; to deny the unfortunate results would be quite another. Unfortunate they are. But the downward tendency observable since the end of the Civil War seems to have been arrested. When the war was over, the Union saved, the curse of slavery gone forever, there came a season of contentment and of lassitude. A nation which had surmounted such dangers seemed to have nothing more to fear. Those who had fought with tongue and pen and rifle might now rest on their laurels. After long continued strain and effort, the wearied nerve and muscle sought repose. It was repose from political warfare only. For the end of the war coincided with the opening of a time of swift material growth and abounding material propensity in which industry and the development of the West absorbed more and more of the energy of the people. Hence a neglect of details of politics such as had never been seen before. . . .

James Bryce,
The American Commonwealth, 1891

DOCUMENT B.

We have had an era of material inventions. We now need a renaissance of moral inventions, contrivances to tap the vast currents of moral magnetism flowing uncaught over the face of society. . . . If the tendency to combination is irresistible, control of it is imperative. Monopoly and anti-monopoly . . . represent the two great tendencies of our time: monopoly, the tendency to combination; anti-monopoly, the demand for social control of it. As the man is bent toward business or patriotism, he will negotiate combination or agitate for laws to regulate them. The first is capitalistic and the second is social. The first, industrial; the second, moral. The first promotes wealth; the second, citizenship. Our young men can no longer go west; they must go up or down. Not new land, but new virtue must be the outlet for the future.

Henry Demarest Lloyd,
"Lords of Industry," *North American Review,* June 1884

DOCUMENT C.

Collections of the Library of Congress

DOCUMENT D.

Year by year man's liberties are trampled under foot at the bidding of corporations and trusts, rights are invaded and law perverted. In all ages wherever a tyrant has shown himself he has always found some willing judge to clothe that tyranny in the robes of legality, and modern capitalism has proven no exception to the rule.

You [a federal judge] may not know that the labor movement as represented by the trades unions, stands for right, for justice, for liberty. You may not imagine that the issuance of an injunction depriving men of a legal as well as a natural right to protect themselves, their wives and little ones, must fail of its purpose. Repression or oppression never yet succeeded in crushing the truth or redressing a wrong.

Samuel Gompers,
"Letter on Labor in Industrial Society," *Forum,* September 1894

DOCUMENT E.

Be it enacted by the Senate and House of Representatives of the United States of America in Congress assembled, that the provisions of this act shall apply to any common carriers engaged in the transportation of passengers or property wholly by railroad, . . . from one state or territory of the United States, or the District of Columbia, to any other state or territory of the United States, or the District of Columbia. . . .

Section 3. That it shall be unlawful for any common carrier subject to the provisions of this act to make or give any undue or unreasonable preference or advantage to any particular person, company, firm, corporation, or locality. . . .

Section 4. That it shall be unlawful for any common carrier subject to the provision of this act to charge or receive any greater compensation in the aggregate for the transportation of passengers or of like kind of property, under substantially similar circumstances and conditions, for a shorter than for a longer distance over the same line. . . .

The Interstate Commerce Act, 1887

DOCUMENT F.

By the act of the legislature of 1888, the factory inspectors were required to enforce the law relating to the indenturing of apprentices. . . . The industrial conditions existing at, and previously to, the time of the passage of the Law of 1871 are so completely revolutionized that the old form of apprenticeship has become almost obsolete. Where, in former times, boys were expected to learn a trade in all its features, they are now simply put at a machine or at one branch of the craft, and no understanding exists that they shall be taught any other branch or the use of any other machine. Employers claim that these boys are not apprentices, and even if they so desired, could not teach . . . an apprentice all the intricacies of a trade, for the reason that where the skill and intelligence of a journeyman [trained] workman were once essential, a simple machine now unerringly performs the service, and consequently there is no occasion for an apprentice to learn to do the labor by hand. These were the principal reasons given by employers as to why the law had become inoperative.

Third Annual Report of the Factory Inspectors
of the State of New York for the
Year Ending December 1st, 1888, 1889

DOCUMENT G.

The Chairman: We want to find out how the working people of Fall River [Massachusetts] are living and doing. . . . Just tell us the condition of the operatives there, in your own way.

The Witness: I have been in Fall River about eleven years, though I have been one year absent during that time. As a physician and surgeon, of course, I have been brought into contact with all classes of people there, particularly the laboring classes, the operatives of the city.

With regard to the effect of the present industrial system upon their physical and moral welfare, I should say it was of such a character as to need mending, to say the least. It needs some radical remedy. Our laboring population is made up very largely of foreigners, men, women, and children, who have either voluntarily come to Fall River or who have been induced to come there by the manufactures.

As a class they are dwarfed physically. . . .

They are dwarfed, in my estimation, sir, as the majority of men and women who are brought up in factories must be dwarfed under the present industrial system; because by their long hours of indoor labor and their hard work they are cut off from the benefit of breathing fresh air and from the sights that surround a workman outside a mill. Being shut up all day long in the noise and in the high temperature of these mills they become physically weak.

Testimony of a Physician (Timothy D. Stow),
Report of the Committee of the Senate
Upon the Relations of Labor and Capital, 1890

DOCUMENT H.

We have witnessed, for more than a quarter of a century the struggles of the two great political parties for power and plunder, while grievous wrongs have been inflicted upon the suffering people. We charge that the controlling influences dominating both these parties have permitted the existing dreadful conditions to develop without serious effort to prevent or restrain them.

Neither do they now promise us any substantial reform. They have agreed together to ignore, in the coming campaign, every issue but one. They propose to drown the outcries of a plundered people with the uproar of a sham battle over the tariff, so that capitalists, corporations, national banks, rings, trusts, watered stock, the demonetization of silver and the oppressions of the usurers may all be lost sight of. They propose to sacrifice our homes, lives, and children on the altar of mammon; to destroy the multitude in order to secure corruption funds from the millionaires.

Populist Party Platform, 1892

FOREIGN POLICY, 1865–1914

Ever since the 1790s, U.S. foreign policy had been centered on expanding westward, protecting U.S. interests abroad, and limiting foreign influences in the Americas. The period after the Civil War saw the development of a booming industrial economy, which created the basis for a major shift in U.S. relations with the rest of the world. Instead of a nation that—at least since the War of 1812—had been relatively isolated from European politics, the United States became a world power with territories extending across the Pacific to the Philippines. How and why did the United States acquire an overseas empire and intervene in the affairs of Cuba, Mexico, and other Latin American nations? For the origins of these developments, we must return briefly to the years just after the Civil War.

Seward, Alaska, and the French in Mexico

A leading Republican of the 1850s and 1860s, William H. Seward of New York served under both Abraham Lincoln and Andrew Johnson as their secretary of state (1861–1869). Seward achieved more as secretary of state than anyone since the time of John Quincy Adams (who had helped formulate the Monroe Doctrine in 1823). During the Civil War, Seward helped Lincoln prevent Great Britain and France from entering the war on the side of the South. A strong expansionist, he was unsuccessful in his efforts to convince Congress to annex Hawaii and purchase the Danish West Indies, but he achieved the annexation of Midway Island in the Pacific and gained rights to build a canal in Nicaragua.

The French in Mexico

Napoleon III (nephew of the first Napoleon) had taken advantage of U.S. involvement in the Civil War by sending French troops to occupy Mexico. With the conclusion of the Civil War in 1865, Seward immediately invoked the Monroe Doctrine and threatened U.S. military action unless the French withdrew. Napoleon III backed down, and the French troops left Mexico.

The Purchase of Alaska

For decades, the vast territory of Alaska had been the subject of dispute between two European powers that claimed it: Russia and Great Britain. Russia assumed control and established a small colony for seal hunting, but the territory soon became an economic burden always subject to the threat of a British takeover. Seeking buyers, Russia found Seward to be an enthusiastic champion of the idea of the United States acquiring Alaska by purchase. Due to Seward's lobbying, and also in appreciation of Russian support during the Civil War, Congress in 1867 agreed to purchase Alaska for $7.2 million. It would take many years, however, for Americans to see the value in Alaska and stop referring to it derisively as "Seward's Folly" and "Seward's Icebox."

The "New Imperialism"

As the United States industrialized in the late 19th century, it also intensified its foreign involvement partly because it needed (1) worldwide markets for its growing industrial and agricultural surpluses and (2) sources of raw materials for manufacturing. In addition, many conservatives hoped that overseas territories and adventures might offer an outlet and safety valve for unhappiness at home. They were concerned about the growing violence of labor-management disputes and the unrest of farmers. For the most part, advocates of an expansionist policy hoped to achieve their ends by economic and diplomatic means, not by military action.

International Darwinism

Darwin's concept of the survival of the fittest was applied not only to competition in the business world but also to competition among nations. According to this theory, only the strongest survived, and, depending on the interests of various groups, this meant that the U.S. had to be strong religiously, militarily, and politically. Therefore, in the international arena, the United States had to demonstrate its strength by acquiring territories overseas. Expansionists of the late 19th century extended the idea of manifest destiny so that the potential for U.S. territorial expansion applied not just to North America but to all parts of the world.

Imperialism. Americans were not alone in pursuing a policy of *imperialism,* which meant either acquiring territory or gaining control over the political or economic life of other countries. Many nations in Europe, led by Britain, France, Germany, and Russia, as well as Japan, were involved in gaining possessions and influence in weaker countries, especially in Africa and the Pacific Ocean. Some in the United States believed that the nation had to compete with the imperialistic nations for new territory or it would grow weak and fail to survive.

In the United States, advocates of American expansion included missionaries, politicians, naval strategists, and journalists.

Missionaries. In his book *Our Country: Its Possible Future and Present Crisis* (1885), the Reverend Josiah Strong wrote that people of Anglo-Saxon stock were "the fittest to survive" and that Protestant Americans had a Christian duty to colonize other lands for the purpose of spreading Christianity and Western civilization. Strong's book expressed the thinking of many Protestant congregations, which believed that westerners of the Christian faith had a duty to bring the benefits of their "superior" civilization (medicine, science, and technology) to less fortunate peoples of the world. Many of the missionaries who traveled to Africa, Asia, and the Pacific islands also believed in the racial superiority and supremacy of whites. Mission activities of their churches encouraged many Americans to support active U.S. government involvement in foreign affairs.

Politicians. Many in the Republican party were closely allied with business leaders. Republican politicians therefore generally endorsed the use of foreign affairs to search for new markets. Congressional leaders such as Henry Cabot Lodge of Massachusetts and the Republican governor of New York, Theodore Roosevelt, were eager to build U.S. power through global expansion.

Naval power. U.S. Navy Captain Alfred Thayer Mahan wrote an important book, *The Influence of Sea Power Upon History* (1890), in which he argued that a strong navy was crucial to a country's ambitions of securing foreign markets and becoming a world power. Mahan's book was widely read by prominent American citizens—and also by political leaders in Europe and Japan. Using arguments in Mahan's book, U.S. naval strategists persuaded Congress to finance the construction of modern steel ships and encouraged the acquisition of overseas islands, such as Samoa, to be used as coaling and supply stations so that the new fleet would be a world power. By 1900, the United States had the third largest navy in the world.

Popular press. Newspaper and magazine editors found that they could increase circulation by printing adventure stories about distant and exotic places. Stories in the popular press increased public interest and stimulated demands for a larger U.S. role in world affairs.

Latin America

Beginning with the Monroe Doctrine in the 1820s, the United States had taken a special interest in problems of the Western Hemisphere and had assumed the role of protector of Latin America from European ambitions. Benjamin Harrison's Secretary of State James G. Blaine of Maine played a principal role in extending this tradition.

Blaine and the Pan-American Conference (1889). Blaine's repeated efforts to establish closer ties between the United States and its southern neighbors bore fruit in 1889 with the meeting of the first Pan-American Conference in Washington. Representatives from various nations of the Western Hemisphere decided to create a permanent organization for international cooperation on trade and other issues. Blaine had hoped to bring about reductions in tariff rates. Although this goal was not achieved, the foundation was established for the larger goal of hemispheric cooperation on both economic and political issues. The Pan-American Union continues today as part of the Organization of American States, which was established in 1948.

Cleveland, Olney, and the Monroe Doctrine. One of the most important uses of the Monroe Doctrine in the 19th century concerned a boundary dispute between Venezuela and a neighboring territory—the British colony of Guiana. In 1895 and 1896, President Cleveland and Secretary of State Richard Olney insisted that Great Britain agree to arbitrate the dispute. At first, the British said the matter was not the business of the United States. Cleveland and Olney, however, argued that the Monroe Doctrine applied to the situation, and if the British did not arbitrate, the United States stood ready to back up its argument with military force.

Deciding that U.S. friendship was more important to its long-term interests than winning a boundary dispute in South America, the British finally agreed to U.S. demands. As it turned out, the arbitrators ruled mainly in favor of Britain, not Venezuela. Even so, Latin American nations appreciated U.S. efforts to protect them from European domination. Most important, the Venezuela boundary dispute marked a turning point in U.S.–British relations. From 1895 on, Britain would cultivate U.S. friendship rather than continuing its former hostility. The friendship would prove vital for both nations throughout the coming century.

The Spanish-American War

A principal target of American imperialism was the nearby Caribbean area. Expansionists from the South had coveted Cuba as early as the 1850s. Now, in the 1890s, large American investments in Cuban sugar, Spanish misrule of Cuba, and the Monroe Doctrine all provided justification for U.S. intervention in the Caribbean's largest island.

Causes of War

In the 1890s, American public opinion was being swept by a growing wave of *jingoism*—an intense form of nationalism calling for an aggressive foreign policy. Expansionists demanded that the United States take its place with the imperialist nations of Europe as a world power. Not everyone favored such a policy. Presidents Cleveland and McKinley were among many who thought military action abroad was both morally wrong and economically unsound. Nevertheless, specific events combined with background pressures led to overwhelming popular demand for war against Spain.

Cuban revolt. Bands of Cuban nationalists had been fighting for ten years to overthrow Spanish colonial rule. In 1895, they adopted the strategy of sabotaging and laying waste Cuban plantations in order either to force Spain's withdrawal or involve the United States in their revolution. Spain responded by sending the autocratic General Valeriano Weyler and over 100,000 troops to suppress the revolt.

Yellow press. Actively promoting war fever in the United States were sensationalistic city newspapers with their bold and lurid headlines of crime, disaster, and scandal. "Yellow journalism," as this type of newspaper reporting was called, went to new extremes as two New York newspapers—Joseph Pulitzer's New York *World* and William Randolph Hearst's New York *Journal*—printed exaggerated and false accounts of Spanish atrocities in Cuba. Believing what they read daily in their newspapers, many Americans urged Congress and the president to intervene in Cuba to put a stop to the atrocities and suffering.

De Lôme letter (1898). One story that caused a storm of outrage was a Spanish diplomat's letter that was leaked to the press and printed on the front page of Hearst's New York *Journal*. Written by the Spanish minister to the United States, Dupuy de Lôme, the letter was highly critical of President McKinley. Many considered it an official Spanish insult against the U.S. national honor.

Sinking of the *Maine*. Less than one week after the de Lôme letter made headlines, a far more shocking event occurred. On February 15, 1898, the U.S. battleship *Maine* was at anchor in the harbor of Havana, Cuba, when it suddenly exploded, killing 260 Americans on board. The yellow press accused Spain of deliberately blowing up the ship, even though experts later concluded that the explosion was probably an accident.

McKinley's war message. Following the sinking of the *Maine,* President McKinley issued an ultimatum to Spain demanding that it agree to a ceasefire in Cuba. Spain agreed to this demand, but U.S. newspapers and a majority in Congress kept clamoring for war. McKinley yielded to the public pressure in April by sending a war message to Congress. He offered four reasons for the United States to intervene in the Cuban revolution on behalf of the rebels:

1. "Put an end to the barbarities, bloodshed, starvation, and horrible miseries" in Cuba

2. Protect the lives and property of U.S. citizens living in Cuba

3. End "the very serious injury to the commerce, trade, and business of our people"

4. End "the constant menace to our peace" arising from the disorders in Cuba

Teller Amendment. Responding to the president's message, Congress passed a joint resolution on April 20 authorizing war. Part of the resolution, the Teller Amendment, declared that the United States had no intention of taking political control of Cuba and that, once peace was restored to the island, the Cuban people would control their own government.

Fighting the War

The first shots of the Spanish-American War were fired in Manila Bay in the Philippines, thousands of miles from Cuba. The last shots were fired only a few months later in August. So swift was the U.S. victory that Secretary of State John Hay called it "a splendid little war."

The Philippines. Theodore Roosevelt, McKinley's assistant secretary of the navy, was an expansionist who was eager to show off the power of his country's new, all-steel navy. Anticipating war and recognizing the strategic value of Spain's territories in the Pacific, Roosevelt had ordered a fleet commanded by Commodore George Dewey to the Philippines. This large group of islands had been under Spanish control ever since the 1500s.

On May 1, shortly after war was declared, Commodore Dewey's fleet opened fire on Spanish ships in Manila Bay. The Spanish fleet was soon pounded into submission by U.S. naval guns. The fight on land took longer. Allied with Filipino rebels, U.S. troops captured the city of Manila on August 13.

Invasion of Cuba. More troublesome than the Philippines was the U.S. effort in Cuba. An ill-prepared, largely volunteer force landed in Cuba by the end of June. Here the most lethal enemy proved to be not Spanish bullets but tropical diseases. More than 5,000 American soldiers died of malaria, typhoid, and dysentery, while less than 500 died in battle.

Attacks by both American and Cuban forces succeeded in defeating the much larger but poorly led Spanish army. Next to Dewey's victory in Manila Bay, the most celebrated event of the war was a cavalry charge up San Juan Hill in Cuba by the Rough Riders, a regiment of volunteers led by Theodore Roosevelt, who had resigned his Navy post to take part in the war. Roosevelt's volunteers were aided in victory by veteran regiments of African Americans. Less heroic but more important than the taking of San Juan Hill was the success of the U.S. Navy in destroying the Spanish fleet at Santiago Bay on July 3.

Without a navy, Spain realized that it could not continue fighting, and in early August asked for U.S. terms of peace.

Annexation of Hawaii

For decades before the war, the Pacific islands of Hawaii had been settled by American missionaries and entrepreneurs. U.S. expansionists had long coveted the islands and, in 1893, American settlers had aided in the overthrow of the Hawaiian monarch, Queen Liliuokalani. President Cleveland, however, had opposed Republican efforts to annex Hawaii. Then the outbreak of war and fight for the Philippines gave Congress and President McKinley the pretext to complete annexation in July 1898. The Hawaiian islands became a territory of the United States in 1900. Hawaii became the fiftieth state in the Union in August 1959.

Controversy Over the Treaty of Peace

Far more controversial than the war itself were the terms of the treaty of peace signed in Paris on December 10, 1898. It provided for (1) recognition of Cuban independence, (2) U.S. acquisition of two Spanish islands—Puerto Rico in the Caribbean and Guam in the Pacific, and (3) U.S. acquisition of the Philippines in return for payment to Spain of $20 million. Since the avowed purpose of the U.S. war effort was to liberate Cuba, Americans accepted this provision of the treaty. They were not prepared, however, for the idea of taking over a large Pacific island nation, the Philippines.

The Philippine question. Controversy over the Philippine question took many months longer to resolve than the brief war with Spain. Opinion both in Congress and the public at large became sharply divided between imperialists who favored annexing the Philippines and anti-imperialists who opposed it. In the Senate, where a two-thirds vote was required to ratify the Treaty of Paris, anti-imperialists were determined to defeat the treaty because of its provision for taking over the Philippines. They argued that, for the first time, the United States would be taking possession of a heavily populated area whose people were of a different race and culture. Such action, they thought, violated the principles of the Declaration of Independence by depriving Filipinos of the right to "life, liberty, and the pursuit of happiness," and also would entangle the United States in the political conflicts of Asia.

On February 6, 1899, the imperialists prevailed and the Treaty of Paris (and Philippine annexation) was ratified by an extremely close vote of 57 to 27. The anti-imperialists fell just two votes short of defeating the treaty.

The people of the Philippines were outraged that their hopes for national independence from Spain were now being denied by the United States. Filipino nationalist leader Emilio Aguinaldo had fought alongside U.S. troops during the Spanish-American War. Now he led bands of guerrilla fighters in a war against U.S. control. It took U.S. troops three years and cost thousands of lives on both sides before the insurrection finally ended in 1902.

Other Results of the War

Imperialism remained a major issue in the United States even after ratification of the Treaty of Paris. An Anti-Imperialist League, led by William Jennings Bryan, rallied opposition to further acts of expansion in the Pacific.

Insular Cases. One question concerned the constitutional rights of the Philippine people: Did the Constitution follow the flag? In other words, did the provisions of the U.S. Constitution apply to whatever territories fell under U.S. control, including the Philippines and Puerto Rico? Bryan and other anti-imperialists argued in the affirmative, while leading imperialists argued in the negative. The issue was resolved in favor of the imperialists in a series of Supreme Court cases (1901–1903) known as the insular (island) cases. The Court ruled that constitutional rights were *not* automatically extended to territorial possessions and that the power to decide whether or not to grant such rights belonged to Congress.

Cuba and the Platt Amendment (1901). Previously, the Teller Amendment to the war resolution of 1898 had more or less guaranteed U.S. respect for Cuba's sovereignty as an independent nation. Nevertheless, U.S. troops remained in Cuba from 1898 until 1901. In the latter year, Congress made the withdrawal of troops conditional upon Cuba's acceptance of certain terms. These terms were included in an amendment to an army appropriations bill—the Platt Amendment of 1901. Bitterly resented by Cuban nationalists, the Platt Amendment required Cuba to agree

1. never to sign a treaty with a foreign power that impaired its independence

2. never to build up an excessive public debt

3. to permit the United States to intervene in Cuba's affairs to preserve its independence and maintain law and order

4. to allow the U.S. to maintain naval bases in Cuba, including one at Guantanamo Bay

A Cuban convention reluctantly accepted these terms, adding them to its country's new constitution. In effect, the Platt Amendment made Cuba a U.S. protectorate; in other words, its foreign policy would be, for many years, subject to U.S. oversight and control.

Election of 1900. The Republicans renominated President McKinley, along with war hero and New York Governor Theodore Roosevelt for vice president. The Democrats, as they had in 1896, nominated William Jennings Bryan, who again argued for free silver. With most Americans accepting the recently enacted gold standard, Bryan vigorously attacked the growth of American imperialism. While many Americans questioned imperialism, they saw the new territory, including the Philippines, acquired during the war as an accomplished fact. The deciding issue was the growing national economic prosperity, which convinced the majority to give McKinley a larger margin of victory than in 1896.

Recognition of U.S. power. One positive consequence of the Spanish-American War was its effect on the way both Americans and Europeans thought about U.S. power. The decisive U.S. victory in the war filled Americans with national pride. Southerners shared in this pride and became more attached to the Union after their bitter experience in the 1860s. At the same time, France, Great Britain, and other European nations came to recognize that the United States was a first-class power with a strong navy and a new willingness to take an active role in international affairs.

Open Door Policy in China

Europeans were further impressed by U.S. involvement in global politics as a result of John Hay's policies toward China. As McKinley's secretary of state, Hay was alarmed that the Chinese empire, weakened by political corruption and failure to modernize, was falling under the control of various outside powers. In the 1890s, Russia, Japan, Great Britain, France, and Germany had all established *spheres of influence* in China, meaning that they could dominate trade and investment within their sphere (a particular port or region of China) and shut out competitors. To prevent the United States from losing access to the lucrative China trade, Hay dispatched a diplomatic note in 1899 to nations holding spheres of influence. He asked them to accept the concept of an Open Door, by which all nations would have equal trading privileges in China. The replies to Hay's note were evasive, but because no nation rejected the concept, Hay declared that all had accepted the Open Door policy. The press hailed Hay's initiative as a diplomatic triumph.

Boxer Rebellion (1900). As the 19th century ended, nationalism and *xenophobia* (hatred and fear of foreigners) were on the rise in China. In 1900, a secret society of Chinese nationalists—the Society of Harmonious Fists, or Boxers—attacked foreign settlements and murdered dozens of Christian missionaries. To protect American lives and property, U.S. troops participated in an international force that marched into Peking (Beijing) and quickly succeeded in crushing the rebellion of the Boxers. China was forced to pay a huge sum in indemnities, which further weakened the imperial regime.

Hay's second round of notes. Hay feared that the expeditionary force in China might attempt to occupy the country and destroy its independence. In 1900, therefore, he wrote a second note to the imperialistic powers stating U.S. commitment to (1) preserve China's territorial integrity as well as (2) safeguard "equal and impartial trade with all parts of the Chinese empire." Hay's first and second notes set U.S. policy on China not only for the administrations of McKinley and Theodore Roosevelt but also for future presidents. In the 1930s, this Open Door policy for China would strongly influence U.S. relations with Japan.

Hay's notes in themselves did not deter other nations from exploiting the situation in China. For the moment, European powers were kept from grabbing larger pieces of China by the political rivalries among themselves.

Theodore Roosevelt's Big-Stick Policy

In 1901, only a few months after being inaugurated president for a second time, McKinley was fatally shot by an anarchist (person who opposed all government). Succeeding him in office was the Republican vice president— the young expansionist and hero of the Spanish-American War, Theodore Roosevelt. Describing his foreign policy, the new president had once said that it was his motto to "speak softly and carry a big stick." The press therefore applied the label "big stick" to Roosevelt's aggressive foreign policy. By acting boldly and decisively in a number of situations, Roosevelt attempted to build the reputation of the U.S. as a world power. Imperialists applauded his every move, but critics of the big-stick policy disliked breaking from the tradition of noninvolvement in global politics.

The Panama Canal

As a result of the Spanish-American War, the new American empire stretched from Puerto Rico in the Caribbean to the Philippines in the Pacific. As a strategic necessity for holding on to these far-flung islands, the United States needed a canal through Central America to connect the Atlantic and Pacific oceans.

Revolution in Panama. Roosevelt was eager to begin the construction of a canal through the narrow but rugged terrain of the isthmus of Panama. He was frustrated, however, by the fact that Colombia controlled this isthmus and refused to agree to U.S. terms for digging the canal through its territory. Losing patience with Colombia, Roosevelt supported a revolt in Panama in 1903. With U.S. backing, the rebellion succeeded immediately and almost without bloodshed. The first act of the new government of independent Panama was to sign a treaty (the Hay-Bunau-Varilla Treaty of 1903) granting the United States long-term control of a canal zone.

Hay-Pauncefote Treaty (1901). One other obstacle to a canal built and operated by the United States had been removed earlier by the signing in 1901 of a treaty with Great Britain. The British had agreed to abrogate (cancel) an earlier treaty of 1850 in which any canal in Central America was to be under joint British-U.S. control. Now, as a result of the Hay-Pauncefote Treaty, the United States could begin to dig the canal without British involvement.

Building the canal. Started in 1904, the Panama Canal was completed in 1914. Hundreds of laborers lost their lives in the effort. The work was completed thanks in great measure to the skills of two Army colonels—George Goethals, the chief engineer of the canal, and Dr. William Gorgas, whose efforts eliminated the mosquitoes that spread deadly yellow fever.

Most Americans approved of Roosevelt's determination to build the canal. Many, however, were unhappy with the high-handed tactics employed to secure the Canal Zone. Latin Americans were especially resentful. To compensate, Congress finally voted in 1921 to pay Colombia an indemnity of $25 million for its loss of Panama.

The Roosevelt Corollary to the Monroe Doctrine

Another application of Roosevelt's big-stick diplomacy involved Latin American nations that were in deep financial trouble and could not pay their debts to European creditors. In 1902, for example, the British dispatched warships to Venezuela to force that country to pay its debts. In 1904, it appeared that European powers stood ready to intervene in Santo Domingo (the Dominican Republic) for the same reason. Rather than let Europeans intervene in Latin America—a blatant violation of the Monroe Doctrine—Roosevelt declared in December 1904 that the United States would intervene instead, whenever necessary. This policy became known as the Roosevelt Corollary to the Monroe Doctrine. It meant that the United States would send gunboats to a Latin American country that was delinquent in paying its debts. U.S. sailors and marines would then occupy the country's major ports to manage the collection of customs taxes until European debts were satisfied.

Over the next 20 years, U.S. presidents used the Roosevelt Corollary to justify sending U.S. forces into Haiti, Honduras, the Dominican Republic, and Nicaragua. The long-term result of such interventions was poor U.S. relations with the entire region of Latin America.

East Asia

As the 20th century began, Japan and the United States were both relatively new imperialist powers in East Asia. Their relationship during Theodore Roosevelt's presidency, though at first friendly, grew increasingly competitive.

Russo-Japanese War. Imperialist rivalry between Russia and Japan led to a war between these nations (1904–1905), which Japan was winning. To end the war, Theodore Roosevelt arranged for a diplomatic conference between representatives of the two foes at Portsmouth, New Hampshire, in 1905. Although both Japan and Russia agreed to the Treaty of Portsmouth, Japanese nationalists blamed the United States for not giving their country all that they wanted from Russia.

"Gentlemen's Agreement." A major cause of friction between Japan and the United States concerned the laws of California, which discriminated against Japanese Americans. San Francisco's practice of requiring Japanese American children to attend segregated schools was considered a national insult in Japan. In 1908, President Roosevelt arranged a compromise by means of an informal understanding, or "gentlemen's agreement." The Japanese government secretly agreed to restrict the emigration of Japanese workers to the United States in return for Roosevelt persuading California to repeal its discriminatory laws.

Great White Fleet. To demonstrate U.S. naval power to Japan and other nations, Roosevelt sent a fleet of battleships on an around-the-world cruise (1907–1909). The great white ships made an impressive sight, and the Japanese government warmly welcomed their arrival in Tokyo Bay.

Root-Takahira Agreement (1908). An important executive agreement was concluded between the United States and Japan in 1908. Secretary of State Elihu Root and Japanese Ambassador Takahira exchanged notes pledging the following: (1) mutual respect for each nation's Pacific possessions and (2) support for the Open Door policy in China.

Peace Efforts

The purpose of the great white fleet and all other applications of Roosevelt's big-stick policy was to maintain the peace between rival nations. The president consistently promoted peaceful solutions to international disputes. For his work in settling the Russo-Japanese War, Roosevelt was awarded the Nobel Peace Prize in 1906. In the same year, he helped arrange and direct the Algeciras Conference in Spain, which succeeded in settling a conflict between France and Germany over claims to Morocco. The president also directed U.S. participation at the Second International Peace Conference at the Hague in 1907, which discussed rules for limiting warfare.

William Howard Taft and Dollar Diplomacy

Roosevelt's successor, William Howard Taft (1909–1913), did not carry a big stick. He adopted a foreign policy that was mildly expansionist but depended more on investors' dollars than on the navy's battleships. His policy of trying to promote U.S. trade by supporting American enterprises abroad was given the name *dollar diplomacy.*

Dollar Diplomacy in East Asia and Latin America

Taft believed that private American financial investment in China and the nations of Central America would lead to greater stability there, while at the same time promoting U.S. business interests. His policy, however, was thwarted by one major obstacle: growing anti-imperialism both in the United States and overseas.

Railroads in China. Taft first tested his policy in China. Wanting U.S. bankers to be included in a British, French, and German plan to invest in railroads in China, Taft succeeded in securing American participation in an agreement signed in 1911. In the northern province of Manchuria, however, the United States was excluded from an agreement between Russia and Japan to build railroads there. In direct defiance of the U.S. Open Door policy, Russia and Japan agreed to treat Manchuria as a jointly held sphere of influence.

Intervention in Nicaragua. To protect American investments, the United States intervened in Nicaragua's financial affairs in 1911, and sent in marines when a civil war broke out in 1912. The marines remained, except for a short period, until 1933.

The Lodge Corollary

Henry Cabot Lodge, a Republican senator from Massachusetts, was responsible for another action that alienated both Latin America and Japan. A group of Japanese investors wanted to buy a large part of Mexico's Baja Peninsula, extending south of California. Fearing that Japan's government might be secretly scheming to acquire the land, Lodge introduced and the Senate in 1912 passed a resolution known as the Lodge Corollary to the Monroe Doctrine. The resolution stated that non-European powers (such as Japan) would be excluded from owning territory in the Western Hemisphere. President Taft opposed the corollary, which also offended Japan and angered Latin American countries.

Woodrow Wilson and Moral Diplomacy

In his campaign for president in 1912, the Democratic candidate Woodrow Wilson called for a *New Freedom* in government and promised a moral approach to foreign affairs. Wilson said he opposed imperialism and the big-stick and dollar-diplomacy policies of his Republican predecessors.

Moral Diplomacy

In his first term as president (1913–1917), Wilson had limited success applying a high moral standard to foreign relations. He and Secretary of State William Jennings Bryan hoped to demonstrate that the United States respected other nations' rights and would support the spread of democracy.

Righting past wrongs. Hoping to demonstrate that his presidency was opposed to self-interested imperialism, Wilson took steps to correct what he viewed as wrongful policies of the past.

1. The Philippines. Wilson won passage of the Jones Act of 1916, which (1) granted full territorial status to that country, (2) guaranteed a bill of rights and universal male suffrage to Filipino citizens, and (3) promised Philippine independence as soon as a stable government was established.

2. Puerto Rico. An act of Congress in 1917 granted U.S. citizenship to all the inhabitants and also provided for limited self-government.

3. The Panama Canal. Wilson persuaded Congress in 1914 to repeal an act that had granted U.S. ships an exemption from paying the standard canal tolls charged other nations. Wilson's policy on Panama Canal tolls angered American nationalists like Roosevelt and Lodge but pleased the British, who had strongly objected to the U.S. exemption.

Conciliation treaties. Wilson's commitment to the ideals of democracy and peace was fully shared by his famous secretary of state, William Jennings Bryan. Bryan's pet project was to negotiate treaties in which nations pledged to (1) submit disputes to international commissions and (2) observe a one-year cooling-off period before taking military action. Bryan arranged with Wilson's approval, 30 such conciliation treaties.

Military Intervention in Latin America

Wilson's commitment to democracy and anticolonialism had a blind spot with respect to the countries of Central America and the Caribbean. He went far beyond both Roosevelt and Taft in his use of U.S. marines to straighten out financial and political troubles in the region. Throughout his presidency, he kept marines in Nicaragua and ordered U.S. troops into Haiti in 1915 and the Dominican Republic in 1916. He argued that such intervention was necessary to maintain stability in the region and protect the Panama Canal.

Conflict in Mexico

Wilson's moral approach to foreign affairs was severely tested by a revolution and civil war in Mexico. Wanting democracy to triumph there, he refused to recognize the military dictatorship of General Victoriano Huerta, who had seized power in Mexico in 1913 by arranging to assassinate the democratically elected president.

Tampico incident. To aid a revolutionary faction that was fighting Huerta, Wilson asked for an arms embargo against the Mexican government and sent a fleet to blockade the port of Vera Cruz. In 1914, several American seamen went ashore at Tampico where they were arrested by Mexican authorities and soon released. Huerta refused to apologize, as demanded by a U.S. naval officer, and Wilson in retaliation ordered the U.S. Navy to occupy Vera Cruz. War between Mexico and the United States seemed imminent. It was averted, however, when South America's ABC powers—Argentina, Brazil, and Chile—offered to mediate the dispute. This was the first dispute in the Americas to be settled through joint mediation.

Pancho Villa and the U.S. expeditionary force. Huerta fell from power in late 1914 and was replaced by a more democratic regime led by Venustiano Carranza. Almost immediately, the new government was challenged by a band of revolutionaries loyal to Pancho Villa. Hoping to destabilize his opponent's government, Villa led raids across the U.S.–Mexican border and murdered a

U.S. TERRITORIES AND PROTECTORATES, 1917

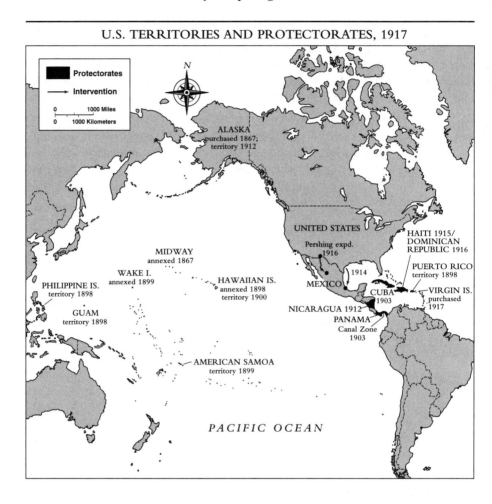

number of people in Texas and New Mexico. In March 1916, President Wilson ordered General John J. Pershing to pursue Villa into Mexico. This expeditionary force, as it was called, was in northern Mexico for months without being able to capture Villa. President Carranza eventually protested the American presence in Mexico. In January 1917, the growing possibility of U.S. entry into World War I caused Wilson to withdraw Pershing's troops.

HISTORICAL PERSPECTIVES: WAS IMPERIALISM DRIVEN ONLY BY ECONOMIC MOTIVES?

Much of the early writing on U.S. emergence as a world power at the start of the 20th century stressed economic motives as the principal reason for the imperialistic direction of U.S. policy.

Whether explaining the Spanish-American War or later actions, historians such as William Appelman Williams and Walter La Feber focused on U.S. desires for overseas markets, raw materials, and investments.

This economic explanation of U.S. imperialism has been questioned on two levels. First, with respect to the Spanish-American War, historians note that business interests were at first opposed to U.S. intervention in Cuba because they feared that it would disrupt commerce. They later would support the war as a stabilizing influence, but at what point did bankers and large manufacturers change their view? Some historians argue that most businesspeople supported the war only *after* it had actually started.

Second, critics of the economic interpretation of imperialism stress the importance of noneconomic motives. They point out that there were both humanitarian and nationalistic reasons for the decision to send U.S. troops to Cuba in 1898. Influenced by shocking stories in the yellow press, American public opinion had no economic reasons for demanding that the United States go to war. The prowar sentiment seemed to express genuine humanitarian impulses—and also nationalistic outrage over the sinking of the *Maine*. Other historians, studying the motives of nationalist leaders like Theodore Roosevelt and Henry Cabot Lodge, have concluded that their chief interest was in establishing U.S. power on the world stage. In securing U.S. control of the Philippines, Roosevelt's role was crucial, and he was motivated by strategic considerations (establishing a naval base in the Pacific), not by economics. On the other hand, those stressing economic motives argue that, even if Roosevelt had not ordered Dewey to Manila Bay, the Philippines would sooner or later have become a target of U.S. imperialist ambitions.

Other historians believe that a new generation of foreign-policy makers had come to power around 1900. These talented leaders—chiefly Theodore Roosevelt and Woodrow Wilson—were critical of the mediocre leadership in Washington in the post-Civil War years and were eager to take bold new directions. Historians taking this view portray Theodore Roosevelt as a realist who saw diplomacy as a question of balance-of-power politics, as opposed to the idealist, Woodrow Wilson, who approached foreign policy as a matter of morals and legality.

The historian Richard Hofstadter interpreted the Spanish-American War from the perspective of social psychology. He argued that the popular movement for war resulted from a psychic crisis in the nation. In Hofstadter's view, the American people were expressing aggression built up by economic depressions, the closing of the frontier, and the rise of big business on the one hand and labor radicalism on the other.

Economic motives are always important and cannot be discounted in a balanced interpretation of foreign policy. Nevertheless, we now know that there were other, perhaps equally important, factors in explaining the Spanish-American War and later U.S. interventions in Latin America and Asia.

KEY NAMES, EVENTS, AND TERMS

William Seward

Napoleon III

Mexico

Alaska purchase (1867)

"new imperialism"

international Darwinism

Josiah Strong, *Our Country: Its Possible Future and Current Crisis*

Alfred Thayer Mahan, *The Influence of Sea Power Upon History*

Pan-American Conference (1889)

James Blaine

Richard Olney

Venezuela boundary dispute

Cuba

jingoism

Valeriano Weyler

yellow journalism

Spanish-American War

De Lôme Letter

Maine

Teller Amendment

Philippines

George Dewey

Theodore Roosevelt

Rough Riders

Hawaii; Liliuokalani

Puerto Rico; Guam

Philippine annexation

Emilio Aguinaldo

Anti-Imperialist League

insular cases

Platt Amendment (1901)

John Hay

spheres of influence

Open Door policy

xenophobia

Boxer Rebellion

big-stick policy

Hay-Pauncefote Treaty (1901)

Panama Canal

George Goethals

William Gorgas

Roosevelt Corollary

Santo Domingo

Russo-Japanese War

Treaty of Portsmouth (1905)

gentlemen's agreement

great white fleet

Root-Takahira Agreement (1908)

Algeciras Conference (1906)

William Howard Taft

dollar diplomacy

Nicaragua

Henry Cabot Lodge

Lodge Corollary

Woodrow Wilson

New Freedom

moral diplomacy

Jones Act (1916)

Mexican civil war

Victoriano Huerta

Tampico incident

ABC (Argentina, Brazil, Chile) powers

Pancho Villa

Venustiano Carranza

expeditionary force

John J. Pershing

MULTIPLE-CHOICE QUESTIONS

1. By the end of the 19th century, jingoism in the United States was encouraged by all of the following EXCEPT
   (A) European imperialism
   (B) international Darwinism
   (C) yellow journalism
   (D) naval views of Alfred Thayer Mahan
   (E) new immigrants

2. Which of the following statements best defines the Open Door policy?
   (A) The United States would encourage greater immigration from Europe and Asia.
   (B) The United States would seek spheres of influence in China.
   (C) Japan would not be permitted to trade in China.
   (D) All nations should have equal trading rights in China.
   (E) All nations should have equal trading rights in all parts of the world.

3. Which of the following DOES NOT correctly describe how a territory was added to the United States?
   (A) Hawaii annexed by Congress
   (B) Alaska purchased from Russia
   (C) the Philippines annexed by treaty
   (D) Cuba annexed by Congress
   (E) Florida purchased from Spain

4. All of the following concerned U.S.-Japanese relations EXCEPT the
   (A) Teller Amendment

   (B) Gentlemen's Agreement
   (C) Treaty of Portsmouth
   (D) Lodge Corollary
   (E) great white fleet

5. Which of the following was an IMMEDIATE cause of the Spanish-American War?
   (A) Cuban nationalism
   (B) U.S. expansionism
   (C) yellow journalism
   (D) the sinking of the *Maine*
   (E) business need for raw materials and new markets

6. Which of the following best explains the influence of yellow journalism on U.S. foreign policy in the 1890s?
   (A) Sensational news stories stirred the anger of the American public.
   (B) Newspapers failed to report news about Congress.
   (C) Most editorials favored China and criticized Japan.
   (D) Political cartoons ridiculed "mugwump" politics.
   (E) Publishers of New York dailies suppressed news that favored Cuban revolutionaries.

7. The Roosevelt Corollary to the Monroe Doctrine called for
   (A) prohibiting foreign nations from purchasing land in the Western Hemisphere.
   (B) investing in the development of Latin America
   (C) intervening in Latin American nations that could not pay their debts to European creditors
   (D) building a U.S. naval base in Cuba

(E) pledging never to interfere in another nation's foreign affairs

8. Which statement accurately summarizes Theodore Roosevelt's policy on the Panama Canal?

(A) Roosevelt waited for Colombia to agree to a fair price for the Canal Zone.

(B) Roosevelt gave military support to Panama's revolt against Colombia.

(C) Panama's government persuaded Roosevelt to give U.S. assistance for building a canal.

(D) Roosevelt signed a treaty in which Colombia agreed to create Panama as a separate nation.

(E) Roosevelt was able to develop strong Latin American support for his canal project.

9. Woodrow Wilson's foreign policy differed from that of Theodore Roosevelt and William Howard Taft by its emphasis on

(A) U.S. investment in Latin America

(B) the application of moral principles to foreign affairs

(C) sending troops to intervene in a neighboring country's politics

(D) an open door policy

(E) building a strong navy

10. In 1917, countries shaded on the above map were

(A) subject to U.S. military intervention

(B) participants in the Spanish American War

(C) the only nations that attended the Pan-American Conference

(D) territories annexed by the United States after the Spanish-American War

(E) recipients of economic aid under dollar diplomacy

ESSAY QUESTIONS

1. Analyze the responses to TWO of the following to Secretary of State John Hay's view that the Spanish-American War was "a splendid little war":

   William Jennings Bryan

   Theodore Roosevelt

   Alfred Thayer Mahan

   Emilio Aguinaldo

2. Discuss whether or not U.S. foreign policy from 1890–1914 was principally guided by economic motives.

3. Compare and contrast the foreign policies of Theodore Roosevelt and Woodrow Wilson toward Latin America.

4. Assess the importance of TWO of the following in the U.S. decision to declare war against Spain in 1898.

   yellow journalism

   sinking of the *Maine*

   U.S. business interests

   Cuban revolution

5. In what ways did the United States' relationship with Japan become more competitive after 1900?

DOCUMENTS AND READINGS

Following are primary source documents from the period 1885 to 1900. They include passages from: a Protestant minister's book arguing for the national destiny of the United States (A); a U.S. senator's argument for expansionism (B); an anti-imperialist protest against U.S. policy in the Philippines (C); and President McKinley's justification of that policy (D).

DOCUMENT A.   THE ANGLO-SAXON PEOPLE

The Reverend Josiah Strong's best-selling book *Our Country* was translated into several languages and sold 170,000 copies. This excerpt from the book shows how nationalism and international Darwinism were closely associated.

> Mr. [Charles] Darwin is not only disposed to see, in the superior vigor of our people, an illustration of his favorite theory of natural selection, but even intimates that the world's history thus far has been simply preparatory for our future, and tributary to it. He says: "There is apparently much truth in the belief that the wonderful progress of the United States, as well as the character of the people, are the results of natural selection; for the more energetic, restless and courageous men from all parts of Europe have emigrated during the last ten or twelve generations to that great country, and have there succeeded best. . . ."

There is abundant reason to believe that the Anglo-Saxon race is to be, is, indeed, already becoming, more effective here than in the mother country. . . .

It may be easily shown, and is of no small significance, that the two great ideas of which the Anglo-Saxon is the exponent are having a fuller development in the United States than in Great Britain. There the union of Church and State tends strongly to paralyze some of the members of the body of Christ. Here there is no such influence to destroy spiritual life and power. Here, also, has been evolved the form of government consistent with the largest possible civil liberty. Furthermore, it is significant that the marked characteristics of this race are being here emphasized most. Among the most striking features of the Anglo-Saxon is his money-making power—a power of increasing importance in the widening commerce of the world's future. We have seen . . . that, although England is by far the richest nation of Europe, we have already outstripped her in the race after wealth, and we have only begun the development of our vast resources.

Josiah Strong,
Our Country, 1885

DOCUMENT B.   *"COMMERCE FOLLOWS THE FLAG"*

After teaching history at Harvard, Henry Cabot Lodge entered Massachusetts politics in 1880, was elected to the U.S. House of Representatives in 1887, and then to the Senate in 1893, where he served until his death in 1924. In his first term, Senator Lodge quickly established a reputation as a champion of an expansionist foreign policy. The following excerpt is taken from an article written by Lodge in 1895.

Washington withdrew us from the affairs of Europe, but at the same time he pointed out that our true line of advance was to the West. He never for an instant thought that we were to remain stationary and cease to move forward. He saw, with prophetic vision, as did no other man of his time, the true course for the American people. He could not himself enter into the promised land, but he showed it to his people, stretching from the Blue Ridge to the Pacific Ocean. We have followed the teachings of Washington. We have taken the great valley of the Mississippi and pressed on beyond the Sierras. We have a record of conquest, colonization, and territorial expansion unequalled by any people in the nineteenth century. . . .

There is a very definite policy for American statesmen to pursue in this respect if they would prove themselves worthy inheritors of the principles of Washington and [John Quincy] Adams. We desire no extension to the south, for neither the population nor the lands of Central or South America would be desirable additions to the United States. But from the Rio Grande to the Arctic Ocean there should be but one flag and one country. Neither race nor climate forbids this extension, and every consideration of national growth and national welfare demands it. In the interests of our commerce and of our fullest development we should build the Nicaragua canal,* and for the protection of that canal and for the sake of our commercial supremacy in the Pacific we should control the Hawaiian Islands and maintain our influence in Samoa. England has studded the West Indies with strong places which are a standing menace to our Atlantic seaboard. We should have among those islands at least one strong naval station, and when the Nicaragua canal is built, the island of Cuba, still sparsely settled and of almost unbounded fertility, will become to us a necessity. Commerce follows the flag, and we should build up a navy strong enough to give protection to Americans in every quarter of the globe and sufficiently powerful to put our coasts beyond the possibility of successful attack.

Henry Cabot Lodge,
"Our Blundering Foreign Policy,"
March 1895

DOCUMENT C.   "SLAUGHTER OF THE FILIPINOS"

To protest U.S. occupation of the Philippines, a number of antiexpansionist groups were organized in different states. In 1899 representatives from these leagues gathered in Chicago to form a national association, the American Anti-Imperialist League. The following is from the league's platform.

We hold that the policy known as imperialism is hostile to liberty and tends toward militarism, an evil from which it has been our glory to be free. We regret that it has become necessary in the land of Washington and Lincoln to reaffirm that all men, of whatever race or color, are entitled to life, liberty, and the pursuit of happiness. We maintain that governments derive their just powers from the consent of the governed. We insist that the subjugation of any people is "criminal aggression" and open disloyalty to the distinctive principles of our government.

---

*In the 1890s, Nicaragua was generally considered a more likely route than Panama for building a canal through Central America.

We earnestly condemn the policy of the present national admin- istration in the Philippines. It seeks to extinguish the spirit of 1776 in those islands. We deplore the sacrifice of our soldiers and sailors, whose bravery deserves admiration even in an unjust war. We denounce the slaughter of the Filipinos as a needless horror. We protest against the extension of American sovereignty by Spanish methods.

We demand the immediate cessation of the war against liberty, begun by Spain and continued by us. We urge that Congress be promptly convened to announce to the Filipinos our purpose to concede to them the independence for which they have so long fought and which of right is theirs.

The United States have always protested against the doctrine of international law which permits the subjugation of the weak by the strong. A self-governing state cannot accept sovereignty over an unwilling people. The United States cannot act upon the ancient heresy that might makes right.

Platform of the
American Anti-Imperialist League,
October 17, 1899

DOCUMENT D.   *A PRESIDENT'S DECISION*

Speaking to a church group, President William McKinley gave the follow- ing account of his decision to keep the Philippines under U.S. control.

I walked the floor of the White House night after night until midnight; and I am not ashamed to tell you, gentlemen, that I went down on my knees and prayed Almighty God for light and guidance more than one night. And one night late it came to me this way— I don't know how it was, but it came: (1) that we could not give them back to Spain—that would be cowardly and dishonorable; (2) that we could not turn them over to France or Germany—our commercial rivals in the Orient—that would be bad business and discreditable; (3) that we could not leave them to themselves—they were unfit for self-government—and they would soon have anarchy and misrule there worse than Spain's was; and (4) that there was nothing left for us to do but to take them all, and to educate the Filipinos, and uplift and civilize and Christianize them, and by God's grace do the very best we could by them. . . .

William McKinley,
speech to a Methodist Church group,
November 1899

ANALYZING THE DOCUMENTS

1. How would you characterize Josiah Strong's views in Document A? Are they nationalist, racist, or both? Explain.

2. How many of the expansionist goals listed by Henry Cabot Lodge in Document B were realized by 1905?

3. Do you agree with President McKinley, in Document D, that he had only four alternatives in dealing with the Philippines? Can you think of some other options?

4. "For a complete explanation of U.S. actions in Cuba and the Philippines in the 1890s, one would have to give equal weight to four motives: racism, nationalism, commercialism, and humanitarianism."

Using the documents as evidence, discuss whether you agree or disagree with the above statement.

THE PROGRESSIVE ERA, 1901–1918

I am, therefore, a Progressive because we have not kept up with our own changes of conditions, either in the economic field or in the political field. We have not kept up as well as other nations have. We have not adjusted our practices to the facts of the case. . . .

Woodrow Wilson, campaign speech, 1912

Industrialization, immigration, and urban expansion were the major elements in the dramatic growth that the United States experienced during the last quarter of the 19th century. Accompanying this growth were both old and new concerns and problems about the lives of many Americans. (Growth and associated problems are covered in Chapters 17, 18, and 19.) By the turn of the century, a reform movement had developed that included a wide range of groups and individuals with a common desire to improve life in the industrial age. Their ideas and work became known as *progressivism,* because they wanted to build on the existing society, making moderate political changes and social improvements through government action. Most Progressives were not revolutionaries but shared the goals of limiting the power of big business, improving democracy for the people, and strengthening social justice. This chapter will examine the origins, efforts, and accomplishments of the Progressive era. It should be recognized that while the Progressives did not cure all of America's problems, they improved the quality of life, provided a larger role for the people in their democracy, and established a precedent for a more active role for the federal government.

Origins of Progressivism

Although the Progressive movement had its origins in the state reforms of the early 1890s, it acquired national momentum only with the dawn of a new century and the unexpected swearing into office of a young president, Theodore Roosevelt, in 1901. So enthusiastic did middle-class Americans become about the need to adjust to changing times that their reformist impulse gave a name to an era: the Progressive era. It lasted through the Republican

424

presidencies of Roosevelt (1901–1909) and William Howard Taft (1909–1913), and the first term of the Democrat, Woodrow Wilson (1913–1917). U.S. entry into World War I in 1917 diverted public attention away from domestic issues and brought the era to an end—but not before major regulatory laws had been enacted by Congress and various state legislatures.

Attitudes and Motives

Entering a new century, most Americans were well aware of how their country was rapidly changing. A once relatively homogeneous, rural society of independent farmers was becoming an industrialized nation of mixed ethnicity centered in the growing cities. For decades, middle-class Americans had been alarmed by the rising power of big business, the increasing gap between rich and poor, the violent conflict between labor and capital, and the dominance of corrupt political machines in the cities. Most disturbing to minorities were the racist, Jim Crow laws in the South that relegated African Americans to the status of second-class citizens. Crusaders for women's suffrage added their voices to the call for political reform and greater democracy.

The groups participating in the Progressive movement were extremely diverse. There were Protestant church leaders who championed one set of reforms, African Americans proposing other reforms, union leaders seeking public support for their goals, and feminists lobbying their state legislatures for votes for women. Loosely linking their reform efforts under a single label, Progressive, was a belief that changes in society were badly needed and that government was the proper agency for correcting social and economic ills.

Who were the Progressives? Unlike the Populists of the 1890s, whose strength came from rural America, citizens active in the Progressive movement were chiefly middle-class residents of U.S. cities. The urban middle class had steadily grown in the final decades of the 19th century. In addition to doctors, lawyers, ministers, and storekeepers (the heart of the middle class in an earlier era), there were now thousands of white-collar office workers and middle managers employed in banks, manufacturing firms, and other businesses. Members of this business and professional middle class took their civic responsibilities seriously. They were disturbed about what might happen to American democracy from such conditions as unrest among the poor, excesses of the rich, corruption in government, and an apparent decline in morality.

A missionary spirit inspired certain aspects of middle-class progressivism. Protestant churches preached against vice and taught a code of social responsibility, which included caring for the poor and the less fortunate and insisting on honesty in public life. The Social Gospel popularized by Walter Rauschenbusch (see Chapter 18) was an important element in Protestant Christians' response to the problem of urban poverty.

Without strong leadership, the diverse forces of reform could not have overcome conservatives' resistance to change. Fortunately for the Progressives, a number of dedicated and able leaders entered politics at the turn of the century to challenge the status quo. Theodore Roosevelt and Robert La Follette in the Republican party and William Jennings Bryan and Woodrow Wilson in the Democratic party demonstrated a vigorous style of political leadership that had been sorely lacking from national politics during the Gilded Age.

What was the Progressives' philosophy? The reform impulse was hardly new. In fact, many historians see progressivism as just one more phase in a reform tradition going back to the Jeffersonians in the early 1800s, the Jacksonians in the 1830s, and the Populists in the 1890s. Without doubt, the Progressives—like American reformers before them—were committed to democratic values and shared in the belief that honest government and just laws could improve the human condition.

A revolution in thinking occurred at the same time as the Industrial Revolution. Charles Darwin, in his *Origin of Species,* presented the concept of evolution, which had an impact well beyond simply justifying the accumulation of wealth (see Chapter 17). The way people thought and reasoned was challenged, and the prevailing philosophy of romantic transcendentalism in America gave way to a balanced *pragmatism.* In the early 20th century, William James and John Dewey were two leading American advocates of this new philosophy. They defined "truth" in a way that many Progressives found appealing. James and Dewey argued that the "good" and the "true" could not be known in the abstract as fixed and changeless ideals. Rather, they said, people should take a pragmatic, or practical, approach to morals, ideals, and knowledge. They should experiment with ideas and laws and test them in action until they found something that seemed to work well for the better ordering of society.

Progressive thinkers adopted the new philosophy of pragmatism because it enabled them to challenge fixed notions that stood in the way of reform. For example, they rejected laissez-faire theory as impractical. The old standard of rugged individualism no longer seemed viable in a modern society dominated by impersonal corporations.

Scientific management. Another idea that gained widespread acceptance among Progressives came from the practical studies of Frederick W. Taylor. By using a stopwatch to time the output of factory workers, Taylor discovered ways of organizing people in the most efficient manner—the scientific management system. Many Progressives believed that government too could be made more efficient if placed in the hands of experts and scientific managers. They objected to the corruption of political bosses partly because it was antidemocratic and partly because it was an inefficient way to run things.

The Muckrakers

Before the public could be roused to action, it first had to be well informed about the "dirty" realities of party politics and the scandalous conditions in factories and slums. Newspaper and magazine publishers found that their middle-class readers loved to read about underhanded schemes in politics. Therefore, in-depth, investigative stories came to characterize much of the journalistic reporting of the era. Writers specializing in such stories were referred to as muckrakers by President Theodore Roosevelt.

Origins. One of the earliest muckrakers was Chicago reporter Henry Demarest Lloyd, who in 1881 wrote a series of articles for the *Atlantic Monthly* attacking the practices of the Standard Oil Company and the railroads. Published in book form in 1894, Lloyd's *Wealth Against Commonwealth* fully exposed the corruption and greed of the oil monopoly but failed to suggest how to control it.

Magazines. An Irish immigrant, Samuel Sidney McClure, founded *McClure's Magazine* in 1893, which became a major success by running a series of muckraking articles by Lincoln Steffens (*Tweed Days in St. Louis,* 1902) and another series by Ida Tarbell (*The History of the Standard Oil Company,* also in 1902). Combining careful research with sensationalism, these articles set a standard for the deluge of muckraking that followed. Popular 10- and 15-cent magazines such as *McClure's, Collier's,* and *Cosmopolitan* competed fiercely to outdo their rivals with shocking exposés of political and economic corruption.

Books. The most popular series of muckraking articles were usually collected and published as best-selling books. Articles on tenement life by Jacob Riis, one of the first photojournalists, were published as *How the Other Half Lives* (1890). Lincoln Steffens' *The Shame of the Cities* (1904) also caused a sensation by describing in detail the corrupt deals that characterized big-city politics from Philadelphia to Minneapolis.

Many of the muckraking books were novels. Two of Theodore Dreiser's novels, *The Financier* and *The Titan,* portrayed the avarice and ruthlessness of an industrialist. Fictional accounts such as Frank Norris' *The Octopus* (on the tyrannical power of railroad companies) and *The Pit* (grain speculation) were more effective than many journalistic accounts in stirring up public demands for government regulations.

Decline of muckraking. The popularity of muckraking books and magazine articles began to decline after 1910 for several reasons. First, writers found it more and more difficult to top the sensationalism of the last story. Second, publishers were expanding and faced economic pressures from banks and advertisers to tone down their treatment of business. Third, by 1910 corporations were becoming more aware of their public image and developing a new specialty: the field of public relations. Nevertheless, muckraking had a lasting effect on the Progressive era. It exposed inequities, educated the public about corruption in high places, and prepared the way for corrective action.

Political Reforms in Cities and States

The cornerstone of Progressive ideology was faith in democracy. Progressives believed that, given a chance, the majority of voters would elect honest officials instead of the corrupt officials handpicked by boss-dominated political machines.

Voter Participation

Progressives advocated a number of methods for increasing the participation of the average citizen in political decision-making.

Australian, or secret, ballot. Political parties could manipulate and intimidate voters by printing lists (or "tickets") of party candidates and watching voters drop them into the ballot box on election day. In 1888, Massachusetts was the first state to adopt a system successfully tried in Australia of issuing ballots printed by the state and requiring voters to mark their choices secretly within the privacy of a curtained booth. By 1910, voting in all states was done this way.

Direct primaries. In the late 19th century, it was the common practice of Republicans and Democrats to nominate candidates for state and federal offices in state conventions dominated by party bosses. In 1903, the Progressive governor of Wisconsin, Robert La Follette, introduced his state to a new system for bypassing politicians and placing the nominating process directly in the hands of the voters. This method for nominating party candidates by majority vote was known as the direct primary. By 1915, some form of the direct primary was used in every state. The system's effectiveness in overthrowing boss rule was limited, as politicians devised ways of confusing the voters and splitting the antimachine vote. Some southern states even used the primary system to exclude African Americans from voting.

Direct election of U.S. senators. Before the Progressive era, U.S. senators had been chosen not by the people but by majority vote of the state legislatures. Progressives believed this was a principal reason that the Senate had become a millionaires' club dominated by big business. Nevada in 1899 was the first state to give the voters the opportunity to elect U.S. senators directly. By 1912, a total of 30 states had adopted this Progressive reform, and in 1913, adoption of the Seventeenth Amendment required that all U.S. senators be elected by popular vote.

Less successful were the Progressives' efforts to reform the state legislatures, which largely remained under the control of political bosses and machines.

Initiative, referendum, and recall. If politicians in the state legislatures balked at obeying the "will of the people," then Progressives proposed two methods for forcing them to act. Amendments to state constitutions offered voters (1) the *initiative*—a method by which voters could compel the legislature to consider a bill and (2) the *referendum*—a method that allowed citizens to vote on proposed laws printed on their ballots.

A third Progressive measure, the *recall,* enabled voters to remove a corrupt or unsatisfactory politician from office by majority vote before that official's term had expired.

Between 1889, when South Dakota adopted the initiative and referendum, and 1918 (the end of World War I), a total of 20 states—most of them west of the Mississippi—offered voters the initiative and the referendum, while 11 states offered the recall.

Social welfare. Urban life in the Progressive era was improved not only by political reformers but also by the efforts of settlement house workers (see Chapter 18) and other civic-minded volunteers. Jane Addams, Frances Kelly, and other leaders of the social justice movement found that they needed political support in the state legislatures for meeting the needs of immigrants and the working class. They lobbied vigorously and with considerable success for better schools, juvenile courts, liberalized divorce laws, and safety regulations for tenements and factories. Believing that criminals could learn to become effective citizens, reformers fought for such measures as a system of parole, separate reformatories for juveniles, and limits on the death penalty.

Municipal Reform

City bosses and their corrupt alliance with local businesses (trolley lines and utility companies, for example) were the first target of Progressive leaders. In Toledo, Ohio, in 1897, a self-made millionaire with strong memories of his origins as a workingman became the Republican mayor. Adopting "golden rule" as both his policy and his middle name, Mayor Samuel M. "Golden Rule" Jones delighted Toledo's citizens by introducing a comprehensive program of municipal reform, including free kindergartens, night schools, and public playgrounds. Another Ohioan, Tom L. Johnson, devoted himself to the cause of tax reform and three-cent trolley fares for the people of Cleveland. As Cleveland's mayor from 1901–1909, Johnson fought valiantly—but without success—for public ownership and operation of the city's public utilities and services (water, electricity, and trolleys).

Controlling public utilities. Reform leaders arose in other cities throughout the nation seeking to break the power of the city bosses and take utilities out of the hands of private companies. By 1915 fully two-thirds of the nation's cities owned their own water systems. As a result of the Progressives' efforts, many cities also came to own and operate gas lines, electric power plants, and urban transportation systems.

Commissions and city managers. New types of municipal government were another Progressive innovation. In 1900, Galveston, Texas, was the first city to adopt a commission plan of government, in which voters elected the heads of city departments (fire, police, and sanitation), not just the mayor. Ultimately proving itself more effective than the commission plan was a system first tried in Dayton, Ohio, in 1913, in which an expert manager was hired by an elected city council to direct the work of the various departments of city government. By 1923, more than 300 cities had adopted the manager-council plan of municipal government.

State Reform

At the state level, reform governors battled corporate interests and championed such measures as the initiative, the referendum, and the direct primary to give the common people control of their own government. In New York, Charles Evans Hughes battled fraudulent insurance companies. In California, Hiram Johnson successfully fought against the economic and political power of the Southern Pacific Railroad. In Wisconsin, Robert La Follette established a strong personal following as the governor (1900–1904) who won passage of the "Wisconsin Idea"—a series of Progressive measures that included a direct primary law, tax reform, and regulation of railroad rates.

Temperance and prohibition. Whether or not to shut down saloons and prohibit the drinking of alcohol was one issue over which the champions of reform were sharply divided. While urban Progressives recognized that saloons were often the neighborhood headquarters of political machines, they generally had little sympathy for the temperance movement. Rural reformers, on the other hand, thought they could clean up morals and politics in one stroke by abolishing liquor. The drys (prohibitionists) were determined and well organized. By 1915, they had persuaded the legislatures of two-thirds of the states to prohibit the sale of alcoholic beverages.

Political Reform in the Nation

While Progressive governors and mayors were battling conservative forces in the state houses and city halls, three presidents—Roosevelt, Taft, and Wilson—sought broad reforms and regulations at the national level.

Theodore Roosevelt's Square Deal

Following President McKinley's assassination in September 1901, Theodore Roosevelt went to the White House at the age of 42, the youngest president in U.S. history and also the most athletic. He was unusual not simply because of his age and vigor but also because he believed that the president should do much more than lead the executive departments. He thought it was the president's job to set the legislative agenda for Congress as well. Thus, by the accident of McKinley's death, the Progressive movement suddenly shot into high gear under the dynamic leadership of an activist, reform-minded president.

"Square Deal" for labor. Presidents in the 19th century had consistently taken the side of business in its conflicts with labor—Hayes in the railroad strike of 1877, Cleveland in the Pullman strike of 1894. Roosevelt, however, in the first economic crisis of his presidency, demonstrated that he favored neither business nor labor but insisted on a *Square Deal* for both. The crisis involved a strike of anthracite coal miners through much of 1902. If the strike continued, many Americans feared that—without coal—they would freeze to death when winter came. Roosevelt took the unusual step of trying to mediate the labor dispute by calling a union leader and coal mine owners to the White House. The mine owners' stubborn refusal to compromise angered the president. To ensure the delivery of coal to consumers, he threatened to take over the mines with federal troops. The owners finally agreed to accept the findings of a special commission, which granted a 10 percent wage increase and a nine-hour day to the miners (but did not grant union recognition).

Voters overwhelmingly approved Roosevelt and his Square Deal by electing him by a landslide in 1904.

Trust-busting. Roosevelt further increased his popularity by being the first president since the passage of the Sherman Antitrust Act in 1890 to enforce that poorly written law. The trust that he most wanted to bust was a combination of railroads known as the Northern Securities Company. Reversing its position in earlier cases, the Supreme Court in 1904 upheld Roosevelt's action in breaking up the railroad monopoly. Roosevelt later directed his attorney general to take antitrust action against Standard Oil and more than 40 other large corporations. Roosevelt did make a distinction between breaking up "bad trusts," which harmed the public and stifled competition, and regulating "good trusts," which through efficiency and low prices dominated a market.

Railroad regulation. President Roosevelt also took the initiative in persuading a Republican majority in Congress to pass two laws that significantly strengthened the regulatory powers of the Interstate Commerce Commission (ICC). Under the Elkins Act (1903), the ICC had greater authority to stop railroads from granting rebates to favored customers. Under the Hepburn Act (1906), the commission could fix "just and reasonable" rates for railroads.

Consumer protection. *The Jungle,* a muckraking book by Upton Sinclair, described in horrifying detail the conditions in the Chicago stockyards and meatpacking industry. The public outcry following the publication of Sinclair's novel caused Congress to enact two regulatory laws in 1906:

1. The *Pure Food and Drug Act* forbade the manufacture, sale, and transportation of adulterated or mislabeled foods and drugs.

2. The *Meat Inspection Act* provided that federal inspectors visit meatpacking plants to ensure that they met minimum standards of sanitation.

Conservation. As a lover of the wilderness and the outdoor life, Roosevelt made an enthusiastic champion of the cause of conservation. In fact, Roosevelt's most original and lasting contribution in domestic policy may have been his efforts to protect the nation's natural resources. Three actions stood out as particularly important.

1. During his presidency, Roosevelt made repeated use of the Forest Reserve Act of 1891 to set aside 150 million acres of federal land as a national reserve that could not be sold to private interests.

2. In 1902, Roosevelt won passage of the Newlands Reclamation Act, a law providing money from the sale of public land for irrigation projects in western states.

3. In 1908, the president publicized the need for conservation by hosting a White House conference on the subject. Following this conference, a National Conservation Commission was established under Gifford Pinchot of Pennsylvania, whom Roosevelt had earlier appointed to be the first director of the U.S. Forest Service.

Taft's Presidency

The good-natured William Howard Taft had served in Roosevelt's cabinet as secretary of war. Honoring the two-term tradition, Roosevelt refused to seek reelection and picked Taft to be his successor. The Republican party readily endorsed Taft as its nominee for president in 1908 and, as expected, defeated for a third time the Democrats' campaigner, William Jennings Bryan.

More trust-busting and conservation. Taft continued Roosevelt's Progressive policies. As a trustbuster, Taft ordered the prosecution of almost twice the number of antitrust cases as his predecessor. Among these cases was one against U.S. Steel, which included a merger approved by then President Theodore Roosevelt. An angry Roosevelt viewed Taft's action as a personal attack on his integrity. As a conservationist, he established the Bureau of Mines, added large tracts in the Appalachians to the national forest reserves, and also set aside federal oil lands (the first president to do so).

Two other Progressive measures were at least equal in importance to legislation enacted under Roosevelt. The Mann-Elkins Act of 1910 gave the Interstate Commerce Commission the power to suspend new railroad rates and oversee telephone, telegraph, and cable companies. The Sixteenth Amendment, ratified by the states in 1913, authorized the U.S government to collect an income tax. (This reform was originally proposed by the Populists in their 1892 platform.) Progressives heartily approved the new tax because, at first, it applied only to the very wealthy.

Split in the Republican party. Progressives in the Republican party were unimpressed with Taft's achievements. In fact, they became so disenchanted with his leadership that they accused him of betraying their cause and joining the conservative wing of the party. These were their reasons:

1. Payne-Aldrich Tariff. During his 1908 campaign, Taft had promised to lower the tariff. Instead, conservative Republicans in Congress passed the Payne-Aldrich Tariff in 1909, which raised the tariff on most imports. Taft angered Progressives in his party not only by signing the tariff bill but by making a public statement in its defense.

2. Pinchot-Ballinger Controversy. The Progressives liked and respected the chief of the Forest Service, Gifford Pinchot, as a dedicated conservationist. On the other hand, they distrusted Taft's secretary of the interior, Richard Ballinger, especially after he opened public lands in Alaska for private development. In 1910, when Pinchot criticized Ballinger, Taft stood by his cabinet member and fired Pinchot for insubordination. Conservatives applauded; Progressives protested.

3. House Speaker Joe Cannon. Progressive Republicans became even angrier with the president when he failed to support their effort to reduce the dictatorial powers of Congress' leading conservative, Speaker of the House Joseph Cannon.

4. Midterm elections. Fighting back against his Progressive critics, Taft openly supported conservative candidates for Congress in the midterm elections of 1910. It was a grievous mistake. Progressivism was now at high tide, and Progressive Republicans from the Midwest easily defeated the candidates endorsed by Taft. After this election, the Republican party was split wide open between two opposing groups: a conservative faction loyal to Taft and a Progressive faction. The latter group of Republicans fervently hoped that their ex-president and hero, Theodore Roosevelt, would agree to become their candidate again in 1912.

Rise of the Socialist Party

A third party developed in the first decade of the 1900s that was dedicated to the welfare of the working class. Originally called the Socialist Labor party in 1897, it changed its name in 1901 to the Socialist Party of America. The Socialist platform called for more radical reforms than the Progressives favored: public ownership of the railroads, utilities, and even of major industries such as oil and steel.

Eugene V. Debs. One of the founders of the Socialist party, Eugene Debs, was the party's candidate for president in five elections—the first in 1900, the last in 1920. A former railway union leader who adopted socialism while jailed for the Pullman strike, Debs was an outspoken critic of business and a champion of labor.

Influence. On such issues as workers' compensation and minimum wage laws, Progressives and some Socialists joined forces. For the most part, however,

Progressives wanted to distance themselves from the ideas of Socialists, since the majority of voters favored only mild reforms, not radical causes. Eventually, however, some Socialist ideas were accepted: public ownership of utilities, the eight-hour workday, and pensions for employees.

The party reached its peak in the presidential election of 1912 when Debs received over 900,000 votes—6 percent of the total.

The Election of 1912

Reform efforts dominated a campaign that involved four notable presidential candidates.

Candidates. President Taft was renominated by the Republicans after his supporters excluded Theodore Roosevelt's delegates from the party's convention. Progressive Republicans then formed a new party and nominated Theodore Roosevelt. (Roosevelt's claim that he was as strong as a bull moose gave the new Progressive party its nickname: the Bull Moose party.) After lengthy balloting, Democrats united behind Woodrow Wilson, a newcomer who had first been elected to office in 1910 as governor of New Jersey. The Socialist party, gaining strength, again nominated Eugene V. Debs.

Campaign. With Taft enjoying little popularity and Debs considered too radical, the election came down to a battle between Theodore Roosevelt and Woodrow Wilson. Roosevelt called for a New Nationalism, with more government regulation of business and unions, women's suffrage, and more social welfare programs. Wilson pledged a New Freedom, which would limit both big business and big government, bring about reform by ending corruption, and revive competition by supporting small business.

Results. With the Republicans split, Wilson won easily with 435 electoral votes (Roosevelt received 88, Taft 8, and Debs none). The Democrats gained control of Congress, although Wilson was a minority president with 41 percent of the popular vote (Roosevelt got 27 percent, Taft 23 percent, and Debs 6 percent). The overwhelming support for the Progressive presidential candidates ensured that reform efforts would continue under Wilson, while the failure of the Progressive party to elect local candidates gave evidence that the new party would not last. But the idea contained in Roosevelt's New Nationalism—of strong federal government regulations helping the people—did have a lasting influence for much of the century (see, in Chapter 24, the New Deal, and, in Chapter 28, the Great Society).

Woodrow Wilson's Progressive Program

Wilson, who grew up in Virginia during the Civil War, was only the second Democrat elected president since the war (Cleveland was the other), and the first southerner to occupy the White House since Zachary Taylor. A complex man, Wilson was idealistic, intellectual, righteous, and inflexible. Like Roosevelt, he believed that a president should actively lead Congress and, when necessary, appeal directly to the people to rally their support for his legislative program.

In his inaugural address in 1913, the Democratic president pledged again his commitment to a New Freedom. To bring back conditions of free and fair competition in the economy, Wilson attacked "the triple wall of privilege": tariffs, banking, and trusts.

Tariff reduction. Wasting no time to fulfill a campaign pledge, Wilson on the first day of his presidency called a special session of Congress to lower the tariff. Past presidents had always sent written messages to Congress, but Wilson broke this longstanding tradition by addressing Congress in person about the need for lower tariff rates to bring consumer prices down. Passage of the Underwood Tariff in 1913 substantially lowered tariffs for the first time in over 50 years. To compensate for the reduced tariff revenues, the Underwood bill included a graduated income tax rate of from 1 to 6 percent.

Banking reform. Wilson's next major initiative concerned the banking system and the money supply. He was persuaded that the gold standard was inflexible and that banks, rather than serving the public interest, were too much influenced by stock speculators on Wall Street. The president again went directly to Congress in 1913 to propose a plan for building both stability and flexibility into the U.S. financial system. Rejecting the Republican proposal for a private national bank, he proposed a national banking system with 12 district banks supervised by a Federal Reserve Board. After months of debate, Congress finally passed the Federal Reserve Act in 1914. Ever since, Americans have purchased goods and services using the Federal Reserve Notes (dollar bills) issued by the federally regulated banking system.

Business regulation. Two major pieces of legislation in 1914 completed Wilson's New Freedom program:

1. Clayton Antitrust Act. This act greatly strengthened the provisions in the Sherman Antitrust Act for breaking up monopolies. Most important for organized labor, the new law contained a clause exempting unions from being prosecuted as trusts.

2. Federal Trade Commission. The new regulatory agency was empowered to investigate and take action against any "unfair trade practice" in every industry except banking and transportation.

Other reforms. Wilson was at first opposed to any legislation that seemed to favor special interests, such as farmers' groups and labor unions. He was finally persuaded, however, to extend his reform program to include the following Progressive measures:

1. Federal Farm Loan Act. In 1916, 12 regional federal farm loan banks were established to provide farm loans at low interest rates.

2. Child Labor Act. This measure, long favored by settlement house workers and labor unions alike, was enacted in 1916. It prohibited the shipment in interstate commerce of products manufactured by children under 14 years old. The Supreme Court, however, found this act to be unconstitutional in the 1918 case of *Hammer v. Dagenhart.*

African Americans in the Progressive Era

In championing greater democracy for the American people, leaders of the Progressive movement thought only in terms of the white race. African Americans were, for the most part, ignored by Progressive presidents and governors. President Wilson, with a strong southern heritage and many of the racist attitudes of the times, acquiesced to the demands of southern Democrats and permitted the segregation of federal workers and buildings.

The status of African Americans had declined steadily since the days of Reconstruction. With the Supreme Court's "separate but equal" decision in *Plessy v. Ferguson* (1896), racial segregation had been the rule in the South and, unofficially, in much of the North as well. Ironically and tragically, the Progressive era coincided with years when thousands of blacks were lynched by racist mobs. Progressives did nothing about segregation and lynching for two reasons: (1) They shared in the general prejudice of their times. (2) They considered other reforms (such as lower tariffs) to be more important than antilynching laws because such reforms benefited everyone in American society, not just one group.

Of course, African American leaders strongly disagreed and took action on their own to alleviate conditions of poverty and discrimination.

Two Approaches: Washington and Du Bois

Economic deprivation and exploitation was one problem; denial of civil rights was another. Which problem was primary was a difficult question that became the focus of a debate between two African American leaders: Booker T. Washington and W. E. B. Du Bois.

Washington's stress on economics. By far the most influential African American at the turn of the century was the head of the Tuskegee Institute in Alabama, Booker T. Washington. In his Atlanta Exposition speech in 1895, Washington argued that blacks' needs for education and economic progress were of foremost importance, and that they should concentrate on learning industrial skills for better wages. Only after establishing a secure economic base, said Washington, could African Americans hope to realize their other goal of political and social equality. (See Chapter 16.)

Du Bois' stress on civil rights. Unlike Washington, who had been born into slavery on a southern plantation, W. E. B. Du Bois was a northerner with a college education, who became a distinguished scholar and writer. In his book *The Souls of Black Folk* (1903), Du Bois criticized Booker T. Washington's approach and demanded equal rights for African Americans. He argued that political and social rights were a prerequisite for economic independence.

Washington's pragmatic approach to economic advancement and Du Bois' militant demands for equal rights framed a debate in the African American community that continued throughout much of the 20th century.

Urban Migration

At the close of the 19th century, about nine out of ten African Americans lived in the South. In the next century, this ratio steadily shifted toward the North. The migration began in earnest between 1910 and 1930 when about a million people traveled north to seek jobs in the cities. Motivating their decision to leave the South were: (1) deteriorating race relations, (2) destruction of their cotton crops by the boll weevil, and (3) job opportunities in northern factories that opened up when white workers were drafted in World War I. The Great Depression in the 1930s slowed migration, but World War II renewed it. Between 1940 and 1970, over 4 million African Americans went north. Although many succeeded in improving their economic conditions, the newcomers to northern cities also faced racial tension and discrimination.

Civil Rights Organizations

Increased racial discrimination during the Progressive era was one reason that a number of civil rights organizations were founded in the first decade of the 20th century.

1. In 1905, W. E. B. Du Bois met with a group of black intellectuals in Niagara Falls, Canada, to discuss a program of protest and action aimed at securing equal rights for blacks. They and others who later joined the group became known as the *Niagara Movement.*

2. On Lincoln's birthday in 1908, Du Bois, other members of the Niagara Movement, and a group of white progressives founded the National Association for the Advancement of Colored People (NAACP). Their mission was no less than to abolish all forms of segregation and to increase educational opportunities for African American children. By 1920, the NAACP was the nation's largest civil rights organization, with over 100,000 members.

3. Another organization, the National Urban League, was formed in 1911 to help those migrating from the South to northern cities. The league's motto, "Not Alms But Opportunity," reflected its emphasis on self-reliance and economic advancement.

Women, Suffrage, and the Progressive Movement

The Progressive era was a time of increased activism and optimism for a new generation of feminists. By 1900, the older generation of suffrage crusaders led by Susan B. Anthony and Elizabeth Cady Stanton had passed the torch to younger women. Although the younger generation of men were generally more liberal than their elders, not all male Progressives enthusiastically endorsed the women's movement. President Wilson, for example, refused to support the suffragists' call for a national amendment until late in his presidency.

The Campaign for Women's Suffrage

Carrie Chapman Catt, an energetic reformer from Iowa became the new president of the National American Woman Suffrage Association (NAWSA) in 1900. Catt argued for the vote as a broadening of democracy which would empower women, thus enabling them to more actively care for their families in an industrial society. At first, Catt continued NAWSA's drive to win votes for women at the state level before changing strategies and seeking a suffrage amendment to the U.S. Constitution.

Militant suffragists. A more militant approach to gaining the vote was adopted by some women, who took to the streets with mass pickets, parades, and hunger strikes. Their leader, Alice Paul of New Jersey, broke from NAWSA in 1916 to form the National Woman's party. From the beginning, Paul focused on winning the support of Congress and the president for an amendment to the Constitution.

Nineteenth Amendment (1920). The dedicated efforts of women on the home front in World War I finally persuaded a majority in Congress and President Wilson to adopt a women's suffrage amendment. Its ratification as the Nineteenth Amendment in 1920 guaranteed women's right to vote in all elections at the local, state, and national levels. Following the victory of her cause, Carrie Chapman Catt organized the League of Women Voters, a civic organization dedicated to keeping voters informed about candidates and issues.

Other Issues

Although gaining the vote received the most attention in the Progressive era, women activists also campaigned for other rights. Some progress was achieved in securing educational equality, liberalizing marriage and divorce laws, reducing discrimination in business and the professions, and recognizing women's rights to own property.

HISTORICAL PERSPECTIVES: REFORM OR REACTION?

Historians have generally agreed that the Progressive movement was a response to industrialization and urbanization. They do not agree, however, on whether the Progressives were truly seeking to

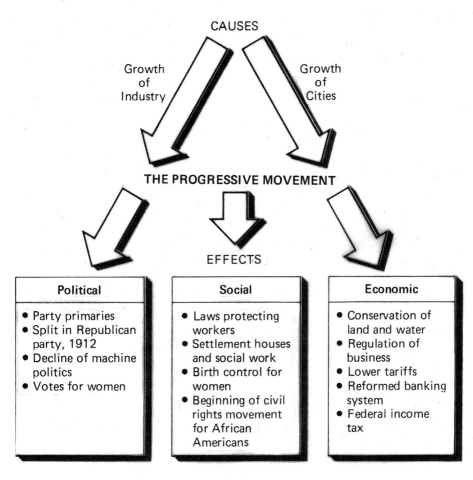

Causes and Effects of the Progressive Movement

move society in new directions or whether they were reacting *against* new trends and attempting to maintain society as it once was.

Progressives, of course, saw themselves as genuine reformers, and for many years, historians accepted this view. Historians said that Progressives were simply acting in the tradition of earlier reformers: the Jeffersonians, Jacksonians, and Populists. William Allen White argued that the Progressives adopted the complete Populist package of reforms except for free silver. Historian Arthur M. Schlesinger, Jr., thought that U.S. history moved in a liberal-conservative cycle and that progressivism was a predictable phase in that cycle following the conservatism of late-19th century politics.

Another, complementary view of the Progressives depicts them not as democratic champions of "the people" but as modernizers who wanted to apply rational, scientific methods to the operations of social and political institutions. Samuel P. Hay's study of municipal reform, for example, shows that Progressive leaders were an educated, upper-class elite working to make government more efficient under the direction of skilled experts.

Those historians who view Progressives as conservatives in disguise—or even as reactionaries—stress how disturbed these citizens were by labor strife, by the agrarian discontent of the Populists, and by signs of revolutionary ferment among the urban masses. Gabriel Kolko argues that the business elite, far from being opposed to government regulation, in fact wanted regulation as a means of stabilizing industry. Kolko points out that the regulation of the meatpacking industry, although inspired by muckraking literature, worked for the benefit of the large meatpackers, who lobbied behind the scenes for government controls.

Most historians agree that the middle class, not the working class, were chiefly involved in the Progressive movement. But what was the main motive for their reforms? Did they act out of sympathy for the workers or out of fear of a Socialist revolution? George Mowry in the early 1950s characterized the Progressive movement as a reaction of middle-class professionals and small-business owners to pressures both from above (large corporations) and from below (labor unions). In this view, which Richard Hofstadter expanded upon, the middle class is shown attempting to maintain its traditional leadership of society by directing reform. The neglect of unions and African Americans by Progressives is seen as further evidence that the reformers were conservative at heart.

On the other hand, some historians argue that middle-class motives for reform might have been an expression of that group's strong sense of social conscience. The Protestant churches had cultivated a sense of responsibility and justice. The muckrakers' articles stirred their readers' conscience and aroused genuine feelings of guilt with respect to the poor and outrage with respect to dishonest politics.

KEY NAMES, EVENTS, AND TERMS

Progressive movement	Henry Demarest Lloyd	direct primary
pragmatism	Standard Oil Company	Robert La Folette
William James	Lincoln Steffans	direct election of senators;
John Dewey	Ida Tarbell	Seventeenth Amendment
Frederick W. Taylor	Jacob Riis	initiative; referendum; recall
scientific management	Theodore Dreiser	social welfare
muckrakers	Australian ballot	municipal reform

Samuel M. Jones
Tom L. Johnson
Charles Evans Hughes
Hiram Johnson
Theodore Roosevelt; Square Deal
anthracite coal miners' strike (1902)
trust-busting
Elkins Act (1903)
Hepburn Act (1906)
Upton Sinclair, *The Jungle*
Pure Food and Drug Act (1906)
Meat Inspection Act (1906)
conservation
Newlands Reclamation Act (1902)

Gifford Pinchot
William Howard Taft
Mann-Elkins Act (1910)
federal income tax; Sixteenth Amendment
Payne-Aldrich Tariff (1909)
Joseph Cannon
Socialist Party of America
Eugene V. Debs
Bull Moose party
New Nationalism
New Freedom
Underwood Tariff (1913)
Federal Reserve Act (1914)
Federal Reserve Board
Clayton Antitrust Act (1914)
Federal Trade Commission

Federal Farm Loan Act (1916)
urban migration
Niagara Movement
Booker T. Washington
W. E. B. Du Bois
National Association for the Advancement of Colored People
National Urban League
Carrie Chapman Catt
National American Woman Suffrage Association
Alice Paul
National Woman's party
Nineteenth Amendment
League of Women Voters

MULTIPLE-CHOICE QUESTIONS

1. Which of the following best defines the Progressive movement?
   (A) working-class response to big business
   (B) conservative reaction to immigration
   (C) middle-class response to urbanization and industrialization
   (D) Populist response to falling farm prices
   (E) Republican response to muckraking

2. All of the following reforms were adopted during the Progressive era EXCEPT
   (A) stronger antitrust law
   (B) protection of national forests
   (C) lower tariff rates
   (D) regulation of meatpacking industry
   (E) federal antilynching law

3. Which of the following was NOT a reason for the split in the Republican party in 1912?
   (A) Democratic control of the White House
   (B) Taft's tariff policy
   (C) Progressives' fight against House Speaker Joseph Cannon
   (D) conservatives' nomination of William Howard Taft
   (E) popularity of Theodore Roosevelt

4. Which of the following was LEAST likely to support a proposal for a direct primary?
   (A) Robert La Follette
   (B) Joseph Cannon
   (C) Woodrow Wilson

(D) Theodore Roosevelt

(E) William Jennings Bryan

5. Most Progressive politicians opposed the election of

(A) Theodore Roosevelt in 1904

(B) William Howard Taft in 1908

(C) Theodore Roosevelt in 1912

(D) William Howard Taft in 1912

(E) Woodrow Wilson in 1912

6. The passage of the Federal Reserve Act in 1913 was important because it

(A) ended the power of the Second Bank of the United States

(B) permitted a flexible money supply

(C) allowed the president to set interest rates

(D) made up revenues lost by the Underwood Tariff

(E) established forest and oil reserves in the West

7. Woodrow Wilson's campaign for New Freedom won the 1912 presidential election over Theodore Roosevelt and his New Nationalism. Which of the following statements is accurate?

(A) Roosevelt would have won if Eugene Debs had not been a candidate.

(B) African American support helped Wilson and the Democrats enact their program.

(C) New Nationalism would still influence the federal government for the next 60 years.

(D) Wilson encouraged cooperation between government and big business.

(E) Social Darwinism inspired the programs of both Wilson and Roosevelt.

8. W. E. B. Du Bois disagreed with Booker T. Washington's

(A) stress on civil rights

(B) suggestion that economic issues were more important than civil rights

(C) advocacy of Progressive reforms

(D) reasons for founding the Tuskegee Institute

(E) attitude toward emancipation of slaves

9. "It is vitally necessary to move forward and to shake off the dead hand ... of the reactionaries; and yet there is apt to be a lunatic fringe among the votaries of any forward movement."

In the context of political activists, who would Theodore Roosevelt most likely refer to as the "lunatic fringe"?

(A) supporters of the Social Gospel

(B) suffragists

(C) the NAACP

(D) conservationists

(E) Socialists

10. Of the following individuals, who would have been most likely to agree with the policy depicted in the cartoon on page 443?

(A) Woodrow Wilson

(B) Robert La Follette

(C) Eugene V. Debs

(D) William Howard Taft

(E) Henry George

Collections of the Library of Congress

ESSAY QUESTIONS

1. Compare and contrast Woodrow Wilson's New Freedom approach to regulation with Theodore Roosevelt's New Nationalism approach.

2. Assess the contributions of TWO of the following to the influence and reforms of the Progressive movement:

   middle class

   muckrakers

   philosophy of pragmatism

   presidential leadership

3. Progressives believed that greater democracy was the key to solving society's problems. Identify TWO problems that Progressives addressed and, for each, describe a democratic reform that was designed to deal with the problem.

4. Compare and contrast Booker T. Washington and W. E. B. Du Bois regarding their objectives and methods.

5. Analyze the extent to which the Progressives were concerned with the interests and values of the middle class and neglected the interests of the working class.

Some historians contend that there was no single Progressive movement but rather a number of separate reform efforts on a variety of issues. The following readings reflect this diversity but also may reveal a common belief in democracy and high moral purpose that gave a common impulse to the politics of the era.

DOCUMENT A.   VOTES FOR WOMEN

After a lifetime devoted to women's suffrage, Susan B. Anthony wrote the following summation of her mission.

> Until woman has obtained "that right protective of all other rights—the ballot," this agitation must still go on, absorbing the time and energy of our best and strongest women. Who can measure the advantages that would result if the magnificent abilities of these women could be devoted to the needs of government, society, home, instead of being consumed in the struggle to obtain their birthright of individual freedom? Until this can be gained we can never know, we cannot even prophesy, the capacity and power of woman for the uplifting of humanity.
>
> It may be delayed longer than we think; it may be here sooner than we expect; but the day will come when man will recognize woman as his peer, not only at fireside but in the councils of the nation.

> Susan B. Anthony,
> *Arena Magazine*, 1897

DOCUMENT B.   PLEDGE FOR TEMPERANCE

More women of the early 20th century campaigned for temperance and prohibition than for suffrage. Millions of women and men were persuaded by the Woman's Christian Temperance Union (WCTU) to take the following pledge.

> We believe that God created both man and woman in His own image, and, therefore, we believe in one standard of purity for both men and women, and in equal rights of all to hold opinions and to express the same with equal freedom.
>
> We believe in a living wage; in an eight-hour day; in courts of conciliation and arbitration; in justice as opposed to greed of gain; in "peace on earth and goodwill to men."

We therefore formulate and, for ourselves, adopt the following pledge, asking our sisters and brothers of a common danger and a common hope to make common cause with us in working its reasonable and helpful precepts into the practice of everyday life:

I hereby solemnly promise, *God helping me,* to abstain from all distilled, fermented, and malt liquors, including wine, beer, and cider, and to employ all proper means to discourage the use of and traffic in the same.

National Woman's Christian
Temperance Union,
Annual Leaflet, 1902

DOCUMENT C. CHILD LABOR

By 1900, some progress had been made in limiting the employment of children in factories and mines. Florence Kelley was an associate of Jane Addams and a co-leader of the settlement house movement in Chicago. Appointed chief factory inspector for Illinois, she delivered a report in 1906 clarifying the existing problems and calling for renewed efforts to end the abuses.

These, I believe are the gravest obstacles at the present time to the enforcement of the child labor law [in Illinois]: first, the general hypocrisy of the American people, believing that child labor is evil, and that, therefore, we do not tolerate it—when there are working children on the streets before our eyes, every working day in the year, in every manufacturing city; second, the failure to make the work of enforcing the law a desirable and recognized profession into which the ablest men will willingly go.

The trouble is ourselves. We get exactly the sort of care for the children through the officials that the community determines they shall have; and we register our indifference in accepting such printed records as we have now, obscuring the actual conditions of the working children in nearly all the states.

The next step which we need to take is to insist that this is a national evil, and we must have a national law abolishing it.

Florence Kelley,
"Obstacles to the Enforcement of
Child Labor Legislation," 1906

DOCUMENT D. CIVIL RIGHTS FOR AFRICAN AMERICANS

The following excerpt expresses the views of the leading champion of the Niagara Movement, W. E. B. Du Bois.

> We repudiate the monstrous doctrine that the oppressor should be the sole authority as to the rights of the oppressed. The Negro race in America, stolen, ravished, and degraded, struggling up through difficulties and oppression, needs sympathy and receives criticism; needs help and is given mob violence; needs justice and is given charity; needs leadership and is given cowardice and apology; needs bread and is given a stone. This nation will never stand justified before God until these things are changed.
>
> .... Of the above grievances we do not hesitate to complain, and to complain loudly and insistently. To ignore, overlook, or apologize for these wrongs is to prove ourselves unworthy of freedom. Persistent, manly agitation is the way to liberty, and toward this goal the Niagara Movement has started and asks the cooperation of all men of all races.

Principles of the Niagara Movement,
July 1905

ANALYZING THE DOCUMENTS

1. Why does Susan B. Anthony in Document A call the ballot a right that is "protective of all other rights"? In what way does this view parallel the beliefs of male Progressives?

2. Do you find a Progressive purpose and theme in Document B, the Pledge for Temperance?

3. Based on the documents and your knowledge of the period, write an essay on the following question: To what extent did the Progressive movement represent a unified effort by all groups in society to correct abuses in society and government?

WORLD WAR I, 1914–1918

It breaks his heart that kings must murder still,
That all his hours of travail here for men
Seem in vain. And who will bring white peace
That he may sleep upon his hill again?

Vachel Lindsay, "Abraham Lincoln
Walks at Midnight," 1914

The sequence of events leading from peace in Europe to the outbreak of a general war occurred with stunning rapidity:

- SARAJEVO, JUNE 28, 1914: A Serbian terrorist assassinates Austrian Archduke Francis Ferdinand—the heir apparent to the throne of the Austro-Hungarian empire—and his wife.

- VIENNA, JULY 23: The Austrian government issues an ultimatum threatening war against Serbia and invades that country four days later.

- BERLIN, AUGUST 1: As Austria's ally, the German government under Kaiser Wilhelm I declares war against Russia, an ally of Serbia.

- BERLIN, AUGUST 3: Germany declares war against France, an ally of Russia, and immediately begins an invasion of neutral Belgium because it offers the fastest route to Paris.

- LONDON, AUGUST 4: Great Britain, as an ally of France, declares war against Germany.

In the United States, the American people were shocked that the European nations were actually at war. True, since 1898, the United States had acted as a major power by intervening in the Caribbean and asserting an Open Door policy in China (Chapter 20). Yet it strongly held to the tradition begun by Washington and Jefferson of not allying the nation with any European power or becoming involved in a war on the other side of the Atlantic. President Wilson's first response to the outbreak of the European war was therefore predictable. He issued a declaration of U.S. neutrality and called upon the American people to support his policy by not taking sides. In trying to steer a neutral course, however, Wilson soon found that it was difficult—if not

OPPOSING SIDES IN WORLD WAR I

impossible—to protect U.S. trading rights and maintain a policy that favored neither the Allied Powers (Great Britain, France, and Russia) nor the Central Powers (Germany, Austria-Hungary and the Ottoman Empire/Turkey). During a relatively short period (1914–1919), the United States and its people rapidly moved through a wide range of roles: first as a contented neutral country, next as a country waging a war for peace, then as a victorious world power, and finally, as an alienated, isolationist nation.

Neutrality

In World War I (as in the War of 1812), the trouble for the United States arose from the efforts of the belligerent powers to stop supplies from reaching the enemy. Having the stronger navy, Great Britain was the first to declare a naval blockade against Germany by mining the North Sea and seizing ships—including U.S. ships—attempting to run the blockade. President Wilson protested British seizure of American ships as a violation of a neutral nation's right to freedom of the seas.

Submarine Warfare

Germany's one hope for challenging British power at sea lay with a new naval weapon, the submarine. In February 1915, Germany answered the British blockade by announcing a blockade of its own and warned that ships attempting to enter the "war zone" (waters near the British Isles) risked being sunk on sight by German submarines.

Lusitania **crisis.** The first major crisis challenging U.S. neutrality and peace was the torpedoing and sinking of a British passenger liner, the *Lusitania,* on May 7, 1915. Most of the passengers drowned, including 128 Americans. Wilson responded by sending Germany a strongly worded diplomatic message warning that Germany would be held to "strict accountability" if it continued its policy of sinking unarmed ships. Secretary of State William Jennings Bryan objected to this message as too warlike and resigned from the president's cabinet.

Other sinkings. In August 1915, two more Americans lost their lives at sea as the result of a German submarine attack on another passenger ship, the *Arabic.* This time, Wilson's note of protest prevailed upon the German government to pledge that no other unarmed passenger ships would be sunk without warning (that is, without time being allowed for passengers to get into lifeboats).

Germany kept its word until March 1916 when a German torpedo struck an unarmed merchant ship, the *Sussex,* injuring several American passengers. Wilson threatened to cut off U.S. diplomatic relations with Germany—a step preparatory to war. Once again, rather than risk U.S. entry into the war on the British side, Germany backed down. Its reply to the president, known as the *Sussex* pledge, promised not to sink merchant or passenger ships without giving due warning. For the remainder of 1916, Germany was true to its word.

Economic Links With Britain and France

Even though the United States was officially a neutral nation, its economy became closely tied to that of the Allied powers, Great Britain and France. In early 1914, before the war began, the United States had been in a business recession. Soon after the outbreak of war, the economy rebounded in part because of orders for war supplies from the British and the French. By 1915, U.S. businesses had never been so prosperous.

In theory, U.S. manufacturers could have shipped supplies to Germany as well, but the British blockade effectively prevented such trade. Wilson's policy did not deliberately favor the Allied powers. Nevertheless, because the president more or less tolerated the British blockade while restricting Germany's submarine blockade, U.S. economic support was going to one side (Britain and France) and not the other. Between 1914 and 1917, U.S. trade with the Allies quadrupled while its trade with Germany dwindled to the vanishing point.

Loans. In addition, when the Allies found they could not finance the purchase of everything they needed, the U.S. government permitted J. P. Morgan and other bankers to extend as much as $3 billion in secured credit to Great Britain and France. These loans maintained U.S. prosperity, and at the same time they sustained the Allies' war effort.

Public Opinion

If Wilson's policies unintentionally favored Britain, so did the attitudes of the majority of Americans. In August 1914, as Americans read in their newspapers about German armies marching ruthlessly through Belgium, they perceived Germany as a cruel bully whose armies were commanded by a mean-spirited autocrat, Kaiser Wilhelm. This view of German ruthlessness was reinforced by the sinking of the *Lusitania* in 1915.

Ethnic influences. In 1914, first- and second-generation immigrants made up over 30 percent of the U.S. population. They were glad to be out of the fighting and strongly supported neutrality. Even so, their sympathies were committed to their nationality of origin. When Italy joined the Allies in 1915, Italian Americans began cheering on the Allies in their desperate struggle to fend off German assaults on the Western Front (entrenched positions in France).

German Americans, on the other hand, strongly sympathized with the struggles of their "homeland." Another large ethnic group, the Irish Americans, hated Britain because of its oppressive rule of Ireland. Their sympathies were openly committed to the Central Powers.

Still, the great majority of native-born Americans wanted Britain and France to win the war. Positive U.S. relations with France since the Revolutionary War bolstered public support for the French. Americans also tended to sympathize with Britain and France because of their democratic governments. President Wilson himself, as a person of Scotch-English descent, had long admired the British political system.

British war propaganda. Not only did Britain command the seas but it also commanded the war news that was cabled daily to U.S. newspapers and magazines. Fully recognizing the importance of influencing U.S. public opinion, the British government made sure the American press was well supplied with stories of German soldiers committing atrocities in Belgium and the German-occupied part of eastern France.

The War Debate

After the *Lusitania* crisis, a small but vocal minority of influential Republicans from the East—including Theodore Roosevelt—argued for U.S. entry into the war against Germany. The majority of Americans, however, were thankful for a booming economy and peace.

Preparedness

Eastern Republicans like Roosevelt were the first to recognize that the U.S. Army and Navy were hopelessly unprepared for a major war. They clamored for "preparedness" (greater defense expenditures) soon after the European war broke out. Leading the campaign was the National Security League, organized by a group of business leaders to promote preparedness and to extend direct U.S. aid to the Allies, if needed.

At first, President Wilson opposed the call for preparedness, but in late 1915, he changed his policy and urged Congress to approve an ambitious expansion of the armed forces. The president's proposal provoked a storm of controversy, especially among Democrats who until then were largely opposed to military increases. After a nationwide speaking tour on behalf of preparedness, Wilson finally convinced Congress to pass the National Defense Act in June 1916, which increased the regular army to a force of nearly 175,000. A month later, Congress approved the construction of more than 50 warships (battleships, cruisers, destroyers, and submarines) in just one year.

Opposition to War

Many Americans, especially in the Midwest and West, were adamantly opposed to preparedness, fearing that it would soon lead to U.S. involvement in the war. The antiwar activists included Populists, Progressives, and Socialists. Leaders among the peace-minded Progressives were William Jennings Bryan, Jane Addams, and Jeannette Rankin—the latter the first woman to be elected to Congress. Woman suffragists actively campaigned against any military buildup (although later, after the U.S. declaration of war in 1917, they would loyally support the war effort).

The Election of 1916

President Wilson was well aware that, as a Democrat, he had won election to the presidency in 1912 only because of the split in Republican ranks between Taft conservatives and Roosevelt Progressives. Despite his own Progressive record, Wilson's chances for reelection did not seem strong after Theodore Roosevelt declined the Progressive party's nomination for president in 1916 and rejoined the Republicans. (Roosevelt's decision virtually destroyed any chance of the Progressive party surviving.) Charles Evans Hughes, a Supreme Court justice and former governor of New York, became the presidential candidate of a reunited Republican party.

"He kept us out of war." The Democrats adopted as their campaign slogan: "He kept us out of war." The peace sentiment in the country, Wilson's record of Progressive leadership, and Hughes' weakness as a candidate combined to give the president the victory in an extremely close election. Democratic strength in the South and West had overcome Republican dominance in the East.

Peace Efforts

Wilson made repeated efforts to fulfill his party's campaign promise to keep out of the war. Before the election, in 1915, he had sent his chief foreign policy adviser, Colonel Edward House of Texas, to London, Paris, and Berlin to negotiate a peace settlement. This mission, however, had been unsuccessful. Other efforts at mediation also were turned aside by both the Allies and the Central Powers. Finally, in January 1917, Wilson made a speech to the Senate declaring U.S. commitment to the idea of "peace without victory."

Decision for War

In April 1917, only one month after being sworn into office a second time, President Wilson went before Congress to ask for a declaration of war against Germany. What had happened to change his policy from neutrality to war?

Unrestricted Submarine Warfare

Most important in the U.S. decision for war was a sudden change in German military strategy. The German high command had decided in early January 1917 to resume unrestricted submarine warfare. They recognized the risk of the United States entering the war but believed that, by cutting off supplies to the Allies, Germany could win the war before Americans could react. Germany communicated its decision to the U.S. government on January 31. A few days later, Wilson broke off U.S. diplomatic relations with Germany.

Immediate Causes

Wilson still hesitated, but a series of events in March 1917 as well as the president's hopes for arranging a permanent peace in Europe convinced him that U.S. participation in the war was now unavoidable.

Zimmermann Telegram. On March 1, U.S. newspapers carried the shocking news of a secret offer made by Germany to Mexico. Intercepted by British intelligence, a telegram to Mexico from the German foreign minister, Arthur Zimmermann, proposed that Mexico ally itself with Germany in return for Germany's pledge to help Mexico recover lost territories: Texas, New Mexico, and Arizona. The Zimmermann Telegram aroused the nationalist anger of the American people and convinced Wilson that Germany fully expected a war with the United States.

Russian Revolution. Applying the principle of moral diplomacy, Wilson wanted the war to be fought for a worthy purpose: the triumph of democracy. It bothered him that one of the Allies was Russia, a nation governed by an autocratic czar. This barrier to U.S. participation was suddenly removed on March 15, when Russian revolutionaries overthrew the czar's government and proclaimed a republic. (Only later in November would the revolutionary government be taken over by Communists.)

Renewed submarine attacks. In the first weeks of March, German submarines sank five unarmed U.S. merchant ships.

Declaration of War

On April 2, 1917, President Wilson stood before a special session of senators and representatives and solemnly asked that Congress recognize a state of war existed between Germany and the United States. His speech condemned Germany's submarine policy as "warfare against mankind" and declared: "The world must be made safe for democracy." On April 6, an overwhelming majority in Congress voted for a declaration of war, although a few pacifists, including Robert La Follette and Jeanette Rankin, defiantly voted no.

Mobilization

U.S. mobilization for war in 1917 was a race against time. It was understood that Germany was preparing to deliver a knockout blow to end the war on German terms. On land, Germany planned a major offensive against Allied lines on the Western Front; at sea, the unleashed power of German submarines could now do serious damage to British sources of supply. Could the United States mobilize its vast economic resources fast enough to make a difference? That was the question Wilson and his advisers confronted in the critical early months of U.S. involvement in war.

Industry and Labor

Since it would take many months to train U.S. troops, the first American contribution to the Allies would be in shipping needed supplies: chiefly munitions (rifles and gunpowder) and food. For this purpose, Wilson created a number of war agencies staffed by volunteers. For example:

Bernard Baruch, a Wall Street broker, volunteered to use his extensive contacts in industry to help win the war. Under his direction, the War Industries Board set production priorities and established centralized control over raw materials and prices.

Herbert Hoover, a distinguished engineer, took charge of the Food Administration, which encouraged American households to eat less meat and bread so that more food could be shipped abroad for the French and British troops. The conservation drive paid off; in two years, U.S. overseas shipment of food tripled.

Harry Garfield volunteered to head the Fuel Administration, which directed efforts to save coal. Nonessential factories were closed, and daylight saving time went into effect for the first time.

Former president William Howard Taft helped arbitrate disputes between workers and employers as head of the National War Labor Board. Labor won concessions during the war that had earlier been denied. Wages rose, the eight-hour day became more common, and union membership increased.

Finance

Paying for something as costly as war is always a huge problem. Wilson's war government managed to raise $33 billion in two years by a combination of loans and taxes. It conducted four massive drives to convince Americans to put their savings into federal government Liberty Bonds. Congress also increased both personal income and corporate taxes and placed an excise tax on luxury goods.

Public Opinion and Civil Liberties

The U.S. government used techniques of both patriotic persuasion and legal intimidation to ensure public support for the war effort. Progressive journalist George Creel took charge of a propaganda agency called the Committee on Public Information, which enlisted the voluntary services of artists, writers, vaudeville performers, and movie stars to depict the heroism of the "boys" (U.S. soldiers) and the villainy of the kaiser. The vast amount of war propaganda created under Creel's direction consisted of films, posters, pamphlets, and volunteer speakers—all urging Americans to watch out for German spies and to "do your bit" for the war.

War hysteria and patriotic enthusiasm too often provided an excuse for nativist groups to take out their prejudices on "disloyal" minorities. One such group, the American Protective League, mounted "Hate the Hun" campaigns and used vigilante action in attacking all things German—from the performing of Beethoven's music to the cooking of sauerkraut.

Espionage and Sedition acts. A number of socialists and pacifists took the risk of criticizing the government's war policy. After the passage of the Espionage Act in 1917 and the Sedition Act in 1918, the penalty for speaking out in this way was often a stiff prison sentence. The Espionage Act provided for imprisonment of up to 20 years for persons who either tried to incite rebellion in the armed forces or obstruct the operation of the draft. The Sedition Act went much further by prohibiting anyone from making "disloyal" or "abusive" remarks about the U.S. government. About 2,000 people were prosecuted under these laws, half of whom were convicted and jailed. Among them was the Socialist leader, Eugene Debs, who was sentenced to ten years in federal prison for speaking against the war.

Case of *Schenck v. United States.* The Supreme Court upheld the constitutionality of the Espionage Act in a case involving a man who had been imprisoned for distributing pamphlets against the draft. In 1919, Justice Oliver Wendell Holmes concluded that the right to free speech could be limited when it represented a "clear and present danger" to the public safety.

Armed Forces

As soon as war was declared, thousands of young men voluntarily enlisted for military service. The largest number of recruits, however, were conscripted (drafted) into the army by a system requiring all men between 21 and 30 (and later between 18 and 45) to register with the government for possible induction.

Selective Service Act (1917). The system of "selective service" was devised by Secretary of War Newton D. Baker as a democratic method for ensuring that all groups in the population would be called into service. Under the Selective Service Act, passed by Congress in June 1917, about 2.8 million men were eventually called by lottery. The draftees provided over half the total of 4.7 million Americans who were issued a uniform during the war. Of these, more than 2 million were transported overseas to join the British and the French in the trenches on the Western Front.

African Americans. Racial segregation applied to the army as it did to civilian life. Almost 400,000 African Americans served in World War I in segregated units. Only a few were permitted to be officers, and all were barred from the Marine Corps. Nevertheless, W. E. B. Du Bois believed that the record of service by African Americans, fighting to "make the world safe for democracy," would earn them equal rights at home when the war ended. (His hopes, however, would be bitterly disappointed.)

Effects on American Society

All groups in American society—business and labor, women and men, immigrants and native-born—were required to adjust to the unusual demands of a wartime economy.

More jobs for women. As men were drafted into the army, the jobs they vacated were often taken by women, thousands of whom entered the workforce for the first time. Their contributions to the war effort, both as volunteers and wage earners, finally convinced President Wilson and Congress to support the Nineteenth Amendment.

Migration of Mexicans and African Americans. Job opportunities in wartime America, together with the upheavals of the revolution in Mexico, caused thousands of Mexicans to cross the border to work in agriculture and mining. Most were employed in the Southwest, but a significant number also traveled to the Midwest for factory jobs. African Americans also took advantage of job opportunities opened up by the war and migrated north.

Fighting the War

By the time the first U.S. troops were shipped overseas in late 1917, millions of European soldiers on both sides had already been killed by murderous artillery barrages, machine-gun fire, and poison gas attacks. A second revolution in Russia by Bolsheviks (or Communists) took that nation out of the war. With no Eastern Front to divide its forces, Germany could now concentrate on one all-out push to break through Allied lines in France.

Naval Operations

Germany's policy of unrestricted submarine warfare was having its intended effect. Merchant ships bound for Britain were being sunk at a staggering rate: 900,000 tons of shipping was lost in just one month (April 1917). U.S. response to this Allied emergency was to undertake a record-setting program of ship construction. The U.S. Navy also implemented a convoy system of armed escorts for groups of merchant ships. By the end of 1917, the system was working well enough to ensure that Britain and France would not be starved into submission.

American Expeditionary Force

Unable to imagine the grim realities of trench warfare, U.S. troops were eager for action. The idealism of both the troops and the public is reflected in the popular song of George M. Cohan that many were singing:

> Over there, over there,
> Send the word, send the word over there
> That the Yanks are coming,
> The Yanks are coming,
> The drums rum-tumming ev'ry where—

The American Expeditionary Force (AEF) was commanded by General John J. Pershing. The first U.S. troops to see action were used to plug weaknesses in the French and British lines, but by the summer of 1918, as American forces arrived by the hundreds of thousands, the AEF assumed independent responsibility for one segment of the Western Front.

Last German offensive. Enough U.S. troops were in place in the spring of 1918 to hold the line against the last ferocious assault by German forces. At Château-Thierry on the Marne River, Americans stopped the German advance (June 1918) and struck back with a successful counterattack at Belleau Wood.

Drive to victory. In August, September, and October, an Allied offensive along the Meuse River and through the Argonne Forest (the Meuse–Argonne offensive) succeeded in driving an exhausted German army backward toward the German border. U.S. troops participated in this drive at St. Mihiel—the southern sector of the Allied line. On November 11, 1918, the Germans signed an armistice in which they agreed to surrender their arms, give up much of their navy, and evacuate occupied territory.

U.S. casualties. After only a few months of fighting, U.S. combat deaths totaled nearly 49,000. Many more thousands died of disease, including a flu epidemic in the training camps, bringing the total U.S. fatalities in World War I to 112,432.

Making the Peace

During the war, Woodrow Wilson never lost sight of his ambition to shape the peace settlement when the war ended. In January 1917 he had said that the United States would insist on a "peace without victory." A year later (January 1918), he presented to Congress a detailed list of war aims, known as the Fourteen Points.

The Fourteen Points

Several of the president's Fourteen Points related to specific territorial questions: for example, the return of Alsace and Lorraine to France and the German evacuation of Belgium in the west and of Romania and Serbia in the east. Of greater significance were the following broad principles for securing the peace:

- Recognition of freedom of the seas
- An end to the practice of making secret treaties
- Reduction of national armaments
- An "impartial adjustment of all colonial claims"
- Self-determination for the various nationalities within the Austro-Hungarian empire
- "A general association of nations ... for the purpose of affording mutual guarantees of political independence and territorial integrity to great and small states alike"

The last point was the one that Wilson valued the most. The international peace association that he envisioned would soon be named the League of Nations.

The Treaty of Versailles

The peace conference following the armistice took place in the Palace of Versailles outside Paris, beginning in January 1919. Every nation that had fought on the Allied side in the war was represented. Before this, no U.S. president had ever traveled abroad to attend a diplomatic conference, but to defend his Fourteen Points, President Wilson decided that his personal participation at Versailles was vital. Republicans criticized him for being accompanied to Paris by several Democrats, but only one Republican, whose advice was never sought.

The Big Four. Other heads of state at Versailles made it clear that their nations wanted both revenge against Germany and compensation in the form of indemnities and territory. They did not share Wilson's idea of a peace without victory. David Lloyd George of Great Britain, Georges Clemenceau of France, and Vittorio Orlando of Italy met with Wilson almost daily as the Big Four. After months of argument, the president reluctantly agreed to compromise on most of his Fourteen Points. He insisted, however, that the other delegations accept his plan for a League of Nations.

Peace terms. When the peace conference adjourned in June 1919, the Treaty of Versailles included the following terms:

1. Germany was disarmed and stripped of its colonies in Asia and Africa. It was also forced to admit guilt for the war, accept French occupation of the Rhineland for 15 years, and pay a huge sum of money in reparations to Great Britain and France.

2. Applying the principle of self-determination, territories once controlled by Germany, Austria-Hungary, and Russia were taken by the Allies, independence was granted to Estonia, Latvia, Lithuania, Finland, and Poland, and the new nations of Czechoslovakia and Yugoslavia were established.

3. Signers of the treaty would join an international peacekeeping organization, the League of Nations. Article X of the covenant (charter) of the League called on each member nation to stand ready to protect the independence and territorial integrity of other nations.

The Battle for Ratification

Returning to the United States, President Wilson had to win approval of two-thirds of the Senate for all parts of the Treaty of Versailles, including the League of Nations covenant. Republican senators raised objections to the League, arguing that U.S. membership in such a body might interfere with U.S. sovereignty and might also cause European nations to interfere in the Western Hemisphere (a violation of the Monroe Doctrine).

Increased partisanship after the war. Wilson was partly to blame for his trouble in winning Senate ratification. He had made the mistake in October 1918 of asking the American people to vote Democratic in the midterm elections as an act of patriotic loyalty. This political appeal had backfired badly. In the 1918 election, Republicans had won a solid majority in the House and a majority of two in the Senate. Now in 1919 Wilson needed Republican cooperation in the Senate for the Treaty of Versailles to be ratified. Instead, he faced the determined hostility of a leading Senate Republican, Henry Cabot Lodge.

EUROPE AFTER WORLD WAR I (1919)

Opponents: irreconcilables and reservationists. Senators opposed to the Treaty of Versailles were divided into two groups. The irreconcilable faction, consisting of about a dozen Republican senators, could not accept U.S. membership in the League, no matter how the covenant was worded. The reservationist faction, a larger group led by Senator Lodge, said they could accept the League if certain reservations were added to the covenant. Wilson had the option of either accepting Lodge's reservations or fighting for the treaty as it stood. He chose to fight.

Wilson's western tour and breakdown. Believing that his policy could prevail if he could personally rally public support, Wilson boarded a train and went on an arduous speaking tour to the West to make speeches for the League of Nations. On September 25, 1919, he collapsed after delivering a speech in Colorado. He returned to Washington and a few days later suffered a massive stroke from which he never fully recovered.

Rejection of the treaty. The Senate voted twice on the treaty question in November 1919. The treaty was defeated both times, with and without reservations. In 1920, a number of Democrats joined the reservationist Republicans in voting for the treaty *with* reservations. The ailing Wilson directed his loyal supporters to reject any reservations, and they joined with the irreconcilables in defeating the treaty.

Not until after Wilson left office in 1921 did the United States officially end the war and make a separate peace with Germany. It never ratified the Treaty of Versailles, nor did it ever join the League of Nations.

Postwar Problems

Americans had trouble adjusting from the patriotic fervor of wartime to the economic and social stresses of postwar uncertainties.

Demobilization

During the war, 4 million American men had been taken from civilian life and the domestic economy. Now, suddenly, they were back home and out of uniform. Not all the returning soldiers could find jobs right away, but many who did took employment from the women and African Americans who, for a short time, had thrived on war work. The business boom of wartime also went flat, as factory orders for war production fell off. With European farm products back on the market, U.S. farmers suffered from falling prices. In the cities, consumers went on a buying spree leading to inflation and a short boom in 1920. The spree did not last. In 1921, business plunged into a recession, and 10 percent of the American workforce was unemployed.

The Red Scare

In 1919, there was widespread unhappiness with the peace process and also growing fears of socialism fueled by the Communist takeover in Russia and labor unrest at home. The anti-German hysteria of the war years turned suddenly into anti-Communist hysteria known as the Red Scare.

Palmer raids. A series of unexplained bombings caused Attorney General A. Mitchell Palmer to establish a special office under J. Edgar Hoover to gather information on radicals. Palmer also ordered mass arrests of anarchists, Socialists, and labor agitators. From November 1919 through January 1920, over 6,000 people were arrested, based on limited criminal evidence. Most of the suspects were foreign born, and 500 of them, including the outspoken radical Emma Goldman, were deported.

The scare faded almost as quickly as it arose. Palmer warned of huge riots on May Day, 1920, but they never took place. His loss of credibility, coupled with rising concerns about civil liberties, caused the hysteria to recede.

Labor Conflict

In a nation that valued free enterprise and rugged individualism, a large part of the American public regarded unions with distrust. Their antiunion attitude softened during the Progressive era. Factory workers and their unions were offered a square deal under Theodore Roosevelt and protection from lawsuits under the Clayton Antitrust Act of 1914. During the war, unions made important gains. In the postwar period, however, a series of strikes in 1919 as well as fear of revolution turned public opinion against unions.

Strikes of 1919. The first major strike of 1919 was in Seattle in February. Some 60,000 unionists joined shipyard workers in a peaceful strike for higher pay. Troops were called out, but there was no violence. In Boston, in September, police went on strike to protest the firing of a few police officers who tried to unionize. Massachusetts Governor Calvin Coolidge sent in the National Guard to break the strike. Also in September, workers for the U.S. Steel Corporation struck. State and federal troops were called out and, after considerable violence, the strike was broken in January 1920.

Race Riots

The migration of African Americans to northern cities during the war increased racial tensions. Whites resented the increased competition for jobs and housing. During the war, race riots had erupted, the largest in East St. Louis, Illinois, in 1917. In 1919, racial tensions led to violence in many cities. The worst riot was in Chicago, where 40 people were killed and 500 were injured. Conditions were no better in the South, as racial prejudice and fears of returning African American soldiers led to an increase in racial violence and lynchings by whites.

HISTORICAL PERSPECTIVES: WILSON'S DECISION FOR WAR

Analysis of U.S. involvement in World War I focuses on two questions: (1) Why did the United States go to war, and (2) How did the peace treaty fail? Central to answering both questions is an understanding of the leadership and personality of Woodrow Wilson. Historical interpretations of Wilson from the 1920s to our own times are widely divergent.

Less than ten years after the war ended, revisionist historians led by Harry Elmer Barnes offered highly critical studies of Wilson's policies and motives. They argued that Wilson had strong pro-British sympathies, that his policies favored Britain throughout the period of neutrality, and that the interests of U.S. bankers and arms manufacturers in making war profits were ultimately behind Wilson's decision for war. This critical view of Wilson remained popular through much of the 1930s when a majority of Americans looked back upon World War I as a tragic mistake.

In the 1940s, after U.S. entry into World War II, historians adopted a "realist" perspective on Wilson. They now saw the decision for war as a necessary and unavoidable response to German submarine attacks. They also looked positively on Wilson's commitment to the League of Nations as a pioneering step toward the formation of the United Nations in 1945. The diplomat and historian George F. Kennan argued that Wilson was a realist in foreign policy, who recognized the dire consequences to U.S. security if Germany were permitted to overthrow the balance of power in Europe.

Arthur S. Link, a leading biographer of Wilson, has portrayed him as a gifted leader who responded appropriately to both British and German violations of U.S. neutral rights and who was forced by events outside his control into a war he did not want. Link also believes that the primary motivation for Wilson's war message of 1917 was his desire for the United States to play a leading role in the peacemaking process.

Other historians, including Arno J. Mayer and Gordon Levin, believe that Wilson skillfully combined his democratic ideals with consideration for U.S. economic and strategic interests. They point out how the president's efforts to ensure free trade and self-determination and to end colonialism and militarism served the purpose of advancing liberal capitalism. According to Levin, Wilson's motivations went beyond economics. His championing of the League of Nations transcended narrow U.S. self-interest and reflected a vision of a new world order based on collective security.

KEY NAMES, EVENTS, AND TERMS

neutrality	mobilization	Big Four
submarine warfare	George Creel	David Lloyd George
Lusitania	war agencies	Georges Clemenceau
Sussex pledge	Espionage Act (1917)	Vittorio Orlando
Allied powers	Sedition Act (1918)	League of Nations
Central Powers	*Schenck v. United States*	Henry Cabot Lodge
propaganda	Selective Service Act	reservationists
preparedness	Bolsheviks	irreconcilables
Jeannette Rankin	American Expeditionary	Red Scare
Edward House	Force	Palmer raids
Zimmermann telegram	Fourteen Points	Emma Goldman
Russian Revolution	Treaty of Versailles	strikes; race riots

MULTIPLE-CHOICE QUESTIONS

1. "German submarine warfare was the single most important factor in causing the United States to enter World War I."

   Evidence supporting this position includes all of the following EXCEPT

   (A) the sinking of the *Lusitania*

   (B) the Zimmermann Telegram

   (C) the *Sussex* pledge

   (D) Wilson's decision to break off diplomatic relations with Germany

   (E) Wilson's war message to Congress, April 1917

2. Which of the following was NOT involved in Woodrow Wilson's decision to ask Congress for a declaration of war?

   (A) the influence of Henry Cabot Lodge

   (B) the Russian Revolution

   (C) Germany's autocratic government

   (D) sympathy for the democracies of Britain and France

   (E) Germany's plans for military victory

3. The generalization BEST supported by information in the graph is that

   (A) World War I had little effect on U.S. government finances

   (B) the U.S. government financed its participation in World War I entirely from tax receipts

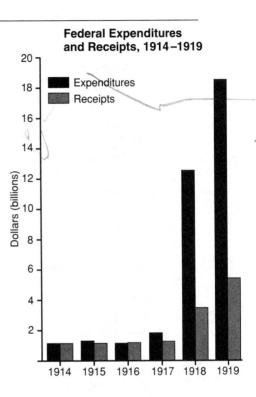

Federal Expenditures and Receipts, 1914–1919

- Expenditures
- Receipts

Dollars (billions)

1914 1915 1916 1917 1918 1919

   (C) from 1914 to 1919, the U.S. government debt increased dramatically

   (D) the U.S. government paid for war costs chiefly by selling bonds

   (E) total U.S. expenditures in the years 1917 and 1918 exceeded $20 billion

4. Which of the following could NOT be an explanation for Woodrow Wilson's reelection in 1916?

   (A) Henry Cabot Lodge's opposition to the League of Nations

(B) the Democratic campaign slogan: "He kept us out of war."

(C) prosperity resulting from increased exports to Britain

(D) Wilson's policy of neutrality

(E) a decline in support for the Socialist party

5. Which of the following is a correct statement about the United States during the years 1919 and 1920?

(A) The Democratic party controlled the White House and Congress.

(B) Republicans were united in their opposition to the Treaty of Versailles.

(C) Socialism and labor unions gained respect from the majority.

(D) The president was partially incapacitated by illness.

(E) There was a marked improvement in race relations.

6. Those who question whether U.S. policy from 1914–1916 was truly neutral point to

(A) the sinking of unarmed ships by German submarines

(B) the president's prejudices on racial issues

(C) increased U.S. trade with Britain and France

(D) the reelection of President Wilson

(E) Germany's secret diplomacy with Mexico

7. The Treaty of Versailles was defended by President Wilson on the grounds that

(A) large war reparations would satisfy the Allies

(B) it represented the best thinking of the world's political leaders

(C) it provided for a League of Nations committed to preserving the peace

(D) Germany deserved to be treated harshly

(E) there was nothing wrong with the treaty

8. Which of the following was a major effect of World War I on American society in 1917 and 1918?

(A) migration of African Americans to the North

(B) reduction in income taxes

(C) increase in amount of consumer goods

(D) increase in unemployment rate

(E) entry of large numbers of women into the military

9. A historian writing about Woodrow Wilson's foreign policy after the Armistice would be LEAST interested in examining

(A) the Zimmerman Telegram

(B) the Treaty of Versailles

(C) the covenant of the League of Nations

(D) the memoirs of Henry Cabot Lodge

(E) Senate debates of 1919

10. Going into war, Wilson said: "The world must be made safe for democracy." Someone wishing to argue that democracy in the United

States was *less* safe after World War I would point to

(A) the Senate debate on the Treaty of Versailles

(B) Wilson's speeches for the League of Nations

(C) the Red Scare

(D) the Republican control of Congress

(E) adoption of the Nineteenth Amendment

ESSAY QUESTIONS

1. How did German policy from January 1917 onward cause the United States to declare war?

2. Discuss how President Wilson could argue that his foreign policy was still committed to peace after he asked Congress for a declaration of war.

3. Assess the influence of United States' involvement in World War I on TWO of the following:

African Americans   women

civil liberties   business

4. To what extent were Woodrow Wilson's illness and his refusal to compromise responsible for the defeat of the Treaty of Versailles in the U.S. Senate?

5. Compare and contrast U.S. foreign policy from 1914–1917 with U.S. foreign policy from 1801–1812.

DOCUMENT-BASED QUESTION (DBQ)

In your answer to the following question, write an essay that integrates your interpretations of Documents A–H *and* your knowledge of history.

"The ideals used to justify U.S. involvement in World War I disguised the real reasons for Wilson's change in policy from neutrality to war and, in fact, violated the traditional values of the American nation."

Assess the reasons for the change in U.S. policy in 1917, AND whether these reasons were consistent with traditional American values.

DOCUMENT A.

Now, the real significance of this [campaign for preparedness] is that we have all at once, in the midst of a terrifying cataclysm, abjured our faith in many things American. We no longer believe, as for 140 years, in the moral power of an America unarmed and unafraid; we believe suddenly that the influence of the United States is to be measured only by the numbers of our soldiery and our dreadnoughts—our whole history to the contrary notwithstanding.

Next, the preparedness policy signifies an entire change in our attitude toward the military as to whom we inherited from our forefathers suspicions and distrust. A cardinal principle of our polity has always been the subordination of the military to the civil authority as a necessary safeguard for the republic.

Oswald Garrison Villard,
Annals of the American Academy of
Political and Social Science, July 1916

DOCUMENT B.

Value of United States Imports and Exports, 1914–1920

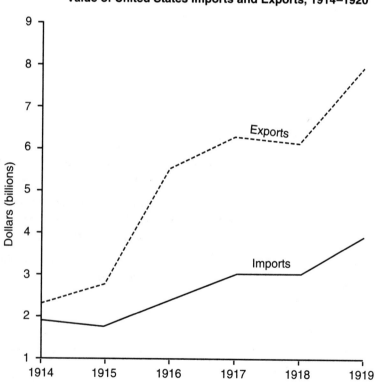

U.S. Bureau of the Census, *Historical Statistics of the United States,* Part 1, 1975.

DOCUMENT C.

We are glad, now that we see the facts with no veil of false pretense about them, to fight thus for the ultimate peace of the world and for the liberation of its peoples, the German peoples included: for the rights of nations great and small and the privilege of men everywhere to choose their way of life and of obedience. The world must be made safe for democracy. Its peace must be planted upon the tested foundations of political liberty. We have no selfish ends to serve. We desire no conquest, no dominion. We seek no indemnities for ourselves, no material compensation for the sacrifices we shall freely make. We are but one of the champions of the rights of mankind. We shall be satisfied when those rights have been made as secure as the faith and the freedom of nations can make them.

President Woodrow Wilson,
War Message to Congress, April 2, 1917

DOCUMENT D.

We are taking a step today that is fraught with untold danger. We are going into war upon the command of gold. We are going to run the risk of sacrificing millions of our countrymen's lives in order that other countrymen may coin their lifeblood into money. . . . We are about to do the bidding of wealth's terrible mandate. By our act we will make millions of our countrymen suffer, and the consequences of it may well be that millions of our brethren must shed their lifeblood, millions of broken-hearted women must weep, millions of children must suffer with cold, and millions of babes must die from hunger, and all because we want to preserve the commercial right of American citizens to deliver munitions of war to belligerent nations.

Senator George W. Norris,
Speech in the U.S. Senate, April 4, 1917

DOCUMENT E.

Corbis-Bettmann

DOCUMENT F.

. . . Tolerance arises from the existence of varying types of doers, all willing to respect one another's special competence. It is not too extreme to assert that in wartime (as in peacetime) some of the most heroic deeds are performed by those who do not (and, if called upon, would not) take up arms in defense of the cause. There are other forms of bravery than the purely military one. Let us be reasonable.

In bringing the gift of freedom to the distant unemancipated, shall we betray so precious a cause by brute denial of freedom to those of our own blood and tradition, to our own freedom lovers within the gate? What a sorry, tragical miscarriage of wisdom!

Norman Thomas,
The New Republic, May 26, 1917

DOCUMENT G.

We ask that good Americans . . . uphold the hands of the government at every point efficiently and resolutely against our foreign and domestic foes, and that they constantly spur the government to speedier and more effective action. Furthermore, we ask that, where government action cannot be taken, they arouse an effective and indignant public opinion against the enemies of our country, whether these enemies masquerade as pacifists, or proclaim themselves the enemies of our allies, or act through organizations such as the I.W.W. and the Socialist Party machine, or appear nakedly as the champions of Germany. Above all, we ask that they teach our people to spurn any peace save the peace of overwhelming victory in the war to which we have set our hands.

Theodore Roosevelt,
Pledge of Loyalty, September 11, 1917

DOCUMENT H.

We entered this war because violations of right had occurred which touched us to the quick and made the life of our own people impossible unless they were corrected and the world secured once for all against their recurrence. What we demand in this war, therefore, is nothing peculiar to ourselves. It is that the world be made fit and safe to live in; and particularly that it be made safe for every peace-loving nation which, like our own, wishes to live its own life, determine its own institutions, be assured of justice and fair dealings by the other peoples of the world, as against force and selfish aggression. All the peoples of the world are in effect partners in this interest, and for our own part we see very clearly that unless justice be done to others it will not be done to us.

Woodrow Wilson,
Speech to Congress on the Fourteen Points, January 8, 1918

A NEW ERA: THE 1920s

My candle burns at both ends;
It will not last the night;
But ah, my foes, and oh, my friends—
It gives a lovely light!

Edna St. Vincent Millay, "First Fig," 1920

The armistice ending World War I was two years in the past in November 1920 when the American people—women as well as men—went to the polls to cast their votes for president. Their choice was between two men from Ohio: Governor James Cox, a Democrat who urged the adoption of the League of Nations, and Senator Warren G. Harding, a Republican who was unclear about where he stood on every issue. The only memorable phrase in Harding's campaign was his assertion that the American people wanted a "return to normalcy." Harding apparently was right, because he was elected by a landslide. It was a sign that the idealism and activism that had characterized the prewar years of the Progressive era were over.

Republican Control

Through the 1920s, three Republican presidents would control the executive branch. Congress too was solidly Republican through a decade in which U.S. business boomed, while farmers and unions struggled.

Business Doctrine

The great leader of the progressive wing of the Republican party, Theodore Roosevelt, died in 1919. This loss, combined with public disillusionment over the war, allowed the return of the old-guard (conservative) Republicans. Unlike the Republicans of the Gilded Age, however, Republican leadership in the 1920s did not preach laissez-faire economics but rather accepted the idea of limited government regulation as an aid to stabilizing business. The regulatory commissions established in the Progressive era were now administered by appointees who were more sympathetic to business than to the general public. The prevailing idea of the Republican party was that the nation would benefit if business and the pursuit of profits took the lead in developing the economy.

470

The Presidency of Warren Harding

Harding had been a newspaper publisher in Ohio before entering politics. He was handsome and well-liked among the Republican political cronies with whom he regularly played poker. His abilities as a leader, however, were less than presidential. When the Republican national convention of 1920 deadlocked, the party bosses decided "in a smoke-filled room" to deliver the nomination to Harding as a compromise choice.

A few good choices. Harding recognized his limitations and hoped to make up for them by appointing able men to his cabinet. He appointed the former presidential candidate and Supreme Court justice Charles Evans Hughes to be secretary of state; the greatly admired former mining engineer and Food Administration leader Herbert Hoover to be secretary of commerce; and the Pittsburgh industrialist and millionaire Andrew Mellon to be secretary of the treasury. When the Chief Justice's seat on the Supreme Court became vacant, Harding filled it by appointing former President William Howard Taft.

The one surprise decision of Harding's presidency was his pardoning of Socialist leader Eugene Debs and winning his release from federal prison. (While a prisoner for violating the Espionage Act in wartime, Debs had nevertheless won 920,000 votes in the 1920 election as the Socialist candidate for president.) Harding's pardoning of Debs was prompted by the president's generous spirit—certainly not by ideology, since Harding was a conservative.

Domestic policy. Harding did little more than sign into law the measures adopted by the Republican Congress. He approved (1) a reduction in the income tax, (2) an increase in tariff rates under the Fordney-McCumber Tariff Act of 1922, and (3) establishment of the Bureau of the Budget, with procedures for all government expenditures to be placed in a single budget for Congress to review and vote on.

Scandals and death. Curiously, Harding's postwar presidency was marked by scandals and corruption similar to those that had occurred under an earlier postwar president, Ulysses S. Grant. Having appointed some excellent officials, Harding also selected a number of incompetent and dishonest men to fill important positions, including Secretary of the Interior Albert B. Fall and Attorney General Harry M. Daugherty. In 1924, Congress discovered that Fall had accepted bribes for granting oil leases near Teapot Dome, Wyoming. Daugherty also took bribes for agreeing not to prosecute certain criminal suspects.

Shortly before these scandals were uncovered, however, Harding died suddenly in August 1923 while traveling in the West. He was never implicated in any of the scandals.

The Presidency of Calvin Coolidge

Harding's vice president and successor, Calvin Coolidge, had won popularity in 1919 as the Massachusetts governor who broke the Boston police strike.

He was a man of few words who richly deserved the nickname "Silent Cal." Coolidge once explained why silence was good politics. "If you don't say anything," he said, "you won't be called on to repeat it." Also unanswerable was the president's sage comment: "When more and more people are thrown out of work, unemployment results." Coolidge summarized both his presidency and his era in the phrase: "The business of America is business."

The Election of 1924. After less than a year in office, Coolidge was the overwhelming choice of the Republican party as their presidential nominee in 1924. The Democrats nominated a conservative lawyer from West Virginia, John W. Davis, and tried to make an issue of the Teapot Dome scandal. Unhappy with conservative dominance of both parties, liberals formed a new Progressive party led by its presidential candidate, Robert La Follette of Wisconsin. Coolidge won the election easily, but the Progressive ticket did extremely well for a third party in a conservative era. La Follette received nearly 5 million votes, chiefly from discontented farmers and laborers.

Vetoes and inaction. Coolidge believed in limited government that stood aside while business conducted its own affairs. Little was accomplished in the White House except keeping a close watch on the budget. Cutting spending to the bone, Coolidge vetoed even the acts of the Republican majority in Congress. He would not allow bonuses for World War I veterans and vetoed a bill (the McNary-Haugen Bill of 1928) to help farmers cope with falling crop prices.

Hoover, Smith, and the Election of 1928

Coolidge declined to run for the presidency a second time. The Republicans therefore turned to an able leader with a spotless reputation, self-made millionaire and Secretary of Commerce Herbert Hoover. Hoover had served three presidents (Wilson, Harding, and Coolidge) in administrative roles but had never before campaigned for elective office. Nevertheless, in 1928, he was made the Republican nominee for president.

Hoover's Democratic opponent was the governor of New York, Alfred E. Smith. As a Roman Catholic and an opponent of prohibition, Smith appealed to many immigrant voters in the cities. Many Protestants, however, were openly prejudiced against Smith.

Republicans boasted of "Coolidge Prosperity," which Hoover promised to extend. He even suggested (ironically, as it proved) that poverty would soon be ended altogether. Hoover won in a landslide and even took a large number of the electoral votes in the South. In several southern states—including Texas, Florida, and Virginia—the taste of prosperity and general dislike for Smith's religion outweighed the voters' usual allegiance to the Democratic party.

Mixed Economic Development

Politics took a backseat in the 1920s, as Americans concentrated on adapting to economic growth and social change. The decade began with a brief postwar recession (1921), entered a lengthy period of business prosperity (1922–1928), and ended in economic disaster (October 1929) with the nation's worst stock market crash. During the boom years, unemployment was generally below 4 percent. The standard of living for most Americans improved significantly. Indoor plumbing and central heating became commonplace. By 1930, two-thirds of all homes had electricity. Real income for both the middle class and the working class increased substantially.

The prosperity, however, was far from universal. In fact, during the 1920s as many as 40 percent of U.S. families in both rural and urban areas had incomes in the poverty range—they struggled to live on less than $1,500 a year. Farmers in particular did not share in the booming economy.

Causes of Business Prosperity

The business boom—led by a spectacular rise of 64 percent in manufacturing output between 1919 and 1929—resulted from several factors.

Increased productivity. There was greater use of research, as with the expanded application of Frederick W. Taylor's time-and-motion studies and principles of scientific management. The manufacturing process was made more efficient by the adoption of improved methods of mass production. In 1914, Henry Ford had perfected a system for manufacturing automobiles by means of an assembly line. Instead of losing time moving around a factory as in the past, Ford's workers remained at one place all day and performed the same simple operation over and over again at rapid speed. In the 1920s, most major industries adopted the assembly line and realized major gains in worker productivity.

Energy technologies. Another cause of economic growth was the increased use of oil and electricity, although coal was still used for the railroads and to heat most homes. Increasingly, oil was used to power factories and to provide gasoline for the rapidly increasing numbers of automobiles. By 1930, oil would account for 23 percent of U.S. energy (up from a mere 3 percent in 1900). Electric motors in factories and new appliances at home increased electrical generation over 300 percent during the decade.

Government policy. Government at all levels in the 1920s favored the growth of big business by offering corporate tax cuts and doing almost nothing to enforce the antitrust laws of the Progressive era.

Farm Problems

Farmers did not share in the Coolidge prosperity. Their best years had been 1916–1918, when crop prices had been kept artificially high by (1) wartime demand in Europe and (2) the U.S. government's wartime policy of guaranteeing a minimum price for wheat and corn. When the war ended, so did farm prosperity. Farmers who had borrowed heavily to expand during the war were now left with a heavy burden of debt. New technologies (chemical fertilizers, gasoline tractors) helped farmers increase their production in the 1920s, but did not solve their problems. In fact, productivity only served to increase their debts, as growing surpluses produced falling prices.

Labor Problems

Wages rose during the 1920s, but the union movement went backward. Membership in unions declined 20 percent, partly because most companies insisted on an *open shop* (keeping jobs open to nonunion workers). Some companies also began to practice welfare capitalism—voluntarily offering their employees improved benefits and higher wages in order to remove the need for organizing unions. In the South, efforts to unionize the textile industry were violently resisted by police, state militia, and local mobs.

In an era that so strongly favored business, union efforts at strikes usually failed. The United Mine Workers, led by John L. Lewis, suffered setbacks in a series of violent and ultimately unsuccessful strikes in Pennsylvania, West Virginia, and Kentucky. Conservative courts routinely issued injunctions against strikes and nullified labor laws aimed at protecting workers' welfare.

A New Culture

The Census of 1920 reported that, for the first time, more than half of the American population lived in urban areas. The culture of the cities was based on popular tastes, morals, and habits of mass consumption that were increasingly at odds with the strict religious and moral codes of rural America.

The Jazz Age

High school and college youth expressed their rebellion against their elders' culture by dancing to jazz music. Brought north by African American musicians, jazz became a symbol of the "new" and "modern" culture of the cities. The proliferation of phonographs and radios made this new style of music available to a huge (and chiefly youthful) public.

Consumerism

Electricity in their homes enabled millions of Americans to purchase the new consumer appliances of the decade—refrigerators, vacuum cleaners, and washing machines. Automobiles became more affordable and sold by the millions, making the horse-and-buggy era a thing of the past. Advertising expanded as business found that consumers' demand for new products could be manipulated by appealing to their desires for status and popularity. Stores increased sales of the new appliances and automobiles by allowing customers to buy on credit. Chain stores proliferated. Their greater variety of products were attractively displayed and often priced lower than the neighborhood stores, which they threatened to displace.

Impact of the automobile. More than anything else, the automobile changed the pattern of American life. By 1929, a total of 26.5 million automobiles were registered, compared to 1.2 million in 1913. The enormous increase in automobile sales meant that, by the end of the decade, there was an average of nearly one car per American family. In economic terms, the production of automobiles replaced the railroad industry as the key promoter of economic growth. Other industries—steel, glass, rubber, gasoline, and highway construction—now depended on automobile sales. In social terms, the automobile affected all that Americans did: shopping, traveling for pleasure, commuting to work, even courting (or "dating") the opposite sex. Of course, there were new problems as well: traffic jams in the cities, injuries and deaths on roads and highways.

Entertainment. Newspapers had once been the only medium of mass communication and entertainment. In the 1920s, a new medium—the radio—suddenly appeared. The first commercial radio station went on the air in 1920 and broadcast music to just a few thousand listeners. By 1930 there were over 800 stations broadcasting to 10 million radios—about a third of all U.S. homes. The organization of the National Broadcasting Company (NBC) in 1924 and the Columbia Broadcasting System (CBS) in 1927 provided networks of radio stations that enabled people from one end of the country to the other to listen to the same programs: news broadcasts, sporting events, soap operas, quiz shows, and comedies.

The movie industry centered in Hollywood, California, became big business in the 1920s. Going to the movies became a national habit in cities, suburbs, and small towns. Sexy and glamorous movie stars such as Greta Garbo and Rudolf Valentino were idolized by millions. Elaborate movie theater "palaces" were built for the general public. With the introduction of talking (sound) pictures in 1927, the movie industry reached new heights. By 1929, over 80 million tickets to the latest Hollywood movies were sold each week.

Popular heroes. In an earlier era, politicians like William Jennings Bryan, Theodore Roosevelt, and Woodrow Wilson had been popularly viewed as heroic figures. In the new age of radio and movies, Americans radically shifted their viewpoint and adopted as role models the larger-than-life personalities celebrated on the sports page and the movie screen. Every sport had its superstars who were nationally known. In the 1920s, people followed the knockouts of heavyweight boxer Jack Dempsey, the swimming records of Gertrude Ederle, the touchdowns scored by Jim Thorpe, the homeruns hit by Babe Ruth, and the golf tournaments won by Bobby Jones.

Of all the popular heroes of the decade, the most celebrated was a young aviator who, in 1927, thrilled the nation and the entire world by flying nonstop across the Atlantic from Long Island to Paris. Americans listened to the radio for news of Charles Lindbergh's flight and welcomed his return to the United States with ticker tape parades larger than the welcome given to the returning soldiers of World War I.

Gender Roles, Family, and Education

The passage of the Nineteenth Amendment did not change either women's lives or U.S. politics as much as had been anticipated. Voting patterns in the election of 1920 showed that women did not vote as a bloc, but adopted the party preferences of the men in their families. With few exceptions, for example, wives of Republican husbands voted Republican.

Women at home. The traditional separation of labor between men and women continued into the 1920s. Most middle-class women expected to spend their lives as homemakers and mothers. The introduction into the home of such laborsaving devices as the washing machine and vacuum cleaner eased but did not substantially change the daily routines of the homemaker.

Women in the labor force. Participation of women in the workforce remained about the same as before the war. Employed women usually lived in the cities, were limited to certain categories of jobs as clerks, nurses, teachers, and domestics, and received lower wages than men.

Revolution in morals. Probably the most significant change in the lives of young men and women of the 1920s was their revolt against sexual taboos. Some were influenced by the writings of the Austrian psychiatrist Sigmund Freud, who stressed the role of sexual repression in mental illness. Others, who perhaps had never heard of Freud, took to premarital sex as if it were—like radio and jazz music—one of the inventions of the modern age. Movies, novels, automobiles, and new dance steps (the fox-trot and the Charleston) also encouraged greater promiscuity. The use of contraceptives for birth control was still against the law in almost every state. Even so, the work of Margaret Sanger and other advocates of birth control achieved growing acceptance in the twenties.

A special fashion that set young people apart from older generations was the flapper look. Influenced by movie actresses as well as their own desires for independence, young women shocked their elders by wearing dresses hemmed at the knee (instead of the ankle), "bobbing" (cutting short) their hair, smoking cigarettes, and driving cars. High school and college graduates also took office jobs until they married. Then, as married women, they were expected to abandon the flapper look, quit their jobs, and settle down as wives and mothers.

Divorce. As a result of women's suffrage, state lawmakers were now forced to listen to feminists, who demanded changes in the divorce laws to permit women to escape abusive and incompatible husbands. Liberalized divorce laws were one reason that one in six marriages ended in divorce by 1930—a dramatic increase over the one-in-eight ratio of 1920.

Education. Widespread belief in the value of education, together with economic prosperity, stimulated more state governments to enact compulsory school laws. By the end of the 1920s, the number of high school graduates had doubled to over 25 percent of the school-age young adults.

Religion

Divisions among Protestants reflected the tensions in society between the traditional values of rural areas and the modernizing forces of the cities.

Modernism. A range of influences, including the changing role of women, the Social Gospel movement, and scientific knowledge, caused large numbers of Protestants to define their faith in new ways. Modernists took a historical and critical view of certain passages in the Bible and believed they could accept Darwin's theory of evolution without abandoning their religious faith.

Fundamentalism. Protestant preachers in rural areas condemned the modernists and taught that every word in the Bible must be accepted as literally true. A key point in fundamentalist doctrine was that creationism (the idea that God had created the universe in seven days, as stated in the Book of Genesis) explained the origin of all life. Fundamentalists blamed the liberal views of modernists for causing a decline in morals.

Revivalists on the radio. Ever since the Great Awakening of the early 1700s, there had been periodic religious revivals in America. Revivalists of the 1920s preached a fundamentalist message but did so for the first time making full use of the new instrument of mass communication, the radio. The leading radio evangelists were Billy Sunday, who drew large crowds as he attacked drinking, gambling, and dancing; and Aimee Semple McPherson, who condemned the twin evils of communism and jazz music from her pulpit in Los Angeles.

The Literature of Alienation

Scorning religion as hypocritical and bitterly condemning the sacrifices of wartime as a fraud perpetrated by money interests were the dominant themes of the leading writers of the postwar decade. This disillusionment caused the writer Gertrude Stein to call these writers a "lost generation." The novels of F. Scott Fitzgerald, Ernest Hemingway, and Sinclair Lewis, the poems of Ezra Pound and T. S. Eliot, and the plays of Eugene O'Neill expressed disillusionment with the ideals of an earlier time and with the materialism of a business-oriented culture. Fitzgerald and O'Neill took to a life of drinking, while Eliot and Hemingway expressed their unhappiness by moving into exile in Europe.

Art

The widely held belief in scientific efficiency and business was reflected in many areas. A new profession, industrial design, developed; it was devoted to making products look as well as they functioned. In architecture, Frank Lloyd Wright expanded on the idea of his mentor Louis Sullivan in applying *functionalism* (form follows function). Many architects followed this philosophy in building a generation of skyscrapers with little decoration. A more critical view of the impact of this new technology and urban life is found in the stark paintings of Edward Hopper and Georgia O'Keeffe.

Harlem Renaissance

By 1930, almost 20 percent of African Americans lived in the North, as migration from the South continued. In the North, African Americans still faced discrimination in housing and jobs, but for most, there was at least some improvement in their earnings and material standard of living. The largest African American community developed in the Harlem section of New York City. With a population of almost 200,000 by 1930, Harlem became famous in the 1920s for its concentration of talented actors, artists, musicians, and writers. So promising was their artistic achievement that it was referred to as the Harlem Renaissance.

Poets and musicians. The leading Harlem poets included Countee Cullen, Langston Hughes, James Weldon Johnson, and Claude McKay. Commenting on the African American heritage, their poems expressed a range of emotions, from bitterness and resentment to joy and hope.

The Jazz Age resulted from the broad popularity among whites and African Americans of jazz music and artists such as Duke Ellington and Louis Armstrong. African American artists received acclaim in many areas, including the great blues singer Bessie Smith, and the multitalented singer and actor Paul Robeson. Yet while they might perform before integrated audiences in Harlem, they often found themselves and their audiences segregated in much of the rest of the nation.

Marcus Garvey. In 1916, the United Negro Improvement Association (UNIA) was brought to Harlem from Jamaica by a charismatic immigrant, Marcus Garvey. Garvey advocated individual and racial pride for African Americans and developed political ideas of black nationalism. Going beyond the efforts of W. E. B. Du Bois, Garvey established an organization for black separatism, economic self-sufficiency, and a back-to-Africa movement. Garvey's sale of stock in the Black Star Steamship line led to federal charges of fraud. In 1925, he was tried, convicted, and jailed. Later, he was deported to Jamaica and his movement collapsed.

W. E. B. Du Bois and other African American leaders disagreed with Garvey's back-to-Africa idea but endorsed his emphasis on racial pride and self-respect. In the 1960s, Garvey's thinking helped to inspire a later generation to embrace the cause of black pride and nationalism.

Cultures in Conflict

The dominant social and political issues of the 1920s expressed sharp divisions in U.S. society between the young and the old, between urban modernists and rural fundamentalists, between prohibitionists and antiprohibitionists, and between nativists and the foreign-born.

Fundamentalism and the Scopes Trial

More than any other single event, a much-publicized trial in Tennessee focused the debate between religious fundamentalists in the rural South and modernists of the northern cities. Tennessee was one of several southern states that made it illegal to teach Darwin's theory of evolution in the public schools. To challenge the constitutionality of such laws, the American Civil Liberties Union persuaded a Tennessee biology teacher, John Scopes, to teach the theory of evolution to his high school class. For doing so, Scopes was duly arrested and brought to trial in 1925.

The trial. The entire nation followed the Scopes trial both in their newspapers and on the radio. Defending Scopes was the famous lawyer Clarence Darrow. Representing the fundamentalists was three-time Democratic candidate for president William Jennings Bryan, who testified as an expert on the Bible. In the most sensational moment of the trial, Bryan was made to look foolish by Darrow's clever questioning. Soon afterward, Bryan died of a stroke.

Aftermath. As expected, Scopes was convicted, but the conviction was later overturned on a technicality. Laws banning the teaching of evolution remained on the books for years, although they were rarely enforced. The northern press asserted that Darrow and the modernists had thoroughly discredited fundamentalism. To this day, however, the basic question of religion and the public schools remains controversial and unresolved.

Prohibition

Another controversy that helped define the 1920s concerned people's conflicting attitudes toward the Eighteenth Amendment. Wartime concerns to conserve grain and maintain a sober workforce moved Congress to pass this amendment, which strictly prohibited the manufacture and sale of alcoholic beverages, including liquors, wines, and beers. It was ratified in 1919. The adoption of the Prohibition amendment and a federal law enforcing it (the Volstead Act, 1919) were the culmination of many decades of crusading by temperance forces.

Defying the law. By no means did Prohibition stop people from drinking alcohol either in public places or at home. In fact, especially in the cities, it became fashionable to defy the law by going to clubs or bars known as speakeasies, where bootleg (smuggled) liquor was sold. City police were paid to look the other way. Even elected officials like President Harding served alcoholic drinks to guests. Liquors, beers, and wines were readily available from bootleggers who smuggled them from Canada or made them in their garages or basements.

Rival groups of gangsters, including a Chicago gang headed by Al Capone, fought for control of the lucrative bootlegging trade. Organized crime became big business. The millions made from the sale of illegal booze allowed the gangs to expand their other illegal activities involving prostitution, gambling, and narcotics.

Political discord and repeal. Most Republicans publicly supported the "noble experiment" of Prohibition (although in private, many politicians would drink). Democrats divided on the issue, with southerners supporting it and northern city politicians calling for repeal. Supporters of the Eighteenth Amendment pointed to declines in alcoholism and alcohol-related deaths, but as the years passed, they gradually weakened in the face of growing public resentment and clear evidence of increased criminal activity. With the coming of the Great Depression, economic arguments for repeal were added to the others. In 1933, the Twenty-first Amendment repealing the Eighteenth was ratified, and millions celebrated the new year by toasting the end of Prohibition.

Nativism

The world war had interrupted the flow of immigrants to the United States, but as soon as the war ended, immigration shot upward. Over a million foreigners entered the country between 1919 and 1921. Like the immigrants of the prewar period, the new arrivals were mainly Catholics and Jews from eastern and southern Europe. Once again, nativist prejudices of native-born Protestants were aroused. Workers feared competition for jobs. Isolationists wanted minimal contact with Europe and saw the immigrants as radicals who might foment revolution. In this climate of antiforeign reaction, public demands for restrictive legislation were quickly acted upon by Congress.

Quota laws. Congress passed two laws that severely limited immigration by setting quotas based on nationality. The first quota act of 1921 limited immigration to 3 percent of the number of foreign-born persons from a given nation counted in the 1910 Census (a maximum of 357,000). To ensure that the law would discriminate against immigrants from southern and eastern Europe, Congress passed a second quota act in 1924 that set quotas of 2 percent based on the Census of 1890 (before the arrival of most of the "new" immigrants). Although there were quotas for all European and Asian nationalities, the law chiefly restricted those groups considered "undesirable" by the nativists. By 1927, the quota for all Asians and eastern and southern Europeans had been limited to 150,000, with all Japanese immigrants barred. With these acts, the traditional United States policy of unlimited immigration ended.

Canadians and Latin Americans were exempt from restrictions. This fact enabled almost 500,000 Mexicans to migrate legally to the Southwest during the 1920s.

Case of Sacco and Vanzetti. Although liberal American artists and intellectuals were few in number, they were a vocal minority who protested against racist and nativist prejudices. They rallied to the support of two Italian immigrants, Nicola Sacco and Bartolomeo Vanzetti, who in 1921 had been convicted in a Massachusetts court of committing robbery and murder. Liberals protested that the two men were innocent, and that they had been accused, convicted, and sentenced to die simply because they were poor Italians and anarchists (who were against all government). After six years of appeals and national and international debates over the fairness of their trial, Sacco and Vanzetti were executed in 1927.

Ku Klux Klan

The most extreme expression of nativism in the 1920s was the resurgence of the Ku Klux Klan. Unlike the original Klan of the 1860s and 1870s, the new Klan founded in 1915 was as strong in the Midwest as in the South. Northern branches of the KKK directed their hostility not only against blacks but also against Catholics, Jews, foreigners, and suspected Communists. The new Klan used modern advertising techniques to grow to 5 million members by 1925. It drew most of its support from lower-middle-class white Protestants in small cities and towns.

Tactics. The Klan employed various methods for terrorizing and intimidating anyone targeted as "un-American." Dressed in white hoods to disguise their identity, Klan members would burn crosses and apply vigilante justice, punishing their victims with whips, tar and feathers, and even the hangman's noose. In its heyday in the early 1920s, the Klan developed strong political influence. In Indiana and Texas, its support became crucial for candidates hoping to win election to state and local offices.

Decline. At first, the majority of native-born white Americans appeared to tolerate the Klan because it vowed to uphold high standards of Christian morality and drive out bootleggers, gamblers, and adulterers. Beginning in 1923, however, investigative reports in the northern press revealed that fraud and corruption in the KKK were rife. In 1925, the leader of Indiana's Klan, Grand Dragon David Stephenson, was convicted of murder. After that, the Klan's influence and membership declined rapidly. Nevertheless, it continued to exist and remained a force for white supremacy into the 1960s.

Foreign Policy: The Fiction of Isolation

Despite U.S. refusal to join the League of Nations, it would be a mistake to characterize U.S. foreign policy in the postwar years as isolationist. It is certainly true that widespread disillusionment with the war, Europe's postwar problems, and communism in the Soviet Union (as Russia was renamed) made Americans fearful of being pulled into another foreign war. Nevertheless, the makers of U.S. foreign policy did not retreat to the isolationism of the Gilded Age. Instead, they actively pursued arrangements in foreign affairs that would advance American interests while also maintaining world peace.

Disarmament and Peace

The Republican presidents of the 1920s tried to promote peace and also scale back expenditures on defense by arranging treaties of disarmament. The most successful disarmament conference—and the greatest achievement of Harding's presidency—was held in Washington, D.C., in 1921.

Washington Conference (1921). Secretary of State Charles Evans Hughes initiated talks on naval disarmament, hoping to stabilize the size of the U.S. Navy relative to that of other powers and to resolve conflicts in the Pacific. Representatives to the Washington Conference came from Belgium, China, France, Great Britain, Italy, Japan, the Netherlands, and Portugal. Three agreements to relieve tensions resulted from the discussions:

1. Five-Power Treaty. Nations with the five largest navies agreed to maintain the following ratio with respect to their largest warships, or battleships: the United States, 5; Great Britain, 5; Japan, 3; France, 1.67; Italy, 1.67. Britain and the United States also agreed not to fortify their possessions in the Pacific, while no limit was placed on the Japanese.

2. Four-Power Treaty. The United States, France, Great Britain, and Japan agreed to respect one another's territory in the Pacific.

3. Nine-Power Treaty. All nine nations represented at the conference agreed to respect the Open Door policy by guaranteeing the territorial integrity of China.

Kellogg-Briand Pact. American women took the lead in a peace movement committed to outlawing future wars. (For her efforts on behalf of peace, Jane Addams was awarded the Nobel Peace Prize in 1931.) The movement achieved its greatest success in 1928 with the signing of a treaty arranged by U.S. Secretary of State Frank Kellogg and the French foreign minister Aristide Briand. Almost all the nations of the world signed the Kellogg-Briand Pact, which renounced the aggressive use of force to achieve national ends. This international agreement would prove ineffective, however, since it (1) permitted defensive wars and (2) failed to provide for taking action against violators of the agreement.

Business and Diplomacy

Republican presidents believed that probusiness policies brought prosperity at home and at the same time strengthened U.S. dealings with other nations. Thus, they found it natural to use diplomacy to advance American business interests in Latin America and other regions.

Latin America. Mexico's constitution of 1917 mandated government ownership of all that nation's mineral and oil resources. U.S. investors in Mexico feared that their properties might be confiscated. A peaceful resolution protecting their interests was negotiated by Coolidge's ambassador to Mexico, Dwight Morrow, in 1927.

Elsewhere in Latin America, U.S. troops remained in Nicaragua and Haiti but were withdrawn from the Dominican Republic in 1924. While U.S. military influence was reduced, the economic impact of the U.S. on its neighbors increased, as American investments in Latin America doubled between 1919 and 1929.

Middle East. The oil reserves in the Middle East were now recognized as a major source of potential wealth. British oil companies had a large head start in the region, but Secretary of State Hughes succeeded in winning oil-drilling rights for U.S. companies.

Tariffs. Passed by Congress in 1922, the Fordney-McCumber Tariff increased the duties on foreign manufactured goods by 25 percent. It was protective of U.S. business interests in the short run, but destructive in the long run. Because of it, European nations were slow to recover from the war and had difficulty repaying their war debts to the United States. They responded to the high U.S. tariffs by imposing tariffs of their own on American imports. Ultimately, these obstacles to international trade weakened the world economy and were one reason for the Great Depression.

War Debts and Reparations

Before World War I, the United States had been a debtor nation, importing more than it exported. It emerged from the war as a creditor nation, having lent more than $10 billion to the Allies. Harding and Coolidge insisted that Britain and France pay back every penny of their war debts. The British and French objected. They pointed out that they suffered much worse losses than the Americans during the war, that the borrowed money had been spent in the United States, and that high U.S. tariffs made it more difficult to pay the debts. To be sure, the Treaty of Versailles required Germany to pay $30 billion in reparations to the Allies. But how were Britain and France to collect this money? Germany was bankrupt, had soaring inflation, and was near anarchy.

Dawes Plan. Charles Dawes, an American banker who would become Coolidge's vice president, negotiated a compromise that was accepted by all sides in 1924. The Dawes Plan established a cycle of payments flowing from the United States to Germany and from Germany to the Allies. U.S. banks would lend Germany huge sums to rebuild its economy and pay reparations to Britain and France. In turn, Britain and France would use the reparations money to pay their war debts to the United States. This cycle helped to ease financial problems on both sides of the Atlantic. After the stock market crash of 1929, however, U.S. bank loans stopped and the prosperity propped up by the Dawes Plan collapsed.

Legacy. Ultimately, Finland was the only nation to repay its war debts in full. The unpaid debts of the other nations left bad feelings on all sides. Many Europeans resented what they saw as American greed, while Americans saw new reasons to follow an isolationist path in the 1930s.

HISTORICAL PERSPECTIVES: HOW CONSERVATIVE WERE THE 1920s?

Even to writers and historians of the time, the 1920s seemed to be a unique decade—a period of social fun and business boom wedged between two calamities, World War I and the Great Depression. Frederick Lewis Allen wrote about the decade as soon as it ended. In his popular history *Only Yesterday* (1931), Allen gave support to the ideas of the leading social critics of the 1920s, H. L. Mencken and Sinclair Lewis. He portrayed the period as one of narrow-minded materialism in which the middle class abandoned progressive reforms, embraced conservative Republican policies, and either supported or condoned reactionary forces: nativism, racism, and fundamentalism. The historian Arthur Schlesinger, Jr., generally accepted this view of the twenties, seeing it within the framework of his cyclical view of history. Schlesinger argued that the politics of the decade represented a conservative reaction to the liberal reforms of the Progressive era.

Revisionist historians questioned whether the 1920s truly was a sharp break with the Progressive past and argued that the period was a continuation of earlier protest movements such as Populism. Richard Hofstadter and other "consensus" writers distinguished between two middle classes: a new urban group with modern values and an older middle class with traditional values. William Leuchtenberg in *The Perils of Prosperity* (1958) portrayed the traditionalists as threatened by changes reflected in cultural pluralism and modern ideas.

A third assessment takes a more positive view of the traditionalists. Some historians, including Alan Brinkley in the 1980s, argue that people in the "old" middle class, including fundamentalists and nativists, were understandably trying to protect their own economic and social self-interests. At the same time, they were seeking to preserve individual and community freedom in face of the modernist movement toward centralized bureaucratic and national control. This effort to maintain local control and independence from big government is seen as continuing from the 1920s to the present.

Given the extreme and deeply felt differences between the modernists and the traditionalists, some historians have wondered why there was not more conflict in the twenties.

One explanation, which has grown from the 1960s to the present, is the importance of the *consumer culture*. Historians, including Stuart Ewen and Roland Marchand, have in diverse ways shown how the influence of growing materialism and prosperity caused people to accept increased bureaucratic control of their lives. They place varying emphasis on the ways in which material affluence, consumer goods, advertising, and a homogeneous mass culture have redefined the social and political values of the United States. While these historians differ greatly on the positive and negative influence of the consumer culture, its importance is evident. With this view, we come almost full circle to the assessments of Mencken, Lewis, and Allen of a society centered on materialism and consumption.

KEY NAMES, EVENTS, AND TERMS

Warren Harding	fundamentalism	Louis Armstrong
Fordney-McCumber Tariff Act (1922)	revivalists: Billy Sunday; Aimee Semple McPherson	Bessie Smith
Bureau of the Budget	Gertrude Stein	Paul Robeson
Teapot Dome	Lost Generation	Marcus Garvey
Calvin Coolidge	F. Scott Fitzgerald	Scopes trial
Herbert Hoover	Ernest Hemingway	Clarence Darrow
Alfred E. Smith	Sinclair Lewis	Prohibition; Volstead Act (1919)
business prosperity	Ezra Pound	organized crime
Henry Ford	T. S. Eliot	immigration quota laws (1921, 1924)
assembly line	Frank Lloyd Wright	Sacco and Vanzetti
open shop	functionalism	Ku Klux Klan
welfare capitalism	Edward Hopper	disarmament
jazz age	Georgia O'Keeffe	Washington Conference (1921)
consumerism: autos, radio, movies	Harlem Renaissance	Kellogg-Briand Treaty (1928)
Charles Lindberg	Countee Cullen	war debts
Sigmund Freud	Langston Hughes	reparations
Margaret Sanger	James Weldon Johnson	Dawes Plan (1924)
modernism	Claude McKay	
	Duke Ellington	

MULTIPLE-CHOICE QUESTIONS

1. All of the following were notable trends and movements of the 1920s EXCEPT
   (A) increase in union membership
   (B) increase in productivity
   (C) urbanization
   (D) consumerism
   (E) business prosperity

2. Which of the following was the LEAST important consideration in U.S. foreign policy during the 1920s?
   (A) repayment of debts by European nations
   (B) negotiating disarmament treaties
   (C) developing strong alliances
   (D) promoting worldwide peace efforts
   (E) promoting U.S. business interests

3. During the 1920s, the group who generally did NOT prosper were
   (A) owners of small businesses
   (B) farmers
   (C) Wall Street brokers
   (D) professionals
   (E) residents of western cities

4. Which of the following was the focus of a dispute between modernists and traditionists in the 1920s?
   (A) Ford assembly lines
   (B) Washington Conference
   (C) Scopes trial
   (D) Teapot Dome Scandal
   (E) welfare capitalism

5. The sentiment expressed in the cartoon on page 487 most directly influenced the passage of
   (A) laws restricting immigration
   (B) the Eighteenth Amendment
   (C) protective tariff legislation
   (D) antitrust laws
   (E) disarmament treaties

6. Which of the following had contrasting points of view on events and issues of the 1920s?
   (A) Calvin Coolidge—Herbert Hoover
   (B) Charles Lindbergh—Henry Ford
   (C) William Jennings Bryan—Clarence Darrow
   (D) Billy Sunday—Aimee Semple McPherson
   (E) Sinclair Lewis—F. Scott Fitzgerald

7. Which source would be most important to a historian investigating the effects of the protective tariff from 1922–1930?
   (A) memoirs of Henry Ford
   (B) Commerce Department statistics on imports and exports
   (C) editorial pages of major city newspapers
   (D) election data from the various states
   (E) encyclopedia articles on modern commerce

8. Prohibition led to all of the following EXCEPT
   (A) defiance of the law by large numbers of people

Corbis-Bettmann

(B) rise of organized crime

(C) divisions in the Democratic party

(D) widespread smuggling

(E) greater tolerance among temperance reformers

9. "We in America today are nearer to the final triumph over poverty than ever before in the history of any land." This statement by the presidential candidate Herbert Hoover in 1928 could BEST be supported by

(A) the speeches of Al Smith

(B) statistics on the U.S. automobile industry

(C) the novels of Sinclair Lewis

(D) graphs on farm income

(E) editorials on Sacco and Vanzetti

10. "Isolationism characterized U.S. foreign policy in the 1920s." Which of the following might be used to refute the above claim?

(A) Harding's championing of the League of Nations

(B) landslide victory of Herbert Hoover in 1928

(C) U.S. leadership in calling the Washington Conference

(D) U.S. military and naval buildup

(E) increased U.S. military intervention in Latin America

ESSAY QUESTIONS

1. Discuss, with respect to TWO of the following, the increase in social conflict during the economic prosperity of the 1920s:

   religious fundamentalism

   Ku Klux Klan

   Prohibition

   nativism

2. "Economic growth and an improved standard of living in the 1920s benefited only a minority of the American people." Argue either for or against the validity of this interpretation.

3. Discuss the factors that contributed to the rebirth and rapid growth of the Ku Klux Klan in the early 1920s.

4. Compare and contrast Woodrow Wilson's domestic policies with those of Calvin Coolidge.

5. Analyze the extent that TWO of the following reflect unilateral action taken by the United States in the 1920s to advance American interests and world peace:

   Kellogg-Briand Pact

   tariffs

   war debts and reparations

   Washington Conference

DOCUMENTS AND READINGS

The 1920s were marked by varied and intense social and cultural conflicts. The following readings represent a spectrum of opinion and advocacy, from a justification of the Ku Klux Klan to Margaret Sanger's arguments for birth control. No matter what the cause or question—be it immigration, race, or women's rights—the authors of these documents expressed religious and national ideals that had their origins in Puritanism and democratic rhetoric. Looking in the other direction, forward from the 1920s to our own time, the controversy over several of these issues continues unabated.

DOCUMENT A.　THE KLAN AND AMERICANISM

In the following excerpt from a magazine article, the Imperial Wizard of the Ku Klux Klan, Hiram W. Evans, justified his movement by appealing to traditional values of American patriotism and Protestant Christianity.

The greatest achievement so far has been to formulate, focus, and gain recognition for an idea—the idea of preserving and developing America first and chiefly for the benefit of the children of the pioneers who made America, and only and definitely along the lines of the purpose and spirit of those pioneers. The Klan cannot claim to have created this idea—it has long been a vague stirring in the souls of the plain people. But the Klan can fairly claim to have given it purpose, method, direction. . . .

Thus the Klan goes back to the American racial instincts, and to the common sense which is their first product, as the basis of its beliefs and methods. The fundamentals of our thought are convictions, not mere opinions. We are pleased that modern research is finding scientific backing for these convictions. We do not need them ourselves; we know that we are right in the same sense that a good Christian knows that he has been saved and that Christ lives—a thing which the intellectual can never understand. These convictions are no more to be argued about than is our love for our children; we are merely willing to state them for the enlightenment and conversion of others.

There are three of these great racial instincts, vital elements in both the historic and the present attempts to build an America which shall fulfill the aspirations and justify the heroism of the men who made the nation. These are the instincts of loyalty to the white race, to the traditions of America, and to the spirit of Protestantism, which has been an essential part of Americanism ever since the days of Roanoke and Plymouth Rock. They are condensed into the Klan slogan: "Native, white, Protestant supremacy."

Hiram W. Evans,
North American Review, 1926

DOCUMENT B.   DEFEATING RACE PREJUDICE

A major contributor to the Harlem Renaissance was James Weldon Johnson, a poet, college professor, and head of the NAACP for over ten years. In a magazine article in 1928, Johnson argued that white prejudice was being challenged for the first time by the artistic accomplishments of African Americans.

. . . [T]here is a common, widespread, and persistent stereotyped idea regarding the Negro, and it is that he is here only to receive; to be shaped into something new and unquestionably better. The common idea is that the Negro reached America intellectually, culturally, and morally empty, and that he is here to be filled—filled with education, filled with religion, filled with morality, filled with culture. In a word, the stereotype is that the Negro is nothing more than a beggar at the gate of the nation, waiting to be thrown the crumbs of civilization.

Through his artistic efforts the Negro is smashing this immemorial stereotype faster than he has ever done through any other method he has been able to use. He is making it realized that he is the possessor of a wealth of natural endowments and that he has long been a generous giver to America. He is impressing upon the national mind the conviction that he is an active and important force in American life; that he is a creator as well as a creature; that he has given as well as received; that he is the potential giver of larger and richer contributions.

In this way the Negro is bringing about an entirely new national conception of himself; he has placed himself in an entirely new light before the American people. I do not think it too much to say that through artistic achievement the Negro has found a means of getting at the very core of the prejudice against him by challenging the Nordic superiority complex. A great deal has been accomplished in this decade of "renaissance."

James Weldon Johnson,
Harper's, November, 1928

DOCUMENT C. *WOMEN AND BIRTH CONTROL*

During the 1920s, Margaret Sanger led the effort to make birth-control information available to women. The following reading is from one of her books on the subject.

The problem of birth control has arisen directly from the efforts of the feminine spirit to free itself from bondage. Woman herself has wrought that bondage through her reproductive powers, and while enslaving herself has enslaved the world. . . . Within her is wrapped up the future of the race—it is hers to make or mar. . . . For ages she has been deprived of the opportunity to meet this obligation. She is now emerging from her helplessness. Even as no one can share the suffering of the overburdened mother, so no one can do this work for her. Others may help, but she and she alone can free herself.

The basic freedom of the world is woman's freedom. A free race cannot be born of slave mothers. A woman enchained cannot choose but give a measure of that bondage to her sons and daughters. No woman can call herself free who does not own and control her body. No woman can call herself free until she can choose consciously whether she will or will not be a mother.

Margaret Sanger,
Woman and the New Race, 1920

DOCUMENT D.   *REFORMING THE DIVORCE LAWS*

The divorce rate almost doubled in the 20 years from 1909 to 1929. Proponents of reform argued that the laws should reflect the realities of failed marriages and not prolong the problems or sufferings of those involved.

Divorce by mutual consent does not necessarily mean that both parties are equally anxious for the decree, but it does mean that they have not parted angrily or furtively. Yet the latter is the [technique] prescribed by law. It would almost seem as though our lawmakers delighted in putting a premium upon indecency and cruelty. Which action, for instance, is the more decent: for a man to "light out" without warning to his wife, leaving her perhaps without sufficient funds, and exposed to the pity of all the neighbors, or for him to discuss his plans with her and break up the home in a dignified fashion?

The current legal theory seems to be that divorce is not to be allowed until one party—the presumably innocent one—shall have been deeply wounded. The underlying Puritanic principle would seem to be that no human being shall find his salvation in freedom until he has walked through the valley of the shadow of death. But is it not pitifully apparent that every man and woman—with the exception of the very shallow—who feels his marriage going to pieces, walks through the valley of the shadow of death? Why must the law, like a heartless surgeon, drive the knife still deeper?

Stephen Ewing,
Harper's Monthly, July 1928

ANALYZING THE DOCUMENTS

1. Why did the Klan slogan "Native, white, Protestant supremacy" draw support from millions of Americans in the years following World War I?

2. How would the views of James Weldon Johnson compare with those of (a) Booker T. Washington and (b) W. E. B. Du Bois?

3. What do you think Margaret Sanger's reaction would have been to the ideas about divorce expressed in Stephen Ewing's magazine article?

4. "Major social issues of the 1990s have their origins in the conflicts and controversies of the 1920s."

Drawing upon the documents, your impressions of contemporary life, and your knowledge of history, explain the extent to which you either agree or disagree with the above statement.

THE GREAT DEPRESSION
AND THE NEW DEAL,
1929–1939

Once I built a tower, to the sun.
Brick and rivet and lime,
Once I built a tower,
Now it's done,
Brother, can you spare a dime?

"Brother, Can You Spare a Dime?"
E. Y. Harburg and Jay Gorney, 1932

When the new Democratic president, Franklin D. Roosevelt, said in his 1933 inaugural address, "the only thing we have to fear is fear itself," he struck a note that the millions who listened to him on the radio could well understand. In 1933, after having experienced nearly four years of the worst economic depression in U.S. history, the American people were gripped by fear for their very survival.

In the past, banks and businesses had periodically plunged into a crisis, or "panic," that was usually of brief duration. In the previous century, there had been financial panics in 1819, 1837, 1857, 1873, and 1893. Only the last two of these economic crises had led to long-term depressions extending beyond a year. Usually, if banks closed for lack of funds or stock market prices dropped off suddenly, there would be a serious economic downturn for several months followed by recovery and eventual prosperity. These ups and downs were thought to be nothing more than the natural pulse of a free enterprise economy. They constituted what was called a business cycle.

This depression of the 1930s seemed much different. It lasted far longer, caused more business failures and unemployment, and affected more people— both of the middle class and the working class—than any other preceding period of hard times. This was in fact, not just an ordinary depression, but the *Great Depression.* Before it was over, two presidents—Herbert Hoover and Franklin Roosevelt—would devote 12 years to seeking the elusive path toward recovery.

Causes and Effects of the Depression, 1929–1933

What caused a spectacular business boom of the 1920s to collapse in October 1929?

Wall Street Crash

The ever-rising stock prices had become both a symbol and a source of wealth during the prosperous 1920s. A "boom" was in full force both in the United States and in the world economy in the late 1920s. On the stock exchange on Wall Street in New York City, stock prices had kept going up and up for 18 months from March 1928 to September 1929. On September 3, the Dow Jones Industrial Average of major stocks had reached an all-time high of 381. An average investor who bought $1,000 worth of such stocks at the time of Hoover's election (November 1928) would have doubled his or her money in less than a year. Millions of people did invest in the boom market of 1928—and millions lost their money in October 1929, when it collapsed.

Black Thursday and Black Tuesday. Although stock prices had fluctuated greatly for several weeks preceding the crash, the true panic did not begin until a Thursday in late October. On this Black Thursday—October 24, 1929—there was an unprecedented volume of selling on Wall Street, and stock prices plunged. The next day, hoping to stave off disaster, a group of bankers bought millions of dollars of stocks in an effort to stabilize prices. The strategy worked for only one business day, Friday. The selling frenzy resumed on Monday. On Black Tuesday, October 29, the bottom fell out, as millions of panicky investors ordered their brokers to sell, when there were practically no buyers to be found.

From that day on, prices on Wall Street kept going down and down. By late November, the Dow Jones index had fallen from its September high of 381 to 198. Three years later, stock prices would finally hit bottom at 41, less then one-ninth of their peak value.

Causes of the Crash

While the collapse of the stock market in 1929 may have triggered economic turmoil, it alone was not responsible for the Great Depression. The depression throughout the nation and the world was the result of a combination of factors that matured during the 1920s.

Uneven distribution of income. Wages had risen relatively little compared to the large increases in productivity and corporate profits. Economic success was not shared by all, as the top 5 percent of the richest Americans received over 33 percent of all income.

Stock market speculation. Many people in all economic classes believed that they could get rich by "playing the market." People were no longer investing their money in order to share in the profits of a company—they were speculating that the price of a stock would go up and that they could sell it for a quick profit. *Buying on margin* allowed people to borrow most of the cost of the stock, making down payments as low as 10 percent. Investors depended that the price of the stock would increase so that they could repay the loan. When stock prices dropped, the market collapsed, and many lost everything they had borrowed and invested.

Excessive use of credit. A belief of both consumers and business that the economic boom was permanent led to increased installment buying. Advertising stimulated consumers' desire for the exciting new appliances and cars that were being produced.

Overproduction of consumer goods. Business growth, aided by increased productivity and use of credit, had produced a volume of goods that workers with stagnant wages could not continue to purchase.

Weak farm economy. The prosperity of the 1920s never reached farmers, who had suffered from overproduction, high debt, and low prices since the end of World War I. As the depression continued through the 1930s, severe weather and a long drought added to farmers' difficulties.

Government policies. During the 1920s, the government had complete faith in business and did little to control or regulate it. Congress enacted high tariffs which protected U.S. industries but hurt farmers and international trade. Years of neglect and bad practices would prove difficult for the government to correct.

Global economic problems. Nations had become more interdependent because of international banking, manufacturing, and trade. Europe had never completely recovered from World War I, but the United States failed to recognize Europe's problems. It insisted that all of its wartime loans to European nations be repaid in full, but at the same time its tariff policies greatly reduced the sale of European goods in America. War reparations burdened Germany throughout the 1920s. Some relief came with U.S. loans under the Dawes Plan, but with the market collapse in 1929, these loans were suspended. Europe's difficulties contributed to the depression in the United States, which in turn became the worldwide Great Depression.

Effects

It is difficult to imagine the pervasive impact of the Great Depression. While in retrospect it can be seen that the economic decline reached bottom in 1932, complete recovery came only with the beginning of another world war, in 1939. The Great Depression's influence on American thinking and policies has even extended beyond the lifetimes of those who experienced it.

Various economic statistics serve as *indicators* that track the health of a nation's economy. The U.S. Gross National Product—the value of all the goods and services produced by the nation in one year—dropped from $104 billion to $56 billion in four years, while the nation's income declined by over 50

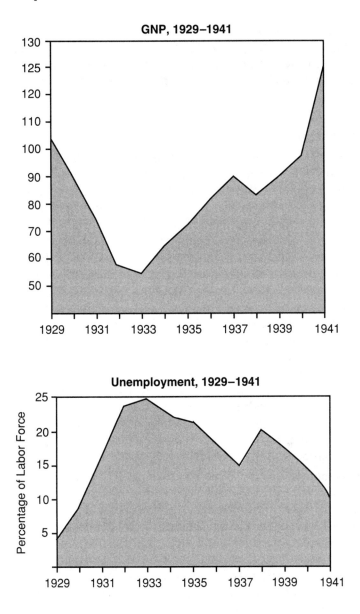

GNP, 1929–1941

Unemployment, 1929–1941

Percentage of Labor Force

percent. Some 20 percent of all banks closed, wiping out 10 million savings accounts. By 1933, the number of unemployed had reached 13 million people, or 25 percent of the workforce, not including farmers.

Politically, Republican domination of government was at an end. The power of the federal government would increase greatly, as the people accepted dramatic, far-reaching changes in policies.

The social effects of the depression were felt by all classes. Those who had never fully shared in the prosperity of the 1920s, such as farmers and African Americans, had increased difficulties. Poverty and homelessness increased, as did the stress on families, as people searched for work. Mortgage foreclosures and evictions became commonplace.

Hoover's Policies

At the time of the stock market crash, nobody could foresee how long the downward slide would last. President Hoover was wrong—but hardly alone—in thinking that prosperity would soon return. The president believed the nation could get through the difficult times if the people took his advice about exercising voluntary action and restraint. Hoover urged businesses not to cut wages, unions not to strike, and private charities to increase their efforts for the needy and the jobless. Until the summer of 1930, he hesitated to ask Congress for legislative action on the economy, afraid that government assistance to individuals would destroy their self-reliance. Gradually, President Hoover came to recognize the need for more direct government action. However, he took the traditional view that public relief should come from state and local governments, not the federal government.

Responding to a Worldwide Depression

Repercussions from the crash on Wall Street were soon felt in the financial centers of Europe. Through trade and the Dawes Plan for the repayment of war debts, European prosperity was closely tied to that of the United States. Hoover's first major decision concerning the international situation was one of the worst mistakes of his presidency.

Hawley-Smoot Tariff (1930). In June 1930, the president signed into law a schedule of tariff rates that was the highest in history. The Hawley-Smoot Tariff passed by the Republican Congress set tax increases ranging from 31 percent to 49 percent on foreign imports. Its political purpose was to satisfy U.S. business leaders who thought a higher tariff would protect their markets from foreign competition. In retaliation for the U.S. tariff, however, European countries enacted higher tariffs of their own against U.S. goods. The effect was to reduce trade for all nations, meaning that both the national and international economies sank further into depression.

Debt moratorium. By 1931, conditions became so bad both in Europe and the United States that the Dawes Plan for collecting war debts could no longer continue. Hoover therefore proposed a moratorium (suspension) on the payment of international debts. Britain and Germany readily accepted, but France balked. The international economy suffered from massive loan defaults, and banks on both sides of the Atlantic scrambled to meet the demands of the many depositors withdrawing their money.

Domestic Programs: Too Little, Too Late

By 1931, Hoover was convinced that some government action was needed to pull the U.S. economy out of its doldrums. He therefore supported and signed into law programs that offered assistance to indebted farmers and struggling businesses.

Federal Farm Board. The Farm Board was actually created in 1929, before the stock market crash, but its powers were later enlarged to meet the economic crisis. The board was authorized to help farmers stabilize prices by temporarily holding surplus grain and cotton in storage. The program, however, was much too modest to handle the continued overproduction of farm goods.

Reconstruction Finance Corporation (RFC). This federally funded, government-owned corporation was created by Congress early in 1932 as a measure for propping up faltering railroads, banks, life insurance companies, and other financial institutions. The president reasoned that emergency loans from the RFC would help to stabilize these key businesses. The benefits would then "trickle down" to smaller businesses and ultimately bring recovery. Democrats scoffed at this measure, saying it would only help the rich.

Despair and Protest

By 1932, millions of unemployed workers and impoverished farmers were in a state bordering on desperation. Some decided to take direct action to battle the forces that seemed to be crushing them.

Unrest on the farms. In many communities, farmers banded together to stop banks from foreclosing on their farms and evicting them from their homes. Farmers in the Midwest formed the Farm Holiday Association, which attempted to reverse the drop in prices by stopping the entire crop of grain harvested in 1932 from reaching the market. The effort collapsed after some violence.

Bonus march. Also in the desperate summer of 1932, a thousand unemployed World War I veterans marched to Washington, D.C., to demand immediate payment of the bonuses promised them at a later date (1945). They were eventually joined by thousands of other veterans who brought their wives and children and camped in improvised shacks near the Capitol. Congress failed to pass the bonus bill they sought. When two veterans were killed in a clash with police, Hoover ordered the army to break up the encampment. General Douglas MacArthur, the army's chief of staff, used tanks and tear gas to destroy the shantytown and drive the veterans from Washington. The incident caused many Americans to regard President Hoover as heartless and uncaring.

The Election of 1932

The depression's worst year, 1932, happened to be a presidential election year. The disheartened Republicans renominated Hoover, who warned that a Democratic victory would only result in worse economic problems.

Democrats. At their convention, the Democrats nominated New York Governor Franklin D. Roosevelt for president and Speaker of the House John Nance Garner of Texas for vice president. As a candidate, Roosevelt pledged a "new deal" for the American people, the repeal of Prohibition, aid for the unemployed, and cuts in government spending.

Results. In voters' minds, the only real issue was the depression, and which candidate—Hoover or Roosevelt—could do a better job of ending the hard times. Almost 60 percent of them concluded that it was time for a change. The Roosevelt-Garner ticket carried all but six traditional Republican states in the Northeast. Desperate for change, many Socialists deserted their candidate, Norman Thomas, to support Roosevelt. Not only was the new president to be a Democrat but both houses of Congress were to have large Democratic majorities.

Hoover as "lame-duck" president. For the four months between Roosevelt's election and his inauguration in March 1933, Hoover was still president. Hoover was a "lame duck," however, powerless to cope with the depression, which continued to get worse. He offered to work with the president-elect through the long period, but Roosevelt declined, not wanting to be tied to any of the Republican president's ideas. The Twentieth Amendment (known as the *lame-duck amendment*), passed in February 1933 and ratified by October 1933, shortened the period between presidential election and inauguration. The amendment set a new date, January 20, for the start of a president's term in office.

Franklin D. Roosevelt's New Deal

The new president was a distant cousin of President Theodore Roosevelt and was married to Theodore's niece, Eleanor. More than any other president, Franklin Delano Roosevelt—popularly known by his initials, F.D.R.—expanded the size of the federal government, altered its scope of operations, and greatly enlarged the powers of the presidency. He would dominate the nation and the U.S. government for an unprecedented stretch of time, 12 years and two months. He would prove to be one of the most influential world leaders of the 20th century.

F.D.R.: The Man

Franklin Roosevelt was the only child of a wealthy New York family. He personally admired cousin Theodore and followed in his footsteps as a New York state legislator and then as U.S. assistant secretary of the navy. Unlike Republican Theodore, however, Franklin was a Democrat. In 1920 he was the Democratic nominee for vice president. He and James Cox, the presidential candidate, lost badly in Warren G. Harding's landslide victory.

Disability. In the midst of a promising career, Roosevelt was paralyzed by polio in 1921. Although he was wealthy enough to retire, he labored instead to resume his career in politics and eventually regained the full power of his upper body, even though he could never again walk unaided and required the assistance of crutches, braces, and a wheelchair. Roosevelt's greatest strengths were his warm personality, his gifts as a speaker, and his ability to work with and inspire people. In 1928, campaigning from a car and in a wheelchair, F.D.R. was elected governor of New York. In this office, he instituted a number of welfare and relief programs to help the jobless.

Eleanor Roosevelt. Roosevelt's wife, Eleanor, emerged as a leader in her own right. She became the most active first lady in history, writing a newspaper column, giving speeches, and traveling the country. Though their personal relationship was strained, Eleanor and Franklin Roosevelt had a strong mutual respect. She served as the president's social conscience and influenced him to support minorities and the less fortunate.

New Deal Philosophy

In his campaign for president in 1932, Roosevelt offered vague promises but no concrete programs. He did not have a detailed plan for ending the depression, but he was committed to action and willing to experiment with political solutions to economic problems.

The three R's. In his acceptance speech at the Democratic convention in 1932, Roosevelt had said: "I pledge you, I pledge myself, to a new deal for the American people." He had further promised in his campaign to help the "forgotten man at the bottom of the economic pyramid." During the early years of his presidency, it became clear that his New Deal programs were to serve three R's: *relief* for people out of work, *recovery* for business and the economy as a whole, and *reform* of American economic institutions.

Brain Trust and other advisers. In giving shape to his New Deal, President Roosevelt relied on a group of advisers who had assisted him while he was governor of New York. Louis Howe was to be his chief political adviser. For advice on economic matters, Roosevelt turned to a group of university professors, known as the Brain Trust, which included Rexford Tugwell, Raymond Moley, and Adolph A. Berle, Jr.

The people that Roosevelt appointed to high administrative positions were the most diverse in U.S. history, with a record number of African Americans, Catholics, Jews, and women. His secretary of labor, for example, was Frances Perkins, the first woman ever to serve in a president's cabinet.

The First Hundred Days

With the nation desperate and close to the brink of panic, the Democratic Congress looked to the new president for leadership, which Roosevelt was eager to provide. Immediately after being sworn into office on March 4, 1933, Roosevelt called Congress into a hundred-day-long special session. During this brief period, Congress passed into law every request of President Roosevelt, enacting more major legislation than any single Congress in history. So numerous were the new laws and agencies that they were commonly referred to by their initials: WPA, AAA, CCC, NRA.

Bank holiday. In early 1933, banks were failing at a frightening rate, as depositors flocked to withdraw funds. As many banks failed in 1933 (over 5,000) as had failed in all the previous years of the depression. To restore confidence in those banks that were still solvent, the president ordered the banks closed for a bank holiday on March 6, 1933. He went on the radio to explain that the banks would be reopened after allowing enough time for the government to reorganize them on a sound basis.

Repeal of Prohibition. The new president kept a campaign promise to enact repeal of Prohibition and also raised needed tax money by having Congress pass the Beer-Wine Revenue Act, which legalized the sale of beer and wine. Later in 1933, the ratification of the Twenty-first Amendment repealed the Eighteenth Amendment, bringing Prohibition to an end.

Fireside chats. Roosevelt went on the radio on March 12, 1933, to present the first of many fireside chats to the American people. The president assured his listeners that the banks which reopened after the bank holiday were now safe. The public responded as hoped, with the money deposited in the reopened banks exceeding the money withdrawn.

Financial recovery programs. As the financial part of his New Deal, the new president persuaded Congress to enact the following measures:

■ The Emergency Banking Relief Act authorized the government to examine the finances of banks closed during the bank holiday and reopen those judged to be sound.

■ The Federal Deposit Insurance Corporation (FDIC) guaranteed individual bank deposits up to $5,000.

■ The Home Owners Loan Corporation (HOLC) provided refinancing of small homes to prevent foreclosures.

■ The Farm Credit Administration provided low-interest farm loans and mortgages to prevent foreclosures on the property of indebted farmers.

Programs for relief for the unemployed. A number of programs created during the Hundred Days related to the needs of the millions of unemployed workers.

■ The Federal Emergency Relief Administration (FERA) offered outright grants of federal money to states and local governments that were operating soup kitchens and other forms of relief for the jobless and homeless. The director of FERA was Harry Hopkins, one of the president's closest friends and advisers.

- The Public Works Administration (PWA), directed by Secretary of the Interior Harold Ickes, allotted money to state and local governments for building roads, bridges, dams, and other public works. Such construction projects were a source of thousands of jobs.

- The Civilian Conservation Corps (CCC) employed young men on projects on federal lands and paid their families small monthly sums.

- The Tennessee Valley Authority (TVA) was a huge experiment in regional development and public planning. As a government corporation, it hired thousands of people in one of the nation's poorest regions, the Tennessee Valley, to build dams, operate electric power plants, control flooding and erosion, and manufacture fertilizer. The TVA sold electricity to residents of the region at rates that were well below those previously charged by a private power company.

Industrial recovery program. The key measure in 1933 to combine immediate relief and long-term reform was the National Recovery Administration (NRA). Directed by Hugh Johnson, the NRA was an attempt to guarantee reasonable profits for business and fair wages and hours for labor. With the antitrust laws temporarily suspended, the NRA could help each industry (such as steel, oil, and paper) set codes for wages, hours of work, levels of production, and prices of finished goods. The law creating the NRA also gave workers the right to organize and bargain collectively. The complex program operated with limited success for two years before the Supreme Court declared the NRA unconstitutional (*Schechter v. U.S.*).

Farm production control program. Farmers were offered a program similar in concept to what the NRA did for industry. The Agricultural Adjustment Administration (AAA) encouraged farmers to reduce production (and thereby boost prices) by offering to pay government subsidies for every acre they plowed under. The AAA met the same fate as the NRA. It was declared unconstitutional in a 1935 Supreme Court decision.

Other Programs of the First New Deal

Congress adjourned briefly after its extraordinary legislative record in the first Hundred Days of the New Deal. Roosevelt, however, was not finished devising new remedies for the nation's ills. In late 1933 and through much of 1934, the Democratic Congress was easily persuaded to enact the following:

- The Civil Works Administration (CWA) was added to the PWA and other New Deal programs for creating jobs. This agency hired laborers for temporary construction projects sponsored by the federal government.

■ The Securities and Exchange Commission (SEC) was created to regulate the stock market and to place strict limits on the kind of speculative practices that had led to the Wall Street crash in 1929.

■ The Federal Housing Administration (FHA) gave both the construction industry and homeowners a boost by insuring bank loans for building new houses and repairing old ones.

■ Another new law took the United States off the gold standard in an effort to halt deflation (falling prices). The value of the dollar was set at $35 per ounce of gold (but no longer were paper dollars redeemable in gold).

The Second New Deal

Roosevelt's first two years in office were largely focused on achieving one of the three R's: recovery. Democratic victories in the congressional elections of 1934 gave the president the popular mandate he needed to seek another round of laws and programs. In the summer of 1935, the so-called second New Deal was launched. This batch of new legislation concentrated on the other two R's: relief and reform.

Relief Programs

Harry Hopkins became even more prominent in Roosevelt's administration with the creation in 1935 of a new relief agency, which Hopkins headed.

Works Progress Administration (WPA). Much larger than the relief agencies of the first New Deal, the WPA spent billions of dollars between 1935 and 1940 to provide people with jobs. After its first year of operation under Hopkins, it employed 3.4 million men and women who had formerly been on the relief rolls of state and local governments. It paid them double the relief rate but less than the going wage for regular workers. Most WPA workers were put to work constructing new bridges, roads, airports, and public buildings. Unemployed artists, writers, and actors were paid by the WPA to paint murals, write histories, and perform in plays.

One part of the WPA, the National Youth Administration (NYA), provided part-time jobs to help young people stay in high school and college or until they could get a job with a private employer.

Resettlement Administration (RA). Placed under the direction of one of the Brain Trust, Rexford Tugwell, the Resettlement Administration provided loans to sharecroppers, tenants, and small farmers. It also established federal camps where migrant workers could find decent housing.

Reforms

The reform legislation of the second New Deal reflected Roosevelt's belief that industrial workers and farmers needed to receive more government help than members of the business and privileged classes.

National Labor Relations (Wagner) Act (1935). This major labor law of 1935 replaced the labor provisions of the National Industrial Recovery Act, after that law was declared unconstitutional. The Wagner Act guaranteed a worker's right to join a union and a union's right to bargain collectively. It also outlawed business practices that were unfair to labor. A new agency, the National Labor Relations Board (NLRB), was empowered to enforce the law and make sure that workers' rights were protected.

Rural Electrification Administration (REA). This new agency provided loans for electrical cooperatives to supply power in rural areas.

Federal taxes. A revenue act of 1935 significantly increased the tax on incomes of the wealthy few. It also increased the tax on large gifts from parent to child and on capital gains (profits from the sale of stocks or other properties).

The Social Security Act

The reform that, for generations afterward, would affect the lives of nearly all Americans was the passage in 1935 of the Social Security Act. It created a federal insurance program based upon the automatic collection of taxes from employees and employers throughout people's working careers. The Social Security trust fund would then be used to make monthly payments to retired persons over the age of 65. Also receiving benefits under this new law were workers who lost their jobs (unemployment compensation), persons who were blind or otherwise disabled, and dependent children and their mothers.

The Election of 1936

The economy was improved but still weak and unstable in 1936 when the Democrats nominated Roosevelt for a second term. Because of his New Deal programs and active style of personal leadership, the president was now enormously popular among workers and small farmers. Business, however, generally disliked and even hated him because of his regulatory programs and prounion measures such as the Wagner Act.

Alf Landon. Challenging Roosevelt was the Republican nominee for president, Alfred (Alf) Landon, the progressive-minded governor of Kansas. Landon criticized the Democrats for spending too much money but in general accepted most of the New Deal legislation.

Results. Roosevelt swamped Landon, winning every state except Maine and Vermont and more than 60 percent of the popular vote. Behind their president's New Deal, the Democratic party could now count on the votes of a new coalition of popular support. Through the 1930s and into the 1960s, the Democratic coalition would consist of the Solid South, white ethnic groups in the cities, midwestern farmers, and labor unions. In addition, new support for the Democrats came from African Americans, mainly in northern cities, who left the Republican party of Lincoln because of Roosevelt's New Deal.

Opponents of the New Deal

Opinion polls and election results showed that a large majority of Americans supported Roosevelt. Nevertheless, his New Deal programs were extremely controversial and became the target of vitriolic attacks by liberals, conservatives, and demagogues.

Liberal Critics

Socialists and extreme liberals in the Democratic party criticized the New Deal (especially the first New Deal of 1933–1934) for doing too much for business and too little for the unemployed and the working poor. They charged that the president failed to address the problems of ethnic minorities, women, and the elderly.

Conservative Critics

More numerous were those on the right who attacked the New Deal for giving the federal government too much power. These critics charged that relief programs such as the WPA and labor laws such as the Wagner Act bordered on socialism or even communism. Business leaders were alarmed by (1) increased regulations, (2) the second New Deal's prounion stance, and (3) the financing of government programs by means of borrowed money—a practice known as deficit financing. Conservative Democrats, including former presidential candidates Alfred E. (Al) Smith and John W. Davis, joined with leading Republicans in 1934 to form an anti-New Deal organization called the American Liberty League. Its avowed purpose was to stop the New Deal from "subverting" the U.S. economic and political system.

Demagogues

Several critics played upon the American people's desperate need for immediate solutions to their problems. Using the radio to reach a mass audience, they proposed simplistic schemes for ending "evil conspiracies" (Father Coughlin), guaranteeing economic security for the elderly (Dr. Townsend), and redistributing the wealth (Huey Long).

Father Charles E. Coughlin. This Catholic priest attracted a huge popular following in the early 1930s through his weekly radio broadcasts. Father Coughlin founded the National Union for Social Justice, which called for issuing an inflated currency and nationalizing all banks. His attacks on the New Deal became increasingly anti-Semitic and Fascist until his superiors in the Catholic Church ordered him to stop his broadcasts.

Dr. Francis E. Townsend. Before the passage of the Social Security Act, a retired physician from Long Beach, California, became an instant hero to millions of senior citizens by proposing a simple plan for guaranteeing a secure income. Dr. Francis E. Townsend proposed that a 2 percent federal sales tax be used to create a special fund, from which every retired person over 60 years old would receive $200 a month. By spending their money promptly, Townsend argued, recipients would stimulate the economy and soon bring the depression to an end. The popularity of the Townsend Plan persuaded Roosevelt to substitute a more moderate plan of his own, which became the Social Security system.

Huey Long. From Roosevelt's point of view, the most dangerous of the depression demagogues was the "Kingfish" from Louisiana, Senator Huey Long. Immensely popular in his own state, Long became a prominent national figure by proposing a "Share Our Wealth" program that promised a minimum annual income of $5,000 for every American family, to be paid for by taxing the wealthy. In 1935, Huey Long challenged Roosevelt's leadership of the Democratic party by announcing his candidacy for president. Both his candidacy and his populist appeal were abruptly ended when he was killed by an assassin.

The Supreme Court

Of all the challenges to Roosevelt's leadership in his first term in office, the conservative decisions of the U.S. Supreme Court proved the most frustrating. In two cases in 1935, the Supreme Court effectively killed both the NRA for business recovery and the AAA for agricultural recovery by deciding that the laws creating them were unconstitutional. Roosevelt interpreted his landslide reelection in 1936 as a popular mandate to end the obstacles posed by the Court.

Court-reorganization plan. President Roosevelt did not have an opportunity to appoint any Justices to the Supreme Court during his first term. He hoped to remove the Court as an obstacle to the New Deal by proposing a judicial-reorganization bill in 1937. Critics called it a "Court-packing" bill. It proposed that the president be authorized to appoint to the Supreme Court an additional justice for each current justice who was older than a certain age (70.5 years). In effect, the bill would have allowed Roosevelt to add up to six more justices to the Court—all of them presumably of liberal persuasion.

Reaction. Republicans and many Democrats were outraged by what they saw as an attempt to tamper with the system of checks and balances. They accused the president of wanting to give himself the powers of a dictator. Roosevelt did not back down—and neither did the congressional opposition. For the first time in Roosevelt's presidency, a major bill that he proposed went down to decisive defeat by a defiant Congress. Even a majority of Democratic senators refused to support him on this controversial measure.

Aftermath. Ironically, while Roosevelt was fighting to "pack" the Court, the justices were already backing off their former resistance to his program. In 1937, the Supreme Court upheld the constitutionality of several major New Deal laws, including the Wagner (Labor) Act and Social Security acts. Also, as it happened, several justices retired during Roosevelt's second term, enabling him to appoint a majority on the Court and thereby ensure judicial support for his reforms.

Rise of Unions

Two New Deal measures—the National Industrial Recovery Act of 1933 and the Wagner Act of 1935—caused a lasting change in labor-management relations by legalizing labor unions. Union membership, which had slumped badly under the hostile policies of the 1920s, shot upward. It went from less than 3 million in the early 1930s to over 10 million (more than one out of four nonfarm workers) by 1941.

Formation of the C.I.O.

As unions grew in size, tensions and conflicts between rival unions grew in intensity. The many different unions that made up the American Federation of Labor (A.F. of L.) were dominated by skilled white male workers and were organized according to crafts. A group of unions within the A.F. of L. wanted union membership to be extended to all workers in an industry regardless of their race and sex, including those who were unskilled. In 1935, the industrial unions, as they were called, joined together as the Committee of Industrial Organizations (C.I.O.). Their leader was John L. Lewis, president of the United Mine Workers union. In 1936, the A.F. of L. suspended the C.I.O. unions. Renamed the *Congress* of Industrial Organizations, the C.I.O. broke away from the A.F. of L. and became its chief rival. It concentrated on organizing unskilled workers in the automobile, steel, and southern textile industries.

Strikes

Even though collective bargaining was now protected by federal law, many companies still resisted union demands. Strikes were therefore a frequent occurrence in the depression decade.

Automobiles. At the huge General Motors plant in Flint, Michigan, in 1937, the workers insisted on their right to join a union by participating in a sit-down strike (literally sitting down at the assembly line and refusing to work). Neither the president nor Michigan's governor agreed to the company's request to intervene with troops. Finally, the company yielded to striker demands by recognizing the United Auto Workers union (U.A.W.). Union organizers at the Ford plant in Michigan, however, were beaten and driven away.

Steel. In the steel industry, the giant U.S. Steel Corporation voluntarily recognized one of the C.I.O. unions, but smaller companies resisted. On Memorial Day, 1937, a demonstration by union picketers at Republic Steel in Chicago ended in four deaths, as the police fired into the crowd. Despite initial resistance, however, almost all the smaller steel companies agreed to deal with the C.I.O. by 1941.

Fair Labor Standards Act

A final political victory for organized labor in the 1930s also represented the last major reform of the New Deal. In 1938, Congress enacted the Fair Labor Standards Act, which provided a host of regulations on businesses in interstate commerce. It established:

- a minimum wage (initially fixed at 40 cents an hour)
- a maximum workweek of 40 hours and time and a half for overtime
- child-labor restrictions on those under 16

Recall that the Supreme Court had declared unconstitutional an earlier law of 1916 prohibiting child labor. In 1941, however, in the case of *U.S. v. Darby Lumber Co.,* the Supreme Court reversed its earlier ruling by upholding the child-labor provisions of the Fair Labor Standards Act.

Last Phase of the New Deal

Passage of the Fair Labor Standards Act was not only the last but also the only major reform of Roosevelt's second term. The New Deal lost momentum in the late 1930s for both economic and political reasons.

Recession, 1937–1938

From 1933 to 1937 (Roosevelt's first term), the economy showed signs of gradually pulling out of its nosedive. Banks were stable, business earnings were moving up, and unemployment, though still bad at 15 percent, had declined from the 25 percent figure in 1933. In the winter of 1937, however, the economy once again had a backward slide and entered into a recessionary period.

Causes. Government policy was at least partly to blame. The new Social Security tax reduced consumer spending at the same time that Roosevelt was curtailing expenditures for relief and public works. In reducing spending for relief, the president hoped to balance the budget and reduce the national debt.

Keynesian economics. The writings of the British economist John Maynard Keynes taught Roosevelt that he had made a mistake in attempting to balance the budget. According to Keynesian theory, deficit spending was acceptable because in difficult times the government needed to spend well above its tax revenues in order to initiate economic growth. Deficit spending would be like "priming the pump" to increase investment and create jobs. Roosevelt's economic advisers adopted this theory in 1938 with positive results. As federal spending on public works and relief went up, so too did employment and industrial production.

Weakened New Deal

Although the economy improved, there was no boom and problems remained. After the Court-packing fight of 1937, the people and Congress no longer automatically followed F.D.R., and the 1938 elections brought a reduced Democratic majority in Congress. A coalition of Republicans and conservative Democrats blocked further New Deal reform legislation. Also, beginning in 1938, fears about the aggressive acts of Nazi Germany diverted attention from domestic concerns toward foreign affairs.

Life During the Depression

Millions of people who lived through the Great Depression and hard times of the 1930s never got over it. They developed a "depression mentality"—an attitude of insecurity and economic concern that would always remain, even in times of prosperity.

Women

During the depression, added pressures were placed on the family as unemployed fathers searched for work, and declining incomes presented severe challenges for mothers in the feeding and clothing of their children. To supplement the family income, more women sought work, and their percentage of the total labor force increased. Women were accused of taking jobs from men, even though they did not get the heavy factory jobs that were lost to all, and most men did not seek the types of jobs available to women. Even with Eleanor Roosevelt championing women's equality, many New Deal programs allowed women to receive lower pay than men.

Dust Bowl Farmers

As if farmers did not already have enough problems, a severe drought in the early 1930s ruined crops in the Great Plains. This region became a *dust bowl,* as poor farming practices coupled with high winds blew away millions of tons of dried topsoil. With their farms turned to dust, thousands of "Okies" from Oklahoma and surrounding states migrated westward to California in search of farm or factory work that often could not be found. The novelist John Steinbeck wrote about their hardships in his classic study of economic heartbreak, *The Grapes of Wrath* (1939).

African Americans

Racial discrimination continued in the 1930s with devastating effects on African Americans, who were the last hired, first fired. Their unemployment rate was higher than the national average. Often, despite their extreme poverty, jobless African Americans were excluded from state and local relief programs. Hard times increased racial tensions, particularly in the South where lynchings continued. Civil rights leaders could get little support from President Roosevelt, who feared the loss of white southern Democratic votes.

Improvements. The New Deal did provide some relief for African Americans, who found low-paying jobs with the WPA and the CCC (even though these jobs were often segregated). African Americans also received moral support from Eleanor Roosevelt and Secretary of the Interior Harold Ickes in a famous incident in 1939. The distinguished African American singer Marian Anderson had been refused the use of Constitution Hall in Washington, D.C., by the all-white Daughters of the American Revolution. Eleanor Roosevelt and Ickes promptly arranged for Anderson to give a special concert at the Lincoln Memorial.

Over one hundred African Americans were appointed to middle-level positions in federal departments by President Roosevelt. One of them, Mary McLeod Bethune, had been a long-time leader of efforts for improving education and economic opportunities for women. Invited to Washington to direct a division of the National Youth Administration, she established the Federal Council on Negro Affairs for the purpose of increasing African American involvement in the New Deal.

Fair Employment Practices Committee. An executive order in 1941 set up a committee to assist minorities in gaining jobs in defense industries. President Roosevelt took this action only after A. Philip Randolph, head of the Railroad Porters Union, threatened a march on Washington to demand equal job opportunities for African Americans.

Native Americans

John Collier, a long-time advocate of Native American rights, was appointed commissioner of the Bureau of Indian Affairs in 1933. He established conservation and CCC projects on reservations and gained Native American involvement in the WPA and other New Deal programs.

Indian Reorganization (Wheeler-Howard) Act (1934). Collier succeeded in winning Roosevelt's support for a major change in policy. The Dawes Act of 1887, which had encouraged Native Americans to be independent farmers, was repealed in 1934 with the passage of the Indian Reorganization Act. This measure returned lands to the control of tribes and supported the preservation of Native American cultures. Despite this major reform, critics later accused the New Deal of being paternalistic and withholding control from Native Americans.

Mexican Americans

Mexican Americans also suffered from discriminatory practices in the 1930s. In California and the Southwest, they had been a principal source of agricultural labor in the 1920s. During the depression, however, high unemployment and drought in the Midwest caused a dramatic growth in white migrant workers who pushed west in search of work. Discrimination in New Deal programs and competition for jobs forced many thousands of Mexican Americans to return to Mexico.

HISTORICAL PERSPECTIVES: WAS THE NEW DEAL REVOLUTIONARY OR CONSERVATIVE?

Roosevelt's New Deal was unique. In later decades, there would be nothing quite like it in terms of either the challenges faced or the legislative record achieved. Recognizing its scope, historians have debated whether the New Deal represented a revolutionary break with the past or an evolutionary outgrowth of earlier movements.

The first detailed historical interpretations tended to see the New Deal in a positive light as a continuation of the Progressive reform movement. In the late 1950s, Arthur M. Schlesinger, Jr., explained it in terms of his theory of a recurring political cycle from a period of liberal reforms to a period of conservative reaction and back again to reform.

Some liberal historians such as Carl Degler went further and characterized the New Deal as a third American Revolution that went far beyond earlier reforms. They argued that such measures as the NRA, the WPA, and the Social Security Act represented nothing less than a redefinition of the role of government in American society. In his *Age of Reform* (1955), Richard Hofstadter agreed that the New Deal had ventured beyond traditional reform movements. It was unique, he said, because it concentrated not on regulating corporate abuses as in the past but on providing social-democratic guarantees for different groups in such forms as Social Security, housing credits, and minimum wage laws.

Revisionists of the 1960s and 1970s proposed different ways of viewing the New Deal. William E. Leuchtenburg in *Franklin D. Roosevelt and the New Deal* (1963) depicted a "halfway revolution" that helped some (farmers and labor unions), ignored others (African Americans), and implemented changes without being either completely radical or conservative. Leuchtenburg believed Roosevelt did the best he could given both his own personal ideas and the political realities of the time. A highly critical interpretation came from New Left scholars (radical thinkers of the 1970s), who argued that the New Deal was a missed opportunity that did not do enough to meet society's needs. They saw New Deal measures as conservative in purpose, aimed at preserving capitalism from a worker revolution. New Left historians have been criticized for judging the New Deal in terms of the 1970s rather than the 1930s.

In recent years, some historians have questioned whether it is useful to characterize the New Deal as either conservative on the one hand or revolutionary on the other. They see the New Deal as nothing more or less than a political response to various groups. In their view, Roosevelt and his political advisers had no central plan but simply responded to the different needs of special interests (farmers, business, labor, and elderly). In defense of Roosevelt, they ask: If the nation in general and the South in particular was essentially conservative, then how far could the New Deal go in improving race relations? If the government bureaucracy was relatively small in the 1930s, how could it be expected to implement massive new programs?

KEY NAMES, EVENTS, AND TERMS

Great Depression
stock market; Wall Street
Black Tuesday (October 29, 1929)
Dow Jones index
income distribution
buying on margin
Gross National Product
Herbert Hoover
Hawley-Smoot Tariff (1930)
debt moratorium
Farm Board
Reconstruction Finance Corporation
bonus march (1932)
Franklin D. Roosevelt
Eleanor Roosevelt
Twentieth Amendment ("lame-duck")
first New Deal
relief, recovery, reform
Brain Trust
Frances Perkins

Hundred Days
bank holiday
repeal of Prohibition
fireside chats
Federal Deposit Insurance Corporation
Public Works Administration
Harold Ickes
Civilian Conservation Corps
Tennessee Valley Authority
National Recovery Administration
Schechter v. U.S.
Securities and Exchange Commission
Federal Housing Administration
second New Deal
Works Progress Administration
Harry Hopkins
National Labor Relations (Wagner) Act (1935)
Social Security Act (1935)

Father Charles Coughlin
Francis Townsend
Huey Long
Supreme Court reorganization plan
Congress of Industrial Organizations
John L. Lewis
sit-down strike
Fair Labor Standards Act (1938)
new Democratic coalition
John Maynard Keynes
depression mentality
drought; dust bowl; Okies
John Steinbeck, *The Grapes of Wrath*
Marian Anderson
Mary McLeod Bethune
Fair Employment Practices Committee
A. Philip Randolph
Indian Reorganization (Wheeler-Howard) Act (1934)

MULTIPLE-CHOICE QUESTIONS

1. In combating the depression, President Herbert Hoover favored all of the following EXCEPT
   (A) federal relief programs for the unemployed

(B) state and local relief programs
(C) businesses maintaining wages and employment
(D) private volunteer efforts

(E) emergency financing for banks and railroads

2. "The New Deal brought sweeping changes in American politics and society." Each of the following actions supports this statement EXCEPT

(A) Roosevelt's use of federal deficit spending

(B) a majority of African Americans voting for Democratic candidates

(C) passage of the Social Security Act

(D) increased spending by consumers

(E) increased power of labor unions

3. The New Deal legislation that has had the widest impact over the past 60 years is the

(A) Wagner Act

(B) National Industrial Recovery Act (NRA)

(C) Banking Act (FDIC)

(D) National Housing Act (FHA)

(E) Social Security Act

4. "Economic indicators during Hoover's presidency reached new lows." Which of these indicators went UP instead of down?

(A) farm prices

(B) unemployment

(C) national income

(D) GNP

(E) earnings

5. Of the following, the greatest threat to Franklin D. Roosevelt and the New Deal was:

(A) Huey Long

(B) A. Philip Randolph

(C) Father Coughlin

(D) Mary McLeod Bethune

(E) Herbert Hoover

6. Which of the following pairs of people is closely identified with the bonus march?

(A) Herbert Hoover and Douglas MacArthur

(B) Franklin Roosevelt and Eleanor Roosevelt

(C) Harry Hopkins and Frances Perkins

(D) John L. Lewis and John Maynard Keynes

(E) Alf Landon and Al Smith

7. All of the following were passed or created by Congress during the second New Deal EXCEPT

(A) the Social Security Act

(B) the Wagner Act

(C) the Works Progress Administration

(D) the Resettlement Administration

(E) the National Recovery Administration

8. All of the following played a role in causing the Great Depression EXCEPT

(A) uneven distribution of wealth

(B) weak farm economy

(C) overproduction of consumer goods

(D) low tariffs

(E) practice of buying stocks with borrowed money

9. The New Deal implemented theories of John Maynard Keynes that stressed the importance of
   (A) a balanced federal budget
   (B) deficit spending for "pump priming"
   (C) a laissez-faire policy toward business
   (D) "trickle-down" economic theory
   (E) high-tariff protectionism

10. In response to conservative rulings of the Supreme Court, President Roosevelt took action that resulted in
    (A) his first major legislative defeat
    (B) passage of a law reorganizing the judicial branch
    (C) his reelection in 1936
    (D) New Deal laws being declared unconstitutional
    (E) enactment of legislation known as the third New Deal

ESSAY QUESTIONS

1. Compare and contrast Herbert Hoover's economic policies with those of Franklin Roosevelt.

2. Analyze the role of TWO of the following in explaining the causes of the Great Depression:

   farm problems

   income distribution

   world trade and finance

   government policy

3. "Those on the right criticized the New Deal for attempting too much, while those on the left criticized it for not doing enough."
   Illustrate this statement with reference to the views from each side.

4. To what extent did Roosevelt's first New Deal favor business, while his second New Deal favored labor?

5. Select TWO New Deal agencies or commissions and assess how well each satisfied the three R's of relief, recovery, and reform.

DOCUMENTS AND READINGS

The first three decades of the 20th century saw major changes in the status of women. World War I increased the number of women working outside the home, the Nineteenth Amendment brought the vote, and the twenties added the flapper look and greater independence for some. With the election of a new president in 1932, women gained their strongest supporter ever in the White House: Eleanor Roosevelt.

The depression presented new challenges for women in their struggle to survive economically and advance socially and politically. The following readings, including excerpts from an oral history (Document D), present the views and experiences of women of different backgrounds. They reflect some of the thinking of society in general and women in particular during this turbulent period.

DOCUMENT A.   VIEW FROM THE WHITE HOUSE

For many Americans, it was hard to accept the fact that a First Lady would articulate personal opinions on political questions and at times differ from the president. For others, however, Eleanor Roosevelt in her speeches and writing, including a newspaper column, provided unparalleled inspiration. The following excerpt from her autobiography tells how she approached the problem of speaking out independently from the White House.

> As time went by, I found that people no longer considered me a mouthpiece for my husband but realized that I had a point of view of my own with which he might not at all agree. Then I felt freer to state my own views. However, I always used some care, and sometimes, for example, I would send Franklin one of my columns about which I was doubtful. The only change he would ever suggest was occasionally in the use of a word, and that was simply a matter of style. Of course, this hands-off policy had its advantages for him, too; for it meant that my column could sometimes serve as a trial balloon. If some idea I expressed strongly—and with which he might agree—caused a violent reaction, he could honestly say that he had no responsibility in the matter and that the thoughts were my own.
>
> Though Franklin himself never tried to discourage me and was undisturbed by anything I wanted to say or do, other people were frequently less happy about my actions. I knew, for instance, that many of my racial beliefs and activities in the field of social work caused Steve Early and Marvin McIntyre [F.D.R.'s political advisers] grave concern. They were afraid that I would hurt my husband politically and socially, and I imagine they thought I was doing many things without Franklin's knowledge and agreement. On occasion they blew up to him and to other people. I knew it at the time, but there was no use in my trying to explain, because our basic values were very different. . . .

Eleanor Roosevelt,
This I Remember, 1949

DOCUMENT B.   SHOULD WOMEN GIVE UP THEIR JOBS?

Even though most women in the thirties were limited to such occupations as nursing and domestic work, some still complained that women workers should step aside so that men could have work to support their families. Here is one feminist's response to that argument.

The hard times have brought out a fresh crop of protests against the earning of money by women, especially married women, unless they are compelled to do it. We are told over and over that every salaried woman who could live without her job ought to give it up in favor of the jobless.

An argument can be made for this, from the standpoint of the Golden Rule. But, if it is sound, it does not apply to woman only. No one suggests that every man who could live without his job ought to retire in favor of the jobless. On the contrary, if a rich man's son, sure of inheriting enough for himself and his family, goes to work for a salary, he is universally praised. But if that young man's sister, married or single, does the same, she is blamed.

School boards are even urged to dismiss all married women from the teaching force; but it is never suggested that all male teachers ought to be dismissed who could live without their pay.

A young scoffer once told a distinguished clergyman that the religion he preached might be very good for old women, but would not do for men. The clergyman answered, "Sir, either the religion that I preach is true or it is not true. If it is true, it is good for everybody. If it is not true, it is neither good for old women nor for anybody else."

All believers in human rights should set themselves against these attempts to impose a rule. . . . Either it applies to both sexes, or it does not apply at all.

Alice Stone Blackwell,
"May Woman Earn?" January 1931

DOCUMENT C.   *SINGING FOR "THE GOOD OLD UNION"*

Women played an active role in the labor movement, both as the majority of workers in the garment industry and textile mills and as working companions of their husbands, brothers, and fathers in other industries. This popular song of the labor movement was written in 1931 by Florence Reece.

Come all of you good workers,
Good news to you I'll tell
Of how the good old union
Has come in here to dwell

Chorus:
Which side are you on?
Which side are you on?
Which side are you on?
Which side are you on?

My daddy was a miner
And I'm a miner's son,
And I'll stick with the union
Till every battle's won

They say in Harlan County
There are no neutrals there;
You'll either be a union man
Or a thug for J. H. Blair

Oh, workers, can you stand it?
Oh, tell me how you can.
Will you be a lousy scab
Or will you be a man?

Don't scab for the bosses,
Don't listen to their lies.
Us poor folks haven't got a chance
Unless we organize.

Florence Reece,
"Which Side Are You On?" 1931

DOCUMENT D. ONE WOMAN'S DECISION

Remembering the depression, a Mexican American woman in Texas gave the following oral account of her struggle to earn a living and educate her children.

They won't let me work on WPA. I have to fight. The place where I went to put my application, they tell me that I cannot work because I'm not citizen. I say, "How come I not citizen? I born and raised here and my father and mother. What else do you want?"

The lady call a man who say, "But you lost your citizenship when you married your husband. He is a citizen of Mexico."

I ask him, "You mean I get job only if I divorce him? What am I to be, and what are my kids to be? Give me paper to explain it to the judge why I divorce this man, because he is not a citizen."

And the man says: "I can't do that."

I am mad and I say back to him: "Then explain it to me how my kids gonna eat? How I'm gonna feed them?"

So he said he'd think about it. "No time to think about it," I told him. "I want answer quick, because I'm not gonna let my kids starve to death."

Then—two, three days later—they sent me a card to report to work. He wrote to Dallas or something, and they send papers for me to sign. I go to work in the sewing room and get thirty dollars a month, and I make so many pants that they give me a raise to forty dollars a month.

When the WPA stop, we go back to the fields until I press my foot down. I tell my husband, "This is it. No more field work. We have to educate the kids. We have to stay in one place and think about them now. . . ."

We have a big fight, but I win. I told him if he wanted to go on the field to go. I stay with the kids.

And that's when I start to work in the houses, you know. I have to do housework, have to do whatever come in. They pay one dollar a day, practically nothing . . . but it is enough. And I settled down in the town and since my oldest son go to school, I don't go back to the fields ever. I know my kids need the education.

My husband used to say it cost too much, but I didn't pay any attention to him. I say, "The door is open. You can walk out and walk in whenever you want, but *I am not going to the fields.*"

> "Nico Rodriguez's Story" in Jeane Westin, *Making Do: How Women Survived the '30s*

ANALYZING THE DOCUMENTS

The conditions of the depression made many women realize that they could no longer accept the economic and social limitations that had been placed upon them.

1. What are some of the common stereotypes of women before World War II that are reflected in these readings?

2. Do you observe any similarities between Eleanor Roosevelt and Nico Rodriguez in the ways they faced and dealt with their individual problems?

3. In the 1930s, while women successfully resisted efforts to push them from the workplace, what job inequalities still remained to be surmounted?

DIPLOMACY AND WORLD WAR II, 1929–1945

We seek peace—enduring peace. More than an end to war, we want an end to the beginnings of all wars.

Franklin D. Roosevelt, April 13, 1945

President Roosevelt's fervent desire for peace was hardly unusual. World War I, after all, was meant to be a "war to end all wars" and, as Woodrow Wilson had said, a war "to make the world safe for democracy." After that war, U.S. diplomacy had been partly responsible for almost all nations agreeing to the Kellogg-Briand Pact of 1928, in which they pledged not to use military force for aggressive ends. Through the 1920s, the League of Nations (without the U.S.) had met continuously in Geneva, Switzerland, to ensure that peace prevailed.

In 1933, however, few people believed that the fragile peace established by the Treaty of Versailles would hold up for long. In Asia, Japan was threatening China, while in Europe, the Nazi party under Adolf Hitler came to power in Germany with promises of reasserting German nationalism and militarism. In the United States, worries about the depression overshadowed concerns about a second world war. Even if war did break out, most Americans were determined not to send troops abroad again.

As we know, however, a second world war did occur, and the United States played a major role in fighting it. How and why U.S. foreign policy under Presidents Hoover and Roosevelt changed from disengagement to neutrality and from neutrality to total involvement is the subject of this chapter.

Herbert Hoover's Foreign Policy

Hoover concurred with the prevailing opinion of the American people that the United States should not enter into firm commitments to preserve the security of other nations. Such an opinion, in the 1930s, would be labeled "isolationism." Hoover viewed peace conferences and treaties as moral efforts and opposed using economic sanctions against aggressors, believing such a policy would lead to military involvement.

JAPANESE AGGRESSION IN ASIA IN THE 1930s

Japanese Aggression in Manchuria

In the early 1930s, Japan posed the greatest threat to world peace. Defying both the Open Door policy and the covenant of the League of Nations, Japanese troops marched into Manchuria in September 1931, renamed the territory Manchukuo, and established a puppet government.

Despite its commitment to taking action against blatant aggression, the League of Nations did nothing except to pass a resolution condemning Japan for its actions in Manchuria. The Japanese delegation then walked out of the League, never to return. In the Manchuria crisis, the League, through its failure to take action, showed its inability to maintain peace. Its warnings would never be taken seriously by potential aggressors.

Stimson Doctrine. U.S. response to Japan's violation of the Open Door policy was somewhat stronger than the League's response—but no more effective in deterring further aggression. Secretary of State Henry Stimson declared in 1932 that the United States would honor its treaty obligations under the Nine-Power Treaty (1922) by refusing to recognize the legitimacy of any regime like "Manchukuo" that had been established by force. The League of Nations readily endorsed the Stimson Doctrine and issued a similar declaration.

Latin America

Hoover actively pursued friendly relations with the countries of Latin America. In 1929, even before being inaugurated, the president-elect went on a goodwill tour of the region. As president, he ended the interventionist policies of Taft and Wilson by (1) arranging for U.S. troops to leave Nicaragua by 1933 and (2) negotiating a treaty with Haiti to remove all U.S. troops by 1934.

Franklin Roosevelt's Policies, 1933–1938

In his first term, Roosevelt's concentration on dealing with the economic crisis at home kept him from giving much thought to shaping foreign policy. He did, however, extend Hoover's efforts at improving U.S. relations with Latin America by initiating a good-neighbor policy.

Good-Neighbor Policy

In his first inaugural address in 1933, Roosevelt promised a "policy of the good neighbor" toward other nations of the Western Hemisphere. What were his reasons for wanting to improve relations by taking a noninterventionist course in Latin America? First, interventionism in support of dollar diplomacy no longer made economic sense, since U.S. businesses during the depression lacked the resources to invest in foreign operations. Second, the rise of militarist regimes in Germany and Italy prompted Roosevelt to seek Latin America's cooperation in defending the region from potential danger. The president acted on his good-neighbor policy in the following ways:

Pan-American conferences. At Roosevelt's direction, the U.S. delegation at the Seventh Pan-American Conference in Montevideo, Uruguay, in 1933, pledged never again to intervene in the internal affairs of a Latin American country. In effect, Franklin Roosevelt repudiated the policy of his older cousin, Theodore, who had justified intervention as a corollary to the Monroe Doctrine. Another Pan-American conference was held in Buenos Aires, Argentina, in 1936. Roosevelt himself attended the conference. He personally pledged to submit future disputes to arbitration and also warned that if a European power such as Germany attempted "to commit acts of aggression against us," it would find "a Hemisphere wholly prepared to consult together for our mutual safety and our mutual good."

Cuba. Cubans had long resented the Platt Amendment, which had made their country's foreign policy subject to U.S. approval. In 1934, President Roosevelt persuaded Congress to nullify the Platt Amendment, retaining only the U.S. right to keep its naval base at Guantanamo Bay.

Mexico. Mexico tested U.S. patience and commitment to the good-neighbor policy in 1938 when its president, Lázaro Cárdenas, seized oil properties owned by U.S. corporations. Roosevelt rejected corporate demands to intervene and encouraged American companies to negotiate a settlement.

Economic Diplomacy

Helping the U.S. economy was the chief motivation for Roosevelt's policies toward other foreign policy issues in his first term.

London Economic Conference (1933). During Hoover's last months in office, he had agreed to allow U.S. participation in an international economic conference called by the League of Nations. Initially, President Roosevelt supported the efforts of the conference. But when proposals were made to stabilize currencies, Roosevelt feared that this would hurt his own plans for recovery, and he withdrew his support. The conference then ended without reaching any agreement.

Recognition of the Soviet Union. The Republican presidents of the 1920s had refused to grant diplomatic recognition to the Communist regime that ruled the Soviet Union. Roosevelt promptly changed this policy by granting recognition in 1933. His reason for doing so, he said, was to increase U.S. trade and thereby boost the economy.

Philippines. Governing the Philippines cost money. As an economy measure, Roosevelt persuaded Congress to pass the Tydings-McDuffie Act in 1934, which provided for the independence of the Philippines by 1946 and the gradual removal of U.S. military presence from the islands. In 1935, the Philippine people elected a president under a new constitution, even though the United States was still nominally in control of the territory.

Reciprocal Trade Agreements. Acting in the tradition of progressive Democrats like William Jennings Bryan and Woodrow Wilson, President Roosevelt favored lower tariffs as a means of increasing international trade. In 1934, Congress enacted a plan suggested by Secretary of State Cordell Hull, which gave the president power to reduce U.S. tariffs up to 50 percent for nations that reciprocated with comparable reductions for U.S. imports.

Events Abroad: Fascism and Aggressive Militarism

The worldwide depression soon proved to have alarming repercussions for world politics. Combined with nationalist resentments after World War I, economic hardships gave rise to military dictatorships in Italy in the 1920s and Japan and Germany in the 1930s. Eventually, in 1940, Japan, Italy, and Germany signed a treaty of alliance which formed the Axis Powers.

Italy. A new regime seized power in Italy in 1922. Benito Mussolini led Italy's Fascist party, which attracted dissatisfied war veterans, nationalists, and those afraid of rising communism. Dressed in black shirts, the Fascists marched on Rome and installed Mussolini in power as "Il Duce" (the Leader). Fascism—the idea that people should glorify their nation and their race through an aggressive show of force—became the dominant ideology in European dictatorships in the 1930s.

Germany. The Nazi party was the German equivalent of Italy's Fascist party. It arose in the 1920s in reaction to deplorable economic conditions after the war and national resentments over the Treaty of Versailles. The Nazi leader, Adolf Hitler, used bullying tactics against Jews as well as Fascist ideology to increase his popularity with disgruntled, unemployed German workers. Hitler seized the opportunity presented by the depression to play upon anti-Semitic hatreds. With his personal army of "brown shirts," Hitler gained control of the German legislature in early 1933.

Japan. Nationalists and militarists in Japan increased their power in the 1920s and 1930s. As economic conditions worsened, they persuaded Japan's nominal ruler, the emperor, that the best way to ensure access to basic raw materials (oil, tin, and iron) was to invade China and Southeast Asia and thereby give Japan control over what their leaders proclaimed to be the Greater East Asia Co-Prosperity Sphere.

American Isolationists

Public opinion in the United States was also nationalistic but expressed itself in an opposite way from fascism and militarism. Disillusioned with the results of World War I, American isolationists wanted to make sure that the United States would never again be drawn into a foreign war. Japanese aggression in Manchuria and the rise of fascism in Italy and Germany only increased the determination of isolationists to avoid war at all costs. Isolationist sentiment was strongest in the Midwest and among Republicans.

Revisionist history of World War I. Widely accepted in the early 1930s was the idea that U.S. entry into World War I had been a terrible mistake. This view was bolstered in Congress by an investigating committee led by Senator Gerald Nye of North Dakota. The Nye committee concluded in 1934 that the main reason for U.S. participation in the world war was to serve the greed of bankers and arms manufacturers. This committee's work influenced isolationist legislation in the following years.

Neutrality acts. Isolationist senators and representatives in both parties held a majority in Congress through 1938. To ensure that U.S. policy would be strictly neutral if war broke out in Europe, Congress adopted a series of neutrality acts, which Roosevelt signed with some reluctance. Each law applied to nations that the president proclaimed to be at war.

- The *Neutrality Act of 1935* authorized the president to prohibit all arms shipments and to forbid U.S. citizens to travel on the ships of belligerent nations.

- The *Neutrality Act of 1936* forbade the extension of loans and credits to belligerents.

- The *Neutrality Act of 1937* forbade the shipment of arms to the opposing sides in the civil war in Spain.

Spanish civil war. The outbreak of civil war in Spain in 1936 was viewed in Europe and the United States as an ideological struggle between the forces of fascism, led by General Francisco Franco, and the forces of republicanism, called Loyalists. Roosevelt and most Americans sympathized with the Loyalists but, because of the Neutrality Acts, could do nothing to aid them. Ultimately, in 1939, Franco's Fascists prevailed and established a military dictatorship.

America First Committee. In 1940, after World War II had begun, the isolationists became alarmed by Roosevelt's pro-British policies. To mobilize American public opinion against war, they formed the America First Committee and engaged speakers like Charles Lindbergh to travel the country warning against the folly of getting involved a second time in Europe's troubles.

Prelude to War

In the years 1935 to 1938, a series of aggressive actions by the Fascist dictatorships made democratic governments in Britain and France extremely nervous. It was known that Hitler was creating an air force more powerful than anything they could match. Hoping to avoid open conflict with Germany, the democracies adopted a policy of appeasement—allowing Hitler to get away with relatively small acts of aggression and expansion. The United States went along with the British and French policy.

Appeasement. The following events showed how unprepared the democracies were to challenge Fascist aggression.

1. Ethiopia, 1935. In a bid to prove fascism's military might, Mussolini ordered Italian troops to invade Ethiopia. The League of Nations and the United States objected but did nothing to stop the Italian aggressor, which succeeded in conquering the African country after a year of bitter fighting.

2. Rhineland, 1936. This region in western Germany was supposed to be permanently demilitarized, according to the terms of the Versailles Treaty. Hitler openly defied the treaty by ordering German troops to march into the Rhineland.

AXIS AGGRESSION IN THE 1930s

■ Germany and Italy (Axis Powers)	(1935) Date of Annexation, Occupation, or Invasion	0 100 200 Miles / 0 100 200 Kilometers

3. China, 1937. Full-scale war between Japan and China erupted in 1937 as Japan's troops invaded its weaker neighbor. A U.S. gunboat in China, the *Panay*, was bombed and sunk by Japanese planes. Japan's apology for the sinking was quickly accepted by the U.S. government.

4. Sudetenland, 1938. In Europe, Hitler insisted that Germany had a right to take over a strip of land in Czechoslovakia, the Sudetenland, where most people were German-speaking. To maintain peace, Roosevelt encouraged the British prime minister, Neville Chamberlain, and the French president, Édouard Daladier, to meet with Hitler and Mussolini in Munich. At this conference in September 1938, the British and French leaders agreed to allow Hitler to take the Sudetenland unopposed. The word "Munich" has since become synonymous with appeasement.

U.S. response. Roosevelt recognized the dangers of Fascist aggression but was limited by the isolationist feelings of the majority of Americans. When Japan invaded China in 1937, he tested public opinion by making a speech proposing that the democracies act together to "quarantine" the aggressor. Public reaction to the speech was overwhelmingly negative, and Roosevelt dropped the quarantine idea as politically unwise.

Preparedness. Like Wilson in 1916, Roosevelt managed to argue for neutrality and U.S. security at the same time by proposing an arms buildup. Congress went along with his request in late 1938 by increasing the military and naval budgets by nearly two-thirds. Some isolationists accepted the increased defense spending, thinking it would be used only to protect against possible invasion of the Western Hemisphere.

From Neutrality to War, 1939–1941

In March 1939, Hitler broke the Munich agreement by sending troops to occupy all of Czechoslovakia. After this, it became clear that Hitler's ambitions had no limit and that war was probably unavoidable.

Outbreak of War in Europe

Now recognizing the failure of appeasement, Britain and France pledged to fight if Poland was attacked. They had always assumed that they could count on the Soviet leader, Joseph Stalin, to oppose Hitler, since communism and fascism were ideological enemies. The democracies were therefore shocked in August 1939 when Stalin and Hitler signed a nonaggression pact. Secretly, the Soviet and German dictators agreed to divide Poland between them.

Invasion of Poland. On September 1, 1939, German tanks and planes began a full-scale invasion of Poland. Keeping their pledge, Britain and France declared war against Germany—and soon afterward, they were also at war with its Axis allies, Italy and Japan. World War II in Europe had begun.

Blitzkrieg. Poland was the first to fall to Germany's overwhelming use of air power and fast-moving tanks—a type of warfare called *blitzkrieg* (lightning war). After a relatively inactive winter, the war was resumed in the spring of 1940 with Germany attacking its Scandinavian neighbors to the north and its chief enemy, France, to the west. Denmark and Norway surrendered in a few days, France in only a week. By June 1940, the only ally that remained free of German troops was Great Britain.

Changing U. S. Policy

Now that war had actually begun, most Americans were alarmed by news of Nazi tanks, planes, and troops conquering one country after another. They were strongly opposed to Hitler but still hoped to keep their country out of the war. President Roosevelt believed that British survival was crucial to U.S. security. He therefore chipped away at the restrictive neutrality laws until practically nothing remained to prevent him from giving massive aid to Britain. By 1940, most Americans accepted the need to strengthen U.S. defenses, but giving direct aid to Britain was widely debated.

"Cash and carry." The British navy still controlled the seas. Therefore, if the United States ended its arms embargo, it could only aid Britain, not Germany. Roosevelt persuaded Congress in 1939 to adopt a less restrictive Neutrality Act, which provided that a belligerent could buy U.S. arms if it used its own ships and paid cash. Technically, "cash and carry" was neutral, but in practice, it strongly favored Britain.

Selective Service Act (1940). Without actually naming Germany as the potential enemy, Roosevelt pushed neutrality back one more step by persuading Congress to enact a law for compulsory military service. The Selective Training and Service Act of September 1940 provided for the registration of all American men between the ages of 21 and 35 and for the training of 1.2 million troops in just one year. There had been a military draft in the Civil War and World War I but only when the United States was officially at war. Isolationists strenuously opposed the peacetime draft, but they were now outnumbered as public opinion shifted away from strict neutrality.

Destroyers-for-bases deal. In September 1940, Britain was under constant assault by German bombing raids. German submarine attacks threatened British control of the Atlantic. Roosevelt could not sell U.S. destroyers to the British outright without alarming the isolationists. He therefore cleverly arranged a trade. Britain received 50 older but still serviceable U.S. destroyers in exchange for giving the United States the right to build military bases on British islands in the Caribbean.

The Election of 1940

Adding to public suspense over the war was uncertainty over a presidential election. Might Franklin Roosevelt be the first president to break the two-term tradition and seek election to a third term? For months, the president gave an ambiguous reply, causing frenzied speculation and rumor-mongering in the press. At last, he announced that, in those critical times, he would not turn down the Democratic nomination if it was offered. Most Democrats were delighted to renominate their most effective campaigner. During the campaign, Roosevelt made the rash pronouncement: "Your boys are not going to be sent into any foreign wars."

Wendell Willkie. The Republicans had a number of veteran politicians who were eager to challenge the president. Instead, the surprise nominee had never before run for public office. The popular choice of the Republicans was

Wendell Willkie, a lawyer and utility executive with a magnetic personality. Although he criticized the New Deal, Willkie largely agreed with Roosevelt on preparedness and giving aid to Britain short of actually entering the war. His strongest criticism of Roosevelt was the president's decision to break the two-term tradition established by George Washington.

Results. Roosevelt won election for a third time with 54 percent of the popular vote—a smaller margin than in 1932 and 1936. Important factors in the president's reelection were (1) a strong economic recovery based on defense purchases and (2) fear of war causing voters to stay with the more experienced leader.

Arsenal of Democracy

Roosevelt viewed Germany's conquest of most of Europe as a direct threat both to U.S. security and to the future of democratic governments everywhere. After his reelection, he believed that he was in a stronger position to end the appearance of U.S. neutrality and give material aid to Britain. In a December 1940 fireside chat to the American people, he explained his thinking and concluded: "We must be the great arsenal of democracy."

Four Freedoms. Addressing Congress on January 6, 1941, the president delivered a speech that proposed lending money to Britain for the purchase of U.S. war materials and justified such a policy because it was in defense of "four freedoms." He said the United States must stand behind those nations that were committed to freedom of speech, freedom of religion, freedom from want, and freedom from fear.

Lend-Lease Act. Roosevelt proposed ending the cash-and-carry requirement of the Neutrality Act and permitting Britain to obtain all the U.S. arms it needed on credit. The president said it would be like lending a neighbor a garden hose to put out a fire. Isolationists in the America First Committee campaigned vigorously against the lend-lease bill. By now, however, majority opinion had shifted toward aiding Britain, and the Lend-Lease Act was signed into law in March 1941.

Atlantic Charter. With the United States actively aiding Britain, Roosevelt could foresee the possibility that the United States might soon be drawn into the war. He arranged for a secret meeting in August with British Prime Minister Winston Churchill aboard a ship off the coast of Newfoundland. The two leaders drew up a document known as the Atlantic Charter that affirmed what their peace objectives would be when the war ended. They agreed that the general principles for a sound peace would include self-determination for all people, no territorial expansion, and free trade.

Shoot-on-sight. In July 1941, the president extended U.S. support for Britain even further by protecting its ships from submarine attack. He ordered the U.S. Navy to escort British ships carrying lend-lease materials from U.S.

shores as far as Iceland. On September 4, the American destroyer *Greer* was attacked by a German submarine it had been hunting. In response, Roosevelt ordered the Navy to attack all German ships on sight. In effect, this meant that the United States was now fighting an undeclared naval war against Germany.

Disputes With Japan

Meanwhile, through 1940 and 1941, U.S. relations with Japan were becoming increasingly strained as a result of Japan's invasion of China and ambitions to extend its conquests to Southeast Asia. Beginning in 1940, Japan was allied with Germany and Italy as one of the Axis powers. Hitler's success in Europe provided an opportunity for Japanese expansion into the Dutch East Indies, British Burma, and French Indochina—territories still held as colonies by European nations.

U.S. economic action. When Japan joined the Axis in September 1940, Roosevelt responded by prohibiting the export of steel and scrap iron to all countries except Britain and the nations of the Western Hemisphere. His action was aimed at Japan, which protested that it was an "unfriendly act." In July 1941, Japanese troops occupied French Indochina. Roosevelt then froze all Japanese credits in the United States and also cut off Japanese access to vital materials, including U.S. oil.

Negotiations. Both sides realized that Japan needed oil to fuel its navy and air force. If the U.S. embargo on oil did not end, Japan would be forced to extend its conquests by taking the oil resources in the Dutch East Indies. At the same time, Japan's invasion of China was a blatant violation of the Open Door policy, to which the United States was still committed. Roosevelt and Secretary of State Cordell Hull insisted that Japan pull its troops out of China, which Japan refused to do. The Japanese ambassador to the United States tried to negotiate a change in U.S. policy regarding oil. Agreement, however, seemed most unlikely. In October, a new Japanese government headed by General Hideki Tojo made a final attempt at negotiating an agreement. Neither side, however, changed its position.

Roosevelt's military advisers hoped that an armed confrontation with Japan could be delayed until U.S. armed forces in the Pacific were sufficiently strong. Japan, on the other hand, believed that quick action was necessary due to its limited oil supplies.

Pearl Harbor

The U.S. fleet in the Pacific was anchored at Pearl Harbor, Hawaii. On Sunday morning, December 7, 1941, while most American sailors were still asleep in their bunks, Japanese planes from aircraft carriers flew over Pearl Harbor bombing every ship in sight. The surprise attack lasted less than two hours. In that time, 2,400 Americans were killed (including over 1,100 when the battleship *Arizona* sank), almost 1,200 were wounded, 20 warships were sunk or severely damaged, and approximately 150 airplanes were destroyed.

Partial surprise. The American people were stunned by the attack on Pearl Harbor. High government officials, however, knew that an attack somewhere in the Pacific was imminent because they had broken the Japanese codes. They did not know the exact target and date for the attack, which many felt would be in the Philippines, the Dutch East Indies, or Malaya.

Declaration of war. Addressing Congress on the day after Pearl Harbor, Roosevelt described the seventh of December as "a date that will live in infamy." He asked Congress to declare "that since the unprovoked and dastardly attack by Japan on December 7, 1941, a state of war has existed between the United States and the Japanese Empire." On December 8, Congress acted immediately by declaring war, with only one dissenting vote. Three days later, Germany and Italy honored their treaty with Japan by declaring war on the United States.

World War II: The Home Front

In December 1941, the battlefront in Europe had shifted from the west to the east. Breaking his nonaggression pact with Stalin, Hitler had ordered an invasion of the Soviet Union. Thus, the principal Allies fighting Nazi Germany from 1942–1945 were Britain, the United States, and the Soviet Union. The three Allied leaders—Churchill, Roosevelt, and Stalin—agreed to concentrate on the war in Europe before shifting their resources to counter Japanese advances in the Pacific.

Industrial Production

As in World War I, the U.S. government organized a number of special agencies to mobilize U.S. economic and military resources for the wartime crisis. Early in 1942, the War Production Board (WPB) was established to manage war industries. Later the Office of War Mobilization (OWM) set production priorities and controlled raw materials. The government used a cost-plus system, in which it paid war contractors the costs of production plus a certain percentage for profit.

Stimulated by wartime demand and government contracts, U.S. industries did a booming business, far exceeding their production and profits of the 1920s. The depression was over, vanquished at last by the coming of war. By 1944, unemployment had practically disappeared.

War-related industrial output in the United States was astonishing. By 1944, it was twice that of all the Axis powers combined. Instead of automobiles, tanks and fighter planes rolled off the assembly lines. So efficient were production methods that Henry Kaiser's giant shipyard in California could turn out a new ship in just 14 days.

Wages, prices, and rationing. One federal agency, the Office of Price Administration (OPA), regulated almost every aspect of civilians' lives by freezing prices, wages, and rents and rationing such commodities as meat, sugar, gasoline, and auto tires.

Unions. Labor unions and large corporations agreed that while the war lasted, there would be no strikes. Workers became disgruntled, however, as their wages were frozen while corporations made large profits. John L. Lewis therefore called a few strikes of coal unions. The Smith-Connally Anti-Strike Act of 1943, passed over Roosevelt's veto, empowered the government to take over war-related businesses whose operations were threatened by a strike. In 1944, Roosevelt had occasion to use this law when he ordered the army to operate the nation's railroads for a brief period.

Financing the war. The government paid for its huge increase in spending ($100 billion spent on the war in 1945 alone) by (1) increasing the income tax and (2) selling war bonds. For the first time, most Americans were required to pay an income tax, and in 1944, the practice was begun of automatically deducting a withholding tax from paychecks. Borrowing money by selling $135 billion in war bonds supplemented the tax increase. In addition, the shortage of consumer goods made it easier for Americans to save.

The War's Impact on Society

Every group in the U.S. population adjusted in different ways to the unique circumstances of wartime. The increase in factory jobs caused millions to leave rural areas for industrial jobs in the Midwest and on the Pacific Coast, especially California. Entirely new communities arose around the construction of new factories and military bases. A number of new defense installations were located in the South because of that region's warm climate and low labor costs.

African Americans. Attracted by jobs in the North and West, over 1.5 million African Americans left the South. In addition, a million young men left home to serve in the armed forces. Whether as soldiers or civilians, all faced continued discrimination and segregation. White resentment in urban areas led to dozens dying in race riots in New York and Detroit during the summer of 1943. Civil rights leaders encouraged African Americans to adopt the "Double V" slogan—V for victory over fascism abroad and V for victory for equality at home.

Membership in the NAACP increased during the war. Another civil rights organization, the Congress of Racial Equality (CORE), was formed in 1942 to work more militantly for African American interests. One judicial victory was achieved in the Supreme Court case of *Smith v. Allwright* (1944), which ruled that it was unconstitutional to deny membership in political parties to African Americans as a way of excluding them from voting in primaries.

Mexican Americans. Many Mexican Americans worked in defense industries, and over 300,000 served in the military. A 1942 agreement with Mexico allowed Mexican farmworkers, known as *braceros,* to enter the United States in the harvest season without going through formal immigration procedures. The sudden influx of Mexican immigrants into Los Angeles stirred white resentment and led to the so-called zoot suit riots in the summer of 1943, in which whites and Mexican Americans battled on the streets.

Native Americans. Native Americans also contributed to the war effort. Approximately 25,000 served in the military, and thousands more worked in defense industries. Having left the reservations, more than half never returned.

Japanese Americans. More than any other ethnic group, Japanese Americans suffered from their association with a wartime enemy. Almost 20,000 native-born Japanese Americans served loyally in the military. Nevertheless, following the attack on Pearl Harbor, Japanese Americans were suspected of being potential spies and saboteurs, and a Japanese invasion of the West Coast was considered imminent by many. In 1942, these irrational fears as well as racism prompted the U.S. government to order over 100,000 Japanese Americans on the West Coast to leave their homes and reside in the barracks of internment camps. Japanese Americans living in other parts of the U.S., including Hawaii, did not come under this order. In the case of *Korematsu v. U.S.* (1944), the Supreme Court upheld the U.S. government's internment policy as justified in wartime. Years later, in 1988, the federal government agreed that an injustice had been done and awarded financial compensation to those still alive who had been interned.

Women. The war also changed the lives of women. Over 200,000 served in the military in noncombat roles. Once again, as in World War I, an acute labor shortage caused women to take jobs vacated by men in uniform. Almost 5 million women entered the workforce, many of them working in industrial jobs in the shipyards and defense plants. A song about "Rosie the Riveter" was used to encourage women to take defense jobs. The pay they received, however, was well below that of male factory workers.

Propaganda. The government's war propaganda was everywhere. The posters, songs, and news bulletins had many purposes: to maintain public morale, to encourage people to sacrifice and conserve resources, and to increase war production. The Office of War Information controlled news about troop movements and battles. Movies, radio, and popular music all supported and reflected a cheerful, patriotic view of the war.

The Election of 1944

With the war consuming most of people's attention, the presidential election of 1944 had less interest than usual.

Again, F.D.R. Many felt that, in the war emergency, there should be no change in leadership. The president therefore sought and received the Democratic nomination for the fourth time. There was a change, however, in the Democrats' choice of a vice presidential running mate. Party leaders felt that Roosevelt's third-term vice president, Henry Wallace, was too radical and unmanageable. With Roosevelt's agreement, they replaced Wallace with Harry S. Truman, a Missouri senator with a national reputation for having conducted a much-publicized investigation of war spending. Although Roosevelt publicly denied medical problems, those near him recognized the uncertainty of his health.

Thomas Dewey. The Republicans nominated the 42-year-old governor of New York, Thomas Dewey, who had a strong record of prosecuting corruption and racketeering. The Republican candidate was unable to offer any real alternative to Roosevelt's leadership or generate enthusiasm for change.

Results. Winning 53 percent of the popular vote and an overwhelming 432–99 victory in the electoral college, the president was elected to an unprecedented fourth term. As it proved, however, F.D.R. would live for less than three months after his inauguration. Most of his term would be served by Truman.

World War II: The Battlefronts

The fighting of World War II was waged on two fronts, or "theaters of operation." In the Pacific, Japanese forces in 1942 reached the height of their power, occupying the Philippines, the Dutch East Indies, and islands of the South Pacific. In Europe, much of the fighting in the first year of war was between the Germans and the Soviets, as the latter fought desperately to prevent the conquest of Russia.

Fighting Germany

The high tide of the German advance ended in 1942, partly as a result of U.S. entry into the war but mainly because of a Soviet victory at Stalingrad in the winter of the year.

Defense at sea, attacks by air. Coordinating their military strategy, the British and Americans concentrated on two objectives in 1942: (1) overcoming the menace of German submarines in the Atlantic and (2) beginning bombing raids on German cities. The protracted naval war to control the shipping lanes was known as the Battle of the Atlantic. German submarines sank over 500 Allied ships in 1942. Gradually, however, the Allies developed ways of containing the submarine menace through the use of radar, sonar, and the bombing of German naval bases.

From North Africa to Italy. The Allies had the daunting task of driving German occupying forces out of their advance positions in North Africa and the Mediterranean. They began their North Africa campaign, Operation Torch, in November 1942. Led by U.S. General Dwight Eisenhower and British General

Bernard Montgomery, Allied forces succeeded in taking North Africa from the Germans by May 1943.

The next U.S.-British target was the Mediterranean island of Sicily, which they occupied in the summer of 1943, preparatory to an invasion of Italy. Mussolini fell from power during the summer, but Hitler's forces rescued him and gave him nominal control of northern Italy. In fact, German troops controlled much of Italy at the time that the Allies invaded the peninsula in September 1943. The Germans put up a determined resistance to the Allied offensive, holding much of northern Italy until their final surrender in May 1945.

From D day to victory in Europe. The Allied drive to liberate France began on June 6, 1944, with the largest invasion by sea in history. On D day, as the invasion date was called, British, Canadian, and U.S. forces under the command of General Eisenhower secured several beachheads on the Normandy coast. After this bloody but successful attack, the Allied offensive moved rapidly to roll back German occupying forces. By the end of August, Paris was liberated. By September, Allied troops had crossed the German border for a final push toward Berlin. The Germans launched a desperate counterattack in Belgium in December 1944 in the Battle of the Bulge. After this setback, however, Americans reorganized and resumed their advance.

German surrender and discovery of the Holocaust. Since 1942, Allied bombing raids over Germany had reduced that nation's industrial capacity and ability to continue fighting. Recognizing that the end was near, Hitler committed suicide on April 30, 1945. The unconditional surrender of the Nazi armies took place a week later, on May 7.

As U.S. troops advanced through Germany, they came upon German concentration camps and witnessed the horrifying extent of the Nazi's program of genocide against the Jews and others. Americans and the world were shocked to learn that as many as 6 million Jewish civilians had been systematically murdered by Nazi Germany.

Fighting Japan

In Europe, British, Soviet, and U.S. forces were jointly responsible for defeating Germany, but in the Pacific, it was largely the U.S. armed forces that challenged the Japanese. After the Pearl Harbor attack, Japan succeeded in achieving control of much of East Asia and Southeast Asia. By early 1942, Japanese troops occupied Korea, eastern China, the Philippines, British Burma and Malaya, French Indochina (Vietnam, Cambodia, and Laos), the Dutch East Indies (Indonesia), and most of the Pacific islands west of Midway Island.

Turning point, 1942. The war in the Pacific was dominated by naval forces battling over a vast area. Two naval battles in the late spring of 1942 proved to be a turning point in halting the Japanese advance. On May 7–8, in the Battle of the Coral Sea, U.S. aircraft carriers stopped a Japanese invasion of Australia. Next, June 4–7, in the decisive Battle of Midway, the interception and decoding of Japanese messages enabled U.S. forces to destroy four Japanese carriers and 300 planes.

Island-hopping. Now began the long campaign to get within striking distance of Japan's home islands by seizing strategic islands in the Pacific. Naval commanders adopted a strategy called "island-hopping," in which they bypassed strongly held Japanese islands and isolated them with naval and air power. This strategy, adopted by Admiral Chester Nimitz, allowed Allied forces to move rapidly toward Japan. Vowing to return to the Philippines (conquered by Japan in early 1942), General Douglas MacArthur commanded army units in the southern Pacific.

Major battles. The naval battle that prepared the way for U.S. reoccupation of the Philippines was the largest naval battle in history. At the Battle of Leyte Gulf in October 1944, the Japanese navy was virtually destroyed. For the first time in the war, the Japanese used *kamikaze* pilots to make suicide attacks on U.S. ships. Kamikazes also inflicted major damage in the colossal Battle of Okinawa (April to June 1945). Before finally succeeding in taking this island near Japan, U.S. forces suffered 50,000 casualties and killed 100,000 Japanese.

Atomic bombs. After Okinawa, a huge invasion force stood ready to attack Japan. Extremely heavy casualties were feared. By this time, however, the United States had developed a frightfully destructive new weapon. The top-secret Manhattan Project had begun in 1942. Directed by the physicist J. Robert Oppenheimer, the project employed over 100,000 people and spent $2 billion to develop a weapon whose power came from the splitting of the atom. The atomic bomb, or A-bomb, was successfully tested on July 16, 1945, at Alamogordo, New Mexico. The new president, Harry Truman, and his wartime allies called on Japan to surrender unconditionally or face "utter destruction." When Japan gave an unsatisfactory reply, Truman consulted with his advisers and decided to use the new weapon on two Japanese cities. On August 6, an A-bomb was dropped on Hiroshima, and on August 9, a second bomb was dropped on Nagasaki. About 250,000 Japanese died, either immediately or after a prolonged period of suffering, as a result of the two bombs.

Japan surrenders. Within a week after the second bomb fell, Japan agreed to surrender if the Allies would agree to allow the emperor to remain on the throne as a titular (powerless) head of state. Japan's formal surrender was received by General MacArthur on September 2, 1945 in Tokyo harbor aboard the battleship *Missouri*.

Wartime Conferences

During the war, the Big Three (leaders of the United States, the Soviet Union, and Great Britain) arranged to confer secretly to coordinate their military strategies and to lay the foundation for peace terms.

Casablanca. The first conference involved only two of the Big Three. In January 1943, Roosevelt and Churchill agreed to invade Sicily and to demand "unconditional surrender" from the Axis powers.

Teheran. The Big Three—Roosevelt, Churchill, and Stalin—met for the first time in the Iranian city of Teheran in November 1943. They agreed that the British and Americans would begin their drive to liberate France in the spring of 1944 and that the Soviets would invade Germany and eventually join the war against Japan.

Yalta. In February 1945, the Big Three conferred again at Yalta, a resort town on the Black Sea coast of the Soviet Union. Their agreement at Yalta would prove to have long-term significance. After victory in Europe was achieved, Roosevelt, Churchill, and Stalin agreed that

- Germany would be divided into occupation zones

- there would be free elections in the liberated countries of Eastern Europe (even though Soviet troops now controlled this territory)

- the Soviets would enter the war against Japan, which they did on August 8, 1945—just as Japan was about to surrender

- the Soviets would control the southern half of Sakhalin island and the Kurile Islands in the Pacific and would also have special concessions in Manchuria

- a new world peace organization (the future United Nations) would be formed at a conference in San Francisco.

Death of President Roosevelt. When the president returned from Yalta and informed Congress of his agreement with Churchill and Stalin, it was apparent that his health had deteriorated. On April 12, 1945, while resting in a vacation home in Georgia, an exhausted Franklin Roosevelt died suddenly. News of his death shocked the nation almost as much as Pearl Harbor. Harry S. Truman entered the presidency unexpectedly to assume enormous responsibilities as commander in chief of a war effort that had not yet been won.

Potsdam. In late July, after Germany's surrender, only Stalin remained as one of the Big Three. Truman was the U.S. president, and Clement Attlee had just been elected the new British prime minister. The three leaders met in Postsdam, Germany (July 17–August 2, 1945) and agreed (1) to issue a warning to Japan to surrender unconditionally, and (2) to hold war-crime trials of Nazi leaders.

The War's Legacy

The most destructive war in the history of the world had profound effects on all nations, including the United States.

Costs

Approximately 300,000 Americans lost their lives either in Europe or the Pacific, and 800,000 were wounded. Excluding the Civil War, more Americans died in World War II than in all other U.S. wars combined. The dollar cost was over $320 billion, a sum ten times greater than spending for World War I. Deficit spending during the last years of the depression was almost negligible compared to the deficits incurred during the war. Federal spending increased 1,000 percent between 1939 and 1945. By war's end, the national debt had reached the staggering figure of $250 billion, five times what it had been in 1941.

The United Nations

Unlike the rejection of the League of Nations following World War I, Congress readily accepted the peacekeeping organization that was conceived during World War II and put in place immediately after the war. Meeting in 1944 at Dumbarton Oaks near Washington, D.C., Allied representatives from the United States, the Soviet Union, Great Britain, and China proposed an international organization to be called the United Nations. Then in April 1945, delegates from 50 nations assembled in San Francisco, where they took only eight weeks to draft a charter for the United Nations. The Senate quickly voted to accept U.S. involvement in the U.N. On October 24, 1945, the U.N. came into existence when the majority of member-nations ratified its charter.

Expectations

In a final speech, which he never delivered, Franklin Roosevelt wrote: "The only limit to our realization of tomorrow will be the doubts of today." There were doubts, to be sure, about the new world order to emerge from World War II. Initially at least, there were also widely shared hopes that life would be better and more prosperous after the war than before. While other combatants, such as China, France, Germany, Great Britain, Italy, Japan, and the Soviet Union, had suffered extensive damage from the war, the cities of the United States had remained unscarred. Without a doubt, the United States in 1945 was at once the most prosperous and the most powerful nation in the world. It had played a major role in defeating the Fascist dictators. Now people looked forward with some optimism to both a more peaceful and more democratic world. Unfortunately, the specters of the Soviet Union and the A-bomb would soon dim these expectations of a brighter tomorrow.

HISTORICAL PERSPECTIVES: COULD PEARL HARBOR HAVE BEEN AVOIDED?

At first it seemed that U.S. entry into World War II was simply a reaction to Japan's attack on Pearl Harbor. Probing more deeply, some historians placed part of the blame for the outbreak of World War II on U.S. policies in the late 1930s. They argued that U.S.

isolationism emboldened the Fascist dictators and also left U.S. territories vulnerable to attack through military unpreparedness.

In the late 1940s, revisionists wrote that the Pearl Harbor attack could have been avoided if the diplomacy of Roosevelt and Secretary of State Hull had been less inflexible. Charles A. Beard took the extreme view that Roosevelt intended the embargo on raw materials to force Japan into war. Many of the revisionists believed that Roosevelt wanted the United States in the war because of his anti-Fascist beliefs and pro-British sympathies.

Later revisionist criticisms of the 1950s and 1960s asked why naval authorities at Pearl Harbor were unprepared for an attack since the United States had broken the Japanese code. Presumably, officials knew that a Japanese attack was coming but could not determine precisely when and where it would be.

For many, the definitive study of Pearl Harbor is Gordon W. Prange's *At Dawn We Slept* (1981). While Prange believes the government could have done better predicting and preparing for an attack, he finds no evidence of a secret plot to allow Pearl Harbor to happen. His key point is that the Japanese had brilliantly planned and executed an attack that was inconceivable to most Americans at that time.

Taking the opposite position is John Toland's *Infamy: Pearl Harbor and Its Aftermath* (1982). Toland argues that Roosevelt had advance knowledge of the attack but withheld any warning so that a surprise attack would bring the United States into the war. A major problem with this argument is that the author presents no direct evidence for his conclusion.

In assessing the divergent views on the Pearl Harbor attack, we should differentiate between historical *analysis* of how and why events occurred and historical *judgment* of a leader's underlying motives. In the latter type of history, a writer's personal biases are apt to play a stronger role.

KEY NAMES, EVENTS, AND TERMS

Manchuria (Manchukuo)	Cordell Hull	neutrality acts
Stimson Doctrine	fascism	Spanish Civil War (1936–
good-neighbor policy	Italian Fascist party; Benito	1939)
Pan-American conferences	Mussolini	Francisco Franco
(1933, 1936)	German Nazi party; Adolf	America First Committee
London Economic	Hitler	appeasement
Conference (1933)	Axis Powers	Ethiopia
Soviet Union, recognized	isolationism	Rhineland
Tydings-McDuffie Act	Nye Committee	Czechoslovakia

Sudetenland	Atlantic Charter	Holocaust
Munich	Pearl Harbor	Battle of Midway
quarantine speech	Office of Price Administration	Chester Nimitz
Poland; *blitzkrieg*	*Smith v. Allwright*	Douglas MacArthur
cash and carry	*Korematsu v. U.S.*	Manhattan Project
Selective Training and Service Act (1940)	Harry S. Truman	J. Robert Oppenheimer
destroyers-for-bases deal	Battle of the Atlantic	atomic bomb
Wendell Willkie	Dwight Eisenhower	Hiroshima; Nagasaki
four freedoms speech	D day	Big Three
Lend-Lease Act (1941)	Battle of the Bulge	Yalta
		United Nations

MULTIPLE-CHOICE QUESTIONS

1. Which of the following phrases accurately describes Roosevelt's good-neighbor policy?
   - (A) search for improved relations with Canada
   - (B) abandonment of the Open Door policy in China
   - (C) U.S. pledge not to intervene in Latin America
   - (D) diplomatic recognition of the Soviet Union
   - (E) commitment to the democracies of Europe

2. "It was like lending a garden hose to a neighbor whose house was burning."

   This statement by President Roosevelt is consistent with all of the following U.S. policies EXCEPT
   - (A) the Neutrality Acts
   - (B) the destroyers-for-bases deal
   - (C) the Lend-Lease Act
   - (D) the Atlantic Charter
   - (E) "sink-on-sight"

3. Which of the following was an expression of isolationism in the 1930s?
   - (A) Roosevelt's "quarantine" speech
   - (B) the good-neighbor policy
   - (C) the Nye Committee
   - (D) recognition of the Soviet Union
   - (E) "cash and carry" policy

4. In the 1930s, the foreign policies of Japan and the United States were chiefly in conflict over
   - (A) U.S. control of the Philippines
   - (B) Japanese invasion of China
   - (C) U.S. isolationism
   - (D) ideological differences
   - (E) internment of Japanese Americans

5. On the home front, U.S. involvement in World War II brought about
   - (A) increased labor violence

(B) increased spending on consumer goods

(C) increased employment of women

(D) strict limits on corporate profits

(E) an end to deficit spending by the federal government

6. In *Korematsu v. U.S.* the Supreme Court upheld the government's practice of

(A) placing quotas on Japanese immigration

(B) embargoing trade with Japan

(C) providing financial compensation for victims of discrimination

(D) placing Japanese Americans in internment camps

(E) drafting men into the armed services in peacetime

7. Consequences of Truman's decision to use the atomic bomb against Japan included all of the following EXCEPT

(A) the surrender of Japan

(B) the end of World War II

(C) full-scale invasion of Japan by U.S. troops

(D) destruction of two Japanese cities

(E) the deaths of thousands of civilians

8. At which of the following conferences did Stalin agree to hold free elections in the countries of Eastern Europe?

(A) London

(B) Casablanca

(C) Teheran

(D) Yalta

(E) San Francisco

9. Which is an accurate characterization of how U.S. foreign policy changed from 1938 to early 1941?

(A) from neutrality to support for Britain

(B) from isolationism to neutrality

(C) from intervention in Latin America to the good-neighbor policy

(D) from hostility to Japan to diplomatic efforts to appease Japan

(E) from pro-German policies to anti-Japanese policies

10. From 1942 to 1945, the United States was allied with

(A) Great Britain only

(B) Great Britain and the Soviet Union

(C) France, Spain, and the Soviet Union

(D) Italy and Great Britain

(E) no other nation

ESSAY QUESTIONS

1. Discuss the view that a different U.S. foreign policy could have prevented the outbreak of World War II.

2. Assess President Roosevelt's efforts to deal with the dangers of fascism and lead the nation away from a policy of isolationism in the context of TWO of the following:

   Panay incident

   cash and carry

   quarantine speech

   destroyers-for-bases deal

3. Compare and contrast U.S. reaction to war in Europe in 1914 with its reaction in 1939.

4. Analyze the discrimination TWO of the following groups faced during World War II, despite their patriotism:

   African Americans

   Japanese Americans

   Mexican Americans

   women

5. Argue either for or against this statement: "President Truman's decision to use the atomic bomb was completely justified."

DOCUMENT-BASED QUESTION (DBQ)

"To a greater or lesser extent, three factors were involved in explaining U.S. response to Japanese and German aggression: (a) economics, (b) national security, and (c) democratic values."

Drawing upon the documents that follow as well as your knowledge of history, write an essay explaining how these factors influenced Franklin Roosevelt's foreign policy from 1937 to 1941.

DOCUMENT A.

I am compelled and you are compelled, to look ahead. The peace, the freedom and the security of 90 per cent of the population of the world is being jeopardized by the remaining 10 per cent who are threatening a breakdown of all international order and law.

Surely the 90 per cent who want to live in peace under law and in accordance with moral standards that have received almost universal acceptance through the centuries, can and must find some way to make their will prevail. . . .

Franklin D. Roosevelt,
Speech in Chicago, "Quarantine the Aggressors,"
October 5, 1937

DOCUMENT B.

The Commandant of the Third Naval District expressed "hearty accord" with President Roosevelt's proposal to increase the nation's naval strength by a huge and extraordinary appropriation of public funds. "A navy second to none," said he, was needed as a "contribution to world peace," and he denounced "all foolish nations which through mistaken ideas of altruism were unprepared to defend themselves when attacked."

In the stock markets [according to the New York *Herald Tribune,* December 30], "intermittent buying in aircrafts, steels, and a selected assortment of heavy industrials pushed prices substantially higher, demand apparently being based on expectations of large rearmament expenditures by the national government."

Council on Foreign Relations,
The United States in World Affairs,
1937 (Harper & Brothers, 1938)

DOCUMENT C.

If Hitler wins in Europe—if the strength of the British and French armies and navies is forever broken—the United States will find itself alone in a barbaric world—a world ruled by Nazis, with "spheres of influence" assigned to their totalitarian allies. However different the dictatorships may be, racially, they all agree on one primary objective: *"Democracy must be wiped from the face of the earth."*

The world will be placed on a permanent war footing. Our country will have to pile armaments upon armaments to maintain even the illusion of security. We shall have no other business, no other aim in life, but primitive self-defense. We shall exist only under martial law—or the law of the jungle. . . .

Advertisement, *The New York Times,*
June 10, 1940

DOCUMENT D.

I cannot ask the American people to put their faith in me without recording my conviction that some form of selective service is the only democratic way in which to secure the trained and competent manpower we need for national defense.

Also, in the light of my principle, we must honestly face our relationship with Great Britain. We must admit that the loss of the British Fleet would greatly weaken our defense. This is because the British Fleet has for years controlled the Atlantic, leaving us free to concentrate in the Pacific. If the British Fleet were lost or captured, the Atlantic might be dominated by Germany, a power hostile to our way of life, controlling in that event most of the ships and shipbuilding facilities of Europe.

This would be calamity for us. We might be exposed to attack on the Atlantic. Our defense would be weakened until we could build a navy and air force strong enough to defend both coasts. Also, our foreign trade would be profoundly affected. That trade is vital to our prosperity. But if we had to trade with a Europe dominated by the present German trade policies, we might have to change our methods to some totalitarian form. This is a prospect that any lover of democracy must view with consternation.

Wendell Willkie,
Acceptance Speech at the Republican National Convention,
August 17, 1940

DOCUMENT E.

Brown Brothers

DOCUMENT F.

Our national policy is this:

First, by an impressive expression of the public will and without regard to partisanship, we are committed to all-inclusive national defense.

Second, by an impressive expression of the public will and without regard to partisanship, we are committed to full support of all those resolute people everywhere who are resisting aggression and are thereby keeping war away from our hemisphere. By this support we express our determination that the democratic cause shall prevail, and we strengthen the defense and the security of our own nation. . . .

Let us say to the democracies: "We Americans are vitally concerned in your defense of freedom. We are putting forth our energies, our resources and our organizing powers to give you the strength to regain and maintain a free world. We shall send you in ever-increasing numbers, ships, planes, tanks, guns. That is our purpose and our pledge."

Franklin D. Roosevelt,
Speech to Congress, "Four Freedoms,"
January 6, 1941

DOCUMENT G.

The Effect of World War II on Industry			
	1939	**1940**	**1941**
Index of manufacturing output (1939 = 100)	100	116	154
Corporate profits before taxes (billions of dollars)	6.4	9.3	17.0
Corporate profits after taxes (billions of dollars)	5.0	6.5	9.4
Business failures	14,768	13,619	11,848

Adapted from Gilbert C. Fite, Jim E. Reese,
An Economic History of the United States (1959)

DOCUMENT H.

The United States is better situated from a military standpoint than any other nation in the world. Even in our present condition of unpreparedness no foreign power is in a position to invade us today. If we concentrate on our own defenses and build the strength that this nation should maintain, no foreign army will ever attempt to land on American shores.

War is not inevitable for this country. Such a claim is defeatism in the true sense. No one can make us fight abroad unless we ourselves are willing to do so. No one will attempt to fight us here if we arm ourselves as a great nation should be armed. Over 100 million people in this nation are opposed to entering the war. If the principles of democracy mean anything at all, that is reason enough for us to stay out.

Charles A. Lindbergh,
Speech in New York City, "America First,"
April 23, 1941

TRUMAN AND THE COLD WAR, 1945–1952

Communism holds that the world is so deeply divided into opposing classes that war is inevitable.
Democracy holds that free nations can settle differences justly and maintain lasting peace.

President Harry S. Truman,
Inaugural Address, January 20, 1949

World War II dramatically changed the United States from an isolationist country into a military superpower and leader in world affairs. After World War II, most of the Americans at home and the millions coming back from military service wished to return to normal domestic life and enjoy the revitalized national economy. However, during the Truman presidency, the growing conflict between the Communist Soviet Union and the United States—a conflict that came to be known as the Cold War—would dampen the nation's enjoyment of the postwar boom.

Postwar America

The 15 million American soldiers, sailors, and marines returning to civilian life in 1945 and 1946 faced the problem of finding jobs and housing. Many feared that the end of the war might mean the return of economic hard times. Happily, the fears were not realized because the war years had increased the per-capita income of Americans. Much of that income was tucked away in savings accounts, since wartime shortages meant there had been few consumer goods to buy. Pent-up consumer demand for autos and housing combined with government road-building projects quickly overcame the economic uncertainty after the war and introduced an era of unprecedented prosperity and economic growth. By the 1950s, Americans enjoyed the highest standard of living achieved by any society in history.

GI Bill—Help for Veterans

The Servicemen's Readjustment Act of 1944, popularly known as the GI Bill of Rights, proved a powerful support during the transition of 15 million veterans to a peacetime economy. More than half the returning GIs (as the men and women in uniform were called) seized the opportunity afforded by the GI Bill to continue their education at government expense. Over 2 million GI's attended college, which started a postwar boom in higher education. The veterans also received over $16 billion in low-interest, government-backed loans to buy homes and farms and to start businesses. By focusing on a better educated workforce and also promoting new construction, the federal government stimulated the postwar economic expansion.

Baby Boom

One sign of the basic confidence of the postwar era was an explosion in marriages and births. Younger marriages and larger families resulted in 50 million babies entering the U.S. population between 1945 and 1960. As the *baby-boom* generation gradually passed from childhood to adolescence to adulthood, it would profoundly affect the nation's social institutions and economic life in the last half of the 20th century. Initially, the baby boom tended to focus women's attention on raising children and homemaking. Nevertheless, the trend of more women in the workplace continued. By 1960, one-third of all married women worked outside the home.

Suburban Growth

The desperate need for housing after the war resulted in a construction boom. William J. Levitt led in the development of postwar suburbia with his building and promotion of Levittown, a project of 17,000 mass-produced, low-priced family homes on Long Island, New York. Low interest rates on mortgages that were both government-insured and tax deductible made the move from city to suburb affordable for almost any family of modest means. In a single generation, the majority of middle-class Americans became suburbanites. For many older, inner cities, the effect of the mass movement to suburbia was little short of disastrous. By the 1960s, cities from Boston to Los Angeles became increasingly poor and racially divided.

Rise of the Sunbelt

Uprooted by the war, millions of Americans made moving a habit in the postwar era. A warmer climate, lower taxes, and economic opportunities in defense-related industries attracted many GI's and their families to the Sunbelt states from Florida to California. By transferring tax dollars from the Northeast and Midwest to the South and West, military spending during the Cold War helped finance the shift of industry, people, and ultimately political power from one region to the other.

Postwar Politics

Harry S. Truman, a moderate Democratic senator from Missouri, replaced the more liberal Henry Wallace as FDR's vice president in the 1944 election.

Thrust into the presidency after Roosevelt's death in April 1945, Truman matured into a decisive leader whose basic honesty and unpretentious style appealed to average citizens. President Truman attempted to continue in the New Deal tradition of his predecessor.

Economic Program and Civil Rights

Truman's proposals for full employment and for civil rights for African Americans ran into opposition from more conservative Congresses.

Employment Act of 1946. In September 1945, during the same week that Japan formally surrendered, Truman urged Congress to enact a series of progressive measures, including national health insurance, an increase in the minimum wage, and a bill to commit the U.S. government to maintaining full employment. After much debate, the watered-down version of the full-employment bill was enacted as the Employment Act of 1946. It created the Council of Economic Advisers to counsel both the president and Congress on means of promoting national economic welfare. Over the next seven years, conservative Congresses and the beginning of the Cold War would hinder the passage of most of Truman's domestic program.

Inflation and strikes. Truman asked Congress to continue the price controls of wartime in order to hold inflation in check. Instead, southern Democrats joined with Republicans in relaxing the controls of the Office of Price Administration. The result was an inflation rate of almost 25 percent in the first year and a half of peace.

Workers and unions wanted wages to catch up after years of wage controls. Over 4.5 million workers went on strike in 1946. Strikes by railroad and mine workers threatened the national safety. Truman took a tough approach to this challenge, seizing the mines and using soldiers to keep them operating until the United Mine Workers finally called off its strike.

Civil rights. Truman was the first modern president to use the powers of his office to challenge racial discrimination. Bypassing southern Democrats who controlled key committees in Congress, the president used his executive powers to establish the Committee on Civil Rights in 1946. He also strengthened the civil rights division of the Justice Department, which aided the efforts of black leaders to end segregation in schools. Most important, in 1948 he ordered the end of racial discrimination in the departments of the federal government and all three branches of the armed forces. The end of segregation within the military also changed life on military bases, many of which were in the South.

Recognizing the odds against passage of civil rights legislation, Truman nevertheless urged Congress to create a Fair Employment Practices Commission that would prevent employers from discriminating against the hiring of African Americans. Southern Democrats blocked the legislation.

Republican Control of the Eightieth Congress

Unhappy with inflation and strikes, voters were in a conservative mood in the fall of 1946 when they elected Republican majorities in both houses of Congress. Under Republican control, the Eightieth Congress attempted to pass two tax cuts for upper-income Americans, but Truman vetoed both measures. More successful were Republican efforts to amend the Constitution and roll back some of the New Deal gains for labor.

Twenty-second Amendment (1951). Reacting against the fact that Roosevelt had been elected president four times, the Republican-dominated Congress proposed a constitutional amendment to limit a president to a maximum of two full terms in office. The Twenty-second Amendment was ratified by the states in 1951.

Taft-Hartley Act (1947). In 1947, Congress passed the probusiness Taft-Hartley Act. Truman vetoed the measure as a "slave-labor" bill, but Congress overrode his veto. The one purpose of the Republican-sponsored law was to check the growing power of unions. Its provisions included

- outlawing the closed shop (contract requiring workers to join a union *before* being hired)

- permitting states to pass "right to work" laws outlawing the union shop (contract requiring workers to join a union *after* being hired)

- outlawing secondary boycotts (the practice of several unions giving support to a striking union by joining a boycott of a company's products)

- giving the president the power to invoke an 80-day cooling-off period before a strike endangering the national safety could be called.

For years afterward, unions sought without success to secure the repeal of the Taft-Hartley Act. It was a major issue dividing Republicans and Democrats into the 1950s.

The Election of 1948

As measured by opinion polls, Truman's popularity was at a low point as the 1948 campaign for the presidency began. Republicans were confident of victory, especially after both a liberal faction and a conservative faction in the Democratic party abandoned Truman to organize their own third parties. Liberal Democrats, who thought Truman's aggressive foreign policy threatened world peace, formed a new Progressive party that nominated former vice president Henry Wallace. Southern Democrats also bolted the party in reaction to Truman's support for civil rights. Their States' Rights party, better known as the Dixiecrats, chose J. Strom Thurmond of South Carolina as its presidential candidate.

The Republicans once again nominated New York Governor Thomas E. Dewey, who looked so much like a winner from the outset that he conducted an overly cautious and unexciting campaign. Meanwhile, the man without a chance toured the nation by rail, attacking the "do-nothing" Republican Eightieth Congress with "give-'em-hell" speeches. The feisty Truman confounded the polling experts with a decisive victory over Dewey (a 2 million majority in the popular vote and 303–189 electoral votes). The president had succeeded in reuniting Roosevelt's New Deal coalition, except for four southern states that went to Thurmond and the Dixiecrats.

The Fair Deal

Fresh from victory, Truman launched an ambitious reform program, which he called the *Fair Deal*. In 1949, he urged Congress to enact national health care insurance, federal aid to education, civil rights legislation, funds for public housing, and a new farm program. Conservatives in Congress managed to block most of the proposed reforms, except for an increase in the minimum wage (from 40 to 75 cents an hour) and the inclusion of more workers under Social Security.

Most of the Fair Deal bills were defeated for two reasons: (1) Truman's political conflicts with Congress and (2) the pressing foreign policy concerns of the Cold War. Nevertheless, liberal defenders of Truman give him credit for at least maintaining the New Deal reforms of his predecessor and making civil rights part of the liberal agenda.

Origins of the Cold War

The Cold War dominated international relations from the late 1940s to the collapse of the Soviet Union in 1991. The conflict centered around the intense rivalry between two superpowers, the Communist empire of the Soviet Union and the leading Western democracy, the United States. Competition between these powers and their allies was usually conducted by means short of armed conflict but, in several instances, the Cold War took the world dangerously close to a nuclear war.

Among historians there is intense debate over how and why the Cold War began. Many analysts see Truman's policies as a reasonable response to Soviet efforts to increase Communist influence in the world. Critics, however, argue that Truman misunderstood and overreacted to Russia's historic need to secure its borders. Conservative critics at the time, however, increasingly attacked his administration as being weak or "soft" on communism.

U.S.-Soviet Relations to 1945

The wartime alliance between the United States and the Soviet Union against the Axis powers was actually a temporary halt in their generally poor relations of the past. The Bolshevik Revolution that established a Communist government in Russia in 1917 had been immediately viewed as a threat to all capitalistic countries. In the United States, it led to the Red Scare of 1919. The

United States refused to recognize the Soviet Union until 1933. Even then, after a brief honeymoon period of less than a year, Roosevelt's advisers concluded that Joseph Stalin and the Communists could not be trusted. Confirming their view was the notorious Nonaggression Pact of 1939, in which Stalin and Hitler agreed to divide up Eastern Europe.

Allies in World War II. In 1941, Hitler's surprise invasion of the Soviet Union and Japan's surprise attack on Pearl Harbor led to a U.S.–Soviet alliance of convenience—but not of mutual trust. Stalin bitterly complained that the British and Americans waited until 1944 to open a second front in France. The postwar conflicts over Central and Eastern Europe were already evident in the negotiations of the Big Three (Britain, the Soviet Union, and the U.S.) at Yalta and Potsdam in 1945. Roosevelt hoped that personal diplomacy might keep Stalin in check, but when Truman came to power, he quickly became suspicious of Soviet acts and intentions.

Postwar cooperation—the U.N. The founding of the United Nations in the fall of 1945 was one hopeful sign for the future. The General Assembly of the United Nations was created to provide representation to all member nations, while the 15-member Security Council was given the primary responsibility within the UN for maintaining international security and authorizing peacekeeping missions. The five major allies of wartime—the United States, Great Britain, France, China, and the Soviet Union—were granted permanent seats and veto power in the U.N. Security Council. Optimists hoped that these nations would be able to reach agreement on international issues. In addition, the Soviets went along with a U.S. proposal to establish an Atomic Energy Commission in the United Nations. They rejected, however, a plan proposed by Bernard Baruch for regulating nuclear energy and eliminating atomic weapons. Rejection of the Baruch Plan was interpreted by some American leaders as proof that Moscow did not have peaceful intentions.

The United States also offered the Soviets participation in the new International Bank for Reconstruction and Development (World Bank) created at the Bretton Woods Conference in 1944. The bank's initial purpose was to fund rebuilding of a war-torn world. The Soviets, however, declined to participate because they viewed the bank as an instrument of capitalism. The Soviets did join the other Allies in the 1945–1946 Nuremberg trials of 22 top Nazi leaders for war crimes and violations of human rights.

Satellite states in Eastern Europe. Distrust turned into hostility beginning in 1946, as Soviet forces remained in occupation of the countries of central and Eastern Europe. Elections were held by the Soviets—as promised by Stalin at Yalta—but the results were manipulated in favor of Communist candidates. One by one, from 1946 to 1948, Communist dictators, most of them loyal to Moscow, came to power in Poland, Romania, Bulgaria, Albania, Hungary, and Czechoslovakia. Apologists for the Soviets argued that Russia needed buffer states or satellites (nations under the control of a great power), as a protection against another Hitler-like invasion from the West.

The U.S. and British governments were alarmed by the Soviet takeover of Eastern Europe. They regarded Soviet actions in this region as a flagrant violation of self-determination, genuine democracy, and open markets. The British especially wanted free elections in Poland, whose independence had been the issue that started World War II.

Occupation zones in Germany. At the end of the war, the division of Germany and Austria into Soviet, French, British, and U.S. zones of occupation was meant to be only temporary. In Germany, however, the eastern zone under Soviet occupation gradually evolved into a new Communist state, the German Democratic Republic. The conflict over Germany was at least in part a conflict over differing views of national security and economic needs. The Soviets wanted a weak Germany for security reasons and large war reparations for economic reasons. The United States and Great Britain refused to allow reparations from their western zones because both viewed the economic recovery of Germany as important to the stability of Central Europe. The Soviets, fearing a restored Germany, tightened their control over East Germany. Also, since Berlin lay within their zone, they attempted to force the Americans, British, and French to give up their assigned sectors of the city.

Iron Curtain. "I'm tired of babying the Soviets," Truman told Secretary of State James Byrnes in January 1946. News of a Canadian spy ring stealing atomic secrets for the Soviets and continued Soviet occupation of northern Iran further encouraged a get-tough policy in Washington.

In March 1946, in Fulton, Missouri, Truman was present on the speaker's platform as former British Prime Minister Winston Churchill declared: "An iron curtain has descended across the continent" of Europe. The iron-curtain metaphor was later used throughout the Cold War to refer to the Soviet satellite states of Eastern Europe. Churchill's "iron curtain" speech called for a partnership between Western democracies to halt the expansion of communism. Did the speech anticipate the Cold War—or help to cause it? Historians still debate this question.

Containment in Europe

Early in 1947, Truman adopted the advice of three top advisers in deciding to "contain" Soviet aggression. His containment policy, which was to govern U.S. foreign policy for decades, was formulated by the secretary of state, General George Marshall; the undersecretary of state, Dean Acheson; and an expert on Soviet affairs, George F. Kennan. In an influential article, Kennan had written that only "a long-term, patient but firm and vigilant containment of Russian expansive tendencies" would eventually cause the Soviets to back off their Communist ideology of world domination and live in peace with other nations.

Did the containment policy attempt to do too much? Among the critics who argued that it did was the journalist Walter Lippmann, who had coined the term "Cold War." Lippmann argued that some areas were vital to U.S. security, while others were merely peripheral; some governments deserved U.S. support, but others did not. American leaders, however, had learned the lesson of Munich and appeasement well and felt that Communist aggression, wherever it occurred, must be challenged.

The Truman Doctrine

Truman first implemented the containment policy in response to two threats: (1) a Communist-led uprising against the government in Greece and (2) Soviet demands for some control of Turkey's Dardanelles. In what became known as the Truman Doctrine, the president asked Congress in March 1947 for $400 million in economic and military aid to assist the "free people" of Greece and Turkey against "totalitarian" regimes. While Truman's alarmist speech may have oversimplified the situation in Greece and Turkey, it gained bipartisan support from Republicans and Democrats in Congress.

The Marshall Plan

After the war, Europe lay in ruins, short of food and deep in debt. The harsh winter of 1946–1947 further demoralized Europeans, who had already suffered through years of depression and war. Discontent encouraged the growth of the Communist party, especially in France and Italy. The Truman administration feared that the western democracies might actually vote the Communists into power.

In June 1947, George Marshall outlined an extensive program of U.S. economic aid to help the nations of Europe revive their economies, and at the same time strengthen democratic governments. In December, Truman submitted to Congress a $17 billion European Recovery Program, better known as the Marshall Plan. In 1948, $12 billion in aid was approved for distribution to the countries of Western Europe over a four-year period. The Soviet Union and its Eastern European satellites were also offered Marshall Plan aid, but they refused to take part, fearing that their countries might then become dependent on the United States.

Effects. The Marshall Plan worked exactly as Marshall and Truman had hoped. The massive infusion of U.S. dollars helped Western Europe achieve self-sustaining growth by the 1950s and ended any real threat of Communist political successes in that region. It also bolstered U.S. prosperity by greatly increasing U.S. exports to Europe. At the same time, however, it deepened the rift between the non-Communist West and the Communist East.

The Berlin Airlift

The first major crisis of the Cold War focused on Berlin. In June 1948, the Soviets cut off all access by land to the German city. Truman dismissed any plans to withdraw from Berlin, but he also rejected any idea of using force to open up the roads through the Soviet-controlled eastern zone. Instead, he ordered U.S. planes to fly in supplies to the people of West Berlin. Day after day, week after week, the massive airlift continued. At the same time, Truman sent 60 bombers capable of carrying atomic bombs to bases in England. The world waited nervously for the outbreak of war, but Stalin decided not to challenge the airlift. (Truman's stand on Berlin was partly responsible for his victory in the 1948 election.)

By May 1949, the Soviets finally opened up the highways to Berlin, thus bringing their 11-month blockade to an end. A major long-term consequence of the Berlin crisis was the creation of two Germanies: the Federal Republic of Germany (West Germany, a U.S. ally) and the German Democratic Republic (East Germany, a Soviet satellite).

NATO and National Security

Ever since Washington's farewell address of 1796, the United States had avoided permanent alliances with European nations. Truman broke with this tradition in 1949 by recommending that the United States join a military defense pact to protect Western Europe. The Senate readily gave its consent. Ten European nations joined the United States and Canada in creating the North Atlantic Treaty Organization (NATO), a military alliance for defending all members from outside attack. Truman selected General Eisenhower as NATO's first Supreme Commander and stationed U.S. troops in Western Europe as a deterrent against a Soviet invasion. Thus, the containment policy led to a military buildup and major commitments abroad. The Soviet Union countered in 1955 by forming the Warsaw Pact, a military alliance for the defense of the Communist states of Eastern Europe.

National Security Act (1947). The United States had begun to modernize its military capability in 1947 by passing the National Security Act. It provided for (1) a centralized Department of Defense (replacing the War Department) to coordinate the operations of the Army, Navy, and Air Force; (2) the creation of the National Security Council (NSC) to coordinate the making of foreign policy in the Cold War, and (3) the creation of the Central Intelligence Agency (CIA) to employ spies to gather information on foreign governments. In 1948, the Selective Service System and a peacetime draft were instituted.

Atomic weapons. After the Berlin crisis, teams of scientists in both the Soviet Union and the United States were engaged in an intense competition— or *arms race*—to develop superior weapons systems. For a period of just four years (1945–1949), the United States was the only nation to have the atomic bomb. It also developed in this period a new generation of long-range bombers for delivering nuclear weapons.

The Soviets tested their first atomic bomb in the fall of 1949. Truman then approved the development of a bomb a thousand times more powerful

EUROPE AFTER WORLD WAR II: THE COLD WAR

than the A-bomb that had destroyed Hiroshima. In 1952, this hydrogen bomb (or H-bomb) was added to the U.S. arsenal. Earlier, in 1950, the National Security Council had recommended, in a secret report known as NSC-68, that the following measures were necessary for fighting the Cold War:

- quadruple U.S. government defense spending to 20 percent of GNP
- form alliances with non-Communist countries around the world
- convince the American public that a costly arms buildup was imperative for the nation's defense

Evaluating U.S. policy. Critics of NATO and the defense buildup argued the Truman only intensified Russian fears and started an unnecessary arms race. Time would prove, however, that NATO was one of the most successful military alliances in history. In combination with the deterrent power of nuclear weapons, NATO effectively checked Soviet expansion in Europe and thereby maintained an uneasy peace until the Soviet Union collapsed in 1991.

Cold War in Asia

The success of the containment policy in Europe proved difficult to duplicate in Asia. Following World War II, the old imperialist system crumbled in India and Southeast Asia, as former colonies became new nations. Because these nations had different cultural and political traditions and also bitter memories of Western colonialism, they were less responsive to U.S. influence. Ironically, the Asian nation that became most closely tied to the U.S. defense system was its former enemy, Japan.

Japan

Unlike Germany, Japan was solely under the control of the United States. General Douglas MacArthur took firm charge of the reconstruction of Japan. Seven Japanese generals, including Premier Hideki Tojo, were tried for war crimes and executed. Under MacArthur's guidance, the new constitution adopted in May 1947 set up a parliamentary democracy. It retained Emperor Hirohito as the ceremonial head of state, but the emperor gave up his claims to divinity. The new constitution also renounced war as an instrument of national policy and provided for only limited military capability. As a result, Japan depended on the military protection of the United States.

U.S.-Japanese Security Treaty. The occupation of Japan ended in 1951 with the signing of a peace treaty in which Japan agreed to surrender its claims to Korea and islands in the Pacific. A second treaty also signed and ratified in 1951 ended formal occupation of Japan but also provided for U.S. troops to remain in military bases in Japan for that country's protection against external enemies (communism). Japan became a strong ally and prospered under the American shield.

The Philippines and the Pacific

On July 4, 1946, in accordance with the act passed by Congress in 1934, the Philippines became an independent republic, but the United States retained important naval and air bases there throughout the Cold War. This, together with U.S. control of the United Nations trustee islands taken from Japan at the end of the war, began to make the Pacific Ocean look like an American lake.

China

Since coming to power in the late 1920s, Chiang Kai-shek (Jiang Jie-shi) had used his command of the Nationalist, or Kuomintang, party to control China's central government. During World War II, the United States had given massive military aid to Chiang to prevent all of China from being conquered by Japan. As soon as the war ended, a civil war dating back to the 1930s was renewed between Chiang's Nationalists and the Chinese Communists led by Mao Zedong. The Nationalists were losing the loyalty of millions of Chinese because of runaway inflation and widespread corruption, while the well-organized Communists successfully appealed to the poor landless peasants.

U.S. policy. The Truman administration sent George Marshall in 1946 to China to negotiate an end to the civil war, but his compromise fell apart in a few months. By 1947, Chiang's armies were in retreat. Truman seemed unsure of what to do, after ruling out a large-scale American invasion to rescue Chiang. In 1948, Congress voted to give the Nationalist government $400 million in aid, but 80 percent of the U.S. military supplies ended up in Communist hands because of corruption and the collapse of the Nationalist armies.

Two Chinas. By the end of 1949, all of mainland China had fallen to the Communist forces. The only refuge for Chiang and the Nationalists was the island once under Japanese rule, Formosa (Taiwan). There, Chiang established his government, which still claimed to be the only legitimate government for all of China. The United States continued to support Chiang and refused to recognize Mao Zedong's regime in Beijing (the People's Republic of China) until 30 years later, in 1979.

In the United States, Republicans were especially alarmed by the "loss of China" to the Communists and blamed the Democrats as wholly responsible for the disaster. In 1950, the two Communist dictators, Stalin and Mao, signed a Sino-Soviet pact, which seemed to provide further proof of a worldwide Communist conspiracy.

The Korean War

After the defeat of Japan, its former colony Korea was divided at the 38th parallel by the victors. Soviet armies occupied Korean territory north of the line, while U.S. forces occupied territory to the south. By 1949 both armies were withdrawn, leaving the North in the hands of the Communist leader Kim Il Sung and the South under the conservative nationalist Syngman Rhee.

Invasion. On June 25, 1950, the North Korean army surprised the world, even possibly Moscow, by invading South Korea. Truman took immediate action, applying his containment policy to this latest crisis in Asia. He called for a special session of the U.N. Security Council. Taking advantage of a temporary boycott by the Soviet delegation, the Security Council under U.S. leadership authorized a U.N. force to defend South Korea against the invaders. Although other nations participated in this force, U.S. troops made up most of the U.N. forces sent to help the South Korean army. Commanding the expedition was General Douglas MacArthur. Congress supported the use of U.S. troops in the Korean crisis but failed to declare war, accepting Truman's characterization of U.S. intervention as merely a "police action."

Counterattack. At first the war in Korea went badly, as the North Koreans pushed the combined South Korean and American forces to the tip of the peninsula. However, General MacArthur reversed the war by a brilliant amphibi-

THE KOREAN WAR

0 50 100 Miles
0 50 100 Kilometers

SOVIET UNION

MANCHURIA

Tumen River

CHINA

Yalu River

Farthest Advance of U.N. Troops

NORTH KOREA

SEA OF JAPAN

• Pyongyang

Cease-Fire Line, July 27, 1953

38°

38° Parallel

• Seoul
• Inchon

SOUTH KOREA

Farthest Advance of the North Korean Troops

YELLOW SEA

Pusan

ous assault at Inchon behind the North Korean lines. U.N. forces then proceeded to destroy much of the North Korean army, advancing northward almost as far the Chinese border. MacArthur failed to heed China's warnings that it would resist threats to its security. In November 1950, masses of Chinese troops crossed the border into Korea, overwhelmed U.N. forces in one of the worst defeats in U.S. military history, and drove them out of North Korea.

Truman versus MacArthur. MacArthur managed to stabilize the fighting near the 38th parallel. At the same time, he called for an expanded war, including the bombing and invasion of mainland China. As commander in chief, Truman cautioned MacArthur about making public statements that suggested criticism of official U.S. policy. The general spoke out anyway. In April 1951, Truman with the support of the Joint Chiefs of Staff recalled MacArthur for insubordination.

MacArthur returned home to a hero's welcome. Most Americans understood his statement, "There is no substitute for victory," better than the president's containment policy and concept of "limited war." Truman and the Democrats were viewed by many as appeasers for not trying to destroy communism in Asia.

Armistice. In Korea, the war was stalemated along a front just north of the 38th parallel. At Panmunjom, peace talks began in July 1951. The police action dragged on for another two years, however, until an armistice was finally signed in 1953 during the first year of Eisenhower's presidency. Before the fighting ended, more than 54,000 Americans had died in Korea.

Political consequences. From the perspective of the grand strategy of the Cold War, Truman's containment policy in Korea worked. It stopped Communist aggression without allowing the conflict to develop into a world war. The Truman administration used the Korean War as justification for dramatically expanding the military, funding a new jet bomber (the B-52), and stationing more U.S. troops in overseas bases.

The Republicans, however, were far from satisfied. In fact, the stalemate in Korea and the loss of China provided Republican politicians with plenty of material to characterize Truman and the Democrats as "soft on communism." They attacked leading Democrats as members of "Dean Acheson's Cowardly College of Communist Containment." (In 1949 Acheson had replaced George Marshall as secretary of state.)

The Second Red Scare

Curiously, just as a Red Scare had followed U.S. victory in World War I, a second Red Scare followed U.S. victory in World War II. The Truman administration's tendency to see a Communist conspiracy behind civil wars in Europe and Asia contributed to the belief that there were also Communist conspirators and spies in the U.S. State Department, the U.S. military, and all institutions in American society.

Security and Civil Rights

In 1947, the Truman administration—under pressure from Republican critics—set up a Loyalty Review Board to investigate the background of more than 3 million federal employees. Thousands of officials and civil service employees either resigned or lost their jobs in a probe that went on for four years (1947–1951).

Prosecutions under the Smith Act. In addition, the leaders of the American Communist party were jailed for advocating the overthrow of the U.S. government. In the case of *Dennis et al. v. United States* (1951), the Supreme Court upheld the constitutionality of the Smith Act of 1940, which made it illegal to advocate or teach the overthrow of the government by force or to belong to an organization with this objective.

McCarran Internal Security Act (1950). Over Truman's veto, Congress passed the McCarran Internal Security Act, which (1) made it unlawful to advocate or support the establishment of a totalitarian government, (2) restricted the employment and travel of those joining Communist-front organizations, and (3) authorized the creation of detention camps for subversives.

Un-American activities. In the House of Representatives, the Un-American Activities Committee (HUAC), originally established in 1939 to seek out Nazis, was reactivated in the postwar years to find Communists. The committee not only investigated government officials but also looked for Communist influence in such organizations as the Boy Scouts and in the Hollywood film industry. Actors, directors, and writers were called before the committee to testify. Those who refused to testify were tried for contempt of Congress. Others were blacklisted from the industry.

The American Civil Liberties Union and other opponents of these internal security measures argued that the First Amendment protected the free expression of unpopular political views and membership in political groups, such as the Communist party.

Espionage Cases

The fear of a Communist conspiracy bent on world conquest was supported by a series of actual cases of Communist espionage in Great Britain, Canada, and the United States. The methods used to identify Communist spies, however, raised serious questions about whether the government was going too far and violating civil liberties in the process.

Hiss case. Whittaker Chambers, a confessed Communist, became a star witness for the House Un-American Activities Committee in 1948. His testimony, along with the investigative work of Richard M. Nixon, a young Congressman from California, led to the trial of Alger Hiss, a prominent official in the State Department who had assisted Roosevelt at the Yalta Conference. Hiss denied the accusations that he was a Communist and had given secret documents to Chambers. In 1950, however, he was convicted of perjury and sent to prison. Many Americans could not help wondering whether the highest levels of government were infiltrated by Communist spies.

Rosenberg case. When the Soviets tested their first atomic bomb in 1949, many Americans were convinced that spies had helped them to steal the technology from the United States. Klaus Fuchs, a British scientist who had worked on the Manhattan Project, admitted giving A-bomb secrets to the Russians. An FBI investigation traced another spy ring to Julius and Ethel Rosenberg in New York. After a controversial trial in 1951, the Rosenbergs were found guilty of treason and executed for the crime in 1953. Civil rights groups raised questions about whether anticommunist hysteria had played a role in the conviction and punishment of the Rosenbergs.

The Rise of Joseph McCarthy

Joseph McCarthy, a Republican senator from Wisconsin, used the growing concern over communism in his reelection campaign. In a speech in 1950, he charged that 205 Communists were still working for the State Department. This sensational accusation was widely publicized in the American press. McCarthy then rode the wave of anticommunist feelings to make himself one of the most powerful men in America. His power was based entirely on people's fear of the damage McCarthy could do if his accusing finger pointed their way.

McCarthy's tactics. Senator McCarthy used a steady stream of unsupported accusations about Communists in government to keep the media focus on himself and to discredit the Truman administration. Working-class Americans at first loved his "take the gloves off," hard-hitting remarks, which were often aimed at the wealthy and privileged in society. While many Republicans disliked McCarthy's ruthless tactics, he was primarily hurting the Democrats before the election of Eisenhower in 1952. He became so popular, however, that even President Eisenhower would not dare to defend his old friend, George Marshall, against McCarthy's untruths.

Army-McCarthy hearings. Finally, in 1954, McCarthy's "reckless cruelty" was exposed on television. A Senate committee held televised hearings on Communist infiltration in the Army, and McCarthy was seen as a bully by millions of viewers. In December, Republicans joined Democrats in a Senate censure of McCarthy. The "witchhunt" for Communists (McCarthyism) had played itself out. Three years later, McCarthy died a broken man.

Truman in Retirement

The second Red Scare, the stalemate in Korea, the loss of China, and scandals surrounding several of Truman's advisers made his prospects of reelection unlikely. Truman decided to return to private life in Missouri—a move that he jokingly called his "promotion." In the election of 1952, Republicans blamed Truman for "the mess in Washington." In time, however, even Truman's critics came to respect his many tough decisions and, in retrospect, admire his direct and frank character.

HISTORICAL PERSPECTIVES: WHO STARTED THE COLD WAR?

Among U.S. historians, the traditional, or orthodox, view of the origins of the Cold War is that the Soviet government under Stalin started the conflict by subjugating the countries of Eastern Europe in the late 1940s. For having failed to understand the Soviets' aggressive intentions, Franklin Roosevelt is severely criticized for his agreement at Yalta. The traditional view holds that the Truman Doctrine, Marshall Plan, and NATO finally checked Soviet expansion in Europe. The United States in the Cold War (as in both world wars) was viewed as the defender of the "free world."

In the 1960s, during the time of public unhappiness over the Vietnam War, revisionist historians began to argue that the United States was primarily responsible for starting the Cold War. These historians praised Roosevelt for his understanding of Russia's historical needs for security on its eastern borders. Truman, on the other hand, was blamed for antagonizing the Soviets with his blunt challenge of their actions in Poland and the Balkans. A few revisionists, such as Gar Alperovitz (*The Decision to Use the Atomic Bomb,* 1995), even concluded that Truman had dropped atomic bombs on Japan primarily to send a message to Stalin to remove his troops from Eastern Europe. Other revisionists have also argued that U.S. capitalism's need for open markets in Europe and Asia was the main reason for the U.S. government's anticommunist policies.

In recent years, postrevisionist historians have seen the Cold War as the unintended result of a series of misunderstandings on both sides. Each action by one side to increase its security was judged as an act of aggression by the other side. A prime example of this vicious circle was the arms race in nuclear weapons.

Obviously, the recent collapse of the Soviet Union will have a major effect on later historical interpretations of the origins of the Cold War. Only in the early 1990s did historians begin to have access to many of the secret, top-security documents from the 1940s filed in government offices in Moscow and Washington.

KEY NAMES, EVENTS, AND TERMS

Servicemen's Readjustment Act (GI Bill) (1944)	States-Rights party (Dixiecrats)	Truman Doctrine
baby boom	J. Strom Thurmond	Marshall Plan
suburban growth	Thomas Dewey	Berlin airlift
Sunbelt	Fair Deal	East Germany; West Germany
Harry Truman	Cold War	North Atlantic Treaty Organization
Employment Act of 1946	Soviet Union	National Security Act (1947)
Council of Economic Advisers	United Nations	arms race; NSC-68
inflation; strikes	World Bank	U.S.-Japanese Security Treaty
Committee on Civil Rights	Communist satellites	Douglas MacArthur
Twenty-second Amendment	Iron Curtain	Chinese civil war
Taft-Hartley Act (1947)	Winston Churchill	Chiang Kai-shek
Progressive party	George Kennan	Taiwan
Henry Wallace	Dean Acheson	Mao Zedong
	containment policy	People's Republic of China

Joseph Stalin	*Dennis et al. v. United States*	Alger Hiss
Kim Il Sung	Smith Act (1940)	Whittaker Chambers
Syngman Rhee	McCarran Internal Security	Rosenberg case
Korean War; U.N. police	Act (1950)	Joseph McCarthy
action	House Un-American Activities	
38th parallel	Committee	

MULTIPLE-CHOICE QUESTIONS

1. U.S. economic expansion after World War II was encouraged by all of the following EXCEPT
   (A) Office of Price Administration
   (B) veterans' loans
   (C) increased savings from the war years
   (D) high demand for consumer goods
   (E) increase in per capita income

2. President Truman's domestic policies included support for all of the following EXCEPT
   (A) a full-employment bill
   (B) increase in the minimum wage
   (C) national health care insurance
   (D) desegregating the armed forces
   (E) the Taft-Hartley Act

3. Which of the following was NOT a major issue between the Soviet Union and the United States in the postwar years 1945–1950?
   (A) establishment of Communist governments in Eastern Europe
   (B) occupation zones in Japan
   (C) access to Berlin
   (D) Marshall Plan aid
   (E) development and control of atomic weapons

4. "In these circumstances, it is clear that the main element of any United States policy toward the Soviet Union must be that of a long-term, patient, but firm and vigilant containment of Russian expansive tendencies. It is important to note, however, that such a policy has nothing to do with outward histrionics, with threats or blustering or superfluous gestures of outward 'toughness.' "

   This statement is taken from
   (A) President Roosevelt's speech at the Yalta conference
   (B) Winston Churchill's "Iron Curtain" speech
   (C) George Marshall's introduction to his Marshall Plan
   (D) George Kennan's article, "The Sources of Soviet Conduct"
   (E) General MacArthur's letter to Congressman Joseph Martin

5. The primary purpose of the Marshall Plan was to
   (A) end the rift between the United States and the Soviet Union

(B) establish a uniform world currency

(C) aid the economic recovery of war-devastated Europe

(D) set up a military alliance of anticommunist nations

(E) hinder the economic recovery of nations under Soviet control

6. Which U.S. action is NOT correctly paired with an event in international politics?

(A) airlift—Soviet blockade of Berlin

(B) troops sent to Korea—Churchill's Iron Curtain speech

(C) Truman Doctrine—civil war in Greece

(D) Marshall Plan—growing popularity of communism in Western Europe

(E) development of hydrogen bomb—A-bomb tested in Soviet Union

7. Which of the following was NOT an issue during the Korean War?

(A) whether to expand the war by attacking China

(B) whether North Korea had committed aggression

(C) whether Congress should have declared war

(D) the removal of General Douglas MacArthur

(E) the policies of containment and "limited war"

8. Which of the following contributed the LEAST to the growth of the Red Scare in the 1950s?

(A) loss of atomic bomb secrets to the Soviets

(B) Army-McCarthy hearings

(C) Alger Hiss case

(D) fall of China to the Communists

(E) investigations by the House Un-American Activities Committee

9. Which of the following BEST describes Truman's foreign policy from 1945 to 1952?

(A) reluctance to involve the United States in foreign conflicts

(B) willingness to negotiate differences with the Soviet Union

(C) aggressive use of U.S. troops in Europe and Asia

(D) commitment to containing Communist expansion

(E) extending foreign aid only with U.N. approval

10. The principal reason for the defeat of most Fair Deal programs was

(A) opposition by Republicans in Congress

(B) outbreak of the Second Red Scare

(C) McCarthy's accusations

(D) Truman's lack of experience in domestic policy

(E) Dewey's speeches in the election of 1948

ESSAY QUESTIONS

1. How did Truman's Fair Deal go beyond the reforms of the New Deal of the 1930s?

2. Analyze the impact of TWO of the following on American–Soviet relations during the Truman presidency:

   atomic weapons

   Marshall Plan

   Berlin blockade

   North Atlantic Treaty Organization

3. To what extent were the hostilities that developed between the United States and the Soviet Union from 1946 and 1952 inevitable?

4. Analyze the effects of the Cold War on TWO of the following from 1946 to 1952:

   civil liberties

   election politics

   government size and spending

5. Analyze the causes of the second Red Scare and Joseph McCarthy's rise to power.

DOCUMENTS AND READINGS

The following documents are from the critical years 1945 to 1947 and deal with the following questions: (1) What were the causes of the Cold War? and (2) Why was the containment policy developed?

DOCUMENT A.   TELEGRAM FROM MOSCOW

In early 1946, George Kennan, a State Department expert in Moscow, sent the following "long telegram" to his superiors in Washington, offering an explanation of Soviet behavior. He argued that a combination of history and Communist ideology was behind the Soviet takeover of Eastern Europe. Later, in 1947, Kennan developed his theories into the containment policy. (Note: Because this document was written as a telegram, words in brackets [the, a] were omitted in the original.)

At the bottom of the Kremlin's neurotic view of world affairs is [the] traditional and instinctive Russian sense of insecurity. Originally, this was [the] insecurity of [a] peaceful people trying to live on [a] vast exposed plain in [the] neighborhood of fierce nomadic peoples. To this was added, as Russia came into contact with [an] economically advanced West, fear of more competent, more powerful, more highly organized societies in that area. But this latter type of insecurity was one which afflicted rather Russian rulers than

Russian people; for Russian rulers have invariably sensed that their rule was relatively archaic in form, fragile and artificial in its psychological foundation, unable to stand comparison for contact with political systems of Western countries. For this reason they have always feared foreign penetration, feared direct contact between [the] Western world and their own, feared what would happen if Russians learned [the] truth about [the] world without or if foreigners learned [the] truth about the world within. And they have learned to seek security only in [a] patient but deadly struggle for total destruction of [a] rival power, never in compacts and compromises with it. . . .

After establishment of [the] Bolshevist regime, Marxist dogma, rendered even more truculent and intolerant by Lenin's interpretation, became [a] more perfect vehicle for [the] sense of insecurity with which [the] Bolsheviks, even more than previous Russian rulers, were afflicted. In this dogma, with its basic altruism of purpose, they found justification for their instinctive fear of [the] outside world, for the dictatorship without which they did not know how to rule, for cruelties they did not dare not inflict, for sacrifices they felt bound to demand. In the name of Marxism they sacrificed every single ethical value in their methods and tactics. . . .

George Kennan,
Telegram from Moscow, February 22, 1946

DOCUMENT B. THE TRUMAN DOCTRINE

In March 1947, President Truman delivered a speech before a joint session of Congress in which he asked for $400 million in aid for Greece and Turkey. He also called on the American people to take up a new mission to assist free peoples of the world against the totalitarianism of Communist governments.

One of the primary objectives of the foreign policy of the United States is the creation of conditions in which we and other nations will be able to work out a way of life free from coercion. This was a fundamental issue in the war with Germany and Japan. Our victory was won over countries which sought to impose their will, and their way of life, upon other nations.

To insure the peaceful development of nations, free from coercion, the United States has taken a leading part in establishing the United Nations. The United Nations is designed to make possible lasting freedom and independence for all its members. We shall not realize our objectives, however, unless we are willing to help free peoples to maintain their free institutions and their national integrity against aggressive movements that seek to impose upon them totalitarian regimes. This is no more than a frank recognition that totalitarian regimes imposed upon free people, by direct or indirect aggression, undermine the foundations of international peace and hence the security of the United States.

The peoples of a number of countries of the world have recently had totalitarian regimes forced upon them against their will. The government of the United States has made frequent protests against coercion and intimidation, in violation of the Yalta Agreement, in Poland, Rumania, and Bulgaria. I must also state that in a number of other countries there have been similar developments. . . .

I believe that it must be the policy of the United States to support free peoples who are resisting attempted subjugation by armed minorities or by outside pressures.

I believe that we must assist free peoples to work out their own destinies in their own way.

I believe that our help should be primarily through economic and financial aid, which is essential to economic stability and orderly political process.

The seeds of totalitarian regimes are nurtured by misery and want. They spread and grow in the evil soil of poverty and strife. They reach their full growth when the hope of a people for a better life has died.

We must keep that hope alive.

The free peoples of the world look to us for support in maintaining their freedoms.

If we falter in our leadership, we may endanger the peace of the world—and we shall surely endanger the welfare of our own Nation.

Great responsibilities have been placed upon us by the swift movement of events.

I am confident that the Congress will face these responsibilities squarely.

President Harry S Truman,
Congressional Record, 80th Congress,
1st Session, March 12, 1947

DOCUMENT C.   *SOVIET REACTION TO THE MARSHALL PLAN*

At first the Soviet Union seemed interested in participating in the Marshall Plan, but it later turned down offers of U.S. aid, as did the other Communist states of Eastern Europe. In September 1947, Soviet deputy foreign minister Andrei Vyshinsky attacked the United Marshall Plan before the United Nations.

As is now clear, the Marshall Plan constitutes in essence merely a variant of the Truman Doctrine adapted to the conditions of postwar Europe. In bringing forward this plan, the United States Government apparently counted on the cooperation of the Governments of the United Kingdom and France to confront the European countries in need of relief with the necessity of renouncing their inalienable right to dispose of their economic resources and to plan their national economy in their own way. The United States also counted on making all these countries directly dependent on the interests of American monopolies, which are striving to avert the approaching depression by an accelerated export of commodities and capital to Europe. . . .

It is becoming more and more evident to everyone that the implementation of the Marshall Plan will mean placing European countries under the economic and political control of the United States and direct interference by the latter in the internal affairs of those countries.

Moreover, this Plan is an attempt to split Europe into two camps and, with the help of the United Kingdom and France, to complete the formation of a *bloc* of several European countries hostile to the interests of the democratic countries of Eastern Europe and most particularly to the interests of the Soviet Union.

An important feature of this Plan is the attempt to confront the countries of Eastern Europe with a *bloc* of Western European States including Western Germany. The intention is to make use of Western Germany and German heavy industry (the Ruhr) as one of the most important economic bases for American expansion in Europe, in disregard of the national interests of the countries which suffered from German aggression.

Andrei Vyshinsky,
Speech to General Assembly of the
United Nations, September 18, 1947

DOCUMENT D.   OPPOSITION TO THE CONTAINMENT POLICY

In July 1947, George Kennan explained the thinking behind the containment policy in an article that he signed "By Mr. X." Shortly afterward, the journalist Walter Lippmann presented his reasons for predicting that a containment policy would not be practical. In a series of articles in the New York *Herald Tribune,* Lippmann anticipated problems that would arise later in trying to apply the containment policy to the Korean and Vietnam wars and to developing nations in Africa and Latin America.

Now the strength of the western world is great, and we may assume that its resourcefulness is considerable. Nevertheless, there are weighty reasons for thinking that the kind of strength we have and the kind of resourcefulness we are capable of showing are peculiarly unsuited to operating a policy of containment.

How, for example, under the Constitution of the United States, is Mr. X going to work out an arrangement by which the Department of State has the money and military power always available in sufficient amounts to apply "counterforce" at constantly shifting points all over the world? Is he going to ask Congress for a blank check on the Treasury and for a blank authorization to use the armed forces? Not if the American constitutional system is to be maintained. . . . A policy of shifts and maneuvers may be suited to the Soviet system of government, which, as Mr. X tells us, is animated by patient persistence. It is not suited to the American system of government.

It is even more unsuited to the American economy which is unregimented and uncontrolled, and therefore cannot be administered according to a plan. Yet a policy of containment cannot be operated unless the Department of State can plan and direct exports and imports. . . . Mr. X is surely mistaken, it seems to me, if he thinks that a free and undirected economy like our own can be used by the diplomatic planners to wage a diplomatic war against a planned economy [Soviet Union] at a series of constantly shifting geographical and political points. . . .

I find it hard to understand how Mr. X could have recommended such a strategic monstrosity. . . . Mr. X says that the United States should aim to win a series of victories which will cause the Russians to "yield on individual sectors of the diplomatic front." And then what? When the United States has forced the Kremlin to "face frustration indefinitely" there will "eventually" come "either the breakup or the gradual mellowing of the Soviet power."

There is, however, no rational ground for confidence that the United States could muster "unalterable counterforce" at all the individual sectors. The Eurasian continent is a big place, and the military power of the United States, though it is very great, has certain limitations which must be borne in mind if it is to be used effectively. . . . The planners of American diplomatic policy must use the kind of power we do have, not the kind we do not have. . . .

American military power is peculiarly unsuited to a policy of containment which has to be enforced persistently and patiently for an indefinite period of time. . . . [T]he genius of American military power does not lie in holding positions indefinitely. That requires a massive patience by great hordes of docile people. American military power is distinguished by its mobility, its speed, its range and its offensive striking force. It is, therefore, not an efficient instrument for a diplomatic policy of containment. It can only be the instrument of a policy which has as its objective a decision and a settlement. . . . But it is not designed for, or adapted to, a strategy of containing, waiting, countering, blocking, with no more specific objective than the eventual "frustration" of the opponent.

The Americans would themselves probably be frustrated by Mr. X's policy long before the Russians were.

Walter Lippmann,
The Cold War: A Study in U.S. Foreign Policy, 1947

ANALYZING THE DOCUMENTS

1. Some historians consider Kennan's "Long Telegram" one of the most important documents of the Cold War. How could it have contributed to the development of the Cold War?

2. Those close to Truman said that the Truman Doctrine speech was the "most important thing that had happened since Pearl Harbor." What was the significance of this speech?

3. What arguments in Vyshinshy's attack on the Marshall Plan were probably propaganda and which may have reflected genuine concerns of the Soviet Union?

4. For what constitutional, economic, military, and political reasons does Lippmann think that the containment policy was ill-suited to the United States?

5. Using the documents provided and your knowledge of the era, write an essay on the following question: Was Soviet domination of the countries in Eastern Europe the main cause of the Cold War?

27

THE EISENHOWER YEARS, 1952–1960

*We conclude that in the field of public education the doctrine of
"separate but equal" has no place. Separate educational facilities are
inherently unequal.*

Earl Warren, *Brown v. Board of Education
of Topeka,* May 17, 1954

The 1950s have the popular image of the "happy days," when the nation prospered and teens enjoyed the new beat of rock and roll music. To a certain extent, this nostalgic view of the fifties is correct—but limited. The decade started with a war in Korea and the incriminations of McCarthyism. From the point of view of African Americans, what mattered about the 1950s was not so much the music of Elvis Presley but the resistance of Rosa Parks and Martin Luther King, Jr., to segregation in the South. While middle-class suburbanites enjoyed their chrome-trimmed cars and tuned in "I Love Lucy" on their new television sets, the Cold War and threat of nuclear destruction loomed in the background.

Eisenhower Takes Command

Much as Franklin Roosevelt dominated the 1930s, President Dwight ("Ike") Eisenhower personified the 1950s. The Republican campaign slogan, "I Like Ike," expressed the genuine feelings of millions of middle-class Americans. They liked his winning smile and trusted and admired the former general who had successfully commanded Allied forces in Europe in World War II.

The Election of 1952

In 1952, the last year of Truman's presidency, Americans were looking for relief from the Korean War and an end to political scandals commonly referred to as "the mess in Washington." Republicans looked forward with relish to their first presidential victory in 20 years. In the Republican primaries, voters had a choice between the Old Guard's favorite, Senator Robert Taft of

Ohio, and the war hero, Eisenhower. Most of them liked "Ike," who went on to win the Republican nomination. Conservative supporters of Taft balanced the ticket by persuading Eisenhower to choose Richard Nixon for his running mate. This young California senator had made a name for himself attacking Communists in the Alger Hiss case.

The Democrats nominated Adlai Stevenson, popular governor of Illinois, whose wit, eloquence, and courage in facing down McCarthyism appealed to liberals.

Campaign highlights. As a nonpolitician, Eisenhower had a spotless reputation for integrity that was almost spoiled by reports that his running mate, Richard Nixon, had used campaign funds for his own personal use. Nixon was almost dropped from the ticket. He managed to save his political future, however, by effectively using the new medium of television to defend himself. In his so-called Checkers speech, Nixon won the support of millions of viewers by tugging at their heartstrings. With his wife and daughters around him, he emotionally vowed never to return the gift of their dog, Checkers, which the whole family loved.

What really put distance between the Republicans and the Democrats was Eisenhower's pledge during the last days of the campaign to go to Korea and end the war. The Eisenhower-Nixon ticket went on to win over 55 percent of the popular vote and an electoral college landslide of 442 to Stevenson's 89.

Domestic Policies

As president, Eisenhower adopted a style of leadership that emphasized the delegation of authority. He filled his cabinet with successful corporate executives who gave his administration a businesslike tone. His secretary of defense, for example, was Charles Wilson, the former head of General Motors. Eisenhower was often criticized by the press for spending too much time golfing and fishing and perhaps entrusting important decisions to others. Later research showed, however, that behind the scenes Eisenhower was in charge.

Modern Republicanism. Eisenhower was a fiscal conservative whose first priority was balancing the budget after years of deficit spending. Although his annual budgets were not always balanced, he came closer to curbing federal spending than any of his successors. As a moderate on domestic issues, he accepted most of the New Deal programs as a reality of modern life and even extended some of them. During Eisenhower's two terms in office, Social Security was extended to 10 million more citizens, the minimum wage was raised, and additional public housing was built. In 1953, Eisenhower consolidated the administration of welfare programs by creating the Department of Health, Education, and Welfare (HEW) under Oveta Culp Hobby, the first woman in a Republican cabinet. For farmers, a soil-bank program was initiated as means of reducing farm production and thereby increasing farm income.

On the other hand, Eisenhower opposed the ideas of federal health care insurance and federal aid to education.

As the first Republican president since Hoover, Eisenhower called his balanced and moderate approach "modern Republicanism." His critics called it "the bland leading the bland."

Interstate highway system. The most permanent legacy of the Eisenhower years was the passage in 1956 of the Highway Act, which authorized the construction of 42,000 miles of interstate highways linking all the nation's major cities. When completed, the U.S. highway system became a model for the rest of the world. The justification for new taxes on fuel, tires, and vehicles was to improve national defense. At the same time, this immense public works project created jobs, promoted the trucking industry, accelerated the growth of the suburbs, and contributed to a more homogeneous national culture. The emphasis on cars, trucks, and highways, however, hurt the railroads and ultimately the environment. Little attention was paid to public transportation, on which the old and the poor depended.

Prosperity. Eisenhower's domestic legislation was modest. During his years in office, however, the country enjoyed a steady growth rate, with an inflation rate averaging a negligible 1.5 percent. Although the federal budget had a small surplus only three times in eight years, the deficits fell in relation to the national wealth. For these reasons, some historians rate Eisenhower's economic policies the most successful of any modern president's. Between 1945 and 1960, the per-capita disposable income of Americans more than tripled. By the mid-1950s, the average American family had twice the real income of a comparable family during the boom years of the 1920s. The postwar economy gave Americans the highest standard of living in the world.

The Election of 1956

Toward the end of his first term, Eisenhower suffered a heart attack in 1955 and had major surgery in 1956. Democrats questioned whether his health was strong enough for election to a second term. Four years of peace and prosperity, however, made Ike more popular than ever, and the Eisenhower-Nixon ticket was enthusiastically renominated by the Republicans. The Democrats again nominated Adlai Stevenson. In this political rematch, Eisenhower won by an even greater margin than in 1952. It was a personal victory only, however, as the Democrats retained control of both houses of Congress.

Eisenhower and the Cold War

Most of Eisenhower's attention in both his first and second terms focused on foreign policy and various international crises arising from the Cold War. The experienced diplomat who helped to shape U.S. foreign policy throughout Eisenhower's presidency was Secretary of State John Foster Dulles.

Dulles' Diplomacy

Dulles had been critical of Truman's containment policy as too passive. He advocated a "new look" to U.S. foreign policy that took the initiative in challenging the Soviet Union and the People's Republic of China. He talked of "liberating captive nations" of Eastern Europe and encouraging the Nationalist government of Taiwan to assert itself against "Red" (Communist) China. Dulles pleased conservatives—and alarmed many others—by declaring that, if the United States pushed Communist powers to the brink of war, they would back down because of American nuclear superiority. His hard line became known as "brinkmanship." In the end, however, Eisenhower prevented Dulles from carrying his ideas to an extreme.

Massive retaliation. Dulles advocated placing greater reliance on nuclear weapons and air power and spending less on conventional forces of the army and navy. In theory, this would save money ("more bang for the buck"), help balance the federal budget, and increase pressure on potential enemies. In 1953, the United States developed the hydrogen bomb, which could destroy the largest cities. Within a year, however, the Soviets caught up with a hydrogen bomb of their own. To some, the policy of massive retaliation looked more like a policy for mutual extinction. Nuclear weapons indeed proved a powerful deterrent against the superpowers fighting an all-out war between themselves, but such weapons could not prevent small "brushfire" wars from breaking out in the developing nations of Southeast Asia, Africa, and the Middle East.

Unrest in the Third World

The collapse of colonial empires after World War II may have been the single most important development of the postwar era. Between 1947 and 1962, dozens of colonies in Asia and Africa gained their independence. In Asia, India and Pakistan became new nations in 1947 and the Dutch East Indies became the independent country of Indonesia in 1949. In Africa, Ghana threw off British colonial rule in 1957, and a host of other nations followed. These new, Third World countries (in contrast to the industrialized nations of the Western bloc and the Communist bloc) often lacked stable political and economic institutions. Their need for foreign aid from either the United States or the Soviet Union often made them into pawns of the Cold War.

Covert action. Part of the new look in Eisenhower's conduct of U.S. foreign policy was the growing use of covert action. Undercover intervention in the internal politics of other nations seemed less objectionable than employing U.S. troops and also proved less expensive. In 1953 the CIA played a major role in helping to overthrow a government in Iran that had tried to nationalize the holding of foreign oil companies. The overthrow of the elected government allowed for the return of Reza Pahlavi as shah (monarch) of Iran. The shah in return provided the West with favorable oil prices and made enormous purchases of American arms.

In Guatemala, in 1954, the CIA overthrew a leftist government that threatened American business interests. U.S. opposition to communism seemed to drive Washington to support corrupt and often ruthless dictators, especially in Latin America. This tendency produced growing anti-American feeling, which became manifest when angry crowds in Venezuela attacked Vice President Nixon's motorcade during his goodwill tour of South America in 1958.

Asia

During Eisenhower's first year in office, some of the most serious Cold War challenges concerned events in East Asia and Southeast Asia.

Korean armistice. Soon after his inauguration in 1953, Eisenhower kept his election promise by going to Korea to visit U.N. forces and see what could be done to stop the war. He understood that no quick fix was possible. Even so, diplomacy, the threat of nuclear war, and the sudden death of Joseph Stalin in March 1953 finally moved China and North Korea to agree to an armistice and an exchange of prisoners in July 1953. The fighting stopped and most (but not all) U.S. troops were withdrawn. Korea would remain divided near the 38th parallel, and despite years of futile negotiations, no peace treaty was ever concluded between North Korea and South Korea.

Fall of Indochina. After losing their Southeast Asian colony of Indochina to Japanese invaders in World War II, the French made the mistake of trying to retake it. Wanting independence, native Vietnamese and Cambodians resisted. French imperialism had the effect of increasing support for nationalist and Communist leader Ho Chi Minh. By 1950, the anticolonial war in Indochina became part of the Cold War rivalry between Communist and anticommunist powers. Truman's government started to give U.S. military aid to the French, while China and the Soviet Union aided the Viet Minh guerrillas led by Ho Chi Minh. In 1954, a large French army at Dien Bien Phu was trapped and forced to surrender. After this disastrous defeat, the French tried to convince Eisenhower to send in U.S. troops, but he refused. At the Geneva Conference of 1954, France agreed to give up Indochina, which was divided into the independent nations of Cambodia, Laos, and Vietnam.

Division of Vietnam. By the terms of the Geneva Conference, Vietnam was to be temporarily divided at the 17th parallel until a general election could be held. The new nation remained divided, however, as two hostile governments took power on either side of the line. In North Vietnam, Ho Chi Minh established a Communist dictatorship. In South Vietnam, a government emerged under Ngo Dinh Diem, whose support came largely from anticommunist, Catholic, and urban Vietnamese, many of whom had fled from Communist rule in the

North. The general election to unite Vietnam was never held, largely because South Vietnam's government feared that the Communists would win.

From 1955 to 1961, the United States gave over $1 billion in economic and military aid to South Vietnam in an effort to build a stable, anticommunist state. In justifying this aid, President Eisenhower made an analogy to a row of dominoes. According to this *domino theory* (later to become famous), if South Vietnam fell under Communist control, one nation after another in Southeast Asia would also fall, until Australia and New Zealand were in dire danger.

SEATO. To prevent the "fall" to communism of South Vietnam, Laos, and Cambodia, Dulles put together a regional defense pact called the Southeast Asia Treaty Organization (SEATO). Agreeing to defend one another in case of an attack within the region, eight nations signed the pact in 1954 (the United States, Great Britain, France, Australia, New Zealand, the Philippines, Thailand, and Pakistan).

The Middle East

In the Middle East, the United States had the difficult balancing act of maintaining friendly ties with the oil-rich Arab states while at the same time supporting the new state of Israel. The latter nation was created in 1948 under U.N. auspices, after a civil war in the British mandate territory of Palestine left the land divided between the Israelis and the Palestinians. Israel's neighbors, including Egypt, had fought unsuccessfully to prevent the Jewish state from being formed.

Suez crisis. Led by the Arab nationalist General Gamal Nasser, Egypt asked the United States for funds to build the ambitious Aswan Dam project on the Nile River. The United States refused, in part because Egypt threatened Israel's security. Nasser turned to the Soviet Union to help build the dam. The Soviets agreed to provide limited financing for the project. Seeking another source of funds, Nasser precipitated an international crisis in July 1956 by seizing and nationalizing the British- and French-owned Suez Canal. Loss of the canal threatened Western Europe's supply line to Middle Eastern oil. In response to this threat, Britain, France, and Israel carried out a surprise attack against Egypt and retook the canal.

A furious Eisenhower, who had been kept in the dark by his old allies the British and French, sponsored a U.N. resolution condemning the invasion of Egypt. Under pressure from the United States and world public opinion, the invading forces withdrew. After the Suez crisis, Britain and France would never again play the role of major powers in world affairs.

Eisenhower Doctrine. The United States quickly replaced Britain and France as the leading Western influence in the Middle East, but it faced a

MIDDLE EAST AREAS OF CONFLICT, 1948–1990

growing Soviet influence in Egypt and Syria. In a policy pronouncement later known as the *Eisenhower Doctrine,* the United States in 1957 pledged economic and military aid to any Middle Eastern country threatened by communism. Eisenhower first applied his doctrine in Lebanon in 1958 by sending 14,000 marines to that country to prevent the outbreak of a civil war between Christians and Muslims.

OPEC and oil. In Eisenhower's last year in office, 1960, the Arab nations of Saudi Arabia, Kuwait, Iraq, and Iran joined Venezuela to form the Organization of Petroleum Exporting Countries (OPEC). Oil was shaping up to be a critical foreign policy issue. The combination of growing Western dependence on Middle East oil, spreading Arab nationalism, and a conflict between Israelis and Palestinian refugees would trouble American presidents in the coming decades.

U.S.-Soviet Relations

In terms of U.S. security, nothing was more crucial than U.S. diplomatic relations with its chief political and military rival, the Soviet Union. Throughout Eisenhower's presidency, the relations between the two superpowers fluctuated regularly from periods of relative calm to periods of extreme tension.

Spirit of Geneva. After Stalin's death in 1953, Eisenhower called for a slowdown in the arms race and presented to the United Nations an *atoms for peace* plan. The Soviets too showed signs of wanting to reduce Cold War tensions. They withdrew their troops from Austria (once that country had agreed to be neutral in the Cold War) and also established peaceful relations with Greece and Turkey. By 1955, a desire for improved relations on both sides resulted in a summit meeting in Geneva, Switzerland, between Eisenhower and the new Soviet premier, Nikolai Bulganin. At this conference, the U.S. president proposed that the superpowers agree to "open skies" over each other's territory—open to aerial photography by the opposing nation—in order to eliminate the chance of a surprise nuclear attack. The Soviets rejected the proposal. Nevertheless, the "spirit of Geneva," as the press called it, produced the first thaw in the Cold War. Even more encouraging, from the U.S. point of view, was a speech by the new Soviet leader Nikita Khrushchev in early 1956 in which he denounced the crimes of Joseph Stalin and supported "peaceful coexistence" with the West.

Hungarian revolt. The relaxation in the Cold War encouraged workers in East Germany and Poland to demand reforms from the Communist governments of these countries. In October 1956 a popular uprising in Hungary actually succeeded in overthrowing a government backed by Moscow. It was replaced briefly by more liberal leaders who wanted to pull Hungary out of the Warsaw Pact, the Communist security organization. This was too much for the Kremlin, and Khrushchev sent in Soviet tanks to crush the freedom fighters and restore control over Hungary. The United States took no action in the crisis. Eisenhower feared that if he sent troops to aid the Hungarians, it would touch off a world war in Europe. In effect, by allowing Soviet tanks to roll into Hungary, the United States gave de facto recognition to the Soviet sphere of influence in Eastern Europe and ended Dulles' talk of "liberating" this region. Soviet suppression of the Hungarian revolt also ended the first thaw in the Cold War.

***Sputnik* shock.** In 1957, the Soviet Union shocked the United States and surprised the world by launching the first satellites, *Sputnik I* and *Sputnik II,* into orbit around the earth. Suddenly, the technological leadership of the United States was open to question. To add to American embarrassment, U.S. rockets designed to duplicate the Soviet achievement failed repeatedly.

What was responsible for this scientific debacle? Some blamed the schools and "inadequate" instruction in the sciences. In 1958, Congress responded with the National Defense and Education Act (NDEA), which authorized giving hundreds of millions in federal money to the schools for science and foreign language education. Congress in 1958 also created the National Aeronautics and Space Administration (NASA), to direct the U.S. efforts to build missiles and explore outer space. Billions were appropriated to compete with the Russians in the space race.

Fears of nuclear war were intensified by *Sputnik,* since the missiles that launched the satellites could also deliver thermonuclear warheads anywhere in the world in minutes, and there was no defense against them.

Second Berlin crisis. "We will bury capitalism," Khrushchev boasted. With new confidence and pride based on *Sputnik,* the Soviet leader pushed the Berlin issue in 1958 by giving the West six months to pull its troops out of West Berlin before turning over the city to the East Germans. The United States refused to yield. To defuse the crisis, Eisenhower invited Khrushchev to visit the United States in 1959. At the presidential retreat of Camp David in Maryland, the two agreed to put off the crisis and scheduled another summit conference in Paris for 1960.

U-2 incident. The friendly "spirit of Camp David" never had a chance to produce results. Two weeks before the planned meeting in Paris, the Russians shot down a high-altitude U.S. spy plane—the U-2—over the Soviet Union. The incident exposed a secret U.S. tactic for gaining information. After its open-skies proposals had been rejected by the Soviets in 1955, the United States had decided to conduct regular spy flights over Soviet territory to find out about its enemy's missile program. Eisenhower took full responsibility for the flights—*after* they were exposed by the U-2 incident—but his honesty proved a diplomatic mistake. Khrushchev had little choice but to denounce Eisenhower and call off the Paris summit.

Communism in Cuba

Perhaps more alarming than any other Cold War development during the Eisenhower years was the loss of Cuba to communism. A bearded revolutionary, Fidel Castro, overthrew the Cuban dictator Fulgencio Batista in 1959. At first, no one knew whether Castro's politics would be better or worse than those of his ruthless predecessor. Once in power, however, Castro nationalized American-owned businesses and properties in Cuba. Eisenhower retaliated by cutting off U.S. trade with Cuba. Castro then turned to the Soviets for support. He also revealed that he was a Marxist and soon proved it by setting up a Communist totalitarian state. With communism only 90 miles off the shores of Florida, Eisenhower authorized the CIA to train anticommunist Cuban exiles to retake their island, but the decision to go ahead with the scheme was left up to the next president, Kennedy.

Eisenhower's Legacy

After leaving the White House, Eisenhower claimed credit for checking Communist aggression and keeping the peace without the loss of American lives in combat. He also started the long process of relaxing tensions with the Soviet Union. In 1958, he initiated the first arms limitations by voluntarily suspending above-ground testing of nuclear weapons.

"Military-industrial complex." In his farewell address as president, Eisenhower spoke out against the negative impact of the Cold War on U.S. society. He warned the nation to "guard against the acquisition of unwarranted influence . . . by the military-industrial complex." If the outgoing president was right, the arms race was taking on a momentum and logic of its own. It seemed to some Americans in the 1960s that the United States was in danger of going down the path of ancient republics and, like Rome, turning into a military, or imperial, state.

The Civil Rights Movement

While Eisenhower was concentrating on Cold War issues, events of potentially revolutionary significance were developing in the relations between African Americans and other Americans.

Origins of the Movement

The baseball player Jackie Robinson had broken the color line in 1947 by being hired by the Brooklyn Dodgers as the first African American to play on a major league team. President Truman had integrated the armed forces in 1948 and introduced civil rights legislation in Congress. These were the first well-publicized indications that race relations after World War II were changing. As the 1950s began, however, African Americans in the South were still by law segregated from whites in schools and in most public facilities. They were also kept from voting by poll taxes, literacy tests, grandfather causes, and intimidation. Social segregation left most of them poorly educated, while economic discrimination kept them in a state of poverty.

Changing demographics. The origins of the modern civil rights movement can be traced back to the movement of millions of African Americans from the rural South to the urban centers of the South and the North. In the North, African Americans, who joined the Democrats during the New Deal, had a growing influence in party politics in the 1950s.

Changing attitudes in the Cold War. The Cold War also played an indirect role in changing both government policies and social attitudes. The U.S. reputation for freedom and democracy was competing against Communist ideology for the hearts and minds of the peoples of Africa and Asia. Against this global background, racial segregation and discrimination stood out as glaring wrongs that needed to be corrected.

Desegregating the Schools

The NAACP had been working through the courts for decades trying to overturn the Supreme Court's 1896 decision, *Plessy v. Ferguson,* which allowed segregation in "separate but equal" facilities. In the late 1940s, the NAACP won a series of cases involving higher education.

Brown decision. One of the great landmark cases in Supreme Court history was argued in the early 1950s by a team of NAACP lawyers led by Thurgood Marshall. In the case of *Brown v. Board of Education of Topeka,* they argued that segregation of black children in the public schools was unconstitutional because it violated the Fourteenth Amendment's guarantee of "equal protection of the laws." In May 1954, the Supreme Court agreed with Marshall and overturned the *Plessy* case. Writing for a unanimous Court, Chief Justice Earl Warren ruled that (1) "separate facilities are inherently unequal" and unconstitutional and (2) segregation in the schools should end with "all deliberate speed."

Resistance in the South. States in the Deep South fought the Supreme Court's decision with a variety of tactics, including the temporary closing of the public schools. In Arkansas in 1956, Governor Orval Faubus used the state's National Guard to prevent nine African American students from entering Little Rock Central High School, as ordered by a federal court. President Eisenhower then intervened. While the president did not actively support desegregation and had reservations about the *Brown* decision, he understood his constitutional responsibility to uphold federal authority. Eisenhower ordered federal troops to stand guard in Little Rock and protect black students as they walked to school. He thus became the first president since Reconstruction to use federal troops to protect the rights of African Americans.

Montgomery Bus Boycott

Segregation of public transportation also came under attack as a result of one woman's refusal to take a back seat. In Montgomery, Alabama, in 1955, Rosa Parks was too tired after a long day at work to move to the back of the bus to the section reserved for African Americans. Her arrest for violating the segregation law sparked a massive African American protest in Montgomery in the form of a boycott against riding the city buses. The Reverend Martin Luther King, Jr., minister of the Baptist church where the boycott started, soon emerged as the inspiring leader of a nonviolent movement to achieve integration. The protest touched off by Rosa Parks and the Montgomery boycott eventually triumphed when the Supreme Court in 1956 ruled that segregation laws were unconstitutional.

Federal Laws

Signed into law by President Eisenhower, two civil rights laws of 1957 and 1960 were the first such laws to be enacted by the U.S. Congress since Reconstruction. They were modest in scope, providing for a permanent Civil Rights Commission and giving the Justice Department new powers to protect the voting rights of blacks. Despite this legislation, southern officials still used an arsenal of obstructive tactics to discourage African Americans from voting.

Nonviolent Protests

What the government would not do, the African American community did for itself. In 1957, Martin Luther King, Jr., formed the Southern Christian Leadership Conference (SCLC), which organized ministers and churches in the South to get behind the civil rights struggle. In February 1960, college students in Greensboro, North Carolina, started the sit-in movement after being refused service at a segregated Woolworth's lunch counter. To call attention to the injustice of segregated facilities, students would deliberately invite arrest by sitting in restricted areas. The Student Nonviolent Coordinating Committee (SNCC) was formed a few months later to keep the movement organized. In the 1960s African Americans used the sit-in tactic to integrate restaurants, hotels, buildings, libraries, pools, and transportation throughout the South.

The actions of the Supreme Court, Congress, and President Eisenhower marked a turning point in the civil rights movement—as did the Montgomery bus boycott. Progress was slow, however. In the 1960s, a growing impatience among many African Americans would be manifested in violent confrontations in the streets.

Popular Culture in the Fifties

Among white suburbanites, the 1950s were marked by conformity to social norms. Consensus about political issues and conformity in social behavior were safe harbors for Americans troubled by the foreign ideology of communism. At the same time, they were the hallmarks of a consumer-driven mass economy.

Consumer Culture and Conformity

Television, advertising, and the middle-class move to the suburbs contributed mightily to the growing homogeneity of American culture.

Television. Little more than a curiosity in the late 1940s, television suddenly became a center of family life in millions of American homes. By 1961, there were 55 million TV sets, about one for every 3.3 Americans. Television programming in the fifties was dominated by three national networks, which presented viewers with a bland menu of situation comedies, westerns, quiz shows, and professional sports. Such critics as FCC chairman Newton Minnow called television a "vast wasteland" and worried about the impact on children of a steady dose of five or more hours of daily viewing. Yet the culture portrayed on television—especially for third and fourth generations of white ethnic Americans—provided a common content for their common language.

Advertising. In all the media (television, radio, newspapers, and magazines), aggressive advertising by name brands also promoted common material wants, and the introduction of suburban shopping centers and the plastic credit card in the 1950s provided a quick means of satisfying them. The phenomenal proliferation of McDonald's yellow arches on the roadside was one measure of how successful were the new marketing techniques and standardized products as the nation turned from "mom and pop" stores to franchise operations.

Paperbacks and records. Despite television, Americans read more than ever. Paperback books, an innovation in the 1950s, were selling almost a million copies a day by 1960. Popular music was revolutionized by the mass marketing of inexpensive long-playing (LP) record albums and stacks of 45 rpm records. Teenagers fell in love with rock and roll music, a blend of African American rhythm and blues with white country music, popularized by the gyrating Elvis Presley.

Corporate America. In the business world, conglomerates with diversified holdings began to dominate such industries as food processing, hotels, transportation, insurance, and banking. For the first time in history, more American workers held white-collar jobs than blue-collar jobs. To work for one of *Fortune* magazine's top 500 companies seemed to be the road to success. Large corporations of this era promoted teamwork and conformity, including a dress code for male workers of a dark business suit, white shirt, and a conservative tie. The social scientist William Whyte documented this loss of individuality in his book *The Organization Man* (1956).

Big unions became more powerful after the merger of the AF of L and the CIO in 1955. They also became more conservative, as blue-collar workers began to enjoy middle-class incomes.

For most Americans, conformity was a small price to pay for the new affluence of a home in the suburbs, a new automobile every two or three years, good schools for the children, and maybe a vacation at the recently opened Disneyland (1955).

Religion. Organized religions expanded dramatically after World War II with the building of thousands of new churches and synagogues. Will Herberg's book *Protestant, Catholic, Jew* (1955) commented on the new religious tolerance of the times and the lack of interest in doctrine, as religious membership became a source of both individual identity and socialization.

Women's Roles

The baby boom and running a home in the suburbs made homemaking a full-time job for millions of women. In the postwar era, the traditional view of a woman's role as caring for home and children was reaffirmed in the mass media and in the best-selling self-help book, *Baby and Child Care* (1946) by Dr. Benjamin Spock.

At the same time, evidence of dissatisfaction was growing, especially among well-educated women of the middle class. More married women, especially as they reached middle age, entered the workforce. Yet male employers in the 1950s saw female workers primarily as wives and mothers, and women's lower wages reflected this attitude.

Social Critics

Not everybody approved of the social trends of the 1950s. In *The Lonely Crowd* (1958), Harvard sociologist David Riesman criticized the replacement of "inner-directed" individuals in society with "other-directed" conformists. In *The Affluent Society* (1958), the economist John Kenneth Galbraith wrote about the failure of wealthy Americans to address the need for increased social spending for the common good. (Galbraith's ideas were to influence the Kennedy and Johnson administrations in the next decade.) The sociologist C. Wright Mills portrayed dehumanizing corporate worlds in *White Collar* (1951) and threats to freedom in *The Power Elite* (1956).

Novels. Some of the most popular novelists of the fifties wrote about the individual's struggle against conformity. J. D. Salinger provided a classic commentary on "phoniness" as viewed by a troubled teenager in *The Catcher in the Rye* (1951). Joseph Heller satirized the stupidity of the military and war in *Catch-22* (1961).

"Beatniks." A group of rebellious writers and intellectuals made up the so-called Beat generation of the 1950s. Led by Jack Kerouac (*On the Road,* 1957) and poet Allen Ginsberg ("Howl," 1956), they advocated spontaneity, use of drugs, and rebellion against societal standards. The Beatniks of the fifties would become models for the youth rebellion of the sixties.

HISTORICAL PERSPECTIVES: A SILENT GENERATION?

Among intellectuals, a commonly held view of the 1950s was that Americans had become complacent in their political outlook— a "silent generation" presided over by a grandfatherly and passive President Eisenhower. Liberal academics believed that McCarthyism had stopped any serious or critical discussion of the problems in American society. Eisenhower's policies and their general acceptance by most voters seemed a bland consensus of ideas that would bother no one. Liberal critics contrasted the seeming calm of the fifties with the more "interesting" social and cultural revolution of the next decade.

In recent years, historians' view of the 1950s has become more respectful. Historical research into the Eisenhower papers has revealed a president who used a hidden-hand approach to leadership. Behind the scenes, he was an active and decisive administrator who was in full command of his presidency. His domestic policies achieved sustained economic growth, and his foreign policy relaxed international tensions. Such accomplishments no longer look boring after decades of economic dislocations and stagnant or declining incomes.

Reflecting this more generous view of Eisenhower is William O'Neill's *American High: The Years of Confidence, 1945–1960* (1987). O'Neill argues that Eisenhower led a needed and largely successful economic and social postwar "reconstruction." He and other historians now emphasize that the 1950s prepared the way for *both* the liberal reforms of the 1960s and the conservative politics of the 1980s. Achievements of women, African Americans, and other minorities in a later era were made possible by changes in the fifties. Furthermore, the integration of Catholics, Jews, and other white ethnics into American society during the postwar years made it possible for Kennedy to be elected the first Irish Catholic president in 1960.

Once considered an era in which America was adrift, the 1950s is now being regarded nostalgically as an all-too-brief golden age in U.S. history.

KEY NAMES, EVENTS, AND TERMS

Dwight Eisenhower	Ho Chi Minh	*Sputnik*
Richard Nixon	Vietnam	National Aeronautics and
modern Republicanism	domino theory	Space Administration
Oveta Culp Hobby	Southeast Asia Treaty	U-2 incident
soil-bank program	Organization (1954)	Fidel Castro
Highway Act (1956);	Suez Canal crisis (1956)	Cuba
interstate highway system	Eisenhower Doctrine	military-industrial complex
John Foster Dulles;	Organization of Petroleum	civil rights
"brinksmanship"	Exporting Countries (OPEC)	Jackie Robinson
massive retaliation	"spirit of Geneva"	NAACP
Third World	open-skies crisis	desegregation
Iran	Nikita Khrushchev	*Brown v. Board of Education*
covert action	peaceful coexistence	*of Topeka*
Indochina	Hungarian revolt	Earl Warren
Geneva Conference	Warsaw Pact	Little Rock crisis

Rosa Parks

Montgomery bus boycott

Martin Luther King, Jr.

civil rights acts of 1957, 1960

Civil Rights Commission

Southern Christian Leadership Conference

nonviolent protest

sit-in movement

Student Nonviolent Coordinating Committee

corporate America

consumer culture

David Riesman, *The Lonely Crowd*

John Kenneth Galbraith, *The Affluent Society*

Beatniks

MULTIPLE-CHOICE QUESTIONS

1. President Eisenhower's "modern Republicanism" can best be described as

   (A) a return to the economic policies of Coolidge and Hoover

   (B) a general acceptance of the New Deal programs and a balanced budget

   (C) an effort to shift taxes from the wealthy to lower income Americans

   (D) opposition to all liberal causes, including civil rights

   (E) the return of social and welfare programs to the states

2. John Foster Dulles' "new look" to U.S. foreign policy included all of the following EXCEPT

   (A) taking Communist nations to the brink of war to force them to back down

   (B) threatening massive retaliation with nuclear weapons to prevent Soviet aggression

   (C) supporting the liberation of "captive" nations

   (D) recognizing the Communist government of China

   (E) reducing conventional forces of the U.S. Army and Navy

3. U.S. intervention in Iran in 1953 and in Guatemala in 1954 are examples of

   (A) the use of covert action by the CIA

   (B) the application of the Eisenhower Doctrine

   (C) U.S. efforts to stop the proliferation of nuclear weapons

   (D) the use of U.S. troops to support democratic governments

   (E) the policy of brinkmanship

4. "We declare that however acute the ideological differences between the two systems—the socialist and the capitalist—we must solve questions in dispute among states not by war, but by peaceful negotiation."

   This statement by Nikita Khrushchev in 1957 expressed the idea of

   (A) massive retaliation

   (B) de-Stalinization

   (C) inevitability of the triumph of communism

(D) peaceful coexistence

(E) cultural revolution

5. Which of the following represented a major crisis during Eisenhower's presidency?

(A) Cuban missile crisis

(B) invasion of South Korea

(C) Spirit of Camp David

(D) British, French, and Israeli invasion of Egypt

(E) blockade of Berlin

6. In the case of *Brown v. Board of Education of Topeka,* the Supreme Court ruled that

(A) segregated facilities must be equal

(B) African Americans and whites must have equal access to public transportation

(C) racially segregated schools are inherently unequal and unconstitutional

(D) nonviolent protests are protected by the First Amendment

(E) voting rights must apply equally to whites and African Americans

7. The Montgomery bus boycott and Greensboro lunch counter sit-ins are examples of

(A) enforcement by the Justice Department of the *Brown* decision

(B) President Eisenhower's use of federal troops to end segregation

(C) court-initiated efforts to end racial discrimination

(D) failures of nonviolent direct action by the NAACP

(E) protests against segregation coming from the African American community

8. During the 1950s, all of the following contributed to a more homogeneous culture EXCEPT

(A) building of the interstate highway system

(B) the Beat generation

(C) television programming

(D) spread of franchise operations

(E) growth of the suburbs

9. The United States during the Eisenhower years was characterized by

(A) decreased spending for defense

(B) breakup of conglomerates

(C) increased tension between Protestants, Catholics, and Jews

(D) increased middle-class affluence

(E) radical protests on college campuses

10. All of the following represented a criticism of the society and conformity of the 1950s EXCEPT

(A) David Reisman's *The Lonely Crowd*

(B) William Whyte's *The Organization Man*

(C) John Kenneth Galbraith's *The Affluent Society*

(D) David Halberstam's *The Best and the Brightest*

(E) C. Wright Mills' *The Power Elite*

ESSAY QUESTIONS

1. To what extent did President Eisenhower continue the containment policy of Harry Truman?

2. Analyze the relative influence of African Americans and the federal government in TWO of the following civil rights cases:

   Brown v. Board of Education of Topeka

   Little Rock Central High School

   Montgomery bus boycott

3. Discuss the consequences of TWO of the following on Cold War tensions:

   Geneva summit meeting

   Sputnik launching

   U-2 incident

   Fidel Castro's Cuban revolution

4. To what extent were the 1950s an era of conformity and complacency?

5. How did television affect American culture and politics in the 1950s?

DOCUMENTS AND READINGS

Were the 1950s an era of conformity and consensus, as commonly believed? The combination of voices sampled in these pages can be interpreted as reflecting conformity—and also as supporting a contrary view of the decade.

DOCUMENT A. *MCCARTHY ON THE COMMUNIST THREAT*

Senator Joseph McCarthy of Wisconsin became a national figure in 1950 after repeatedly charging that the State Department was infested with Communists. The following remarks were typical of his rhetoric and thinking.

Today, we are engaged in a final, all-out battle between communistic atheism and Christianity. The modern champions of communism have selected this as the time. And, ladies and gentlemen, the chips are down—they are truly down.

Six years ago . . . there was within the Soviet orbit 180 million people. Lined up on the antitotalitarian side there were in the world at that time roughly 1,625 million people. Today, only six years later, there are 800 million under the absolute domination of Soviet Russia—an increase of over 400 percent. On our side, the figure has shrunk to around 500 million. In other words, in less than six years the odds have changed from 9 to 1 in our favor to 8 to 5 against us. This indicates the swiftness of the tempo of Communist victories and American defeats in the cold war. As one of our outstanding historical figures once said, "When a great democracy is destroyed, it will not be because of enemies from without, but rather because of enemies from within."

The reason why we find ourselves in a position of impotency is not because our only powerful potential enemy has sent men to invade our shores, but rather because of the traitorous actions of those who have been treated so well by this Nation. It has not been the less fortunate or members of minority groups who have been selling this Nation out, but rather those who have had all the benefits that the wealthiest nation on earth has had to offer—the finest homes, the finest college education, and the finest jobs in government we can give.

This is glaringly true in the State Department. There the bright young men who are born with silver spoons in their mouths are the ones who have been worst. . . . In my opinion the State Department, which is one of the most important government departments, is thoroughly infested with Communists.

I have in my hand 57 cases of individuals who would appear to be either card-carrying members or certainly loyal to the Communist Party, but who nevertheless are still helping to shape our foreign policy.

One thing to remember in discussing the Communists in our Government is that we are not dealing with spies who get 30 pieces of silver to steal the blueprints of a new weapon. We are dealing with a far more sinister type of activity because it permits the enemy to guide and shape our policy. . . .

Senator Joseph McCarthy,
Congressional Record, February 20, 1950

DOCUMENT B.   *DANGERS OF A GARRISON STATE*

In his farewell address to the American people in 1961, President Eisenhower warned against the increasing influence of the military and of costly scientific technologies.

A vital element in keeping the peace is our military establishment. Our arms must be mighty, ready for instant action, so that no potential aggressor may be tempted to risk his own destruction.

Our military organization today bears little relation to that known by my predecessors in peacetime, or indeed by the fighting men in World War II or Korea.

Until the latest of our world conflicts, the United States had no armaments industry. American makers of plowshares could, with time and as required, make swords as well. But now we can no longer risk emergency improvision of national defense; we have been compelled to create a permanent armaments industry of vast proportions. Added to this, three and a half million men and women are directly engaged in the defense establishment. We annually spend on military security more than the net income of all United States corporations.

This conjunction of an immense military establishment and a large arms industry is new in American experience. The total influence—economic, political, even spiritual—is felt in every city, every state house, every office of the federal government. We recognize the imperative need for this development. Yet we must not fail to comprehend its grave implications. Our toil, resources, and livelihood are all involved; so is the very structure of our society.

In the councils of government, we must guard against the acquisition of unwarranted influence, whether sought or unsought, by the military-industrial complex. The potential for the disastrous rise of misplaced power exists and will persist.

We must never let the weight of this combination endanger our liberties or democratic processes. We should take nothing for granted. Only an alert and knowledgeable citizenry can compel the proper meshing of the huge industrial and military machinery of defense with our peaceful methods and goals, so that security and liberty may prosper together.

Akin to, and largely responsible for, the sweeping changes in our industrial-military posture has been the technological revolution during the recent decades.

In this revolution, research has become central; it also becomes more formalized, complex, and costly. A steadily increasing share is conducted for, by, or at the direction of, the federal government.

Today, the solitary inventor, tinkering in his shop, has been overshadowed by task forces of scientists in laboratories and testing fields. In the same fashion, the free university, historically the fountainhead of free ideas and scientific discovery, has experienced a revolution in the conduct of research. Partly because of the huge costs involved, a government contract becomes virtually a substitute for intellectual curiosity. For every old blackboard there are now hundreds of new electronic computers.

The prospect of domination of the nation's scholars by federal employment, project allocations, and the power of money is ever present and is gravely to be regarded.

Yet, in holding scientific research and discovery in respect, as we should, we must also be alert to the equal and opposite danger that public policy could itself become the captive of a scientific-technological elite.

It is the task of statemanship to mold, to balance, and to integrate these and other forces, new and old, within the principles of our democratic system—ever aiming toward the supreme goals of our free society.

President Dwight D. Eisenhower,
Farewell Address, January 17, 1961

DOCUMENT C. *THE DAMAGE CAUSED BY SEGREGATION*

In 1954, the Supreme Court headed by Chief Justice Earl Warren ruled that "separate but equal" public schools were "inherently unequal." The landmark decision was controversial not only because of its conclusion but also because of its use of intangible and psychological evidence.

In approaching this problem, we cannot turn the clock back to 1868 when the [14th] Amendment was adopted, or even to 1896 when *Plessy v. Ferguson* was written. We must consider public education in the light of its full development and its present place in American life throughout the Nation. Only in this way can it be determined if segregation in public schools deprives these plaintiffs of the equal protection of the laws.

Today, education is perhaps the most important function of state and local governments. Compulsory school attendance laws and the great expenditures for education both demonstrate our recognition of the importance of education to our democratic society. It is required in the performance of our most basic public responsibilities, even service in the armed forces. It is the very foundation of good citizenship. Today it is a principal instrument in awakening the child to cultural values, in preparing him for later professional training, and in helping him to adjust normally to his environment. In these days, it is doubtful that any child may reasonably be expected to succeed in life if he is denied the opportunity of an education. Such an opportunity, where the state has undertaken to provide it, is a right which must be made available to all on equal terms.

We come then to the question presented: Does segregation of children in public schools solely on the basis of race even though the physical facilities and other "tangible" factors may be equal, deprive the children of the minority group of equal education opportunities? We believe that it does.

In *Sweatt v. Painter, supra,* in finding that a segregated law school for Negroes could not provide them equal educational opportunities, this court relied in large part on "those qualities which are incapable of objective measurement but which make for greatness in a law school." In *McLaurin v. Oklahoma State Regents, supra,* the court, in requiring that a Negro admitted to a white graduate school be treated like all other students, again resorted to intangible consideration: ". . . his ability to study, to engage in discussions and exchange views with other students, and in general, to learn his profession." Such considerations apply with added force to children in grade and high schools. To separate them from others of similar age and qualifications solely because of their race generates a feeling of inferiority as to their status in the community that may affect their hearts and minds in a way unlikely ever to be undone. The effect of this separation on their educational opportunities was well stated by a finding in the Kansas case by a court which nevertheless felt compelled to rule against the Negro plaintiffs:

Segregation of white and colored children in public schools has a detrimental effect upon the colored children. The impact is greater when it has the sanction of law; for the policy of separating the races is usually interpreted as denoting the inferiority of the Negro group. A sense of inferiority affects the motivation of a child to learn. Segregation with the sanction of law, therefore, has a tendency to [retard] the educational and mental development of Negro children and to deprive them of some of the benefits they would receive in a racial[ly] integrated school system.

Whatever may have been the extent of psychological knowledge at the time of *Plessey v. Ferguson,* this finding is amply supported by modern authority. Any language in *Plessy v. Ferguson* contrary to this finding is rejected.

We conclude that in the field of public education the doctrine of "separate but equal" has no place. Separate educational facilities are inherently unequal. Therefore, we hold that the plaintiffs and others similarly situated for whom the actions have been brought are, by reasons of segregation complained of, deprived of the equal protection of the laws guaranteed by the Fourteenth Amendment.

Supreme Court,
Brown v. Board of Education of Topeka, May 17, 1954

DOCUMENT D. *SUBURBAN CONFORMITY*

In novels and poetry, critics of society are often able to hit their target harder than the nonfiction writer. Malvina Reynolds in "Little Boxes" attacked middle-class suburban life in humorous but memorable song.

Little Boxes

Little boxes on the hillside, little boxes made of ticky tacky,
Little boxes on the hillside, little boxes all the same,
There's a green one and a pink one, and a blue one and a yellow one,
And they're all made out of ticky tacky, and they all look just the same.

And the people in the houses
All went to the university,
Where they were put in boxes
And they came out all the same,
And there's doctors and lawyers,
And business executives,
And they're all made out of ticky tacky
And they all look just the same.

And they all play on the golf course
And drink their martinis dry
And they all have pretty children
And the children go to school,
And the children go to summer camp
And then to the university,
Where they are put in boxes
And they come out all the same. . . .

Malvina Reynolds,
"Little Boxes," 1962

ANALYZING THE DOCUMENTS

1. What tactics or strategies of what became known as "McCarthyism" can you find in the senator's 1950 speech? Why might he be called a "populist"?

2. Identify the dangers that President Eisenhower warned Americans against in his farewell address. Were these dangers a result of the Cold War?

3. What intangible or psychological evidence did the Supreme Court use to strike down "separate but equal"? Why was this kind of evidence controversial?

4. In "Little Boxes," what or who is implicitly blamed for the growing conformity in American society?

5. The four documents express views on a number of issues, but to some degree, each contains a criticism of postwar American society. Which of the concerns can be traced to the effects of the Cold War? Do these documents support the view that the 1950s were essentially an era of conformity and consensus?

PROMISES AND TURMOIL: THE 1960s

> *Let the word go forth from this time and place, to friend and foe*
> *alike, that the torch has been passed to a new generation of*
> *Americans—born in this century, tempered by war, disciplined by a*
> *hard and bitter peace, proud of our ancient heritage. . . . Let every*
> *nation know, whether it wishes us well or ill, that we shall pay any*
> *price, bear any burden, meet any hardship, support any friend,*
> *oppose any foe to assure the survival and success of liberty.*
>
> John F. Kennedy, Inaugural Address, January 20, 1961

The 1960s were in many ways both the best and the worst of times. On the one hand, the postwar economic prosperity peaked in the 1960s. At the same time, racial strife, a controversial war in Vietnam, and student radicalism started to tear the country apart. The proud superpower began to learn its limits both in the jungles of Vietnam and on the streets at home.

John F. Kennedy's New Frontier

The decade began with an election that proved symbolic of the changes that were to come.

The Election of 1960

President Eisenhower had not been able to transfer his popularity to other Republicans, and the Democrats retained control of Congress through Eisenhower's last two years in office.

Nixon. At their convention in 1960, the Republicans unanimously nominated Richard Nixon for president. During his eight years as Eisenhower's vice president, Nixon had gained a reputation as a statesman in his diplomatic travels to Europe and South America. In a visit to Moscow, he stood up to Nikita Khrushchev in the so-called kitchen debate (which took place in a model of an American kitchen) over the relative merits of capitalism and communism. Still a young man at 47, the Republican candidate was known to be a tough and seasoned campaigner.

593

Kennedy. Through the early months of 1960, several Democrats believed they had a chance to secure the nomination of their party. Liberal Democrats still liked Adlai Stevenson of Illinois, and southern Democrats supported the Senate majority leader, Lyndon B. Johnson of Texas. In the primaries, however, a charismatic, wealthy, and youthful 43-year-old senator from Massachusetts, John F. Kennedy, defeated his rivals. Going into the convention, he had just enough delegates behind him to win the nomination. To balance the ticket, the New Englander chose a Texan, Lyndon B. Johnson, to be his vice presidential running mate—a choice that proved critical in carrying southern states in the November election.

Campaign. The new medium of television was perhaps the most decisive factor in the close race between the two youthful campaigners, Nixon and Kennedy. In the first of four televised debates—the first such debates in campaign history—Kennedy appeared on screen as more vigorous and comfortable than the pale and tense Nixon. On the issues of the day, Kennedy attacked the Eisenhower administration for the recent recession and for permitting the Soviets to take the lead in the arms race. As it proved, what Kennedy called a "missile gap" was actually in the U.S. favor, but his charges seemed plausible after Sputnik. As the first Catholic presidential candidate since Al Smith (1928), Kennedy's religion became an issue in the minds of some voters. Religious loyalties helped Nixon in rural Protestant areas but helped Kennedy in the large cities.

Results. In one of the closest elections in U.S. history, Kennedy defeated Nixon by a little over 100,000 popular votes, and by a slightly wider margin of 303 to 219 in the electoral college. Many Republicans, including Nixon, felt the election had been stolen by Democratic political machines in states like Illinois and Texas by stuffing ballot boxes with "votes" of the deceased.

Domestic Policy

At 43, Kennedy was the youngest candidate ever to be elected president. Youthful energy and a sharp wit gave a new, personal style to the presidency. In his inaugural address, Kennedy spoke of "the torch being passed to a new generation" and promised to lead the nation into a New Frontier. The Democratic president surrounded himself with both tough-minded pragmatists like Secretary of Defense Robert McNamara, and liberal academics like economist John Kenneth Galbraith. For the sensitive position of attorney general, the president chose his younger brother, Robert Kennedy. The youthful couple in the White House, John Kennedy and his attractive wife, Jacqueline ("Jackie"), brought style, glamor, and an appreciation of the arts to the White House. The press loved Kennedy's witty news conferences, and soon his administration was likened to the mythical kingdom of Camelot and the court of King Arthur.

New Frontier programs. The promises of the New Frontier proved difficult to keep. Kennedy called for aid to education, federal support of health care, urban renewal, and civil rights, but his domestic programs languished in Congress. While few of them became law during his thousand-day administration, most were passed later under President Johnson.

On economic issues, Kennedy had some success. He faced down big steel executives over an inflationary price increase and achieved a price rollback. In addition, the economy was stimulated by increased spending for defense and space exploration, as the president committed the nation to land on the moon by the end of the decade.

Foreign Affairs

With his domestic programs often blocked, Kennedy increasingly turned his attention to foreign policy issues. In 1961, he set up the Peace Corps, an organization that recruited young American volunteers to give technical aid to developing countries. Also in 1961, another foreign aid program, the Alliance for Progress, was organized to promote land reform and economic development in Latin America. Congress was also persuaded to pass the Trade Expansion Act of 1962, which authorized tariff reductions with the recently formed European Economic Community (Common Market) of Western European nations.

Bay of Pigs invasion (1961). Kennedy made a major blunder shortly after entering office. He gave his approval to a Central Intelligence Agency scheme planned under the Eisenhower administration to use Cuban exiles to overthrow Fidel Castro's regime in Cuba. In April 1961 the CIA-trained force of Cubans landed at the Bay of Pigs in Cuba but failed to set off a general uprising as planned. Trapped on the beach, the anti-Castro Cubans had little choice but to surrender after Kennedy rejected the idea of using U.S. forces to save them. Castro used the failed invasion to get even more aid from the Soviet Union and to strengthen his grip on power.

Berlin Wall. Trying to shake off the embarrassment of the Bay of Pigs defeat, Kennedy agreed to meet Soviet premier Khrushchev in Vienna in the summer of 1961. Khrushchev seized the opportunity in Vienna to threaten the president by renewing Soviet demands that U.S. troops be pulled out of Berlin. Kennedy refused. In August, the East Germans, with Soviet backing, built a wall around West Berlin. Its purpose was to stop East Germans from fleeing to West Germany. As the wall was being built, Soviet and U.S. tanks faced off in Berlin. Kennedy called up the reserves, but he made no move to stop the completion of the wall. In 1963, the president traveled to West Berlin to assure its residents of continuing U.S. support. To cheering crowds, he proclaimed: "Freedom has many difficulties and democracy is not perfect, but we have never had to put up a wall to keep our people in. . . . As a free man, I take pride in the words, *'Ich bin ein Berliner'* [I am a Berliner]."

The Berlin Wall stood as a gloomy symbol of the Cold War until it was torn down by rebellious East Germans in 1989.

THE CARIBBEAN AND CENTRAL AMERICA

Cuban missile crisis (1962). The most dangerous challenge from the Soviets came in October 1962. U.S. reconnaissance planes discovered that the Russians were building underground sites in Cuba for the launching of offensive missiles that could reach the United States in minutes. Kennedy responded by announcing to the world that he was setting up a naval blockade of Cuba until the weapons were removed. A full-scale nuclear war between the superpowers seemed likely if Soviet ships challenged the U.S. naval blockade. After days of tension, Khrushchev finally agreed to remove the missiles from Cuba in exchange for Kennedy's pledge not to invade the island nation.

The Cuban missile crisis had a sobering effect on both sides. Soon afterward, a telecommunications hot line was established between Washington and Moscow to make it possible for the leaders of the two countries to talk directly during a crisis. In 1963, the Soviet Union and the United States—along with nearly one hundred other nations—signed the Nuclear Test Ban Treaty to end the testing of nuclear weapons in the atmosphere. This first step in controlling the testing of nuclear arms was offset by a new round in the arms race for developing missile and warhead superiority.

Flexible response. A different Cold War challenge were the many "brush-fire wars" in Africa and Southeast Asia, in which insurgent forces were often aided by Soviet arms and training. Such conflicts in the Congo (later renamed Zaire) in Africa and in Laos and Vietnam in Southeast Asia convinced the Kennedy administration to adopt a policy of flexible response. Moving away from Dulles' idea of massive retaliation and reliance on nuclear weapons, Kennedy and McNamara decided to increase spending on conventional (non-nuclear) arms and mobile military forces. While the flexible-response policy reduced the risk of using nuclear weapons, it also increased the temptation to send elite special forces, such as the Green Berets, into combat in third world countries like South Vietnam.

Assassination in Dallas

After just two and a half years in office, President Kennedy's "one brief, shining moment" was cut short on November 22, 1963, in Dallas, Texas, as two bullets from an assassin's rifle found their mark. After the shocking news of Kennedy's murder, millions of stunned Americans were fixed to their televisions for days and even witnessed the killing of the alleged assassin, Lee Harvey Oswald, just two days after the president's assassination. The Warren Commission, headed by Chief Justice Earl Warren, concluded that Oswald was the lone assassin. For years afterward, however, unanswered questions about the events in Dallas produced dozens of conspiracy theories pointing to possible involvement by organized crime, Castro, the CIA, and the FBI. For many Americans, the tragedy in Dallas and doubts about the Warren Commission marked the beginning of a loss of credibility in government.

In retrospect. At the time, John Kennedy's presidency inspired many idealistic young Americans to take seriously his inaugural message and to "ask not what your country can do for you—ask what you can do for your country." More recently, however, his belligerent Cold War rhetoric has drawn criticism from historians. Nevertheless, the Kennedy legend endured for years and cast a spell on American politics through the 1960s and 1970s.

Lyndon Johnson's Great Society

Two hours after the Kennedy assassination, Lyndon Johnson took the oath of office as president aboard an airplane at the Dallas airport. On the one hand, as a native of rural west Texas and a graduate of a teacher's college, he seemed less polished and sophisticated than the wealthy, Harvard-educated, well-mannered Kennedy. On the other hand, Johnson was a much more experienced lawmaker and politician. He had started out in politics during the depression as a devoted follower of Roosevelt's New Deal.

As the new president, Johnson was determined to expand the social reforms of the New Deal. Having spent almost 30 years in Congress, he knew how to get things done. Shortly after taking office, Johnson persuaded Congress to pass (1) an expanded version of Kennedy's civil rights bill and (2) Kennedy's proposal for an income tax cut. The latter measure sparked an increase in jobs, consumer spending, and a long period of economic expansion in the sixties.

The War on Poverty

Michael Harrington's best-selling book on poverty, *The Other America* (1962), helped to focus national attention on the 40 million Americans still living in poverty. Johnson responded by declaring in 1964 an "unconditional war on poverty." The Democratic Congress gave the president almost everything that he asked by creating the Office of Economic Opportunity (OEO) and providing this antipoverty agency with a billion-dollar budget. The OEO sponsored a wide variety of self-help programs for the poor, such as Head Start for preschoolers, the Job Corps for vocational education, literacy programs, and legal services. The controversial Community Action Program allowed the poor to run antipoverty programs in their own neighborhoods.

Like the New Deal, some of Johnson's programs produced results, while others did not. Nevertheless, before being cut back to pay for the far more costly Vietnam War, the War on Poverty did significantly reduce the number of American families living in poverty.

The Election of 1964

Johnson and his running mate, Senator Hubert Humphrey of Minnesota, went into the 1964 election with a clearly liberal agenda. In contrast, the Republicans nominated a staunch conservative, Senator Barry Goldwater of Arizona, who advocated ending the welfare state, including TVA and Social Security. A TV ad by the Democrats pictured Goldwater as a dangerous extremist, who would be quick to involve the United States in nuclear war.

Johnson won the election by a landslide, taking 61 percent of the popular vote—a higher figure than FDR's landslide of 1936. In addition, Democrats now controlled both houses of Congress by better than a two-thirds margin. A Democratic president and Congress were in a position to pass the economic and social reforms originally proposed by President Truman in the 1940s.

Great Society Reforms

The list of Johnson's legislative achievements in 1965 and 1966 is long and includes new programs that would have lasting effects on U.S. society:

- Medicare, a health insurance program for those 65 and older

- Medicaid, government-paid health care for the poor and the disabled

- the Elementary and Secondary Education Act, providing aid especially to poor school districts

- a new immigration law, abolishing the discriminatory quotas based on national origins passed in the 1920s and greatly increasing opportunities for Asians and Latin Americans to emigrate to the United States

- the National Foundation on the Arts and the Humanities, providing federal funding for worthy creative and scholarly projects

- two new cabinet departments: the Department of Transportation (DOT), and the Department of Housing and Urban Development (HUD)
- increased funding for higher education
- increased funding for public housing and crime prevention

Congress also passed programs to regulate the automobile industry, in response to Ralph Nader's book *Unsafe at Any Speed* (1965). Clean air and water laws were enacted in part as a response to Rachel Carson's exposé of pesticides, *Silent Spring* (1962). First lady Lady Bird Johnson contributed to improving the environment with her Beautify America campaign.

Evaluating the Great Society. Johnson's Great Society has been criticized for its unrealistic promises to eliminate poverty and for creating a centralized welfare state that was inefficient and very costly. On the other hand, defenders of his domestic policy point out that it gave vitally needed assistance to millions of Americans who had previously been forgotten or ignored—the poor, the disabled, and the elderly. Johnson would hurt his peaceful War on Poverty by escalating a real war in Vietnam—a war that resulted in higher taxes and inflation.

Civil Rights Acts of 1964 and 1965

Ironically, a southern president succeeded in persuading Congress to enact the most important civil rights laws since Reconstruction. Even before the 1964 election, Johnson managed to persuade both a majority of Democrats and some Republicans in Congress to pass the 1964 Civil Rights Act, which made segregation illegal in all public facilities, including hotels and restaurants, and gave the federal government additional powers to enforce school desegregation. This act also set up the Equal Employment Opportunity Commission to end racial discrimination in employment. Also in 1964, the Twenty-fourth Amendment was ratified. It abolished the practice of collecting a poll tax, one of the measures that, for decades, had discouraged poor persons from voting.

In 1965, the brutality in Selma, Alabama, against the voting rights marches led by Martin Luther King moved the Congress to pass the Voting Rights Act of 1965. This act ended literacy tests and provided federal registrars in areas in which blacks were kept from voting. The impact was most dramatic in the Deep South, where African Americans could vote for the first time since the Reconstruction era.

Civil Rights and Conflict

The civil rights movement gained momentum during the Kennedy and Johnson presidencies. A very close election in 1960 influenced President Kennedy not to press the issue of civil rights, lest he alienate white voters. But the defiance of the governors of Alabama and Mississippi to federal court rulings on integration forced a showdown. In 1962, James Meredith, a young African American air force veteran, attempted to enroll in the University of Mississippi. A federal court guaranteed his right to attend. Supporting Meredith and the court order, Kennedy sent in 400 federal marshals and 3,000 troops to control mob violence and protect Meredith's right to attend class.

A similar incident occurred in Alabama in 1963. Governor George Wallace tried to stop an African American student from entering the University of Alabama. Once again, President Kennedy sent troops to the scene, and the student was admitted.

The Leadership of Dr. Martin Luther King, Jr.

Throughout the Deep South, civil rights activists and freedom riders who traveled through the South registering African Americans to vote and integrating public places were met with beatings, bombings, and murder by white extremists. Recognized nationally as the leader of the civil rights movement, Dr. Martin Luther King, Jr., remained committed to nonviolent protests against segregation. In 1963, he and his followers were jailed in Birmingham, Alabama, for what local authorities judged to be an illegal march. The jailing of King, however, proved to be a milestone in the civil rights movement because most Americans believed King to have been jailed unjustly. From his jail cell, King wrote an essay, "Letter From a Birmingham Jail," in which he argued:

> . . . [W]e need emulate neither the "do-nothingism" of the complacent nor the hatred and despair of the black nationalist. For there is the more excellent way of love and nonviolent protest. I am grateful to God that, through the influence of the Negro church, the way of nonviolence became an integral part of our struggle. . . .
>
> One day the South will know that when these disinherited children of God sat down at lunch counters, they were in reality standing up for what is best in the American dream and for the most sacred values in our Judaeo-Christian heritage, thereby bringing our nation back to those great wells of democracy which were dug deep by the founding fathers in their formulation of the Constitution and the Declaration of Independence. . . .

The episode moved President Kennedy to support a tougher civil rights bill.

March on Washington (1963). In August 1963, King led one of the largest and most successful demonstrations in U.S. history. About 200,000 blacks and whites took part in the peaceful March on Washington in support of the civil rights bill. The highlight of the demonstration was Dr. King's impassioned "I Have a Dream" speech, which appealed for the end of racial prejudice and ended with everyone in the crowd singing "We Shall Overcome."

March to Montgomery (1965). When a voting rights march from Selma to Montgomery, Alabama, in 1965 was met with police beatings, President

Johnson sent in the troops to protect Dr. King and other civil rights demonstrators. Johnson also sponsored a powerful voting rights bill. Nevertheless, young African Americans were losing patience with the slow progress toward equality and the continued violence against their people by white extremists.

Black Muslims and Malcolm X

Seeking a new cultural identity based on Africa and Islam, the Black Muslim leader Elijah Muhammad preached black nationalism, separatism, and self-improvement. The movement had already attracted thousands of followers by the time a young man serving a prison sentence became a convert and adopted the name Malcolm X. Leaving prison in 1952, Malcolm X acquired a reputation as the movement's most controversial voice. He criticized King as "an Uncle Tom" (subservient to whites) and advocated self-defense—using black violence to counter white violence. He eventually left the Black Muslims to found a more conciliatory Organization of Afro-American Unity, but before he could pursue his ideas, he was assassinated by black opponents in 1965. *The Autobiography of Malcolm X* remains an engaging testimony to one man's development from a petty criminal into a major leader.

Black Power and Race Riots

The radicalism of Malcolm X influenced the thinking of young blacks in civil rights organizations such as the Student Nonviolent Coordinating Committee (SNCC) and the Congress of Racial Equality (CORE). Stokely Carmichael, the chairman of SNCC, repudiated nonviolence and advocated "black power" (especially economic power) and racial separatism. In 1966, the Black Panthers were organized by Huey Newton, Bobby Seale, and other militants as a revolutionary socialist movement advocating self-rule for American blacks.

Riots. The Panthers' frequently shouted slogans—"Get whitey" and "Burn baby, burn"—made whites suspect that black extremists and revolutionaries were behind the race riots that erupted in black neighborhoods of major cities from 1964 through 1968. In the summer of 1965, for example, riots in the Watts section of Los Angeles resulted in the deaths of 34 people and the destruction of over 700 buildings. There is little evidence, however, that the Black Power movement was responsible for the violence. A federal investigation of the many riots, the Kerner Commission, concluded in late 1968 that racism and segregation were chiefly responsible and that the United States was becoming "two societies, one black, one white—separate and unequal." By the mid-sixties, the issue of civil rights had spread far beyond *de jure* segregation practiced under the law in the South and now included the de facto segregation and discrimination caused by racist attitudes in the North and West.

Murder in Memphis. Martin Luther King, Jr., received the Nobel Peace Prize in 1964, but his nonviolent approach was under increasing pressure from all sides. His effort to use peaceful marches in urban centers of the North, such as Chicago, met with little success. King also broke with President Johnson over the Vietnam War because that war was beginning to drain money from social programs. In April 1968, the nation again went into shock over the news that King, while standing on a motel balcony in Memphis, Tennessee, had been shot and killed by a white man. Massive riots erupted in 168 cities across the country, leaving at least 46 people dead. The violence did not reflect the ideals of the murdered leader, but it did reveal the anger and frustrations among African Americans in both the North and the South.

The Warren Court and Individual Rights

As Chief Justice of the Supreme Court from 1953 to 1969, Earl Warren had an impact on the nation comparable to that of John Marshall in the early 1800s. Warren's decision in the desegregation case of *Brown v. Board of Education of Topeka* (1954) was by far the most important case of the 20th century involving race relations. Then in the 1960s the Warren Court made a series of decisions that had a profound effect on the criminal justice system, the political system of the states, and the definition of individual rights. Before Warren's tenure as chief justice, the Supreme Court had concentrated on protecting property rights. During and after his tenure, the Court shifted its attention to cases involving the protection of individual rights.

Criminal Justice

Among the many decisions of the Warren Court concerning a defendant's rights, these were most important:

- *Mapp v. Ohio* (1961) ruled that illegally seized evidence cannot be used in court against the accused.

- *Gideon v. Wainwright* (1963) required that state courts provide counsel (services of an attorney) for indigent (poor) defendants.

- *Escobedo v. Illinois* (1964) required the police to inform an arrested person of his or her right to remain silent.

- *Miranda v. Arizona* (1966) extended the ruling in *Escobedo* to include the right to a lawyer being present during questioning by the police.

Reapportionment

Before 1962, it was common for at least one house of a state legislature (usually the state senate) to be based upon the drawing of district lines that strongly favored rural areas to the disadvantage of large cities. The Warren Court's decision in the landmark case of *Baker v. Carr* (1962) declared such practices to be unconstitutional. In *Baker* and later cases, the Court established the principle of "one man, one vote," meaning that election districts would have to be redrawn to provide equal representation for all of a state's citizens.

Freedom of Expression and Privacy

Other rulings by the Warren Court extended the rights mentioned in the First Amendment to protect the radical actions of demonstrators and students and to permit greater latitude under freedom of the press, to ban religious activities from public schools, and to guarantee adults' rights to use contraceptives.

- *Yates v. United States* (1957) said that the First Amendment protected radical and revolutionary speech, even by Communists, unless it was a "clear and present danger" to the safety of the country.

- *Engel v. Vitale* (1962) ruled that state laws requiring prayers and Bible readings in the public schools violated the First Amendment's provision for separation of church and state.

- *Griswold v. Connecticut* (1965) ruled that, in recognition of a citizen's right to privacy, a state could not prohibit the use of contraceptives by adults. (This privacy case provided the foundation for later cases establishing a woman's right to an abortion.)

The Warren Court's defense of the rights of unpopular groups and of the freedoms of accused "criminals" provoked a storm of controversy. Critics even called for the impeachment of Earl Warren. Both supporters and critics, however, could agree that the decisions of the Warren Court caused a profound and pervasive revolution in the interpretation of constitutional rights.

Social Revolutions and Cultural Movements

In the early and mid-1960s, various liberal groups began to identify with blacks' struggle against oppressive controls and laws. The first such group to rebel against established authority were college and university students.

Student Movement and the New Left

In 1962, at a meeting of the newly formed Students for a Democratic Society (SDS) in Port Huron, Michigan, a group of radical students led by Tom Hayden issued a declaration of purposes known as the Port Huron Statement. It called for university decisions to be made through participatory democracy, so that students would have a voice in decisions affecting their lives. Activists and intellectuals who supported Hayden's ideas became known as the New Left.

The first major student protest took place in 1964 on the Berkeley campus of the University of California. Calling their cause the Free Speech Movement, Berkeley students demanded an end to university restrictions on student political activities. By the mid-1960s, students across the country were protesting a variety of university rules, including those against drinking and dorm visits by members of the opposite sex. They also demanded a greater voice in the government of the university. Student demonstrations grew with the escalation of U.S. involvement in the Vietnam War. Hundreds of campuses were disrupted or closed down by antiwar protests.

The most radical fringe of the SDS, known as the Weathermen, embraced violence and vandalism in their attacks on American institutions. In the eyes of most Americans, the Weathermen's extremist acts and language discredited the early idealism of the New Left.

Counterculture

The political protests of the New Left went hand in hand with a new counterculture that was expressed by young people in rebellious styles of dress, music, drug use, and, for some, communal living. The apparent dress code of the "hippies" and "flower children" of the sixties included long hair, beards, beads, and jeans. The folk music of Joan Baez and Bob Dylan gave voice to the younger generation's protests, while the rock and roll music of the Beatles, the Rolling Stones, Jim Morrison, and Janis Joplin provided the beat and lyrics for the counterculture. As a result of experimenting with hallucinogenic drugs such as LSD, some young people became addicts and destroyed their lives. In 1969, they had one final fling at the Woodstock Music Festival in upper New York State. This gathering of thousands of "hippies" reflected the zenith of the counterculture. The movement's excesses and the economic uncertainties of the times led to its demise in the 1970s.

In retrospect. The generation of baby boomers that came of age in the 1960s believed fervently in the ideals of a democratic society. They hoped to slay the dragons of unresponsive authority, poverty, racism, and war. Unfortunately, many became impatient in their idealistic quest and turned to radical solutions and self-destructive behavior. Their methods tarnished their own democratic values and discredited their cause in the eyes of older Americans.

Sexual Revolution

One aspect of the counterculture that continued beyond the 1960s was a change in many Americans' attitudes toward sexual expression. Traditional beliefs about sexual conduct had originally been challenged in the late 1940s and 1950s by the pioneering surveys of sexual practice conducted by Alfred Kinsey. His research indicated that premarital sex, marital infidelity, and homosexuality were more common than anyone had suspected. Medicine (antibiotics for venereal disease) and technology (the introduction of the birth control pill in 1960) also played a role in tempting people to engage in casual sex with a number of partners. Moreover, overtly sexual themes in advertisements, popular magazines, and movies made sex appear to be just one more consumer product.

How deeply the so-called sexual revolution changed the behavior of the majority of Americans is open to question. There is little doubt, however, that the new mores weakened the earlier restrictions on premarital sex, contraception, abortion, and homosexuality. Later, in the 1980s, there was a general reaction against the loosened moral codes as a result of an increase in illegitimate births, especially among teenagers, an increase in crimes of rape and sexual abuse, and the deadly outbreak of AIDS (acquired immune deficiency syndrome).

The Women's Movement

Increased education and employment of women in the 1950s, the civil rights movement, and the sexual revolution all contributed to a renewal of the women's movement in the 1960s. Betty Friedan's book *The Feminine Mystique* (1963) gave the movement a new direction by encouraging middle-class women to seek fulfillment in professional careers rather confining themselves to the roles of wife, mother, and homemaker. In 1966, Friedan helped to found the National Organization for Women (NOW), which adopted the activist tactics of other civil rights movements to secure equal treatment of women. By this time, Congress had already enacted two antidiscriminatory laws: the Equal Pay Act of 1963 and the Civil Rights Act of 1964. These measures prohibited discrimination in employment and compensation on the basis of gender.

Campaign for the ERA. Feminists' greatest legislative victory was achieved in 1972 when Congress passed the Equal Rights Amendment (ERA). This proposed constitutional amendment stated: "Equality of rights under the law shall not be denied or abridged by the United States or by any state on account of sex." Although NOW and other groups campaigned hard for the ratification of the ERA, it just missed acceptance by the required 38 states. It was defeated in the 1970s in part because of a growing conservative reaction to radical feminists.

Achievements. Even without the ERA, the women's movement accomplished fundamental changes in employment and hiring practices. In increasing numbers, women moved into professions previously dominated by men: business, law, medicine, and politics. Although women still experienced the "glass ceiling" in the corporate world, American society at the beginning of the 21st century was less and less a man's world.

The Vietnam War—to 1969

There were many divisive issues in the 1960s, but none was more tragic than the war in Vietnam. Some 2.7 million Americans served in the conflict and 58,000 died in an increasingly costly and hopeless effort to prevent South Vietnam from falling to communism.

Early Stages

When the decade began, Vietnam was hardly mentioned in the election debates of 1960 between Nixon and Kennedy. U.S. involvement was minimal at that time, but every year thereafter, it loomed larger and eventually dominated the presidency of Lyndon Johnson and the thoughts of the nation.

Buildup under Kennedy. President Kennedy adopted Eisenhower's domino theory that, if Communist forces overthrew South Vietnam's government, they would quickly overrun other countries of Southeast Asia—Laos, Cambodia, Thailand, Malaysia, and Indonesia. Kennedy therefore continued U.S. military aid to South Vietnam's regime and significantly increased the number of military "advisers," who trained the South Vietnamese army and guarded weapons and facilities. By 1963, there were more than 16,000 U.S. troops in South Vietnam, but their role at this time was support, not combat. They provided training and supplies for South Vietnam's armed forces and helped create "strategic hamlets" (fortified villages).

Unfortunately, South Vietnam's government under Ngo Dinh Diem was far from popular. It continued to lose the support of peasants in the countryside, while in the capital city of Saigon, Buddhists set themselves on fire in the streets as an act of protest against Diem's policies. Kennedy began to question whether the South Vietnamese could win "their war" against Communist insurgents. Just two weeks before Kennedy himself was assassinated in Dallas, Diem was overthrown and killed by South Vietnamese generals. It was later learned that Diem's assassination was carried out with the knowledge of the Kennedy administration.

Tonkin Gulf Resolution. Lyndon Johnson became president just as things began to fall apart in South Vietnam. The country had seven different governments in 1964. During the U.S. presidential campaign, Republican candidate Barry Goldwater attacked the Johnson administration for giving only weak support to South Vietnam's fight against the Vietcong (Communist guerrillas). In August 1964, President Johnson and Congress took a fateful turn in policy. Johnson made use of a naval incident in the Gulf of Tonkin off Vietnam's coast to secure congressional authorization for U.S. forces going into combat. Allegedly, North Vietnamese gunboats had fired on U.S. warships in the Gulf of Tonkin. The president persuaded Congress that this aggressive act was sufficient reason for a military response by the United States. Congress voted its approval of the Tonkin Gulf Resolution, which basically gave the president, as commander in chief, a blank check to take "all necessary measures" to protect U.S. interests in Vietnam.

Critics later called the full-scale use of U.S. forces in Vietnam an illegal war, because the war was not declared by Congress, as is required by the Constitution. Congress, however, did not have this concern and did not withdraw its resolution. Until 1968, most Americans supported the effort to contain communism in Southeast Asia. Johnson was caught in a political dilemma to which there was no good solution. How could he stop the defeat of a weak and unpopular government in South Vietnam without making it into an American war—a war whose cost would doom his Great Society programs? If he pulled out, he would be seen as weak and lose public support.

Escalating the War

In 1965, the U.S. military as well as most of the president's foreign policy advisers recommended expanding operations in Vietnam to save the Saigon government. After a Vietcong attack on the U.S. base at Pleiku in 1965, Johnson authorized Operation Rolling Thunder, a prolonged air attack using B-52 bombers against targets in North Vietnam. In April the president decided to use U.S. combat troops for the first time to fight the Vietcong. By the end of 1965, there were over 184,000 U.S. troops in South Vietnam, and most of them were engaged in a combat role. Johnson continued a step-by-step escalation of U.S. involvement in the war. Hoping to win a war of attrition, American generals used search-and-destroy tactics, which only further alienated the peasants. By the end of 1967, the United States had over 485,000 troops in Vietnam (the peak was 540,000 in March 1969), and 16,000 Americans had already died in the conflict. Nevertheless, General William Westmoreland, commander of the U.S. forces in Vietnam, assured the American public that he could see "light at the end of the tunnel."

Controversy

Misinformation from military and civilian leaders combined with Johnson's reluctance to speak frankly with the American people on the scope and the costs of the war created what the media called a credibility gap. Johnson always hoped that a little more military pressure would bring the North Vietnamese to the peace table. The most damaging knowledge gap, however, may have been within the inner circles of government. Years later, Robert McNamara in his memoirs concluded that the leaders in Washington had failed to understand either the enemy or the nature of the war.

Hawks versus doves. The supporters of the war, the "hawks," believed that the war was an act of Soviet-backed Communist aggression against South Vietnam and that it was part of a master plan to conquer all of Southeast Asia. The opponents of the war, the "doves," viewed the conflict as a civil war fought by Vietnamese nationalists and some Communists who wanted to unite their country by overthrowing a corrupt Saigon government.

Some Americans opposed the war because of its costs in lives and money. They believed the billions spent in Vietnam could be better spent on the problems of the cities and the poor in the United States. By far the greatest opposition came from students on college campuses who, after graduation, would become eligible to be drafted into the military and shipped off to Vietnam.

In November 1967, the antiwar movement was given a political leader when scholarly Senator Eugene F. McCarthy of Minnesota became the first antiwar advocate to challenge Johnson for the 1968 Democratic presidential nomination.

Tet offensive. On the occasion of their Lunar New Year (Tet) in January 1968, the Vietcong launched an all-out, surprise attack on almost every provincial capital and American base in South Vietnam. Although the attack took a fearful toll in the cities, the U.S. military counterattacked, inflicted much heavier losses on the Vietcong, and recovered the lost territory. Even so, in political terms, the American military victory proved irrelevant to the way the Tet offensive was interpreted at home. The destruction viewed by millions on the TV news appeared as a colossal setback for Johnson's Vietnam policy. Thus, for the Vietcong and North Vietnamese, Tet was a tremendous political victory in demoralizing the American public. In the New Hampshire primary in February, the antiwar McCarthy took 42 percent of the vote against Johnson.

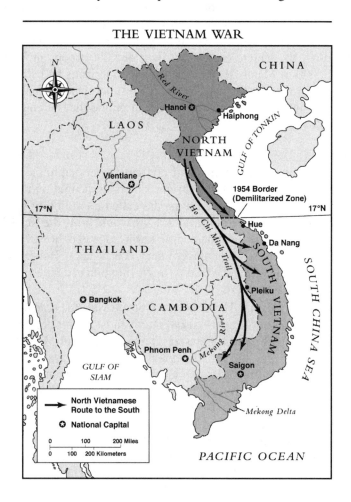

THE VIETNAM WAR

L.B.J. withdraws. The Joint Chiefs of Staff responded to Tet by re-questing 200,000 more troops to win the war. By this time, however, the group of experienced Cold War diplomats who advised Johnson had turned against further escalation of the war. On March 31, 1968, President Johnson went on television and told the American people that he would limit the bombing of North Vietnam and negotiate a peace. He then surprised everyone by announcing that he would not run again for president.

In May 1968 peace talks between North Vietnam, South Vietnam, and the United States started in Paris, but they were quickly deadlocked over minor issues. The war continued, and tens of thousands more died. But the escalation of the number of U.S. troops in Vietnam had stopped, and under the next administration would be reversed.

Coming Apart at Home, 1968

Few years in U.S. history were as troubled or violent as 1968. The Tet offensive and the withdrawal of Johnson from the presidential race were fol-lowed by the senseless murder of Martin Luther King, Jr., and destructive riots in cities across the country. As the year unfolded, Americans wondered if their nation was coming apart from internal conflicts over the war issue, the race issue, and the generation gap between the baby boomers and their parents.

Second Kennedy Assassination

In 1964 Kennedy's younger brother, Robert Kennedy, had become a senator from New York. Four years later, he decided to enter the presidential race after McCarthy's strong showing in New Hampshire. Bobby Kennedy was more effective than McCarthy in mobilizing the traditional Democratic blue-collar and minority vote. On June 5, 1968, he won a major victory in California's primary, but immediately after his victory speech, he was shot and killed by a young Arab nationalist who opposed Kennedy's support for Israel.

The Election of 1968

After Robert Kennedy's death, the election of 1968 turned into a three-way race between two conservatives—George Wallace and Richard Nixon—and one liberal, Vice President Hubert Humphrey.

Democratic convention at Chicago. When the Democrats met in Chicago for their party convention, it was clear that Hubert Humphrey had enough delegates to win the nomination. As vice president, he had loyally supported Johnson's domestic and foreign policies. He controlled the convention, but the antiwar demonstrators were determined to control the streets. Chicago's mayor Richard Daley had the police out in mass, and the resulting violence went out on television across the country as a "police riot." Humphrey left the convention as the nominee of a badly divided Democratic party, and early opinion polls showed he was a clear underdog in a nation sick of disorder and protest.

White backlash and George Wallace. The growing hostility of many whites to federal desegregation, antiwar protests, and race riots was tapped by Governor George Wallace of Alabama. He was the first politician of contemporary, late-20th-century America to marshal the general resentment against the Washington establishment ("pointy-head liberals," as he called them) and the two-party system. He ran for president as the self-nominated candidate of the American Independent party, hoping to win enough electoral votes to throw the election into the House of Representatives.

Return of Richard Nixon. Many observers thought Richard Nixon's political career had ended in 1962 after his unsuccessful run for governor of California. In 1968, however, a new, more confident, and less negative Nixon announced his candidacy and soon became the front-runner in the Republican primaries. He was also the favorite of the party regulars and had little trouble securing his nomination at the Republican convention. For his running mate, he selected Governor Spiro Agnew of Maryland, whose rhetoric was similar to that of George Wallace. Nixon was a "hawk" on the Vietnam War and ran on the slogans of "peace with honor" and "law and order."

Results. Wallace and Nixon started strong, but the Democrats began to catch up, especially in northern urban centers, as Humphrey preached to the faithful of the old New Deal coalition. On election night, Nixon defeated Humphrey by a very close popular vote but took a substantial majority of the electoral vote (301 to 191), ending any threat that the three-candidate election would end up in the House of Representatives.

The significance of the 1968 election is clear in the combined total of Nixon's and Wallace's popular vote of almost 57 percent. Apparently, most Americans wanted time out to heal the wounds inflicted on the national psyche by the upheavals of the sixties. Supporters of Nixon and Wallace had had enough of protest, violence, permissiveness, the counterculture, drugs, and federal intervention in social institutions. Elections in the 1970s and 1980s would confirm that the tide was running against New Deal liberalism in favor of the conservatives.

HISTORICAL PERSPECTIVES: THE LESSONS OF VIETNAM

The U.S. war in Vietnam eventually became the nation's longest—and also the first war in which the United States failed to achieve its military objective. What went wrong? Critics of the war argued that the United States failed in Vietnam because neither the government nor the military understood the nature of the war. Eisenhower, Kennedy, Johnson, and Nixon viewed the conflict strictly in Cold War terms as an act of aggression by the Communist "monolith" to take over another part of the world, instead of a civil war in which a former colony was trying to gain its independence from Western colonialism. Former Secretary of Defense Robert McNamara, in his book *In Retrospect: The Tragedy and Lessons of Vietnam* (1995) laments that members of the Johnson administration lacked Asian experts to advise them on the formulation of Vietnam policy.

Another conclusion was advanced by General William Westmoreland and other military leaders of the era. They blamed the civilian government for placing restrictions on the conduct of the war that prevented the military from winning it. In their view, the war could have been won if only the U.S. military had been permitted to take the offensive and bring the war to a swift conclusion. The generals blamed the media for turning the American people against the war. Westmoreland and others argued that the telecasts of the Tet offensive forced a change in the conduct of the war, just at the point that the U.S. military was beginning to win it.

Many observers have attempted to extract lessons from Vietnam, hoping that the mistakes of the past can be avoided in the future. To many critics of the war, it appeared that the most important mistake was attempting to impose an unsatisfactory regime on a country of no clear importance to U.S. interests. If this was so, an obvious lesson was that the United States should not go into a war if its vital national interests are not at stake. Another possible lesson is that the president and Congress should not lead the nation into war unless they are confident that they can rally and sustain the support of the American people behind the effort.

In an article in the journal *Foreign Affairs* (Spring 1985), David Fromkin and James Chace reviewed the full range of lessons that supposedly could be derived from the Vietnam disaster. They concluded that the Vietnam experience, unlike the appeasement at Munich in the 1930s, was so complex and unique that it provided no reliable lessons for future policy-makers in deciding whether or not to intervene militarily in another country.

KEY NAMES, EVENTS, AND TERMS

John F. Kennedy	Bay of Pigs	Lyndon Johnson
Jacqueline Kennedy	Berlin Wall	Great Society
New Frontier	Cuban missile crisis (1962)	War on Poverty
Peace Corps	flexible response	Michael Harrington, *The Other America*
Alliance for Progress	Nuclear Test Ban Treaty	
Trade Expansion Act (1962)	Warren Commission	Barry Goldwater

Medicare; Medicaid	Congress of Racial Equality	New Left
Elementary and Secondary Education Act (1965)	Stokely Carmichael	counterculture
	Black Panthers	sexual revolution
Ralph Nader, *Unsafe at Any Speed*	Watts riots	women's movement
	Kerner Commission	Betty Friedan, *The Feminine Mystique*
Rachel Carson, *Silent Spring*	Warren Court	
Lady Bird Johnson	*Brown v. Board of Education of Topeka*	National Organization for Women
Civil Rights Act of 1964		
Equal Employment Opportunity Commission	*Gideon v. Wainwright*	Equal Pay Act (1963)
	Edcobedo v. Illinois	Equal Rights Amendment
Twenty-fourth Amendment	*Miranda v. Arizona*	Vietnam War
Voting Rights Act of 1965	reapportionment	Tonkin Gulf Resolution
James Meredith	*Baker v. Carr*	Tet offensive
Martin Luther King, Jr.	"one man, one vote"	hawks and doves
March on Washington; "I Have a Dream" speech	*Yates v. United States*	Eugene McCarthy
	separation of church and state	Robert Kennedy
Black Muslims		George Wallace
Malcolm X	*Engel v. Vitale*	Hubert Humphrey
Student Nonviolent Coordinating Committee	Students for a Democratic Society	

MULTIPLE-CHOICE QUESTIONS

1. Which of the following does NOT accurately describe the Kennedy administration?

(A) Much of his domestic program was held up by Congress.

(B) The U.S. space program was committed to landing astronauts on the moon.

(C) Defense spending and the number of nuclear weapons were cut.

(D) The Trade Expansion Act set up a tariff-reduction process.

(E) Kennedy used presidential pressure to control inflationary price increases.

2. Which of the following resulted in the greatest threat of nuclear war during the Kennedy administration?

(A) Reaction to the Alliance for Progress in Latin America

(B) U.S. military aid to South Vietnam

(C) The outbreak of a war in the Middle East

(D) A U.S. naval blockade of Cuba

(E) Civil wars in the Congo and Laos

3. President Johnson's Great Society programs included all of the following EXCEPT

(A) federal aid to poor elementary and high school districts

(B) ratification of the Equal Rights Amendment to guarantee equality for women

(C) federal health insurance for the elderly and medical care for the poor and disabled

(D) federal funding of self-help programs for the poor

(E) passage of civil rights laws to promote equal opportunity for all Americans

4. Which of the following is NOT a correct association of a person with a policy?

(A) Barry Goldwater—medical care for the poor and elderly

(B) Michael Harrington—reduction of poverty in America

(C) Ralph Nader—regulation of automobile industry

(D) Rachel Carson—protection of the environment

(E) Martin Luther King, Jr.— federal protection of voting rights

5. The Black Muslims and the Black Power movement advocated

(A) equal opportunity and social integration

(B) voting rights and nonviolent protest

(C) multicultural education for whites and blacks

(D) increased participation of African Americans in national politics

(E) separatism and self-rule for African Americans

6. Which of the following was NOT a ruling of the Warren Court?

(A) All election districts must provide equal representation for voters.

(B) The courts must provide lawyers for poor defendants.

(C) Police must advise suspects of their right to remain silent.

(D) The right to life of an unborn child is guaranteed by the Fourteenth Amendment.

(E) State-required prayers and Bible readings in public schools violate the First Amendment.

7. Betty Friedan's book *The Feminine Mystique*

(A) advocated no-fault divorce and open marriages

(B) argued that many women could not have fulfilling lives if limited to a traditional role in the home

(C) proposed federal protection of the special needs of wives and mothers

(D) resulted in the passage of the Equal Rights Amendment

(E) supported premarital sex, abortion, and gay rights

8. The Tonkin Gulf Resolution

(A) supported Barry Goldwater's suggestion to bomb North Vietnam

(B) expressed the prowar feeling of the majority of Americans

(C) authorized the president to take all necessary steps to defend U.S. forces and interests in Vietnam

(D) approved the overthrow of the Diem government in Vietnam

(E) authorized the use of up to 500,000 U.S. troops in Vietnam

9. Which phrase best describes President Johnson's policy in Vietnam?

    (A) gradual withdrawal of U.S. forces

    (B) gradual military escalation to force North Vietnam to negotiate

    (C) total unwillingness to discuss peace terms

    (D) placing strict limits on U.S. military involvement

    (E) threatening the use of nuclear weapons

10. The Tet offensive resulted in all of the following EXCEPT

    (A) the military defeat of U.S. forces in South Vietnam

    (B) significant military losses by the Vietcong

    (C) reduced public support for Johnson's conduct of the war

    (D) increased public support in the primaries for antiwar Senator Eugene McCarthy

    (E) U.S. diplomats advising Johnson against further escalation of the war

ESSAY QUESTIONS

1. Analyze the ways that TWO of the following reformed United States society during the 1960s:

Great Society legislation

Civil Rights acts of 1964 and 1965

Warren Court decisions

2. Explain how TWO of the following contributed to the social revolutions of the 1960s:

civil rights movement

counterculture

women's movement

war in Vietnam

3. Assess the influence of TWO of the following on the civil rights movement of the 1960s:

Martin Luther King, Jr.

Malcolm X

Black Power movement

4. Compare and contrast President Johnson's policy in Vietnam with the policies of Presidents Eisenhower and Kennedy.

5. To what extent did radicalism and violence affect the political and social developments of the 1960s?

DOCUMENT-BASED QUESTION (DBQ)

Assess the view that President Johnson's Vietnam policies failed for both political and military reasons.

Use the documents and your knowledge of the period from 1960 to 1969 to construct your response.

DOCUMENT A.

Whereas naval units of the communist regime in Vietnam . . . have deliberately and repeatedly attacked United States Naval vessels lawfully present in international waters . . . and

Whereas these attacks are part of a deliberate and systematic campaign of aggression that the Communist regime in North Vietnam has been waging against its neighbors. . . . Now therefore, be it Resolved by the Senate and the House of Representatives of the United States of America in Congress assembled, That: The Congress approves and supports the determination of the President, as Commander-in-Chief, to take all necessary measures to repel any armed attack against the forces of the United States and to prevent further aggression. . . .

The United States is . . . prepared, as the President determines, to take all necessary steps, including the use of armed force, to assist any member . . . of the Southeast Asia Collective Defense Treaty requesting assistance in defense of its freedom. . . .

U.S. Congress,
Gulf of Tonkin Resolution, August 7, 1964

DOCUMENT B.

A mature great power will make measured and limited use of its power. It will eschew [shun] the theory of a global and universal duty which not only commits it to unending wars of intervention but intoxicates its thinking with the illusion that it is a crusader for righteousness, that each war is a "war to end all war." Since in this generation we have become a great power, I am in favor of learning to behave like a great power, of getting rid of the globalism which would not only entangle us everywhere but is based on the totally vain notion that if we do not set the world in order, no matter what the price, we cannot live in the world safely.

Walter Lippmann,
Great Decisions, 1966

DOCUMENT C.

We will stay because a just nation cannot leave to the cruelties of its enemies a people who have staked their lives and independence on America's solemn pledge—a pledge which had grown through the commitment of three American Presidents.

We will stay because in Asia—and around the world—are countries whose independence rests, in large measure, on confidence in America's word and in American protection. To yield to force in Viet-Nam would weaken that confidence, would undermine the independence of many lands, and would whet the appetite of aggression. We would have to fight in one land, and then we would have to fight in another—or abandon much of Asia to the domination of Communists.

Lyndon B. Johnson,
State of the Union Message,
January 12, 1966

DOCUMENT D.

Opponents of the administration's policies point out that the many Saigon governments have been military dictatorships.

None of the many Saigon governments were elected by the Vietnamese people. The United States refused to permit the elections provided by the Geneva Agreement of 1954 and installed Ngo Diem. South Vietnam had been ruled by military dictatorship supported by United States' dollars ever since. Opposed by the majority of the people of South Vietnam, it has changed 14 times since January 1964.

An Appeal to the Conscience of the
American People; Handbill [n.d.]

DOCUMENT E.

Bettmann/CORBIS

DOCUMENT F.

Every American instinct makes us want to jump in with both feet and get this unpleasant job over with—as quickly as possible.

Traditional oriental patience makes them willing to extend the struggle unto generation after generation, if necessary.

We are fighting the war with the commodity most precious to us—and held much cheaper by the enemy—the lives of men.

And toward what objective?

Negotiation.

I submit to you that it is not possible for us to lose the war. We are too strong. But it is more than possible to lose the negotiation. And the longer it is delayed, the more likely we are to lose it. . . .

So—how do we end the war in Vietnam? . . .

We must fight it with least cost to ourselves and at the greatest cost to the enemy. We must change the currency in this game from men to material.

America's greatest strength in this military situation is our air and naval power. We must use it strategically. We must use it decisively. We must use it now. . . .

I do not think it will be necessary to use nuclear weapons to accomplish this task. But I would not rule out any strength that we have, if the situation demanded it. . . .

General Curtis LeMay,
Congressional Record, April 10, 1967

DOCUMENT G.

Until we Americanized the war by our own intervention it was essentially a civil war. South Vietnamese, provoked by repressive acts of the Saigon government, revolted against Diem. We intervened with money, "advisors," bombers and weapons at a time when even our own government did not claim that North Vietnam was sending forces south. According to a speech of Senator Mansfield in 1966, "When the sharp increase in military effort began in early 1965, it was estimated that only about 400 North Vietnamese soldiers were among the enemy force in the South which totaled 140,000 at that time." Today our government claims that North Vietnam has about 100,000 troops in the South. Meanwhile we have an occupation force of 500,000 ground troops in the South supported by over 70,000 foreign allied troops, plus the Pacific Naval and Air Command.

Professional and Faculty Committee on the
Vietnam Moratorium, Advertisement in newspapers,
November–December, 1969

DOCUMENT H.

We are confronted with a situation in which a very patient enemy had been led to believe that we are sorely divided, and that if he will only fight long enough and make clever plans for offenses from time to time, we will become weary of war and we will give over the country in a veil of surrender or under some face-saving method and get out. I believe that is what this protracted debate has been accomplishing. . . .

I think the major achievement of the enemy has been to frighten so many people in this country into wanting to get out, into negotiating, into believing that we cannot win, into believing that we are losing and we have to just withdraw unilaterally.

Senator John Tower of Texas,
Congressional Record,
March 7, 1968

DOCUMENT I.

While determined to pursue Mr. Kennedy's policy in Vietnam, President Johnson was nevertheless obsessed with his program of domestic achievement, the Great Society. Although he expanded American military commitment, he pursued a policy at home of business as usual. . . .

Despite congressional endorsement for military action, as firm as that provided Truman, Eisenhower, and Kennedy, President Johnson was determined to keep the war limited and publicly announced that he would sanction no expansion of it. That locked American military forces into a defensive strategy, as anyone versed in military history knows that a force on the offensive has advantages over one on the defensive. . . .

As the war dragged on without decisive military action, the mood of Congress changed, a reflection of public attitudes strongly influenced by the news media, particularly television.

General William Westmoreland (Retired),
The Vietnam War, 1979

29

LIMITS OF A
SUPERPOWER, 1969–1980

*If, when the chips are down, the world's most powerful nation, the
United States, acts like a pitiful, helpless giant, the forces of
totalitarianism and anarchy will threaten free nations and free
institutions throughout the world.*

Richard Nixon, Address to the Nation, April 30, 1970

In 1969, television viewers around the world witnessed the astonishing sight of two American astronauts walking on the moon's surface. This event, followed by a series of other successes for the U.S. space program, represented some of the high points of the era. Offsetting these technological triumphs, however, were shocking revelations about White House participation in the Watergate crime, a stagnant economy, and the fall of South Vietnam to communism. Increased foreign economic competition, oil shortages, rising unemployment, and high inflation made Americans aware that even the world's leading superpower would have to adjust to a fast-changing, less manageable world.

Richard Nixon's Foreign Policy

In his January 1969 inaugural address, President Nixon promised to bring Americans together after the turmoil of the 1960s. Suspicious and secretive by nature, however, Nixon soon began to isolate himself in the White House and create what Arthur Schlesinger, Jr., called an "imperial presidency." Nixon's first interest was international relations, not domestic policy. Together with his national security adviser, Henry Kissinger (later to become secretary of state during Nixon's second term), President Nixon fashioned a realistic foreign policy that generally succeeded in reducing the tensions of the Cold War.

Vietnam

When Nixon took office, more than half a million U.S. troops were in Vietnam. His principal objective was to find a way to reduce U.S. involvement in the war while at the same time avoiding the appearance of conceding defeat.

In a word, Nixon said the United States was seeking nothing less than "peace with honor."

"Vietnamization." Almost immediately, the new president began the process called "Vietnamization." He announced that he would gradually withdraw U.S. troops from Vietnam and give the South Vietnamese the money, the weapons, and the training that they needed to take over the full conduct of the war. Under this policy, U.S. troops in South Vietnam went from over 540,000 in 1969 to under 30,000 in 1972. Extending the idea of disengagement to other parts of Asia, the president proclaimed the *Nixon Doctrine,* declaring that in the future Asian allies would receive U.S. support but without the extensive use of U.S. ground forces.

Opposition to Nixon's war policies. Nixon's gradual withdrawal of forces from Vietnam at first reduced the number of antiwar protests. In April 1970, however, the president expanded the war by using U.S. forces to invade Cambodia in an effort to destroy Vietnamese Communist bases in that country. A nationwide protest against this action on U.S. college campuses resulted in the killing of four youths by National Guard troops at Kent State in Ohio and two black students at Jackson State in Mississippi. In reaction to the escalation of the war, the U.S. Senate (but not the House) voted to repeal the Gulf of Tonkin Resolution.

Also in 1970, the American public was shocked to learn about a 1968 massacre of women and children by U.S. troops in the Vietnamese village of My Lai. Further fueling the antiwar sentiment was the publication by *The New York Times* of the Pentagon Papers, a secret government history documenting the mistakes and deceptions of government policy-makers in dealing with Vietnam. The papers had been turned over, or "leaked," to the press by Daniel Ellsberg, a former Defense Department analyst.

Peace talks, bombing attacks, and armistice. On the diplomatic front, Nixon had Kissinger conduct secret meetings with North Vietnam's foreign minister, Le Duc Tho. Kissinger announced in the fall of 1972 that "peace is at hand," but this announcement proved premature. When the North Vietnamese failed to compromise, Nixon ordered massive bombing of North Vietnam (the heaviest air attacks of the long war) to force a settlement. After several weeks of B-52 bomber attacks, the North Vietnamese agreed to an armistice, in which the United States would withdraw the last of its troops and get back over 500 prisoners of war (POWs). The Paris Accords of January 1973 also promised a cease-fire and free elections. In fact, however, the armistice did not end the war between the North and the South and left tens of thousands of enemy troops in South Vietnam.

The armistice finally allowed the United States to extricate itself from a war that had claimed over 58,000 American lives. The $118 billion spent on the war began the inflationary cycle that racked the U.S. economy for years afterward.

Détente With China and the Soviet Union

Nixon and Kissinger strengthened the U.S. position in the world by taking advantage of the rivalry between the two Communist giants, China and the Soviet Union. Their diplomacy was praised for bringing about *détente*—a deliberate reduction of Cold War tensions. Even after Watergate ended his presidency in disgrace, Nixon's critics would admit that his conduct of foreign affairs had enhanced world peace.

Visit to China. Nixon knew that only an outspoken critic of communism like himself could take the bold step of improving relations with "Red" China (Mao Zedong's Communist regime) without being condemned as "soft" on communism. After a series of secret negotiations with Chinese leaders, Nixon astonished the world in February 1972 by traveling to Beijing to meet with Mao. His visit initiated diplomatic exchanges that ultimately led to U.S. recognition of the Communist government in 1979.

Arms control with the U.S.S.R. Nixon used his new relationship with China to put pressure on the Soviets to agree to a treaty limiting antiballistic missiles (ABMs), a new technology that would have expanded the arms race. At the conclusion of the first round of Strategic Arms Limitations Talks (SALT I), U.S. diplomats secured Soviet consent to a freeze on the number of ballistic missiles carrying nuclear warheads. While this agreement did not end the arms race, it was a significant step toward reducing Cold War tensions and bringing about détente.

Nixon's Domestic Policy

Throughout the 1970s, the Democrats continued to hold majorities in both houses of Congress. The Republican president had to live with this reality and obtain some concessions from Congress through moderation and compromise. At the same time, Nixon laid the foundation for a shift in public opinion toward conservatism and for Republican gains that would challenge and overthrow the Democratic control of Congress in the 1980s and 1990s.

The New Federalism

Nixon tried to slow down the growth of Johnson's Great Society programs by proposing the Family Assistance Plan, a reform of the welfare system. The Democratic majority in Congress easily defeated this initiative. The Republican president did succeed, however, in shifting some of the responsibility for social programs from the federal to the state and local levels. In a program known as revenue sharing, or the New Federalism, Congress approved giving local governments $30 billion in block grants over five years to address local needs as they saw fit (instead of specific uses of federal money being controlled by Washington). Republicans hoped revenue sharing would check the growth of the federal government and return responsibility to the states, where it had rested before the New Deal.

Nixon attempted to bypass Congress by impounding (not spending) funds appropriated for social programs. Democrats protested that such action was an abuse of executive powers. The courts agreed with the president's critics, arguing that it was a president's duty to carry out the laws of Congress, whether or not he agreed with them.

Nixon's Economic Policies

Starting with a recession in 1970, the U.S. economy throughout the seventies faced the unusual combination of economic slowdown and high inflation—a condition referred to as *stagflation* (*stag*nation plus in*flation*). To slow inflation, Nixon at first tried to cut federal spending. When this policy contributed to a recession and unemployment, however, he adopted Keynesian economics and deficit spending in order not to alienate middle-class and blue-collar Americans. In August 1971, he surprised the nation by imposing a 90-day wage and price freeze. Next, he took the dollar off the gold standard, which helped to devalue it relative to foreign currencies. This action, combined with a 10 percent surtax on all imports, improved the U.S. balance of trade with foreign competitors.

By the election year of 1972, the recession was over. Also in that year, Congress approved automatic increases for Social Security benefits based on the annual rise in the cost of living. This measure protected seniors, the poor, and the disabled from the worst effects of inflation but also contributed to budget problems in the future.

Southern Strategy

Having received just 43 percent of the popular vote in 1968, Nixon was well aware of being a minority president. He devised a political strategy to form a Republican majority by appealing to the millions of voters who had become disaffected by antiwar protests, black militants, school busing to achieve racial balance, and the excesses of the youth counterculture. Nixon referred to these conservative Americans as the "silent majority." Many of them were Democrats, such as southern whites, Catholic ethnics, blue-collar workers, and recent suburbanites who were dismayed by the liberal drift of their party.

To win over the South, the president asked the federal courts in that region to delay integration plans and busing orders. He also nominated two southern conservatives (Clement Haynsworth and G. Harold Carswell) to the Supreme Court. The Senate refused to confirm them, and the courts rejected his requests for delayed integration. Nevertheless, his strategy played well with southern white voters. At the same time, Nixon authorized Vice President Spiro Agnew to make verbal assaults against both war protesters and the liberal press.

The Burger Court

Four resignations of older justices from the Supreme Court gave Nixon the opportunity to replace liberal, activist members of the Warren court with more conservative, strict constructionist justices. In 1969 he appointed Warren E. Burger of Minnesota as chief justice to succeed the retiring Earl Warren. After the two conservative nominees were rejected by Congress, the president then compromised by selecting a more moderate Harry Blackmun (who would write the proabortion ruling in *Roe v. Wade,* 1973). His next two appointments, Lewis Powell and William Rehnquist, were both approved. Ironically, in the last days of his Watergate agony, the Court that Nixon tried to shape would fail him by denying his claims to executive privilege and ordering him to turn over the Watergate tapes (*United States v. Nixon,* 1974).

The Election of 1972 South turns republican

The success of Nixon's southern strategy became evident in the presidential election of 1972 when the Republican ticket won majorities in every southern state. Nixon's reelection was practically assured by (1) his foreign policy successes in China and the Soviet Union, (2) the removal of George Wallace from the race by an assassin's bullet that paralyzed the Alabama populist, and (3) the nomination by the Democrats of a very liberal, antiwar, antiestablishment candidate, Senator George McGovern of South Dakota.

McGovern's campaign quickly went off track. After some indecision, he dropped his vice presidential candidate, Senator Thomas Eagleton of Missouri, when it was discovered that he had undergone electroschock treatment for depression. On election day, Nixon overwhelmed McGovern in a landslide victory that carried every state but Massachusetts and won 60.8 percent of the popular vote. The Democrats still managed to keep control of both houses of Congress. Nevertheless, the voting patterns for Nixon indicated the start of a major political realignment of the Sunbelt and suburban voters forming a new Republican majority. Nixon's electoral triumph in 1972 made the Watergate revelations and scandals of 1973 all the more surprising.

Watergate

The tragedy of Watergate went well beyond the public humiliation of Richard Nixon and the conviction and jailing of 26 White House officials and aides. Watergate had a paralyzing effect on the political system in the mid-1970s, a critical time both at home and overseas, when the country needed respected, strong, and confident leadership.

White House Abuses

In June 1972, a group of men hired by Nixon's reelection committee were caught breaking into the offices of the Democratic national headquarters in the

Watergate complex in Washington, D.C. This break-in and attempted bugging were only part of a series of illegal activities and "dirty tricks" conducted by the Nixon administration and the Committee to Re-Elect the President (CREEP).

Earlier, Nixon had ordered wiretaps on government employees and reporters to stop news leaks such as one that had exposed the secret bombing of Cambodia. The president's aides created a group, called the "plumbers," to stop leaks as well as to discredit opponents. Before Watergate, the "plumbers" had burglarized the office of the psychiatrist of Daniel Ellsberg, the person behind the leaking of the Pentagon Papers, in order to obtain information to discredit Ellsberg. The White House had also created an "enemies list" of prominent Americans who opposed Nixon, the Vietnam War, or both. People on this list were investigated by government agencies, such as the IRS. The illegal break-in at Watergate reflected the attitude in the Nixon administration that any means could be used to promote the national security—an objective that was often confused with protecting the Nixon administration from its critics.

Watergate Investigation

There was no solid proof that President Nixon ordered any of these illegal activities. After months of investigation, however, it became clear that Nixon did engage in an illegal cover-up to avoid scandal. Tough sentencing of the Watergate burglars by federal judge John Sirica led to information about the use of money and a promise of pardons by the White House staff to keep the burglars quiet. A Senate investigating committee headed by Democrat Sam Ervin of North Carolina brought the abuses to the attention of Americans through televised hearings. A highlight of these hearings was the testimony of a White House lawyer, John Dean, who linked the president to the cover-up. Nixon's top aides, H. R. Haldeman and John Ehrlichman, resigned to protect him and were later indicted, as were many others, for obstructing justice.

The discovery of a taping system in the Oval Office led to a year-long struggle between Nixon, who claimed executive privilege for the tapes, and investigators, who wanted the tapes to prove the cover-up charges. The Nixon administration received another blow in the fall of 1973, when Vice President Agnew was forced to resign for having taken bribes when governor of Maryland.

Other Developments in 1973

Although the Watergate affair absorbed most of Nixon's attention during his shortened second term, other developments at home and abroad were also important.

War Powers Act. Further discrediting Nixon was the news that he had authorized 3,500 secret bombing raids in Cambodia, a neutral county. Congress used the public uproar over this information to attempt to limit the president's powers over the military. In November 1973, after a long struggle, Congress finally passed the War Powers Act over Nixon's veto. This law required Nixon and any future president to report to Congress within 48 hours after taking military action. It further provided that Congress would have to approve any military action that lasted more than 60 days.

October war and oil embargo. In world politics, probably the most important event of 1973 was the outbreak of another war in the Middle East. On October 6, on the Jewish holy day of Yom Kippur, the Syrians and Egyptians launched a surprise attack on Israel in an attempt to recover the lands lost in the Six-Day War of 1967. President Nixon ordered the U.S. nuclear forces on alert and airlifted almost $2 billion in arms to Israel to stem their retreat. The tide of battle quickly shifted in favor of the Israelis, and the war was soon over.

The United States was made to pay a huge price for supporting Israel. The Arab members of the Organization of Petroleum Exporting Countries (OPEC) placed an embargo on oil sold to Israel's supporters. The embargo caused a worldwide oil shortage and long lines at gas stations in the United States. Even worse was the impact on the U.S. economy, which now suffered from runaway inflation, the loss of manufacturing jobs, and a lower standard of living for blue-collar workers. Consumers switched from big American-made cars to smaller, more fuel-efficient Japanese cars, which cost U.S. automobile workers over 225,000 jobs. Congress responded by enacting a 55-miles-per-hour speed limit to save gasoline and approved an oil pipeline to be built in Alaska to tap American oil reserves. No government program, however, seemed to bolster the sluggish economy or stem high inflation rates, which continued to the end of the decade.

Resignation of a President

In 1974, Nixon made triumphal visits to Moscow and Cairo, but at home his reputation continued to slide. In October 1973, the president fired Archibald Cox, the special prosecutor assigned to the Watergate investigations, and the U.S. attorney general resigned in protest. The start of impeachment hearings in the House encouraged Nixon to reveal some transcripts of the Watergate tapes in April 1974, but it took a Supreme Court decision in July to force him to turn over the tapes to the courts and Congress. Meanwhile, the House Judiciary Committee voted three articles of impeachment: (1) obstruction of justice, (2) abuse of power, and (3) contempt of Congress.

The conversations recorded on the tapes shocked friends and foes alike. The transcript of one such White House conversation clearly implicated Nixon in the cover-up only days after the Watergate break-in. Faced with certain impeachment in the House and a trial in the Senate, Richard Nixon chose to resign on August 9, 1974. His appointed vice president Gerald Ford then took the oath of office as the first unelected president in U.S. history.

Significance. To some, the final outcome of the Watergate scandal (Nixon leaving office under pressure) proved that the U.S. constitutional system of checks and balances worked as it was intended. For others, the scandal underlined the dangerous shift of power to the presidency that began with Franklin Roosevelt and expanded during the Cold War. Without doubt, Watergate contributed to a growing loss of faith in the federal government.

Gerald Ford in the White House

Before Nixon chose him to replace Vice President Agnew in 1973, Gerald Ford had served in Congress for years as a representative from Michigan and as the Republican minority leader of the House. Ford was a likeable and unpretentious man, but his ability to be president was questioned by many in the media.

Pardoning of Nixon

In his first month in office, President Ford lost the goodwill of many by granting Nixon a full and unconditional pardon for any crime that he might have committed. The pardon was extended even before any formal charges or indictment had been made by a court of law. Ford was accused of making a "corrupt bargain" with Nixon, but he explained that the purpose of the pardon was to end the "national nightmare," instead of prolonging it for months, if not years. Critics were angered that the full truth of Nixon's deeds never came out, while the former president's aides (including Haldeman and Ehrlichman) were convicted and served prison terms.

Investigating the CIA

During Ford's presidency (1974–1977), the Democratic Congress continued to search for abuses in the executive branch, especially in the CIA. This intelligence agency was accused of engineering the assassination of foreign leaders, among them the Marxist president of Chile, Salvador Allende. Ford appointed former Texas Congressman George H. Bush to reform the agency.

Failure of U.S. Policy in Southeast Asia

President Ford was unable to get additional funds from Congress for the South Vietnamese, who in 1974 were facing strong attack from Communist forces.

Fall of Saigon. In April 1975, the U.S.-supported government in Saigon fell to the enemy, and Vietnam became one country under the rule of the Communist government in Hanoi (North Vietnam's capital). Just before the final collapse, the United States was able to evacuate about 150,000 Vietnamese who had supported the United States and now faced certain persecution. The fall of South Vietnam marked a low point of American prestige overseas and confidence at home.

Genocide in Cambodia. Also in 1975, the U.S.-supported government in neighboring Cambodia fell to the Khmer Rouge, a radical Communist faction that conducted genocide against over a million of its own people. In an attempt to compensate for the failure of U.S. policy in Southeast Asia, President Ford ordered an attack on a Cambodian naval base that had captured the U.S. merchant ship *Mayaguez*. The action helped free the 39 crewmen, but 38 marines died in the assault.

Future of Southeast Asia. The fall of Cambodia seemed to fulfill Eisenhower's domino theory, but in fact the rest of Southeast Asia did not fall to communism. Instead, such nations as Singapore, Thailand, and Malaysia emerged as the "little tigers" of the vigorously growing Asian (Pacific Rim) economy. Some argued that U.S. support of South Vietnam was not a waste, because it bought time for other nations of East Asia and Southeast Asia to develop and better resist communism.

The Economy and Domestic Policy

On domestic matters, Ford proved less accommodating and more conservative than Nixon. His chief concern was bringing inflation under control. He urged voluntary measures on the part of businesses and consumers, including the wearing of WIN buttons (Whip Inflation Now). Not only did inflation continue, but the economy also sank deeper into recession, with the unemployment rate reaching over 9 percent. Ford finally agreed to a Democratic package to stimulate the economy, but he vetoed 39 other Democratic bills.

Bicentennial celebration. In 1976, the United States celebrated its 200th birthday. Americans' pride in their history helped to put Watergate and Vietnam behind them. Even the lackluster presidency of Gerald Ford served the purpose of restoring candor and humility to the White House.

The Election of 1976

Watergate still cast its gloom over the Republican party in the 1976 elections. President Ford was challenged for the party's nomination by Ronald Reagan, a former actor and ex-governor of California, who enjoyed the support of the more conservative Republicans. Ford won the nomination in a close battle, but the conflict with Reagan hurt him in the polls.

Emergence of Jimmy Carter. A number of Democrats competed for their party's nomination, including a little-known former governor of Georgia, James Earl (Jimmy) Carter. With Watergate still on voters' minds, Carter had success running as an outsider against the corruption in Washington. His victories in open primaries reduced the influence of more experienced Democratic politicians. After watching his huge lead in the polls evaporate in the closing days of the campaign, Carter managed to win a close election (287 electoral votes to 241 for Ford) by carrying most of the South and getting an estimated

97 percent of the African American vote. In the aftermath of Watergate, the Democrats also won strong majorities in both houses of Congress.

Jimmy Carter's Presidency

The informal style of Jimmy Carter signaled an effort to end the imperial presidency. On his inaugural day, he walked down Pennsylvania Avenue to the White House instead of riding in the presidential limousine. Public images of the president carrying his own luggage may have impressed average Americans. Veteran members of Congress, however, always viewed Carter as an outsider, who depended too much on his politically inexperienced advisers from Georgia. Even Carter's keen intelligence and dedication to duty may have been partly a liability in causing him to pay close attention to all the details of government operations. Critics observed that, when it came to distinguishing between the forest and the trees, Carter was a "leaf man."

Foreign Policy

The hallmark of Carter's foreign policy was human rights, which he preached with Wilsonian fervor to the world's dictators.

Human rights diplomacy. Carter appointed Andrew Young, an African American, to serve as U.S. ambassador to the United Nations. Young championed the cause of human rights by denouncing the oppression of the black majority in South Africa and Rhodesia (Zimbabwe). In Latin America, human rights violations by the military governments of Argentina and Chile caused Carter to cut off U.S. aid to those countries.

Panama Canal. The Carter administration attempted to correct inequities in the original Panama Canal Treaty of 1903 by negotiating a new treaty. In 1978, after long debate, the Senate ratified a treaty that would gradually transfer operation and control of the Panama Canal from the United States to the Panamanians, a process to be completed by the year 2000. Opponents would remember Carter's "give away" of the canal in the 1980 election.

Camp David Accords (1978). Perhaps Carter's single greatest achievement as president was arranging a peace settlement between Egypt and Israel. In 1977, Egyptian President Anwar Sadat took the first courageous step toward Middle East peace by visiting Israeli Prime Minister Menachem Begin in Jerusalem. President Carter followed this bold initiative by inviting Sadat and Begin to meet again at the presidential retreat in Camp David, Maryland. With Carter acting as an intermediary, the two leaders negotiated the Camp David Accords (September 1978), which provided a framework for a peace settlement between their countries.

Later, as a result of a peace treaty concluded in 1979, Egypt became the first Arab nation to recognize the nation of Israel. In return, Israel withdrew its troops from the Sinai territory taken from Egypt in the Six-Day War of

1967. The treaty was opposed by the Palestine Liberation Organization (PLO) and most of the Arab world, but it proved the first step in the long road to a negotiated peace in the Middle East.

Iran and the hostage crisis. The Middle East was also the setting for Carter's greatest frustration and defeat. In 1979, Islamic fundamentalists in Iran, led by the Ayatollah Khomeini, overthrew the shah's dictatorial government. The shah had kept the oil flowing for the West during the 1970s, but his autocratic rule and policy of westernization had alienated a large part of the Iranian population.

With the ayatollah and fundamentalists in power, Iranian oil production ground to a halt, causing the second worldwide oil shortage of the decade and another round of price increases. U.S. impotence in dealing with the crisis became more evident in November 1979 when Iranian militants seized the U.S. embassy in Teheran and held more than 50 members of the American staff as prisoners and hostages. The hostage crisis dragged out through the remainder of Carter's presidency. In April 1980, Carter approved a rescue mission, but the breakdown of the helicopters over the Iranian desert forced the United States to abort the mission. For many Americans, Carter's unsuccessful attempts to free the hostages became a symbol of a failed presidency.

Cold War. President Carter attempted to continue the Nixon-Ford policy of détente with China and the Soviet Union. In 1979, the United States ended its official recognition of the Nationalist Chinese government of Taiwan and completed the first exchange of ambassadors with the People's Republic of China. At first, détente also moved ahead with the Soviet Union with the signing in 1979 of a SALT II treaty, which provided for limiting the size of each superpower's nuclear delivery system. The Senate never ratified the treaty, however, as a result of a renewal of Cold War tensions over Afghanistan.

In December 1979, Soviet troops invaded Afghanistan—an aggressive action that ended a decade of improving U.S.-Soviet relations. The United States feared that the invasion might lead to a Soviet move to control the oil-rich Persian Gulf. Carter reacted by (1) placing an embargo on grain exports and the sale of high technology to the Soviet Union and (2) boycotting the 1980 Olympics in Moscow. After having campaigned for arms reduction, Carter now had to switch to an arms buildup.

Domestic Policy: Dealing With Inflation

At home, the biggest issue was the growing inflation rate. At first Carter tried to check inflation with measures aimed at conserving oil energy and reviving the U.S. coal industry. The compromises that came out of Congress, however, failed either to reduce the consumption of oil or to check inflation. In 1979–1980, inflation seemed completely out of control and reached the unheard of rate of 13 percent.

Troubled economy. Inflation slowed economic growth as consumers and businesses could no longer afford the high interest rates that came with high prices. The chairman of the Federal Reserve Board, Paul Volcker, hoped to break the back of inflation by pushing interest rates even higher, to 20 percent in 1980. These rates especially hurt the automobile and building industries, which laid off tens of thousands of workers. Inflation also pushed middle-class taxpayers into higher tax brackets, which led to a "taxpayers' revolt." Government social programs that were indexed to the inflation rate helped to push the federal deficit to nearly $60 billion in 1980. Many Americans had to adjust to the harsh truth that, for the first time since World War II, their standard of living was on the decline.

Loss of Popularity

Intelligence, effort, and integrity were not enough to get Jimmy Carter through the Iranian hostage crisis and worsening economic crisis. In 1979, in what the press called Carter's "national malaise" speech, he blamed the problems of the United States on a "moral and spiritual crisis" of the American people. By that time, however, many Americans blamed the president for weak and indecisive leadership. By the election year 1980 his approval rating had fallen to only 23 percent. In seeking a second term, the unpopular president was clearly vulnerable to political challenges from both Democrats and Republicans.

American Society in Transition

Social changes in the 1970s were of potentially even greater significance than politics. By the end of the decade, for the first time, half of all Americans lived in the fastest-growing sections of the country—the South and the West. Unlike the previous decade, which was dominated by the youth revolt, Americans were conscious in the seventies that the population was aging. The fastest growing age group was senior citizens over 65.

The country's racial and ethnic composition was also changing noticeably in the final decades of the 20th century. By 1990, minority groups made up 25 percent of the population. The Census Bureau predicted that, by 2050, as much as half the population would be Hispanic American, African American, or Asian American. Cultural pluralism was replacing the melting pot as the model for U.S. society, as diverse ethnic and cultural groups strove not only to end discrimination and improve themselves but also to celebrate their unique values and traditions.

Growth of Immigration

Before the 1960s, most immigrants to the United States had come from Europe and Canada. By the 1980s, 47 percent of immigrants came from Latin

America, 37 percent from Asia, and less than 13 percent from Europe and Canada. In part, this dramatic shift was caused by the arrival of refugees leaving Cuba and Vietnam after the Communist takeovers of these countries. Of far greater importance was the impact of the Immigration Act of 1965, which ended the ethnic quota acts of the 1920s favoring Europeans and thereby opened the United States to immigrants from all parts of the world.

Illegal immigrants. How many immigrants entered the United States illegally every year could only be estimated, but by the mid-1970s, the immigration commission concluded that as many as 12 million foreigners were in the U.S. illegally. The rise in illegal immigrants from countries of Latin America and Asia led to the Immigration Reform and Control Act of 1986, which penalized employers for hiring illegal immigrants while also granting amnesty to illegal immigrants arriving by 1982. Even so, many Americans concluded that the nation had lost control of its own borders, as both legal and illegal immigrants continued to flock to the United States at an estimated million persons a year.

Demands for Minority Rights

One aspect of the protest movements of the 1960s that continued into later decades was the movement by different minorities to gain both relief from discrimination and recognition for their contributions to U.S. society.

Hispanic Americans. Most Hispanic Americans before World War II lived in the southwestern states, but in the postwar years new arrivals from Puerto Rico, Cuba, and South and Central America increasingly settled in the East and Midwest. Mexican workers, after suffering deportation during the Great Depression, were encouraged to come to the United States in the 1950s and 1960s to take low-paying agricultural jobs. They were widely exploited before the long series of boycotts led by Cesar Chavez and the United Farm Workers Organization finally gained collective bargaining rights for farm workers in 1975. Chicano (Mexican American) activists also won a federal mandate for bilingual education requiring schools to teach Hispanic children in both English and Spanish. In the 1980s, a growing number of Hispanic Americans were elected to public office, including mayors of such large cities as Miami and San Antonio. The Census Bureau reported that, in 2000, Hispanics, including Cubans, Puerto Ricans, and other Latin Americans, had become the country's largest minority group.

Native American movement. In the 1950s, the Eisenhower administration had made an unsuccessful attempt to encourage Native Americans to leave reservations and assimilate into urban America. Native American leaders resisted the loss of cultural identity that would have resulted from such a policy.

To achieve self-determination and revival of tribal traditions, the American Indian Movement (AIM) was founded in 1968. Militant actions soon followed, including AIM's takeover of the abandoned prison on Alcatraz Island in San Francisco Bay in 1969. AIM members also occupied Wounded Knee, South Dakota, in 1973, site of the infamous massacre of Native Americans by the U.S. cavalry in 1890.

The movement had a number of successes both in Congress and the courts. Congress' passage of the Indian Self-Determination Act of 1975 gave reservations and tribal lands greater control over internal programs, education, and law enforcement. Native Americans also used the federal courts successfully to regain property or compensation for treaty violations. Widespread unemployment and poverty on reservations was attacked by improving education, through the Tribally Controlled Community College Assistance Act of 1978, and also by building industries and gambling casinos on reservations, under the self-determination legislation.

Native Americans also gained the support of public opinion, as the story of their historic oppression was given a sympathetic retelling in such popular films as *Dances With Wolves* (1990). By 1990, a growing Native American population numbered 1.5 million, with about half the people living on tribal reservations.

Asian Americans. Americans of Asian birth and descent had become the fastest growing ethnic minority by the 1980s. The largest group of Asian Americans were of Chinese ancestry, followed by Filipinos, Japanese, Indians, Koreans, and Vietnamese. A strong dedication to education resulted in Asian Americans being well represented in the best colleges and universities. In some parts of the country, however, Asian Americans suffered from discrimination, envy, and Japan-bashing, while the less educated immigrants earned well below the national average.

Gay liberation movement. In 1969, a police raid on the Stonewall Inn, a gay bar in New York City, sparked both a riot and the gay rights movement. Gay activists urged homosexuals to be open about their identity and to work to end discrimination and violent abuse. By the mid-1970s, homosexuality was no longer classified as a mental illness and the federal Civil Service dropped its ban on employment of homosexuals. In 1993, President Clinton attempted to end discrimination against gays and lesbians in the military, but settled for the compromise "don't-ask, don't-tell" policy.

The Environmental Movement

The participation of 20 million citizens in the first Earth Day in 1970 reflected the nation's growing concerns over pollution and the destruction of the natural environment. It also was a vivid example of the increased questioning of technological progress in the last decades of the 20th century. Massive oil spills around the world, such as the *Exxon Valdez* tanker accident in Alaska in 1989, reinforced fears about the deadly combination of human error and modern technology. Public opinion also turned against building additional nuclear power plants after an accident at the Three Mile Island power plant in Pennsylvania (1979) and the deadly explosion of the Chernobyl nuclear reactor in the Soviet Union (1986).

Protective legislation. Conservationists demanded laws that would protect against pollution and destruction of the environment. In 1970, Congress passed the Clean Air Act and created the Environmental Protection Agency (EPA) and followed this legislation in 1972 with the Clean Water Act. In 1980, the Superfund was created to clean up toxic dumps, such as Love Canal in Niagara Falls, New York.

The protest movements by diverse groups in American society seemed to produce more social stress and fragmentation. Combined with a slowing economy and a declining standard of living, these forces left many Americans feeling angry and bitter. A conservative reaction to the liberal policies of the New Deal and the Great Society was gaining strength in the late 1970s and would prove a powerful force in the politics of the next decade.

HISTORICAL PERSPECTIVES: END OF THE IMPERIAL PRESIDENCY?

The Cold War, and the Vietnam War in particular, caused a growing concern over the expansion and abuse of power by the office of the president. Critics in the 1970s saw parallels between the decline of the Roman Republic and the rise of the powerful emperor system of the Roman Empire during its expansion and the developments in the political system of the United States during its emergence as a superpower after World War II. The abuse of power under Richard Nixon and the Watergate scandals confirmed many Americans' fears. A few even at first misjudged Nixon's mobilization of the armed forces during the Middle East October War of 1973 as an attempted coup d'état to take over the government.

Arthur Schlesinger, Jr. argued in his book *The Imperial Presidency* (1973) that the United States' exercise of world leadership had gradually undermined the original intent of the Constitution and the war powers of Congress. Cold War presidents had used national security, the need for secrecy, executive privilege, and the mystique of the high office to concentrate power into the White House. The end of the Vietnam War, the resignation of Richard Nixon, and the War Powers Act of 1973 seemed to end the dangers of the imperial presidency. Presidents Ford and Carter proved comparatively weak presidents, and by the 1990s power had clearly shifted back to the Congress, as the Founders had intended. However, the U.S. political system would continue to be challenged on how to provide strong leadership in world affairs. Arthur Schlesinger, Jr. concluded that the U.S. continued to need a strong president, but one working *within* the limits of the Constitution.

KEY NAMES, EVENTS, AND TERMS

Richard Nixon
Henry Kissinger
Vietnamization
Nixon Doctrine
Kent State
My Lai
Pentagon Papers
Paris Accords of 1973
détente
China visit
Soviet Union; Strategic Arms Limitation Talks
New Federalism
stagflation
southern strategy
Warren Burger
George McGovern
Watergate; articles of impeachment
United States v. Nixon

War Powers Act (1973)
Middle East War (1973)
OPEC; oil embargo
Gerald Ford
Cambodia; Khmer Rouge
Bicentennial
James Earl (Jimmy) Carter
human rights
Panama Canal treaty (1978)
Camp David Accords (1978)
Anwar Sadat; Menachem Begin
Iran; hostage crisis
Afghanistan invasion
cultural pluralism
Immigration Act (1965)
Immigration Reform and Control Act (1986)
Hispanic Americans
Cesar Chavez

American Indian Movement
Indian Self-Determination Act (1975)
Asian Americans
gay liberation movement
environmental movement
Earth Day (1970)
nuclear accidents: Three Mile Island, Chernobyl
Clean Air Act (1970)
Environmental Protection Agency
Clean Water Act (1972)
Environmental Superfund

MULTIPLE-CHOICE QUESTIONS

1. Which of the following BEST reflected President Nixon's policy of "Vietnamization"?
   - (A) massive bombing of North Vietnam by American air power
   - (B) full-scale invasion of Cambodia to end the Communist threat
   - (C) gradual withdrawal of American armed forces from Vietnam
   - (D) turning the war in South Vietnam over to United Nations forces
   - (E) stopping all American military and economic aid to South Vietnam

2. Richard Nixon's conduct of foreign affairs emphasized all of the following EXCEPT
   - (A) playing off Communist China against Communist Russia
   - (B) reduction of tension between the United States and Communist countries
   - (C) a use of the balance of power diplomacy to achieve stability in the world
   - (D) a renewed arms race in ballistic and antiballistic missiles
   - (E) providing economic and military assistance to other nations, but not large numbers of American troops

3. The Paris Accords of 1973 included all of the following EXCEPT
   - (A) the United States would withdraw the rest of its troops from South Vietnam
   - (B) the United States would end all economic and military aid to South Vietnam
   - (C) the United States would get back all prisoners in enemy hands
   - (D) North Vietnam could keep some of its troops in South Vietnam
   - (E) a promise of a cease-fire and free elections

4. Under the program of New Federalism, President Nixon sought to
   - (A) shift the responsibility for social programs from the federal to state and local governments
   - (B) end the Great Society assistance programs for the working poor
   - (C) attack inflation with a series of voluntary guidelines for business and labor
   - (D) slow down desegregation by turning over busing decisions to the state courts
   - (E) bring social programs all together under more efficient federal bureaucracy

5. Richard Nixon's strategy to build a Republican majority for 1972 included all of the following EXCEPT
   - (A) hard-hitting attacks by Vice President Spiro Agnew on liberals and the media

(B) gaining support in the South by slowing down court-ordered busing for desegregation

(C) appointment of southern conservatives to the Supreme Court

(D) appealing to the "silent majority"

(E) establishing positive relationships with the national media and liberal press

6. What caused Richard Nixon to resign in 1974?

(A) He violated the War Powers Act passed by Congress.

(B) He ordered the "Saturday night massacre."

(C) The White House tapes proved he was guilty of obstruction of justice.

(D) He ordered his staff to keep an "enemies list" and use "dirty tricks."

(E) He took bribes while governor of Maryland.

7. President Gerald Ford lost the most support from the American public for

(A) allowing the fall of South Vietnam to the Communists

(B) his ineffective WIN campaign against inflation

(C) becoming the first unelected president of the United States

(D) the loss of American lives in the *Mayaquez* affair

(E) his pardon of Richard Nixon

8. The main guiding principle of President Carter's foreign policy was

(A) détente

(B) human rights

(C) support of Israel

(D) lower gas prices

(E) containment of communism

9. The U.S. economy in the late 1970s was characterized by all of the following EXCEPT

(A) low interest rates

(B) oil shortages and increased oil prices

(C) massive layoffs of workers

(D) runaway inflation rates

(E) recession

10. The U.S. policy of détente with the Soviet Union ended because of

(A) the development of the MX missile

(B) the U.S. recognition of the People's Republic of China

(C) the Soviet invasion of Afghanistan

(D) the failure of Congress to ratify SALT II

(E) boycott of the Olympics in Moscow

ESSAY QUESTIONS

1. Analyze the foreign policy accomplishments of the Nixon administration from 1969 to 1974.

2. What were the abuses and illegal activities that became known as Watergate, and what impact did they have on domestic politics in the 1970s?

3. Describe and account for the economic problems that the United States experienced in the 1970s.

4. Why were the presidencies of Gerald Ford and Jimmy Carter perceived as weak and ineffectual? Assess the va-

lidity of those perceptions, taking into account both their domestic and foreign policies.

5. In what ways was American society changing in the 1970s and 1980s, and why were these changes taking place?

DOCUMENTS AND READINGS

The optimism of the 1950s and early 1960s gave way to the protests and "cultural wars" of the 1970s and 1980s. The following readings to some extent question America's power, policies, or cultural values. They also reflect the growing sense of limits for the world's most powerful nation.

DOCUMENT A. *NIXON'S GRAND STRATEGY IN THE COLD WAR*

Early in his career, Richard Nixon had established himself as a strong anticommunist. As president he used that reputation to allow him to take risks, such as his visit to Communist China, to achieve a more stable world.

> Never once in my career have I doubted that the Communists mean it when they say that their goal is to bring the world under Communist control. Nor have I ever forgotten Whittaker Chambers' chilling comment that when he left communism, he had the feeling he was leaving the winning side. But unlike some anticommunists who think we should refuse to recognize or deal with the Communists lest in doing so we imply or extend an ideological respectability to their philosophy and their system, I have always believed that we can and must communicate and, when possible, negotiate with Communist nations. . . .
>
> I felt that we had allowed ourselves to get in a disadvantageous position vis-à-vis the Soviets. They had a major presence in Arab states of the Middle East, while we had none; they had Castro in Cuba; since the mid-1960's they had supplanted the Chinese as the principal military suppliers of North Vietnam; and except for Tito's Yugoslavia they still totally controlled Eastern Europe and threatened the stability and security of Western Europe.
>
> There were, however, a few things in our favor. The most important and interesting was the Soviet split with China. There was also some evidence of growing, albeit limited, independence in some

of the satellite nations. There were indications that the Soviet leaders were becoming interested in reaching an agreement on strategic arms limitation. They also appeared to be ready to hold serious talks on the anomalous situation in Berlin, which, almost a quarter century after the war had ended, was still a divided city and a constant source of tension, not just between the Soviets and the United States, but also between the Soviets and Western Europe. We sensed that they were looking for a face-saving formula that would lessen the risk of confrontation in the Mideast. And we had some solid evidence that they were anxious for an expansion of trade.

It was often said that the key to a Vietnam settlement lay in Moscow and Peking rather than in Hanoi. Without continuous and massive aid from either or both of the Communist giants, the leaders of North Vietnam would not have been able to carry on the war for more than a few months. Thanks to the Sino-Soviet split, however, the North Vietnamese had been extremely successful in playing off the Soviets and the Chinese against each other. . . . Aside from wanting to keep Hanoi from going over to Peking, Moscow had little stake in the outcome of the North Vietnamese cause, especially as it increasingly worked against Moscow's own major interests vis-à-vis the United States. While I understood that the Soviets were not entirely free agents where their support for North Vietnam was concerned, I nonetheless planned to bring maximum pressure to bear on them in this area.

Richard Nixon,
RN: Memoirs of Richard Nixon, 1978

DOCUMENT B.   *THE REVIVAL OF THE WOMEN'S MOVEMENT*

A key objective of the modern women's movement was equal pay for equal work. In the following selection, Gloria Steinem, a leader in the women's movement and founder of *Ms.,* a magazine promoting women's issues, speaking before a Senate hearing on the Equal Rights Amendment, addressed the concerns about mothers becoming full-time workers.

American mothers spend more time with their homes and children than those of any other society we know about. In the past, joint families, servants, a prevalent system in which grandparents raised the children, or family field work in the agrarian system— all these factors contributed more to child care that the labor-saving devices of which we are so proud.

The truth is that most American children seem to be suffering from too much Mother, and too little Father. Part of the program of Women's Liberation is a return of fathers to their children. If laws permit women equal work and pay opportunities, men will then be relieved of their role of sole breadwinner. Fewer ulcers, fewer hours of meaningless work, equal responsibility for his own children: these are a few of the reasons that Women's Liberation is Men's Liberation, too.

As for the psychic health of the children, studies show that the quality of time spent by parents is more important than the quantity. The most damaged children were not those whose mothers worked, but those whose mothers preferred to work but stayed home out of role-playing desire to be a "good mother."

Gloria Steinem,
Hearing, The "Equal Rights"
Amendment, 1970

DOCUMENT C.

from *Herblock: A Cartoonist's Life*
(Times Books, 1998)

DOCUMENT D.   *A NATIONAL CRISIS OF CONFIDENCE*

In the midst of the oil crisis, the Iranian hostage crisis, and some of the worst inflation in the nation's history, President Jimmy Carter, after conferring with various experts for ten days, delivered a remarkable speech on nationwide network television. While the speech did little to help Carter's popularity, it revealed the loss of confidence that many in the nation witnessed in the late 1970s.

The erosion of our confidence in the future is threatening to destroy the social and the political fabric of America. . . .

Our people are losing faith, not only in government itself but in their ability as citizens to serve as the ultimate rulers and shapers of our democracy. As a people we know our past and we are proud of it. Our progress has been part of the living history of America, even the world. We always believed that we were part of a great movement of humanity itself called democracy, involved in the search for freedom, and that belief has always strengthened us in our purpose. But just as we are losing our confidence in the future, we are also beginning to close the door on our past.

In a nation that was proud of hard work, strong families, close-knit communities, and our faith in God, too many of us now tend to worship self-indulgence and consumption. Human identity is no longer defined by what one does, but by what one owns. But we've discovered that owning things and consuming things does not satisfy our longing for meaning. We've learned that piling up material goods cannot fill the emptiness of lives which have no confidence or purpose.

The symptoms of this crisis of the American spirit are all around us. For the first time in the history of our country a majority of our people believe that the next five years will be worse than the past five years. Two-thirds of our people do not even vote. The productivity of American workers is actually dropping, and the willingness of Americans to save for the future has fallen below that of all people in the Western world.

As you know, there is a growing disrespect for government and for churches and for schools, the news media, and other institutions. This is not a message of happiness or reassurance, but it is the truth and it is a warning.

These changes did not happen overnight. They've come upon us gradually over the last generation, years that were filled with shocks and tragedy.

We were sure that ours was a nation of the ballot, not the bullet, until the murders of John Kennedy and Robert Kennedy and Martin

Luther King, Jr. We were taught that our armies were always invincible and our causes were always just, only to suffer the agony of Vietnam. We respected the Presidency as a place of honor until the shock of Watergate.

We remember when the phrase "sound as a dollar" was an expression of absolute dependability, until ten years of inflation began to shrink our dollar and our savings. We believed that our Nation's resources were limitless until 1973, when we had to face a growing dependence on foreign oil. . . .

What you see too often in Washington and elsewhere around the country is a system of government that seems incapable of action. You see a Congress twisted and pulled in every direction by hundreds of well-financed and powerful special interests. You see every extreme position defended to the last vote, almost to the last breath by one unyielding group or another. You often see a balanced and a fair approach that demands sacrifice, a little sacrifice from everyone, abandoned like an orphan without support and without friends. . . .

Jimmy Carter,
Public Papers of the Presidents of the United States, 1979

ANALYZING THE DOCUMENTS

1. What was Nixon's grand strategy for improving relations with the Soviet Union and at the same time ending the war in Vietnam?

2. According to Steinem, why would equal pay for equal work be good for children and men, as well as women? How accurate was her 1970 prediction of the benefits of working mothers?

3. Analyze the way the Watergate tapes and the media contributed to the resignation of President Nixon.

4. According to Carter, what were the causes of the problems of the late 1970s and the general loss of confidence in the government?

5. Not all issues have a clearly conservative or liberal side to them. However, based on your overall knowledge of the times, try to assess the point of view of each author. On the issue involved in each source, was the opinion conservative, moderate, or liberal? What evidence would you use to support your conclusion?

THE CONSERVATIVE
RESURGENCE,
1980–PRESENT

In this present crisis, government is not the solution to our problem;
government is the problem.

President Ronald Reagan, Inaugural Address, January 20, 1981

The history of the United States since 1980 is not a focus of the Advanced Placement U.S. History examination. The exam will probably have only a couple of multiple-choice questions from this chapter, and the College Board assures students that no DBQ or essay question "will deal exclusively with this period." However, an understanding of the last two decades of the 20th century provides perspective for the postwar years, especially for the Cold War and domestic politics and policies. This final chapter will survey the key events from 1980 both for exam preparation and to complete our review of U.S. history.

Among the important changes during the 1980s and 1990s were the collapse of communism in Eastern Europe, the breakup of the Soviet Union, and the end of the Cold War. In the post-Cold War world, older ethnic and religious conflicts reemerged to threaten the peace with civil wars and terrorism. On the domestic scene, the conservative agenda of the Reagan administration (1981–1989)—for a stronger military, lower taxes, fewer social programs, and traditional cultural values—helped the Republicans become the majority party, which by 2003 controlled the White House and both houses of Congress.

The Rise of Conservatism

Even though Barry Goldwater was defeated in a landslide in the election of 1964, his campaign for the presidency marked the beginning of the resurgence of conservatism. The policies of presidents Nixon and Ford and the writings of the political commentator William F. Buckley, Jr., and the economist Milton Friedman gave evidence in the 1970s of a steady shift to the right, away from the liberalism of the sixties. By 1980, a loose coalition of economic and political conservatives, religious fundamentalists, and political action committees

(PACs) had become a potent force for change. These groups were opposed to big government, New Deal liberalism, gun control, feminism, gay rights, welfare, affirmative action, sexual permissiveness, abortion, and drug use, which, in their view, were responsible for undermining family and religious values, the work ethic, and national security.

Leading Issues

By 1980, various activists had taken the lead in establishing a conservative agenda for the nation, which included such diverse causes as lower taxes, improved morals, and reduced emphasis on affirmative action.

Taxpayers' revolt. In 1978, California voters led the revolt against high taxes by passing Proposition 13, a measure that sharply cut property taxes. Nationally, conservatives promoted economist Arthur Laffer's belief that tax cuts would promote economic growth. Two Republican members of Congress, Jack Kemp and William Roth, proposed legislation to reduce federal taxes by 30 percent, which became the basis for the Reagan tax cuts.

Moral revival. Moral decay was a weekly theme of televangelists such as Pat Robertson, Oral Roberts, and Jim Bakker, who by 1980 had a combined weekly audience of between 60 and 100 million viewers. Religion became an instrument of electoral politics, when the Moral Majority, founded by Virginia evangelist Jerry Falwell, financed campaigns to unseat liberal members of Congress. Religious fundamentalists attacked "secular humanism" as a godless creed taking over public education and also campaigned for the return of prayers and the teaching of the Biblical account of creation in the public schools. The legalization of abortion in the *Roe v. Wade* (1973) decision sparked the right-to-life movement that joined together Catholics and fundamentalist Protestants, who believed that human life began at the moment of conception.

"Reverse discrimination." In 1965, President Johnson had committed the U.S. government to a policy of affirmative action to ensure that underprivileged minorities and women would have equal access to education, jobs, and promotions. Suffering through years of recession and stagflation in the 1970s, many white males blamed their troubles on the "reverse discrimination" imposed by the government's support of racial and ethnic quotas. The Supreme Court ruled in their favor in the landmark case of *Regents of the University of California v. Bakke* (1978), by deciding that college admissions could not be based on race alone. After this decision, conservatives intensified their campaign to end all quotas and preferential treatment based on race and ethnic background.

Ronald Reagan and the Election of 1980

Ronald Reagan, a well-known movie and television actor, gained fame among Republicans as an effective political speaker in the 1964 Goldwater campaign. He went on to be elected the governor of California, the nation's most populous state. In 1976 Reagan came close to taking the party's nomination from President Ford. By this time, he was widely recognized as the most effective spokesperson for conservative positions. Handsome and vigorous in his late sixties, he proved a master of the media and was seen by millions as a likable and sensible champion of average Americans.

Campaign for president, 1980. Senator Edward Kennedy's challenge to President Carter for the Democratic nomination left Carter battered in the polls. As the Republican nominee, Reagan attacked the Democratic party's big-government solutions to problems and the loss of U.S. prestige abroad. (Throughout the campaign, American hostages remained in the hands of Iranian radicals.) Reagan also pointed to a "misery index" of 28 (rate of inflation added to the rate of unemployment) and concluded his campaign by asking a huge television audience, "Are you better off now than you were four years ago?" The voters' rejection of Carter's presidency and the growing conservative mood gave Reagan 51 percent of the popular vote and almost 91 percent of the electoral vote. Carter received 41 percent of the popular vote, while a third candidate, John Anderson (a moderate Republican running as an independent), received 8 percent.

Significance. Reagan's election broke up a key element of the New Deal coalition by taking over 50 percent of the blue-collar vote. For the first time since 1954, the Republicans gained control of the Senate by defeating 11 liberal Democrats targeted by the Moral Majority. The Republicans also gained 33 seats in the House, which when combined with the votes of conservative southern Democrats would give them a working majority on many key issues. Political analysts marked the 1980 election as the end of a half century of Democratic dominance of Congress.

The Reagan Revolution

On the very day that Reagan was inaugurated, the Iranians released the 52 American hostages, giving his administration a positive start. Two months later, the president survived a serious gunshot wound from an assassination attempt. Reagan handled the crisis with such humor and charm that he emerged from the ordeal as an even more popular leader. He pledged that his administration would lower taxes, reduce government spending on welfare, build up the U.S. armed forces, and create a more conservative federal court. He delivered on all four promises—but there were some costs.

Supply-Side Economics ("Reaganomics")

The Reagan administration advocated supply-side economics, arguing that tax cuts reduced government spending, would increase investment by the private sector, and lead to increased production, jobs, and prosperity. This approach contrasted with the Keynesian economics long favored by the Democrats, which relied on government spending to boost consumer income and demand. The supply-side theory reminded critics of the "trickle-down" economics of the 1920s, in which wealthy Americans prospered, and some of their increased profits and spending benefited the middle class and the poor.

Len Boro/Rothco

Federal tax reduction. The legislative activity early in Reagan's presidency reminded some in the media of FDR's Hundred Days. Congress passed most of the tax cuts that Reagan asked for, including a 25 percent decrease in personal income taxes over three years. Cuts in the corporate income tax, capital gains tax, and gift and inheritance taxes guaranteed that a large share of the tax relief went to upper-income taxpayers. Under Reagan, the top income tax rate was reduced to 28 percent. At the same time, small investors were also helped by a provision that allowed them to invest up to $2,000 a year in Individual Retirement Accounts (IRAs) without paying taxes on this money.

Spending cuts. With the help of conservative southern Democrats ("boll weevils"), the Republicans cut over $40 billion from domestic programs, such as food stamps, student loans, and mass transportation. These savings were offset, however, by a dramatic increase in military spending. No cuts in Medicare or Social Security were passed, but the Social Security system was made more solvent by legislation that raised the retirement age and taxed benefits paid to upper-income recipients.

Deregulation

Following up on the promise of "getting government off the backs of the people," the Reagan administration reduced federal regulations on business and industry—a policy of deregulation begun under Carter. Restrictions were eased on savings and loan institutions, mergers and takeovers by large corporations, and environmental protection. To help the struggling American auto industry, regulations on emissions and auto safety were also reduced. Secretary of the

Interior James Watt opened federal lands for increased coal and timber production and offshore waters for oil drilling.

Labor Unions

Despite having once been the president of the Screen Actors Guild, Reagan took a tough stand against unions. He fired thousands of striking federal air traffic controllers for violating their contract and decertified their union (PATCO). Many businesses followed this action by hiring striker replacements in labor conflicts. These antiunion policies along with the loss of manufacturing jobs hastened the decline of union membership among nonfarm workers from over 30 percent in 1962 to only 12 percent in the late 1990s. In addition, the recession of 1982 and foreign competition had a dampening effect on workers' wages.

Recession and Recovery

In 1982, the nation suffered the worst recession since the 1930s. Banks failed and unemployment reached 11 percent. At the same time, however, the recession along with a fall in oil prices reduced the double-digit inflation rate of the late 1970s to less than 4 percent. As the policies of Reaganomics took hold, the economy rebounded and beginning in 1983 entered a long period of recovery. The recovery, however, only widened the income gap between rich and poor. While upper-income groups and "yuppies" (young urban professionals) enjoyed higher incomes and material benefits from a deregulated marketplace, the standard of living of the middle class remained stagnant or declined during the 1980s and early 1990s. In the late 1990s, the middle class gained back some of its losses.

Social Issues

President Reagan followed through on his pledge to appoint conservative judges to the Supreme Court by nominating Sandra Day O'Connor, the first woman on the Court, as well as Antonin Scalia and Anthony Kennedy. Led by a new chief justice, William Rehnquist, the Supreme Court scaled back affirmative action in hiring and promotions and limited *Roe v. Wade* by allowing states to impose certain restrictions on abortion, such as requiring minors to notify their parents before having an abortion.

The Election of 1984

The return of prosperity, even if not fully shared by all Americans, restored public confidence in the Reagan administration. At their convention in 1984, Republicans nominated their popular president by acclamation. Among Democrats, Jesse Jackson became the first African American politician to make a strong run for the presidency by seeking the support of all minority groups under the banner of the *rainbow coalition*. The Democratic majority, however, nominated Walter Mondale, Carter's vice president, to be their presidential candidate and Representative Geraldine Ferraro of New York to be the first woman to run for vice president.

Reagan easily defeated the liberal Mondale, taking every state except Mondale's home state of Minnesota. Two-thirds of white males voted for Reagan. Analysis of voting returns indicated that only two groups still favored the Democrats: African Americans and those earning less than $12,500 a year.

Budget and Trade Deficits

By the mid-1980s, Reagan's tax cuts combined with large increases in military spending were creating federal deficits of over $200 billion a year. Over the course of Reagan's two terms as president, the national debt tripled from about $900 billion to almost $2.7 trillion. The tax cuts, designed to stimulate investments, seemed only to increase consumption, especially of foreign-made luxury and consumer items. As a result, the U.S. trade deficit reached a staggering $150 billion a year. The cumulative trade imbalance of $1 trillion during the 1980s contributed to a dramatic increase in the foreign ownership of U.S. real estate and industry. In 1985, for the first time since the World War I era, the United States became a debtor nation.

In an effort to keep the federal deficit under control, Congress in 1985 passed the Gramm-Rudman-Hollings Balanced Budget Act, which provided for across-the-board spending cuts. Court rulings and later congressional changes kept this legislation from achieving its full purpose, but Congress was still able to reduce the deficit by $66 billion from 1986 to 1988.

Impact of Reaganomics

President Reagan's two terms reduced restrictions on a free-market economy and left more money in the hands of investors and higher income Americans. Reagan's policies also succeeded in containing the growth of the New Deal-Great Society welfare state. Another legacy of the Reagan years were the huge federal deficits, which were to change the context of future political debates. With yearly deficits running between $200–$300 billion, it no longer seemed reasonable for either Democrats or Republicans to propose new social programs, such as universal health coverage. Instead of asking what new government programs might be needed, Reaganomics changed the debate to issues of what government programs to cut and by how much.

Foreign Policy During the Reagan Years

Reagan started his presidency determined to restore the military might and superpower prestige of the United States and to intensify the Cold War competition with the Soviet Union. He called the Soviet Communists "the evil empire" and "focus of evil in the modern world." Reagan was prepared to use military force to back up his rhetoric. During his second term, however, he proved flexible enough in his foreign policy to respond to significant changes in the Soviet Union and its satellites in Eastern Europe.

Renewing the Cold War

Increased spending for defense and aid to anticommunist forces in Latin America were the hallmarks of Reagan's approach to the Cold War during his first term.

Military buildup. The Reagan administration spent billions to build new weapons systems, such as the B-1 bomber and the MX missile, and to expand the U.S. Navy from 450 to 600 ships. The administration also increased spending on the Strategic Defense Initiative (SDI), an ambitious plan for building a high-tech system of lasers and particle beams to destroy enemy missiles before they could reach U.S. territory. Critics called the SDI "Star Wars" and argued that the costly program would only escalate the arms race and could be overwhelmed by the Soviets building more missiles. Although Congress made some cuts in the Reagan proposals, the defense budget grew from $171 billion in 1981 to over $300 billion in 1985.

Central America. In the Americas, Reagan supported "friendly" right-wing dictators to keep out communism and also worked to overthrow Marxist regimes such as the Sandinistas that had taken over Nicaragua in 1979. Large amounts of U.S. military aid went to the "contras," antileftist rebels in Nicaragua who fought the Sandinistas in an attempt to seize power. In 1985, Democrats opposed to the administration's policies in Nicaragua passed the Boland Amendment prohibiting further aid to the contras.

In El Salvador, meanwhile, the Reagan administration spent nearly $5 billion to support the Salvadoran government against a coalition of leftist guerrillas. Many Americans protested the killing of more than 40,000 civilians, including American missionaries, by right-wing "death squads" with connections to the El Salvador army.

Grenada. On the small Caribbean island of Grenada, a coup led to the establishment of a pro-Cuban regime. In October 1983, President Reagan ordered a small force of marines to invade the island in order to prevent the establishment of a strategic Communist military base in the Americas. The invasion quickly succeeded in reestablishing a friendly government in Grenada.

Iran-contra affair. If Grenada was the notable military triumph of Reagan's presidency, his efforts to aid the Nicaraguan contras involved him in a serious blunder and scandal. The so-called Iran-contra affair had its origins in U.S. troubles with Iran. Since 1980, Iran and Iraq had been engaged in a bloody war. Reagan aides came up with the plan—kept secret from the American public—of selling U.S. antitank and antiaircraft missiles to Iran's government for its help in freeing the Americans held hostage by a radical Arab group. In 1986, another Reagan staff member had the "great idea" to use the profits of the arms deal with Iran to fund the contras in Nicaragua.

President Reagan denied that he had knowledge of the illegal diversion of funds—illegal in that it violated both the Boland Amendment and congressional budget authority. The picture that emerged from a televised congressional investigation was of an uninformed, hands-off president who was easily manipulated by his advisers. Reagan suffered a sharp, but temporary, drop in the popularity polls. He would leave office with his reputation intact as one of the most popular presidents of the 20th century.

Lebanon, Israel, and the PLO

Reagan's foreign policy suffered a series of setbacks in the Middle East. In 1982, Israel (with U.S. approval) invaded southern Lebanon to stop PLO terrorists from raiding Israel. Soon the United States became involved in helping to evacuate the PLO to a safe haven and in providing peacekeeping forces to Lebanon in an effort to contain that country's bitter civil war. In April 1983, an Arab suicide squad bombed the U.S. embassy in Beirut, killing 63 people. A few months later, another Arab terrorist drove a bomb-filled truck into the U.S. Marines barracks, killing 241 servicemen. In 1984, Reagan pulled U.S. forces out of Lebanon, with little to show for the effort and loss of lives.

Secretary of State George Schultz pushed for a peaceful settlement of the Palestinian-Israeli conflict by setting up a homeland for the PLO in the West Bank territories occupied by Israel since the 1967 war. Under American pressure, PLO leader Yassir Arafat agreed in 1988 to recognize Israel's right to exist.

Improved U.S.-Soviet Relations

The Cold War intensified in the early 1980s as a result of both Reagan's arms buildup and the Soviet deployment of a larger number of missiles against NATO countries. In 1985, however, a dynamic reformer, Mikhail Gorbachev, became the new Soviet leader. Gorbachev attempted to change Soviet domestic politics by introducing two major reforms: (1) *glasnost,* or openness, to end political repression and move toward greater political freedom for Soviet citizens, and (2) *perestroika,* or restructuring of the Soviet economy by introducing some free-market practices. To achieve his reforms, Gorbachev had to end the costly arms race and deal with a deteriorating Soviet economy.

In 1987, after two earlier attempts, Gorbachev and Reagan agreed to remove and destroy all intermediate-range missiles (the INF agreement). In 1988, Gorbachev further reduced Cold War tensions by starting the pullout of Soviet troops from Afghanistan. He also cooperated with the United States in putting diplomatic pressure on Iran and Iraq to end their war. By the end of Reagan's second term, relations between the two superpowers had so improved that the end of the Cold War seemed at hand.

Assessing Reagan's policy. The Reagan administration would claim that its military buildup forced the Soviet Union to concede defeat and abandon the Cold War. Others would give credit to George Kennan's containment policies and to Gorbachev's initiative. Regardless of what caused the Soviets to change their policy, President Reagan must be credited with responding to the opportunity to end the Cold War. By the time Reagan's second term came to a close in 1988, many Americans wished he could continue for another four years, but the constitutional limit forced him into retirement. Ronald Reagan's combination of style, humor, and patriotism had won over the electorate. As a leader, he changed the politics of the nation for at least a generation by bringing many former Democrats into the Republican party.

President George H. Bush and the End of the Cold War

The Cold War had threatened the very existence of the planet and of humankind. At the same time, ever since 1945, it had given clear purpose and structure to U.S. foreign policy. What would be the U.S. role in the world *after* the Cold War? George H. Bush, a former ambassador to the United Nations and director of the CIA (and the father of President George W. Bush), became the first president to define the U.S. role in the new era.

The Election of 1988

The Democrats regained control of the Senate in 1986 and hoped that the Iran-contra scandal and the huge deficits under Reagan would hurt the Republicans in the presidential race of 1988. Michael Dukakis, governor of Massachusetts, won the Democratic nomination and balanced the ticket by selecting Senator Lloyd Bentsen of Texas as his running mate. The Republican candidates were Reagan's vice president, George H. Bush, and a young Indiana senator, Dan Quayle. Bush was no Reagan in front of the camera, but he quickly overtook an expressionless Dukakis by charging that the Democrat was soft on crime (for furloughing criminals) and weak on national defense. Bush also appealed to voters by promising not to raise taxes: "Read my lips—no new taxes."

The Republicans won a decisive victory in November by a margin of 7 million votes. Once again, the Democrats failed to win the confidence of most white middle-class voters. Nevertheless, the voters sent mixed signals by returning larger Democratic majorities to both the House and the Senate. Americans evidently believed in the system of checks and balances, but unfortunately it often produced legislative gridlock in Washington.

The Collapse of Soviet Communism and the Soviet Union

The first years of the Bush administration were dominated by dramatic changes in the Communist world.

Tiananmen Square. In China during the spring of 1989, prodemocracy students demonstrated for freedom in Beijing's Tiananmen Square. Television cameras from the West broadcast the democracy movement around the world. Under the cover of night, the Chinese Communist government crushed the protest with tanks, killing hundreds and ending the brief flowering of an open political environment in China.

Eastern Europe. Challenges to communism in Eastern Europe produced more positive results. Gorbachev declared that he would no longer support the various Communist governments of Eastern Europe with Soviet armed forces. Starting in Poland in 1989 with the election of Lech Walesa, the leader of the once outlawed Solidarity movement, the Communist party fell from power in one country after another—Hungary, Czechoslovakia, Bulgaria, and Romania. The Communists in East Germany were forced out of power after protesters tore down the Berlin Wall, the hated symbol of the Cold War. In October 1990, the two Germanys, divided since 1945, were finally reunited with the blessing of both NATO and the Soviet Union.

Breakup of the Soviet Union. The swift march of events and the nationalist desire for self-determination soon overwhelmed Gorbachev and the Soviet Union. In 1990 the Soviet Baltic republics of Estonia, Latvia, and Lithuania declared their independence. After a failed coup against Gorbachev by Communist hard-liners, the remaining republics dissolved the Soviet Union in December 1991, leaving Gorbachev a leader with no country. Boris Yeltsin, president of the Russian Republic, joined with nine former Soviet republics to form a loose confederation, the Commonwealth of Independent States (CIS). Yeltsin disbanded the Communist party in Russia and attempted to establish a democracy and a free-market economy.

End of the Cold War. Sweeping agreements to dismantle their nuclear weapons were one tangible proof that the Cold War had ended. Bush and Gorbachev signed the START I agreement in 1991, reducing the number of nuclear warheads to under 10,000 for each side. In late 1992, Bush and Yeltsin agreed to a START II treaty, which reduced the number of nuclear weapons to just over 3,000 each. The treaty also offered U.S. economic assistance to the troubled Russian economy.

Even as Soviet communism collapsed, President Bush, a seasoned diplomat, remained cautious. Instead of celebrating final victory in the Cold War, Americans grew concerned about the outbreak of civil wars and violence in the former Soviet Union. In Eastern Europe, Yugoslavia started to disintegrate in 1991, and a civil war broke out in the provinces of Bosnia and Herzegovina in 1992. At home, the end of the Cold War raised questions about whether the need still existed for heavy defense spending and large numbers of U.S. military bases.

Invasion of Panama

Since the outbreak of the Cold War in the 1940s, U.S. intervention in foreign conflicts had been consistently tied to the containment of communism. In December 1989, U.S. troops were used for a different purpose, as Bush ordered the invasion of Panama to remove the autocratic General Manuel Noriega. The alleged purpose of the invasion was to stop Noriega from using his country as a drug pipeline to the United States. U.S. troops remained until elections established a more creditable government.

Persian Gulf War

President Bush's hopes for a "new world order" of peace and democracy were challenged in August 1990 when Iraq's dictator, Saddam Hussein, invaded oil-rich but weak Kuwait and threatened Western oil sources in Saudi Arabia and the Persian Gulf. President Bush successfully built a coalition of United Nations members to put pressure on Hussein to withdraw from Kuwait. A U.N. embargo against Iraq, however, had little effect. Bush won congressional approval for a military campaign to roll back Iraq's act of aggression. In January 1991, in a massive operation called Desert Storm, over half a million Americans were joined by military units from 28 other nations. Five weeks of relentless air strikes were followed by a brilliant ground war conducted by U.S. General Norman Schwarzkopf. After only 100 hours of fighting on the ground, Iraq was forced to concede defeat.

Some Americans were disappointed that the United States stopped short of driving Saddam Hussein from power in Iraq. Nevertheless, after the victory, Bush enjoyed a boost in his approval rating to nearly 90 percent.

Domestic Problems

President Bush's political future seemed secure based on his foreign policy successes, but a host of domestic problems dogged his administration.

Nomination of Clarence Thomas. The president's nomination of Clarence Thomas to the Supreme Court to replace the retiring Thurgood Marshall proved extremely controversial. Thomas's conservative views on judicial issues were attacked by African American organizations, and charges of sexual harassment against him were widely believed by millions of women. Nevertheless, the Senate confirmed Thomas' nomination.

Taxes and the economy. Americans were shocked to learn that the government's intervention to save weak savings and loan institutions and to pay insured depositors for funds lost in failed S&L's would cost the taxpayers over $250 billion. Also disturbing was the idea that federal budget deficits of over

$250 billion a year added over $1 trillion to the national debt during the Bush presidency. Thousands of Republican voters felt betrayed when, in 1990, Bush violated his campaign pledge of "no new taxes" by agreeing to accept the Democratic Congress' proposed $133 billion in new taxes. The unpopular tax law increased the top income tax rate to 31 percent and raised federal excise taxes on beer, wine, cigarettes, gasoline, and luxury cars and boats. Most damaging of all for Bush's reelection prospects was a recession starting in 1990 that ended the Reagan era of prosperity, increased unemployment, and decreased average family income.

Political inertia. President Bush began his administration calling for "a kinder, gentler America" and declaring himself the "education president." He did sign into law the Americans With Disabilities Act (1990), which prohibited discrimination against citizens with physical and mental disabilities in hiring, transportation, and public accommodation. Outside of this accomplishment, the president offered little in the way of domestic policy. In the midst of recession, he emphasized cuts in federal programs. This seemed to offer little hope to growing numbers of Americans left behind by the "Reagan revolution."

The Clinton Years, 1993–2001: Prosperity and Partisanship

During the last years of the 20th century, the United States enjoyed a period of unrivaled economic growth and technological innovation. The end of the Cold War allowed Americans to focus more on economic and domestic issues. But, during this period, American politics became more divided, bitter, and scandal-driven.

Anti-Incumbent Mood

A stagnant economy, huge budget deficits, and political deadlock fueled a growing disillusionment with government, especially as practiced in the nation's capital. The movement to impose term limits on elected officials gained popularity on the state level, but the Supreme Court ruled in *U.S. Term Limits Inc. v. Thorton* (1995) that the states could not limit the tenure of federal lawmakers without a constitutional amendment.

Another reflection of Americans' disillusionment with Washington politics was the ratification in 1992 of the Twenty-seventh Amendment. First proposed by James Madison in 1789, this amendment prohibited members of Congress from raising their own salaries. Future raises could not go into effect until the next session of Congress.

The Election of 1992

As expected, George H. Bush was nominated by the Republicans for a second term. After a long career in public service, the president seemed tired and out of touch with average Americans, who were more concerned about their paychecks than with Bush's foreign policy successes.

William Jefferson Clinton. Among Democrats, Bill Clinton, the youthful governor of Arkansas, emerged from the primaries as his party's choice for president. The first member of the baby-boom generation to be nominated for president, Clinton proved an articulate and energetic campaigner. He presented himself as a moderate "New Democrat," who focused on economic issues such as jobs, education, and health care, which were important to the "vital center" of the electorate. The strategy was known among his political advisers as: "It's the economy, stupid!"

H. Ross Perot. Ross Perot, a Texas billionaire, entered the 1992 race for president as an independent. Able to use his own resources to finance a series of TV commercials, Perot appealed to millions with his anti-Washington, anti-deficit views. On election day, Perot captured nearly 20 percent of the popular vote for the best third-party showing since Theodore Roosevelt and the Bull Moose campaign of 1912.

Results. Despite the serious challenge from Perot, the front-runners still divided up all the electoral votes: 370 for Clinton (and 43 percent of the popular vote), 168 for Bush (37 percent of the popular vote). Clinton and his running mate, Senator Albert Gore of Tennessee, did well in the South and recaptured the majority of the elderly and blue-collar workers from the Republicans. In addition, the Democrats again won control of both houses of Congress. The new Congress better reflected the diversity of the U.S. population. Among its 66 minority members and 48 women was Carol Moseley-Braun of Illinois, the first African American woman to be elected to the Senate.

Clinton's First Term   (1993–1997)

The early years of Bill Clinton's presidency were marked by controversies over his cabinet nominations, his failed effort to lift the ban on homosexuals in the military, scandals in the White House travel office, and his connection to the failed Whitewater real estate deal in Arkansas.

Setbacks. During the first two years of the Clinton administration, the Republicans, by filibustering in the Senate, were able to kill the president's economic stimulus package, campaign-finance reform, environmental bills, and health care reform. The president's use of his wife, Hilary Rodham Clinton, as the chief architect of his program for universal health coverage backfired. The Clintons' complicated proposal for managed health care ran into determined opposition from the insurance industry and small business organizations. By the end of 1994, the Republicans had managed to stop all the Democrats' proposals for health care reform.

Early accomplishments. The Democratic Congress started out in 1993 by passing the Family and Medical Leave Act and the "motor-voter" law that enabled citizens to register to vote as they received their driver's licenses. The Brady Handgun bill, which mandated a five-day waiting period for the purchase of handguns, was enacted. In 1994, Congress enacted Clinton's Anti-Crime Bill, which provided $30 billion in funding for more police protection and crime-prevention programs. The legislation also banned the sale of most assault weapons, which angered the gun lobby. After protracted negotiation and compromise, Congress passed a deficit-reduction budget that included $255 billion in spending cuts and $241 billion in tax increases. Incorporated in this budget were the president's requests for increased appropriations for education and job training. Clinton also won a notable victory by signing the North American Free Trade Agreement (NAFTA), which created a free-trade zone with Canada and Mexico. Despite these accomplishments, Clinton's apparent waffling on policies and eagerness to compromise seemed to confirm his negative image, as "Slick Willie."

Republicans Take Over Congress

In the midterm elections of November 1994, the Republicans gained control of both houses of Congress for the first time since 1954. They benefited from the perception that the Democratic Congress was inept and dedicated to increasing taxes and federal regulations. President Clinton adjusted to his party's defeat by declaring in his 1995 State of the Union address, "The era of big government is over."

Zealous Reformers. Newt Gingrich, the newly elected Speaker of the House, led the Republicans in an attack on federal programs and spending outlined in their campaign manifesto, "Contract with America." While the president and moderates agreed with the goal of a balanced budget, Clinton proposed a "leaner, not meaner" budget. This confrontation resulted in two shutdowns of the federal government in late 1995, which many Americans blamed on an overzealous Congress. Antigovernment reformers were not helped by the mood after the bombing in 1995 of a federal building in Oklahoma City by militia-movement extremists. The bombing took 169 lives, the worst act of terrorism in the nation's history until the attacks on September 11, 2001.

Balanced Budget. Finally, in the 1996 election year, Congress and the president compromised on a budget that left Medicare and Social Security benefits intact, limited welfare benefits to five years under the Personal Responsibility and Work Opportunity Act, set some curbs on immigrants, increased the minimum wage, and balanced the budget. The spending cuts and tax increases made during Clinton's first term, along with record growth in the economy, helped to eliminate the deficit in federal spending in 1998 and produced the first federal surplus since 1969. In his battle with the Republican Congress, President Clinton captured the middle ground by successfully characterizing the Republicans as extremists, and by taking over their more popular positions, such as balancing the budget and reforming welfare. He was also aided in the 1996 election by a fast-growing economy that had produced over 10 million new jobs.

The Election of 1996

Senator Bob Dole of Kansas, the majority leader of the Senate, became Clinton's Republican opponent. His campaign, which proposed a 15 percent tax cut, never captured the voters' imagination. Character attacks and massive campaign spending by both sides did little to bring more people to the polls, and the turnout dropped below 50 percent of eligible voters.

The Clinton-Gore ticket won with 379 electoral votes (49.2 percent of the popular vote), while Dole and his running mate, Jack Kemp, captured 159 electoral votes (40.8 percent of the popular vote). Ross Perot ran again, but had little impact on the election. President Clinton became the first Democrat since Franklin Roosevelt to be reelected president. The Republicans could celebrate retaining control of both houses of Congress, which they had not done since the 1920s.

Clinton's Second Term: Prosperity and Poisonous Politics

During President Clinton's second term (1997–2001), the United States enjoyed the longest peacetime economic expansion in its history, with annual growth rates of over 4 percent. Technological innovations in computers, the Internet, and wireless communications fueled increased national productivity (a gain of over 5 percent in 1999) and made "e- (or electronic) commerce" part of American life. After years of heavy competition with Europe and Asia, American businesses had become proficient in cutting costs, which both increased their profitability and held down the U.S. inflation rate to 2–3 percent a year. Investors were rewarded with record gains in the stock market (over 22 percent average annual gains in Standard and Poor's Index of 500 leading stocks). The number of households worth $1 million or more quadrupled in the 1990s, to over 8 million, or one in 14 households. The unemployment rate fell from 7.5 percent in 1992 to a 30-year low of 3.9 percent in 2000, and the unemployment of African Americans and Hispanics was the lowest on record. During the peak of prosperity from 1997–1999, average and lower-income Americans experienced the first gains in real income since 1973. However, the economic boom was over by 2001, and both investors and wage earners faced another recession.

Issues of the Surplus. The prosperity of the late 1990s shifted the debate in Washington to what to do with the federal government's surplus revenues, projected to be $4.6 trillion over the first ten years of the 21st century. In 1997 Congress and the president did compromise on legislation that cut taxes on estates and capital gains, and gave tax credits for families with children and for higher education expenses. As Clinton's second term progressed, the struggle between the Democratic president and the Republican Congress intensified. The Republicans pressed for more tax revenue cuts, such as the elimination of the "death tax" (estate taxes) and the "marriage penalty" (taxes on two-income families), while the president held out for using the projected surplus to support Social Security, expand Medicare, and reduce the national debt.

Investigations and Impeachment. From the early days of the Clinton presidency, President Clinton, his wife, Hillary, cabinet members, and other associates had been under investigation by Congress and by congressionally appointed independent prosecutors (a legacy of the independent prosecutor law of the Watergate era). Some Democrats viewed these investigations as a "right-wing conspiracy" to overturn the elections of 1992 and 1996. After long and expensive investigations, the Clintons were not charged with illegalities in the Whitewater real estate deal, the firings of White House staff ("Travelgate"), or the political use of FBI files ("Filegate"). However, independent prosecutor Kenneth Starr charged that President Clinton, during his deposition in a civil suit about alleged sexual harassment while governor of Arkansas, had lied about his relations with a young woman who had served as a White House intern.

Impeachment. In December 1998, the House voted to impeach the president on two counts, perjury and obstruction of justice. Members of both parties and the public condemned Clinton's reckless personal behavior, but popular opinion did not support the largely Republican attempt to remove him from office. In the fall elections, Democrats gained House seats and Newt Gingrich resigned as speaker. In February 1999, after a formal trial in the Senate, neither impeachment charge was upheld even by a Senate majority, much less the two-thirds vote needed to remove a president from office. However, the Republicans damaged Clinton's reputation by making him the first president to be impeached since 1868. A weary Congress in 2000 allowed the controversial law establishing the independent prosecutor's office to lapse.

Foreign Policy in the Clinton Administration

The end of the Cold War, while taking away the Soviet threat, exposed dozens of long-standing ethnic, religious, and cultural conflicts in a world of 190 nations. During Clinton's first term, Secretary of State Warren Christopher conducted a low-key foreign policy, which critics thought lacked coherent purpose. In 1997 Madeleine K. Albright became the first women to serve as secretary of state. She proved more assertive in the use of American power, but questions still remained about the role of the United States, especially the use of its armed forces for peacekeeping in foreign nations' internal conflicts.

Peacekeeping. The first deaths of U.S. soldiers in humanitarian missions during the Clinton administration came in the civil war in Somalia in 1993. In 1994, after some reluctance, the president sent 20,000 troops into Haiti to restore its elected president, Jean-Bertrand Aristide, after a military coup and deteriorating economic conditions had caused an exodus of Haitians to Florida. The United States also played a key diplomatic role in negotiating an end to British rule and the armed conflict in Nothern Ireland in 1998.

Europe. Under President Boris Yeltsin, Russia struggled with attempted economic reforms and rampant corruption. In 2000 his elected successor, Vladimir Putin, had to deal with the physical breakdown of systems, such as Russia's space station, and the accidental sinking of a nuclear submarine, which killed all on board. Relations with the United States were strained by Russia's brutal repression of the civil war in Chechnya, the admittance in 1999 of the Czech Republic, Hungary, and Poland to NATO, and by Russia's support of Serbia in the Balkan wars of the 1990s. In the latter, Serbian dictator Solobodan Milosevic carried out a series of armed conflicts to suppress independence movements in the former Yugoslav provinces of Slovenia, Croatia, Bosnia, and Kosovo. Hundreds of thousands of members of ethnic and religious minorities were killed in a process that was labeled "ethnic cleansing." A combination of diplomacy, bombing, and troops from NATO countries, including the United States, stopped the bloodshed first in Bosnia in 1995 and again in Kosovo in 1999. The Serbian people themselves removed Milosevic from power in the 2000 election, and an international tribunal tried him for the crime of genocide. These Balkan wars proved to be the worst conflict Europe had seen since World War II, and were a troubling reminder of how World War I had started.

Asia. Nuclear proliferation became a growing concern in the 1990s, when North Korea stepped up its nuclear reactor and missile programs, and India and Pakistan tested nuclear weapons for the first time in 1998. North Korea agreed to halt the development of nuclear weapons after direct negotiations with the Clinton administration, but later secretly restarted the program. In 1995, 20 years after the fall of Saigon to the Communists, the United States established diplomatic relations with Vietnam. The Clinton administration continued to sign trade agreements with China through his second term, hoping to improve diplomatic relations and encourage reform within China, despite protests from human rights activists and labor unions at home, and Chinese threats to the still-independent island nation of Taiwan.

Middle East. Iraqi leader Saddam Hussein's continued defiance of UN weapons inspectors led to the suspension of all inspections in 1998. President Clinton responded with a series of air strikes against Iraq, but Hussein remained in power, as support for U.S. economic sanctions declined in Europe and the Middle East. The United States continued to assist in the Israeli-Palestinian peace process, which resulted in the return of home rule to the Palestinians in the Gaza strip and parts of the West Bank territories, and the signing of a peace treaty with King Hussein of Jordan in 1994. The peace process slowed after the assassination of Israeli Prime Minister Yitzak Rabin in 1995, and it broke down late in 2000 over issues of Israeli security and control of Jerusalem. Renewed violence in Israel also provoked a new round of anti-American sentiment in the Islamic world.

Globalization. The surging increases in trade, communications, and the movement of capital around the world during this era were key parts of the process of *globalization*. Globalization promoted the development of global and regional economic organizations. The World Trade Organization (WTO) was established in 1994 to oversee trade agreements, enforce trade rules, and settle disputes. The powerful International Monetary Fund (IMF) and the World Bank made loans to and supervised the economic policies of poorer nations with debt troubles. The European Union (EU) became a unified market of 15 nations, 12 of which adopted a single currency, the euro, in 2002. The EU planned to grow to 25 European nations, and promised to become an economic superpower of the 21st century. The Group of Seven (G-7), the world's largest industrial powers (Canada, France, Germany, Italy, Japan, the United Kingdom, and the United States), which controlled two-thirds of the world's wealth, remained the leading economic powers, but China and India enjoyed rapid development. The growing gap between the rich and poor nations of the world caused tensions, especially over the debts the poor nations owed to powerful banks and the richest nations. Workers and unions in the richest nations often resented globalization, however, because they lost their jobs to cheaper labor markets in the developing world.

A CHANGING AMERICAN SOCIETY

According to the 2000 census, the resident population of the United States was 281.4 million, making it the third most populous nation in the world. The 32.7-million-person increase since 1990 represented a growth rate of 13.2 percent over the decade. The fastest-growing regions of the United States in the 1990s continued to be centered in the West (19.7 percent) and in the South (17.3 percent), while slower growth took place in the Midwest (7.9 percent) and the Northeast (5.9 percent). The South, the most populous region with over 100 million people, and the West would continue to enjoy the shift of congressional representatives and electoral votes to their regions, which had helped to make them the centers of political power. The 2000 census reported that more than 80 percent of U.S. residents lived in the nation's 280 metropolitan areas, which included cities and their surrounding suburbs.

Race and origins. In the 2000 census, Americans could identify their origins by two or more races for the first time, which 6.8 million people did. The white-only population, while growing in numbers, continued to decline as a percentage of the population, from 87.5 percent in 1970 to 75.1 percent in 2000. This was largely a result of lower birthrates and shifts in sources of immigration. The percentage of black-only population was 12.3 in 2000, up from 11.1 in 1970. However, the Hispanic population, whose origins may be of any race, was the fastest-growing segment of the population. In 2000, for the first time, Hispanics emerged as the largest minority group in the nation, with 12.5 percent of the U.S. population. Asian Americans also represented another fast-growing part of society, with a population of over 10 million.

By 2000, 10.4 percent of the population was foreign born, the largest percentage since the 1930 census, but well below the levels of foreigh-born population that the United States had in the 1870s through the 1920s. Immigration accounted for 27.8 percent of the population increase the 1990s, and was a key stimulus to the economic growth during the decade. Without immigration, it is predicted that the United States could experience a negative population growth by 2030.

Aging and the family. As the United States becomes more ethnically diverse, the population is also "graying," with a steady increase in life expectancy. By 2000, 35 million people were over 65 (12.3 percent), but the fastest-growing segment of the population was those 85 and over. As the baby-boom generation ages, there is growing concern about health care, prescription drugs, senior housing, and Social Security. It is extimated that in 2030 that there will be only about two workers for every person receiving Social Security.

The decline of the traditional family and the growing number of single-parent families had become another national concern. The number of families headed by a female with no husband soared from 5.5 million (10.7 percent) in 1970 to 12.8 million (17.6 percent) in 2000. Single women headed an alarming 47.2 percent of black families in 2000, but the same trend was also evident in white and Hispanic households with children under 18. Children in these families often grew up in poverty and without adequate support.

Income and wealth. In many ways, Americans were achieving the American dream. Homeownership continued to climb during the prosperity of the 1990s to 67.4 percent of all households, up from 62.9 percent in 1970. Per-capita money income in constant (inflation-adjusted) dollars rose dramatically, from $12,275 in 1970 to $22,199 in 2000. However, the distribution of income varied widely by race, gender, and education. For example, the median income in 2000 was $53,256 for white families, $35,054 for Hispanic families, and $34,192 for black families. High school graduates earned only half the income of their college-educated counterparts.

Even more pronounced was the growing concentration of wealth among the richest Americans. In 1999 the top fifth of American households earned over half of all income, up from 44.2 percent in 1977. All other categories saw their share of income decline. The average after-tax income actually declined between 1977 and 1997 for the lowest three-fifths of households. The United States entered the 21st century as the richest country in the world. But of all the leading industrialized nations, it also had the lartgest gap between lowest and highest paid workers and the greatest concentration of wealth among the top-earning households. Some critics of the change called it the new Gilded Age.

Average Income, by Household Group, 1977 and 1999					
Household Groups	**Share of All Income**		**Average After-Tax Income (Estimated)**		**Change**
	1977	1999	1977	1999	
One-fifth with lowest income	5.7%	5.2%	$10,000	$8,800	−12.0%
Next lowest one-fifth	11.5%	9.7%	$22,100	$20,000	−9.5%
Middle one-fifth	16.4%	14.7%	$32,400	$31,400	−3.1%
Next highest one-fifth	22.8%	21.3%	$42,600	$45,100	+5.9%
One-fifth with highest income	44.2%	50.4%	$74,000	$102,300	+38.3%
1 Percent with highest income	*7.3%*	*12.9%*	*$234,700*	*$515,600*	*+119.7%*

Figures do not equal 100 because of rounding.
Source: Congressional Budget Office

The Lone Superpower in a New Century

The United States entered the 21st century in a position of unrivaled economic and military dominance in the world, yet it was vulnerable to new kinds of attacks. The first election of the new century gave the new president, George W. Bush, the opportunity to pursue the conservative domestic and foreign policies of the administrations of his father and Ronald Reagan.

Disputed Election of 2000

Vice President Al Gore easily captured the presidential nomination of the Democratic party. Gore selected Senator Joseph Lieberman of Connecticut for his vice president, the first Jewish American to run for national office. Governor George W. Bush of Texas, eldest son of former President George H. Bush, gained the nomination of the Republican party, and selected Dick Cheney, his father's secretary of defense, as his running mate. Both candidates fought over the moderate and independent vote, Gore as a champion of "working families" and Bush running as a "compassionate conservative." Ralph Nader, the candidate for the liberal Green party, ran a distant third, but in one of the closest presidential elections in United States history, he may have made the difference in states like Florida.

Gore received over 500,000 more popular votes nationwide than Bush, out of over 105 millions votes cast, but victory hinged on who won Florida's 25 electoral votes. Bush led by only 537 popular votes in Florida after a partial recount, but Democrats asked for an additional manual recount, because many punch-card ballots were undercounted. The Supreme Court of Florida ordered

PRESIDENTIAL ELECTION 2000, ELECTORAL VOTES BY STATE

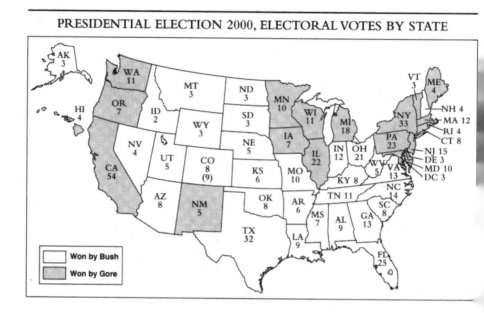

hand recounts of the votes, but the Republicans appealed the decision in the federal courts. In the case *Bush v. Gore*, the U.S. Supreme Court, in a split 5-4 decision, essentially made George W. Bush president. The court majority ruled that the varying standards used in Florida's hand recount violated the equal-protection clause of the 14th Amendment, and that there was not enough time left to conduct a lawful recount. Vice President Gore ended the election crisis by accepting the Supreme Court's ruling. Governor Bush won with 271 electoral votes against Gore's 266 (one Democratic elector abstained), in the closest victory since the disputed election of 1876.

The Rise of Southern Republicans

The election of George W. Bush in 2000 and the congressional elections in 2002 confirmed the impact of the Reagan Revolution on domestic politics. Ronald Reagan's presidency legitimized the Republican party among conservative white southerners, who had solidly supported the Democratic party since the days of the Reconstruction. Southern conservatives had increasingly voted for Republican presidential candidates since the campaign of Barry Goldwater in 1964, but it was not until the 1980s and 1990s that a majority voted for Republicans in House and Senate races. The results transformed American politics, and were the dynamic behind the conservative resurgence of the era. Southern conservatives like Gingrich, Dick Armey, Tom DeLay, and Trent Lott took over the leadership of the Republican party in the Congress, and, especially after the 1994 election, made the party more conservative and partisan. The shift of white conservative voters in the South clearly cost the Democrats their control of Congress, which dated back to the New Deal. The former Confederate states bacame a Republican stronghold for the first time since Reconstruction. The "Solid South" was now Republican, and helped to transform the party of Lincoln into the party of Ronald Reagan.

Domestic Policies and Problems

President Bush, although not the choice of the majority of voters, aggressively pushed his conservative agenda: tax cuts, federal aid to faith-based service organizations, school choice, privatization of Social Security and Medicare, opposition to *Roe v. Wade*, drilling for oil and gas in the Alaska wildlife refuge, and voluntary environmental standards.

Republican tax cut. In 2001, Congress passed a $1.35 trillion tax cut, spread over ten years. The bill gave all taxpayers an immediate $300 or $600 rebate, reduced all tax brackets, and increased both child credit and limits for IRA and 401(k) contributions. Many Democrats attacked the bill for giving half of the tax cuts to the top 2 percent of income-earners, by lowering the top tax bracket from 39.5 to 35 percent and eliminating estate taxes of the wealthy over a ten-year period. When the tax cut was passed, the government was running a surplus, and the stock market was at one of its highs.

Education reform. In 2002 President Bush signed a bipartisan education bill, the No Child Left Behind Act. The act aimed to improve student performance and close the gap between well-to-do and poor students in the public schools through nationwide testing of all students, student transfer rights to better public schools, improved reading programs, and training of high-quality teachers. Later in 2002, the Supreme Court in a 5–4 decision ruled that local government funding of school vouchers for religious schools did not violate the "establishment of religion" clause of the First Amendment. These victories for school-choice advocates put more pressure on public schools to raise student performance or lose funding.

Recession of 2001. The technology boom of the 1990s came to an end in 2000. The stock market crashed, and the Dow Jones Industrial Average fell by 38 percent from its highs in 2000 to its lows in 2002. The country experienced in 2001 its first recession since the early 1990s. By 2002, the unemployment rate had climbed to 6 percent, the highest in eight years, while the number of people living in poverty increased for the first time in eight years. The Federal Reserve fought the recession by cutting interest rates to 1.25 percent, the lowest in 50 years. The recession, along with Bush's tax cuts and increased defense spending, turned the surplus of the past Clinton budgets into more than a $400-billion annual deficit by 2004.

Corporate corruption. Fraud and dishonesty committed by business leaders also hurt the stock market and consumer confidence in the economy.

Large corporations, such as Enron and WorldCom, had "cooked their books" (falsified earnings and profits), with the help of accounting companies and lenders. Public opinion forced the president and Congress to call for strengthening the regulatory powers of the Securities and Exchange Commission and jail time for those convicted of these white-collar crimes. Revelations of corporate corruption gave new life to a congressional bill to stop the flood of special-interest money into political campaigns. The law that passed banned unlimited donations, known as "soft money," to political parties. However, it did not stop advertising by special interest groups.

The War on Terrorism

Terrorism and nations suspected of supporting it dominated U.S. foreign policy after September 11, 2001. George W. Bush entered the White House with no foreign policy experience, but surrounded himself with veterans of prior Republican administrations. General Colin Powell, his secretary of state, became the first African American to hold the position. President Bush's confident and aggressive approach won over his fellow Americans, but promoted criticism of the United States around the world and even among allies.

Roots of terrorism. The United States was faulted by many in the Arab world for siding with Israel in the deadly cycle of Palestinian terror-bombings and Israeli reprisals that killed hundreds of innocent people. However, the causes of anti-Americanism often went deeper. After World War I, the Ottoman Empire, the last of the Islamic empires, was replaced in the Middle East by Western-style secular nation-states. Religious fundamentalists decried modernization and the corruption of "the House of Islam," an ancient Islamic ideal of a realm governed by the precepts of the Qur'an. The stationing of American troops in the Middle East after the Persian Gulf War was seen as another violation of their lands. Resurgent Islamic fundamentalism, along with poor economies and despotic political conditions in the Middle East, provided extremists with a fertile breeding ground for new recruits. The former included Osama bin Laden and his associates in al Qaeda ("the Base") who preached *jihad*, or holy war, against the "Jews and Crusaders."

The bombing of the World Trade Center in New York City in 1993 brought home for the first time the threat posed by these extremists. In 1998, the United States responded to the terrorist bombing of two U.S. embassies in Kenya and Tanzania by bombing al Qaeda camps in Afghanistan and the Sudan. Osama bin Laden had been identified as a leader and financial supporter of this terrorism, and under U.S. pressure he fled to Afghanistan. There he allied himself with the Taliban, the Islamic extremists who ruled the country.

September 11, 2001. The terrorist attacks on the twin towers of the World Trade Center in New York, the Pentagon in Washington, D.C., and the downing of a fourth plane in Pennsylvania, which altogether claimed over 3000 lives, galvanized public opinion as nothing had done since the attack on Pearl Harbor in 1941. President Bush aggressively pursued al Qaeda and Osama bin Laden ("Wanted: Dead or Alive") and gained the support of Congress and most nations, including Pakistan and Russia, to pursue and root out terrorists. In the United States, the assets of groups suspected of supporting terrorism were frozen, suspects were rounded up, and an executive order set up secret hearings and military tribunals to try foreigners accused of terrorism. After this watershed event, most Americans accepted background checks, airport and border searches, detentions, and new police powers, but some questioned the loss of privacy and civil liberties.

War in Afghanistan. After the Taliban refused to turn over bin Laden and his associates, their government was quickly overthrown in the fall of 2001 by a combination of U.S. bombing, anti-Taliban Northern Alliance troops, and American Special Forces. Into 2003, U.S. and Afghan forces continued to pursue the remnants of al Qaeda in the mountains bordering Pakistan, but they failed to capture bin Laden. Afghanistan remained unstable and divided by tribal conflicts and Taliban sympathizers.

Homeland security. First the Democrats, then the president, called for a new cabinet position for domestic defense. The Homeland Security Department combined over 20 federal agencies with 170,000 employees, including Customs, Immigration and Naturalization, the Coast Guard, and the Secret Service, in one of the largest government reorganizations since the creation of the Department of Defense after World War II. Many in Congress questioned why the FBI and the CIA were left out of the new department. In 2004 a bipartisan national commission on terrorism also criticized the FBI and the CIA, as well as the Defense Department, for failing to work together to "connect the dots" and uncover the September 11 plot. Under pressure from the families of 9/11 victims, Congress finally passed most of the commission's recommendations, including creating a Director of National Intelligence to coordinate the intelligence activities of often-competing bureaucracies.

Changing foreign policy. The Bush administration worked with European nations and Russia to expand the European Union and NATO, helped admit China to the World Trade Organization, and brokered conflicts between the nuclear powers of India and Pakistan. However, the Bush administration also refused to join the Kyoto accord to prevent global warming, walked out of the United Nations conference on racism, and abandoned the 1972 Anti-Ballistic Missile Treaty with Russia. Critics questioned whether the administration valued negotiation and cooperation with the nations of the world, or followed a unilateralist approach of the world's only military superpower. The threat of weapons of mass destruction in the hands of terrorists gave the Bush foreign policy team cause to question prior foreign policies. President Bush argued that the old policies of containment and nuclear deterrence were no longer effective in a world of stateless terrorists. To protect itself from its new foes, America would have to strike first.

Results of Midterm Elections

President Bush and the Republicans successfully made the war on terrorism the main issue of the congressional elections of 2002. The Republicans took control of the Senate again and strengthened their majority in the House. For the first time since the 1950s, the Republicans controlled both houses of Congress and the White House, and conservatives carried the Supreme Court on most issues.

President Bush used the election returns to push through another round of tax cuts, which included the elimination of taxes on stock dividends for investors and the reduction of taxes for married couples. Opponents argued that half of the tax cuts went to the richest 10 percent of the population, and the cuts were irresponsible during wartime. Congress also fulfilled a campaign promise of President Bush to provide prescription drug coverage for seniors.

War in Iraq

In his first State of the Union address, in January 2002, President Bush singled out Iraq, along with North Korea and Iran, as the "axis of evil." American intelligence found no link between Iraq's Saddam Hussein and the September 11 attacks, but the Bush administration pursued a preemptive attack on Iraq before Saddam Hussein could build and distribute "weapons of mass destruction" (nuclear and biological) to terrorists. Critics of the policy, overseas and at home, charged that the real purpose of a war was "regime change," and that the administration failed to work with its allies and the United Nations. Late in 2002, Secretary of State Powell negotiated an inspection plan with the UN Security Council, which Iraq accepted. In the following months, UN inspectors failed to find weapons of mass destruction in Iraq.

In 2003, President Bush declared that Iraq had not complied with numerous UN resolutions since 1991, and "the game was over." Without winning support of the UN Security Council, the United States launched the war on March 19, with an air attack. In less than four weeks, a combination of U.S. and British armed forces in "Operation Iraqi Freedom" overran Iraqi defenses, captured the capital, Baghdad, and ended Hussein's dictatorship. However, the defeat of the Iraq army and the capture of Saddam Hussein in December 2003 did not end the violence.

Diverse groups of Iraqi insurgents, many of them followers of the former dictator, and foreign fighters, some with connections to al Qaeda, tried to stop the political and physical reconstruction of Iraq. By mid-2005, more than 1,700 American soldiers had been killed and over 13,000 wounded in Iraq.

The Bush administration faced criticism, especially from abroad, for going to war with faulty intelligence about "weapons of mass destruction," which were never found. The conduct of the war was also questioned for an inadequate number of U.S. troops sent to Iraq, a failure to create a viable Iraqi army and police force, and the abusive treatment of prisoners held by U.S. forces. However, President Bush defended the war as part of his campaign against terrorism and goal of bringing democracy to the Middle East. The reconstruction of Iraq gained ground in 2005 when the Iraqis held their first free election and created a national assembly, which selected a prime minister, cabinet ministries, and a committee to write a new constitution. The Sunni minority that ruled Iraq under Saddam Hussein also began working with the Shiite majority and the Kurds in the new government, which lessened chances of civil war among the factions in Iraq.

Elections of 2004

America entered the 2004 elections divided not only over the war in Iraq, but also by the limited economic recovery, tax cuts and the deficit, and social issues such as gay marriage, abortion, and the role of religion in public institutions. The Democrats were optimistic as they faced an incumbent president with an approval rating of only 50 percent. Democratic voters in the primaries selected Senator John Kerry of Massachusetts as their presidential candidate, and he chose a rival in the primaries, Senator John Edwards of North Carolina, as his running mate. Senator Kerry attacked President Bush for his handling of the war in Iraq, favoring drug and insurance companies, pushing tax cuts for the wealthy, and running up huge federal deficits.

President Bush ran on his popular image as a strong and consistent leader in the war and a compassionate conservative at home. He successfully painted his opponent as a "flip-flopper" on defense issues and a "tax-and-spend liberal." The Bush-Cheney campaign successfully energized its conservative base on issues such as tax cuts, gay marriage, abortion, and the liberal media. Bush also benefited from the feeling that a wartime president and his team should have the opportunity to finish the job in Iraq.

In the November 2004 election, unlike the election of 2000, George W. Bush won both the popular vote and a clear electoral-college vote majority. President Bush defeated Senator Kerry by about 3.5 million votes (51 percent), and captured 286 electoral votes to his opponent's 252. The country remained divided, much as it was in 2000. (See the electoral vote map on page 662.) Republicans won by heavy majorities in the South and the Western heartland (adding Iowa and New Mexico in 2004), while the Democrats retained the urban Northeast (adding New Hampshire in 2004) and the West Coast states. Republicans also expanded their majorities in the Senate and House, and continued to gain on the state level, especially in the South, which left the party in the strongest position it had enjoyed since the 1920s.

Both parties agreed that the Republicans used volunteers more successfully than the Democrats in registering and getting out their voters. Some analysts interpreted the election results as revealing a deep cultural divide between sophisticated, diverse, and international-minded coastal urban centers that voted Democratic, and more traditional, religious, and nationalistic rural and small-town areas that went Republican. Democrats were left to wonder why low- and middle-income workers continued seemingly to go against their own economic interests and vote Republican for moral issues, such as gay marriages.

In his second term, President Bush interpreted the election not only as a mandate to continue his foreign policy, but also to replace part of the Social Security system with private investment accounts. This was part of an effort to move Americans from dependence on government programs toward what he called an "ownership society." The president, with the support of a 55-vote Republican majority in the Senate, was also in a position to fill federal court vacancies with conservative judges. By 2005, the conservative political resurgence of the 1980s and 1990s seemed nearly complete.

HISTORICAL PERSPECTIVES: FREEDOM AND FEDERALISM

It is too early to understand fully the importance of events from the last two decades of the 20th century, but certain trends are apparent. Basic concepts such as "freedom" and "rights" were being reshaped by conservative politics. In the decades after the New Deal and World War II, freedom was associated with economic security and the enjoyment of equal rights, which were largely guaranteed by federal government laws and court interpretations of constitutional amendments. In the 1980s and 1990s, freedom was frequently defined as the absence of "big" government and federal regulations. Eric Foner, in *The Story of American Freedom* (1999), attributed this change to reactions to forced desegregation in the 1950s and 1960s, liberal court rulings banning prayer in schools, and laws and court decisions allowing free speech and abortion rights. Many conservative commentators equated freedom with unregulated capitalism. Foner argued, for example, that the freedom of speech issues in the 1990s were raised not by radicals, but by corporate interests fighting limits on campaign financing and restrictions on the concentrated ownership of the media.

President Reagan had resurrected the states' right debate in his 1980 Inaugural Address (Document A, p. 672). As Congress shifted more responsibilities back to the states, conservative majorities on the Supreme Court in the 1990s also reasserted the states' sovereignty and the immunity of the states to federal laws. Whether the states or the federal government can better protect the rights of citizens often depends on how one defines such basic concepts as "freedom," and on one's view of the history of federal–state conflicts from the time of Hamilton and Jefferson through the modern civil rights movement. In the early 21st century, it seems fairly certain that the balance between the powers of the federal government and the state governments will remain a central issue for the nation and for students of its history.

KEY NAMES, EVENTS, AND TERMS

conservatism

religious fundamentalism

political action committees (PACs)

abortion rights; *Roe v. Wade*

reverse discrimination

Regents of University of California v. Bakke

Ronald Reagan

supply-side economics (Reaganomics)

Sandra Day O'Connor; William Rehnquist

budget and trade deficits

"evil empire"

Strategic Defense Initiative (Star Wars)

Nicaragua; Sandinistas; Iran-contra affair

Middle East; Palestine Liberation Organization

Mikhail Gorbachev; *glasnost, perestroika*

George H. Bush, Dan Quayle

Soviet Union breakup; end of Cold War

Boris Yeltsin

Panama invasion (1989)

Saddam Hussein

Persian Gulf War (1991)

Operation Desert Storm

Americans With Disabilities Act (1990)

William (Bill) Clinton, Albert Gore

North American Free Trade Agreement (NAFTA)

Oklahoma City bombing

e-commerce

Clinton impeachment and trial

Madeleine K. Albright

Yugoslavia breakup; Balkan Wars: Bosnia, Kosovo; "ethnic cleansing"

nuclear proliferation

globalization

World Trade Organization

European Union (EU); euro

metropolitan areas

George W. Bush, Dick Cheney

Bush v. Gore

education reform; No Child Left Behind Act

corporate corruption

campaign-finance reform

terrorism, war on

September 11, 2001 attacks on the U.S.

al Qaeda; Osama bin Laden

Afghanistan

"axis of evil"

Homeland Security Department

Iraq; "weapons of mass destruction"

"regime change"

preemptive strike

UN inspections

Colin Powell

Iraq war; Operation Iraqi Freedom

MULTIPLE-CHOICE QUESTIONS

1. The conservative movement by 1980 was supported by all of the following EXCEPT
   (A) Moral Majority
   (B) advocates of gun control
   (C) opponents of affirmative action
   (D) critics of "secular humanism"
   (E) citizens against increased taxes

2. All of the following were part of Reaganomics EXCEPT
   (A) cuts of benefits from Medicare and Social Security to seniors
   (B) a dramatic reduction in personal income taxes
   (C) deregulation of business and industry
   (D) tough stand against federal labor unions, such as PATCO
   (E) the theory of supply-side economics

3. Ronald Reagan's greatest strength or achievement as president was
   (A) the reduction of federal deficits
   (B) his hands-on administration of the federal government
   (C) initiating the improvement of relations with the Soviet Union
   (D) his ability to communicate traditional values and restore confidence
   (E) increasing the standard of living of middle-class Americans

4. All of the following were true of the Iran-contra affair EXCEPT

   (A) Reagan advisers tried to exchange American hostages for a weapons deal
   (B) antitank and antiaircraft missiles were sold to Iran
   (C) funds were used to support rebels against Saddam Hussein
   (D) the arms deal violated the law and congressional restrictions
   (E) Democrats hoped that the scandal would help them in the 1988 election

5. President George H. Bush received his greatest public approval for
   (A) the appointment of the first African American to the Supreme Court
   (B) his conduct of foreign affairs in the Middle East
   (C) his landmark legislation to improve American education
   (D) holding the line against tax increases
   (E) the invasion of Grenada

6. The election of Bill Clinton in 1992 was most closely associated with the slogan or phrase:
   (A) "It's the economy, stupid!"
   (B) "Government is not the solution, it is the problem."
   (C) "Teflon president"
   (D) "Read my lips—no new taxes."
   (E) "baby-boomers" and "yuppies"

7. Which of the following was NOT true of the American economy during the Reagan and George H. Bush administrations?

(A) The upper 20 percent of households gained a larger share of the national income.

(B) The national debt increased over four times of what is was in 1980.

(C) The median family income remained stagnant.

(D) The United States became a debtor nation for the first time since World War I.

(E) Deregulation reduced the competitiveness of American business.

8. Bill Clinton's popularity during his presidency can be attributed mainly to

(A) willingness to take on unpopular causes, such as gay rights

(B) successes in foreign affairs and peacekeeping

(C) improving economic conditions for average Americans

(D) ability to work with Congress

(E) incremental approach to legislation

9. The extreme partisanship of the Clinton era is illustrated by all of the following EXCEPT:

(A) shutdowns of the federal government

(B) debates over tax cuts

(C) investigations by independent prosecutors

(D) impeachment and trial of Clinton

(E) NAFTA and Chinese trade agreements

10. Which of the following problems during the Clinton presidency presented the most serious possibility of developing into an international crisis?

(A) conflict in northern Ireland

(B) civil war in Somalia

(C) nuclear weapons program in North Korea

(D) civil war in the Balkans

(E) terrorism in Yemen

11. For the nation in the last two decades of the 20th century

(A) the fastest population growth was centered in the Northeast and Midwest states

(B) the increased birthrate contributed to a younger median age

(C) a growing percentage of adults and children lived in nuclear families

(D) Hispanic Americans became the fastest growing and largest minority group

(E) the reduction in violent crime contributed to smaller prison populations

12. The growing strength of the Republican party in Congress and on the national level in the 1980s and 1990s can be primarily attributed to the

(A) campaign finance and election reform championed by Republicans in the 1970s

(B) shift of white conservative voters in the South from the Democratic to the Republican party

(C) conservative fiscal policies and debt reduction under the Reagan and two Bush administrations

(D) improper behavior by and

impeachment of President Bill Clinton

(E) voters' fears of terrorist attacks and interest in homeland security

ESSAY QUESTIONS

1. Analyze the causes of the resurgence of conservative politics in the United States in the 1980s and 1990s.

2. Evaluate the role of TWO of the following in ending the Cold War:

   Ronald Reagan

   Mikhail Gorbachev

   Boris Yeltsin

   George H. Bush

3. Assess the impact of the Reagan administration on the politics and the economy of the United States.

4. To what extent were the peacekeeping efforts of the United States success-

ful in TWO of the following areas during the George H. Bush and Clinton presidencies?

   Middle East

   Europe

   Western Hemisphere

5. Analyze the political decisions and economic changes in the 1990s that helped to create the prosperity experienced during the Clinton presidency.

6. How and why did terrorism become a focus of American foreign policy after the end of the Cold War?

DOCUMENTS AND READINGS

DOCUMENT A.   CRITIQUE OF BIG GOVERNMENT

When Ronald Reagan became the 40th President of the United States at 69 years of age, he was the oldest person to assume the presidency. More important, he was the most conservative politician to occupy the White House in 50 years. In the following selections from his first inaugural address, the president presented his views on the federal government.

These United States are confronted with an economic affliction of great proportion. We suffer from the longest and one of the worst sustained inflations in our national history. It distorts our economic decisions, penalizes thrift, and crushes the struggling young and the fixed-income elderly alike. . . . Those who work are denied a fair return for their labor by a tax system which penalizes successful achievement and keeps us from maintaining full productivity. . . .

In this present crisis, government is not the solution to our problem; government is the problem. From time to time we've been tempted to believe that society has become too complex to be managed by self-rule, that government by an elite group is superior to government for, by, and of the people. Well, if no one among us is capable of governing himself, then who among us has the capacity to govern someone else?

. . . It is my intention to curb the size and influence of the federal establishment and to demand recognition of the distinction between the powers granted to the Federal government and those reserved to the States or to the people. All of us need to be reminded that the Federal government did not create the States; the States created the Federal Government. . . .

. . . It is no coincidence that our present troubles parallel and are proportionate to the intervention and intrusion in our lives that result from unnecessary and excessive growth of government. It is time for us to realize that we're too great a nation to limit ourselves to small dreams. . . .

In the days ahead I will propose removing the roadblocks that have slowed our economy and reduced productivity. . . . It is time to reawaken this industrial giant, to get government back within its means, and to lighten our punitive tax burden. And these will be our first priorities, and on these principles there will be no compromise. . . .

President Ronald Reagan,
Inaugural Address, January 20, 1981

DOCUMENT B.   *AN EVIL EMPIRE*

President Reagan faced opposition to his costly military buildup both at home and overseas. He was also criticized for his undiplomatic statements, such as calling the Soviet Union "an evil empire," a term from the movie *Star Wars* (1977). However, supporters countered that Reagan was right and that his policies brought down communism decades before it would have collapsed on it own.

Yes, let us pray for the salvation of all of those who live in totalitarian darkness—pray they will discover the joy of knowing God. But until they do, let us be aware that while they preach the supremacy of the state, declare its omnipotence over individual man, and predict its eventual domination of all peoples on the Earth, they are the focus of evil in the modern world. . . . But if history teaches anything, it teaches that simple-minded appeasement or wishful thinking about our adversaries is folly. It means the betrayal of our past, the squandering of our freedom.

So, I urge you to speak out against those who would place the United States in a position of military and moral inferiority. . . . So, in your discussions of the nuclear-freeze proposals, I urge you to beware of the temptation of pride—the temptation of blithely declaring yourselves above it all and label both sides equally at fault, to ignore the facts of history and the aggressive impulses of an evil empire, to simply call the arms race a giant misunderstanding and thereby remove yourself from the struggle between right and wrong and good and evil.

I believe we shall rise to the challenge. I believe that communism is another sad, bizarre chapter in human history whose last pages even now are being written. . . .

Yes, change your world. One of our Founding Fathers, Thomas Paine, said, "We have it within our power to begin the world over again."

President Ronald Reagan
Remarks at the Convention of Evangelicals, March 8, 1983

DOCUMENT C. *THE GULF WAR AND THE NEW WORLD ORDER*

As the Cold War came to a conclusion, many Americans questioned what would be the future role of the United States in the world. What would be the role of NATO? the United Nations? The invasion of oil-rich Kuwait by Iraq provided some answers.

The United States, together with the United Nations, exhausted every means at our disposal to bring this crisis to a peaceful end. However, Saddam clearly felt that by stalling and threatening and defying the United Nations, he could weaken the forces arrayed against him.

While the world waited, Saddam Hussein met every overture of peace with open contempt. While the world prayed for peace, Saddam prepared for war. . . .

Saddam was warned over and over again to comply with the will of the United Nations: Leave Kuwait, or be driven out. Saddam has arrogantly rejected all warnings. Instead, he tried to make this a dispute between Iraq and the United States of America.

Well, he failed. Tonight, 28 nations—countries from 5 continents, Europe and Asia, Africa and the Arab League—have forces in the Gulf area standing shoulder to shoulder against Saddam Hussein. These countries had hoped the use of force could be avoided. Regrettably, we now believe that only force will make him leave. . . .

This is an historic moment. We have in this past year made great progress in ending the long era of conflict and cold war. We have before us the opportunity to forge for ourselves and for future generations a new world order—a world where the rule of law, not the law of the jungle, governs the conduct of nations. When we are successful—and we will be—we have a real chance at this new world order, an order in which a credible United Nations can use its peacekeeping role to fulfill the promise and vision of the U.N.'s founders.

President George H. Bush,
Address to the Nation, January 16, 1990

DOCUMENT D. COMPETING IN THE NEW WORLD ECONOMY

Many Democrats, especially those with close ties to labor unions, opposed the North American Free Trade Agreement because they feared U.S. jobs would be exported to Mexico, which had much lower wage scales. President Clinton proved a "new" or centrist Democrat by finally supporting the treaty after resolving some reservations about it. He made the following statement after the Senate narrowly passed the treaty.

Tonight's vote is a defining moment for our nation. At a time when many of our people are hurting from the strains of this tough global economy, we chose to compete, not to retreat, to lead a new world economy, to lead as America has done so often in the past. The debate over NAFTA has been contentious. Men and women of good will raised strong arguments for and against this agreement. But every participant in this debate wanted the same things: more jobs, more security, more opportunity for every American. . . .

NAFTA is a big step, but just the first step in our effort to expand trade and spark an economic revival here and around the world. One legitimate point that the opponents of NAFTA made is that we will do even better in the global economy if we have a training system and retraining system and a job placement system for our workers worthy of the challenges they face. We simply must guarantee our workers the training and education they need to compete in the global marketplace. And I call on the coalition that passed NAFTA to help me early next year to present to Congress and pass a world-class reemployment system that will give our working people the security of knowing that they'll be able always to get the training they need as economic conditions change.

We've faced choices before like the one we faced tonight, whether to turn inward or turn outward. After World War I, the United States turned inward and built a wall of protection around our economy. The result was a depression and ultimately another world war. After the Second World War, we made a very different choice. We turned outward. We built a system of expanded trade and collective security. We rebuilt the economies of our former foes . . . [and] created the great American middle class.

Tonight, with the cold war over, our Nation is facing that choice again. And tonight, I am proud to say, we have not flinched. Tonight the leaders of both parties found common ground in supporting the common good. We voted for the future tonight. We once again showed our strength. We once again showed our self-confidence, even in this difficult time. Our people are winners. And I believe we showed tonight we are ready together to compete and win and to shape the world of the 21st century.

President Bill Clinton,
statement at news conference, November 17, 1993

ANALYZING THE DOCUMENTS

1. What are the explicit and implied criticisms of the federal government contained in Reagan's speech?

2. The containment policy had governed U.S. relations with the Soviet Union since the administration of President Truman. How would you describe President Reagan's policy toward the Soviet Union? Was it the containment policy?

3. Based on the reading and the events of the Gulf War, explain President Bush's concept of the "new world order." How does it increase the significance of the United Nations?

4. Why did President Clinton consider increased training and education as a necessary follow-up to the passage of the North American Free Trade Agreement?

5. The 1980s marked the end of the Cold War and the growth of domestic opposition to the policies of the New Deal and the Great Society. How do these readings reflect on these changes?

6. Does the statistical table on page 661 provide evidence for the analysis of Reagan's policies found in the cartoon on page 645? What other factors could have caused the changes in the distribution of income from 1977 to 1999?

Practice Examination

Section I: Multiple Choice

Time: 55 minutes   80 questions

Directions: Each of the questions or incomplete statements is followed by five answers or completions. Select the best one for each question or statement.

1. The origins of the women's rights movement in the United States may be traced to the
   - (A) Seneca Falls Convention
   - (B) Niagara Movement
   - (C) National Woman's party
   - (D) temperance movement
   - (E) outbreak of World War I

2. The economic policy that looked at colonies to provide raw materials, trade, and riches was called
   - (A) mercantilism
   - (B) manifest destiny
   - (C) gospel of wealth
   - (D) dollar diplomacy
   - (E) imperialism

3. By the end of the 1950s, many saw a growing internal threat to American democracy. President Dwight Eisenhower in his farewell address warned about the dangers of the
   - (A) quest for material goods
   - (B) segregation in the South
   - (C) worldwide threat of communism
   - (D) power of the military-industrial complex
   - (E) decline of family values

4. The primary goal of France in supporting the American Revolution was to
   - (A) assist the spread of the Catholic religion
   - (B) weaken the British Empire
   - (C) control the fur trade
   - (D) regain Canada
   - (E) increase its exports

5. During the Gilded Age, at the end of the 19th century, the question that received the LEAST attention from the Democratic and Republican parties was
   - (A) tariffs
   - (B) regulation of big business
   - (C) money, Greenbacks, and silver
   - (D) agrarian discontent
   - (E) equality for women and minorities

6. The Progressive Movement did little to protect the rights of
   - (A) consumers
   - (B) African Americans
   - (C) women
   - (D) immigrants
   - (E) city dwellers

7. Which of the following are examples of legislation enacted under President Wilson's New Freedom program?
   - (A) Forest Reserve Act and Platt Amendment
   - (B) Newlands Act and Pure Food and Drug Act

677

(C) Underwood Tariff and Federal Reserve Act

(D) Payne-Aldrich Tariff and Teller Amendment

(E) Mann-Elkins Act and Kellogg-Briand Pact

8. "Small islands not capable of protecting themselves are the proper objects for kingdoms to take under their care; but there is something very absurd in supposing a continent to be perpetually governed by an island." These words were written in the 1770s by

(A) William Pitt

(B) Thomas Paine

(C) John Locke

(D) George Washington

(E) Lord North

9. All of the following actions in the English colonies during the early colonial period suggest a tendency toward democracy EXCEPT

(A) Mayflower Compact

(B) Penn's Charter of Privileges

(C) Dominion of New England

(D) Fundamental Orders of Connecticut

(E) Virginia House of Burgesses

10. Of the many reform movements that developed from the 1820s to the Civil War, the one with the most widespread popular support was concerned with

(A) temperance

(B) mental hospitals

(C) slavery

(D) education

(E) women's rights

11. During the Cold War, United States foreign policy was guided by all of the following concepts EXCEPT

(A) containment

(B) domino theory

(C) massive retaliation

(D) flexible response

(E) peaceful coexistence

12. The 1954 Supreme Court decision in *Brown v. Board of Education of Topeka* basically overturned the earlier decision in

(A) *Gideon v. Wainwright*

(B) *Plessy v. Ferguson*

(C) *McCulloch v. Maryland*

(D) *Gibbons v. Ogden*

(E) *Dred Scott v. Sandford*

13. Of the following, the one with the most far-reaching influence on American society's development in the post–World War II period was the

(A) GI Bill

(B) baby boom

(C) Taft-Hartley Act

(D) Fair Deal program

(E) Employment Act

14. Of most significance in the Benjamin West painting of the peace negotiators at the end of the Revolution, shown on page 671, is the

(A) movement away from folk art

(B) exclusion of the French representatives

(C) missing British negotiators, suggesting unresolved problems

(D) absence of women, who were excluded from political decision-making

(E) development of native-born American artists

Courtesy, Winterthur Museum

15. In his interpretations of the Constitution, Chief Justice John Marshall consistently stressed the importance of

    (A) individual rights
    (B) balancing state and federal power
    (C) establishing judicial review
    (D) strict construction
    (E) a strong central government

16. All of the following are associated with the cultural developments of the 1920s EXCEPT

    (A) jazz
    (B) romanticism
    (C) Harlem renaissance
    (D) lost generation
    (E) functionalism

17. The most prominent consideration by Presidents Hoover and Roosevelt in their diplomatic policy in the 1930s was

    (A) economics
    (B) isolationism
    (C) Fascist aggression
    (D) expansionism
    (E) support for democracy

18. In the first half of the 19th century, Emerson, Thoreau, and others wrote about transcendentalism, which included all of the following beliefs EXCEPT that

    (A) materialistic concerns should be challenged
    (B) the pursuit of wealth was questionable
    (C) self-reliance was essential
    (D) independent thinking was vital
    (E) organized institutions were important

19. The post–World War II civil rights movement used all of the following tactics to achieve equality EXCEPT

(A) establishing a third political party

(B) filing lawsuits in federal courts

(C) securing passage of federal equal-rights legislation

(D) organizing boycotts

(E) staging sit-ins

20. Of the many New Deal agencies established by President Franklin Roosevelt in response to the Great Depression, the one that does NOT exist today is the

(A) Tennessee Valley Authority

(B) Civil Works Administration

(C) Federal Housing Administration

(D) Securities and Exchange Commission

(E) Federal Deposit Insurance Corporation

21. The independent farmer as the cornerstone of a strong nation was at the center of government policy for

(A) John Adams

(B) Alexander Hamilton

(C) Thomas Jefferson

(D) Benjamin Franklin

(E) George Washington

22. The two graphs below deal with the antebellum South. Graph A shows the increase in cotton production from 1790 on. A direct correlation with this increase is shown in Graph B, which demonstrates the increase in

(A) textile production

(B) farm machinery production

(C) investment capital

(D) slave population

(E) tobacco farms

23. The Cold War crisis that brought the United States and the Soviet Union into direct confrontation with the threat of nuclear war was

(A) placement of Soviet missiles in Cuba

(B) U-2 spyplane incident

(C) Berlin airlift

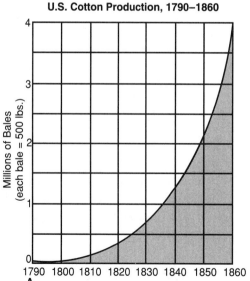

U.S. Cotton Production, 1790–1860

A

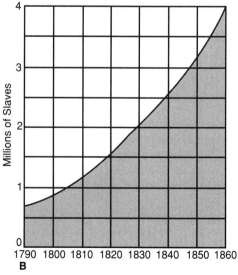

———— in the United States, 1790–1860

B

(D) Berlin Wall

(E) Bay of Pigs invasion

24. With the Revolution of 1800, the Democratic-Republicans and Thomas Jefferson gained control of the national government from the Federalists and

(A) ended neutrality in foreign policy

(B) repealed excise and whisky taxes

(C) eliminated the National Bank

(D) restructured the Supreme Court

(E) stopped debt repayment

25. In the 1920s and 1930s, isolationists often cited the words and warnings of

(A) James Madison

(B) James Monroe

(C) George Washington

(D) Theodore Roosevelt

(E) Woodrow Wilson

26. "Millions for defense, but not one cent for tribute" was the rallying cry by Americans in response to

(A) German submarine attacks

(B) Stamp Act

(C) British impressment

(D) XYZ Affair

(E) Barbary pirates

27. Which of the following is a correct statement about Abraham Lincoln's primary goal at the beginning of the Civil War?

(A) emancipate the slaves

(B) ensure federal supremacy over states' rights

(C) maintain Republican party control of Congress

(D) unite the North and the West

(E) restore the Union

28. When founded, the first political parties, the Federalists and Democratic-Republicans, had clear

positions on all of the following issues EXCEPT

(A) national debt

(B) French Revolution

(C) national bank

(D) tariffs

(E) slavery

29. During the 1920s, there was a dramatic rise in the membership and influence of the

(A) American Federation of Labor

(B) National Association for the Advancement of Colored People

(C) America First Committee

(D) Ku Klux Klan

(E) Socialist party

30. Increased popular interest in religion in America is reflected in all of the following movements EXCEPT

(A) fundamentalism

(B) Social Gospel

(C) Great Awakening

(D) Revivalism

(E) social Darwinism

31. The minority group whose economic status and civil rights were diminished during World War II were

(A) African Americans

(B) Japanese Americans

(C) Mexican Americans

(D) Native Americans

(E) womeniu3104

32. In the map on page 674, which of the land acquisitions by the United States was accompanied by the least turmoil and controversy?

(A) Gadsden Purchase

(B) Oregon country

(C) Texas

(D) Florida

(E) Mexican Cession

LANDS ADDED TO THE U.S. 1783–1853

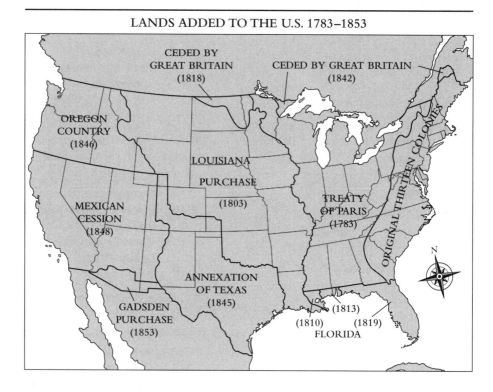

33. In the United States, tariffs have long been debated and policies often changed. Which of the following is an INCORRECT statement of U.S. tariff policy?
    (A) 1789, Hamilton's protective tariff
    (B) 1816, protective tariffs after the War of 1812
    (C) 1828, increases, in "Tariff of Abominations"
    (D) 1888, Cleveland's campaign for tariff reduction
    (E) 1890, McKinley Tariff reductions

34. After over 150 years, the United States tradition of avoiding "entangling European alliances" was ended by participation in the
    (A) Marshall Plan
    (B) United Nations

    (C) North Atlantic Treaty Organization
    (D) World Bank
    (E) occupation of Germany

35. Leading up to the Civil War, all of the following increased tensions between the North and South EXCEPT
    (A) attack on Senator Charles Sumner
    (B) Fugitive Slave Act
    (C) Stowe's *Uncle Tom's Cabin*
    (D) rise of the Know-Nothing party
    (E) John Brown's raid

36. Which of the following political developments during the age of Jackson did the LEAST to promote democracy?
    (A) party nominating conventions
    (B) "kitchen cabinet"

(C) universal manhood suffrage

(D) popular vote for presidential electors

(E) rotation of officeholders and spoils system

37. The early foreign policy of President Franklin Roosevelt was by necessity based on pressing domestic concerns. This is reflected in his actions regarding all of the following EXCEPT the

(A) London Economic Conference

(B) recognition of the Soviet Union

(C) reciprocal trade agreements

(D) Philippine independence

(E) Greater East Asia Co-Prosperity Sphere

38. Intervention by the United States in Latin American affairs was specifically justified by the

(A) Roosevelt Corollary

(B) Monroe Doctrine

(C) writing of Alfred T. Mahan

(D) moral diplomacy of Woodrow Wilson

(E) Open Door Policy

39. The war hawks were a group of young congressmen who called for military action against

(A) Mexico in 1914

(B) Spain in 1819

(C) Great Britain in 1812

(D) Germany in 1917

(E) Japan in 1937

40. All of the following were minority presidents, winning the presidency while receiving less than 50 percent of the total popular vote. Which president won while receiving fewer electoral

and popular votes than one of his opponents?

(A) John Quincy Adams

(B) James Buchanan

(C) Abraham Lincoln

(D) Grover Cleveland

(E) Woodrow Wilson

41. Which of the following sources would be most useful in studying the development of religious freedom during the colonial period?

(A) Massachusetts Circular Letter

(B) Act of Toleration

(C) Halfway Covenant

(D) Fundamental Orders of Connecticut

(E) John Locke's theory of natural law

42. "It is to be regretted that the rich and powerful too often bend the acts of government to their selfish purposes." In defending the rights of the common people during his first term, President Andrew Jackson used these words as part of a message regarding the

(A) Bank of the United States charter veto

(B) nullification crisis

(C) Tariff of Abominations

(D) Supreme Court's Indian removal decision

(E) Maysville road veto

43. In *Schenck v. United States,* the Supreme Court and Justice Oliver Wendell Holmes ruled that free speech could be limited when it represented a "clear and present danger." This ruling was made during

(A) Haymarket Riot period

(B) Red Scare in 1919

(C) Bonus March

(D) World War I

(E) World War II

44. Which of the following was the definitive foreign policy concern of President Woodrow Wilson, over which he was unwilling to make any compromises?

(A) national self-determination

(B) freedom of the seas

(C) moral diplomacy

(D) Fourteen Points

(E) League of Nations

45. In facing their many problems at the end of the 19th century, American farmers were aided by

(A) the Republican party

(B) increased tariffs

(C) limits on crop production

(D) government price supports

(E) the Interstate Commerce Act

46. The major philosophical influence on the American leaders for independence from Great Britain was

(A) Thomas Hobbes' divine-right theory

(B) Plato's *Republic*

(C) Adam Smith's *Wealth of Nations*

(D) John Locke's natural rights theory

(E) Thomas Paine's *Common Sense*

47. The most difficult problem of the depression of the 1930s for President Franklin Roosevelt and his New Deal to correct was

(A) unemployment

(B) banking practices

(C) stock market speculation

(D) agricultural overproduction

(E) public cynicism and apathy

48. War and expansionism by the United States in the 19th century took land from and caused lasting resentment in

(A) Canada

(B) Mexico

(C) Spain

(D) Cuba

(E) Philippines

49. Which of the following decisions or actions by President Franklin Roosevelt caused the greatest controversy and opposition during his presidency?

(A) running for a third term in office

(B) lend-lease program

(C) Supreme Court reorganization plan

(D) bank holiday

(E) Japanese trade embargo

50. During the first half of the 19th century, the fastest growing influence on the nation was

(A) industrialization

(B) racism

(C) nativism

(D) revivalism

(E) sectionalism

51. "During the early 19th century, the United States economy gradually changed from agricultural to industrial." Each of the following developments supports this statement EXCEPT the

(A) growth of the Democratic-Republican party

(B) improvements in transportation

(C) increase in European immigration

(D) incorporation laws

(E) rapid rise in number of patents granted

52. President Franklin Roosevelt achieved a recognized diplomatic success with his
    (A) resolution of the *Panay* incident
    (B) Japanese trade embargo
    (C) quarantine speech
    (D) cash-and-carry program
    (E) good-neighbor policy in Latin America

53. During the Civil War, the United States for the first time in its history had
    (A) a military draft
    (B) women serving in the army
    (C) African Americans serving in the army
    (D) paper money
    (E) excise taxes

54. Reconstruction after the Civil War ended with the
    (A) impeachment of President Andrew Johnson
    (B) passage of the 13th, 14th, and 15th constitutional amendments
    (C) presidential election of 1876
    (D) rise of the Ku Klux Klan
    (E) passage of the civil rights act of 1866

55. The economic issue that was LEAST important in the United States between 1968 and 1980 was
    (A) a balanced federal budget
    (B) growing unemployment
    (C) increasing trade deficits
    (D) high interest rates
    (E) inflation

56. In the 1950s, American society was criticized for its
    (A) declining interest in religion
    (B) increasing number of working mothers
    (C) intellectualism
    (D) conformity and lost individualism
    (E) radicalism and violence

57. At the end of the 19th century, Henry Hobson Richardson and his Romanesque style transformed American
    (A) poetry
    (B) music
    (C) architecture
    (D) literature
    (E) painting

58. The issue that caused the greatest division in American society during the 1960s and 1970s was the
    (A) environmental movement
    (B) sexual revolution
    (C) women's movement
    (D) New Left
    (E) Vietnam War

59. A significant effort to preserve Native American tribal traditions and self-rule was made by the
    (A) Lewis and Clark Expedition
    (B) Dawes Act of 1887
    (C) *Worcester v. Georgia* ruling of Justice John Marshall
    (D) Indian Reorganization Act of 1934
    (E) "termination policy" of Dwight Eisenhower

60. "We must prove ourselves friends, and champions upon terms of equality and honor. . . . I mean the development of constitutional liberty in the world. Human rights, national integrity, and opportunity as against material interests—that, ladies and gentlemen, is the issue which we now have to face." These words, suggesting a

change in American foreign policy, came from President

(A) James Monroe

(B) James Polk

(C) William McKinley

(D) Woodrow Wilson

(E) Dwight Eisenhower

61. At the start of the 20th century, the government policy toward Native Americans centered on the

(A) reservation system

(B) Social Gospel

(C) development of farming skills

(D) assimilation into mainstream American culture

(E) empowerment of tribal councils

62. Which of the following was the LEAST important in the development of slavery in America?

(A) triangular trade

(B) Mason-Dixon line

(C) cotton gin

(D) western expansion to acquire rich farmlands

(E) racism

63. In antebellum southern society, the people who showed the LEAST support for the institution of slavery were

(A) upper-class plantation owners

(B) poor whites

(C) city dwellers

(D) mountain people

(E) farmers

64. The Black Power movement and the Black Muslims of the 1960s and 1970s found inspiration for the ideas of self-help, racial pride, and separatism in the words of

(A) Marcus Garvey

(B) Martin Luther King, Jr.

(C) Booker T. Washington

(D) W. E. B. Du Bois

(E) A. Philip Randolph

65. Justification for the vast differences between the rich and the poor in the late 19th century could be found in the

(A) Jeffersonian tradition

(B) frontier thesis of Frederick Jackson Turner

(C) gospel of wealth

(D) writings of Henry George

(E) social gospel

66. One of the most important actions of Congress preceding the Civil War was the passage of the Kansas-Nebraska Act in 1854, which resulted in

(A) strengthening the Missouri Compromise

(B) uniting the Democratic party

(C) increased support for Stephen Douglas' campaign for president

(D) permitting popular sovereignty to decide whether slavery was to be permitted in the territories

(E) basic agreement between most northerners and southerners

67. During Reconstruction, the Radical Republicans would have described their primary social goal as

(A) domination of the South

(B) extending equal rights to African American freedmen and women

(C) establishing permanent domination by the Republican party

(D) implementing the plans of President Lincoln

(E) guaranteeing control of national economic policy by northern businessmen

68. By the 1890s, all of the following were generally true about the South EXCEPT

(A) education was a priority for state governments

(B) Jim Crow laws were passed in every state

(C) cotton-growing still dominated the economy

(D) conservative Democrats controlled politics

(E) federal laws no longer effectively protected civil rights

69. Of the following, the most important influence on the economy and society of the United States between 1865 and 1914 was

(A) labor unions

(B) national railroad network

(C) the Grange movement

(D) new inventions

(E) unrestricted immigration

70. A major difference between the two periods immediately preceding the world wars was that for most Americans in 1941 there was no

(A) desire to make the world safe for democracy

(B) dislike of the German government

(C) concern for peace

(D) submarine threat

(E) economic relationship with England

71. In the 1840s, President James Polk added territory and secured American borders through separate successful diplomatic negotiations with

(A) Mexico and Spain

(B) Great Britain and Cuba

(C) Mexico and Great Britain

(D) Canada and Mexico

(E) Spain and Great Britain

72. The presidential election that is credited with ending the era of the ideals of Jefferson and Jackson and starting a new age of national politics dominated by big business, urban life, and middle-class values was

(A) 1876, Hayes and Tilden

(B) 1884, Cleveland and Blaine

(C) 1896, McKinley and Bryan

(D) 1904, Roosevelt and Parker

(E) 1912, Wilson, Roosevelt, and Taft

73. The primary goal of President Jefferson's purchase of the Louisiana Territory was to

(A) prevent the British from claiming it

(B) provide more land for American farmers

(C) strengthen the Democratic-Republican party

(D) demonstrate his belief in strict interpretation of the Constitution

(E) acquire New Orleans and gain control of the Mississippi River

74. In the early years of the 20th century, many reform movements increased in strength and support, but one that was weakened because it was associated with violence by some of its members was

(A) equal rights for African Americans

(B) temperance

(C) women's suffrage

(D) socialism

(E) the Grange

75. In the period immediately following World War I, most Americans could agree to support

(A) unions

(B) immigration

(C) withdrawing from foreign alliances

(D) teaching the theory of evolution

(E) prohibition

76. The issue that figured most prominently in the nullification crisis during Jackson's presidency was

(A) slavery

(B) political party rivalries

(C) states' rights

(D) tariff fairness

(E) sectionalism

77. The development of higher education in colonial America was largely the result of efforts by

(A) colonial governments

(B) wealthy patrons

(C) British government

(D) churches

(E) English universities

78. During the 19th century, the organization of labor unions was hampered by all of the following EXCEPT

(A) immigrant workers

(B) economic depressions

(C) labor-saving inventions

(D) laws limiting union rights

(E) differences among skilled and unskilled workers

79. Which of the following people had the LEAST influence on the New Deal and its efforts to find new solutions to the problems of the depression?

(A) Huey Long

(B) Dr. Francis Townsend

(C) John Maynard Keynes

(D) Frances Perkins

(E) Al Smith

80. The 1960 presidential election contest between John Kennedy and Richard Nixon saw for the first time that

(A) personalities, not political party machines, were decisive

(B) televised debates between the candidates could influence voters

(C) religion was the pivotal issue

(D) the "solid" South would vote as a bloc for a Republican

(E) both political parties would nominate candidates who were war veterans

Section II/Part A: Document-Based Question

Time: 45 minutes (preceded by 15-minute reading period)

DIRECTIONS: This question calls for you to develop a logical essay that blends your interpretation of Documents A–H and your knowledge of the period covered in the question. Your essay should utilize pertinent references to some, but not necessarily all, of the documents present as well as your own knowledge of the period.

1. To what extent were the reform efforts of the Progressive Era aimed at maintaining the existing society and to what extent did they bring about radical changes?

DOCUMENT A.

The conscience of the people, in a time of grave national problems, has called into being a new party, born of the nation's sense of justice. We of the Progressive party here dedicate ourselves to the fulfillment of the duty laid upon us by our fathers to maintain the government of the people, by the people and for the people whose foundations they laid. . . .

Political parties exist to secure responsible government and to execute the will of the people. From these great tasks both of the old parties have turned aside. Instead of instruments to promote the general welfare, they have become the tools of corrupt interests which use them impartially to serve their selfish purposes. Behind the ostensible government sits enthroned an invisible government owing no allegiance and acknowledging no responsibility to the people. To destroy this invisible government, to dissolve the unholy alliance between corrupt business and corrupt politics is the first task of statesmanship of the day.

Progressive Party Platform, August 5, 1912

DOCUMENT B.

No one can mistake the purpose for which the Nation now seeks to use the Democratic Party. It seeks to use it to interpret a change in its own plans and point of view. Some old things with which we had grown familiar, and which had begun to creep into the very habit of our thought and of our lives, have altered their aspect as we have latterly looked critically upon them, with fresh awakened eyes; have dropped their disguises and shown themselves alien and sinister. Some new things, as we look frankly upon them, willing to comprehend their real character, have come to assume the aspect of things long believed in and familiar, stuff of our own convictions.

We have itemized with some degree of particularity the things that ought to be altered and here are some of the chief items: A tariff which makes the Government a facile instrument in the hands of private interests; a banking and currency system perfectly adapted to concentrating cash and restricting credits; an industrial system which restricts labor, and exploits natural resources; a body of agriculture never served through science or afforded the facilities of credit best suited to its practical needs.

President Woodrow Wilson,
First Inaugural Address, March 4, 1913

DOCUMENT C.

The Granger Collection, New York

Corbis-Bettmann

DOCUMENT D.

Sir, you have now been President of the United States for six months and what is the result? It is no exaggeration to say that every enemy of the Negro race is greatly encouraged; that every man who dreams of making the Negro race a group of menials and pariahs is alert and hopeful.

A dozen worthy Negro officials have been removed from office, and you have nominated but one black man for office, and he, such a contemptible cur, that his very nomination was an insult to every Negro in the land.

To this negative appearance of indifference has been added positive action on the part of your advisers, with or without your knowledge, which constitutes the gravest attack on the liberties of our people since emancipation. Public segregation of civil servants in government employ, necessarily involving personal insult and humiliation, has for the first time in history been made the policy of the United States government.

W. E. B. Du Bois,
an Open Letter to Woodrow Wilson,
September 1913

DOCUMENT E.

The recognition of shortcomings or inconveniences in government is not by itself sufficient to warrant a change of system. There should be also an effort to estimate and compare the shortcomings and inconveniences of the system to be substituted, for although they may be different they will certainly exist.

Elihu Root,
lecture: "Experiments in Government,"
Princeton University, April 1913

DOCUMENT F.

When one starts to investigate conditions the result is appalling. We are supposed to be progressing, but a little study in comparisons seems to point the other way. For instance, it is a fact that although this country is in its infancy, and has gained in wealth more in fifty years than any other country has in 700 years still we have more poverty in comparison with any of those old countries.

I have always felt that no true state of civilization can ever be realized as long as we continue to have two classes of society. But that is a tremendous problem, and it will take a terrific amount of labor to remedy it. I think myself that we are bound to have a revolution here before these questions are straightened out. We were on the verge of it in the Colorado strike and the reason we did not have it then was not due to the good judgement of public officials, but to that of labor officials, who worked unceasingly to prevent it.

Mother Jones,
Miners' Magazine, April 1915

DOCUMENT G.

The commission is hereby empowered and directed to prevent persons, partnerships, or corporations, except banks, and common carriers subject to the Acts to regulate commerce, from using unfair methods of competition in commerce. If upon such hearing the commission shall be of the opinion that the method of competition in question is prohibited by this Act, it shall make a report in writing in which it shall state its findings as to the facts, and shall issue and cause to be served on such person, partnership, or corporation an order requiring such person, partnership, or corporation to cease and desist from using such methods of competition.

Federal Trade Commission Act,
September 1914

DOCUMENT H.

Culver Pictures

Section II/Parts B and C: Standard Essay Questions

Time: 70 minutes

Directions: Please answer TWO of the questions that follow, *one* from Part B and *one* from Part C. Present your reasoning coherently, using appropriate historical proof. If time allows, check your work when you are finished writing. Be sure to number your answers as the questions are numbered below.

Part B: Select *one* question.
30 minutes writing time and 5 minutes planning are suggested.

2. Assess George Washington's presidency in terms of the influence of the views of Hamilton and Jefferson.

3. Analyze the development of sectionalism in the United States during the first half of the 19th century with reference to TWO of the following:

economic developments
slavery
cultural differences

Part C: Select *one* question.
30 minutes writing time and 5 minutes planning are suggested.

4. The United States is a nation of immigrants with a long history of not welcoming people from other lands. Evaluate this statement with reference to TWO of the following:

frontier theory
immigration quotas
Industrial Revolution
nativism

5. Compare and contrast the prevailing attitudes of the American people following World War I and World War II.

Acknowledgments

Grateful acknowledgment is made to the following sources for permission to use copyrighted materials in this book:

19 *The Log of Christopher Columbus,* translated by Robert H. Fuson, copyright © 1987 by International Marine Publishing Co. Reprinted by permission of The McGraw-Hill Companies.

20 Bartolomé de Las Casas, *History of the Indies,* translated and edited by Andrée Collard, Harper and Row, copyright 1971 by Andrée Collard. Reprinted by permission of Joyce Contrucci.

21–22 David E. Stannard, *American Holocaust,* copyright © 1992 by David A. Stannard. Reprinted by permission of Oxford University Press, Inc.

286–287 Quoted in James M. McPherson, *Marching Toward Freedom,* copyright © 1965. Reprinted by permission of Random House, Inc.

470 Edna St. Vincent Millay, "First Fig," from *Collected Poems*, HarperCollins, copyright 1922, 1950 by Edna St. Vincent Millay. All rights reserved. Reprinted by permission of Elizabeth Barnett, literary executor.

514 Eleanor Roosevelt, *This I Remember*, copyright 1949 by Anna Eleanor Roosevelt, renewed © 1977 by John A. Roosevelt and Franklin A. Roosevelt, Jr. Reprinted by permission of HarperCollins Publishers, Inc.

515–516 Florence Reece, "Which Side Are You On?" copyright © 1947 by Stormking Music Inc. All rights reserved. Reprinted by permission.

516–517 Jean Westin, *Making Do: How Women Survived the '30s*, copyright © 1976. Reprinted by permission of Allyn & Bacon, Simon & Schuster Education Group.

543 Table adapted from data in Gilbert C. Fite and James Reese, *An Economic History of the United States,* copyright © 1959 by Houghton Mifflin Co. Reprinted by permission of Gilbert C. Fite.

592 Words and music by Malvina Reynolds, from the song "Little Boxes," © 1962 by Schroder Music Co. (ASCAP), renewed 1990. Reprinted by permission, all rights reserved.

637–638 *Memoirs of Richard Nixon*, copyright © 1978. Reprinted by permission of Warner Books, Inc., all rights reserved.

Index